THE
SECOND
BATTLE
for
AFRICA

THE SECOND BATTLE

for AFRICA

GARVEYISM, THE US HEARTLAND,
AND GLOBAL BLACK FREEDOM

Erik S. McDuffie

Duke University Press *Durham and London* 2024

Printed in the United States of America on acid-free paper ∞
Project Editor: Michael Trudeau
Designed by Courtney Leigh Richardson
Typeset in Garamond Premier Pro and Montserrat
by Westchester Publishing Services

Library of Congress Cataloging-in-Publication Data
Names: McDuffie, Erik S., [date] author.
Title: The second battle for Africa : Garveyism, the US heartland, and
global Black freedom / Erik S. McDuffie.
Other titles: Garveyism, the US heartland, and global Black freedom
Description: Durham : Duke University Press, 2024. | Includes
bibliographical references and index.
Identifiers: LCCN 2024011096 (print)
LCCN 2024011097 (ebook)
ISBN 9781478031048 (paperback)
ISBN 9781478026839 (hardcover)
ISBN 9781478060062 (ebook)
Subjects: LCSH: Garvey, Marcus, 1887–1940. | Universal Negro
Improvement Association. | Black nationalism—United States—
History—20th century. | Black power—United States—History. | African
Americans—Race identity—History. | African Americans—Civil rights—
History. | BISAC: HISTORY / United States / 20th Century | SOCIAL
SCIENCE / Black Studies (Global)
Classification: LCC E185.61 .M33 2024 (print) | LCC E185.61 (ebook) |
DDC 320.54/60973—DC23/ENG/20240907
LC record available at https://lccn.loc.gov/2024011096
LC ebook record available at https://lccn.loc.gov/2024011097

Cover art: *Top*, Black Student Union march led by eighteen-year-old Terry
Johnson through the west side of Lansing, Michigan, 1971. *Middle*, James
R. and Goldie Stewart and family on the eve of their emigration to Liberia,
Cleveland, Ohio, February 1949. *Bottom*, Revolutionary National Youth
League procession on Randall Street, Monrovia, Liberia, December 31,
2022. Courtesy of Terry Johnson, Roberta Stewart Amos, and Yaya Sesay.

To Mom, Dad, Amaya, Amir, and Melony

Contents

ACS
American Colonization Society

AJG
Amy Jacques Garvey

AJG Papers
Amy Garvey Memorial Collection of Marcus Garvey Special Collections

AN
Amsterdam News (New York)

AOMX / *Autobiography*
The Autobiography of Malcolm X

BS
Betty Shabazz

CCP
Call and Post (Cleveland)

CD
Chicago Defender

CORE
Congress of Racial Equality

CPUSA
Communist Party USA

CWH
Clarence W. Harding Jr.

DD
Daily Defender (Chicago)

DOO
Development of Our Own

EM
Elijah Muhammad

ESC
Earnest Sevier Cox

ESC Papers
Earnest Sevier Cox Papers

FBI
Federal Bureau of Investigation

FHHR
Frederick H. Hammurabi Robb

FOI
Fruit of Islam

FOL
Future Outlook League

HOK
House of Knowledge

JRS
James R. Stewart

JRS D-435
Universal Negro Improvement Association
James R. Stewart Division 435

KKK
Ku Klux Klan

MG
Marcus Garvey

MGI
Marcus Garvey Institute for the Study of African Peoples

MGMI
Marcus Garvey Memorial Institute

MGP
The Marcus Garvey and Universal Negro Improvement Association Papers

MGT-GCC
Muslim Girls Training and General Civilization Class

MMLG
Mittie Maude Lena Gordon

MOJA
Movement for Justice in Africa

MS
Muhammad Speaks

MSTA
Moorish Science Temple of America

MX
Malcolm X

MX Collection
Malcolm X Collection

NAACP
National Association for the Advancement of Colored People

NNW
New Negro World

NOI
Lost-Found Nation of Islam / Nation of Islam

NW
Negro World

NYT
New York Times

OAU
Organization of African Unity

PME
Peace Movement of Ethiopia

PMEW
Pacific Movement of the Eastern World

RAM
Revolutionary Action Movement

SV
Stewart's Voice

TGB
Theodore G. Bilbo

TGB Papers
Theodore G. Bilbo Papers

TWH
Thomas W. Harvey

UNIA
Universal Negro Improvement Association

UNIA Collection CHWM
Universal Negro Improvement Association Collection,
Charles H. Wright Museum of African American History

UNIA Papers RL
Universal Negro Improvement Association Papers, Stuart A. Rose
Manuscript, Archives, and Rare Library

UNIA Papers WRHS
Universal Negro Improvement Association Papers,
Western Reserve Historical Society

UOI
University of Islam

WLS
William L. Sherrill

I must be honest. This book took much longer to complete than I had ever anticipated. Research on this project began in 2009. However, the origins of this book can be traced to my diasporic midwestern beginnings. I am a sixth-generation African American midwesterner. My family has lived in Michigan and Ohio since at least the 1830s. My ancestors and living relatives were ministers, abolitionists, doctors, automobile workers, household laborers, teachers, nurses, and Underground Railroad conductors.

I was born in 1970 in Detroit, Michigan, and raised in suburban Cleveland, Ohio. Growing up, I regularly visited Detroit to see my grandparents, aunts, cousins, uncles, and family members. My grandparents' bungalow house was our family's gathering place. For as long as I can remember, Detroit, Canada, and the automobile industry were central to my life. My maternal grandmother, Margaret Chandler (née Stanley), was born and raised in Toronto. As a young woman, she met my grandfather, Clifford Chandler of Detroit, at a popular Black nightclub in Windsor, Ontario—Detroit's Canadian sister city located across the Detroit River. They eventually married and started a family. My grandfather and seemingly everybody he knew worked at Ford or was in some way connected to the city's automobile industry. My grandmother regularly journeyed to Toronto to see her mother, Marion Stanley, who hailed from the Caribbean island of St. Kitts. I didn't know my great-grandmother very well. But I knew "she was from the islands." As a youngster, I went fishing multiple times every summer for years on the Canadian side of Lake St. Clair with my grandparents, mother, Marion McDuffie (née Chandler), and other family members. Crossing the Detroit River to Canada over the bridge or through the tunnel was quick and easy. You didn't need a passport back then. That was long before 9/11. My father, James McDuffie, was from Columbia, South Carolina.

After serving in the Vietnam War, he migrated to Detroit in 1967 and worked an office job at General Motors before marrying my mom. Soon after I arrived, he became a successful salesman for a Detroit-based automotive supplier. We moved "down" to Ohio when I was three. His aunt, Dorothy Weaks (née McDuffie), migrated from South Carolina to Detroit. Once there, she cleaned white folks' homes and worked as a Detroit Public School bus driver. Regular topics of conversation in Grandma and Papa's home were the Detroit Great Rebellion of 1967, or "the Riot," as my family called it; my grandparents' admiration for Detroit's first Black mayor, Coleman Young; and my grandmother's love for the Detroit Tigers and the "Bad Boys" (Detroit Pistons). There also were somber discussions about the unfolding crack cocaine epidemic and ongoing deindustrialization devastating the city.

I heard stories as a child when visiting my grandparents in Detroit about a midwestern ancestor, John Hatfield, who went to Australia before the Civil War because he wanted to be free and about my grandfather's "communistically inclined" cousin who went to Mexico in the 1960s to evade US racism. I also saw nineteenth-century photos of my ancestors who called Detroit their home. Another turning point in my life came when my parents purchased a vacation home in Puerto Rico. I was seven. It was through countless family trips to the island where I discovered Africa through *bomba*, salsa, rice and beans, *tostones*, and my encounters with the island's immensely proud people and unresolved colonial past and present.

Moving ahead, as an undergraduate at Hamilton College in Central New York State in the early 1990s, I discovered Malcolm X, Marcus Garvey, and the rich history of Black nationalism (Marxism and Black feminism). During a visit to Detroit in the summer before my senior year, I asked my grandfather while we sat on his porch if he remembered Marcus Garvey. I'll never forget my grandfather's response. He smiled. After a pause, he exclaimed: "Ohhhh, yes! Marcus Garvey." My grandfather remembered witnessing massive UNIA parades in Detroit. Then he told an off-color joke about Garvey. . . . Sadly, I don't think I ever followed up with my grandfather about Garvey. I wish I had. Decades later as I researched this book, I stumbled upon a reference in the *Negro World* to an "A. D. Chandler," a prominent Detroit minister who introduced Garvey at a mass UNIA meeting in Detroit in 1923. I was stunned. I knew my great-grandfather, Arthur D. Chandler, was a leading early twentieth-century Black Detroit Baptist minister. I connected the dots. I instantly recalled my conversation years ago about Garvey with my grandfather. How I wish I had asked my grandparents about this history. Sadly, they are long since expired and their house and porch, like countless homes and buildings in Detroit, have been demolished.

I say all this to say that this book is deeply personal. It reflects my own Black diasporic midwestern roots and my attempt to understand the Midwest as a globally impactful, cosmopolitan, transnational center of Black life and Black internationalism, nationalism, and radicalism indelibly shaped by gendered racial capitalism, white supremacy, Black resistance, global events, and the forces of history. I hope this book resonates with readers, especially Black midwesterners.

Urbana, Illinois
July 2024

Acknowledgments

There are so many people I would like to thank. Let me begin by stating that getting to know my subjects constitutes one of the most amazing aspects of writing this book, in particular Muhammad Ahmad (Maxwell Stanford Jr.), Don and (the late) Norma Jeane Freeman, (the late) Donna Cooper Hayford, Deborah Jones, (the late) Steven Jones Jr., Cheryl Morgan, Ilyasah Shabazz, Victor Stewart, and Terance Wilson. Over the years, they have generously shared their knowledge, personal papers, and time with me. Our conversations have helped me to better understand the dynamic histories of Garveyism, the Midwest, Black nationalism, internationalism, and radicalism, Louise Little, Malcolm X, Black Power, and the African world. Getting to know my biographical subjects has made me a better scholar, man, father, partner, son, and global citizen.

The American Council of Learned Societies and National Endowment for the Humanities both generously provided grants for researching this book. My book also benefited from significant support through the University of Illinois at Urbana-Champaign Campus Research Board; Center for Advanced Study, Humanities Research Institute; Office for the Vice Chancellor of Diversity, Equity, and Inclusion; College of Liberal Arts and Sciences; Office for the Vice Chancellor for Research and Innovation; and a Richard and Margaret Romano Professorial Scholarship. Short-term research fellowships from the John Hope Franklin Research Center at Duke University and the Newberry Library came at a crucial time in this book's development.

It is essential that I express my sincerest appreciation to the staff of archives and libraries I visited across the United States and beyond. A special thanks to the staff at the Schomburg Center for Research in Black Culture (Harlem), Moorland-Spingarn Research Center (Washington, DC), Blockson Collection

(Philadelphia), Special Collections and Archives at Fisk University (Nashville), Cleveland Public Library, Detroit Public Library, Library of Congress, National Library of Jamaica, Newberry Library (Chicago), Rubenstein Library (Duke University), The National Archives (Kew, Richmond, United Kingdom), Bentley Historical Library (Ann Arbor, Michigan), George Padmore Library (Accra, Ghana), Africana Collection (Northwestern University), and Manuscripts and Archives (University of Cape Town). I am deeply indebted to Michael Flug, Beverly Cook, and staff at the Carter G. Woodson Library (Chicago); Jennifer Brannock at the Special Collections at the University of Southern Mississippi; Philomena Bloh Sayeh and her colleagues at the Center for National Documents and Records, in Monrovia, Liberia; Randall K. Burkett and the staff at the Stuart A. Rose Manuscript, Archives, and Rare Book Library at Emory University; Ann Sindelar at the Western Reserve History Society Library in Cleveland, Ohio; Celestina Savonius-Wroth of the History, Philosophy, and Newspaper Library and Jennifer Johnson of the Map Library, both at the University of Illinois; and LaNesha DeBardelaben, formerly at the Charles H. Wright Museum of African American History in Detroit, Michigan.

I am honored to join the "unofficial Garvey studies" club. My book has benefited from conversations and engagement with Barbara Bair, Keisha Blain, Horace Campbell, Natanya Duncan, Adam Ewing, Claudrena Harold, Robert A. Hill, Jahi Issa, Kenneth Jolly, Mwariama Kamau, Asia Leeds, Rupert Lewis, Mary Rolinson, James Spady, Ronald Stephens, Ula Taylor, Robert Trent Vinson, Michael West, and many others. It is also delightful to be a part of a new wave of scholarship on the US heartland and Black Midwest. My work has been shaped by exchanges and collaborations with Christy Clark-Pujara, Sara Egge, Keona Ervin, Kristin Hoganson, Ashley Howard, Brad Hunt, Jon Lauck, Martin Manalansan IV, Dan Manett, Crystal Marie Moten, Liesl Olson, Siobhan Somerville, Joe William Trotter Jr., and Terrion Williamson and her Black Midwest Initiative. I also wish to thank the teachers and childcare providers who taught my children and provided me time to complete this book.

This book benefited in innumerable ways from talks, presentations, and conferences at or sponsored by Arizona State University; Carter G. Woodson Institute; Chicago State University; Concordia University (Montreal); DePaul University; Duke University; Hamilton College; Johns Hopkins University; Michigan State University; Newberry Library; Northern Illinois University; Northwestern University; Rutgers University; University of Chicago; University of Illinois at Chicago; University of the West Indies at St. Augustine, Trinidad and Tobago; University of Washington; Vanderbilt University; Washington University in St. Louis; African Studies Association; American Studies

Association; Association for the Study of African American Life and History; Association for the Study of the Worldwide African Diaspora (ASWAD); Berkshire Conference on the History of Women, Genders, and Sexualities; Black Midwestern Symposium; Critical Ethnic Studies Association; Ghana Studies Association; Liberian Studies Association; Midwestern History Association; Organization of American Historians; Society for Historians of American Foreign Relations; and Thomas W. Harvey Memorial Hall (Philadelphia).

International travel and research were some of the most exciting and taxing aspects of this book. My two research trips to Grenada in 2015 and getting to know Terance Wilson were game-changing. Scholars Nicole Phillip-Dowe and John Angus Martin helped make my trips to Grenada most productive. Many thanks to Jenny Hosten and the staff at Jenny's Place in Grand Anse for their amazing accommodations. In Ghana, thank you to Bright Botwe at the Public Records and Archives Administration Department for his research assistance. No words can express my deep appreciation for (the late) Albert Ahwireng, his friendship, and expert guidance in Accra and to Elmina and Cape Coast. Kingston, Jamaica–based Garvey leader and scholar Shani Roper was instrumental in making my 2016 research trip to Jamaica fruitful. Meeting Robyn Maynard and Délice Mugabo at my talk at Concordia University in Montreal in November 2016 was critical to helping me understand the meaning of Louise (Langdon) Little to Black feminist, queer, trans*, activist communities in contemporary Montreal.

Falling in love with Liberia during my six trips to this West African nation has been one of the most incredible experiences of writing this book. I am grateful to the Cape Hotel in Mamba Point, Monrovia, "your home away from home," as the hotel's general manager, Ghassan Rasamny, tells me whenever I check into his hotel. Much love to Cape Hotel staff person Tom Taweh, whose commitment to building a better Liberia is inspirational. I am grateful to Dr. William Allen of the University of Liberia, Helen Roberts-Evans, (the late) Dr. Amos Sawyer, Dr. Philomena Bloh Sayeh, Dr. Togba-Nah Tipoteh, and Dr. Augustine Konneh, as well as to Indiana University–based Liberia scholars Ruth Stone and (the late) Verlon Stone. (The late) Donna Cooper Hayford, Cheryl Morgan, and Victor Stewart welcomed me into their homes and family. Meeting the teachers and children at the James R. Stewart Elementary School in quiet Gbandela, young members of the James R. Stewart Division 435, in particular Emmanuel Mulbah Johnson and Sammitta Entsua, and UNIA president general Michael Duncan and UNIA leader Rosemarie James have been transformative. Big shouts out to the Hill St. Athletic Club of Monrovia, especially Muhammed Odusanya and Alex Quaqua. Running first thing in the morning through the streets of Central Monrovia with these exceptional athletes was always a joy (and sometimes painful).

I would like to thank my colleagues in the Department of African American Studies and the Department of History, in particular Ikuko Asaka, Eugene Avrutin, Ronald Bailey, Teresa Barnes, Marsha Barrett, Merle Bowen, James Brennan, Adrian Burgos, Teri Chettiar, Kenneth Cuno, Jerry Dávila, Augusto Espiritu, Faye Harrison, Marc Hertzman, Kristin Hoganson, Rana Hogarth, Irvin Hunt, Candice Jenkins, Craig Koslofsky, Rosalyn LaPier, Leonard McKinnis, Desirée McMillion, John Meyers, Robert Morrissey, Kevin Mumford, Kemal Nance, Esther Ndumi Ngumbi, Mauro Nobili, Eddie O'Byrn, (the late) Kathryn Oberdeck, Venetria Patton, Dana Rabin, Yuridia Ramírez, John Randolph, Leslie Reagan, Bobby Smith II, Mark Steinberg, Carol Symes, Alexia Williams, and Roderick Wilson. The History Department's writing workshops proved extremely valuable in workshopping portions of my manuscript. I would like to thank other Illinois colleagues: Awad Awad, William Bernhard, Nancy Castro, Jessica Greenberg, Maryam Kashani, Christopher Korose, Korinta Maldonado, Faranak Miraftab, Cynthia Oliver, Junaid Rana, Gilberto Rosas, (the late) Bruce Rosenstock, Ken Salo, Gisela Sin, and Siobhan Somerville. Colleagues in the Center for African Studies—Adéyínká Àlásadé, Maimouna Barro, and Teresa Barnes—have been a joy to work with. This book would not have been possible without the support of the Office of the Vice Chancellor of Research and Innovation: Susan Martinis, (the late) Nancy Ablemann, Melissa Edwards, Maria Gillombardo, Kevin Hamilton, Patricia Jones, Sue Key, Melanie Loots, Tammy Nohren, Cynthia Oliver, Greg Schroeder, and Kim Walters. I would like to thank my colleagues at the University of Delaware during my time there: Erica Armstrong Dunbar, Gretchen Bauer, Arica Coleman, Gabrielle Foreman, Carol Henderson, James Jones, Wunyabari Maloba, Yasser Payne, and George Watson. Much thanks to my former graduate students Courtney Pierre Joseph and Olivia Hagedorn, who are now charting new paths of inquiry about the Diasporic Midwest. Research assistance from Olivia Hagedorn and Amaziah Zuri was mission-critical for this project. I would be remiss if I did not thank my instructors and mentors from my undergraduate days at Hamilton College, where the germinal idea for my book began thirty years ago—Douglas Ambrose, Karen Green, Vicky Green, Maurice Isserman, Christine Johnson, Esther Kanipe, Vincent Odamtten, and Robert Paquette.

Big shout-outs to my ASWAD family: Laura Roseanne Adderley, Leslie Alexander, Jean Allman, Carol Anderson, Curtis Austin, Monique Bedasse, Abena Busia, Kim Butler, Yolanda Covington-Ward, Michael Gomez, Bryce Henson, Leslie James, Sonya Johnson, Laurie Lambert, Minkah Makalani, Yuko Miki,

Jessica Millward, Amrita Chakrabarti Myers, Walter Rucker, Ben Talton, Deborah Thomas, Robert Trent Vinson, and Jason Young. Various chapters, ideas, and parts of the book have greatly benefited from conversations, suggestions, and electronic exchanges with a wide range of academics, independent scholars, and thinkers like Nwando Achebe, Jeffrey Ahlman, Bettina Aptheker, Keisha Blain, Rabbi Capers C. Funnye, Darlene Clark-Hine, Merle Collins, Fassil Demissie, Jacob Dorman, Ashley Farmer, Kevin Gaines, Erik Gellman, Tiffany Gill, Ruth Wilson Gilmore, Marc Goulding, Kali Gross, Frank Guridy, Kelly Harris, Errol Henderson, Sandra Jackson, Robin D. G. Kelley, Haki R. Madhubuti, John Angus Martin, Timothy Nevin, Tiffany Ruby Patterson, Marc Perry, Lara Putnam, Barbara Ransby, Dorothy Roberts, Tracy Denean Sharpley-Whiting, James Spady, James Smethurst, Robyn Spencer, Daniela Steila Quito Swan, Nikki Taylor, (the late) Rosalyn Terborg-Penn, Jeanne Theoharis, Joe William Trotter Jr., Penny Von Eschen, Fanon Wilkins, Rhonda Y. Williams, and Komozi Woodard.

I am especially indebted to Gerald Horne, one of the preeminent Black historians of our time. His productivity, globetrotting, and commitment to internationalist, antiracist, and working-class struggles are legendary. I remain deeply grateful to Eileen Boris for her mentorship and keen editorial eye. The book owes so much to Antoinette Burton, who graciously read multiple drafts of the introduction and whose enthusiasm for my writing about Louise Little is much appreciated. I cannot thank Michael West enough. He read countless portions of the manuscript on short notice, and he is one of the most principled and ethical scholars whom I know.

At Duke University, Gisela Fosado has been an exemplary editor. It is a joy and honor to work with her. Her enthusiasm for my work and sharp, critical eye have enhanced this book in multiple ways. Alejandra Mejía, Michael Trudeau, and Courtney Baker were extremely helpful in moving this book through production. The anonymous readers offered thoughtful and honest criticisms and suggestions for improving and condensing a long manuscript.

I could not have completed this book without the support of dear friends in Champaign-Urbana, like Sara Bartumeus, C. L. Cole, Juan and Carmen Loor, Korinta Maldonado, Rebecca Paez-Rodríguez, Francisco Rodríguez-Suárez, Gilberto Rosas, Nate Schmitz, Gisela Sin, Sam Smith, and Ruth Wyman. I never imagined living in Champaign-Urbana for more than one year. Now, twenty years later, I can't imagine my life without these folks. Special thanks to Robert Trent Vinson and Bryce Henson. "RTV" and "Bro. Bryce" were always there for me to offer fraternal support and spot-on suggestions for the book. Kim Butler will always be my "ASWAD sister." Desirée McMillion is one of my biggest cheerleaders who helped me get through countless difficult days. Thank you, Orlando Plaza and Brian Purnell. You two are like brothers to me. AnneVibe and Clarence Taylor, Tracy Romans, Joe and Allison Ryan, Adriana Bohm, Mary Stricker, Sean Sawyer, Warren Johnson, Christopher Cargile, Lou Duvin, Avrom Feinberg, and Peter Ruggie have remained dear friends, despite hundreds (and in some cases thousands) of miles of separation between me and them.

I have so much love for my parents, James and Marion McDuffie, who laid the foundations for my passions for history, learning, justice, world traveling, and being informed about local and global events. They did everything they could to provide the very best for me. Thank you to my uncle Donald Chandler; my aunts Rose Ann Chandler, Elizabeth Howell, (the late) Gwendolyn Chandler, and Melitha Scherrelle Chandler; and my cousins Ronald Howell Jr., Donald Chandler Jr., William McCant, Willie Deene Davis, and Laniki Yolanda Lawson. It has been an incredible pleasure getting to know my distant relatives from Australia: my cousin Raymond Hatfield and his husband, Don Watkins; my cousin John Hatfield and his wife, Susan; and my good old cousin George Hatfield and his wife, Lorraine.

No words can articulate my love and appreciation for Melony Elizabeth Barrett. We weren't expecting to meet each other. And we come from different worlds. She has been there for me through some exceptionally difficult times. My life has changed exponentially for the better after I met her. There is nothing I can say or do to make up for the time I wish I spent with her while I worked on this book. But I look forward to future days ahead for us, including walking through England, returning to Africa, and traveling to destinations we have yet to imagine.

Finally, I must thank and acknowledge my children, Amaya-Soledad and Amir Wendell Robeson, whom I am very proud of and love very much. I marvel at their resilience and their transformation into two very beautiful and smart people. I dedicate this book to them, the next generation of Black people, who I hope will make this world a better place.

For everything else, I am thankful to almighty God and the ancestors.

INTRODUCTION. A Manifesto on the Making
of the Diasporic Midwest and Garveyism

Once more the white man has outraged American Civilization and dragged the fair name
of the Republic before the Court of Civilized Justice. Another riot has visited the country
and Omaha, Nebraska, has placed her name upon the map of mob violence. . . . The Negro
must organize all over the world, 400,000,000 strong, to administer to our oppressors
their Waterloo. —MARCUS GARVEY, *Negro World*, October 11, 1919

It was Grandmother Louise and Reverend Little . . . who sowed the seeds of insight, dis-
cipline, educational values, and organizational skills in my father, not Elijah Muhammad.
Mr. Muhammad cleared away the weeds and allowed those seeds to flourish and grow.
—ILYASAH SHABAZZ, *Growing Up X*, 2002

This book is a manifesto. It declares the importance of the US Midwest to the
struggle for global Black freedom through Marcus Garvey, Garveyism, the
Universal Negro Improvement Association (UNIA), and its offshoots from
the 1920s onward. The US Midwest, the vast geographic region in the North
American middle, was a center of twentieth-century heavy industry and a crucible of African American life. Through examining the grassroots organizing,
globetrotting, journalism, subjectivities, political and religious beliefs, cultural
work, and institution building of US heartland–linked Black women, men, and
youth inspired by Garvey, this book tells a new story about Garveyism; Black

internationalism, nationalism, and radicalism; the Midwest; Black feminism; and the African Diaspora, the ongoing dispersal of people of African descent throughout the world. At its peak in the early 1920s, the UNIA, then head-quartered in New York, was the largest Black protest organization in history. The organization claimed six million members in the United States, Canada, the Caribbean, Central America, Africa, Europe, and Australia. The UNIA under-stood itself as a provisional government in exile committed to building self-reliant Black institutions, an independent Africa, and a global Black empire capable of protecting the rights and dignity of the African-descended every-where. The Jamaican Black nationalists Marcus Garvey and Amy Ashwood Garvey cofounded the UNIA in 1914 in Kingston, Jamaica. Marcus Garvey served as the UNIA's first president-general.[1] His pan-African vision and call for race pride, armed self-defense, and Black self-determination galvanized the Black masses across the world, not least in the US Midwest.[2]

The Midwest constituted a key stronghold of the UNIA and a generative global crossroads of twentieth-century Black transnational movements. From the 1920s through the 1970s, UNIA divisions (locals) in Chicago, Illinois; Detroit, Michigan; Cleveland, Ohio; Cincinnati, Ohio; Gary, Indiana; Akron, Ohio; St. Louis, Missouri; Youngstown, Ohio; and Pittsburgh, Pennsylvania, constituted some of the largest, most influential, and longest-lasting UNIA out-posts in the world. Through the UNIA, Black midwesterners forged powerful transnational political, cultural, spiritual, and personal linkages with African-descended people globally. My book disrupts the Harlem and Atlantic world-centric view of Garvey and the UNIA. The Midwest's importance to the UNIA would have been no mystery to him. Through his oratory and journalism in *Negro World*, the UNIA's globally circulated newspaper, Garvey from Harlem readily recognized the importance of the Midwest to the UNIA and to the global struggle of African-descended people for life and dignity. He, along with several of his leading lieutenants, regularly traveled from New York to the Mid-west on UNIA-related business. On countless occasions, Garvey's devoted mid-western followers, sometimes in the thousands, came out to hear him speak at UNIA mass events and to march with him in large UNIA street parades in large and small heartland cities. Inspired by his entrepreneurial and pan-African vision, African Americans in heartland cities, towns, and rural areas, like Gar-veyites around the world, established businesses and other institutions with the intention of building autonomous, globally networked Black communi-ties. Midwesterners were not just grassroots supporters of the transnational UNIA. They were some of its most visible leaders. James R. Stewart of Cleveland succeeded Marcus Garvey as the UNIA's president-general shortly after his death in 1940. After becoming the UNIA's new leader, Stewart transferred the transnational UNIA's Parent Body, the organization's executive board, from Harlem to Cleveland. In 1949, he migrated to Liberia with his family. By relocating the seat of the UNIA to Liberia, he fulfilled Garvey's dream of leading the struggle for African redemption from the continent.[3]

The Midwest was critically important to the UNIA and was home to what I have termed the "midwestern Garveyite front"—influential Black formations either based in the heartland or generating strong support there, all of which were inspired by Garveyism and affected the lives of millions of people and all aspects of Black life in and beyond the United States from the 1920s onward.[4] Many of these formations were headquartered or enjoyed strong support in Chicago, Detroit, Cleveland, St. Louis, and Lansing, Michigan. They were colonizationist groups like the Peace Movement of Ethiopia; religious organizations like the Moorish Science Temple of America, Nation of Islam, Clock of Destiny, Shrine of the Black Madonna, and Beth Shalom B'nai Zaken Ethiopian Hebrew Congregation; Afro-Asian solidarity groups like the Pacific Movement of the Eastern World and The Development of Our Own; cultural and community institutions like the House of Knowledge, Third World Press, Malcolm X College, Malcolm X Memorial Foundation, and D-Town Farm; and Black Power groups like the Afro-American Institute, Revolutionary Action Movement, Afro-Set, and Marcus Garvey Institute for the Study of African Peoples. Some formations, such as the Movement for Justice in Africa and the Marcus Garvey Memorial Institute, headquartered in Monrovia, Liberia, during the 1970s, were based overseas but still closely connected to the Midwest. Additionally, the African Hebrew Israelites of Jerusalem, a spiritual organization comprising largely followers from Chicago, is based today in Dimona, Israel. Several Garvey-influenced organizations are still active today and, in some cases, claim tens of thousands of working-class members. Twentieth-century Garvey-influenced Black formations spanned the ideological spectrum. For some people, vigorously reading and studying the writings and teachings of Garvey brought them into the UNIA and its derivatives. For others, the public perception and popular memory of him as a champion and symbol for global Black liberation drew them into Garvey-inspired movements. No matter how people came to Garveyism, they all shared a deep admiration for Garvey, strove to advance the dignity and rights of Black people, and made meaningful interventions in their daily lives in the Midwest and beyond. In terms of social class composition, working-class people composed

FIGURE I.1. Marcus Garvey mural at AAA Party Store by Bennie White, 1993, E. Warren Avenue at Lenox Street, Detroit, Michigan. Library of Congress, Prints and Photographs Division, photograph by Camilo José Vergara.

the bulk of these formations. Given the formations' politics and member-ship, authorities in the United States and elsewhere often looked with alarm at Garvey and his followers for apparently challenging the global color line.

Chicago, Detroit, and Cleveland were major US cities and epicenters of the UNIA and the midwestern Garveyite front, as well as centers of globally con-nected Black communities established as early as the eighteenth century (see an artistic representation of Garvey in figure I.1). Garvey's ideas also influenced Midwest-linked formations, organizers, artists, journalists, students, spiritual leaders, workers, teachers, and world travelers in smaller cities like Omaha, Nebraska; Lansing; Gary; and Youngstown; in rural southwestern Ohio and Central Michigan; and in international locations like Montreal, Toronto, Gre-nada, Liberia, and Ghana. Chronicling the heartland's significance to the Black world provides empirical and theoretical models for writing new histories of Garveyism, the Midwest, and the African Diaspora.

Garveyism in the Diasporic Midwest is exemplified in the story of Louise Little. On one night in early 1925, a group of heavily armed, hooded, torch-bearing Ku Klux Klan members on horseback surrounded her home at 3448 Pinkney Street on the north side of Omaha. Brandishing rifles, the night rid-ers demanded to know the whereabouts of her African American husband,

Map 1.1. The US Midwest.

Reverend Earl Little. They shouted threats. They warned her that "the good Christian white people" of Omaha would no longer tolerate her husband's preaching about the "back to Africa" teachings of Marcus Garvey.[5] Born on the British Caribbean island colony of Grenada, Little had eventually made her way to Montreal and then to Omaha. In interwar Omaha and later in Lansing, she gained a reputation as an able UNIA grassroots organizer committed to advancing what historian Mary Rolinson has called "grassroots Garveyism," the organizational work performed by Garveyites at the local level to achieve Black self-determination everywhere.[6]

On that evening in early 1925, Louise, visibly pregnant, opened her front door and confronted the Klansmen. She told them that her husband was in Milwaukee, Wisconsin, preaching and that she was home alone with three young children. No one exchanged gunfire. After learning that he was not home, the Klansmen galloped away—but not before shattering every window of the house with their rifle butts and screaming racist threats. This incident prompted the incensed but determined Little family to move soon thereafter to Milwaukee, Wisconsin, the next stop in their midwestern journey and quest for the self-determination and dignity of Black people globally through the transnational UNIA.[7]

This harrowing story of Louise Little's brave standoff with white night riders is recounted in the opening of *The Autobiography of Malcolm X*, published in 1965. The unborn child whom she was carrying was her fourth child, Malcolm. Born in Omaha on May 19, 1925, he became best known to the world as Malcolm X. Charismatic and brilliant, he gained an international reputation as the preeminent US Black nationalist following the Second World War through his ministry in the Chicago-based Nation of Islam (NOI), an African American Muslim organization inspired in no small part by Garvey and led by Elijah Muhammad, who admired Garvey. On Malcolm's watch, the NOI emerged as the largest US Black nationalist organization by the early 1960s. His fiery denunciations of American Apartheid, rejection of civil rights liberalism, identification with anticolonial struggles in Africa and Asia, and demand for Black people to secure their human rights "by any means necessary" terrified white America and inspired African Americans and people of color around the world. Reared in a Garveyite family and coming of age in Michigan were foundational to his worldview.[8] The diasporic journeys and grassroots Garveyite organizing of Louise Little and her role in cultivating a Black radical sensibility in her globally renowned son speak to the unique and dynamic interplay between the Midwest and Garveyism in producing the world's largest Black movement and in making the US region a key fulcrum for global Black freedom.

The Diasporic Midwest

St. Clair Drake and Horace Cayton's *Black Metropolis: A Study of Negro Life in a Northern City* (1945) is a starting point for my conceptualization of midwestern Garveyism. Their landmark study examined race and urban life from the Depression through the opening years of the Second World War in "Bronzeville," the dynamic African American neighborhood—a "city within a city"—located on Chicago's South Side.[9] By the early twentieth century, Chicago had become the second largest city in the United States, the second biggest Black urban community on the planet, a national railroad hub, and a global center of heavy industries (steel, meatpacking, and other manufacturing). According to Drake and Cayton, the interplay in Chicago among migration, heavy industry, residential segregation, white anti-Black racial violence, global economic depression, world war, and African American agency explained the process through which Blacks in the Windy City developed a collective consciousness, came to enjoy unprecedented economic and political power, and forged a culturally vibrant, nationally influential community.[10]

While *Black Metropolis* was a community study of the South Side, Drake and Cayton also understood Black Chicago's significance to the global world. In the final paragraph of *Black Metropolis*, they looked cautiously toward the future world on the eve of the postwar period from the vantage point of Chicago:

> So it is really only "One World." The problems that arise on Bronzeville's Forty-seventh Street encircle the globe. But the people of Black Metropolis and of Midwest Metropolis do not feel that this relieves them from maintaining their own constant struggle for a complete democracy as the only way to attain the world we say we want to build. The people of Bronzeville and of Midwest Metropolis and of all their counterparts are intertwined and interdependent. What happens to one affects all. A blow struck for freedom in Bronzeville finds its echo in Chungking and Moscow, in Paris and Senegal. A victory for fascism in Midwest Metropolis will sound the knell of doom for the Common Man Everywhere.[11]

For Drake and Cayton, the struggles of African Americans on the South Side for racial equality were inextricably linked to the fates of hundreds of millions of people across Asia and Africa, who yearned to break the shackles of European colonial subjugation, and of working-class people everywhere as the world emerged from the most destructive war humans had ever witnessed. Framing the status of Black Chicagoans as a barometer for measuring democracy globally, Drake and Cayton contended that the front lines of the unfinished worldwide struggle between fascism and democracy passed directly through the South Side. They argued that the defeat for racial democracy and labor in Chicago would open the floodgates for human inequality and fascism globally. While Drake and Cayton identified Chicago as a global bellwether, they dismissed Garvey and Garveyite groups as a fad of years past among Black South Siders.[12] It is curious that this seminal text in African American urban studies downplayed Garveyism, despite the fact that Drake's father was a Barbados-born UNIA international organizer and that interwar Chicago was home to a massive UNIA local and a thriving midwestern Garveyite front. Drake's and Cayton's middle-class social location and leftist political sympathies may help explain their conclusions.[13]

Drawing from, extending, and inspired by Drake and Cayton's prophetic words and recognition of the South Side's global significance, my book explicates the history of what I call the "Diasporic Midwest." I use the term as an empirical and theoretical framework to extend the study of the African Diaspora by tracing the significance of the American heartland as a germinal hub of Black transnational political activism; to appreciate the possibilities, limitations, gendered contours, and paradoxes of Black nationalism, internationalism, and Black radicalism; to explore the contested and multiple meanings of freedom; and to chart genealogies of Black Power and Black movements through Garveyism. The Diasporic Midwest encompasses the American industrial and rural heartland, a region that includes states north of the Ohio River between the Appalachians and the Rocky Mountains, as a single yet complex and ever-changing geographic, political, historical, material, and discursive formation linked to Africa, the Black Diaspora, and the world.[14] Garveyism provided a powerful vehicle for Black midwesterners, both in urban and rural settings, to forge transnational linkages with the African-descended everywhere and to advance worldwide Black liberation.

Although I use the term "Diasporic Midwest," I am conscious that my subjects neither used the term "diaspora" to describe their social and geographic locations nor in many cases consciously self-identified as midwesterners. Black communities in the geographic region now called the Midwest were from their very beginning connected to the larger African world through migration, trade, politics, culture, and, above all, to what I call the experience of "the dialectic of opportunity and oppression." This dialectic constituted the key distinguishing feature of Black life in the Midwest. For African Americans, the US heartland from the early nineteenth century into the twentieth century came to hold real and symbolic meaning as a land of unparalleled opportunity and freedom, distinct from the racial oppression Blacks faced under slavery and Jim Crow in the South. Historian Joe William Trotter Jr. explores this African American belief in his study of nineteenth- through mid-twentieth-century Black urban life in the Ohio River Valley. The Ohio River constituted the dividing line between slavery and freedom prior to the Civil War and was the boundary between the Jim Crow South and the industrial urban heartland. Read through the lens of the African American prophetic tradition, the Ohio River became the River Jordan, the demarcation between southern slavery and the Promised Land of freedom in the North.[15] In the lead-up to the Civil War and long before twentieth-century Republican and Democratic election rivals, the Midwest was home to key battleground states determining the country's future. The region, known in the antebellum years as the "Old Northwest" and "Great West," was the site of protracted and sometimes deadly struggles for and against slavery. African Americans in heartland cities and rural areas struggled for democracy in the antebellum United States through their community-building and resistance. By the Civil War, the African American perception of the Midwest as a Promised Land was firmly established.

Black Americans continued to enjoy unprecedented economic and political opportunities in the Midwest through the twentieth century and onward. Their economic prosperity and political power were inextricably connected to the region's heavy industrial character. By the early 1900s, the Midwest emerged as the site of the world's most advanced industrial manufacturing. The automobile, steel, rubber, and meatpacking industries made Chicago, Detroit, Cleveland, St. Louis, Pittsburgh, Akron, Gary, and Youngstown the envy of the world, symbols of American prosperity, ingenuity, and opportunity, and a key driver of global economic growth (see figure I.2). By 1920, Chicago, Detroit, and Cleveland ranked as the second, fourth, and fifth largest US cities, respectively. The bulk of the six million African Americans who migrated from the South to the North from 1915 to 1970 came in search of better lives. This new world of mass production, urbanization, and consumer capitalism, together with the Depression, world wars, and decolonization, radicalized and transformed the lives of Blacks in the Midwest who hailed from the region or who migrated there from the Jim Crow South, the Caribbean, and Africa.[16] Blacks in the US heartland enjoyed political rights they could find nowhere else. Unlike in the Jim Crow South and colonial worlds, Black midwesterners could vote and exercise real political power. They earned incomes higher than their counterparts anywhere else. These cities were centers of militant Black labor organizing.[17] Black midwesterners lived in a region that was home to some of the richest biomes and most extensive waterway networks on the planet.[18] They also resided in a region that for centuries was a contested geographic and geopolitical space between Indigenous people and French, Spanish, British, and US continental empires.[19]

At the very same time African Americans found unprecedented opportunities in the Midwest, they lived in a region fraught with virulent racial oppression that rendered them second-class citizens as a racialized minority and subject to persistent state and extralegal violence.[20] The racially hostile heartland was foundational to making the young US republic a white settler continental empire and an emergent center of global racial capitalism. Beginning in the nineteenth century, the Midwest set a national precedent for state-sanctioned and

FIGURE I.2. Depiction of the Ford River Rouge factory in Detroit by the Mexican revolutionary artist and activist Diego Rivera. Diego M. Rivera, Detroit Industry Murals, 1932–1933, frescoes; Detroit Institute of Arts, gift of Edsel B. Ford, 33.10.

extralegal racial discrimination and terror against African Americans, Native Americans, and other people of color.[21] In the antebellum years, the heartland was home to white vigilantes and lynch mobs who roamed the countryside and scoured cities in order to capture and return self-emancipated people to southern slavery and to extinguish Black people.[22] From the twentieth century onward, the Ku Klux Klan, US Nazis, and other right-wing white supremacist formations, the police, and everyday white women, men, and youth terrorized Black folk. In the factories, African American male industrial workers were the last hired and first fired. They experienced super-exploitation and worked the

Map 1.2. The Great Lakes Region.

dirtiest jobs.[23] African American female wage earners in the heartland faced their own distinct challenges. Like elsewhere across the United States and beyond, the bulk of Black midwestern female wage earners toiled as domestic laborers in white people's homes, under the constant threat of sexual assault and verbal abuse.[24] Ideologically, African American midwesterners confronted a prevailing white supremacist discourse in the heartland that framed the region in contradistinction to the US South. This discourse understood the South as an economically backward, politically regressive land of slavery, Jim Crow, and racial terror. Additionally, the dominant midwestern racial discourse framed the heartland as a racially liberal land of limitless opportunity and democratic meritocracy, shrouding the region's deep-seated structural racism and violence.[25] The racist realities of the Midwest were not lost on its Black denizens. The legendary civil rights icon Rosa Parks, who fled in 1957 to Detroit from Montgomery, Alabama, and whose grandfather was a staunch Garveyite, disparaged the Motor City as "the Northern promised land that wasn't" because of its racial terror, residential segregation, and misery for African Americans.[26]

Another unique feature of African American midwestern life was the ability of Black women and men to build long-lasting, grassroots political, cultural, religious, and commercial institutions committed to advancing racial autonomy, race pride, and global Black freedom. The "institution-building impulse in the Midwest" was inextricably connected to the Black midwestern experience of the dialectic of opportunity and oppression.[27] A large portion of Black men in the heartland who joined Garvey-inspired formations worked in heavy industries. Most wage-earning heartland Black women in the UNIA and the midwestern Garveyite front, like elsewhere, toiled backbreaking hours cleaning white women's kitchens. However, a small but significant number of Black midwestern women in the UNIA and the like found employment through these organizations and in African American–owned businesses, providing them with some economic independence from white people and Black men.[28] The unmatched economic and political power of Blacks in the heartland provided them with the unique ability to support the local and transnational work of the UNIA and formations it inspired and to build long-lasting institutions.[29] Taken together, the dialectic of opportunity and oppression, the impulse of institution-building, and the agency of Black midwesterners positioned the region as a center of global struggles for the rights, dignity, and respect of Black people everywhere through the UNIA and neo-Garveyite formations. It is this dynamic but untold story that this book explores.

Interventions: Why the Diasporic Midwest Matters

The Second Battle for Africa makes several interventions in the fields of African American history, African American studies, US midwestern history, women and gender studies, African Diaspora studies, and global history. The Midwest has been critical for centuries to the making of US life, African American history, and Global Africa. From the twentieth century onward, Black movements influenced by Garvey have been central to this ongoing history. These assertions may come as a surprise to some readers, given popular and even scholarly perceptions of the Midwest as "flyover country," a lily-white, provincial, aesthetically unpleasing backwater positioned between the US east and west coasts, and as the "Rust Belt," a postindustrial wasteland.[30] For some observers, midwestern cities such as Cleveland, St. Louis, Chicago, Milwaukee, Youngstown, Gary, Flint (Michigan), and, above all, Detroit, with their shuttered and crumbling factories, population decline, vacant lots, high rates of poverty and gun violence, and abandoned homes, symbolize US industrial decline and the "urban crisis."[31]

Derisive representations of the Midwest as the "Rust Belt" and "flyover country," often tinged with racism, classism, sexism, and US coastal cultural biases, tell us more about the (mis)perceptions of the heartland than about the region's actual histories, complexities, and ongoing importance.[32] The Midwest for much of the twentieth century was to the United States what Silicon Valley became to the country by the millennium: a globally connected powerhouse and symbol of US technological innovation, capitalist accumulation, and modernity. For the first seventy years of the twentieth century, Chicago, Detroit, and Cleveland were among the top ten largest cities in the United States. They prompted millions of people to relocate to the Midwest. Despite facing cascading effects resulting from deindustrialization and other immense challenges beginning after the Second World War, early twenty-first-century midwestern urban and rural communities remain dynamic places and sites for innovative initiatives for building a new, more sustainable and democratic future world.[33]

Recent years have seen a renewed interest among scholars in midwestern life and history. Part of this interest is a response by historians to the neglect of the Midwest by the media, popular misconceptions of the region, and recent political and cultural events. Such events include the 2008 election of Barack Obama of Chicago, the first African American US president; the massive 2012 Chicago teachers' strike led by African American teacher Karen Lewis; the 2014 Flint water crisis; Black Lives Matter protests in Ferguson, Missouri, in 2014 and 2015; the epic 2016 NBA championship victory of the LeBron James–led Cleveland Cavaliers; the Chicago Cubs' World Series title in 2016; the 2016 US presidential election in which Michigan and Wisconsin played a decisive role in securing Donald Trump's narrow electoral victory; the publication of J. D. Vance's *Hillbilly Elegy: A Memoir of a Family and Culture in Crisis* (2016); the unforgettable eight-hour funeral service in Detroit in 2016 for the legendary soul singer Aretha Franklin; unprecedented global protests in 2020 against police brutality and racism, triggered by the police murder of the unarmed African American man George Floyd in Minneapolis, Minnesota; and the 2020 US presidential race in which Wisconsin and Michigan once again proved pivotal to the election outcome.[34] These events, together with ongoing migrations, demographic shifts, and continuing deindustrialization, shone a spotlight on the region.

The founding of the Midwestern Historical Association (MHA) in 2014 by historian Jon Lauck of South Dakota marked a significant step in the revitalization of midwestern history as a major US academic field.[35] Recent publications of several paradigm-shifting regional studies of the Midwest have utilized interdisciplinary approaches from history; ethnic studies; African American studies; gender, women's, and trans* studies; Indigenous studies; environmental studies; and the paradigms of empire, racial capitalism, settler colonialism, whiteness, borderlands, and white supremacy. This work locates the region now understood as the Midwest within a global context, emphasizing the region's critical importance to Indigenous people and European colonialization of the Americas and to the making of US empire and the modern world.[36] Scholars are exploring the origins and meanings of the mythology of the Midwest as "the heartland."[37] This myth not only represents the Midwest as the "geographic center" of the United States.[38] The myth also depicts the region, with its apparent uniformly white, conservative, straight, rural, exceptional, Christian, and provincial character, as the "symbolic center" of post–Second World War US mythologies.[39]

The early 2020s witnessed the emergence of an innovative, multi- and interdisciplinary field that I call "Black midwestern studies." Interest among scholars in African American midwestern life and history is hardly new. What is distinguishing about Black midwestern studies is the way a group of young and established academics, independent scholars, filmmakers, poets, visual artists, and community organizers, many of whom are Black and proudly hail from the Midwest, see themselves as a collective building a new field of study about Black people in the North American middle across varied human geographies and time.[40] These thinkers knowingly and unknowingly stand on the shoulders of Drake and Cayton, who were more than eighty years ahead of the curve with their Black-Chicago-in-the-world perspective. My book, therefore, departs from where *Black Metropolis* left off in uncovering the Black Midwest's global importance through Garveyism.

At its core, *The Second Battle for Africa* obliterates denigrating myths of the region by appreciating the dynamic and complex history of midwestern Garveyism. From the vantage point of Black midwesterners and Garvey-inspired movements, these myths make no sense. The Midwest was never a straight, all-white, middle-class, politically conservative backwater. Instead, the region has been multiracial, cosmopolitan, and globally connected since its beginnings. The African-descended are an essential part of midwestern life. They have always actively pursued forging transnational political, cultural, and personal linkages between the region and the world. Through this work, Black people helped to position the heartland at the front lines in global struggles for democracy and human freedom.

Examining Garveyism in the Diasporic Midwest requires expanding the geographic, analytical, and temporal parameters of the study of Global Africa. In the field of African Diaspora studies today, it is practically a truism to say that migration, mobility, and the circulation and exchange of ideas, commodities, culture, and people, especially through the Middle Passage and voluntary oceanic seafaring and crossings, have come to be understood as critical components of diaspora-making in the modern era. The Middle Passage has come to represent the site of rupture, no return, injury, and transformation.[41] Voluntary oceanic crossings by Blacks during and after slavery, especially by bourgeois or radical (male) spokespersons and intellectuals who enjoyed some degree of economic, political, social, or global status, have been understood as journeys toward self-discovery and freedom.[42] Countless scholars have looked at these phenomena in the Atlantic, Pacific, Indian, and Caribbean basins.[43] Through these studies, we have come to appreciate New York, London, the Caribbean, Charleston and the South Carolina Low Country, Accra, Cartagena, the Chesapeake, Algiers, New Orleans, Cape Town, Dar es Salaam, Montreal, Veracruz, Paris, Dakar, Salvador, Hawai'i, and Rio de Janeiro as important destinations and sites of diaspora-making, exchange, resistance, and community formation.[44] Yet the focus on the Middle Passage and oceanic mobility begs the following questions: Where do the Midwest and other geographic regions located in the middle of continents fit into the worldwide African Diaspora? Why and how have diasporic communities and subjectivities taken different shape in the South Side of Chicago, Gary, and rural southwestern Ohio than in Kingston, São Paulo, and the Futa Toro? Why have regions like the US heartland been seemingly written out of African Diaspora narratives? How does the history of Garveyism and the African world look different when we center the Midwest's distinct contributions to Global Africa and to Garvey-inspired movements?

The Middle Passage and oceanic seafaring are clearly not the perquisites for diaspora-making, and New York and the Atlantic littoral need not be the geographic and analytical foci of the African Diaspora. Instead, living nominally free in the North American middle, one of the world's most prosperous and oppressive places for Blacks, and residing in locales home to several of the world's biggest heavy industries were powerful and distinct forces in diaspora-making. The neglect of the Midwest (and countless other places around the world) in

African Diaspora studies inadvertently frames sites such as Harlem and the Atlantic and Caribbean basins as the standard-bearers of diaspora-making. Cities such as Chicago, Detroit, Cleveland, St. Louis, Lansing, and Gary, located in the North American middle, became, beginning in the late eighteenth century, important destinations for Black people and engines for globally impactful movements. To be clear, slavery was an essential feature of early midwestern Black life. Heartland Garveyites traveled the world. However, the overwhelming bulk of African-descended people who came to the Midwest arrived neither through the Middle Passage nor as oceanic travelers. Most African Americans who settled in the Midwest were poor and working-class people from the South. They came to the North American middle voluntarily in search of a better life. These first Black newcomers made their way to the region by foot, ferried across and traveled down the Ohio River and other midwestern rivers, and took passage on ships on the massive freshwater inland seas that are the Great Lakes. Later, they arrived by train, bus, automobile, and airplane.[45]

The Black midwestern experience of the dialectic of opportunity and oppression fueled this process. In the antebellum years, the dream of escaping southern slavery and living in one of the fastest-growing economic regions brought tens of thousands of Blacks to the Great West. In the twentieth century, living free of Jim Crow and finding a better life through the region's factories or entrepreneurialism did the same. The Diasporic Midwest charges scholars of the African Diaspora to widen their frames of reference and consider what different objects and sites of study offer with regards to diasporic dynamics: its peoples, its cultures, its politics, and its migrations that continue to move in ways that provide invaluable insights and knowledges about Global Africa. From the standpoint of the Diasporic Midwest, Harlem, New Orleans, London, Accra, and Salvador are neither the exemplars of diaspora nor the pinnacles of Blackness. These locales are important. But they are not the alpha and the omega of the African world. For these reasons, the Diasporic Midwest should be useful for scholars who study more commonly looked at sites across the African world to question their own parochialisms and to appreciate the particularities of the sites they research. As historian Minkah Makalani argues, scholars of the African Diaspora must always pay careful attention to locality, temporality, space, and place to the making of diasporic communities and subjectivities.[46] Telling the story of the Diasporic Midwest through Garveyism, then, is useful for expanding canonical narratives about the African Diaspora and for liberating the field from traditional geographic, temporal, gender, national, and class confines.

My book moves the Midwest to the center of analysis in what a new generation of Garvey scholars have called "global Garveyism."[47] Coined by historians Ronald J. Stephens and Adam Ewing, global Garveyism is a framework for looking in new ways and for asking new questions about the history, gender, class, and political contours, geographies, chronologies, and global breadth of Garveyism. Extending and recasting work by pioneering Garvey scholars, Stephens and Ewing credit Garveyites for forging "the largest mass movement in the history of the African Diaspora."[48] In a break from many previous scholars' singular focus on Garvey, Stephens and Ewing contend that Garveyism was far bigger than Garvey and the UNIA. Global Garveyism embodied the revolutionary consciousness and aspirations of the Black masses, rooted in what Black Studies scholar Cedric Robinson called the "Black Radical Tradition" in *Black Marxism: The Making of the Black Radical Tradition* (1983).[49] Stephens and Ewing contend that Garveyism "embodied, at its root, a revolt against the West" that was forged through the struggles of African people against slavery, colonialism, and global white supremacy and for a liberated future Black world through a free Africa.[50] From this perspective, "the history of Garveyism is thus to glimpse something much bigger and much more complex than Garveyism itself: black politics in the making."[51] In addition, the new generation of scholars categorically reject the denouement narrative about Garveyism, a claim that framed Garvey, Garveyism, and the UNIA as fads that ceased to be significant after Garvey's deportation from the United States in 1927 and death in 1940.[52] Recent Garvey scholarship emphasizes how Garvey's legacy lived on across the world long after his departure from the United States, and it passed through a dazzling array of sites—new Black religions, trade unions, leftist formations, the Rastafari, mainstream electoral politics, the NOI, and anticolonial movements. Given its origins, global reach, and enduring mass appeal, "Garveyism concurrently was a window on the past, present, and future of black struggles," observes historian Michael O. West.[53] For these reasons, Garveyism must be understood as critical to the history of pan-Africanism, Black nationalism, Black radicalism, Black internationalism, and worldmaking.[54]

New scholarship on Garvey, Black internationalism, and Black radicalism has opened exciting new areas of inquiry about Black people around the world. However, much work remains to be done. There is a tendency among some scholars to categorically frame Black movements as left-wing projects committed to socialism, secularism, interracialism, and progressive gender politics; to focus on elite Black internationalists of the Atlantic world; and to conceptualize Black internationalism as a byproduct of the global communist left.[55] These conclusions often collapse ideological distinctions among Black internationalists; overlook geographic sites beyond the Atlantic rim where Black internationalism emerged; ignore Garvey; and fail to notice what historians

Benjamin Talton and Monique Bedasse have identified as the "messiness" of Black internationalism—that is, the ways African-descended rulers and people around the world have sometimes exploited and "facilitated the suffering" of Black people and allied themselves with the interests of imperial powers through the guise of ostensibly promoting pan-Africanism and Black radicalism.[56]

Garveyism was the most potent political, cultural, and social force in the twentieth-century Black world. The only real competitor in this regard is the Black Power movement of the 1960s and 1970s, which in multiple ways, in multiple parts of the world, built on Garveyite foundations. The significance of Garveyism lies not so much in the life of Garvey and the organizational life of UNIA and its derivatives. Rather, the power of Garveyism rested in its ability to inspire the African-descended masses to resist dehumanization and oppression and to imagine that another world was possible. Garveyism, perhaps like no other phenomenon, elucidates the brilliance, resilience, creativity, beauty, paradoxes, and complexities of Black people and Black freedom struggles. Arguably, and quiet as it has been kept, no region in the world provides better insight into the power, possibilities, limitations, and legacies of Garveyism, as well as into state responses to Garveyites, than the Diasporic Midwest.

Midwestern Garveyism provides important insights into the complex place of Garveyism within the Black Radical Tradition, the history of Black internationalism, and the contested meaning of freedom among the African-descended. In Garvey's lifetime, countless Blacks affiliated with the Communist Party and other leftist formations had denounced him as a bourgeois imperialist after his rightward political turn, beginning in the early 1920s. From his standpoint, white communists duped Black leftists and used them to advance their own pro-Soviet conspiratorial interests at the expense of Black people. Subsequently, Garvey became staunchly anticommunist.[57]

Among some contemporary scholars, Garvey occupies a curious position in relation to the Black Radical Tradition. Garvey receives only brief attention in Robinson's *Black Marxism* despite the importance of Garvey and the UNIA in propelling Black radicalism from the 1920s onward. His absence in *Black Marxism* speaks to one of the book's greatest ironies. Robinson posits the Black Radical Tradition and Marxism as two discrete revolutionary traditions and understands Marxism, despite its universalist claims, as "a Western construction—a conceptualization of human affairs and historical experiences of European peoples mediated, in turn, through their civilization, their social orders, and their cultures."[58] However, the three key biographical subjects of *Black Marxism*—W. E. B. Du Bois, C. L. R. James, and Richard Wright—were intimately tied to Marxism even as they revised it or broke from the communist left. My intention here is not to downplay the importance of the Black left to Black and global twentieth-century histories. Communist-affiliated Black formations were homes to trailblazing revolutionary Black activist-intellectuals such as Du Bois, Paul and Eslanda Robeson, Claudia Jones, C. L. R. James, Louise Thompson Patterson, and Esther Cooper Jackson, all of whom were some of the tallest trees in our forest. However, it is undeniable that exponentially more African-descended people joined the UNIA and its derivatives than ever enlisted in Black formations associated or friendly with the US Communist Party. So, when we think about Black radicalism, we cannot overlook Garvey, the UNIA, and its offshoots.

Garveyism's complex location in the Black Radical Tradition can be best understood by grounding the former within the long history of Black nationalism. Black nationalism represents a powerful oppositional ideology originating in the eighteenth century as a response of African-descended people in the Americas to enslavement and the ideals of white supremacy. At its core, Black nationalism understands African Americans as a nation within a nation and the African-descended worldwide as one people, linked by the concept of racial unity, entitled to self-determination.[59] Garveyism was inextricably connected to what historian Wilson Jeremiah Moses calls "classical black nationalism," an ideology that peaked in the 1850s and again in the 1920s in response to Garvey. A key feature of classical Black nationalism was the desire to establish an economically and militarily powerful Black nation-state or empire.[60] "Civilizationism" constituted another significant component of classical Black nationalism. Informed by prevailing western beliefs of the time—the superiority of Christianity, biological understandings of race, the virtues of republicanism, and benefits of capitalism—classical Black nationalists believed that New World Blacks possessed the right to civilize and modernize allegedly backward African Indigenes.[61] From this perspective emerged what African American religion scholar Sylvester Johnson has termed "Black settler colonialism." He describes Black settler colonialism as an important political and theological idea articulated before the Civil War by free African Americans who called for self-determination among Blacks in the antebellum United States.[62] Black settler colonialists saw themselves as key agents of African redemption, "an overarching divine plan to bring the race from heathen backwardness to modern civility through Christian domination."[63] Leading nineteenth-century and early twentieth-century Black thinkers on both sides of the Atlantic to varying degrees embraced civilizationism—Martin R. Delany, Frederick Douglass, Edward Wilmot Blyden, Alexander Crummell, Henry McNeal Turner, Booker T. Washington, Mary Church Terrell, Ida B. Wells, W. E. B. Du Bois, J. E. and

Adelaide Casely Hayford, and John Langalibalele Dube—many of whom influenced Garvey.[64] Classical Black nationalism was gendered to the core. Literary scholar Michelle Stephens asserts that Garvey's global vision "was revolutionary and democratic in its imagination of a free, self-governing black proletariat."[65] Still, despite its working-class character, Garveyism "was imperial in its attachment to the gendered hierarchies and patriarchal logic of racial nationalism and limited in its fetishistic use of race thinking as the philosophy undergirding a masculine vision of a multinational and multiracial self-government."[66]

Liberia was key to Black settler colonial schemes from the early nineteenth century onward, including those of Garvey and many of his disciples. New World Black settlers first arrived in 1822 in the West African nation that became the Republic of Liberia. The American Colonization Society (ACS), founded in Washington, DC, in 1816, was critical in financing and organizing Liberian colonization. Composed predominantly of slaveholders, US congresspersons, and prominent white citizens, the ACS viewed free Blacks as an existential threat and believed that colonization was essential for protecting the young white settler republic. The ACS worked with free African Americans in promoting Liberian colonization. While white supremacists backed Liberia, the dream of returning to Africa originated from African Americans themselves who desired to live in a haven from racial oppression. In 1847, Liberia declared independence, making it the second Black republic in the world and the first republic on the African continent, with the motto "The Love of Liberty Brought Us Here." Liberia sparked enormous debate among African Americans.[67] Despite this contention and imposing obstacles, more than sixteen thousand Black Americans resettled in the West African republic during the nineteenth century.[68] Once there, they came to be known as "Americo-Liberians." They forged a nation that became both a symbol of freedom to countless New World Blacks and a settler society predicated on wanton violence against African Indigenes.[69] The settler colonial projects pursued by New World Blacks on the continent, in the view of historian Tunde Adeleke, shared much in common with European imperialists by stripping continental Africans of their sovereignty: "Europeans and black American nationalists constituted two rival groups of imperialists, of unequal force, who converged on Africa in the second half of the nineteenth century."[70] Black settler colonialism and civilizationism were not the exclusive domain of Garveyites. African-descended people in the church, women's clubs, civil rights organizations, and the left upheld notions of western superiority over continental Africans deep into the twentieth century.[71] However, Black nationalists were at the forefront in advancing Black settler colonialism.

The global liberatory vision proffered by midwestern Garveyites and Black nationalists elsewhere provides important insight into what I call "Black diasporic right radicalism," which describes a classical Black nationalist–informed tendency within the Black Radical Tradition, upheld to varying degrees by Black nationalists following Garvey's rightward political turn in the early 1920s. Black diasporic right radicalism emerged as a response to the social environment that Black nationalists encountered, and as leftist forces that were committed to socialism, trade unionism, multiracial internationalism, secularism, decolonization, African sovereignty, and in some cases women's rights gained momentum across the interwar African world. Garveyites' outlook was diasporic and radical, given they were at the front lines in repudiating European colonialism, Jim Crow, peonage, lynching, white cultural hegemony, and other indignities and in calling for the full freedom of Black people globally.[72] Black nationalists understood perhaps better than anyone else white supremacy, slavery, colonialism, and racial oppression and terror as constituent parts of the modern world system, culture, and all dimensions of Black and human existence. The politics of some Black nationalists were right-wing because they embraced settler colonialism, civilizationism, heteropatriarchy, and capitalism as solutions to the problems facing Black people worldwide. Many Black diasporic right radicals upheld a virulent anticommunism. Their willing collaborations with white supremacists stand as the most distinguishing *and* controversial feature of Black diasporic right radicalism. Beginning in the nineteenth century, several Black nationalists collaborated with white supremacists—in many cases openly and unapologetically—in support of racial separation, African redemption, and Black freedom. This was the case with Marcus Garvey, Amy Jacques Garvey, Mittie Maude Lena Gordon, James R. Stewart, Elijah Muhammad, and Malcolm X. Most notably, Black nationalist leader Mittie Maude Lena Gordon of Chicago worked for Liberian colonization for years with US senator Theodore Bilbo of Mississippi, a fierce proponent of segregation, and with leading white supremacist intellectual Earnest Sevier Cox of Virginia. Black nationalists' embrace of capitalism, empire, civilizationism, heteropatriarchy, and biological understandings of race explain why and how Black diasporic right radicals and white supremacists found common ground.[73]

From a contemporary standpoint, Black settler colonialism and Black diasporic right radicals might seem conservative if not outright reactionary. In many ways they were. At the same time, it should be remembered that in the context of the late nineteenth century and early twentieth century, when European colonialism was at its height, Black settler colonialism challenged global white supremacy. Black settler colonialists in theory but also often in practice recognized the humanity of African people and deplored the brutality of European colonial subjugation of Africa. Through calling for African redemption, Garveyites and other Black settler colonialists contested European colonialism and demanded Black freedom. This explains why Garveyism flourished across the African continent and electrified the African masses.[74]

Even more, the working-class composition, program, and global vision of the UNIA and its offshoots fundamentally challenged the gendered racial capitalist global order. This fact was not lost on US white authorities—or on European colonial officials in Africa and the Caribbean.[75] In the United States, white rulers identified Black nationalists, even those who collaborated with white supremacists, as the most significant African American domestic security threat during much of the twentieth century.[76] Federal, state, and local state actors targeted, harassed, punished, incarcerated, and killed Black nationalists to a greater extent than their leftist and civil rights counterparts. Marcus Garvey's deportation is but one example. The Midwest was ground zero for state repression against Black nationalists. This was apparent through Louise Little's incapacitation in a Michigan-operated psychiatric hospital; the incarceration of Mittie Maude Lena Gordon for her alleged pro-Japanese sentiments during the Second World War; Elijah Muhammad and scores of his midwestern Muslim followers being sent to federal prison in the 1940s for defying the US military draft; and the institutionalization of the Cleveland Moorish Science spiritual leader Ahmad El in 1954 in an Ohio mental health state hospital for his racial defiance.

Another way to understand Garvey's centrality to the Black Radical Tradition is to acknowledge the importance of him and UNIA-inspired movements to the making of individuals readily seen today as key figures in Black radicalism who received either passing or no attention in *Black Marxism*—Malcolm X, Claudia Jones, Kwame Nkrumah, Queen Mother Audley and Eloise Moore, Don Freeman, Muhammad Ahmad, Dara Abubakari, General Baker, Amos Sawyer, Nnamdi Azikiwe, Kimathi Mohammed, and Louise Little. These figures, many of whom were midwesterners and who embraced socialism, credited Garvey and neo-Garveyite movements for sparking their political awakenings. Several of them readily acknowledged the importance of Garvey to shaping their politics through their entire lives. In other words, many Black leftists and revolutionary nationalists did not grow out of and dispense with Garveyism as they matured politically and adopted anticapitalist positions. They continued to credit Garvey for inspiration, demonstrating how Black leftists and revolutionary nationalists often found a way to make two seemingly opposite Black politics coexist. Their embrace of Garvey also speaks to one of the most enduring strengths of Garveyism: its ideological malleability. Garveyism seemingly provided disparate groups of Black thinkers, workers, organizers, students, artists, religious followers, and everyday women, men, and youth from around the world and across the political spectrum with a common political vocabulary and reference point.[77] Many of his disciples neither blindly accepted nor embraced all his beliefs. Like Garvey, many Black nationalists upheld incompatible ideas.

I am not suggesting that we collapse ideological distinctions among Blacks in Garvey-inspired and leftist formations or overlook the paradoxes and limitations of Garveyism—or for the Black left for that matter. But we must appreciate how political labels and ideological categories, such as radical, liberal, Garveyite, conservative, nationalist, Marxist, and socialist, among the African-descended have never been neat and tidy.[78] The exigencies and uncertainties of Black life have always required ideological flexibility and creativity, as well as political pragmatism and compromise, among the African-descended. For these reasons, scholars, especially those sympathetic with the Black left, should not dismiss Black nationalist movements as ephemeral, bourgeois, or reactionary. We need to understand that the Black left was not the only site where critical conversations about and political actions against racism, capitalism, imperialism, and, to varying degrees, heteropatriarchy took place. These discussions also occurred within Garvey-inspired movements from the 1920s onward, although often through a different political lexicon and from different social locations from their leftist counterparts.[79]

While some Garveyites embraced Black diasporic right radicalism, others never practiced it or abandoned it for revolutionary nationalist and leftist formulations of Black radicalism. Malcolm's political journey is a case in point. His associations with early Black Power militants in Detroit and global travels helped him to rethink the narrow racial nationalism of the Nation of Islam and to adopt a revolutionary nationalism near the end of his life. The political journeys of Malcolm and other midwestern Black nationalists provide keen insight into the processes through which African-descended militants moved beyond Black diasporic right radicalism and rejected capitalism, sexism, white supremacy, and empire.

In addition, the work and visibility of midwestern Garveyites in relation to Liberia through the twentieth century and onward counter the prevailing scholarly narratives that downplay or ignore the West African republic's key place in Black internationalism.[80] Today, Haiti, the world's first Black republic, garners significantly more attention from scholars interested in nineteenth-century Black internationalism than Liberia.[81] For the twentieth century, Ghana, Tanzania, and Algeria, among other places, far eclipse Liberia in studies of Black internationalism.[82] The invisibility of Liberia is curious, given that the West African republic electrified the Black global political imagination.[83] How do we explain why the world's second Black republic has been largely forgotten in Black internationalism? Part of this answer lies with the unease among scholars about Liberia's origins as a settler nation linked with the racist ACS; the nation's "lack of a revolutionary pedigree . . . like Haiti"; the ruthless treatment of Indigenes by Americo-Liberians; Liberia's apparent cozy diplomatic relationship with the United States, especially during the era of African decolonization; and decades of civil strife and horrific humanitarian suffering following the 1980 military coup.[84] A romantic aura does not surround Liberia as it does Haiti, Ghana, Algeria, and Tanzania. Put another way, Liberia is not sexy to many scholars of Black internationalism.[85] However, scholars have much to learn from Liberia's rich and complicated past. Midwestern Garveyites show us how. Contrary to (mis)perceptions of Liberia as a backward staid nation marginal to global decolonization, African liberation, and Black Power of the 1960s and 1970s, I show the reverse to be true. Take, for example, the life and work of a Chicago UNIA leader, Rev. Clarence W. Harding Jr., in Liberia during the Black Power era. He organized the Marcus Garvey Memorial Institute, a freedom and secondary education school in Monrovia, and worked closely with the Movement for Justice in Africa (MOJA), a Marxist, pan-African organization. Harding and MOJA played a crucial role in making Liberia a hotbed of Black Power, African liberation, and radical Black internationalism. Acknowledging and examining the possibilities, complexities, and paradoxes of Liberia so evident in the work of midwestern Garveyites and Black settler colonialists is precisely what scholars of Black radicalism and internationalism need to pursue when looking at sites around the African world.

The Diasporic Midwest was a key site where Garvey's ideas lived on long after his death. My extended history of the UNIA and its offshoots in the Diasporic Midwest attests to the ways that Black people on both sides of the Atlantic and beyond were critical to refashioning Garveyism to preserve its relevance in a world transformed by global depression, world war, decolonization, and Black Power. I also show how the midwestern Garveyite front gradually emerged, beginning in the 1930s, as the most important site in preserving and advancing Garvey's legacy. Some midwestern Garveyite front groups counted only a handful of members and were ephemeral; others lasted for decades and touched the lives of millions of people. UNIA officials during and long after Garvey's passing sometimes perceived rival groups as imposters and apostates who threatened the UNIA and the well-being of Black people everywhere. For this reason, Garvey and some of his lieutenants often moved quickly to denounce and quash their apparent rivals. Yet more times than naught, grassroots Garveyites and even prominent UNIA leaders in the heartland decided to work with and in some cases defect to new Black formations and sometimes multiracial ones because they saw them as the inheritors of and the best vehicles for advancing Garveyism during new historical conjunctures.

I adopt an intersectional and queer of color framework that interrogates the connections among race, gender, sexualities, and class with midwestern Garveyism. I thereby shed new light on the ideological variance of diasporic feminist praxis; the intersections among race, gender, class, and sexualities in Black movements; and the construction of historical memory through the lives and globetrotting of heartland-linked women within global Garveyism. Existing work on Black internationalism often concentrates exclusively on male spokespersons, while scholarship on Garveyite women tends to look at globally prominent UNIA women based in the Atlantic basin. I shift the focus to the "community feminism" of UNIA female leaders linked to the Midwest: Louise Little, Bessie Bryce, Ethel Collins, Mittie Maude Lena Gordon, Elinor White Neely, Goldie Stewart, Christine Johnson, Betty Shabazz, Alice Windom, Georgina Thornton, Patricia ("Noni") Gee, Mary Mason, Cynthia Hamilton, and Sammitta Entsua. "Community feminism," coined by historian Ula Y. Taylor, describes a distinct Black feminist politics formulated by Garveyite women that rejected masculinist claims of women's intellectual inferiority and subordination to male leadership and argued instead that women were best suited for Black nation-building.[86] Little and most of her heartland-linked Garveyite sisters would not have called themselves "community feminists." What is certain is that they were keenly aware of the multiple oppressions they faced as African-descended women living in the United States and elsewhere. Heartland-linked Garveyite women focused considerable attention on empowering Black women.

Louise Little is especially important to my book. Given her long life, diasporic kinship and journeys, personal tragedies, and resilience, combined with her growing fame as the mother of Malcolm X, she is an anchor in my narrative history of Garveyism in the Diasporic Midwest. Despite her achievements and long life, history was not kind to her. Arguably, her defiance of the gender, racial, and class protocols of her day, together with the masculinist scholarly framings of Malcolm X and Black movements, helps explain her absence from the historical record. As the Guyanese-born writer Jan Carew emphasized, most accounts of Malcolm X ignore his Grenadian mother's brilliance and extraordinary life. Instead, they frame her as a tragic figure who succumbed to mental illness and whose story disappears after her institutionalization.[87] This portrayal is most apparent in *The Autobiography of Malcolm X*, which frames Little as passive and apolitical; it focuses exclusively on her alleged physically abusive marriage, her struggles with mental illness following the gruesome murder of Earl Little at the hands of a lynch mob, and the hardships of a widowed mother, all of which contributed to her institutionalization.[88] The marginality of women in the *Autobiography* can be explained in part by the patriarchal gender politics embraced by Malcolm X and Alex Haley, the writer of the memoir, at the time they conducted the interviews that served as the basis for the text. Malcolm was still in the staunchly patriarchal Nation of Islam. Haley was a conservative Black Republican who had little interest in Black nationalism and pan-Africanism, and he subscribed to traditional gender politics. Similarly, Manning Marable's Pulitzer Prize–winning biography *Malcolm X: A Life of Reinvention* minimizes Louise Little's active role in cultivating Malcolm's political consciousness.[89] Minimizing her importance to Malcolm is not limited to scholars. Despite growing scholarly and popular interest in her life, many Grenadians and Black people around the world remain unaware of Louise's remarkable life and that she was the mother of the internationally renowned US Black nationalist of the 1960s.[90]

Little and other Midwest-based Garveyite women have been erased from historical narratives about Black nationalism, internationalism, and radicalism. Michel-Rolph Trouillot has argued that historical archives and narratives of the past are mediated through struggles for power.[91] Similarly, diasporic feminist scholar Carole Boyce Davies has shown us how some white cold warriors and some Black radical male thinkers wrote Black communist theorist and leader Claudia Jones out of history due to her positionality as a "black radical female subject." Boyce Davies uses the term "black radical female subject" to describe the varied ways Jones defied the political, racial, class, and heteropatriarchal order during the height of the repressive Cold War era.[92]

Like Jones, Little and other heartland Black nationalist women often paid a terrible personal price from state actors for their organizing and lifeways. Recovering Little's story, then, is important not only because she was the mother of Malcolm X. Even more, her life provides a lens for interrogating the connections among memory, knowledge production, and power, as well as for countering prevailing narratives that (re)produce and normalize white supremacy, capitalism, empire, and heteropatriarchy. Given this perspective, her life and legacy demonstrate how gender shaped historical movements from within and how the distinct political and social landscape of the heartland informed the innovative ways women built the UNIA and midwestern Garveyite front and grappled with multiple oppressions within Black movements and society at large.

At the same time, Midwest-based Black nationalist women provide important insight into the underappreciated ideological complexities of diasporic feminist praxis and Black transnational politics. I refer to neither Little nor other Black nationalist women as "black radical female subjects," given the term's association with Jones and the communist left. Calling the African-descended in nationalist and leftist movements "black radical female subjects" would collapse important ideological differences despite some similarities among them. Most Garveyite and Black communist women hailed from working-class backgrounds and were migrants. They regularly encountered male chauvinism from their Black male colleagues and sexism from white men. Appreciating Black freedom in global and intersectional terms, Black nationalist and communist women alike looked to African-descended women as the catalyst for advancing the dignity and rights of Black people everywhere. Still, the politics and social worlds of Black nationalist and communist women were often very different. The former operated in formations committed to racial separatism and co-fraternity among the world's darker races, while the latter joined an international communist movement committed to Black-white solidarity and the Soviet Union. Many midwestern Garveyite women such as Mittie Maude Lena Gordon and Elinor White subscribed to Black diasporic right radicalism. Openly hostile to communism, they also rejected the queer lifeways practiced by many African American leftist women. Some Black leftist women spurned the staunch racial separatism and anticommunism of their Garveyite counterparts. The virulent anticommunism of some heartland Black nationalist women affirms the Black feminist theorist Joy James's observation that "Black women activists and feminists are not uniformly progressive."[93] Yet there were also Black nationalist women such as the NOI educator Christine Johnson of Chicago, Malcolm X ally and world traveler Alice Windom of St. Louis, and the Cleveland Black Power organizer Mary Mason who operated comfortably in multiple political spaces and saw no contradiction in upholding nationalist and leftist politics. Recognizing the ideological differences and complexities among Black female nationalists and leftists shows that "there is no 'master' narrative that frames the concerns of all black women."[94]

Rethinking the life and legacy of Malcolm X through the history of the Diasporic Midwest and Garveyism is my book's final intervention. I reassess his life in relation to Garveyism and the heartland through the *Autobiography* and Louise Little's role in cultivating his Black radical sensibility. Decades after its publication, the memoir, the best-known source about him, remains indispensable for understanding his life. The story also has come to be widely understood as definitive truth.[95] However, the memoir and the popular perception of it do not fully capture his life journey. As discussed, the memoir erases Louise Little's UNIA work and obscures her role in cultivating Malcolm's Black radicalism. The *Autobiography* also frames him as a directionless, self-hating, criminally minded, apolitical person prior to his incarceration in 1946 in a Massachusetts state prison for burglary and before his conversion to Islam in prison and rise to international prominence through the NOI.

The *Autobiography* tells a powerful story. However, the memoir seemingly tells us more about a re-created story that Malcolm X and Alex Haley crafted than about the former's historic life. For years, scholars have challenged the memoir's historical accuracy, speculated about Malcolm's reinvention of his life, and postulated about the impact of Haley's biases on the book.[96] Other work has called attention to the significance of Detroit and Lansing to shaping Malcolm's worldview and radicalism from his childhood years to his death.[97] As noted, scholars are also appreciating Louise Little's profound political influence on her son.

I build off the *Autobiography*, the vast scholarship on Malcolm, growing research on Louise Little, remembrances of him from family and associates, and his papers at the Schomburg Center for Research in Black Culture in Harlem and at the Charles H. Wright Museum of African American History in Detroit to explore the totality of his lived experiences.[98] His imprisonment, years of ministering and residing in New York, marriage to Betty Shabazz, and international travels were important in shaping his politics and subjectivity. However, growing up in a Garveyite family in the racially hostile heartland, maintaining lifelong connections to the region, and Garvey's ideas had an enduring impact on Malcolm's extraordinary and tragically short life. So, in some ways, his life was not exceptional. He shared much in common with other African-descended people and the Black formations in the Diasporic Midwest covered in this book.

Multisited Archives and Oral Histories as Method

This book uses multisited archives and oral history interviews as a historically informed, interdisciplinary, transnational, intersectional method for explicating the history of Garveyism in the Diasporic Midwest. Excavating this untold history is no easy task. There is neither a repository nor a scholarly institute anywhere dedicated to archiving transnational Black midwestern history or Garveyism in the heartland. Given this reality and following the indomitable Black scholar Gerald Horne's marching orders for scholars to take up "a transnational research agenda" for Black history, my book required me to construct a transnational archive of Garveyism in the Diasporic Midwest through original primary research conducted over ten years in nine countries—Canada, Ghana, Grenada, Jamaica, Liberia, South Africa, Trinidad and Tobago, the United

Kingdom, and the United States.[99] I trodded to these countries in part because my subject hailed, resided, or traveled to these nations and because they occupied an important place in global Garveyism. To reconstruct the heartland's significance to the African world, I referred to personal papers, UNIA and African American newspapers such as the *Chicago Defender* and Cleveland *Call and Post*, and mainstream newspapers; organizational records of the UNIA, its offshoots, and non-Garveyite Black formations; Robert A. Hill's magisterial *The Marcus Garvey and Universal Negro Improvement Association Papers*; oral history interviews; and government surveillance files.

Archival collections were an especially important source of information and discovery. For me, like other historians, archival research is often a time of joy and exhilaration. One especially exciting moment stands out. While reviewing the UNIA Records at the Stuart A. Rose Manuscript, Archives, and Rare Book Library at Emory University in Atlanta, Georgia, in 2013, I discovered a letter penned on April 10, 1957, by UNIA Detroit leader William Sherrill to Kwame Nkrumah, the founder of the West African state of Ghana. In the letter, Sherrill thanked Nkrumah for inviting him to attend Ghana's independence ceremonies in Accra on March 6, 1957, and for their private meeting in which both men discussed their admiration for Garvey.[100] I was ecstatic after reading the letter. It highlighted the transnational political linkages between Black midwesterners and their brethren on the continent and to the endurance of Garveyism long after Garvey's death that I sought to explicate in this book.

If archival research constituted a source of joy and discovery, the archive sometimes produced extremely unpleasant sensory and emotional experiences for me. This response was most evident when I spent several weeks reviewing the Theodore G. Bilbo Papers at the McCain Library and Archives at the University of Southern Mississippi in Hattiesburg, Mississippi, and the Earnest Sevier Cox Papers at the David M. Rubenstein Rare Book and Manuscript Library at Duke University in Durham, North Carolina. Combined, these immense collections contain thousands of pages of documents related to Garvey, the UNIA, Peace Movement of Ethiopia, and other mid-twentieth-century US Black nationalist formations. Simply put, the Bilbo and Cox papers are a treasure trove of information about Garvey, Garveyism, and Black nationalism.

The Bilbo and Cox papers, nonetheless, made me sick. I grew queasy as I sat for days in archival reading rooms combing through collections I came to call "the white supremacist heteropatriarchal archive in the history of Black nationalism." In these collections, records of the UNIA and midwestern Garveyite front colonizationist groups are interspersed among documents related to

Bilbo, Cox, prominent segregationists, the Ku Klux Klan, the US Nazi Party, racist white neighborhood protection associations in Chicago, and fanatical white supremacists, anticommunists, fascists, and antisemites from around the world. Additionally, these collections hold hundreds of letters by and between Marcus Garvey, Mittie Maude Lena Gordon, Earnest Cox, Theodore Bilbo, and others. They exchanged pleasantries and discussed their shared beliefs in racial purity and emigration; disgust for civil rights, interracialism, and communism; and heteropatriarchal ideas about the family. Garvey and his disciples probably never thought about their correspondences with Bilbo and Cox ending up one day in the same archival folders with documents from Klansmen and segregationists. However, they knew they were working with some of the most notorious US white supremacists of their day.

Through my review and serious contemplation of the Bilbo and Cox papers, I realized that they shed important insight into the white supremacist, heteropatriarchal archive in the history of Black nationalism and into what scholars have termed the "problem" and "politics of the archive."[101] Black nationalists played an important albeit subordinate role in disrupting and reinforcing white supremacist archival narratives produced by the Bilbo and Cox papers. Through my research in these collections, I came to realize that Black people too sometimes had a hand in shaping problematic archives and in producing knowledge that seemingly contributed to their oppression and to maintaining the global status quo. Reckoning with these uncomfortable truths provides additional insight into the complexities and paradoxes of my subjects, Garveyism, and Black movements, as well as into "Black archival practice."[102] Given these facts, I hope this book serves as a guide for constructing a history of Garveyism in the Diasporic Midwest through in part acknowledging some Black nationalists' involvement in forging problematic archives. I envision my critical reading of the archive as a tool for scholars to probe the multidimensions, possibilities, and limitations of archives and Black global liberatory politics.[103]

To fill the gaps of the archive, I turned to US, Ghanaian, British, and South African government records, with special emphasis on Federal Bureau of Investigation surveillance records. FBI files contain voluminous amounts of information about the UNIA and its offshoots and their individuals and organizational histories. However, these records, like the archive, are not without problems. FBI records are riddled with factual inaccuracies, often telling us more about the (mis)perceptions of and the responses by authorities to Black militancy than they do about the actual lives and struggles of my subjects. For these reasons, I draw heavily from the writings and speeches of my subjects. These sources provide useful insight into their activism and globetrotting, the organizational affairs of Garvey-influenced formations, and the twentieth-century world. However, their writings and speeches, like UNIA organizational records and other archival sources, often provide little deep insight into my subjects' inner lives. And none of my main subjects wrote memoirs except Malcolm X.

Oral history interviews are indispensable sources of information for this book and provide information absent from archives and other sources. Since 2012, I spent hundreds of hours conducting in-person interviews and speaking with more than one hundred subjects, aged eighteen to ninety plus, directly and indirectly linked to the UNIA and the midwestern Garveyite front. I also exchanged countless emails and text messages through WhatsApp and Face-book Messenger with subjects about the Diasporic Midwest, Garveyism, Black history, current events, and more topics than I can ever recall. My interviewees include Terance Wilson of Maydes, Grenada, the third cousin of Malcolm X and the world's premier expert on Langdon family history (the family name of Louise's people in the Caribbean, Canada, and Europe); Deborah Jones and the late Stephen Jones of Grand Rapids, Michigan, the grandchildren of Louise Little and the niece and nephew of Malcolm X, respectively; Ilyasah Shabazz, the third child of Malcolm X and Betty Shabazz; the late Amos Saw-yer, the former interim president of Liberia, mentored in Monrovia during the 1970s by the Chicago UNIA leader Reverend Clarence Harding; and (the late) Donna Cooper Hayford, the daughter of James and Goldie Stewart, who lived outside the Liberian capital. Through these interviews and conversations, my knowledge of the UNIA and the midwestern Garveyite front grew immeasur-ably and in unexpected ways. Interviews and conversations occurred in and at multiple venues on three continents: dining room and kitchen tables in New York, Cleveland, Dayton, Detroit, Woodland Park, Michigan, and Paynesville, Liberia; the homesite of Marcus Garvey in St. Ann's Bay, Jamaica; hotel lob-bies in the Washington, DC, area, Grand Rapids, and Accra; the grave site of C. L. R. James in Tunapuna, Trinidad; restaurants from Chicago to Cleveland to Kalamazoo to Montreal to London; a nursing home in Bedford Hills, Ohio; UNIA halls in Jamaica and Philadelphia; elementary schools in rural Grenada and Liberia; the Malcolm X Memorial Foundation in Omaha; the University of Liberia; the Beth Shalom B'nai Zaken Ethiopian Hebrew Congregation on Chicago's southwest side; the Liberian Ministry of Foreign Affairs in Mon-rovia; a Moorish Science corner storefront on the South Side of Chicago; a hillside in La Digue, Grenada; and the UNIA's Liberty Farm in Grand Bassa County, Liberia. Some interviews lasted fewer than thirty minutes. Several subjects I neither spoke to nor saw again after our conversations. But there were

FIGURE I.3. Deborah Jones and Ilyasah Shabazz, Jackson College, Jackson, Michigan, March 2018. Photo by the author.

several people whom I interviewed multiple times, sometimes in person and by phone, over a span of years and in multiple geographic locations, including in the United States, Grenada, and Liberia. Some subjects became not only indispensable sources of information but also good friends (see figures I.3 and I.4).

Becoming close with subjects sometimes posed a potential ethical conundrum for me. Given that trust and respect between the interviewer and subject are the bedrock of oral history reviews and that institutional review boards require ethical protocols when working with human subjects, I grappled with whether to disclose sensitive and personal information told to me. On more than a few occasions, subjects asked me to stop recording the conversation. I did. Others explicitly told me never to retell guarded information shared with me. Some of this information spoke to the paradoxes of Black movements and to the deepest secrets of women and men involved in Garveyite formations. Through these encounters and taking my subjects' dictates to heart, I developed an ethical approach and interpretative method for using sensitive information acquired from oral history interviews that I came to call the "politics of disclosure." The "politics of disclosure" recognizes the vulnerability of my subjects and strikes an ethical balance between sharing information gathered

FIGURE I.4. Terance Wilson, La Digue, Grenada, March 2015. Photo by the author.

from my subjects and protecting their privacy. Given this approach, I decided that fidelity to my subjects' wishes, securing confidential information, and adhering to ethical scholarly protocols superseded my own interests as a historian even when this information could have strengthened my book's arguments. To be clear, I do utilize some personal and sensitive information from oral history interviews. I discuss this information in the spirit in which my subjects shared it and in ways that are sensitive to their personhood and families. However, I neither draw from nor share information that subjects asked to keep confidential. Some things are not meant to be disclosed.

Midwestern Garveyites recognized public space as a site where racial oppression occurred and was (re)produced and consequently could be contested, reimagined, and transformed. For this reason, I look at parades, public rallies, street marches, and in some case pitched battles between Garveyites and authorities on the streets and in parks and courthouses of Chicago, Detroit, Cleveland, and other places across the heartland as sites of struggle for the "right to the city."[104] Additionally, I understand the Midwest as a geography of resistance where African Americans came to appreciate urban and rural landscapes of the heartland as spaces of potential freedom through Garveyism.[105]

Chapter Outline

The Second Battle for Africa is divided into eight chronologically arranged chapters. The first chapter explores the historical context in which the pre-twentieth-century Diasporic Midwest and Black nationalism took shape and prepared the ground for Garveyism. Chapter 2 discusses the global influence of the Midwest on the transnational UNIA during its heyday in the early 1920s, with special attention on Liberia, Louise Little, and the paradoxes of Garveyite collaborations with white supremacists that persisted for decades. The remaining chapters discuss the unfolding history and broadening impact of the heartland on global Garveyism after the Jamaican Black nationalist leader's deportation from the United States in 1927. Chapter 3 looks at evolving struggles Black midwesterners pursued for building a new world during the global Depression and rise of fascism in Europe in the 1930s through the UNIA and religious and colonizationist midwestern Garveyite front organizations. Chapter 4 probes the history of midwestern Garveyism during the Second World War, while chapter 5 looks at the emergent postwar US Black Freedom Movement and African decolonization in the 1950s through James and Goldie Stewart's repatriation to Liberia; Detroit UNIA leader William Sherrill's journey to Ghana's independence ceremony; Kwame Nkrumah's visit to Chicago; Louise Little's role in precipitating Malcolm's conversion to Islam; and the growth of the Nation of Islam into a national organization. Chapter 6 centers the Nation of Islam and Malcolm to keeping Garvey's ideas alive and to influencing pioneering heartland-linked early Black Power organizations. Chapter 7 surveys the unstudied local and global impact of midwestern Garveyites on the internationalist Black Power and Black Arts Movement from the mid-1960s through the 1970s. The concluding chapter discusses the enduring legacy of Garvey in the new millennium through US heartland–linked formations.

This book is not a comprehensive study of the global impact of the Diasporic Midwest through Garveyism. Such a project would require decades of additional research and multiple volumes. However, this book does represent a significant intervention—one that shifts and rethinks historical narratives that until now have shrouded the critical importance of the Midwest to the making of global Garveyism and to the African world from the nineteenth century onward. There is much we will never know about the work, subjectivities, globetrotting, and dreams of prominent and everyday Black women, men, and youth in the US heartland and beyond who came to love Garvey and looked to him and to themselves as inspirations for building a new world for the African-descended. To be sure, the complex history of Garveyism in the Diasporic Midwest provides theoretical and empirical models for extending the geographical scope of the African Diaspora; internationalizing African American midwestern history; appreciating the possibilities, limitations, and gendered contours of Black nationalism, internationalism, and radicalism; exploring the contested meaning of Black freedom; charting new genealogies of Black Power and Black movements from the nineteenth century to today; and imagining alternative Black futurities beyond the limits of what is considered possible.

1

"WE ARE A NATION WITHIN A NATION"

The Making of the Diasporic Midwest and Black Nationalism before the Twentieth Century

We are a nation within a nation. . . . We must go from our oppressors.
—MARTIN R. DELANY, *The Condition, Elevation, Emigration, and Destiny of the Colored People of the United States* (1852)

John Mercer Langston wanted out of America. He made this point abundantly clear during a vigorous debate about Liberian colonization at the Convention of the Colored Citizens of Ohio, convened in Ohio's state capital, Columbus, on January 10–13, 1849.[1] This gathering was part of the larger Colored Conventions movement, a series of Black political conventions held across North America from 1830 to 1893, which were attended by tens of thousands of African Americans committed to advancing the full freedom of Black people everywhere. Ideologically, these conventions served as generative sites for classical Black nationalism and laid the foundation for twentieth-century US Black nationalism, radicalism, and internationalism.[2]

On the second day of the Convention of the Colored Citizens of Ohio, the twenty-four-year-old Langston addressed the assembly. He was a student at the interracial Oberlin College in Oberlin, Ohio, and already a preeminent African American spokesperson of his day who during Reconstruction became the first Black person elected to the US House of Representatives from Virginia.

He was also the great-uncle of arguably the most important twentieth-century US poet: Langston Hughes.[3] From the convention floor in Columbus, Langston spoke favorably of emigration and objected to the proposed conference resolution opposed to colonization. Criticizing the resolution because "it goes against emigration," he declared: "I for one . . . am willing, dearly as I love my native land, (a land which will not protect me however,) to leave it, and go wherever I can be free." Articulating the struggle in masculinist terms, he called on African Americans to "act as men" and to recognize "the very fact of remaining in this country is humiliating, virtually acknowledging our inferiority to the white man." "We must have a nationality, before we can become anybody."[4] Appreciating Black American freedom in global and manly terms, and using the terms *colonization* and *emigration* interchangeably, Langston understood Black America as an emergent nation within a white racist, slaveholding republic and that quitting the United States was the only viable path for African American (manhood) rights and self-determination. He imagined Liberia as a haven for diasporan Blacks. Other conventioneers disagreed. Ultimately, the convention approved the resolution supporting colonization.[5]

The heated debate at the convention over whether African Americans ought to leave or stay in the United States and the gathering's pursuit of the "religious, political, and social elevation" of Black Americans illustrate how the mid-nineteenth-century Old Northwest, especially Ohio, was already a crucible for Black nationalism. From Columbus, conventioneers forged a globally informed, liberatory politics committed to self-determination, racial autonomy, social justice, community- and institution-building, African redemption, and global Black freedom.[6] This convention also illustrated in clear terms that antebellum US Black nationalist thought was neither settled nor without paradox. Nineteenth-century African Americans fiercely debated emigration and colonization.[7] Pre-twentieth-century Black nationalists in the Midwest and across the United States often embraced Black settler colonialism and civilizationism through claiming a right to return to Africa and to rule over African Indigenes in ways that challenged and reinforced European colonialism.

This chapter charts a genealogy of Black nationalism and a prehistory of global Garveyism for appreciating the making of the Diasporic Midwest as a global epicenter and crossroads of Black nationalism, internationalism, and radicalism from the colonial era to the first Great Migration. Key Black nationalist ideas, debates, issues, and strategies that animated, inspired, and divided twentieth-century Black midwestern movements had already been set into motion long before the UNIA took root in the Midwest and beyond. The dialectic of opportunity and oppression in the Midwest was critical to initiating these forces from the nineteenth century onward. Framing the early Midwest through both the dialectic of opportunity and oppression and a transnational lens rejects portrayals of the pre-twentieth-century US heartland as a bucolic land of meritocracy, racial liberalism, and democracy cloistered from global forces of history.[8]

African Americans found unique economic and political opportunities in the pre-twentieth-century Midwest to enjoy a degree of freedom and to build vibrant communities that they could find nowhere else. As the nineteenth century dawned, Blacks—free and enslaved—came to regard the Old Northwest in general and Ohio in particular as the first Promised Land. This belief was not unfounded. Midwestern states outlawed slavery and the region emerged as an economic powerhouse of the young republic. At the same time, antebellum and postbellum Black midwesterners confronted distinct and virulent forms of racial oppression and violence, with lasting implications for the region, United States, and the world. In response to a shifting local, regional, national, and global color line, Black midwesterners in a diverse array of cities (Cincinnati, Chicago, Detroit, Gary, Lansing, St. Louis, and Cleveland) and in rural areas forged thriving communities and lasting institutions committed to racial autonomy, dignity, and respect prior to the Great Migration. These pre-twentieth-century historical forces positioned the early Diasporic Midwest as a unique, fertile, and complex site for laying the groundwork for Garveyism.

The Pre-Columbian Midwest and Early African Encounters in the North American Middle

The geographic landscape where the Diasporic Midwest took shape and where Garveyism came to thrive was in part a byproduct of glacial activity during the most recent and ongoing geological period, the Quaternary, which began approximately 2.6 million years ago. Globally, this period saw extreme climatic fluctuations and ecological regime shifts. In repeated cycles lasting hundreds of thousands of years, continental ice sheets, up to two miles thick, flowed and receded from the Northwest Territories and Labrador in Canada across the Midwest, covering all or significant portions of Illinois, Wisconsin, Michigan, Iowa, Kansas, Minnesota, Ohio, and North Dakota. These immense glacial flows scoured the bedrock beneath them. As the glaciers melted and retreated approximately twelve thousand years ago, they deposited massive amounts of mineral-rich topsoil, and they released voluminous amounts of water, creating the current configurations of the Great Lakes, the largest freshwater system on the planet.[9] The glaciers helped shape the Mississippi River and its tributary, the Ohio River, the waterway that later became the main artery connecting the East Coast with the Midwest and North American interior.[10] After the last glaciation, temperatures rose across the region, transforming the biomes of the North American middle.[11] Prairies, rolling plains of grasslands, eventually came to dominate vast stretches of the North American middle from Alberta, Saskatchewan, and Manitoba southward through the Dakotas, Nebraska, Iowa, Kansas, and Oklahoma to southern Texas and northern Mexico and from western Indiana westward to the Rocky Mountain foothills. The plains contained some of the planet's most fertile soil.[12] No future midwestern city was better situated than Chicago, given the city's proximity to three of North America's most important biomes.[13] Similarly, the origins, growth, and histories of other midwestern cities and rural areas where twentieth-century Black communities and resistance flourished were intimately tied to the region's geographic location, rich biomes, immense network of waterways, and temperate climate that took their current shape over the past two million years.

The Pre-Columbian North American middle was the homeland of numerous dynamic Indigenous societies before the arrival of Africans and Europeans. No place epitomized this fact better than Cahokia ("City of the Sun"), the largest Native city-state in Pre-Columbian North America north of Mexico. Cahokia was located near present-day East St. Louis, Illinois, in the heart of the "American Bottom," a fertile region where the Missouri, Mississippi, Ohio, and Illinois Rivers converge.[14] At its peak around 1200 ACE, the city counted twenty thousand residents, more than London at the time (see figure 1.1). Cahokia's cultural, political, and economic influence stretched across North America before the city's demise by 1350.[15]

European conquest of and settlement in the Americas, together with the onset of the Atlantic slave trade and New World slavery, initiated the historical forces that eventually brought millions of Black people to the heartland beginning as early as the mid-sixteenth century (see figure 1.2). One of the first Africans to set foot in the region may have been an enslaved servant whose name and background are unknown. He apparently traveled in 1539 through Nebraska with a Spanish expedition from Mexico City led by the French-born Franciscan priest Fray Marcos de Niza.[16] Much remains unknown about the African presence in early middle North America. What is for sure is that Black midwestern history began with the dawning of the post-Contact Americas and more than a half-century before the first Africans arrived in 1619 at Point Comfort, Virginia, an event commonly recognized in African American history as the beginning of slavery in the United States.[17]

FIGURE 1.1. Illustration of Cahokia circa 1200 ACE, Cahokia Mounds State Historic Site, Collinsville, Illinois, November 2020. Photo by the author.

The picture of the African presence in the colonial Midwest becomes clearer with the early history of Detroit. The city that would become the symbol of twentieth-century industrialization and an epicenter of Black nationalism, internationalism, and radicalism began through the expropriation of Native land and the enslavement of Indigenous and African people.[18] This process began in 1701 when French military leader and explorer Antoine de La Mothe, Sieur de Cadillac, established Fort Pontchartrain du Detroit. The fort was strategically located at the narrowest point along the western side of a twenty-eight-mile strait that the French named Rivière du Détroit ("River of the Strait"). It connected Lake St. Clair to Lake Erie of the Great Lakes system to the St. Lawrence River and the Atlantic world.

Slavery was foundational to colonial Detroit.[19] The settlement's first enslaved Black inhabitant was an unnamed French-speaking Catholic woman who died in 1736.[20] The city's African population increased after the British captured Fort Detroit in 1760 in the global conflict between Great Britain and France known as the Seven Years' War. Detroit counted 73 enslaved people in 1773 out of a total population about 1,400. By 1782, the number of enslaved

FIGURE 1.2. *L'Amerique septentrionale*, by Coronelli and published by I. B. Nolin in Paris, 1689. Map Library, University of Illinois at Urbana-Champaign.

people increased to 179. Slavery in Detroit, like elsewhere across the Atlantic world, was violent and oppressive.[21]

Slavery in the early Midwest was hardly peculiar to colonial Detroit. Enslavement and unfree labor were common conditions for a significant portion of the population—Native, African, and European—across the colonial Midwest. Take, for example, Illinois, where writer and poet Arna Bontemps emphasized that "early Illinois was anything but an asylum for liberty," due to the significant number of enslaved people living within what became the Land of Lincoln.[22] This reality of unfreedom set the stage for future Black midwestern life.

The birth of Chicago provides the most well-known example of the Black presence in and diasporic contours of the early Midwest. The city's first nonnative resident and founder was Jean-Baptiste Pointe DuSable, a French-speaking fur trader believed to be of partial Haitian descent (see figure 1.3). He established a lucrative trading post by 1780 on the banks of the Chicago River and resided with his Potawatomie wife, Catherine, earning the respect of Indigenes, British officials, and American settlers alike.[23] Their settlement was in a shift-

FIGURE 1.3. Bust of Jean-Baptiste Pointe DuSable, Chicago, Illinois, July 25, 2023. Photo by the author.

ing transnational imperial borderland. English settler colonial expansion in the region and Indian removal from the Great West were critical to precipitating the fall of France's North American empire, British acquisition of the Midwest, and the birth of the United States.[24] In 1796, DuSable sold his property and eventually made his way to St. Charles, Missouri, where he spent his final years.[25] According to St. Clair Drake and Horace Cayton, DuSable set into motion forces that transformed Chicago within one century into a cosmopolitan, industrial metropolis.[26] Even more, DuSable's place in history illustrates, as historian Courtney Cain points out, that Black transnational migration to the Chicago area is hardly new. Rather, the African-descended from the continent and the Caribbean had been arriving in the Midwest for centuries.[27] Taken together, the histories of pre-Contact America and the colonial North American middle show that the Midwest from its beginning was a gateway for people and was a transnational terrain shaped by rich natural landscapes, human migration, labor, and ingenuity. Some Blacks like DuSable enjoyed wealth and influence. However, most African-descended in the eighteenth-century Midwest lived and toiled as unfree subjects in French and British global empires and in a region where settlers encroached on Indigenes' land. This complex reality of the Midwest as a place of opportunity and oppression for Black people persisted into the coming centuries.

The Northwest Ordinance, Slavery, White Settler Colonialism, and Black Laws

The advent of US rule over the Great West at the turn of the eighteenth century forever shaped the racial, geographic, socioeconomic, and geopolitical landscape of the Diasporic Midwest, with lasting implications for the United States and the world. The Ordinance of 1787 (better known as the Northwest Ordinance), passed on July 13, 1787, by the Articles of Confederation, was key to this process. The Northwest Ordinance established the Northwest Territory, consisting of present-day Ohio, Michigan, Indiana, Illinois, Wisconsin, and parts of Minnesota. The United States acquired this land through the 1783 Treaty of Paris in which Great Britain ceded to the new republic a vast territory from the western side of the Appalachian Mountains from New York southward to Florida and westward to the Mississippi River, doubling the new nation's size.[28] The ordinance outlined a process for statehood and for admitting new states from the Northwest Territory on an equal basis with the original thirteen states. The ordinance also outlawed slavery in the Northwest Territory, ostensibly creating the first free territory in the United States and the largest territory in the Americas closed to slavery.[29] At the time of the ordinance's enactment, a few thousand settlers lived in the Northwest Territory. By 1860, the Old Northwest counted four million inhabitants, 63,000 of whom were African American.[30]

The Northwest Ordinance constituted a major event in the history of the United States, the Americas, and slavery. However, the common (mis)interpretation of the ordinance as a radical antislavery, democratic measure overlooks the ways the legislation was critical to advancing state-directed white settler colonialism in the Great West.[31] The early nineteenth-century Old Northwest emerged as a key site and a national model for ethnic cleansing of Native people that came to be called Indian Removal, most notably the US war of conquest in 1832, known as Black Hawk's War, against the Sauk nation.[32]

The Northwest Ordinance and early nineteenth-century territorial and state legislation in the Midwest played an integral role in the legal and social construction of race and whiteness in the heartland. The ordinance prohibited slavery. However, the legislation promoted state-sanctioned, racialized forms of social control and punishment, notably through a fugitive slave clause and a provision allowing slavery and involuntary servitude for the punishment of crime. The ordinance anticipated the fugitive slave clause in the 1787 US Constitution and a subsequent 1793 federal fugitive slave act.[33] The Northwest Ordinance also presaged the 1850 Fugitive Slave Act, which was critical to inflaming sectional tensions, as well as the Thirteenth Amendment in 1865. Enacted immediately after the Civil War, the Thirteenth Amendment abolished slavery and involuntary servitude except as punishment for a crime. Through legalizing slavery as punishment for a crime, the Thirteenth Amendment helped to lay the foundations for Jim Crow and what Angela Davis, Ruth Wilson Gilmore, and other early twenty-first-century scholars, activists, and movements have called the "prison industrial complex."[34] They use this term to describe, as Gilmore writes, "the expanding use of prisons as catchall solutions to social problems."[35] Understanding the linkages among prisons, racial capitalism, globalization, heteropatriarchy, and US empire, Gilmore and other critics of the prison industrial complex call for its abolition.[36] The Northwest Ordinance both opened the door for abolishing slavery across the Northwest Territory and the United States and also laid the groundwork for the Midwest's development into an economically prosperous white settler region and a center of Black resistance and community-building.

From the Northwest Territory's beginning, white authorities and settlers in the region circumvented the ordinance's prohibition of slavery in the territory.[37] The region's first territorial governor, Arthur St. Clair, a Scottish American slaveholder, American War of Independence general, and former president of the Articles of Confederation Congress, argued that the law applied only to enslaved people brought to the territory after 1787. His reinterpretation of the ordinance galvanized pro-slavery forces and set the stage for future racially discriminatory legislation across the region.[38] Slavery died out in the Old Northwest by the 1840s. However, most antebellum white midwesterners opposed extending equal rights to African Americans and feared Black labor competing with white labor.[39]

The racist politics of white settlers explains the passage of what antebellum midwestern territorial and state legislators called "Black Laws," racially discriminatory legislation against African Americans. Informed by the racist interpretation of the Northwest Ordinance and anticipating Black Codes passed by white southern state governments that sought to preserve white racial control over newly freed persons immediately following the Civil War, the "Black Laws" of the Old Northwest limited the legal rights of African Americans and served as important legal measures for promoting white supremacy and settler colonialism.[40] Ohio set the precedent regionally and across the North in passing racially discriminatory legislation during the antebellum years.[41] In keeping with the Northwest Ordinance, the Ohio state constitution, ratified in 1802 on the eve of statehood the following year, prohibited slavery—a move followed by other states admitted from the Northwest Territory.[42] However, in 1803, the Ohio General Assembly passed a law restricting state militia service to white males. In 1804, the Ohio state government in 1804 passed "An Act to Regulate Black and Mulatto Persons." The law banned African American and mixed-race people from moving to Ohio and prohibited whites from employing African-descended people without a court order. The law criminalized aiding and abetting self-emancipated people.[43] In the coming years, the state banned African American men from serving on juries and Black children from attending public schools.[44] In 1849, the Ohio state legislature repealed "An Act to Regulate Black and Mulatto Persons." Still, the fate of Blacks in the state remained an open question. A white state legislator proclaimed that he envisioned Ohio "for the white man, and the white man only."[45] Other midwestern states such as Illinois and Indiana enacted Black Laws, some of which were more draconian than Ohio laws.[46] White voters in Illinois, Indiana, Michigan, Wisconsin, and Iowa in the 1850s rejected state constitutional referenda to enfranchise Black male voters.[47] These racist laws and white attitudes were foundational to shaping racial oppression and concomitant Black resistance in the Midwest.

Black Community Formations in the Old Northwest

Despite whites' best efforts to prohibit African Americans from settling in the Old Northwest, many Blacks journeyed there as the nineteenth century dawned because they saw the heartland as a beacon of hope. They were not naïve about the region's pervasive racism. But they understood that the Old Northwest's color line offered Blacks more freedom and opportunity than they could find in the South where chattel slavery remained the law of the land.[48] A similar logic informed future generations of Black migrants who fled the Jim Crow South for the heartland and who populated the UNIA and Black nationalist movements spawned by Garveyism.

The African American population in the Midwest steadily increased during the antebellum years. Most Blacks who resided in the pre–Civil War heartland lived in the Lower Midwest, a region populated heavily by white southern migrants who brought their racial and antistatist political views with them.[49] The racial contours of the antebellum Lower Midwest would have profound implications for Black midwestern life from the early nineteenth century onward. In 1800, the region counted 500 free Blacks. Ten years later the population increased to approximately 2,000. By 1820, 6,459 free Blacks and 779,211 whites resided in Ohio, Indiana, and Illinois.[50] Ohio was home to the largest African American population in the Old Northwest. In 1800, the territory counted

337 Blacks. In 1830, the state's Black population increased to 9,568 and grew to 36,673, or 1.6 percent of the state's total population by 1860.[51]

African American migration and community formations in the antebellum Midwest were inextricably connected to the region's status as a free territory and its transformation from a sparsely populated frontier into a fast-growing commercial and manufacturing center, breadbasket, and crossroads of the United States. The Ohio River Valley, a center of US commercial and early industrialization, was the first major site of antebellum Black life in the Old Northwest.[52] No place better represented these developments than Cincinnati. Founded in 1788, the city was strategically located at the crossroads between the North, South, and Great West on the northern bank of the Ohio River near the confluence of the Great and Little Miami Rivers. By the 1820s, Cincinnati earned the nickname the "Queen City," due to its rapid growth into a booming manufacturing and commercial urban frontier center.[53] Cincinnati's total population increased from 2,540 in 1810, to 24,148 in 1830, and then to 161,044 in 1860, making it the seventh-largest US city. It was home to the largest African American urban midwestern population until the late nineteenth century.[54] Cincinnati's proximity to slave states and location a half-mile across the Ohio River from Kentucky made the city an accessible destination for African Americans fleeing southern bondage, even though pro-slavery sentiment was strong among large segments of the city's white denizens. The Queen City's Black population grew from 82 in 1810 to 2,258 in 1829 to 3,371 in 1860, with Blacks never counting for more than 9.4 percent of Cincinnati's total inhabitants. Life was difficult for Black Cincinnatians. They held the worst jobs, experienced residential segregation, and faced racial prejudice, especially from the city's large white ethnic and pro-slavery populations. Public schools barred Black students.[55] Given the size of the city's Black population and their yearnings to be free and the city's proximity to slave states, Cincinnati emerged as a regional hub of abolition and the Underground Railroad, a vast social network of organizers and communities committed to transiting formerly enslaved people to freedom in the North, Canada, Mexico, and elsewhere.[56]

Meanwhile, Cleveland emerged as an anchor of Blacks in northeast Ohio. Founded in 1796 at the confluence of the Cuyahoga River into Lake Erie by white surveyor Moses Cleaveland of Connecticut, the city's founders had grand visions for Cleveland as a major urban trade and transportation hub, due to its proximity to waterways and overland trade routes to distant markets.[57] The city's location in a heavily wooded wilderness earned Cleveland the nickname "the Forest City" as early as the 1830s.[58] A less rigid color line developed in Cleveland than in Cincinnati. Unlike the Queen City, Cleveland was located more than two hundred miles from slave states and counted only a handful of Blacks in the city's first decades. By 1860, 799 African Americans resided in Cleveland out of a total population of 43,417.[59] A large segment of early white settlers hailed from New England, where abolitionism had gained traction.[60] From the antebellum years through the turn of the twentieth century, the Forest City gained a reputation for racial liberalism. In contrast to Cincinnati and in defiance of Ohio state law, Cleveland public schools welcomed African American students. Politically, state lawmakers from northeastern Ohio, due to the lobbying of Cleveland's Black and white abolitionists, were critical to the repeal of Black Laws in 1849.[61] However, Cleveland was "no racial utopia."[62] Beyond the Forest City, Black communities developed in cities across Ohio—Akron, Hamilton, Dayton, Springfield, and Youngstown.[63]

Outside of Ohio, Detroit was home to a growing African American community yearning to be free. Detroit's unique location as a fast-growing port and border city, linked to Canada, the Great Lakes, and the Atlantic world, forever shaped the city's Black community.[64] In 1819, Detroit counted 70 Blacks out of a total population of 1,110 residents. By 1850, the city's Black population increased from 587 in 1850 to 1,403 in 1860 out of a total population of 21,019 and 40,838, respectively.[65] From the 1830s onward, Black Detroiters formed their own institutions. Second Baptist Church, established in 1836, was the first Black-owned church in the Midwest. Securing the freedom and survival of Black Detroiters was central to Second Baptist's mission and to other local pre–Civil War Black religious and mutual aid organizations.[66]

Detroit's geographic location enhanced Black Detroiters' global awareness about and response to slavery and abolitionism across the Atlantic world. Due to both Detroit's proximity to Canada and the city's vibrant Black community, Detroit and the Detroit River borderlands became the busiest international gateway in the United States for formerly enslaved people fleeing to the British territory for freedom (see figure 1.4). Thousands of people crossed the Detroit River to the Canadian side of the border annually during the 1840s and 1850s.[67] Community institutions such as Second Baptist Church, leading Detroit abolitionists such as George DeBaptiste, Henry and Mary Bibb, William Lambert, and everyday Black Detroiters aided self-emancipated people traveling to Canada.[68] Further, British imperial abolition enacted in 1833 cemented the perception among self-emancipated people and abolitionists of Canada as a haven from slavery.[69] By 1860, twenty thousand African-descended people lived in Canada West (present-day Ontario), with thousands residing in Windsor, Sandwich, Puce, Amherstburg, Chatham, and other Canadian towns and settlements near Detroit.[70]

FIGURE 1.4. A view of downtown Detroit, Michigan, and the Detroit River from Windsor, Ontario. Photo by the author.

Antebellum Black Detroiters forged meaningful transnational political and social linkages with their African-descended brethren on the Canadian side of the Detroit River. By the 1840s, hundreds of Blacks participated annually in joyous street parades in Detroit celebrating British Emancipation Day (August 1). This date in 1834 marked the end of slavery in the British Empire.[71] Jubilant Black Detroiters crossed the Detroit River where they participated in annual Emancipation Day festivities with Blacks in Windsor, Detroit's Canadian sister city.[72] These celebrations, which lasted long into the twentieth century, helped to forge arguably the tightest-knit cross-border Black urban community in the world at the time.[73] These public outpourings of transnational political solidarity among Blacks on both sides of the US-Canadian border anticipated massive street parades in early twentieth-century Detroit and around the world, organized by Garveyites in support of African redemption and global Black freedom.

In early Chicago, a growing African American community developed as a result of the city's rapid transformation from a frontier settlement into a major commercial and transportation hub, combined with Blacks' perception of the city as a refuge from southern slavery.[74] Chicago's nascent Black community established churches and mutual aid societies, protected self-emancipated people from slave hunters, provided social services to the underserved local Black community, and delivered the formerly enslaved to freedom in Canada through the Underground Railroad.[75] In 1837, four years after the city's incorporation, Chicago counted 77 Blacks out of 4,066 inhabitants. By 1860, the African American population increased to 955, accounting for less than 1 percent of the city's total population of 109,260.[76] Chicago's rapid economic growth by 1840 forever shaped the city's course of development. In 1846, US Congress passed legislation designating Chicago as an international point of entry, expanding the city's commercial linkages across the Great Lakes and St. Lawrence River systems. In 1848, the completion of the Illinois and Michigan Canal, and the city's first railroad line to the East Coast, secured Chicago's trajectory toward becoming a major Great West metropolis.[77]

Even as African American populations grew in predominantly white cities across the antebellum Midwest, most Blacks in the region lived in rural areas. Blacks established at least 338 farming settlements across the Old Northwest between 1800 and 1860, underscoring their determination to live freely and autonomously from whites. Many Black midwestern settlers were formerly enslaved people. They did not forget about their bonded brethren and sometimes worked in solidarity with cooperative whites and Native communities and served as conductors on the Underground Railroad.[78]

Rural Black women were at the forefront in efforts for delivering fugitive enslaved people through the Underground Railroad. As historian Jazma Sutton shows in her work on antebellum Black women in rural Indiana, African American women involved in the Underground Railroad saw their involvement as an extension of their roles as mothers and protectors of their families.[79] Black midwestern women's leadership in the Underground Railroad demonstrates that they were at the front lines of grassroots resistance and community-building from the earliest days of Black protest in the Old Northwest. This tendency continued into the twentieth-century heartland Black nationalist movements.

Blacks pursued freedom and autonomy through building majority African American communities in the antebellum heartland, revealing how Blacks in the Old Northwest were at the vanguard in forging a particular brand of Black nationalism predicated on constructing all-Black towns. This sensibility was most evident in the founding in 1830 of Brooklyn, Illinois. Located along the Mississippi River in St. Clair County near St. Louis, Brooklyn holds the distinction of being the oldest all-Black town in the United States. Brooklyn originated as an enclave for free Blacks and self-emancipated people who had crossed the Mississippi River from Missouri to Illinois in search of freedom. The aspirations of Brooklyn's first residents resembled those of other "freedom villages," antebellum communities located mostly in the Old Northwest and established by formerly enslaved Black people. According to historian Sundiata Keita Cha-Jua, Brooklyn and "Black-town construction" from the early nineteenth through the early twentieth centuries embodied territorial nationalism, that is, an African American nationalist praxis for living freely from racial oppression through establishing autonomous communities and determining their own future.[80] Despite the dreams and herculean efforts of the village's residents, Brooklyn never became an economically prosperous, self-sustaining city. Setting a precedent for future all-Black towns across the United States and anticipating the challenges facing postindustrial-era Black-majority midwestern cities like Detroit, Cleveland, East St. Louis, and Gary, Indiana, Brooklyn found itself ensnared in a precarious trap. The structures of racial capitalism prevented the village from achieving economic growth and autonomy.[81] Still, Brooklyn's broader historical significance to Black America and Black nationalism should not be dismissed. The village signaled an emerging impulse among African Americans to build all-Black autonomous communities that anticipated Black-town construction in Kansas and elsewhere after the Civil War and the racial separatism pursued by twentieth-century Black midwesterners through the UNIA and neo-Garveyite formations.[82] More broadly, Brooklyn, like other Black antebellum midwestern communities located in predominantly white cities and rural areas, illustrated the importance of the heartland as a unique place in pre-abolition United States and the Black world, where the African-descended took advantage of new and unprecedented possibilities for forging community, freedom, and global sensibilities.

The Rising Tide of Racism, Colored Conventions,
and Liberia

From the 1830s to the Civil War, the African American midwestern response through the Colored Conventions movement to a rising tide of state-sanctioned and extralegal racial oppression and terror was critical to stoking militancy among free Black communities nationwide. This politics both challenged and reinforced the local and global status quo while also laying the foundations for twentieth-century midwestern Garveyism. Ohio continued to lead the Old Northwest and free states in white anti-Black violence in the decades leading up to the Civil War. The 1829 Cincinnati Riot is a case in point. Between August 15 and August 29, 1829, groups of two to three hundred whites, many of whom were working-class Irish migrants, assaulted African Americans and destroyed Black-owned property in the city. Racial animus fueled by job competition and white insecurity triggered this anti-Black pogrom. In a testament to their resolve and in anticipation of the twentieth-century African American response to large-scale, organized white terrorism across the United States, Black Cincinnatians fought back with coordinated armed self-defense. In the end, perhaps as many as 1,500 African Americans—or half the city's Black population—fled the Queen City for refuge in the surrounding area and as far as Canada. White anti-Black mob violence ignited again in Cincinnati in 1836 and 1841.[83] Heavily armed white mobs attacked Blacks and destroyed their property in other Old Northwest cities—Detroit (1833), Cleveland (1837 and 1841), and Dayton (1841).[84]

Additionally, the antebellum Midwest holds the troubling yet often overlooked distinction as a national center of state-sanctioned, white vigilante violence that came to be known as lynching after the Civil War.[85] Arguably, the first lynching in the United States occurred in 1836 in St. Louis when a white mob murdered Francis McIntosh, a free Black sailor, by tying him to a tree and burning his body.[86] The following year, white abolitionist Elijah Lovejoy met his death in Alton, Illinois, at the hands of a lynch mob enraged by his antislavery journalism. The McIntosh and Lovejoy cases garnered national attention among foes of slavery and proponents of the rule of law, including a young aspiring Illinois attorney named Abraham Lincoln.[87] The rural Old Northwest was a racially hostile place for African Americans. In 1839, whites castrated two Black men for allegedly raping two white women in rural Warren County in southwestern Ohio. Rural Indiana and Illinois were sites of lynchings of African Americans in the 1850s.[88]

The Midwest was ground zero for slave catching, especially after the passage of the 1850 Fugitive Slave Act. The controversial US federal law required free states to return self-emancipated people to their southern owners.[89] White bounty hunters scoured the midwestern countryside, towns, and cities in search of ex-slaves.[90] The Great West was the site of events that led to the most infamous slave-hunting legal case in US history—the US Supreme Court *Dred Scott* decision of 1857. Dred and Harriet Scott of St. Louis sued for their freedom on the grounds that they were free because their owner had taken the couple as slaves from Missouri to free territory in the Old Northwest (see figure 1.5). Ultimately, the pro-slavery US Supreme Court Chief Justice Roger Taney of Maryland ruled against the Scotts. Declaring that they were not free, Taney ruled that Blacks had "no rights which the white man was bound to respect" and that the federal government was constitutionally obligated to protect slavery.[91]

FIGURE 1.5. Dred and Harriet Scott statue in front of the Old Courthouse, Gateway Arch National Park, St. Louis, Missouri. Photo by the author.

Dred Scott opened the legal door for further US white settler colonial penetration into the North American interior and to the further subjugation of Black people, stoking national debates around slavery that exploded in civil war.[92]

Outside the Midwest, nearly four million enslaved African Americans by 1860 toiled across the South, producing super-profits for white southern slave owners and their northern investors and fueling industrial capitalism in the US Northeast and Great Britain.[93] Growing resistance by enslaved people in Dixie, most notably the 1831 Nat Turner Rebellion, stoked abolitionism in the North, hardened pro-slavery politics in the South, and enflamed sectional tensions. On the eve of the Civil War, the British and French empires had abolished slavery in their Caribbean holdings, and the US South, Brazil, Cuba, and Puerto Rico were the last major holdouts of slavery in the Americas.[94]

As hellish as conditions were for Blacks in the antebellum Midwest and as a yoke of white supremacy tightened around the necks of enslaved African Americans in the South, Black midwesterners engaged in self-activity and collective resistance on multiple fronts for the full freedom of Blacks everywhere, most notably through the Colored Conventions. The first Colored Convention was held September 20–24, 1830, in Philadelphia at the historic Mother Bethel African Methodist Episcopal (AME) church, cofounded by the venerated abolitionist and religious leaders Richard and Sarah Allen.[95] The horrific racial violence and Black resistance in Cincinnati in 1829 inspired the inaugural Colored Convention.[96] The conference, presided over by Richard Allen, opposed slavery, called for establishing a free Black settlement in Canada, condemned the American Colonization Society (ACS) as a white supremacist front, and demanded the dignity and freedom of Black people everywhere.[97] The primacy of antislavery at this convention signaled how Black nationalism and abolitionism were inextricably and mutually generative and that the African-descended were at the forefront in leading the transnational Abolition movement.[98]

Ohio was important geographic terrain for the Colored Conventions movement. The Buckeye State not only hosted the greatest number of Colored Conventions; it was also critical to radicalizing the national movement's political agenda.[99] Take, for example, the historic National Emigration Convention of Colored People held from August 24 to 26, 1854, in Cleveland.[100] Martin R. Delany organized and presided over the conference. Born free in 1812 in Charlestown, West Virginia, and later based in Pittsburgh, the orator, physician, author, globe-trotter, soldier, and politician was the preeminent champion of African American emigration prior to the Civil War. He called the convention after parting ways with self-emancipated abolitionist Frederick Douglass, who opposed emigration on the grounds that African Americans were entitled to full freedom in the land of their birth.[101] The National Emigration Convention was an exciting affair. One hundred and six delegates from across the United States, including Pennsylvania, Missouri, Kentucky, Ohio, Louisiana, and Mississippi, as well as from Canada, gathered in Cleveland.[102] Committed to charting a new course for the political destiny and survival of African Americans, the conference explicitly called for Black sovereignty.[103] This position reflected Delany's belief that Black political sovereignty and independence were paramount to global Black freedom.[104] This line of thought shaped the ideological parameters of Black nationalism later articulated by Marcus Garvey and his disciples.

"The Political Destiny of the Colored Race," a report written and delivered to the convention by Delany, constituted a highlight of the National Emigration Convention and advanced his call for Black sovereignty. The report, which framed African Americans as a nation within a nation, had a primary objective to provide "a true position" on Black life in the United States. According to him, "A people, to be free, must necessarily be *their own rulers*."[105] African Americans neither had been nor could ever be free in the United States, given that the republic was a white settler colonial state predicated on genocide of Native people, the enslavement of Africans, and the ruthlessness and immorality of the nation's Anglo-Saxon majority. Given this deadly reality, he called for African American emigration to unspecified locations in Central America, South America, and the Caribbean as the "remedy" for Black oppression and degradation in the United States.[106] His report did not mention Liberia. However, he held the West African republic in low regard. In his seminal book, *The Condition, Elevation, Emigration, and Destiny of the Colored People of the United States*, published in 1852, he dismissed Liberia as "a pitiful dependency" of the racist ACS, and he disparaged Americo-Liberians for their mixed racial ancestry and alleged subservience to the ACS.[107] Delany's *Condition* "underlined the link between capitalism and religion and demonstrated how emigration (divinely sanctioned) would advance the capitalist goal of the Black middle class. Emigration was consequently consistent with God's plan," notes Tunde Adeleke.[108] Future Black nationalists often echoed these positions.

Colored Conventions were not without their limitations and paradoxes. Masculinism was deeply embedded in the movement. Black male conventioneers tried to exclude Black women from the conferences, much to the latter's chagrin and opposition.[109] Ultimately, Black women activists such as Mary Ann Shadd Cary and Jane P. Merritt demanded a place at the table for women at Colored Conventions. In doing so, they left "an indelible mark . . . on the history" of the movement.[110] Civilizationism was also apparent within the Colored Conventions movement and among antebellum classical Black nationalists. Take, for instance, Delany's *Official Report of the Niger River Valley Exploring Party*, published in 1861. The report detailed an expedition he led to the Niger River Valley in 1859 in search of a site for an African American settlement. Showing respect for the Indigenous cultures of the Yoruba of modern-day southwestern Nigeria, he called for "*Africa for the African race, and black men to rule them.*"[111] He "developed positive portraits of Africa."[112] Still, Delany "was not absolute and unequivocal in denunciation and rejection of Victorian values and worldview. He would later invoke those same values as prescriptions for 'civilizing' aspects of African culture he characterized as primitive."[113] For him and other classical Black nationalists, New World Blacks were best suited for elevating Africa by bringing Christianity, capitalism, and modernity to the continent. Countless twentieth-century Black nationalists would uphold these beliefs.

Grassroots antebellum back-to-Africa schemes to Liberia endorsed by African Americans in the Midwest provide insight into the way Black Americans from the pre–Civil War years forward sometimes forged complicated alliances with white racists. On March 5, 1850, a group of Black Cincinnatians issued a resolution proclaiming their support for emigrating to "Ohio in Africa," a proposed diasporic settlement in Liberia intended for African American Ohioans. Charles McMicken conceived the idea for the colony. He was the founder of the University of Cincinnati, a staunch supporter of the ACS, and one of the Queen City's wealthiest benefactors who made his fortune through large slaveholding in Louisiana.[114] The resolution understood Black freedom as a struggle for manhood rights and assumed that African Americans possessed the right to settle in the West African republic. Even more, this group willingly worked with a major slaveholder.[115] The paradoxical and unsavory nature of this alliance was not lost on African American Cincinnatians opposed to this scheme. In response to this proposed back-to-Africa plan, a large meeting held on March 21, 1850, at Union Baptist Church, the city's oldest African American house of worship, denounced emigration and the ACS.[116] We surely will never know whether those who collaborated with McMicken in promoting Liberian emigration believed they were betraying Black people or if they were trying to find a pragmatic solution for Black Cincinnatians living under the constant threat of annihilation. What is certain is that intense debate about Liberia was part of a larger question among free Blacks about the best path toward self-determination in which the Midwest was central. Debates about the relation of New World Black freedom to Liberia would continue into the next century. Efforts by some nineteenth-century Blacks to work with renowned racists set the stage for Black diasporic right radicalism in the 1920s.

While the 1850s marked a high point of African American support for emigration to Africa and the Caribbean during the antebellum era, the Civil War and Reconstruction years saw an ebb in support among Blacks for returning to Africa.[117] Nationwide, African Americans saw the Civil War as the Coming of the Lord and as a day of reckoning in which the United States would finally live up to its professed democratic promise. From the war's beginning, enslaved and free African Americans understood like no one else that slavery and emancipation were at the core of the conflict.[118] For this reason, Black men in the Midwest, as well as across the United States, took up arms and put their lives on the line to fight against slavery and the Confederacy and to secure their rights and forty acres and a mule.[119] Even the most steadfast emigrationists such as Martin Delany and John Mercer Langston abandoned their desire to flee America's shores during the war. They came to believe that free and formerly enslaved Blacks could at last enjoy their full freedom in the land of their birth.[120]

These dreams were short-lived. The late nineteenth-century United States witnessed tectonic shifts on the color line. The possibilities for building a multiracial democracy through Reconstruction faded into the ugly and violent reality of disfranchisement, lynching, sharecropping, and Jim Crow by the turn of the twentieth century.[121] The US Supreme Court *Plessy v. Ferguson* decision of 1896 enshrined the constitutionality of the separate but equal legal doctrine for public facilities and services. Globally, the United States emerged as the world's foremost industrial nation and as a nascent superpower. European imperial powers scrambled for colonies in Africa and Asia. These US and world events rekindled earlier debates among Blacks about the merits of returning to Africa and the best paths toward freedom for the African-descended globally.[122] The late nineteenth-century Midwest, Chicago particularly, proved to be a key site where these Black nationalist and diasporic political debates and exchanges occurred.

Chicago, the World's Columbian Exposition, and the Congress on Africa

By the end of the nineteenth century, Chicago emerged as a global center of Black urban life, Black nationalism, internationalism, radicalism, and the Diasporic Midwest. This was most evident in responses from African-descended activists, journalists, scholars, world travelers, and everyday people to two historic international events held in 1893 in Chicago: the World's Columbian Exposition and the Congress on African Ethnology (commonly referred to by contemporaries as the World's Fair and the Congress on Africa, respectively). Black critical engagement with the World's Fair and Congress on Africa signaled Chicago's growing preeminence as a major geographic nexus of diasporic protest and diaspora-making. Black responses to these gatherings also provide insight into the appeal, power, and paradoxes of late nineteenth-century Black nationalism and internationalism shaped by revolutionary political, economic, social, cultural, and technological transformations that prepared the ground for midwestern Garveyism and twentieth-century heartland-based Black movements.

The World's Fair and Congress on Africa took place during Chicago's rapid development into the second-largest city in the United States and into a cosmopolitan, heavy industrial global city by the turn of the twentieth century. Chicago's population exploded between 1870 and 1900 from 298,977 to 1,698,575, due in large part to a massive influx of European immigrants. Chicago's rapid growth, steel mills, stockyards, meatpacking plants, elevated trains, railroad yards, workshops, skyscrapers, and sprawling metropolitan area made the city an envy of the world and a symbol of modernity.[123]

The late nineteenth century marked the beginning of a century-long mass migration of African Americans from the South to the Windy City and their transformation into an urban industrial working class. Their desire to flee the nascent Jim Crow South and to secure a better life in booming Chicago swelled the city's Black population from 3,600 in 1870, to 6,480 in 1880, to 14,852 in 1890, to 30,150 in 1900, and to 44,103 in 1910, making the Windy City home to the largest Black urban population in the Midwest.[124] Spatially, nearly 80 percent of Chicago's Black population in 1910 lived in a small but fast-growing, underserved ghetto on the city's South Side that soon came to be known as the "Black Belt" and "Bronzeville."[125] The institutional development of Chicago's Black community surpassed those of other midwestern cities. Established and new locally based African American cultural organizations, community institutions, churches, women's clubs, and businesses with ties to national organizations flourished in Chicago.[126] On the labor front, Black workers in Illinois and particularly in Chicago were militant trade unionists.[127] Chicago became home to a dynamic community of young African American professionals, entrepreneurs, activists, and cultural workers—among them were journalist and antilynching crusader Ida B. Wells, club woman Fannie Barrier Williams, attorney and journalist Ferdinand Barnett, anarchist and labor organizer Lucy Parsons, entrepreneur Jesse Binga, and journalist Robert S. Abbott.[128] These Black spokespersons, professionals, and cultural institutions were part of the broader New Negro Movement (1890–1935), a national Black protest movement committed to "nation building" and racial uplift, a middle-class ideology that upheld the belief that African American material and moral progress would advance Black freedom. Given their belief that they best represented the race's potential and agents for civilizing the Black masses, Black middle-class advocates of racial uplift espoused self-help and service to the race.[129]

By the eve of the 1893 World's Fair, a confident and self-conscious, militant Black Chicago civil society had emerged eager and prepared to fight for the dignity and respect of the African-descended in the city and globally. The world had never seen anything like the World's Columbian Exposition. From May 1 to October 30, 1893, more than twenty-one million people from around the world, including thousands of African-descended people, visited the fair. With its immense construction of spectacular buildings, cultural exhibits, the world's first Ferris wheel, and large crowds of domestic and international visitors, the World's Fair represented a turning point in US and global history.[130] The event's all-white organizers staged the fair to memorialize Columbus's landing in the Americas and to celebrate US nationalism, imperialism, and capitalism. African Americans were well aware of the event's exclusion of people of color from decision-making, the celebration of European civilization, and the denigrating cultural representations of people of color as savage.[131]

Ida B. Wells was a leading spokesperson in generating local and international Black critical responses to the World's Fair. She coproduced a booklet titled *The Reason Why the Colored American Is Not in the World's Columbian Exhibition*. Published in the summer of 1893, the booklet contained uncompromising essays by Wells, Ferdinand Barnett, and educator Irvine Garland Penn of Cincinnati about lynching, postbellum African American achievements, and the fair's racism.[132] Wells enlisted Frederick Douglass to write the booklet's introduction. Appealing to a global audience, the venerable nineteenth-century Black spokesperson, who had recently served as US minister to Haiti, opened the introduction by emphasizing that African Americans "are not indifferent to the good opinion of the world."[133] In addition to working on *The Reason Why*, Wells collaborated with Douglass in organizing the Haytian Pavilion at the World's Fair. The building, representing the only Black nation at the fair, featured exhibits celebrating the Haitian Revolution and Haiti as symbols of global Black freedom.[134]

The visibility of Wells, Barnett, and other Midwest-based activists in actions around the World's Fair represented a changing of the guard of African American leadership from an older generation of Black spokespersons such as the septuagenarian Douglass to a younger generation. He gained his global reputation during the antebellum years through abolitionism. Wells and her colleagues were born during or after the Civil War. They exhibited a confidence and racial sensibility reflecting this new global historical moment and the unique opportunities and transnational linkages the Windy City afforded them for forging a cosmopolitan Black Chicago.

Similarly, the Congress on Africa signaled late nineteenth-century Chicago's importance as an international destination where African-descended spokespersons from around the world assembled and pursued strategies for global racial uplift. Largely forgotten today, the Congress on Africa was the first gathering of its kind. The meeting anticipated the Pan-African Congress of 1900 in London.[135] The eight-day Congress on Africa, held in downtown Chicago from August 14 to August 21, 1893, in conjunction with the World's Fair, was the brainchild of Frederick Perry Noble, a white, liberal, devout Congregationalist, social reformer, librarian, and author.[136] Reflecting his social convictions and commitment to racial confraternity, interfaith cooperation, and African redemption, the Congress of Africa sought to promote "democracy and Christianity" in Africa and globally.[137] The Congress of Berlin of 1884 and 1885 and a follow-up conference in Brussels in the winter of 1889 and 1890 also informed Noble's vision for the Chicago gathering.[138] He perceived these European imperialist meetings about Africa as elitist conclaves that neither gave the African-descended a "voice" in determining the continent's future nor provided humane protections for African Indigenes.[139] For these reasons, he sought to make the Congress on Africa a large gathering that was representative of the world. Holding the conference during the World's Columbian Exhibition with millions of transatlantic visitors provided a unique global stage for realizing his objectives. One hundred women and men from the United States, Africa, Europe, the Caribbean, and Australia attended the conference. They were artists, Christians, educators, world travelers, diplomats, journalists, legislators, scientists, ministers, missionaries, Muslims, physicians, soldiers, US Civil War veterans, and formerly enslaved people. Veteran and younger national African American leaders participated in the conference; they included Frederick Douglass, Ida B. Wells, John Mercer Langston, Henry McNeal Turner, Alexander Crummell, T. Thomas Fortune, Hallie Q. Brown, Paul Laurence Dunbar, and Booker T. Washington.[140] During the conference proceedings, Turner, a freeborn AME leader, politician, world traveler, and preeminent late nineteenth-century proponent of emigration, "declared that nothing like this congress had ever been held."[141] He was right. The Congress on Africa featured lively sessions on African culture, Jim Crow, postbellum Black American achievements, slavery, colonialism, missionary work in Africa, and the relation of the African Diaspora to Africa.[142]

Emigration emerged as a contentious issue at the Congress on Africa. Recalling fierce debates at the antebellum Colored Conventions and foreshadowing future disagreements among Black spokespersons about the fate of African Americans in the United States, emigration deeply divided the conference attendees.[143] Turner made the most powerful case for Black repatriation back to Africa. Pessimistic about the future prospects for African Americans in the United States due to their "ignoble status" in the Jim Crow South "and their scullion employment in the North," he charged that "nothing but nationalization will work out the elevation of the race."[144] Echoing Black nationalist sentiment articulated by antebellum-era emigrationists and anticipating Marcus Garvey's position two decades later, Turner did not call for all diasporan Blacks to return to Africa. Instead, he believed, like Martin Delany and Edward Wilmot Blyden, that some African Americans ought to emigrate to Africa and that a strong and modern Africa would benefit Black people everywhere. Other conference delegates disagreed. New York journalist T. Thomas Fortune dismissed emigration as a fool's errand.[145] Wells's response at the conference to Fortune's remarks are unknown. However, in her 1892 essay "Afro-Americans and Africa," published in the *AME Church Review*, she made it clear that she believed that African Americans were entitled to their full freedom in the land of their birth. But she also respected the desire of African Americans to return to Africa, and she blasted Black spokespersons such as Fortune for opposing emigration.[146]

The World's Columbian Exhibition and Congress on Africa provide insight into Chicago's growing preeminence as a site of diasporic exchange and transnational activism. These gatherings also elucidate the power and limitations of late nineteenth-century classical Black nationalism and Black settler colonialism. Without question, the African American critical take on the World's Fair led by Wells and Douglass on one level brilliantly challenged the event's celebration of racism, white nationalism, and imperialism. However, Black critical reactions to the fair also evinced civilizationism and tensions between diasporan and continental Africans. This view was most apparent in the response of Douglass to Dahomey Village, a cultural exhibit in the heart of the fairgrounds featuring a reconstructed West African Dahomey village. Replete with dark-skinned Fon Indigenes dressed in traditional attire, topless women, thatched-roof wooden compounds, and African drumming and dancing, the exhibit embarrassed Douglass and other Black critics of the World's Fair. For them, Dahomey Village embodied primitivism.[147] Their reaction signaled the importance of gender, sexualities, and respectability in framing their diasporic imaginations of Africa. For them, traditionally clothed African women affirmed prevailing white, racist imperialist discourses of Black women as hypersexual, undesirable, and immoral, used "to buttress and apologise for the colonial project."[148] In drawing these conclusions, Black critics of the World's Fair echoed prominent late nineteenth-century and early twentieth-century Black spokespersons, male and female, who called for the protection of African and New World Black women from white male sexual violence, economic exploitation, and denigrating cultural representations through adopting Victorian, middle-class, Protestant heteronormative mores that simultaneously contested and affirmed the racist, sexist, imperial order.[149] Even more, Black critical responses to Dahomey Village signaled more broadly how classical Black nationalists believed that New World Blacks were the rightful leaders of Africa, obligated to uplift and civilize their allegedly backward continental brethren.

Civilizationism and Black settler colonialism also played out in paradoxical ways at the Congress on Africa. The conference's response to the Congo Free State is a case in point. Established in 1885, the Congo Free State, a vast, multiethnic, culturally dynamic, resource-rich territory in Central Africa, was the personal property of King Leopold II of Belgium. Belgian colonialism in Congo was so ruthless that it generated an international outcry from missionaries, social reformers, journalists, African American spokespersons, and even some European colonial powers.[150] The Congress of Africa condemned Belgian brutality in Congo.[151] However, the conference called neither for independence nor self-rule of Congo. Instead, conference delegates aspired to establish a humanitarian form of colonialism in Congo and across Africa under the leadership of diasporic settlers and Western-educated Africans. As one conference delegate put it, "So far as the future of Africa depends on able native leadership her brightest star of hope hangs over the United States. Many of our most cultivated and energetic Afro-American citizens are sure . . . to become leaders in Africa."[152] The belief among conference delegates in civilizationism and the progressive character of colonialism spoke to the gathering's overall goal of promoting the "modern interests of the Dark Continent and the [US] South" through "the best features of the Berlin and Brussels . . . conferences" and contemporary African American reform.[153]

The civilizationism and Black settler colonialism upheld by Black critics of the World's Fair and attendees of the Congress on Africa followed a familiar road already well traveled by leading classical Black nationalists such as Delany and Blyden. They collaborated with white supremacists and colonialists for advancing Black freedom and African redemption. In 1874, Delany broke from the Republican Party and ran for Lieutenant Governor of South Carolina as an Independent Republican, a breakaway party supported by conservative white Democrats opposed to Reconstruction.[154] Blyden, who had lived in Liberia for decades, returned to the United States and delivered an address at the ACS annual convention in 1883 in Washington, DC. Praising the ACS for its "unparalleled" efforts and success in "carrying on the work of civilization in Africa," he sincerely believed that Africans on the continent and in diaspora had benefited from "Christian and civilized settlers" working with the organization.[155] Blyden had no compunction about working with white supremacists in bringing civilization, capitalism, and Christianity to Africa.[156] In drawing similar conclusions to Blyden, the Congress on Africa challenged European colonial rule of Africa by acknowledging the humanity of African Indigenes and by demanding their protection. But conference delegates also reinforced the prevailing colonial order by upholding Western superiority and by claiming the right of Diasporan Blacks to rule over allegedly backward continental Africans. This stance foreshadowed the Black settler colonialism embraced by Garveyites.

The World's Columbian Exhibition and Congress of Africa illustrated the rising prominence of late nineteenth-century Chicago as a hub of diasporic exchange and transnational activism. Wells, Douglass, and other Black critics of the World's Fair brought global attention to its racism. The Congress of Africa signaled what was to come for international pan-African conferences. Yet both events revealed the limitations and paradoxes of Black nationalism and Black settler colonialism for addressing the complex issues facing the African-descended.

Black Midwestern Resistance and Community-Building on the Eve of the First World War

Black midwesterners beyond Chicago also embraced New Negro ideology, resisted racial oppression, and forged transnational linkages to the world in response to migration, industrialization, urbanization, and the onset of Jim Crow and Western imperialism in the years immediately before the First World War and the Great Migration. The prewar heartland remained a racially hostile place for Blacks. Illinois witnessed at least twenty-two lynchings between 1891 and 1914.[157] White mob violence against African Americans erupted in the downstate Illinois cities of Decatur (1893), Danville (1903), Springfield (1908), and Cairo (1909). African Americans in these cities, like in Cincinnati during the 1829 unrest there, fought back with guns and galvanized Blacks nationwide into action.[158] The scale and virulence of anti-Black white mob violence in Springfield, Abraham Lincoln's hometown, incensed the historian, sociologist, and activist W. E. B. Du Bois, then based at Atlanta University. Spurred into action by Springfield and ready to build a nationwide, interracial civil rights movement for countering Booker T. Washington's racial accommodationism, Du Bois co-organized the National Association for the Advancement of Colored People in 1909. The New York City–based NAACP would become the largest US civil rights organization and a thorn in Garvey's side.[159]

Despite experiencing virulent racial terror, Black midwesterners in the prewar years, like those who had come before them, stood firm and built dynamic all-Black community institutions committed to the New Negro agenda. These institutions, religious and secular, often linked in concrete ways to Black people across the United States and Global Africa in the years immediately before the First World War and Marcus Garvey's arrival in the United States, were pillars of resistance in Black midwestern communities. Blacks in the heartland established new houses of worship such as Pilgrim Baptist Church in Chicago and Lane Colored Methodist Episcopal in Cleveland. Older Black midwestern churches, such as Detroit's Second Baptist Church, continued to thrive.[160]

Additionally, the turn of the twentieth century saw a proliferation of new, nationally influential Black mutual aid societies, women's clubs, civic and fraternal organizations, and businesses in the heartland. The *Chicago Defender* newspaper is but one example of this trend. Founded in 1905 by Robert Sengstacke Abbott, a Georgia migrant, the *Chicago Defender* became the most influential twentieth-century African American newspaper. Featuring sensationalist stories about racial terror in Dixie, the *Chicago Defender* encouraged Blacks to leave Jim Crow and lynching behind for a new life in the North, especially in Chicago. The newspaper also played an important role in forging transnational linkages between Chicago, Black America, and the world through reporting global news affecting Black people.[161] In Cleveland in 1912, social reformer Jane Edna Hunter of South Carolina established the Phillis Wheatley Home, a Black women's protection association. Within a few years, the organization grew into the largest African American women's protection agency in the country.[162]

Politically, the growth of Black populations and institutions, the absence of Jim Crow voting restrictions, and the shifting national color line created unique opportunities for African Americans in the heartland to begin securing electoral power at the local and state levels by the late nineteenth century. In Cleveland, Harry C. Smith, a journalist and longtime resident of the Forest City, was elected in 1893 to the Ohio legislature. During his six years in office, he successfully lobbied for some of the toughest civil rights legislation in the country.[163] As much success as he found in the Ohio legislature, Smith was part of an older Black elite whose influence within African American communities waned by the turn of the century.[164] The old elite represented by Black Cleveland leaders like Harry Smith and the attorney, writer, and civil rights activist Charles W. Chesnutt generally opposed all-Black institutions and maintained close connections to the city's white liberal establishment. New elites and their Black working-class patrons embraced all-Black institutions and New Negro self-help strategies. The lawyer and journalist Thomas Fleming, elected in 1909 as Cleveland City Council's first African American councilperson, and Jane Edna Hunter fit this profile. On the eve of the First World War, the Great Migration, and the rise of the Garvey movement, Black middle-class and working-class people in the Midwest and across the country firmly upheld New Negro ideology.

The pre-twentieth-century Midwest was a devil's den of state-sanctioned and extralegal racial oppression, violence, and iniquity. The Northwest Ordinance, while ostensibly outlawing slavery in the Great West, set the stage for white settler colonialism, ethnic cleansing of Indigenes, and anti-Black oppression. Black Laws passed by antebellum midwestern state legislatures legalized Black second-class citizenship and set a precedent nationally for racially discriminatory legislation before and after the Civil War. White anti-Black mobs, lynching, and slave catching terrorized African Americans across the Old Northwest, and most Black midwesterners occupied the bottom rung of the labor force. Still, despite facing violence, oppression, and hardships, Black women and men found a little bit more freedom than they had experienced in the South where slavery and then Jim Crow were king. In the early nineteenth century, the Great West was a sparsely populated region. By 1900, the Midwest was a global industrial powerhouse. The African-descended first arrived in what became the Midwest at the dawn of the colonial era. In the ensuing centuries, they began forging a collective Black nationalist identity and long-lasting national and (in some cases) global institutions. Through the Colored Conventions movement, Underground Railroad, abolitionism, Black-town construction, World's Columbian Exhibition, and Congress on Africa, Black midwesterners positioned themselves at the front lines in cultivating classical Black nationalism and transnational political linkages. Black midwestern resistance was not without its paradoxes and limitations. But the activism, community-building, and global visions of Black midwesterners did challenge the color line at home and abroad. So, when Marcus Garvey arrived on the scene in the United States during the First World War, Black midwesterners had already, for more than one century, been leaders in the fight for global Black liberation.

2

STRONGHOLD

The Diasporic Midwest and Heyday of the UNIA

The Omaha Division held its regular mass meeting on Sunday, May 23, at 3:30 p.m. A short program was rendered as follows: Opening services conducted by the president, Mr. Little, assisted by the secretary, M. L. Bolden. A splendid address was delivered by Reverend Moseley. —LOUISE LITTLE, *Negro World*, June 19, 1926

Louise Little was eager. It was June 1917. She was aboard the steamer *Chaleur* in the Carenage, the scenic harbor of St. George's, the capital of the British Caribbean colony of Grenada. The ship was bound for St. John, New Brunswick, Canada, with scheduled stops in Barbados, St. Vincent, St. Lucia, Dominica, St. Kitts, Antigua, and Montserrat.[1] Upon arrival in St. John, she planned to travel to Montreal. She selected the city because her uncle Edgerton Langdon resided there after migrating from Grenada to Canada in 1913. Louise, who was in her early twenties, already possessed a deep sense of racial pride and justice. After she boarded the *Chaleur*, the ship's stewards directed her to sit in the first-class passenger section occupied by white Canadian and colonial elites, given that she had purchased a one-way, first-class ticket. She refused to move. She informed the crew that she preferred to sit below decks with her own people—working-class Black Grenadians and other Afro-Caribbean passengers—forsaking the comforts she would have enjoyed on her long voyage had she traveled in first class with white passengers. She surely felt a sense of satisfaction in her decision as the *Chaleur* steamed past Fort George, a large fortress built in 1667 by enslaved Africans, perched 175 feet above the Carenage, and into the Caribbean Sea.[2] She arrived about two weeks later in St. John. From there, she journeyed to Montreal.[3] It is unclear whether she intended to return to Grenada. What we know is that she never returned home and that her journey from Grenada to Montreal is absent in *The Autobiography of Malcolm X.*

In the coming decades, Louise never forgot from where she came. After enlisting in the UNIA in Montreal, she eventually made her way to the Midwest, where in Omaha, Nebraska, and Lansing, Michigan, she carried out her most important life's work on behalf of the Garvey movement as a grassroots organizer. Once there, she strove to forge autonomous Black communities, to defend herself and family from white racial terror, and to cultivate Garveyite principles of self-reliance, race pride, and self-determination in her children. Her diasporic journeys and grassroots pan-African activism provide a larger window into the dynamic history of midwestern Garveyism and to the making of the Diasporic Midwest during the 1920s.

The Midwest, particularly Chicago, Detroit, and Cleveland, emerged as a stronghold of the transnational UNIA from the First World War to Marcus Garvey's deportation from the United States in 1927. These years marked his rise as the premier international Black leader and the zenith of the UNIA's global strength. The dialectic of opportunity and oppression in the Midwest, combined with Blacks' determination to be free, transformed Black midwestern urban communities into self-conscious communities receptive to Garveyism. This chapter begins with a biographical sketch of Marcus Garvey and a brief organizational history of the UNIA from its founding in 1914 to Garvey's deportation, with an examination of his political journey and gradual political turn toward Black diasporic right radicalism. I then look at how developments in Black communities in early twentieth-century Chicago, Detroit, and Cleveland created the conditions for the transnational UNIA to thrive in the heartland. The chapter then discusses the family history of Louise and Earl Little and the couple's UNIA activism in Omaha and Lansing. Their lives provide insight into grassroots Garveyism in the heartland, the diasporic dimensions of Black midwestern life, the personal costs of activism, and the Garveyite groundings of their son, young Malcolm X.[4] The chapter concludes with a discussion of the emergence of the midwestern Garveyite front, most notably the religious leader Noble Drew Ali and his Chicago-based Moorish Science Temple of America (MSTA). Taken together, the UNIA and midwestern Garveyite front of the 1920s strengthened the foundations of the Diasporic Midwest as a crossroads of Black transnational activism and laid the foundations for future, long-lasting, globally impactful Black political, social, and cultural formations. Even more, 1920s heartland Garveyism reveals the complicated meaning of freedom for early twentieth-century midwestern Black nationalists and the evolution of Black nationalism in a new global historical moment. Building from their nineteenth-century predecessors, the Black nationalism and settler colonialism of heartland Garveyites challenged and abetted the global color line.

The Rise of Marcus Garvey and the UNIA

The path of Marcus Mosiah Garvey to global preeminence and the rise of the transnational UNIA into the largest Black movement in history were byproducts of early twentieth-century global upheavals, the long and complex history of Black struggle, and his own lived experiences. He was born on August 17, 1887, in the town of St. Ann's Bay on Jamaica's north shore.[5] A British colony since 1655, Jamaica by the early nineteenth century emerged as the world's most profitable sugar-producing colony. The island's immense enslaved African population produced massive wealth that helped fuel the Industrial Revolution in England.[6] Enslaved Africans and maroons in Jamaica were exceptionally unruly. Their everyday resistance and epic slave rebellions were partly responsible in forcing British rulers to abolish slavery across the New World British Empire in 1833.[7] The legacy of slavery, abolition, and Black resistance in Jamaica permeated every aspect of the island's life at the time of Garvey's birth. Formerly enslaved people and their descendants strove for independence and dignity through an expanding peasant economy. His family hailed from this community. His parents—Sarah Jane Richards, a domestic servant, and Malchus Garvey, a mason by trade who was an immensely proud man, voracious reader, and punitive father and husband—strove for upward mobility, self-improvement, independence, and dignity in a changing world. They passed these convictions on to their son.[8] Malchus apprenticed his son to a printer in Kingston. Precocious and defiant, the young Marcus led a printer's strike in 1907. Living in Kingston stoked his pan-African consciousness. There, he met the physician, journalist, and politician Joseph Robert Love of the Bahamas, who schooled Garvey in nineteenth-century Black nationalist thought.[9]

Globetrotting was critical to opening young Garvey's eyes to the need for transnational approaches for racial uplift. In 1909, he traveled to Central America and South America where he observed the miserable conditions that tens of thousands of Afro-Caribbean migrant workers endured. In 1912, he relocated to London. There, he encountered a small but dynamic community of

African-descended from the continent and the Caribbean. He worked for the legendary Egyptian-Sudanese activist-journalist Dusé Mohamed Ali's *African Times and Orient Review*. Under his tutelage, Garvey studied African history and pan-Africanism and received an introduction to Islam. He came to appreciate the antiracist power of Black history, and he valorized Ancient Egypt as the birthplace of civilization. Reflecting the conclusions of nineteenth-century classical Black nationalists and the prevailing beliefs in the turn-of-the-century United Kingdom, Garvey forged racialist understandings of civilization and human progress, and he viewed contemporary African Indigenes as backward.[10] A key turning point for him came in 1914 after reading *Up from Slavery*, the autobiography of Booker T. Washington, the formerly enslaved person who founded the historically Black college Tuskegee Institute in Tuskegee, Alabama. A champion of industrial education, Washington became the leading African American spokesperson by the turn of the twentieth century. His self-help credo and Tuskegee Institute mesmerized Garvey. After reading the memoir, he asked himself: "Where is the black man's government? Where is his President, his ambassador, his country, his men of big affairs? I could not find them. . . . And then I declared, 'I will help to make them.'" Transformed by his overseas sojourns and Washington's *Up from Slavery*, Garvey returned to Jamaica ready to lead the race (see figure 2.1).[11]

On July 20, 1914, at the age of twenty-seven, Garvey, with Amy Ashwood Garvey, founded the Universal Negro Improvement and Conservation Association and African Communities (Imperial) League in Kingston. The couple conceived the UNIA as a friendly society for promoting racial uplift and pride through education, entrepreneurialism, and self-improvement. Beyond the Caribbean, the group's transnational program called for "civilizing the Backward tribes of Africa" and for supporting Liberia.[12] These initial objectives, together with the UNIA's original name, reflected Garvey's imperial imaginations, civilizationism, modest political goals, middle-class cultural orientation, and desire to maintain cordial relations with white colonial rulers. Despite his high hopes, the UNIA foundered in Jamaica. In his attempt to gain the support of Booker T. Washington, Garvey journeyed to New York in March 1916. Unbeknownst to Garvey, Washington had died the previous year.[13]

Coming to the United States and the First World War radicalized Garvey. The period between the war and July 1921 signaled the most radical phase in his career. His work during these years established him as the foremost champion of global Black freedom in the minds of African-descended people worldwide. Unprecedented carnage on the battlefield, migrations, strikes, and nationalist unrest in India, Ireland, and China weakened the European colonial grip on

FIGURE 2.1. Marcus Garvey statue in front of St. Ann Parish Library, July 25, 2023, St. Ann's Bay, Jamaica, March 24, 2016. Photo by the author.

Africa, Asia, and the Caribbean. In 1917, the Russian Revolution established the world's first socialist state, the Soviet Union. In the United States, the First World War marked the start of the Great Migration. From 1915 to 1930, one and a half million African Americans migrated from the Jim Crow South to the urban North—New York, Chicago, Philadelphia, Detroit, and Cleveland—in search of a better life free from Jim Crow and poverty. Blacks cautiously believed that the war "would make the world safe for democracy" and would improve their status. Wartime events shattered these hopes. The deadly East St. Louis Riot of 1917, a spike in lynching, a national wave of strikes, and the "Red Summer" of 1919, in which racial unrest exploded in twenty-six cities across the United States, proved to Black people that the world had not changed.[14] Beyond the United States, African-descended populations in Paris, Lagos, Harare, Bulawayo, Johannesburg, and São Paulo swelled as migrants moved to these cities in search of brighter futures.[15]

Like millions of Black people around the world, Garvey felt betrayed by the refusal of the Allies to grant self-determination to colonized people after the war. Residing in Harlem located him in the largest Black urban community in the world and in a center of "New Negro radicalism." The term referred to a more militant New Negro tendency, spawned by racial and labor unrest across the United States and a global Black revolt during and immediately after the war. As a political and cultural movement comprising the UNIA, the Harlem-based African Blood Brotherhood, and other protest groups, as well as news and literary journals, New Negro radicalism promoted a more expansive vision of uplift than formations such as the NAACP and Urban League, and it linked Black American freedom with anticolonial revolts around the world.[16]

Garvey's association in Harlem with organizer, educator, bibliophile, free thinker, and orator Hubert Henry Harrison from St. Croix, known among his contemporaries as the "father of Harlem radicalism," was critical to radicalizing and positioning Garvey on the left-wing side of New Negro radicalism. Harrison was a foremost theoretician and organizer, who was the highest-profile Black person in the US Socialist Party prior to his break from it in 1914.[17] During the First World War, he forged a New Negro radical politics he called "Race First." This politics understood the centrality of racial oppression to the modern world-system and the revolutionary potential of Black mass movements and racial consciousness for ending white supremacy and imperialism. He advanced this politics through several Harlem-based New Negro radical formations he established, most notably the Liberty League. Harrison and the Liberty League, which Garvey joined, provided some of Garvey's earliest speaking platforms in Harlem and invaluable lessons in organization-building. He adopted Harrison's "Race First" as his political mantra.[18] Harrison was not only critical to mentoring and radicalizing Garvey. Harrison played an important role in disseminating Garvey's ideas to the African-descended masses globally after he eclipsed his mentor as the leading New Negro radical leader in Harlem. From 1920 through early 1922, Harrison worked as the unofficial managing editor of *Negro World*. On his watch, the worldwide circulation of *Negro World* increased exponentially, and the newspaper gained a global reputation as the leading radical voice for the Black masses.[19]

The wartime Garvey embraced a politics of revolutionary solidarity with racially and nationally oppressed people from around the world. In a March 1919 editorial published in *Negro World*, he praised the 1917 Russian Revolution.[20] Garvey, unlike Harrison, never endorsed socialism. However, Garvey recognized Soviet Russia as an unprecedented development for the "revolutionary world" in its fight against Western imperialism and the global color line.[21] In addition to lauding the Russian Revolution, Garvey expressed solidarity with nationalist struggles in Ireland, India, Egypt, and elsewhere.[22]

Amid global wartime upheavals and Garvey's encounters in Harlem with New Negro radicals, he built the UNIA from a tiny club counting a few dozen members in 1917 to a transnational mass movement claiming six million members by 1923.[23] The UNIA's historic First International Convention of Negro People of the World, held in New York from August 1 to 31, 1920, signaled a high point of Garvey's New Negro radicalism and mass exuberance for the UNIA. Delegates representing "400,000,000" African-descended people from around the world assembled at the conference. The opening sessions, held in New York's Madison Square Garden, attracted more than twenty-five thousand attendees per day. Before a jubilant audience, Garvey called for "a free and independent Africa."[24] The conference adopted the UNIA's official motto: "One God. One Aim. One Destiny." The landmark Declaration of Rights of the Negro Peoples of the World, adopted at the convention, stands as a lasting achievement. Anticipating post–Second World War African American initiatives at the United Nations, the UNIA manifesto demanded "human rights" and self-determination for Black people globally; proclaimed all Blacks worldwide as "free citizens of Africa"; condemned Jim Crow, lynching, peonage, and colonialism; and designated red, black, and green as the official colors of the race. The tricolor flag signified race pride and the UNIA's aspirations for a free Africa.[25]

From the UNIA's Liberty Hall in Harlem, Garvey created a provisional government for the Black world with a constitution, army, national anthem, newspaper, and statelike bureaucracy, as well as positions—dukes, potentates, and other governmental titles. Given its commitment to self-help and Black capitalism, the UNIA established businesses, including cafeterias, dry cleaners, millineries, groceries, and automobile repair shops. The Black Star Line (BSL) constituted the UNIA's most ambitious commercial venture. Founded in 1919, the BSL was a fleet of UNIA-owned merchant ships that Garvey envisaged as the keystone of his plan for global Black economic independence. The venture failed largely due to mismanagement, undercapitalization, and state harassment. Still, the short-lived venture generated immense pride among—and left indelible memories with—people of African descent globally.[26] In addition to its organizational structure, the UNIA forged a dynamic movement culture. Key to this process was Garvey's philosophy of "African fundamentalism," a civic religion he conceived and incorporated into the UNIA's organizational life. Drawing from a variety of Black religious credos, African fundamentalism claimed God was Black, rejected white supremacy, and demanded the full freedom of Black people.[27] Additionally, Garveyism created a welcoming space for Islam. The UNIA was officially nondenominational, and Garvey remained a Catholic throughout his adult life. However, he and the UNIA appropriated Islamic referents into the organization's rhetoric and symbols. *Negro World*, under the editorship of Dusé Mohamed Ali and others, featured global news about nationalist struggles across the Islamic world under European colonialism. The UNIA's Islamophilia helped to precipitate the (re)introduction of Islam into African American communities in the coming years.[28]

Gender was critical to structuring relations of power within the UNIA. Reflecting the prevailing gender politics of the time and Garvey's sexism, the UNIA embraced socially constructed heteronormative ideas about the alleged "natural" roles of women and men in the public and private spheres. Viewing gender roles in binary and complementary terms, men were to be, the UNIA charged, husbands and fathers who provided for and protected their families. Women were to be faithful wives, nurturing mothers, and caretakers of the home.[29] Given this understanding of gender, the UNIA built an internal organizational structure that understood gender relations as "separate and hierarchal."[30] In accordance with the UNIA constitution, the UNIA divisions elected a "male president," who was in charge of leading the local branch, and a "lady president," who oversaw the division's work among women and children.[31]

Despite the UNIA's masculinism, Garveyite women asserted their voices in leading the organization. As discussed, Amy Ashwood Garvey, Marcus Garvey's first wife, cofounded the UNIA with her future husband. Women such as Amy Jacques Garvey, Marcus Garvey's second wife and an indomitable pan-Africanist in her own right, Henrietta Vinton Davis, and Maymie Turpeau De Mena gained international prominence in the 1920s as powerful spokespersons for the transnational UNIA (see figure 2.2). As community feminists, they contested male chauvinism within the UNIA and took up the pan-African crusade. At the grass roots, Garveyite women performed community service work through the Black Cross Nurses, the UNIA auxiliary that carried out similar duties as the Red Cross.[32]

Meanwhile, Garvey emerged as arguably the most prominent Black political prisoner of the twentieth century prior to the 1960s. White rulers in the United States, Western Europe, and the colonial world perceived him as a subversive threat to the global order. Given these fears, colonial authorities across the Caribbean and Africa monitored Garvey and UNIA activities, and in some cases *Negro World*, given its antiracist, anticolonial politics, was banned.[33] Authorities in the US South and South Africa did the same.[34] Beginning in 1918 in the United States, the Bureau of Investigation (BOI), the predecessor of the Federal Bureau of Investigation, surveilled Garvey and the UNIA through

FIGURE 2.2. Amy Jacques Garvey, circa 1923. Fisk University, John Hope and Aurelia E. Franklin Library, Special Collections, Nashville, Tennessee.

BRILLIANT WIFE—HELPMATE

MRS. AMY JACQUES-GARVEY

fe of the Hon. Marcus Garvey who is directing the affairs of the N. I. A. during her husband's absence. See article on page 5.

agents, informants, and agent provocateurs. The government's case against Garvey gained momentum under J. Edgar Hoover. An ardent racist and staunch anticommunist who became director of the BOI in 1925, he masterminded a scheme to bring down Garvey through charging him with mail fraud for allegedly using the US Postal Service to defraud prospective investors in Black Star Line stock. On February 15, 1922, the Justice Department indicted Garvey and twelve officials of the defunct BSL on twelve counts of mail fraud. Garvey and the UNIA had broken no laws. But Hoover and the Justice Department were determined to silence Garvey.[35] On June 21, 1923, a federal court in New York found Garvey guilty of mail fraud and sentenced him to five years in federal prison. He entered Atlanta Federal Penitentiary on February 8, 1925, for a five-year term.[36] He remained in prison until November 18, 1927, when US president Calvin Coolidge commuted Garvey's sentence. From New Orleans on December 2, 1927, US authorities deported Garvey to Jamaica via Panama. He never returned to the United States.[37] His deportation marked Hoover's first takedown of a major Black leader.[38]

Garvey and his unprecedented UNIA shook the world. However, his classical Black nationalism and Black settler colonialism contained serious paradoxes. His scheme to colonize Liberia in the 1920s is a case in point. The UNIA's work there illustrates both its oppositional and conservative character. Following in the footsteps of nineteenth-century Black nationalists, Garvey imagined Liberia as the base for redeeming the continent and for building his global Black empire. He called for the voluntary emigration of New World Blacks—artisans, educators, missionaries, health workers, scientists, engineers, farmers, and professionals—to Liberia. Once there, they would establish settlements, schools, hospitals, commercial farms, and businesses for developing Liberia and strengthening the continent. Accordingly, a unified, modern Africa under a diasporic-led government, he believed, would rival European nations for geopolitical power and thereby protect the rights and dignity of the African-descended everywhere.[39]

Garvey invested considerable time and the UNIA's organizational resources into promoting his Black settler colonial agenda for Liberia. In 1919, he declared his intention of relocating the UNIA's headquarters from Harlem to Monrovia. During the 1920s, he corresponded with Liberian president Charles B. D. King about the UNIA-sponsored colonization plan. Garvey dispatched four delegations of US-based UNIA officials to Liberia to secure a deal with Monrovia.[40] In 1920, he appointed Gabriel M. Johnson, the mayor of Monrovia, as UNIA High Potentate to head the UNIA division in Monrovia. The local counted about one hundred members, most of whom were Americo-Liberians.[41]

Although initially receptive to Garvey's plan, Monrovia bowed to pressure from Washington and the powerful Firestone Rubber Company (based in Akron, Ohio) to break ties with Garvey. Firestone desired to establish a massive rubber plantation in the Liberian interior. Uneasy with Garvey's connections with the West African republic, Firestone lobbied Washington, DC, officials to pressure Monrovia to accept the company's request for land and to break ties with the UNIA in exchange for a sizable loan from the US government. Desiring to maintain good diplomatic relations with the United States and in need of the loan, the cash-strapped Liberian government agreed to the terms.[42] In 1926, Monrovia granted Firestone a ninety-nine-year lease for one million acres of land for six cents per acre—a steal for the US company— making the property the world's largest rubber plantation. Liberian officials cut ties with the UNIA. Feeling betrayed and viewing the deal as a capitulation by Monrovia to a predatory white corporation, Garvey charged that the agreement would tighten the white imperialist grip on Liberia and Blacks globally. He denounced the Liberian government. The agreement and the resulting recriminations between Liberian officials and Garvey led to the shutdown of the Monrovia UNIA, marking the end of major UNIA operations in West Africa during the interwar years.[43]

Garvey's defeat in Liberia was not simply a byproduct of power politics and diplomatic missteps. It was also the result of the contradictions of his Black settler colonialism and social dynamics within the African Diaspora. Racial unity was at the heart of Garvey's pan-Africanism. He perceived Americo-Liberians as natural allies in his quest to redeem the continent. However, he misunderstood Liberia and its complex place within the wider world. Americo-Liberians, a Black settler class residing in an impoverished, neocolonial state, were determined to maintain their privilege vis-à-vis African Indigenes and remain in good standing with the US government. Given this reality, Liberian elites ultimately wanted nothing to do with Garvey.[44]

Fundamentally, Garvey's civilizationist outlook and imperial ambitions both challenged and reproduced Eurocentric assumptions about the treatment of Indigenous Africans. Garvey pursued his emigration schemes against the backdrop of the Black settler conquest of the last pockets of Indigenous resistance within Liberia. In 1916, the Liberian Frontier Force, Monrovia's Black settler colonial militia, crushed a major rebellion by the Kru, an Indigenous maritime people of the southeastern Liberian coast.[45] During the 1920s, Liberian forces pacified the Kpelle, a Mandé-speaking people in central Liberia.[46] Garvey called for the humane treatment of Indigenous people in Liberia and expressed his righteous anger about the atrocities carried out by European colonizers against their African subjects.[47] But he still believed that New World Blacks were best suited to rule over African Indigenes. So, his Black settler colonialism challenged Western imperialism by calling for African independence and protecting Indigenes. Yet he desired self-determination for Africans as long as they lived under the paternal care of New World Blacks and westernized Africans.

While Garvey's Black settler colonial vision generated immense excitement among Blacks around the world, a small community of Harlem New Negro left-wing radicals, including Hubert Harrison, came to oppose Garvey's imperial machinations and civilizationist framings of worldwide African liberation. According to Minkah Makalani, many Black left-wing radicals viewed empire as inextricably linked to imperialism and capitalism. Given this position, they opposed civilizationism and dismissed Garvey's entrepreneurialism as corrupt and inefficacious. Members of the African Blood Brotherhood envisioned an anticapitalist pan-African federation in league with the Soviet Union and oppressed people everywhere as the best vehicle for advancing decolonization, Black-white unity, socialism, and Black freedom.[48] This vision of global Black liberation, grounded in the belief in Africans as key agents for transformative change, challenged the pro-capitalist line and Eurocentric assumptions about Africa deeply embedded in Garveyism and in classical Black nationalism.

Garvey's growing obsession with racial purity and his collaborations with white supremacists best signaled his retreat from New Negro radicalism and move toward Black diasporic right radicalism. In a 1924 statement, "What We Believe," Garvey declared that the UNIA "believe[d] in the purity of the Negro race and the purity of the white race." Opposing "miscegenation" and "race suicide," he charged that racial separation would enable Blacks to build "a strong and powerful Negro nation in Africa."[49] He directed his ire toward his critics, most notably his archrival during the 1920s—W. E. B. Du Bois. Garvey denounced Du Bois as an elitist, racial sellout and (mis)represented him as an aspirant for miscegenation.[50] In addition to blasting Du Bois and civil rights activists, Garvey excoriated white trade unionists and communists as false allies of Black people.[51]

Garvey's advocacy for emigration and racial purity, together with his opposition to Black-white sex and communism, opened the door for collaborations between the UNIA and white supremacists, most notably his infamous meeting in June 1922 in Atlanta with the Ku Klux Klan Acting Imperial Wizard, Edward Young Clarke. During their summit, they conferred about their respective organizations' commitment to racial purity.[52] Underscoring how Garvey understood the racial struggle in highly gendered terms, he declared after the meeting, "I was speaking to a man who was brutally a white man, and I was speaking to him as a man who was brutally a Negro."[53] These two men—a Black nationalist and white supremacist—found common ground through their shared belief in racial purity *and* hypermasculinity. Framing the struggle for African redemption as a Manichean contest between Black and white men for the racial survival of their respective people, Garvey's manly perspective rendered invisible the unique oppressions faced by Black women and equated Black manhood redemption with the full freedom of Blacks everywhere. In the coming years and taking their cues from Garvey, Black nationalists in the heartland and beyond often articulated freedom in masculinist terms.

Garvey's decision to meet with the Klan was a controversial move among his Black opponents. Du Bois famously decried Garvey as either "a lunatic or a traitor" for conferring with the Invisible Empire.[54] From Garvey's standpoint,

meeting with the KKK made sense. He came to believe that the Klan represented the politics and values of white America, with stronger support in the
North than in the South.[55] The return to normalcy in the early 1920s also helps
explain Garvey's growing preoccupation with racial purity and decision to
meet with the Klan. Imperial powers crushed Soviet-inspired revolts in Europe
and anticolonial uprisings in Asia and Africa. In the United States, a red scare
suppressed radical trade unionism and the fledgling Communist Party. Convinced that the possibilities for world revolution had passed and mindful of US
government scrutiny of him and the UNIA, he distanced the organization from
radicalism.[56] For these reasons, he sought an alliance with what he perceived as
the most powerful organization in the United States, the KKK.

Garvey did not overstate the Klan's power. Counting as many as two million
members nationwide at its height in the early 1920s, the KKK was arguably the
largest white civic organization in the United States.[57] Reestablished in 1915,
the "Second Klan," as this new incarnation of the KKK came to be called, was
mindful of its predecessor's unsavory reputation for racial terrorism. Subsequently, the new Klan sought to rebrand itself as the purveyor of white middle-
class respectability, morality, and patriotism.[58] Despite these efforts, the KKK
remained a violent white supremacist organization.[59]

In addition to meeting with the KKK, Garvey forged close ties with leading
white supremacist intellectuals, most notably Earnest Sevier Cox of Richmond,
Virginia. Born in 1880 in rural eastern Tennessee, Cox was a scholar, Methodist
preacher, and world traveler who made it his life mission to prove white people's
alleged racial superiority since the beginning of time. By the early 1920s, he
acquired an international reputation as a preeminent white supremacist intellectual.[60] In 1923, he founded the White America Society, a clearing house for
white nationalism, and published his most famous book, *White America*. Arguing that civilization proceeded from whites and that racial separation was
the only solution to the US race problem, he championed racial purity, railed
against interracial sex, opposed communism, and advocated African American
colonization to Africa. Garvey figured prominently in Cox's thinking. Viewing
him as a kindred spirit and as the leading Black advocate for emigration, Cox
urged whites to support Garvey.[61] Cox and Garvey began corresponding in
1925 while Garvey was in prison.[62] Cox both championed Garvey's cause for
colonization and also supported efforts to get Garvey released from jail.[63]

Garvey saw Cox as an ally. In correspondence with Cox, Garvey praised
White America as a "masterpiece" and denounced civil rights advocates, particularly Du Bois, as "half breeds" for allegedly promoting miscegenation. Garvey and Cox developed a working relationship.[64] In addition to corresponding

with Cox, Garvey in 1925 invited Cox and his associate John Powell of the Anglo Saxon Club to speak at UNIA meetings in Richmond and Harlem, respectively.[65] Garvey was not alone in forging an enduring association with Cox. Amy Jacques Garvey did too through letters.[66]

Marcus Garvey's collaborations with white supremacists stand as his greatest political mistake. His associations with and support for Cox, combined with his civilizationism and masculinism, spoke vividly to his Black diasporic right radicalism. So while Garvey was critical to championing the global struggle against racism and for African liberation in the years immediately after the First World War, his conservative turn soon thereafter signaled how much his thinking remained rooted in Eurocentric paradigms. From the 1920s onward, his midwestern disciples built dynamic, globally influential Black movements that not only linked the heartland to the African world but also reflected the possibilities and limitations of Garveyism.

The Diasporic Midwest and the UNIA's Heyday

In the years during and immediately after the Great War, Chicago, Detroit, and Cleveland emerged as key hubs of New Negro militancy and the transnational UNIA. This development occurred as Garvey took the United States and world by storm. Harlem was the seat of Garvey's Black empire and the largest UNIA division. The Garvey movement in Harlem took shape as New York's Black population swelled from 91,709 in 1910 to 152,467 in 1920 to 327,706 in 1930.[67] Most Blacks in New York hailed from somewhere else—the US South, the Caribbean, and Africa. There were ten times more foreign-born African-descended people in New York than in any other US city, and forty thousand Caribbean immigrants came to New York between 1900 and 1930. The mixture of foreign and native-born Blacks created a vibrant, distinct ethnic community.[68] The bulk of Harlemites made a living through New York's low-wage service sector, massive garment industry, and informal economy. The New York UNIA reflected the heterogeneity and dynamism of Harlem. Caribbean migrants composed a significant portion of the leadership and rank-and-file of the Harlem UNIA, which counted twenty-five thousand members.[69]

Garvey's message resonated in the US South. There, Blacks lived under Jim Crow, and often outnumbered whites in locales across the South. In southeastern Virginia, and Atlantic southern coastal and Gulf cities like New Orleans, Louisiana; Miami, Tampa, Key West, and Jacksonville in Florida; and Mobile, Alabama, the UNIA attracted longshoremen, seamen, and other working-class people tied to the region's maritime economies. Caribbean migrants in Miami,

New Orleans, and Hampton Roads, Virginia, made their way into the UNIA. Garvey found strong support in inland cities like Atlanta, Georgia; Chattanooga and Knoxville in Tennessee; and Greensboro, North Carolina, as well as across parts of the rural South among sharecroppers, farmers, and professionals who wanted to live free from Jim Crow, develop autonomous African American communities, protect Black women, celebrate Black culture, and pursue African redemption.[70] Garveyism developed in a distinct way on the West Coast. There, Blacks constituted a racial minority. They resided in places where other communities of color—Mexicans, Chinese, Japanese, Filipinos, Indians, and Indigenous people—often outnumbered African Americans. Like elsewhere, Blacks on the West Coast, especially in Los Angeles and the Bay Area, upheld Garveyite principles.[71] But the West Coast racial landscape required them to pursue organizing with other communities of color for advancing both Black nationalism and a "multiracial nationalism" opposed to the global color line.[72]

As Garveyism electrified Black people across the postwar African world, the UNIA in the Diasporic Midwest cemented and impacted the globe in distinct, powerful, and lasting ways due to the experience of the dialectic of opportunity and oppression and the determination of Black midwesterners to be free. Chicago continued witnessing phenomenal growth and global visibility as a symbol of modernity and prosperity. The Windy City's population grew from 2,185,283 in 1910 to 2,701,705 in 1920 and then to 3,376,438 in 1930.[73] The First World War era marked a turning point in the history of Black Chicago. Between 1915 and 1920, fifty thousand African Americans migrated from the South to Chicago. More Blacks relocated to Chicago during the Great Migration than to any other US city. By 1920, Chicago's Black population grew to 109,458 and to 233,903 by 1930, making the city home to the second-largest Black urban population in the United States and world. Like in most midwestern cities, the foreign-born Black population in Chicago was small.[74]

Besides Chicago, perhaps no other Midwestern industrial city embodied the possibility for a better life for Blacks than Detroit. The Ford Motor Company (FMC) symbolized the city's industrial prosperity and innovation. Founded in 1903 by the corporate visionary Henry Ford and based in the Detroit suburb of Dearborn, Michigan, the FMC was the world's largest and wealthiest corporation at the time.[75] Through his invention of the assembly line for mass producing automobiles, Henry Ford revolutionized manufacturing, labor, and the social order. The FMC paid each of its workers a living wage of $5 per week so that they could afford to purchase the cars they produced and partake in mass consumerism. By 1920, Detroit emerged more committed to manufacturing than any other city in the United States. Nearly half of the city's factory workers toiled in the automobile industry. Detroit's population swelled from 285,704 in 1900 to nearly one million in 1920, making Detroit the fourth-largest city in the United States.[76]

Black migrants came to Detroit in search of a freer life through the city's booming automobile industry. The city's African American population increased by twentyfold from 5,471 in 1910 to 40,838 in 1920 to 120,066 in 1930.[77] No US industrial city's Black population grew as quickly as Detroit's.[78] The city's automobile plants and factories indelibly shaped the social relations of Black Detroiters.[79] Black men sought employment in the heavy industries, particularly at the FMC, where 45 percent of the city's Black male wage earners worked. Ford was the only major automaker between the two world wars that hired large numbers of African Americans and paid wages equal to those of whites on the assembly line, making Black Detroit autoworkers some of the highest-paid Black wage earners on the planet.[80]

Cleveland developed into a major US industrial city at the turn of the twentieth century. In 1920, the city counted 796,841 inhabitants, making it the fifth-largest city in the United States.[81] Similar to Chicago and Detroit, hopes for a brighter future through finding good-paying jobs in Cleveland's booming war industries prompted the arrival of thousands of Black southerners to the Lake Erie metropolis. Between 1910 and 1920, the city's Black population swelled from 8,448 to 34,351, making it the largest African American urban community in the state and the fifth largest in the Midwest. By 1930, Cleveland's Black population doubled to 71,133.[82]

While African Americans found unprecedented job opportunities in Chicago, Detroit, and Cleveland, these cities were also sites of extreme misery and racial oppression. The early twentieth century witnessed the ghettoization of and growing racial discrimination against African American populations in the urban North. These facts were abundantly clear in housing. In Chicago, a fast-growing eight-square-mile densely populated, hypersegregated, underserved neighborhood located on the South Side took shape.[83] In Detroit, most Blacks lived in the crowded neighborhood known as "Black Bottom," located near downtown because whites allowed African Americans to live nowhere else.[84] Likewise, by the 1920s, most Black Clevelanders lived in the Central Area—the city's Black belt—located on the east side near downtown.[85]

Economically, African Americans in the urban Midwest occupied the bottom rung of the labor market. This was apparent for Black workers at the FMC in Detroit. Even though Ford hired large numbers of Blacks, he nonetheless was a racist paternalist who also despised unions and socialism. The FMC reserved the dirtiest and hardest factory jobs for Blacks. For Black urban midwestern women, their economic fortunes were equally perilous. Like in other parts of the country, they usually toiled as domestics in white households.[86]

In keeping with the region's distinct history of white anti-Black violence, the heartland remained a hostile place for African Americans during the 1920s. The Chicago "Riot" of July 1919 is a case in point. White mobs invaded the South Side, leaving thirty-eight dead (twenty-three Black and fifteen white).[87] Even more, the Midwest, unlike the Northeast, was a KKK stronghold. One-third of the Klan's national membership resided in the heartland, with Illinois, Ohio, and Indiana representing the largest concentration of its strength.[88] Chicago was home to perhaps fifty thousand Klansmen—the highest number of any US city during the first half of the twentieth century.[89] Interwar Detroit was a dangerous place for African Americans. During these years, Detroit saw an influx of more than seventy-five thousand southern whites from rural Kentucky, Tennessee, and West Virginia, making up approximately 5 percent of the city's total population—a larger percentage than in Chicago, Cleveland, Philadelphia, and New York.[90] Determined to preserve their racial privilege in this midwestern industrial juggernaut, white southern migrants in Detroit joined the KKK and white supremacist organizations such as the Midwest-based Black Legion, a more violent offshoot of the Klan.[91] The KKK may have counted as many as fifty thousand members in the Detroit area and eighty thousand members statewide, making Michigan a national center of the Klan.[92] The KKK was not a presence in Cleveland. But African Americans there still bore the burden of racism and poverty.[93] In terms of intraracial dynamics in the Black urban Midwest, longtime African American middle-class residents often looked on migrants as uncouth embarrassments to the race.[94]

Despite racial terror and poverty, Black midwesterners in the 1920s, like their nineteenth-century forebearers, fought back against their oppressors. In Chicago, local, national, and global historical forces transformed Blacks into what St. Clair Drake and Horace Cayton described as "a self-conscious collectivity" and as "a large segment of the [city's] industrial proletariat."[95] Chicago's dynamic New Negro cultural and commercial scene continued gaining national and international exposure. In Detroit, Paradise Valley, the commercial center of Black Bottom, counted more than three hundred African American–owned businesses.[96] Cleveland's Central Area was home to a powerful NAACP branch and to Jane Edna Hunter's Phillis Wheatley Association, which expanded its work across the country.[97] Politically, Black midwesterners voted. Some African

Americans gravitated toward leftist formations—the African Blood Brotherhood and International Workers of the World.[98] It was this unique world in which Black midwesterners lived that set the stage for Garveyism to take root.

Black migrants in Detroit, Chicago, Cleveland, and other midwestern cities came to see the UNIA as a powerful mass platform for adjusting to their new life in the industrial heartland and to connecting their struggle for freedom, dignity, and community with the aspirations of Black and subjugated people around the world. In the process, the heartland made its mark on global Garveyism. In Chicago, Division 23 (later Division 401), the first UNIA local in the city, was founded in 1920. The South Side–based division claimed more than twenty thousand members, making it the biggest Black movement in Chicago and perhaps one of the largest UNIA divisions in the world (second only to Harlem).[99] UNIA Division 125 (later Division 407) took shape in Detroit in 1920. At its peak in the early 1920s, the Detroit UNIA with its five thousand members, the overwhelming bulk of whom were US born, constituted the largest Black organization in the city and one of the most powerful UNIA branches in the world.[100] The Cleveland UNIA—Division 59 (later Division 133)—was established in 1919. By 1923, the Cleveland UNIA enjoyed its apex, counting around one thousand members. Garvey visited the Forest City several times. In 1920, he spoke to more than four hundred exuberant followers at the Cory Methodist Episcopal Church, a house of worship that opened its doors to recently arrived migrants.[101] Cleveland anchored the Garvey movement in Northeast Ohio, the state's industrial core. Statewide, Ohio counted thirty-one UNIA divisions—the most of any midwestern state. Besides Cleveland, the UNIA thrived in several Ohio cities: Akron, Alliance, Barberton, Cincinnati, Columbus, Dayton, and Youngstown.[102] The state's long history of African American resistance, combined with Black Ohioans' responses to postwar events, explains the UNIA's strength in the Buckeye State. As in other parts of the world, middle-class professionals and small-business owners held formal leadership positions in heartland UNIA locals. However, midwestern Garveyism from its beginning was primarily a working-class migrant movement. Common laborers and domestic workers, most of whom were married, and recently arrived migrants propelled and composed the bulk of UNIA membership in midwestern cities.[103]

Through the transnational UNIA, midwestern Garveyism emerged as a powerful alternative to traditional African American protest groups for self-determination and racial autonomy.[104] Contemporary observers acknowledged this point. According to a Detroit mayoral commission report on local race relations, the Detroit UNIA was "not a mere 'protest' organization." In contrast to the NAACP, Division 125 galvanized the Black masses "to meet injustices and denial of rights by starting all kinds of enterprises of their own with the purpose . . . in becoming so independent of the white people . . . that they can organize a government of their own."[105] Women such as the Alabama-born migrant and lifelong Garveyite Ruth Smith were vital to the local's work.[106] In addition to electrifying Black working-class people in Detroit, Garveyism also forged inroads into segments of the city's pre–Great Migration African American elite, illustrating how the UNIA found some success in building a diasporic, cross-class, multigenerational mass movement in the Motor City for Black empowerment. This was the case with the Reverend Arthur D. Chandler. Hailing from a proud family who had lived in Michigan since the 1830s and who had been active in abolition, Chandler, a former pastor of the prestigious Second Baptist Church, was an outspoken advocate for racial justice. He became a staunch Garveyite. At a mass UNIA meeting in 1923 in Detroit presided over by Garvey, Chandler passionately introduced the UNIA president-general.[107]

The heavy industrial character of midwestern cities also brought a small number of foreign-born Blacks to the region, some of whom played critical roles in raising the region's international profile in the UNIA. This was the case with Garveyite stalwart John Charles Zampty. Born in Trinidad, he came to know Garvey in Panama before making his way to Detroit in 1918, where he worked at Ford for the next forty years. After joining the Detroit UNIA, he was elected in 1923 as the UNIA auditor-general, a position he held into the 1970s.[108] Joseph A. Craigen, a native of British Guiana, was another prominent Detroit UNIA leader. After migrating to Detroit in 1918, he worked at several FMC plants. In the early 1920s, he joined the Detroit UNIA, becoming its president.[109] At the 1924 UNIA International Convention in Harlem, he delivered a speech in which he boasted about "represent[ing] the second greatest division of the association, second only to New York." Emphasizing Black economic opportunity in the Motor City, he asserted that "the economic situation is better [in Detroit] than in the average city, thanks to the Ford factories in which Negroes were employed on equal terms with whites."[110] His remarks recognized the heartland's heavy industrial character as a distinguishing feature of the region. He also understood that Detroit's prominence within the UNIA emanated in no small part from the good wages that rank-and-file members earned in automobile factories, a fact he wanted international UNIA conference delegates in Harlem to know.[111] At the same time, Detroit came to hold an infamous place in the history of Garveyism. Detroit was the last US city Garvey visited as a free person before the BOI arrested him in 1925 in Harlem and jailed him soon thereafter.[112]

Garvey recognized the strong support for the UNIA in the Midwest. At a mass meeting at Liberty Hall in Harlem following his return from Chicago in February 1921, he described the Windy City as "another stronghold of his Universal Negro Improvement Association." The crowd applauded.[113] Given the importance of the heartland to his movement, Garvey made several visits to Chicago, Detroit, Cleveland, Cincinnati, Milwaukee, Pittsburgh, St. Louis, Gary, Youngstown, Columbus, and other midwestern cities beginning as early as 1917.[114] Thousands of ecstatic midwestern Garveyites packed churches and meeting halls to see their president-general whenever he visited their city. He regularly dispatched ranking UNIA officials to the North American middle to galvanize his supporters and to fundraise for the organization. The comparatively high wages earned by Black male industrial workers and African American female domestics allowed them to generously support the transnational UNIA, a trend that persisted for decades.[115]

Through its institutions, program, and dynamic movement culture, Garveyism enabled Blacks to forge community in the urban industrial heartland and to cultivate diasporic sensibilities. Through *Negro World*, which featured pages published in Spanish and French, one could read the periodical's "News and Views of UNIA" page about Garveyite outposts from around the world.[116] UNIA meetings were also important sites for cultivating diasporic sensibilities among midwestern Garveyites. Midwestern UNIA meetings, like elsewhere in the United States, resembled Black southern church services. Meetings began with the singing of "From Greenland's Icy Mountains," the popular nineteenth-century abolitionist hymn adopted by the UNIA as its official opening anthem for all events.[117] The song's opening stanza vividly reveals the essence of African fundamentalism as both a political and religious credo for Black liberation.

> From Greenland's icy mountains, from India's coral strand
> Where Afric's sunny fountains roll down their golden sand
> From many an ancient river, from many a palmy plain
> They call us to deliver their land from error's chain.[118]

Prayer followed the song. Then came fiery sermon-like addresses about African redemption, current events, and Black history, which often were punctuated by spontaneous shouts of amen, applause, and feet stomping. Meetings closed with prayer and the singing of "Ethiopia, Thou Land of Our Fathers," the UNIA's official anthem. As scholar Shana Redmond observes, the anthem "became a transnational text that attempted to unite" the African-descended around the world.[119] For newly arrived southern migrants, UNIA meetings surely provided a welcoming sense of community in hostile new urban surroundings and a link to Black people everywhere.

No Garveyite mass event in the heartland was more important to disseminating Garveyism, to making New Negroes, to building community, and to linking the Midwest to the larger world than UNIA-sponsored street parades. Like in Harlem and locales around the world, Garveyites in the urban heartland proudly marched in colorful street parades witnessed in some cases by thousands of people. UNIA parades were transformative events for some participants and bystanders. The recollection of a Black Clevelander who witnessed Marcus Garvey at a large UNIA parade in the Central Area makes this case: "I remember as a lad in Cleveland during the hungry days of 1921, standing on Central Avenue, watching a parade one Sunday afternoon when thousands of Garvey Legionaries, resplendent in their uniforms marched by. When Garvey rode by in his plumed hat, I got an emotional lift, which swept me above the poverty and prejudice by which my life was limited."[120] This passage is significant. The recollection illustrates how Garveyites transformed the streets of the segregated Central Area into a vibrant public space that symbolically contested white supremacy and the misery of Black Cleveland life. The pageantry and symbolism of the parade stimulated the viewer's racial pride and nurtured his diasporic and nationalist consciousness. He became aware of his connection to a larger Black world through witnessing Garvey and the Universal African Legion, the UNIA's paramilitary unit, proudly march through Central Area streets. The parade, most of all, affirmed the observer's humanity and sense of hope, suggesting that Garveyism was critical to helping Blacks in Cleveland (and for that matter in other midwestern cities) come to understand systemic racial oppression, claim a right to the city, and imagine themselves as a distinct people vying for self-determination and African redemption.

While the dialectic of opportunity and oppression forged common bonds among midwestern Garveyites, so did the close geographic proximity of Chicago, Detroit, and Cleveland. Garveyites in these and other midwestern cities regularly attended UNIA events in other locations.[121] Like countless Black newcomers to the Midwest, it seems plausible that rank-and-file heartland Garveyites regularly visited friends and family in the South, some of whom may have been active UNIA members. Midwestern Garveyites were hardly the only UNIA members to travel to nearby and faraway places. But the heartland's central location in the United States and the close geographic proximity of major midwestern cities to one another helped facilitate well-resourced Garveyites to move about the region, United States, and world.

The unique politics of race, space, and place set midwestern Garveyites apart from their counterparts around the world. However, like the UNIA everywhere, midwestern Garveyites created an organizational culture in which masculinism ran deep. In step with Garvey's authoritarian leadership style, midwestern UNIA male officials often silenced women and men who challenged patriarchal authority, sometimes with catastrophic ramifications for the movement. For example, the Chicago-based veteran militant activist Ida B. Wells initially championed Garvey, but broke from him after he summarily dismissed her advice about formulating a better business plan for the BSL.[122] Her encounter with Garvey's autocratic leadership style was hardly unique. In Cleveland, the branch's male leadership ran Division 59 with a dictatorial grip. As a result, the Cleveland UNIA saw a revolving door of officers and the silencing of dynamic women leaders who refused to acquiesce to male leaders. This was true for Bessie A. Bryce. She was the Cleveland UNIA's executive secretary during the mid-1920s. A charismatic and married community feminist, she refused to acquiesce to the group's male leadership.[123] Over the objections of her grassroots supporters, Louis Van Pelt, the Cleveland UNIA president, forced Bryce out of the group in 1926 on the grounds that she allegedly was cantankerous.[124] Her departure cost the division one of its most respected leaders and prompted a significant number of members to exit the division, weakening it in the process. Bryce's departure signaled what was to come for other midwestern UNIA female leaders.

Despite the masculinism within the Garvey movement, midwestern UNIA women—like their Garveyite sisters around the world—embraced community feminism and attempted to make the UNIA their own. An article in *Negro World* by Lavinia D. M. Smith, a Garveyite and Cleveland public school teacher, illustrates this point. Arguing that no people could rise higher than its women, Smith claimed that women appreciated Garveyism because it "gav[e] Negro women an equal . . . opportunity to stand shoulder to shoulder with the men in the great cause for the redemption of Africa."[125] The UNIA did not always live up to Smith's claims. Still, Garveyism afforded Black women both protection from sexual and economic exploitation, and opportunities to lead a transnational Black movement they could find nowhere else.

While midwestern Garveyites dreamed of freeing Africa, their Black settler colonialism also led them down the same complicated path traveled by their president-general. This was apparent in a speech delivered at a South Side hall by Geraldine F. Smith, a Chicago public school teacher and UNIA member. Framing Garvey as the deliverer of African Americans from racial subjugation that began in 1619, she claimed he possessed a God-ordained plan "whereby we shall take over places of the world four hundred million strong, with one God, one aim, one destiny." Given that "Africa is our God-given home," she declared, "we are going back there [to] possess it" through the UNIA.[126] Clearly, Smith decried the subjugation of the African-descended and European colonial rule over the continent. Yet, like Garvey, Smith understood African redemption and emigration in civilizationist terms.

Upholding Black settler colonialism led grassroots midwestern Garveyites to embrace Black diasporic right radicalism and white supremacists. In his 1925 speech before the UNIA's Liberty Hall in Harlem, the white nationalist John Powell boasted that African American book agents in Detroit had sold seventeen thousand copies of Earnest Cox's *White America* to Blacks and whites in the city.[127] It is impossible to verify this claim, and there is no evidence to confirm whether Powell or Cox ever spoke before UNIA audiences in the heartland. What we know is that Cox received solicitations from Garveyites from the Midwest and around the world for his publications.[128] Their interest in his work reveals again the paradoxes of Black diasporic right radicalism. Through Garveyism, Black midwesterners found a powerful platform for welding their dreams for self-determination and African redemption with their pursuit for community and dignity. The region won Garvey's respect and was home to several of the transnational UNIA's largest divisions. But the Black settler colonialism of midwestern Garveyites proved to be a double-edged sword. While they opposed Jim Crow and colonialism, their Black nationalism prompted some midwestern Garveyites to ally with white supremacists. This complex politics carried on for years to come.

Garvey's Persecution, Political Imprisonment,
and the Midwest

Heartland-based Garveyites played a crucial role in leading the organization as Garvey faced government persecution. His legal troubles and incarceration injected paranoia and instability into the UNIA, amplifying the authoritarian tendencies and insecurities of its president-general.[129] Take, for example, Garvey's sacking of UNIA official William LeVan Sherrill. He was born on May 9, 1894, in Forrest City, Arkansas, located in the Arkansas River Delta, a center of Black support for emigration to Liberia.[130] Coming of age in the Arkansas River Delta and the First World War radicalized him. After joining the UNIA in 1921, Sherrill moved to New York where he enjoyed a meteoric ascension in the UNIA. In 1922, he was elected second assistant president-general and "Leader of American Negroes." Garvey promoted Sherrill to the position of

UNIA acting president-general on the eve of his imprisonment.[131] However, Garvey, soon after arriving in prison, grew increasingly suspicious of Sherrill. From prison, Garvey issued a blistering public statement in which he accused Sherrill of mismanaging the UNIA, financial impropriety, and undermining the work of Amy Jacques Garvey to free her husband. Given their distrust of Sherrill, Marcus Garvey and Amy Jacques Garvey moved to oust Sherrill from his position.[132]

As a power struggle ensued between Garvey and Sherrill, Midwest-based Garveyites were at the forefront in efforts to stabilize the transnational UNIA. Per Garvey's directives from prison, the UNIA held a two-week extraordinary international convention in March 1926 in Detroit.[133] The objective of the conference was to elect new officers to the Parent Body and to reassert Garvey's control over the UNIA. He selected the Motor City as the convention site because the Detroit UNIA backed him, while the New York UNIA aligned with Sherrill. In the end, conference delegates removed Sherrill as UNIA acting president-general. Soon afterward, Garvey appointed Ernest B. Knox of Chicago as the acting leader of the UNIA.[134]

Midwestern Garveyites figured visibly in Garvey's final days in the United States. As he waited in New Orleans for his deportation, he announced Knox as his UNIA representative in the United States. A photograph taken on board the SS *Saramacca*, the ship that deported Garvey from the United States, shows him surrounded by five of his leading lieutenants (see figure 2.3). Except for New Orleans UNIA president J. J. Peters, the other Garveyite officials were based in the Midwest—Joseph A. Craigen of Detroit, S. V. Robertson of Cleveland, Cincinnati UNIA president William Ware, and Ernest Knox of Chicago.

The photograph, as well as the Detroit convention and Garvey's appointment of Knox to ranking UNIA positions, should not be overlooked. When Garvey believed that the UNIA and his authority were on the line, he looked to the Diasporic Midwest, not to the East Coast, for deliverance. This move signaled the beginning of a recurring pattern in the Garvey movement: UNIA organizational crises often created opportunities for well-resourced Midwest-based Black nationalists to secure high-ranking formal leaderships within the UNIA and to set its transnational agenda. The Detroit conference and sacking of Sherrill revealed a contest between Midwest and East Coast Garveyites, particularly those in New York and Philadelphia, for control of the UNIA. Although Garveyites did not explicitly articulate the struggle in terms of nationality, it seems that mutual distrust between African Americans, who dominated UNIA divisions in the US heartland, and Caribbean Garveyites, who composed a sig-

FIGURE 2.3. Minutes before the SS *Saramacca* sailed out of the Port of New Orleans on December 1, 1927, Marcus Garvey posed on deck with a group of UNIA and African Communities League officials, including (*L* to *R*) Joseph A. Craigen, Executive Secretary, Detroit Divisions; S. V. Robertson, President, Cleveland Division; Mr. Garvey; Ernest B. Knox, Garvey's personal representative; William Ware, President, Cincinnati Division; and Dr. J. J. Peters, President, New Orleans Division. Xavier University of Louisiana, Archives and Special Collection, New Orleans.

nificant portion of the New York UNIA, may have helped create discord within the movement. What we can say is that a tug of war between Black nationalists based in the Diasporic Midwest and East Coast for control of the UNIA persisted into the future.

The Littles and Grassroots Midwestern Garveyism

As Marcus Garvey readily acknowledged the US heartland as an epicenter of the UNIA and as several midwesterners gained prominence in the transnational UNIA, thousands of everyday Black people played a critical role in advancing grassroots Garveyism in the Diasporic Midwest. Two people who made this happen were Louise and Earl Little. Their life and times in the region highlight the region's violent racial landscape and transnational connections to shaping the couple's grassroots Garveyism and to preparing the ground for Malcolm X's Black (inter)nationalism later in life. For Louise and Earl Little, like so many Black people across the African Diaspora who embraced Garveyism from the 1920s onward, returning to Africa was more of an aspirational goal than a concrete plan. Still, the desire to free Africa and to unite Black people everywhere burned in the Littles' hearts and inspired them to build the Garvey movement, forge self-reliant Black communities, resist white racial terror, and cultivate Garveyite principles of education, self-improvement, race pride, and justice in their children. The couple's passion for Garveyism, above all, affirms historian Lisa Lindsay's claim about "how much the African diaspora was conceived and experienced through family relations" across time, space, and historical generations.[135] However, *The Autobiography of Malcolm X* and prevailing understandings of the Littles shroud the family's diasporic family story and Louise's Garveyite politics. Given this tendency, my account of the Little family centers the Diasporic Midwest to their story.

Louise and Earl Little, like the bulk of grassroots Garveyites around the world, were not blank slates when they joined the UNIA. They arrived already possessing a strong racial and Black internationalist consciousness shaped by their lived experiences. Louise Little was born on January 2, 1894, in La Digue, Grenada, a village in St. Andrew Parish on the windward (eastern) side of the island. The violent history and legacy of slavery and colonialism in Grenada left an indelible mark on Little's body and consciousness. She was born sixty years after the formal end of slavery in Grenada and across the British Caribbean. Little was the product of rape. Her father, Edward Norton, apparently was a middle-aged loafer and a member of a colonial elite family from Scotland who had a penchant for sexually assaulting African-descended women and girls. Norton raped Little's mother, Edith Langdon, when she was eleven years old, producing her only child, Louise. Louise never knew her father.[136] In the *Autobiography*, Malcolm X decried his unnamed grandfather: "I was among the millions of Negroes who were insane enough to feel that it was some kind of status symbol to be light-complexioned—that one was actually fortunate to be born thus. But, still later, I learned to hate every drop of that white rapist's blood that is in me."[137] Louise informed Malcolm's distaste for his white grandfather. Detesting the crime committed by her father against her mother, Louise was cognizant of the painful history of racialized sexual violence experienced by Black women. With her fair complexion and long black hair, she could have passed for white (see figure 2.4). However, growing up in a family fiercely proud of its African ancestry ensured that Little identified with Black people and their struggle to be free, beliefs she passed on to her children.

FIGURE 2.4. Louise Little passport photo, circa 1917. Hidden Gem LLC Deborah Jones and Shawn Durr.

Little grew up in a tight-knit extended family that Langdon family lore claims was directly linked to West Africa and Islam through her maternal grandparents—Jupiter Langdon and Mary Jane Langdon. Details about their early lives are sketchy, and the *Autobiography* does not mention them. What we do know is that Jupiter Langdon was born around 1825, while Mary Jane Langdon was born around 1848.[138] Langdon family history contends that the couple hailed from modern-day Nigeria and that they were "liberated Africans," African captives freed by the British Royal Navy from slave ships on the Atlantic Ocean, who were often sent to the Caribbean (see figure 2.5).[139] According to Langdon family historian Terance Wilson, Jupiter and Mary Jane were Muslim and Yoruba, the largest African ethnic group on the planet and producers of the one of the world's most dynamic cultures.[140] The historical record has yet to reveal the given names of Jupiter and Mary Jane Langdon, how and when they made it to Grenada, adopted English names, and converted to Christianity, or if they continued speaking or taught Yoruba to their descendants.[141] What we know is that the couple apparently converted to Christianity after arriving in Grenada and gave their six children—Edgerton, Edith, Gertrude, Florence, Reginald, and Avey—non-Muslim names and had them baptized at a nearby

FIGURE 2.5. Grand Anse, Grenada, looking north toward St. George's, Grenada. Photo by the author.

Anglican church.[142] Beyond speculation, what is for certain is that Jupiter was determined to live autonomously from whites after arriving in Grenada. A skilled carpenter, he acquired land in La Digue and built a home on the property on which several generations of the Langdon family lived, including Louise (his final resting place is shown in figure 2.6).[143]

The possibility that Jupiter and Mary Jane Langdon were African-born Muslims requires rethinking Malcolm X's conversion story to Islam as told in the *Autobiography*. According to his memoir, he first learned about the NOI and Elijah Muhammad in 1948 while incarcerated at the Concord Prison outside of Boston from letters from Philbert, Malcolm's older brother. After correspondences with family members, prayer, and experiencing a silent apparition of NOI founder W. D. Fard Muhammad in Malcolm's prison cell, Malcolm converted to Islam. Historian Michael Gomez asserts that Malcolm's "embrace of the Nation of Islam was nothing less than a reclamation of origins, allowing for the symbolic reestablishment of ties to Africa."[144] The conversion to Islam by Malcolm and his siblings, then, seemed to constitute a rupture in Little family history, a rediscovery of Islam as the "natural religion" of African Americans, and a rejection of Christianity and white supremacy.[145] Langdon oral tradition

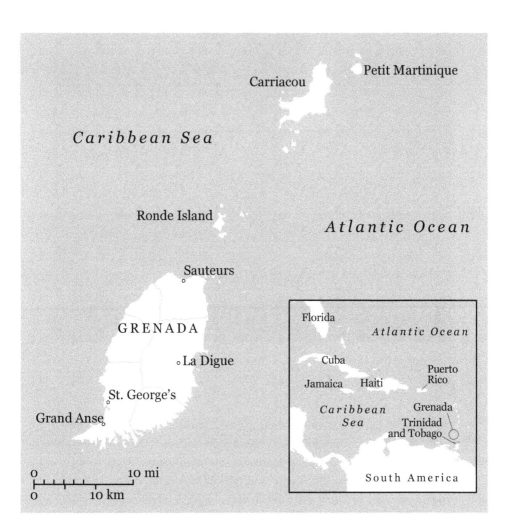

MAP 2.1. Grenada and the Caribbean.

challenges this narrative. Given the importance of family history to the Lang-dons, it seems difficult to imagine that Malcolm was unaware of his maternal great-grandparents' apparent African origins and Muslim faith. If Malcolm knew this history, then his conversion to Islam was in fact a continuation of a longer Islamic family history tied to his West African ancestors.

Just as the *Autobiography* omits Jupiter and Mary Jane Langdon, the memoir provides no discussion of Louise's years growing up in Grenada besides being born there and fathered by a white rapist. Malcolm's memoir also occluded her years in Canada and Garveyite work. What we know is that growing up on

FIGURE 2.6. The grave marker of Jupiter Langdon, La Digue, Grenada. Photo by the author.

the Langdon family property and raising food imparted to Louise the impor-tance of landownership, self-reliance, and independence from whites.[146] Her female relatives played the most important role in raising her. She grew up in a community where women exercised considerable autonomy within the public and private spheres and where children often took the names of their mother's lineage. This was the case with Louise. She was known within the family and La Digue as "Louise Langdon."[147] However, she often used "Norton" as her surname on official documents until her marriage. As a young Black woman in colonial Grenada who possessed few social privileges, she may have strategi-cally used her father's name to leverage the power of his elite racialized and gendered social position. Little was close to her resourceful maternal grand-mother, Mary Jane Langdon, who worked as a domestic, as well as with her aunt Gertrude, a proud, self-reliant seamstress who raised Louise and passed the trade on to her niece.[148]

Growing up in La Digue proved instrumental in instilling Little with a sense of independence, cosmopolitanism, history, and justice. Although it is unclear precisely how much formal education she received, she acquired an excellent education through a nearby school affiliated with Holy Innocents Church, an

Anglican house of worship and her family's church. For a young woman of color living in a colonial society, literacy and formal education were powerful tools for upward mobility. Like with Amy Ashwood Garvey and Amy Jacques Garvey, both of whom attended elite secondary schools for girls in Jamaica, formal education instilled confidence and a sense of independence in Little. She utilized these skills in the UNIA.[149] The rich oppositional culture of La Digue nurtured Little's intellect and sense of social justice for people of color. The memory of epic resistance of the Indigenous Carib people of Grenada to European genocidal wars of extermination during the seventeenth century, as well as the defiance of enslaved Africans, loomed large across the island.[150] Culturally, La Digue was a multilingual community. Little learned to speak English, French, and Patois. Her multilingualism bolstered her cosmopolitanism. By the time she reached early adulthood, Louise was a self-assured, globally minded young Black woman committed to justice whose knowledge of the world emanated largely from her family and community.[151] The limited economic opportunities for the island's Black majority—even modestly comfortable, land-owning Grenadians like the Langdons—explain why she, following in the footsteps of her uncle and thousands of her compatriots, emigrated from Grenada.[152]

Although she possessed a strong racial consciousness before she left Grenada, it was in Montreal, Canada's largest city and home to the country's largest African-descended community, where Louise Little joined the UNIA.[153] She arrived in the city in 1917, the same year the Montreal UNIA took shape. Her uncle Edgerton Langdon, a Garvey enthusiast, introduced his niece to the UNIA.[154] The historical record provides little detail about her involvement in the Montreal UNIA. What we know is that she joined one of the most powerful Garveyite locals in the world, and her uncle and his son, Henry J. Langdon, were actively involved in the division's affairs for decades to come.[155] Personally, living in Montreal and joining the UNIA were transformative for Little. She lived with her uncle Edgerton in the city's Black neighborhood—Little Burgundy—and worked as a seamstress and domestic laborer in white homes. In 1918, she met her future husband, Earl Little, through the Montreal UNIA. They married in Montreal on May 10, 1919.[156]

Earl Little's family history provides additional challenges to commonly held knowledge about Malcolm's background. His paternal family genealogy too is a story of ancestral connections to Africa and Islam, migration, encounters with slavery and racial violence, and resistance. He was born in 1890 in Butler, Georgia, and was raised in the nearby town of Reynolds—both located in the state's Black belt, a citadel of racial terror.[157] Southern whites killed several of his brothers, including one by lynching. According to the *Autobiography*, due to Earl's lived experiences in Jim Crow Georgia, he came to believe "as did Marcus Garvey, that freedom, independence, and self-respect could never be achieved by the Negro in America, and that therefore" Blacks should leave the United States to white people and return to Africa.[158] Earl's determined resistance to racial terror drove him out of Georgia, into the Garvey movement, and eventually to Montreal.[159]

Earl Little's family history provides insight into the diasporic connections among the Midwest, West Africa, and the Islamic world, and it complicates accepted truths about Malcolm X's journey toward Islam. Although completely absent in the *Autobiography* and from most biographical accounts of Malcolm, his paternal family claims a West African Muslim ancestor named Ajar as the Little family progenitor.[160] The paternal great-great-grandfather of Malcolm, Ajar arrived as an enslaved captive to Charleston, South Carolina, in 1815. Born in the Senegambia, he apparently was Bambara, a Mandé-speaking people who trace their ancestry to the medieval Mali Empire of the western Sudan.[161] Little is known about Ajar's journey from West Africa to the United States. What we can say is that his arrival to South Carolina placed him at the epicenter of US slavery and African Muslim communities in British North America and the pre–Civil War United States.[162] According to family lore, he was a "rebellious African" whose fate is unknown.[163] His recalcitrance lived on in his son, Tony, Malcolm's great-grandfather. Ajar's master sold Tony to Allen Little, a white South Carolina slaveholder. That is how Malcolm's paternal family acquired what he later called his "slave name," Little.[164] As a teenager, Malcolm apparently learned about Ajar through his older half-sister Ella Collins, who was a product of Earl Little's first marriage.[165] The possibility that Ajar was a West African–born Muslim provides additional clues to the long history of resistance and Islam in Malcolm's family and its ancestral connections to the continent, challenging common understandings of his turn toward Islam.

Louise and Earl Little departed Montreal by 1920 and made their way to Philadelphia to help build the Garvey movement. Louise was one of eighty-eight thousand people from the Caribbean who migrated to the United States during the early twentieth century.[166] She became a naturalized US citizen. In Philadelphia, she gave birth to her first child, Wilfred. By 1921, the Garvey movement assigned Louise and Earl Little to Omaha, Nebraska, for the purpose of building the organization in this industrial Midwest city. The Littles' life changed forever when they moved to the Diasporic Midwest.[167]

Omaha was Louise and Earl Little's first stop in the American heartland. The city embodied the dialectic of opportunity and oppression. Omaha was a meatpacking center and a railroad hub.[168] The city's Black population doubled from 5,143 to 13,315 in 1920. The foreign-born Black population was small. (Omaha counted approximately 191,000 whites.) Blacks came to Omaha in search of better job opportunities in the stockyards, railroad yards, and meatpacking plants, and a life free of Jim Crow. However, the racial realities of this city dashed many of their dreams. In September 1919, a violent race riot erupted and resulted in the lynching of an African American man and a white mob who burned down the county courthouse, threatened to hang Omaha's white mayor, and attacked Blacks. African Americans fought back with guns.[169] Racial violence and Black resistance in Omaha caught the attention of Marcus Garvey and the Littles. In an editorial about the Omaha riot published in 1919 in *Negro World*, Garvey pointed to this civil unrest as a horrific example of racial oppression on a global scale and the need for Blacks to fight back.[170] No UNIA division existed in Omaha in 1919. However, Black armed self-defense in Omaha impressed the Littles and convinced them to relocate to that city on behalf of the UNIA.[171]

The grassroots activism of Louise and Earl Little in Omaha demonstrates how they understood Garveyism as a tool for building an autonomous Black community, resisting white violence, and forging linkages to the African world. The Omaha UNIA, founded by 1925, counted probably fewer than one hundred members. Earl Little held the presidency, while Louise Little served as secretary and wrote reports published in the globally circulated *Negro World*.[172] The sparse historical records of the Omaha UNIA provide little information into Louise and Earl Little's work there. But what we can tell is that the Littles were at the forefront in community-building.

If the couple dedicated their lives to advancing grassroots Garveyism, then the Littles also willingly put their lives on the line to fight white racial violence. Louise's confrontation with Klansmen outside of the Littles' home in Omaha, as told in the opening of the *Autobiography*, affirms this point. Although this powerful account is mediated through Malcolm X and Alex Haley, frames her in maternalist terms, and omits her involvement in the UNIA, Louise's encounter provides important insight into her militancy and community feminism. The white night riders went to the Littles' home to silence Earl Little for his leadership in the local Garvey movement. However, his success in leading the Omaha UNIA would have been impossible without his wife. Louise must have been scared when the Klansmen approached her home. She could have either run or remained inside the house with her children (their homesite is shown in figure 2.7). Instead, she opened the door, confronted the group of gun-carrying white men, and told them that her husband was out of town preaching. Given that racist whites often saw the Black church and Black ministers as subversive, Louise made no

FIGURE 2.7. The site of the Little family home at 3448 Pinkney Street, Omaha, Nebraska. Photo by the author.

apologies for Earl's Garveyism. Her decision to reveal her pregnant body was a shrewd and risky move. She surely knew that whites had already lynched Black women, including expectant mothers.[173] Given this reality, Louise's decision to show her pregnant body to the Klansmen can be read as a strategic performance that both affirmed and challenged prevailing discourses of Black womanhood, revealing her awareness of the gendered and sexual contours of white supremacy. On the one hand, she portrayed herself as a defenseless, unprotected mother. On the other hand, Little used her body to demand respect and protection of Black womanhood, motherhood, and children. Her actions defied white supremacist, patriarchal, and heteronormative discourses that framed Black women as deviant, unwomanly, and unfit mothers. This effective strategy staved off the attack. Louise's decision to share this story with the young Malcolm X suggests that she wanted him not only to know about the racial violence the family had encountered but also to appreciate his mother's militancy. What is for sure is that there is no evidence that the Littles, in contrast to Garvey, ever contacted white supremacists like Earnest Cox or read his publications. The couple wanted nothing to do with white supremacists, given their horrific encounters with them.

As Louise Little stood up to the Klan, she also defied the patriarchal control of her husband, underscoring her community feminism. The *Autobiography* portrays her as a passive woman victimized by physical and emotional abuse from Earl. Family members tell a different story. They allege that Louise loved Earl, but she stood up to him. They quarreled, sometimes bitterly, but he never physically hit her.[174] The exact nature of Louise and Earl's relationship surely will remain a mystery. But, given her upbringing and fortitude, it seems likely she was just as willing to challenge the patriarchal authority of her husband as she was the racism of white midwesterners.

Arguably, the Littles' nurturing of Black nationalism and internationalism in their children while living in Lansing was the most lasting way that the couple advanced both grassroots Garveyism and community feminism. Like Omaha, Lansing, Michigan's state capital, was a place of opportunity and discrimination for Black people. The city was home to several automobile factories. In 1930, the city counted 1,409 African Americans, or 1.8 percent of the city's total population of 78,397. Most Black men worked in the service economy, while most African American women toiled as domestics. Earl Little worked as a handyman. Louise Little sewed clothes for Black and white clientele.[175] Like other midwestern cities, Lansing was a KKK hot spot.[176] The Littles experienced the wrath of local white supremacy. In 1929, the Black Legionnaires burned down the first home in which the Littles lived in Lansing in retaliation against Earl for allegedly inciting the local Black community. Racist white public school teachers attempted to break Malcolm's spirit, and local whites begrudgingly regarded the Littles as "those smart niggers."[177] Still, the Littles soldiered on. Earl did freelance preaching at local Baptist churches where he exhorted parishioners to learn the teachings of Marcus Garvey. Earl took his children, including Malcolm, to UNIA meetings in nearby Detroit, initiating his close relationship with the city that proved critical to Malcolm's radicalization as an adult.[178]

While Earl remained actively involved in UNIA grassroots organizing in Michigan, the responsibilities of rearing children and tending to a home required Louise to limit her UNIA organizational work. Nonetheless, she was critical to the making of her family into a "proud exemplar of Garveyite dignity" through instilling a Black internationalist perspective in her eight children—Wilfred, Hilda, Philbert, Malcolm, Reginald, Yvonne, Wesley, and Robert.[179] Upon her directives, the children read *Negro World* and *The West Indian*, the newspaper edited by Theophilus A. Marryshow, a Grenadian who later became the leading advocate for the West Indian Federation, a short-lived political union of British colonial territories in the Caribbean from the late 1950s to the early 1960s.[180] She never sent her children to Grenada. However, her Caribbean heritage remained important to her. Some of her children—Wilfred, Hilda, Philbert, Malcolm, and Reginald—bore the names of Louise's relatives in Grenada. "Langdon" was the middle name of her youngest child, Robert, born in 1938 and fathered by a Black man who jilted her.[181] Teaching her children about the Black world and naming them after relatives in Grenada enhanced the children's global awareness and pride and maintained ties of family solidarity between the Diasporic Midwest and the Caribbean. None of this information is chronicled in the *Autobiography*.

For Louise and Earl Little, nothing was more foundational to building a proud, self-reliant Garveyite family than landownership. After their first home in the Lansing area burned down, Earl built by hand a four-room, one-floor house on a six-acre plot owned by him and Louise on the outskirts of the city.[182] The family produced their own food and rented land to Black neighbors. Wilfred Little recalled: "My father and mother were people who were busy working under the philosophy of Marcus Garvey and that's the kind of household that we grew up in."[183] For young Malcolm, coming of age in the racially hostile Midwest and in a close-knit family anchored by two parents, products of the African Diaspora and fierce champions of Garvey, laid the groundwork for his worldview as an adult.

The Emergence of the Midwestern Garveyite Front

From the very onset of the Garvey movement's presence in the heartland, the midwestern Garveyite front emerged concomitantly with the UNIA. Midwest-based Black mass political, religious, and cultural formations inspired by but independent of the UNIA were important, beginning in the 1920s, in stoking Black nationalist consciousness among Black midwesterners and in connecting the Diasporic Midwest to the African world. Chicago was a key terrain in birthing the midwestern Garveyite front in the 1920s. With a large UNIA, dynamic Black community institutions, and a massive southern migrant population yearning to be free, the postwar South Side proved fertile ground for Garveyism to flourish in groups independent of the UNIA, especially religious organizations. Garveyism found a home in mainline Black churches on the South Side, most notably Chicago's Pilgrim Baptist Church pastored by Reverend Junius Caesar Austin, a devout Garveyite. After coming to Pilgrim Baptist Church in 1926, Austin preached the Garveyite principles to his congregation, which grew to nearly fifteen thousand members during his forty-year pastorate.[184]

Although pan-Africanism thrived in some mainstream Black churches in the Windy City and elsewhere, Garveyism found a new home in what scholar

Sylvester Johnson calls "black ethnic religions," or African American religious organizations, heavily shaped by Garveyism, that arose in the United States between the First and Second World Wars. At their core, these "religions posed a central question: what was the original religion of Black people?"[185] The rejection of "Negro" as a descriptor for Black people, history, and identities constituted another important component of Black ethnic religious praxis. As scholar Judith Weisenfeld argues, early twentieth-century Black religions such as Moorish Science, Father Divine's Peace Mission, and the Nation of Islam contended that whites invented the term "Negro" during slavery to rationalize and promote the subjugation and oppression of the African-descended globally.[186] Appreciating African Americans as a distinct people entitled to self-determination and linking people of color globally, these new Black religions proffered new liberated identities to their followers and to the wider African American community.[187] Given this outlook, Black ethnic religions constituted a powerful critique of "both the political aims of White religion and the colonial paradigm of White civilizationism (equating civilization with Europeanness)."[188]

Several Black ethnic religions adopted "Black Israelite" beliefs.[189] According to historian Jacob Dorman, "Black Israelites" were Black ethnic religious practitioners, dating back to the nineteenth century, who believed that the ancient Israelites were Black and ascribed a Black racial identity to a people believed to be the ancestors of all Black people.[190] Edward Wilmot Blyden was the first major Black diasporic thinker who explored the apparent parallels between the Jewish and Black struggles for freedom. He wrote favorably about European Jewish Zionism as a transnational political and spiritual movement committed to freeing Jewish people by unifying them around the world and restoring their professed ancestral home in Palestine.[191] Garvey followed Blyden in embracing a Black Israelite perspective. Although Garvey was prone to making critical statements about Jews, Zionism nonetheless captured his imagination.[192] He regularly wrote and spoke about the apparent similarities between Black and Jewish people and praised the Zionist movement as a powerful model for liberating and unifying African-descended people everywhere. Black Israelite beliefs informed the African Orthodox Church, a UNIA-affiliated religious denomination established in 1921.[193] The ubiquity of Black Israelite beliefs within the Garvey movement explains how Garveyism came to be known by its followers and detractors alike as "Negro Zionism" and "Black Zionism" and how Garvey became the "Black Moses."[194] Black Israelite beliefs of Garvey and the UNIA influenced future neo-Garveyite religious formations. Often referred to pejoratively as "cults" and "sects" due to their working-class composition and Black ethnic religious beliefs, Garvey-informed Black religions emerged as powerful and complex sites of opposition among the African-descended across the United States and world for decades to come.[195]

The Chicago-based Moorish Science Temple of America was the largest African American Muslim formation in the United States from the 1920s through the 1940s.[196] The MSTA was the first African American Muslim mass movement and the precursor to the Nation of Islam. Garvey, Garveyism, and the UNIA were critical to Moorish Science. However, the MSTA reconfigured Garveyism. Embodying the power and limitations of Black nationalism and pan-Africanism, the MSTA signaled the Midwest as a germinal site of enduring Black ethnic religions. Founded in Newark, New Jersey, in 1913 by Noble Drew Ali—born Timothy Drew in North Carolina—the MSTA constructed religious beliefs drawn from Islam, Christianity, Freemasonry, Garveyism, and New Thought.[197] The self-proclaimed "Prophet" relocated to Chicago by 1925, where he incorporated the MSTA and established Temple No. 1, the group's national headquarters. In Chicago the MSTA blossomed.[198]

Key to Moorish Science (and to other Black ethnic religions) was the MSTA's adoption of what literary scholar Bill Mullen terms "Afro-Orientalism"—a unique political and cultural movement informed by exchanges and encounters among African Americans, Africans, and Asians committed to real and imagined Afro-Asian solidarities and to upending the global color line.[199] Through embracing Afro-Orientalism, the MSTA reframed the apparent exoticism and mysticism of Islam and the Eastern world into a powerful subversive discourse and subjectivity that was critical of the racism, imperialism, and materialism of the West.[200]

The Holy Koran of the Moorish Science Temple of America: Circle Seven, the MSTA's most sacred text authored by Drew Ali, embodied Afro-Orientalism.[201] His main argument contended that African Americans were not "Negroes," "Colored Folks," "Black People," or "Ethiopians." Instead, they were "Moors" and hence "Asiatics" because they descended from the ancient tribes of "El" and "Bey" of the kingdom of Moab in the biblical land of Canaan. Moabites, he professed, founded Islam and the holy city of Mecca, and they migrated from Asia to Morocco. He added that Jesus was a prophet, not the Messiah, whom whites had misappropriated to establish Christianity. Islam, then, was the true religion and Allah was the true God of "Moorish Americans." Morocco was their national homeland, while Christianity was the religion of Europeans. By enduring racial oppression in North America, Blacks had forgotten their true religion and nationality and had internalized their inferiority.[202]

Moorish Science constituted a powerful vehicle for promoting self-transformation and racial uplift. Islam, the Prophet preached, restored the true

FIGURE 2.8. Members of the Moorish Science Temple of America, with Noble Drew Ali in a white jacket in the front row, Chicago, Illinois. Schomburg Center for Research in Black Culture, Photographs, and Prints Division, New York, New York.

national identity, decolonized the minds, and secured the dignity of Moorish people. For its adherents, Moorish Science provided a vehicle for gaining autonomy from white Americans and for enjoying equal US citizenship rights. After accepting Moorish Science, MSTA members received "nationality cards," replaced their "slave" names with "national" names such as "El" or "Bey," and observed Muslim dietary rules. Moors discarded Western dress for Islamic-styled fezzes, turbans, and robes. Drew Ali gained notoriety on the South Side for wearing robes and a red fez embroidered with the symbol of Islam: the star and crescent moon. The Prophet called on his followers to practice the principles of "Love, Truth, Peace, Freedom, and Justice." Through their faith and life-way changes, Moors announced and wore their new, liberated identity before the wider world and forged an oppositional community.[203]

The significance of Drew Ali to the history of Black ethnic religions, Black America, and the African Diaspora cannot be overstated (see figure 2.8). According to Michael Gomez, the Moorish Science prophet was the conduit through which pre-twentieth-century Muslim legacies among African Americans survived into the twentieth and twenty-first centuries.[204] Equally important, Drew Ali's significance lies in his attempt "to resolve the rootlessness of the African-derived and the absence of a self-defined group identity by the conceptualization of a Moroccan origin and Asian construct."[205] Drew Ali did not reject the existence of African people per se. Instead, he professed that Africans were progenitors of an influential Asiatic Muslim civilization who migrated to Morocco and America.[206] Through claiming Moab as the ancient homeland of Black Americans, he sought to pinpoint the geographic origins of African Americans and to resolve their long and painful search for an ancestral home that had been seemingly erased by the Middle Passage, New World slavery, colonialism, and Jim Crow. Moreover, Drew Ali linked his followers to the larger African, Islamic, and darker worlds. Because, according to him, all humans except for Europeans were descendants of Asiatic people, the Prophet "formulated a version of Pan-Africanism that expanded the original geographic referents of the ideology to include and unite people of color in Africa, Asia, and America."[207] Future Black ethnic religions, most notably the Nation of Islam, extended these religious claims.

Garveyism loomed large in informing the MSTA's creed. Like the UNIA, the MSTA established businesses. *The Holy Koran of the Moorish Science Temple of America* acknowledged Garvey as a modern-day "forerunner" of the movement sent by Allah.[208] In 1927, Drew Ali visited Garvey while in prison in Atlanta. Garvey reportedly praised the Prophet for his work.[209] As the UNIA splintered during Garvey's imprisonment, many of his followers joined the MSTA, illustrating how they saw in Moorish Science a continuation of Garveyism. However, there were important differences between the UNIA and MSTA. In contrast to the UNIA, the MSTA neither proclaimed itself a government-in-exile nor advocated territorial separation. Drew Ali forged a nationalism focused on building autonomous Black communities through liberating the minds of like-minded people from internalized racism. For these reasons, he was satisfied in building insular Moorish communities in cities where they resided and in maintaining amicable relations with white authorities. The historical record has yet to indicate whether Drew Ali corresponded with white separatists such as Earnest Cox. Given the MSTA's desire to remain in the United States, Cox would have had no use for Drew Ali.[210]

Drew Ali's teachings struck powerful chords among his flock. By 1930, the MSTA claimed as many as thirty thousand members nationwide, with ten thousand dues-paying members in Chicago and strong support in Detroit and Lansing. Like heartland UNIA members, the vast majority of Moorish Americans were poor, recently arrived southern migrants.[211] Moorish Science transformed its believers. Moors gained a reputation among the wider African

American community for clean living, pride, and racial defiance.[212] Even though the Prophet preached interracial harmony and pledged allegiance to the United States, some of his followers believed that Moorish Science provided sovereign immunity from US government authority and that the end of times for white America were near. His untimely death under suspicious circumstances in Chicago on July 20, 1929, fueled perceptions among Moors of Moorish Science as an oppositional movement against white people and power. Some Moors attributed his death to the police who they believed wanted him dead for his apparent racial defiance.[213] The MSTA's creed, together with the controversy surrounding his death, demonstrates that Moorish Science was as much a political phenomenon as it was a religious movement for enabling Black, working-class, southern newcomers in the urban Midwest to (re)claim their humanity, build community, and forge transnational linkages with the Islamic and nonwhite worlds.

While Drew Ali broke new ground in reconceptualizing African American group identity, his Afro-Orientalist thinking revealed long-standing paradoxes in Black nationalist thought, namely civilizationism and masculinism. Like Marcus Garvey, Drew Ali understood racial progress as a civilizationist project. This perspective informed his reinvention of African American group identity as "Moorish." This claim brilliantly refuted white supremacist representations of Blacks as innately inferior by linking them to an ancient "Asiatic" civilization and to Morocco. Yet his thinking revealed ambivalence toward Africa. Like Garvey, the Prophet showed little interest in indigenous African cultures. By claiming Morocco as the African American national homeland and by disassociating Blacks from their West and Central African forebearers, Drew Ali reinvented the past by asserting that societies from which African Americans genealogically hailed contained no significant historical meaning for Moors. This line of thinking extended classical Black nationalist ambivalence toward African Indigenes to its logical ends by rejecting West Africa altogether. Through claiming a glorious non-African genealogy, Moors both contested and replicated Eurocentric devaluation of Africa.

The MSTA's gender politics were no less paradoxical. As historian Marcia Chatelain points out in her study of South Side Black girls in Great Migration–era Chicago, the MSTA practiced a gender politics and offered notions of feminine respectability that both empowered and inhibited Black women and girls.[214] Women, girls, and the family were critical to Drew Ali's teachings. Resembling Garveyite rhetoric about Black women, the Prophet exalted Moorish women as paragons of virtue, beauty, and motherhood, and he called for their protection. By valorizing them, he challenged prevailing cultural representations of Black women as immoral and undesirable, or as unfit and irresponsible mothers.[215]

Moorish Science appealed to Black women and girls in Chicago in part because it provided alternative paths to respectability and leadership opportunities for advancing racial uplift outside of mainstream Black churches, women's clubs, and civic organizations. These groups, often led by longtime middle-class residents, viewed recently arrived Black southern women and girls with contempt. Conversely, the MSTA welcomed Black migrant women and provided Moorish women with economic opportunities and respect they could find nowhere else through the group's businesses and organizational life.[216]

Still, Moorish Science also maintained male domination to the detriment of the MSTA. A sex scandal involving the Prophet rocked the Moorish community and generated national news coverage in the African American press. Immediately following his mysterious death, rumors swirled within the Moorish community that the Prophet engaged in sexual relations with two of his underaged Moorish female secretaries—both of whom he may have married. The state of Illinois filed charges against Drew Ali for violating the 1910 Mann Act after learning about the allegations.[217] The case never went to trial before he died.[218] The possibility that the rumors were true exposed "a seamier side of Moorish Science leadership, an underbelly of licentiousness and exploitation of women and young girls bordering on pedophilia."[219] Whether or not the allegations were true, what is for sure is that the sex scandal sullied his reputation and played a key role in forever splintering the MSTA into rival factions after his death. This would not be the last time that Black ethnic religious male leaders found themselves embroiled in sex scandals. Drew Ali electrified his followers. But his apparently predatory sexual behavior exposed the limitations of Black nationalism for championing global Black freedom.

By the time of both Garvey's deportation from the United States and Drew Ali's death, the Diasporic Midwest constituted a global hub of the transnational UNIA and Black nationalist formations in the Garveyite tradition. Garvey readily acknowledged this fact. The dialectic of opportunity and oppression, global historical forces, and Black agency created the conditions for the UNIA and Moorish Science to take root and flourish in the heartland, especially among thousands of Black newcomers in Chicago, Detroit, and Cleveland. The Midwest was home to prominent Black nationalists, such as Joseph Craigen and Noble Drew Ali, and grassroots Garveyites, such as Louise and Earl Little. Inspired by Garvey, these women and men were serious about freeing Black people around the world. But the meaning of freedom to Garvey and his midwestern disciples was complicated. Their Black settler colonialism contested European colonialism and white supremacy while at the same claiming Black diasporic rule over allegedly backward Africans. By the early 1920s, Garvey retreated from New Negro radicalism and began adopting Black diasporic right radicalism. Patriarchy impeded the UNIA and MSTA. Irrespective of its paradoxes, Garveyism by the late 1920s was deeply entrenched in the Black heartland, and the work of midwestern Black nationalists set the stage for future Black movements. In the next decade, the global Depression and the prospects of a second world war created conditions for the UNIA and Garveyism to endure and to germinate new mass Black movements based in or closely linked to the Diasporic Midwest in ways that challenged and reinforced the global color line.

3

NEW DIRECTIONS

Garveyism in the Heartland during the Great Depression

The Nation of Islam has 21,000,000 trained soldiers ready to take the devils off the earth.
—"400 YOUTHS AT CULT SCHOOL," *Atlanta Daily World*, April 24, 1934

Chicago Black nationalist leader Mittie Maude Lena Gordon meant business. On April 24, 1939, she led a caravan from Chicago of five hundred African American working-class women and men to the steps of the Capitol in Washington, DC. They were members of the Chicago-based Peace Movement of Ethiopia (PME). Founded in 1932 by Gordon, she served as its president. She and her followers traveled to Washington to lobby for the Greater Liberia Act of 1939.[1] Drafted by the arch segregationist US senator Theodore G. Bilbo of Mississippi, the bill called for voluntary mass African American resettlement to Liberia, all to be funded by the US government.[2] Gordon and a small PME delegation met with Bilbo at a scheduled meeting in his Capitol office to discuss the bill. During the meeting, all parties expressed enthusiastic support for the proposed legislation and agreed that racial separation was the only viable solution to racial conflict and to the injustice, misery, and poverty experienced by Blacks in Depression-era America. After the meeting, Bilbo introduced the bill before the Senate, with half of the chamber's gallery filled with Chicago Black nationalists.[3]

Gordon was one of Bilbo's staunchest Black nationalist allies. A powerful orator, entrepreneur, steadfast proponent of repatriation, and disciple of Marcus Garvey, she rivaled Garvey in Depression-era America as the leading Black nationalist through serving as PME president. Inspired by Garveyism, the PME was the largest Black nationalist organization in the world since the UNIA in its heyday and the largest Black nationalist organization ever founded by a woman.[4] The PME, in collaboration with the UNIA, Bilbo, and other white supremacists such as Earnest Sevier Cox, generated significant grassroots support among African Americans across the Midwest and the United States for Liberian colonization. Despite the indefatigable efforts of Gordon and her allies, the Greater Liberia Act never became law.[5]

Garveyism hardly died after Garvey's deportation from the United States in 1927. Garveyism endured worldwide and found new life in the 1930s, not least in the US heartland, through an array of ephemeral and long-lasting religious and colonizationist midwestern Garveyite front formations. Taking up and reconfiguring Black nationalism, acknowledging Garvey as a Black nationalist progenitor, and embracing Afro-Orientalism, these new groups were at the forefront in enabling their followers, most of whom were recently arrived, destitute African American southern migrants, to adjust to midwestern urban life and to pursue dignity and respect through a politics more militant and oppositional than the program proffered by Garvey, the UNIA, and Moorish Science. Depression-era heartland Black nationalists advanced a Black nationalist politics that challenged and reinforced the global color line during the Depression. Multiple factors kept the UNIA going and birthed dynamic new formations in the Garveyite tradition in the 1930s—the dialectic of opportunity and oppression in the heartland, social and political upheavals across the United States spawned by the global economic depression, the rise of fascism in Europe, the Italo-Ethiopian War, Japanese imperial expansion across East Asia, and the agency of everyday Black people. Arguably, Depression-era midwestern Garveyism touched the lives of millions of African-descended in the United States and globally and set the stage for Black transnational protest for decades to come.

The size, mass appeal, militancy, working-class composition, and transnational breadth of heartland Black nationalist movements affirm historian Ernest Allen Jr.'s call to "revise the viewpoint long held by many activists and scholars . . . that the Depression Decade witnessed a strengthening of class consciousness within the African American national community virtually at the full expense of group consciousness and national sentiment."[6] This prevailing interpretation of Depression-era Black America identifies the Black left, not Black nationalist formations, as the primary site of Black radicalism and internationalism during the 1930s. Extending Allen's argument, I contend that the 1930s constituted both another golden era *and* a complex new chapter for Black nationalism in which the Diasporic Midwest was prominent. These years marked the growing ascendance of the midwestern Garveyite front over the UNIA. The Garveyite faithful in religious, colonizationist, Afro-Asian solidarity, and leftist formations moved Black nationalism, internationalism, and radicalism in new directions. They also forged transnational political linkages between the heartland and world. Some midwestern Garveyites embraced Black diasporic right radicalism, leading Black nationalist formations like the PME to ally with white supremacists. The beliefs and practices of some heartland Black nationalists came at tremendous personal cost. White state actors often viewed the activism and lifeways of midwestern Garveyites with alarm and sometimes responded punitively. Despite serious obstacles, Black nationalists in the Diasporic Midwest remained defiant and committed to advancing global Black freedom as the world experienced a catastrophic economic crisis and as the storm clouds of another world war gathered.

The Midwestern UNIA and the Communist Left

The UNIA never again counted millions of members worldwide after its heyday and Garvey's deportation. However, thousands of UNIA members across the Diasporic Midwest and world in the 1930s kept the faith and remained in the Garvey movement. The UNIA in Gary, Indiana, provides a clear example of this resilience. In 1906, the United States Steel Corporation, the world's largest steel manufacturer at the time, established Gary. The city was an experiment in urban industrial planning and the site of the largest steel manufacturing on the planet.[7] By 1920, fifty-four thousand people resided in Gary, which acquired a global reputation as a boomtown.[8] From Gary's beginning, African American southern migrants came in search of a brighter future. By 1930, Gary's Black population grew to nearly eighteen thousand—or about 18 percent of the city's total population. Blacks were 16 percent of the city's steel industry workforce. Black steelworkers earned good wages—or at least more money than they most likely would have earned down south. However, US Steel relegated African American men to the worst jobs, excluded Black women from working in steel mills, and pressured Blacks to stay in line.[9] Blacks in Gary faced substandard housing, ghettoization, job discrimination, and educational inequality.[10] In the early 1920s, the KKK had an estimated 3,000 members in Gary. Indiana was home to perhaps as many as 350,000 KKK members, the largest Klan enclave outside of the South.[11] Gary's harsh racial landscape set the stage for Garveyism to take root.

The Gary UNIA, established by 1921, was for a moment the largest Black organization in the city. Garvey spoke twice in Gary before enthusiastic crowds.[12] The city's geographic location connected Gary to nearby midwestern Garveyite strongholds: Chicago, Detroit, and Milwaukee.[13] By 1927, the Gary UNIA was in disarray due to infighting and the Garvey movement's general decline.[14] However, the Gary UNIA in the 1930s enjoyed a rebound in strength and global visibility under the leadership of Charles L. James. He was a lifelong Black nationalist stalwart, a disciple of Garvey, and the UNIA president-general from 1978 until his death in 1990.[15] Born in 1905 in the British Caribbean colony of Antigua, he migrated to New York in 1922. In Harlem, he joined the UNIA and became one of Garvey's top lieutenants. In 1928, UNIA international organizer Madame Maymie Turpeau De Mena assigned James as president of the Gary UNIA. On his watch, the division grew from a few hundred members to about two thousand. Garveyism lived on in Gary, laying the groundwork for the city's emergence as a Black Power mecca.[16]

The historic all-Black municipality of Robbins, Illinois, provides another example of Garveyism's endurance in the heartland past the 1920s. Located nineteen miles southwest of downtown Chicago, Robbins is the sixth-oldest incorporated African American municipality in the United States and the first US Black town established north of the 40th latitude. (The village today remains the largest all-Black US municipality.) Like nineteenth-century Brooklyn, Illinois, and other all-Black midwestern towns, Robbins spoke to the nationalist aspiration of the village's African American residents for living autonomously from whites. In the 1890s, African American southern migrants—some of whom were formerly enslaved and Civil War veterans—settled in what is today Robbins. Black residents incorporated the village in 1917.[17] Robbins's proximity to Chicago and farmland provided its working-class residents unique opportunities to earn good wages as factory and farm hands, own property and homes, and build their own municipality. The village grew from 431 residents in 1920 to 1,300 by 1940. Robbins never amassed the wealth and power of neighboring white suburbs. Still, the village was a place residents claimed as their own. Robbins's class composition and history made it receptive to Garveyism.[18]

The UNIA in Robbins took shape in early 1920. Garvey visited the village several times. He was intrigued with Black people running their own municipality, underscoring once again how the Diasporic Midwest made a strong impression on the UNIA's president-general. The Robbins UNIA endured long after Garvey's exit from the United States and worked closely with UNIA divisions in the Chicago area and beyond.[19]

Robbins was home to Elinor Robinson White (Neely), a major UNIA official in the village and arguably the most important UNIA leader in the Chicago area from the late 1920s through the mid-1960s.[20] Deeply religious, she became one of Garvey's most trusted confidants, a top figure in the transnational UNIA, and a chronicler of Garveyism. Born in 1900 in Mississippi, she made Robbins her home. Entrepreneurial, she co-owned a grocery store on the South Side with Chicago UNIA official Nathaniel Grissom. Owning her own business, living in an all-Black town, and having a prominent place in the UNIA provided White with a modicum of economic security and middle-class respectability that few Black migrant women of her day enjoyed.[21]

Garveyites in other UNIA midwestern strongholds such as Detroit and Cleveland continued propelling the transnational UNIA in the 1930s. In Detroit, William L. Sherrill, Garvey's one-time nemesis during the 1920s, relocated in 1936 to the Motor City. Sherrill regained Garvey's favor and became president of Detroit's Division 407.[22] Like Elinor White, Sherrill enjoyed some semblance of middle-class respectability and comfort through securing a job in the Wayne County clerk's office and working as the associate editor of the *Michigan Chronicle*, a Detroit-based Black weekly newspaper. His journalism and his unsuccessful bid in 1939 for a seat on the Detroit City Council raised his public profile and helped to prepare the ground for future civil rights and Black Power campaigns in the city.[23]

Garveyism continued bearing fruit in Cleveland during the Depression. The Forest City produced a major but understudied figure in the history of global Garveyism—James R. Stewart. A powerful speaker, strong-willed, and fiercely devoted to Garvey, Garveyism, and the UNIA, Stewart was a classical Black nationalist to the bone. His journey into the UNIA, like those of other midwestern Garveyites, was a story of migration and resilience in the face of racial oppression and opportunity in the US heartland. He was born in 1903 in Moorhead, Mississippi, and reared by his mother in Centreville, Mississippi, in the southwestern corner of the state. His proud family owned a plantation and were formally educated. Racial terror in Mississippi and the possibility of a better life in the North took Stewart and his mother in 1915 to Cleveland.[24] In 1919, he joined the UNIA. It is unknown why he enlisted in the group. But years later, he credited Garveyism for enabling him to appreciate the importance of Liberia to Black America's nationalist aspirations. Liberian repatriation remained at the center of his life and identity.[25] In 1933, he became president of Cleveland Division 133 and four years later was the UNIA commissioner of Ohio, earning Garvey's trust.[26]

Stewart owed his success as a UNIA leader from the Depression onward in no small part to his wife, Goldie Stewart (née Milton), who was as passionate about Garveyism and Liberian colonization as her husband. Born in 1910, she grew up in Ravenna, Ohio, outside of Akron, a KKK hot spot.[27] Goldie's life forever changed in 1929 when she married James Stewart. Marriage brought her into the UNIA.[28] She never held an official position in the UNIA. However, she was a community feminist who gained a reputation within the UNIA as a resourceful woman, faithful wife, and devoted mother to her five children, Anita, Donna, Roberta, James Jr., and Victor.[29] Bearing a resemblance to Louise Little and her grassroots pan-African work, Goldie Stewart instilled Garveyite values in her children and people around her.[30]

Membership in the UNIA and living in the segregated Central Area allowed the Stewarts to carry out their Garveyite work. In 1934, they moved into Cleveland's Liberty Hall, a stately three-storied mansion located at 2200 East 40th Street. For James and Goldie Stewart and their children, the bustling building became a center of their social and political worlds where the local and global conjoined.[31] Taken together, the resurgent Gary UNIA and the lives of Elinor White, William Sherrill, and James and Goldie Stewart illustrate the survival of Garveyism into the 1930s and the ways the Midwest remained a transnational UNIA hot spot.

Although the Midwest remained a stronghold of the UNIA in the 1930s, the emergence of new Black movements galvanized by Depression-era social upheavals and spawned by Garveyism challenged the UNIA's wider influence within African American heartland communities and provided Black midwesterners with viable alternative platforms for fighting for self-determination and forging internationalism. Midwestern Garveyites were keenly aware of this trend. In a meeting in 1935 of the Cleveland UNIA, James Stewart lamented that "old Garveyites are now members of rival organizations."[32] He did not identify the new movements that former Cleveland UNIA members had joined. But he may have had the Future Outlook League (FOL) in mind. Founded in 1935 in the Forest City, the FOL, the largest Black protest organization in Cleveland during the Depression and the Second World War, mobilized Black working-class people through boycotts and pickets, and it worked with communists and trade unions for securing jobs, civil rights, and upward mobility for African Americans.[33]

Midwestern Garveyites also found new homes in the Communist Party and trade unions during the Depression. The unprecedented economic crisis, massive unemployment, hunger, homelessness, racial terror, and the global communist movement's adoption of the "Black Belt Thesis" enabled communists for the first time to gain mass influence in Black America.[34] No event was more important in galvanizing African American mass support in the 1930s for the communist left than the Scottsboro case. The legal case involved nine young Black men, aged twelve to twenty-one, who in March 1931 were falsely accused of raping two white women aboard a freight train en route from Chattanooga to Memphis. Through the Communist Party, Scottsboro came to symbolize Jim Crow, lynching, imperialism, poverty, and racial oppression on a global scale. Due to the success of communists in building a global amnesty movement on behalf of the defendants, the Scottsboro youth were spared the death penalty. Thousands of Black Americans in the 1930s joined the CPUSA and Party-affiliated groups committed to racial equality, jobs, economic justice, housing, food, trade unionism, the cultural arts, international solidarity, colonial independence, peace, and women's rights. Echoing a familiar line, Garvey accused communists of using Scottsboro to advance their own white racial interests at the expense of African Americans.[35]

Despite Garvey's denouncements of communists, some ex-UNIA members in the heartland, like elsewhere around the world, defied him by joining the CPUSA and its affiliates. This was the case with Chicago labor activist Leonidas McDonald, who enlisted in the UNIA in the 1920s but left it by the 1930s. During the Depression, he became a leading trade unionist for the Steel Workers Organizing Committee, and worked with the National Negro Congress (NNC). Founded in 1936 in Chicago and briefly rivaling the NAACP nationally for influence among African Americans, the NNC was a Black united front organization with ties to the communist left and was committed to civil rights, antifascism, trade unionism, and internationalism.[36] McDonald saw no contradiction in advancing Black self-determination through multiracial, leftist formations. But McDonald, like countless ex-UNIA members turned communists, was unwilling to denounce Garvey, whom members credited for initiating their political awakening.[37]

As ex-UNIA members moved to other protest groups, midwestern Garveyites, like their colleagues in UNIA locals around the country, mainly sat on the sidelines. The UNIA's growing Black diasporic right radicalism, exemplified by its stubborn insistence on self-help and entrepreneurialism as solutions for Black people, discouraged the organization from participating in mass actions, supporting trade unionism, and working with communists. Hence, the UNIA overall saw a continued decline in membership. The defection of some Garveyites into the FOL and the CPUSA suggests they continued searching for more militant groups that spoke to their political imaginaries. This movement of Garveyites in and out of the UNIA and the willingness of rival groups to fight for the rights of Black working people, moreover, illustrate that the racial and class identities and politics of 1930s Black midwesterners were hardly fixed, but rather shifting and contingent on both local and global events.

UNIA International Conventions, Ethiopia, and Garvey's Final Years

On the global stage, the Diasporic Midwest remained a nexus of the transnational UNIA and the home to some of Garvey's most loyal constituents following his exit from the United States to his passing in 1940 in London. Living in the Midwest continued affording heartland Garveyites unique opportunities to cultivate transnational political linkages and to keep the UNIA alive during the 1930s. These were no easy tasks. Garvey's deepening Black diasporic right radicalism eroded Black mass support for him and cultivated new Black nationalist and internationalist formations that moved beyond classical Black nationalism.

UNIA international conferences of the 1930s provide important insight into both the underappreciated importance of midwestern Black nationalists in sustaining the UNIA after its heyday and the appeal and limitations of the Garvey movement. The Sixth Annual International Convention of Negro People of the World, held in August 1929 in Kingston, Jamaica, speaks to this point. Residing in Kingston, Garvey called the gathering to establish a new organization in response to financial and legal disputes with the rival Harlem-based UNIA, Inc.[38] A key outcome of the convention was the formation of the Universal Negro Improvement Association and African Communities League, August 1929 of the World, headquartered in Kingston with Garvey as its president-general. This group's establishment marked the first major organizational split within the UNIA.[39]

Despite the Kingston convention's promise, all was not well within the UNIA. After the conference, Garvey excoriated (sometimes through *Negro World*) Earnest Knox, Joseph Craigen, and William Ware, ranking UNIA officials with connections to the Diasporic Midwest, for their alleged misleadership and corruption.[40] They exited the UNIA. Their departure cost the organization veteran Midwest-based leaders who had been critical to keeping the UNIA alive after Garvey's incarceration and deportation, signaling again the destructive impact of the UNIA's authoritarian organizational culture.

Similarly, Garvey's geographic isolation from UNIA loyalists and his responses to Depression-era global events weakened his stature among some of his followers and a new generation of pan-Africanists.[41] Nowhere was his political isolation more apparent than his response to the Italo-Ethiopian War (1935–1936). This conflict was a war of aggression waged by fascist Italy under the leadership of dictator Benito Mussolini against Ethiopia. At the time, Ethiopia was led by Emperor Haile Selassie, who claimed the biblical King Solomon and Queen of Sheba as his ancestors. Mussolini was hell-bent on avenging Italy's humiliating military defeat in 1896 in Ethiopia. Italy invaded Ethiopia on October 3, 1935. By May 1936, Italian forces overwhelmed Ethiopian defenses, slaughtered thousands of civilians, forced Selassie into exile in London, and annexed the Horn of Africa nation.[42]

The fascist Italian conquest of Ethiopia infuriated African-descended people around the world, prompting them to see Black struggles in global terms like never before. Viewing Ethiopia as one of the last two remaining independent African nations and revering Selassie for his sacred importance, Blacks from Harlem to Chicago to London to Kingston called for Ethiopia's defense and Selassie's restoration. This protest marked a shift in Black (inter)nationalist politics. Groups such as the London-based International African Friends of Ethiopia (IAFE), headed by the Trinidadian activist-intellectual C. L. R. James, then a follower of exiled Soviet revolutionary Leon Trotsky; West African nationalist I. T. A. Wallace-Johnson; and Amy Ashwood Garvey, attempted to build grassroots support among Black working-class people for Ethiopia. In a break from classical Black nationalism, the IAFE looked to Africans, not the Diaspora, as the vanguard for global Black freedom.[43]

Garvey's controversial response to the Italo-Ethiopian War through journalism and public speaking revealed the limits of his Black diasporic right radicalism rooted in biological understandings of race and civilizationism. Like Black people everywhere, Italy's wanton conquest of Ethiopia and killing of thousands of innocent African people incensed him. However, he victim-blamed Selassie for Ethiopia's defeat. Framing the war as a clash of civilizations and Selassie as a racial sellout who led a backward, impoverished African nation, Garvey argued that Ethiopia's defeat marked the ascendance of a modern white race over a declining Black race.[44] This position led him to grudgingly admire fascism and Mussolini. He made this position clear in a 1937 interview in London with the Black public historian J. A. Rogers. Garvey boasted that the UNIA "were the first fascists. We had disciplined men, women, and children in training for the liberation of Africa. The Black masses saw that in this extreme nationalism lay their only hope and readily supported it. Mussolini copied fascism from me but the Negro reactionaries sabotaged it."[45] Garvey framed himself as the progenitor of fascism. He also admired Adolf Hitler for his political strength and success in building a powerful Nazi state.[46] As cultural scholar Paul Gilroy observes, the shared hypermasculine values of conquest, aggression, and militarism help explain why Garvey lauded Hitler and Mussolini and drew parallels between the UNIA, fascist Italy, and Nazi Germany.[47] The authoritarian tendencies of classical Black nationalism and Garvey's biological understanding of race also explain why he found common ground with Mussolini and Hitler. Garvey endorsed neither ethnic cleansing nor the persecution of Jews.[48] Nonetheless, his complicated stance on the Italo-Ethiopian War demonstrated the paradoxical ways his hardening Black diasporic right radicalism led him to oppose European imperialism *and* to praise fascist dictators. Many young Black radicals and even some of his supporters found his stance on the conflict "bizarre and incomprehensible."[49]

As Garvey's public stature and health suffered in his final years, he found refuge in the transnational UNIA and enjoyed some of his strongest support from midwestern loyalists. The Second Regional Conference of the UNIA held in August 1937 in Toronto affirms this point (see figure 3.1).[50] This meeting was the most important UNIA international conference during the 1930s. Garvey, who traveled from London to preside over the conference, saw it as critical to reinvigorating the UNIA. The convention brought together 133 delegates from the United States and Canada. The African School of Philosophy, conceived by Garvey and established at the conference, stands as its crowning achievement. He envisioned the school as an ideological institute for training the next generation of UNIA leaders in "African Philosophy," his teachings and philosophy for uplifting the race globally.[51] Serving as principal of the institute, he rigorously instructed his students in Toronto after the conference in leadership training, history, politics, self-improvement, education, ethics, and religion. Garvey conferred upon the ten graduates a "doctorate" in African Philosophy.[52] Six of the ten graduates were based in the Midwest—Charles L. James, Nathaniel Grissom, and Ethel Waddell (Chicago), Elinor White (Robbins), James Stewart (Cleveland), and Theresa Young (Cincinnati).[53]

The prominence of midwesterners in the first graduating class of the School of African Philosophy provides another example of the continued significance of the US heartland to global Garveyism into the 1930s. Like in 1925, when Garvey looked to the extraordinary UNIA international convention in Detroit for regaining control of the UNIA from rivals, he placed significant faith in midwesterners at the 1937 conference in Toronto for restoring the transnational UNIA. Through the School of African Philosophy, he anointed the next generation of UNIA leadership.

Additionally, the UNIA's Second Regional Conference and the geographic proximity of the Diasporic Midwest to Canada created unique opportunities

FIGURE 3.1. The site of the Second Regional UNIA Conference, 355 College St., Toronto, August 24–31, 1937. Photo by the author.

for Garvey to reconnect with his midwestern followers. After the convention, Garvey traveled from Toronto to Windsor, Ontario, with the purpose of meeting with US Garveyites. He remained barred from the United States. But Windsor's location on the Canada-US borderland, a longtime center of Black transnational politics, provided him unique access to the Garveyite stronghold that was Detroit. He spoke at Windsor's Bedford Methodist Episcopal Church before an audience of veteran and ex-UNIA members from Detroit and Chicago who had crossed the Detroit River to see their beloved leader.[54] The group included William Sherrill, the ex-Chicago UNIA leader; the first African American Democratic member of the Illinois senate, William A. Wallace; and Charles C. Diggs Sr., a successful Detroit funeral home proprietor and UNIA supporter who in 1936 became the second African American elected to the Michigan senate.[55]

Garvey, now fifty, had not lost a step since his last visit to nearby Detroit nearly fifteen years earlier. He opened his electrifying address in Windsor by joking that he went to federal prison in 1925 soon after visiting Detroit. The audience laughed. He turned his attention to the UNIA and pointed to the newly established School of African Philosophy as an example of the "new UNIA." He then discussed the Italo-Ethiopian War. He did not explicitly blame Selassie for Ethiopia's defeat. However, Garvey understood fascist Italy's conquest of Ethiopia as a dire warning for Black people's very survival. Reiterating his admiration for fascism, he bragged that Hitler and Mussolini had emulated the UNIA's hypernationalism. Garvey closed his address by emphasizing that "it [was] going to be African philosophy . . . that will save this perishing race of ours." His audience cheered.[56]

We most likely will never know what Sherrill, Wallace, Diggs, and the other midwestern Garveyites who heard Garvey speak that night in Windsor thought about his positions on fascism and the Italo-Ethiopian War. But their exuberance for and willingness to travel to see Garvey illustrate that his laudatory pronouncements about Hitler and Mussolini did not drive them out of the UNIA. If anything, his address strengthened the audience's fidelity to him and signaled their support for a Black (inter)nationalism increasingly out of step with changing times. Garvey cherished and looked to his midwestern supporters for carrying on the UNIA. More broadly, his Windsor address and the prominence of midwesterners in the School of African Philosophy show how the UNIA, combined with the geographic location and racial landscape of the Diasporic Midwest, provided unique opportunities for midwesterners to remain a bedrock of 1930s global Garveyism even as new organizations and changing times eclipsed the UNIA's mass popularity and moved Black transnational politics in new directions.

Nightmare

As thousands of Black women and men in the 1930s Midwest pursued dignity, autonomy, and respect through the UNIA and midwestern Garveyite front organizations, some heartland-based Black nationalists battled for their very lives and the safety of their families in the face of state persecution, political imprisonment, and white racial terror. This was true for Louise Little. *The Autobiography of Malcolm X* identifies the violent death of her husband, Earl, allegedly at the hands of the white supremacist Black Legion on September 28, 1931, in Lansing as the beginning of the "nightmare" in young Malcolm's family life.[57] The facts surrounding Earl's passing remain contested.[58] However, the *Autobiography* is undeniably correct in emphasizing the connections among the traumatic and deleterious impact of Earl's death and Louise's slow-motion mental breakdown with the breakup of the family by white state officials. At the same time, the *Autobiography* both elides Louise's resilience spawned by her Garveyite sensibility, community feminism, Grenadian heritage, self-love, and love for her children, and it overlooks her persecution and institutionalization as a form of political imprisonment.

The unique intersections of race, gender, class, nationality, the law, and power in the Diasporic Midwest help explain the forces that contributed to Louise's nightmarish experiences during the 1930s. Now widowed and the sole provider, she relied on the Garveyite beliefs and lessons she had learned in Grenada to take care of her family in a racially hostile central Michigan during the depths of the Depression. She worked as a domestic for whites, sewed clothing for sale, and forged a support network among Lansing-area Black people, many of whom had been active in the UNIA. Underscoring the continued importance of her Grenadian heritage, she became especially close to two Afro-Caribbean families: the Lyons and McGuires, who lived in nearby Mason, Michigan. Louise held on for eight long years.[59]

Ultimately, Louise was "driven toward madness."[60] The strains of providing for a large family, a failed courtship, and the birth of Little's eighth child by a man who jilted her, together with the discrimination she faced as a Black, single, foreign-born, working-class woman targeted by the state and living in a white supremacist hot spot during the depths of the Depression, overwhelmed her emotionally. The fair-complected Louise lost several jobs after her white employers discovered she was not white. Additionally, she struggled to put food on the table for her children. Rumors in the Black Lansing area about her alleged mental decline swirled after she declined free pork from Henry Doane, a neighbor who raised pigs on his nearby farm. She abstained from pork, given her conversion to Seventh-Day Adventism and observation of its Abrahamic dietary laws.[61] Deeply depressed and out of options, proud and independent Louise was unable to care for herself and provide for her hungry children. She reluctantly took government assistance. Beginning in 1938, white social workers began calling on her home to investigate the well-being of her children after some of them, most notably Malcolm, engaged in shoplifting. Little openly despised the white social workers who came to her home. She believed they wanted to strip her of her children and independence.[62] The Ingham County Probate Court intervened in this affair. Doctors evaluated Little on behalf of the probate court. Using racial, class, and gender-coded language, these evaluations cited her alleged hostility toward relief workers, tendency to talk to herself, recent birth of an "illegitimate" child, refusal to give up her children to foster care, assertion she was of "royal blood," and claim she had been "discriminated against" as evidence of Little's purported insanity and grounds for committing her to the Kalamazoo psychiatric facility.[63] Following these recommendations, probate judge John McClellan deemed her "insane," ordered her to the Kalamazoo Psychiatric Hospital, and placed her younger children, including Malcolm, into foster care.[64]

The institutionalization of Little into a psychiatric hospital should be read as an example of state-sanctioned violence against and political imprisonment of Black women. The work of historian Kali Gross about crime, prosecution, and incarceration of African American women in turn-of-the-twentieth-century Philadelphia provides useful insight into Little's encounter with state violence. Appreciating the justice system as a form of social control that targeted vulnerable, Black working-class women and that framed them as deviant and criminal, "policing and prison practice operated as a self-fulfilling prophecy whereby reformers, criminologists, and prison administrators ultimately invented the very crime class they sought to repress."[65] These descriptions fit Little's experience with social workers and the Michigan family court. Viewing her through racist, sexist, and heteronormative lenses, white doctors, social workers, and court officials interpreted Little's mental breakdown; pride; status as a poor, unmarried, working-class Black woman who recently had a child out of wedlock; and racial defiance as proof of her purported criminality and insanity. Her social location as a Caribbean woman also may help explain why social workers and the courts targeted and punished her. Even though she was a naturalized US citizen, white social workers and court officials nonetheless may have viewed her foreign-born background with contempt and as grounds for her institutionalization. The state through the courts, social workers, and medical professionals punished Louise and her family for their resistance to and determination to live autonomously from white people, subjecting the Littles to trauma, dislocation, and hardship. She was aware of the bitter irony of the state's treatment of her. For years, authorities and the system had done nothing to protect the lives and dignity of Louise and her family from white supremacist violence, poverty, and daily dehumanizing racist microaggressions. Tragically, she entered the Kalamazoo Psychiatric Hospital at the age of forty-two on January 31, 1939. Surely, she and her family could not have imagined that this proud Black woman still in the prime of her life would spend almost twenty-five years in that hospital.[66]

The Nation of Islam

Islam grew even more prominent as a site where Garvey's legacy and midwestern Black nationalism thrived in the 1930s. Moorish Science survived despite the mysterious death of Noble Drew Ali in 1929 and organizational schisms.[67] A fracturing MSTA, the legacy of the UNIA, and 1930s social upheavals created space for the emergence of several new African American Islamic formations in Depression-era America, most notably the Detroit-based Nation of Islam.[68] No Black ethnic religion in the United States better embodied the new directions in 1930s Black nationalism than the NOI. At its core, the Nation forged an innovative Afro-Orientalist, Black diasporic right radical theological response to the unmitigated terrorism and misery that African Americans faced in racist capitalist America.[69] The Nation's globally informed theology provided a powerful spiritual pathway for Black working-class people to adjust, to survive, and to find dignity in the harsh racist, industrial landscape of Depression-era Detroit and Chicago. The NOI's program was more militant than those proffered by the MSTA and UNIA of the 1930s and contrasted with the secular interracialism of communism. Not without its paradoxes, the NOI contested and affirmed the gendered, racial capitalist status quo.

The Depression and Detroit's distinct racial landscape played key roles in setting the stage for the Nation's emergence. The global economic crisis hit Detroit and its automobile industry extraordinarily hard. In 1930, 13.3 percent of the city's labor force was unemployed, the highest rate of unemployment of any major US city. Three years later, 50 percent of the city's 689,000 potential wage workers were unemployed.[70] Like in other US cities, Blacks in Detroit were the first fired and last hired. By 1930, nearly 200,000 Blacks resided in the hypersegregated Black Bottom and Paradise Valley.[71] Police brutality against Black Detroiters remained an epidemic. Bombings by whites of Black homes and churches were common occurrences. The KKK and fascism enjoyed popularity among white Detroiters in the 1930s, most notably through Charles E. Coughlin. Best known as "Father Coughlin" and recognized today as the progenitor of "hate radio," he was a Canadian-born Catholic priest based near Detroit. He used his nationally broadcast radio programs to propagate pro-Nazi views, antisemitism, and racism among millions of aggrieved white listeners across the United States.[72]

Islam was no stranger to interwar Detroit before the Nation came on the scene. Noble Drew Ali found a strong base of support among Black Detroiters. Additionally, 1920s Detroit was home to a small but vibrant South Asian Muslim community comprising mostly male industrial workers, maritime workers, peddlers, students, and small business owners. They came from South Asia and the Middle East to Detroit, like African American southern and European newcomers, searching for a better life through the city's automobile industry. Their presence enhanced the city's multinational character.[73] Key figures in Detroit's South Asian community were Dusé Mohamed Ali, Garvey's mentor who moved from Harlem to the Motor City after editing *Negro World* in the early 1920s, and his friend Dada Amir Haider Khan. Khan was a radical activist-intellectual from Punjab who became a leading champion of Indian independence and international communism.[74] Ali and Khan immersed themselves among Detroit Black nationalists, and Ali knew Noble Drew Ali, preparing the ground for the Nation.[75]

What came to be known as the Lost-Found Nation of Islam began on July 4, 1930, US Independence Day, with the appearance of an enigmatic silk peddler selling African and Asian wares door-to-door in Paradise Valley. His name was Wallace D. Fard Muhammad. He was the NOI's founder. His racial and ethnic background was (and remains) a mystery. But many Black Detroiters at the time believed him to be Arab or Palestinian.[76] In his three-and-a-half-year ministry, he preached a powerful and distinct Black ethnic religious theology blending Islam, Christianity, Garveyism, Moorish Science, Freemasonry, and African American folk beliefs, complete with a cosmogony, creed, theory of history, demonology, and eschatology.[77] He was especially aware of the stature of Drew Ali and Garvey among Black Detroiters.[78]

The Nation's Afro-Orientalist, diasporic, right radical Black ethnic theology represented the NOI's most significant break from mainline African American religions, Garvey, Moorish Science, and Sunni Islam. These beliefs were evident in one of Fard Muhammad's first addresses to the denizens of Paradise Valley in which he self-presented as an Arab Muslim holy man: "My name is W. D. Fard and I came from the Holy City of Mecca. More about myself I will not tell yet, for this time has not come. I am your brother. You have not yet seen me in my royal robes."[79]

Drawing from and moving beyond Moorish Science, Fard Muhammad preached that Allah was the true God and that Islam was the true religion of Blacks. Accordingly, Allah created Black people sixty-six trillion years ago. Described by him as the "Asiatic Black Man" and the "Original Man," Blacks were "the original members of the Tribe of Shabazz from the Lost Nation of Asia."[80] They resided in Mecca and the Nile Valley, where they lived harmoniously and mastered mathematics and science.[81] In a break from Drew Ali, Fard Muhammad identified Arabia and Egypt, not Moab and Morocco, as Blacks' ancestral homelands, thereby connecting them to Islam's historic birthplace and a foundational African civilization.[82] According to Fard Muhammad, Mr. Yacub, a Black, evil god-scientist embittered at Allah, genetically engineered the white race six thousand years ago. Whites were a "race of devils" designed to wreak havoc on and to subjugate Black people. Christianity, slavery, global conquest, colonialism, and world war were a testament to whites' diabolism. Subsequently, whites stole Blacks from Mecca four hundred years ago and brought them to "the wilderness of America" as slaves, where they forgot their true identity.[83] Whites' pervasive use of "tricknology," a science of racist lies and brainwashing, aided in promoting Black "mental slavery."[84] Illustrating the millennial aspect of these beliefs, Fard Muhammad preached racial separation and the relocation of Black people to a physical territory apart from whites as the only solution for African Americans as Judgment Day neared.[85] The precise location of this racial utopia always remained ambiguous in NOI lore. However, Fard Muhammad, unlike Drew Ali, believed that interracial harmony with the irredeemable white man was neither desirable nor possible.[86] The NOI's unique Afro-Orientalism, together with the organization's very name, speaks to the ways the "Lost-Found Nation of Islam" understood Blacks as the first humans and chosen people, tied to the "Asiatic" and Islamic worlds, destined for salvation through Allah. This theology cleverly reversed white supremacist discourses, long upheld by white American churches, that posited Europeans as the embodiment of morality, beauty, intelligence, and humanness.

Lifeway changes constituted a key component of the NOI's creed. Similar to the MSTA, the NOI dispensed with slave names and in coming years adopted "X," the forgotten African family surname, to signify Muslims' self-liberation.[87] Knowledge of self, clean living, good personal hygiene, self-mastery, modest dressing for women, sharp but not ostentatious dressing for men, adherence to the Abrahamic dietary code, and avoidance of what later would be called "soul food" were critical to transforming believers into racially proud, morally righteous Muslims and to differentiating them from unenlightened non-Muslims.[88] Through the "Asiatic Black Man" identity, Wallace D. Fard Muhammad and his successor, Elijah Muhammad, valorized Blackness by crafting a message more in sync with prevailing African American racial consciousness than Moorish Science, whose message remained largely unchanged after Noble Drew Ali's passing.[89]

Fard Muhammad's religious message and institution-building resonated with African Americans in Detroit and Chicago. He established Temple No. 1, the NOI's first headquarters, at 3408 Hastings Street, Paradise Valley's main thoroughfare (see figure 3.2).[90] By 1932, the Nation may have counted as many as eight thousand members in the Motor City and at least four hundred members in Chicago two years later.[91] In Detroit, early NOI members came from the ranks of the city's poorest recent southern newcomers who had migrated to the Motor City in search of the Promised Land. Prior to joining the Nation, many Muslims in Detroit and Chicago possessed little formal education, worked the dirtiest jobs, and had been members of the MSTA and UNIA.[92]

The early NOI produced one of the most important twentieth-century Black nationalists: Elijah Muhammad. Under his guidance, he extended

Fard Muhammad's teachings, eclipsed Noble Drew Ali, and built the NOI into the largest and most globally recognized twentieth-century African American Muslim formation. While his trajectory through the Nation was exceptional, the "Honorable Elijah Muhammad," as Elijah Muhammad later became known, traveled a well-trodden road to interwar Detroit and into the NOI. He was born Elijah Poole in 1897 in the Georgia Black Belt town of Sandersville to a family of sharecroppers. Like fellow Georgian Earl Little, the Peach State, with its lynchings, marginal economic prospects, and suffocating segregation, was a living hell for Elijah Muhammad.[93] In 1923, he quit Georgia. Like thousands of other Black southerners, he headed for Detroit with his young family, where he found work in an automobile plant. By the Depression, he was unemployed and unable to provide for his growing family. Muhammad was not a stranger to either Garveyism or Moorish Science prior to joining the Nation in 1931. He served as an officer in the Detroit UNIA, and he respected Noble Drew Ali before converting to Islam.[94] Due to Elijah's exemplary devotion to Fard Muhammad, he was promoted to a top NOI position—"Minister of Islam"—and was renamed Elijah Karriem, thereby dispensing with his slave name. (He later adopted the surname Mohammed and then Muhammad.)[95] By the late 1930s, he professed that the NOI's founder had revealed only to Elijah Muhammad the former's true identity: that Fard Muhammad was the Mahdi, the prophesized redeemer in Islam who will deliver his chosen people from evil and injustice before the end time.[96] Elijah Muhammad also professed that Fard Muhammad in encounters between only them designated his understudy as "the Messenger of Allah," the disciple who would awaken the "lost found Nation of Islam . . . in the wilderness of North America."[97] After Fard Muhammad's mysterious disappearance in 1934, Elijah Muhammad moved to Chicago. From Temple No. 2 located at 3743 South State Street, he gradually emerged as the Nation's leader, and he dedicated his life to saving Black people by restoring their original identity through Islam.[98]

Just like in the UNIA and other neo-Garveyite Black nationalist organizations, a complex gender ideology undergirded the NOI in ways that promoted and challenged women's subordination. Ula Taylor calls this politics "the promise of patriarchy."[99] Premised on promoting the male-headed nuclear family and Black male protection of Black women, "the promise of patriarchy" proffered an "NOI religious identity that, in theory, shielded women and their children, from Jim Crow violence and the harmful stereotypes that plagued black womanhood."[100] Similar to the UNIA and MSTA, the NOI identified Black women as key agents for uplifting the race through valorizing their roles as mothers and wives, thereby rejecting denigrating cultural representations of Black women.

FIGURE 3.2. Masjid Wali Muhammad, formerly Nation of Islam Temple No. 1, 11529
Linwood Street, Detroit, Michigan. Photo by the author.

While the NOI celebrated Black womanhood and motherhood, the Nation
was patriarchal to its core. The Nation's organizational structure reflected the
promise of patriarchy. In 1931, Fard Muhammad established the Fruit of Islam
(FOI) and Muslim Girls' Training and General Civilization Class (MGT-GCC).
The FOI was an all-male paramilitary organization designed to instruct men to
be responsible breadwinners, while the MGT-GCC taught girls domestic skills
suitable for making them nurturing wives and mothers for the Black nation.[101]

Nation women grappled with the NOI's patriarchal structure and claimed
a place within it, most notably Clara Muhammad (née Evans). The most
important woman in the Nation's entire history, she was a faithful Muslim,
able institution-builder, and the devoted wife of Elijah Muhammad. Like Amy
Jacques Garvey in the UNIA, the Georgia-born "Sister Clara," as she became
affectionally known within the Nation, never held a formal leadership post in
the NOI. However, she used her status as the wife of Elijah Muhammad and
mother of his children to exert influence over the Nation and her husband.[102]
His introduction to the NOI came through her after she went by herself to several meetings where Fard Muhammad preached. Mesmerized by his message,
she concluded that Islam would enable her unemployed husband, who suffered

from depression and alcohol abuse, to turn his life around and to fulfill his manly role as the family provider. Upon his wife's prodding, he joined the Nation and became a new man.[103] In addition to facilitating her husband's entry into the Nation, Sister Clara was critical to establishing the University of Islam (UOI), a national network of elementary and secondary NOI parochial schools. Appreciating the importance of shielding Black children from systemic racism and educational inequality in Detroit public schools, she saw the critical need for an NOI school for instilling Muslim values of self-love, knowledge of self, and race pride in Black children. Through her influence, the NOI in 1934 established the first UOI. The school was in Temple No. 1 and had four hundred students soon after opening.[104] In coming years, UOI schools across the country became central to Muslim life.[105] Her foundational work on behalf of the NOI affirms Ula Taylor's assertion: "What became the Nation of Islam was driven by a woman."[106]

According to sociologist Erdmann Doane Beynon in his 1938 pioneering study of the fledgling Nation in Depression-era Detroit, "Fundamental to [NOI members] is the effort of migrant Negroes to secure a status satisfactory to themselves after their escape from the old southern accommodation of white and Negro."[107] Nowhere was Muslim militancy more apparent than in three high-profile confrontations between the NOI and white state actors in Detroit and Chicago during the 1930s. These clashes illustrate the ways white authorities, the media, and the Black establishment viewed the Nation, like the Garvey movement and Moorish Science Temple of America in their heydays, as transgressive and subversive. The Nation's response to state violence and media misrepresentation counters prevailing misperceptions of the NOI as categorically apolitical, insular, robotic, and patriarchal, showing instead the Nation's creative and spontaneous use of public space, direct action, the media, and the courtroom as a deliberate challenge against racial capitalism, white supremacy, the carceral state, and middle-class respectability.[108]

The Robert Harris case in Detroit marked the first major confrontation between the Nation and the state. Harris was an African American Detroiter accused of murdering his Black roommate on November 20, 1932. Rumors spread that the killing was a human sacrifice and that the suspect was an NOI member. This death triggered an immediate heavy-handed response from the police against the NOI. White Detroit cops raided Temple No. 1. They arrested and jailed several NOI members. The next day, the police jailed Fard Muhammad. The Nation responded. In an event that marked a major event in the Nation's development, five hundred Muslims on November 24, 1932—Thanksgiving Day—marched peacefully and confidently to the police station and court.

Once there, they demanded freedom for Fard Muhammad and other jailed Muslims. Following the march, authorities released the NOI leader and his followers. We can only speculate if protestors and authorities recognized the subversive political symbolism of African American working-class Muslims taking to the streets on Thanksgiving, the US national holiday that celebrates the United States as a divinely sanctioned, exceptional nation and that shrouds the nation's founding through the genocidal white settler conquest of Indigenes. For sure, this NOI-led protest march constituted a political act that resembled communist-led marches for jobs, social relief, and racial justice. Early NOI believers, like those in coming decades, opposed trade unionism and entreaties from communists. Nonetheless, Black Detroit working-class Muslims were convinced they could never secure full freedom through the US government or from whites. Through taking to Detroit's streets and demanding the right to live freely in the Motor City, Muslims for a moment challenged the racial capitalist order, defied Black and white middle-class respectability, and transformed public space.[109]

The Harris incident brought the NOI its first national exposure through the African American and mainstream media and signaled the beginning of decades of state surveillance, repression, and denigrating media representations. The day after the murder, the mainstream *Detroit Free Press* ran a sensationalist front-page article about the case titled "Leader of Cult Admits Slaying at Home 'Altar.'"[110] Another article called the Nation a "voodoo cult" comprising "ignorant and superstitious Detroit Negroes."[111] The African American press criticized the Nation. In a lurid front-page article about the Harris case, the *Chicago Defender* described the Nation as a "queer order" practicing voodoo and Islam.[112] The violent response by authorities to the Harris case and misrepresentations of the NOI by the mainstream and Black media both demonstrate how the Nation was viewed as a menace to society.

The second major clash between the Nation and authorities in Detroit occurred in April 1934, when the city's all-white school board unsuccessfully attempted to shut down the UOI on the spurious grounds that it was uncertified. The school's Black ethnic religious beliefs and working-class character troubled authorities. White police and truant officers raided the school, jailing several teachers and students. Police did not lock up Sister Clara. However, the police jailed her husband the day after the assault.[113] Two days after the raid, five hundred Muslims, including perhaps Sister Clara, marched to the local jail where the police held Elijah Muhammad and other NOI members. Unlike the march on Thanksgiving 1932, police this time viciously beat Muslim female and male marchers. They defended themselves with knives, bricks, and improvised weapons.

In the end, the state dropped its case against the NOI. Still, this confrontation rekindled media and state scrutiny of the NOI as a subversive "cult" and raised the profile of Elijah and Clara Muhammad among Muslims.[114]

The third confrontation between the early NOI and authorities involved a Chicago courtroom revolt on March 5, 1935, in which women were prominent.[115] Forty Muslims, most of whom were women, came to the court in support of Rosetta Hassan, a fellow Muslim who faced criminal charges for allegedly getting into an altercation with a non-Muslim African American woman on a Chicago streetcar.[116] Hassan's supporters sat peacefully in the courtroom. After the judge dismissed the case, Muslims proceeded orderly toward an exit until a white male bailiff attempted to manhandle an NOI member. All hell broke loose. Fists flew.[117] The *Defender* reported that it took nearly one hour before Muslims "were whipped into submission" by one hundred cops and court officials.[118] Forty-four people, including Muslims and law enforcement officers, suffered injuries. One cop died during the melee. The fact that unarmed Muslim women battled gun-carrying white male authorities speaks to these women's courage and to the ways the NOI encouraged Muslim women to defend themselves, even from armed police. Following the incident, the police arrested forty-three Muslims in the courtroom and at Temple No. 2.[119] Soon thereafter, a white male judge sentenced sixteen men to six months and twenty-four women to thirty days in the notorious Cook County Jail for contempt of court. The judge's punishment of Chicago female Muslims contains parallels with Louise Little's legal troubles in the 1930s. Like in her case, authorities viewed Muslim women's defiance as a challenge to the state, white male power, and Black women's prescribed place in America.[120]

Taken together, confrontations between the NOI and authorities in Detroit and Chicago in the 1930s reveal the similar ways various white state actors punished Muslims for their unapologetic racial defiance, Black working-class social character, and religious beliefs. In each altercation, it was white authorities, not the Nation, who initiated violence. Through misrepresenting the NOI, the mainstream press aided in their criminalization. Following the courtroom brawl in Chicago, the mainstream *Chicago Daily Tribune* called attention to Muslims' status as unemployed welfare recipients as further proof of their alleged social pathology warranting the justifiable use of state violence.[121] The *Chicago Defender* offered a more sympathetic take on the courtroom revolt by acknowledging that law enforcement had sparked the altercation. Still, the respectable *Defender* wanted nothing to do with stigmatized Muslim "cultists."[122] As in the Harris case, the white and Black press found common ground through criticizing Black nationalists. This trend continued for decades.

For the early Nation, these confrontations demonstrated the adept use of street protests, the press, and the courtrooms by Muslims for defending their faith, fellow believers, and organization from state violence and media misrepresentation. The state possessed the upper hand in dealing with Muslims. Still, the Nation held their ground, often in the face of heavily armed white authorities and after serving time in jail.[123] State repression emboldened NOI followers. Their religious zeal and racial pride, bearing the stamp of Garveyism and Moorish Science, W. D. Fard Muhammad's teachings, and the aspirations of Black southern working-poor migrants in Detroit and Chicago, positioned the Nation of Islam and the Diasporic Midwest at the front lines of 1930s Black nationalism and internationalism globally.

Colonization, the Peace Movement of Ethiopia, and the Greater Liberia Bill

As thousands of Black midwesterners looked to Islam for spiritual salvation and freedom, an even larger number of African Americans supported mass repatriation to Liberia through the Peace Movement of Ethiopia as the solution to their problems. In the 1930s the PME kept alive the dream of mass African American repatriation to Liberia. In another powerful example of a new Midwest-based Black nationalist organization supplanting the UNIA, the PME emerged as the driving force of mass African American repatriation to Liberia during the Depression. Through Gordon's adept leadership, the PME promoted a Black diasporic right radical politics that contested and reinforced the gendered global color line, signifying once again the Diasporic Midwest's prominent place as an engine for Black nationalism, internationalism, and radicalism.

Gordon's early years prepared the ground for her ascendance as a leading Black nationalist in the 1930s. She was born in 1889 in northwestern Louisiana, and her father, a minister, admired Henry McNeal Turner. As a child, she saw a massive lynch mob pass by her home. From that day forward, she decided to make it her life's mission to free Black people from the yoke of white America.[124] She, like James Stewart, William Sherrill, and Clara Muhammad, migrated to the urban Midwest to pursue her dreams. East St. Louis, an industrial city located across the Mississippi River from St. Louis, was her first stop in the heartland. Gordon experienced white racial terror in East St. Louis. She witnessed the deadly East St. Louis Riot of July 2, 1917, one of the worst incidents of urban racial violence in US history. White mobs invaded the city's Black neighborhoods, leaving at least forty-eight people dead, thirty-nine of whom were African American.[125] This pogrom infuriated Blacks across the country, including Marcus Garvey. On July 8, 1917, at Lafayette Hall in Harlem, he denounced the East St. Louis Riot as a "massacre . . . that will go down in history as one the bloodiest outrages against mankind."[126] We do not know if Gordon was aware of Garvey's speech. What is certain is that her son died from injuries sustained during the massacre, a loss that surely bolstered her Black nationalism.[127]

Gordon's relocation to the South Side of Chicago and enlistment in the Garvey movement by 1920 changed her life. She became an active member of the UNIA along with her second husband, William Gordon of Florida. In the entrepreneurial spirit of Garveyism, the couple established a restaurant on the South Side. Beyond Chicago, she attended the UNIA's Sixth International Convention in Kingston. There, she met Garvey, who encouraged her to become more active in the Chicago UNIA. However, factionalism and sexism at the conference drove her out of the UNIA. She returned home determined to build a Black nationalist organization in the spirit of Garvey but without him at its helm.[128] She realized her wish. On December 7, 1932, the Gordons, together with several associates, founded the Peace Movement of Ethiopia in the couple's home at 4451 South State Street.[129]

In the PME's name, program, and primary objective—"To Return People of African Descent to their Motherland, Africa"—the organization advanced Black diasporic right radicalism through calling for Liberian colonization and bearing the influences of Ethiopianism, the international women's peace movement, and Garveyism.[130] Framing itself as the UNIA's heir, the PME, in its constitution, pledged to follow the "nationalistic principles laid down by the Hon. Marcus Garvey." With its UNIA-like motto ("One God. One Country. One People."), the PME called for "Africa for the Africans," confraternity "among all people of African descent" and "all dark races," and respect for the "National-Hood of all races." The PME also sought to connect its mission to a glorious ancient African past. The image of the Sphinx, the massive Ancient Egyptian monument, adorned PME organizational documents. Highlighting the PME's opposition to Western imperialism, the organization opposed white military force against colonized people.[131] Ex-UNIA members flocked to the PME in Chicago, Detroit, St. Louis, Cleveland, and Gary, and across other parts of the Midwest, South, and East Coast.[132]

While Garveyism found a home in the PME, the organization moved Black nationalism in new directions through advancing a program informed by surging interest in Islam among Black working-class midwesterners. The PME's constitution declared, "We believe in the God of our fore-fathers . . . and ISLAM religion."[133] The PME letterhead featured the Islamic symbol of the star and crescent moon. At PME meetings in Chicago, the Gordons often declared Allah as the one true God of Black people and castigated Christianity as the white man's religion. There is no evidence suggesting the couple converted to Islam. However, they lived in a hotbed of African American Islam, and they were well versed in the teachings of Noble Drew Ali and W. D. Fard Muhammad, whom the couple apparently met.[134] Underscoring the porous organizational boundaries of midwestern Black nationalism, the PME enjoyed support among Muslims. They found common cause with the PME's program, demonstrating the way Islam and Liberian colonization served as a connective tissue among 1930s heartland Black nationalists in the Garveyite tradition.[135]

The PME's key contribution to Black nationalism was its success in reinvigorating the Liberian colonization cause in the wake of the UNIA's organizational decline and in building a grassroots transnational movement proffering repatriation as the solution to the misery, structural racism, and terror experienced by the Black working poor in Depression-era America, especially in the Midwest. This position is evident in the PME's first and most important national action—a petition sent in November 1933 to US president Franklin Delano Roosevelt calling for government-funded, voluntary African American resettlement to Liberia. The group collected 400,000 African American signatories, the bulk of whom were working-class people who lived in midwestern locales.[136] Reflecting the group's heartland base, the document framed petitioners as poor, humble, "law-abiding" African Americans "driven" from the violent Jim Crow South to the urban Midwest. Once there, they experienced unemployment, hunger, homelessness, and cold that left them dependent on government social relief in a racially hostile country that was never their own. Given this reality, the PME charged that colonization and racial separation, not government social welfare programs of the New Deal or communism, offered Blacks the best hope for freedom and opportunity.[137] Roosevelt apparently received the petition but never responded to it directly.[138] By 1939, Gordon and her allies claimed an additional 1,952,200 Black signatories, bringing the total to 2,350,000 names.[139] The PME most likely inflated these figures. Still, it is undeniable that the PME created important space for the Black working poor in Chicago and across the country to pursue Black nationalist and internationalist politics during the depths of the Depression.[140]

Key to the PME's work was its close collaborations with white supremacists. As Keisha Blain points out, PME women in the 1930s worked far more closely with white separatists in pursuing their political goals than Garvey did.[141] Following the precedent set by Garvey in the 1920s when he began collaborating with white separatists, Gordon worked with Earnest Sevier Cox and Theodore

FIGURE 3.3. Mittie Maude Lena Gordon, circa 1933. David M. Rubenstein Rare Book and Manuscript Library, Durham, North Carolina.

Bilbo for Liberian colonization. Cox became her most enduring white racist ally (see figures 3.3 and 3.4). In his first correspondence to Gordon penned in 1934, he praised the PME for "send[ing] a dignified and moving Petition to the President of the United States" and for resurrecting the Liberian colonization cause.[142] In her reply, she expressed the PME's "heartfelt gratitude for your continued interest in the welfare of our people."[143] In addition to sharing common ground on colonization, Gordon, like Cox, opposed miscegenation. She coupled her opposition to interracial sex with a strident anticommunism.[144] In Bilbo's introduction of the Greater Liberia Act before the Senate, he made his case for the bill by citing Gordon's alleged "horror" in witnessing "white women rocking black babies in this country since Communism has been active in establishing itself" in Depression America.[145] His rantings against communism and interracial sex between Black men and white women affirm historian Robin Kelley's conclusion about the ways southern white supremacists linked communism with Black male–white female sex and charged over and over again that African American men joined the CPUSA to gain sexual access to white women.[146]

Personally, Gordon forged an amicable relationship with Cox and Bilbo. Like Garvey's correspondences with white supremacists, Cox and Gordon exchanged pleasantries. He always addressed her as "Mrs. Gordon," while Gordon

FIGURE 3.4. Earnest Sevier Cox, 1959. David M. Rubenstein Rare Book and Manuscript Library, Durham, North Carolina.

usually addressed him as "Col. Cox."[147] Cox defied Jim Crow protocols by addressing her as "Mrs. Gordon." Whites rarely bestowed Black women with the honorific title of "Mrs.," illustrating how Gordon's anticommunism, belief in racial purity, and hatred of Black-white sex afforded her respect from a white supremacist man.

Gordon's repatriation work won significant praise among African Americans across the country, with one anonymous writer for the Baltimore *Afro-American* calling her the "1939 'Moses'" of her people.[148] This title is significant. Only a select few Black leaders had been revered as the Moses of their people—Harriet Tubman, Booker T. Washington, Henry McNeal Turner, and Marcus Garvey.[149] Representing Gordon symbolically as "Moses" illustrates that many African Americans by the 1930s came to view her, not Garvey of yesteryear, as the messianic champion of her people who would lead them to the Promised Land.[150]

In addition to generating strong support for Liberian colonization among Black Americans, Gordon and the PME spurred Garvey and the UNIA into campaigning for mass repatriation to Liberia for the first time since the mid-1920s. Cognizant of the PME's success, Garvey hoped a UNIA-led campaign for the Greater Liberia Act would restore the organization's preeminence among Black Americans.[151] Turning to a familiar strategy, he approached his old racist allies—Bilbo and Cox—to gain federal government support for colonization.[152] Garvey assigned ranking UNIA officials—James Stewart, Thomas Harvey of Philadelphia, and A. L. King of Harlem—to build a UNIA campaign for Liberian repatriation in consultation with Bilbo and Cox.[153] The UNIA's efforts fell flat. Organizational weakness inhibited the group's work, while rivalry among the PME and UNIA prevented them from working collectively. The bill's demise, Garvey's death, and the onset of the Second World War tabled US legislative action on repatriation until after the war. But the campaign for the Greater Liberia Act was hardly a failure. Mass repatriation to Africa remained popular in the 1930s due largely to Gordon and the PME.[154]

If widespread African American support for the Greater Liberia Act illustrated the continued prominence of the Diasporic Midwest as an epicenter of Black nationalism, then the very issue of repatriation revealed deep class and ideological divisions among 1930s African Americans. Leading Black newspapers dismissed the PME's campaign for repatriation as untenable and undesirable as previous Back-to-Africa schemes. Reviling Bilbo for his overt racism, African American liberals and leftists rejoiced in the Greater Liberia Act's demise in the Senate. Many excoriated Gordon and her followers for working with deplorable white racists in pursuit of Liberian colonization.[155] Black Chicago media mogul Claude Barnett referred to Gordon and her PME followers as a "crude, ignorant lot."[156] The *Afro-American* journalist Ralph Matthews characterized the PME as Black America's "lunatic fringe" who ignored Bilbo's unabashed racism and who looked for a "pot of gold" in Liberia.[157]

Insulted, Gordon seethed over attacks from Black middle-class journalists. Echoing Garvey's criticisms of the African American elite, she denounced Black journalists and civil rights proponents as racial sellouts committed to advancing miscegenation and their own self-interests at the expense of the Black masses. She made this case in a 1939 letter to Bilbo, where she contended that Black America comprised two classes—a light-skinned, middle-class intelligentsia led by the NAACP and newspaper editors, and "the second class" composed of the Black masses. She wrote that the Black working class had neither "been satisfied in America" nor been represented by the "intelligencia [*sic*]" who strove for "social equality" and held themselves "distinctly separate" from the masses. They wanted out of the United States, she believed, and the PME was ready to lead them back to Africa.[158] Her claims reveal a class analysis of Black America attuned to colorism and intraracial social tensions. Her response to Black middle-class critics also provides insight into her precarious life in Depression-era Chicago. Like her followers, she struggled to survive and felt the stigma of receiving government social relief. She earned no salary as PME president, and she survived on her husband's meager government relief after the couple's restaurant went out of business.[159] The Black middle class experienced economic precarity and racial discrimination. However, many remained optimistic about the prospects for a better future in the land of their birth and had established roots in the heartland.

At the same time, Gordon's responses to her Black left and liberal critics provide broader insight into the limitations of Black diasporic right radicalism in interrogating the relation between white supremacy and capitalism. Like Garvey, she appreciated the importance of subjugated and superexploited Black people under slavery, colonialism, Jim Crow, and heavy industry to the making of the modern world and Western wealth. However, unlike Black leftists, Gordon believed that capitalism was a fact of life. Given these conclusions, it is not surprising that Gordon, like Garvey, was a staunch anticommunist.

Black nationalists' controversial collaborations with white supremacists in support of the Greater Liberia Act speak again to the idiosyncrasies of Black diasporic right radicalism. Depression-era Black nationalists, like their nineteenth-century predecessors, challenged European settler colonialism in Africa by recognizing the humanity of African Indigenes and their right to live freely from whites. Still, Gordon and the PME believed that Diasporan Blacks possessed the right to rule and to civilize continental Africans.[160]

Gordon sincerely believed that allying with white supremacists in support of Liberian repatriation was in Black people's best interests. Not only Black liberal and leftist opponents of Back-to-Africa schemes cast doubt on this rationale. Some Black nationalists did too. In a 1942 letter to Gordon from Florida PME leader William Ferguson, he questioned collaborating with Bilbo on account of his notorious racism. In her reply, she defended her position: "When we have to depend on the crocodile to cross the stream, we must pat him on the back until we get on the other side." Ferguson got the message. Bilbo was a means to an end.[161] Gordon reasoned that it made pragmatic sense to work with politically powerful white supremacists such as Bilbo and Cox for Black repatriation to Liberia. Gordon, Garvey, and other Black nationalists were hardly naïve about Bilbo's unapologetic racism. But they sought to distinguish the Greater Liberia Act from its Senate sponsor. Desperate times required desperate measures. Blacks were hungry, homeless, and jobless in Depression-era America. The majority of white America, Black nationalists believed, detested African Americans. Black nationalists could look to Nazi Germany to see Christian Europeans making good on their racist and antisemitic promises to exterminate Jews and racial minorities.[162] Leery of the racial sincerity of white liberals and communists, skeptical of the Black elite, opposed to New Deal social relief, and fearful of Black genocide in the United States, Black nationalists believed their interests aligned with well-connected white supremacists who were honest about their racism and supportive of racial separation. Plus, Bilbo and Cox treated Gordon and Garvey with respect they rarely received from Black liberals and communists. For these reasons, Gordon and Garvey willingly worked with arch racists in support of the Greater Liberia Act. Still, at the end of the day, Bilbo and Cox were avowed white supremacists.[163] They took comfort in knowing they had Black allies such as Gordon and Garvey. Arguably, Gordon and Garvey's hostility toward the Black left and civil groups, strident anticommunism, belief in racial purity, and support for colonization provided political cover for white supremacists such as Bilbo and Cox to carry out their dirty work.[164]

While Gordon's Black diasporic right radicalism illustrates the paradoxes of repatriation, her work also provides insight into the PME's complex gender politics. Like the UNIA and its derivatives, the PME encouraged women to take up organizational leadership. In addition to Gordon, the PME's executive board included the Chicago Garveyite Ethel Waddell and PME national organizer Celia Allen.[165] At the same time, the PME promoted a gender politics that circumscribed women to prevailing heteronormative cultural norms. Key to Gordon's popularity among her followers was the coupling of her Moses persona with her adoption of the "motherist frame," a political discourse and identity rooted in normative gender ideologies "that stress the need to fight for equality and justice with the characteristics associated with being a good mother."[166] This politics was evident in the PME song "Battle Hymn of the Peace Movement" written by a thirteen-year-old African American girl and set to the classic Civil War–era song "Battle Hymn of the Republic."

> Mine eyes will see the glory of the returning of Africans
> To the Land of Promise for we'll let her will be done.
> All our brother Africans will meet us on the run,
> Mother Gordon will lead us home.
> (Chorus)
> Mother Gordon is Leading,
> Mother Gordon is Leading,
> Mother Gordon is Leading, and she will lead us home.
> Like the Sphinx o'erlooking Egypt tho never a word it speaks
> We'll follow Mother Gordon's footsteps and always be meek
> For not one step she's taken will ever retreat,
> Mother Gordon will lead us home.
> Our Ambassadors crossed the ocean and brought messages of cheer,
> They replaced the missing link, then they returned back here,
> They gave Mother Gordon the documents and we've nothing to fear,
> Mother Gordon will lead us home.

The Rock of Gibralter has through the ages stood,
The winds and storms about it washed as furiously as they could
Behind our leader we will stand four million strong,
For she will lead us home.[167]

Like the UNIA's anthem "Ethiopia, Thou Land of Our Fathers," the PME's "Battle Hymn of the Peace Movement" constituted a rallying cry for fulfilling the group's Black settler colonial dream. The song rejoiced in the possibility of African Americans repatriating to Africa centuries after being stolen from the continent and after a PME delegation from Chicago returned from Liberia where they attempted to negotiate a land deal for a New World Black settlement in the West African republic.[168] But unlike the UNIA, a woman was at the PME's helm. The hymn captured the motherist and messianic framing of Gordon as the "Moses" of her people. It also celebrated Black motherhood and womanhood and linked her to a tradition of Black women's militancy and prophetic African American Christianity.[169] Yet the motherist frame foreclosed more radical (re)imaginings of Black womanhood and African liberation by tying Gordon's legitimacy as a protest leader to her social location as a mother and wife.

In addition, "Battle Hymn of the Peace Movement" reveals the group's Black Israelite beliefs and affirms what the cultural historian E. Frances White describes as the ways Black nationalists have historically promoted a conservative gender politics through constructing a utopian view of the African past, most notably of Ancient Egypt.[170] The reference in the song to the Sphinx is significant. Here, the Sphinx represents Egypt as a glorious Black civilization. The motherist Gordon would lead her people to freedom and restore the linkage between them and a mythical Promised Land of Africa.[171]

The PME's motherist politics and Black diasporic right radicalism contrasted with Black left feminism forged by Black women affiliated with the US Communist Party from the 1920s onward.[172] Intersectional and global in perspective, Black left feminism is a pathbreaking politics that centers working-class women by combining Communist Party positions on race, gender, and class with Black nationalism and Black left-wing women's lived experiences.[173] In contrast to Gordon and PME women, Black left feminists rejected capitalism, repatriation, narrow racial nationalism, and white supremacy. Many Black left feminists eschewed middle-class respectability and religiosity, forged unconventional marriages, advocated reproductive rights, supported free love, took same-sex and white male romantic partners, relished in queer bohemian underworlds, and globetrotted unaccompanied by a husband. Black left feminists willingly participated in the multiracial, internationalist communist left despite their sometimes vocal criticisms of the CPUSA for neglecting the special needs of Black women. Above all, Black left feminists looked to socialism and the Soviet Union, not to colonization and a glorious African past, for advancing Black and women's liberation.[174]

To be clear, Black nationalist women hardly cowered under patriarchy and lived puritanical lives. Louise Little stood up to her husband and had a child out of wedlock. Amy Ashwood Garvey's short marriage to Marcus Garvey ended because she defied his patriarchal expectations.[175] Amy Jacques Garvey and Marcus Garvey lived on opposite sides of the Atlantic during the final years of their marriage.[176] Black nationalist and leftist women understood Black freedom in global terms. But they upheld distinct gendered visions for global Black liberation.

The death of the Greater Liberia Act in the Senate marked a significant setback for Gordon, the PME, and the emigrationist cause. She probably did not imagine at this moment that she would neither again command as many followers nor ever set foot in Africa. But what we know is that she hardly surrendered. She held her head high, knowing that the PME had galvanized perhaps millions of African Americans for Liberian colonization. The PME's Black diasporic right radicalism was not without serious limitations in countering the gendered global color line. Nonetheless, the PME illustrates both the ways classical Black nationalism survived after Garvey's deportation and the importance of the Diasporic Midwest for fostering a Black (inter)national politics that centered working-class people and that rivaled Black civil rights and leftist formations during the 1930s.

Pro-Japanese Sentiment in the Heartland

Of all the 1930s US Black nationalist movements in the Garveyite tradition, arguably none was more interesting and complicated than the Midwest-based Pacific Movement of the Eastern World (PMEW). Appreciating Japan as the champion of the darker races and advancing Black diasporic right radicalism, the PMEW generated significant grassroots support for the Land of the Rising Sun among Black working-class people across the Depression-era Midwest and the United States. Pro-Japanese sentiment enjoyed widespread support among African Americans following the Russo-Japanese War (1904–1905). African Americans reveled in Russia's humiliating defeat by the Japanese and the rise of Japan as a global superpower.[177] Prominent Black spokespersons—Booker T. Washington, Marcus Garvey, and W. E. B. Du Bois—saw in Japan the champion of the world's darker races and proof that modernity and power were not the sole possessions of white imperial nations.[178] In the interwar years, pro-Tokyo sentiment found a place in the NAACP, UNIA, and other neo-Garveyite groups.[179]

The PMEW was the largest 1930s Black nationalist organization whose prime objective was forging Afro-Asian unity. Founded in 1932, the PMEW called for racial confraternity among the darker races, self-determination for all people, and territorial separation for African Americans. The St. Louis area was the group's center of gravity.[180] This was unsurprising, given the region's fraught racial history and Garvey's immense popularity among Blacks in and around the Gateway City during and long after the UNIA's heyday.[181] The PMEW also enjoyed strong Black grassroots support in the Missouri Bootheel, southern Illinois, Chicago, Detroit, Oklahoma, and Mississippi. Resembling the UNIA's motto, the PMEW's declared, "Asia for the Asians. Africa for the Africans at home and abroad."[182] PMEW established real connections among African Americans and Asians who looked to Japan as the savior for people of color. One of the most important and enigmatic of these figures in the PMEW was the activist and itinerant "Major" Satatoka Takahashi (né Naka Nakane). Born in 1875 in Japan, he migrated around 1900 to Canada, lived in the US Pacific Northwest, and vanished for several years until resurfacing in 1930 at a UNIA meeting in Chicago. There, he claimed to be a retired Japanese army officer, a liaison to the Japanese embassy, and a member of the Kokuryukai, or the Black Dragon Society, a clandestine, ultranationalist organization that championed imperial Japan as the emancipator of people of color worldwide.[183] After arriving in Chicago, he came to know Mittie Maude Lena Gordon, W. D. Fard Muhammad, and Elijah Muhammad. Takahashi worked with Mimo de Guzman (Policarpio Manansala), a prominent pro-Tokyo activist of Philippine origin who posed as Japanese and took the name Ashima Takis. Through Takahashi's charisma and claims, he forged a messianic movement in support of Japan among his African American working-class followers.[184] In addition to his prominence in PMEW, Takahashi helped to organize Development of Our Own (DOO), a pro-Japan Black nationalist group incorporated in 1933 in Lansing with strong support in Detroit, Chicago, and St. Louis.[185]

Even though Asian activists were active in pro-Japan neo-Garveyite groups, African American working-class migrants led them and composed their rank and file. For them, the PMEW's appeal rested in its apparent success in advancing Black self-determination and racial equality in the United States through winning the support of imperial Japan.[186] These beliefs animated General Lee Butler of Mississippi, a leader of the East St. Louis PMEW.[187] Reflecting once again the willingness of grassroots Black nationalists in Chicago, Detroit, and elsewhere to move across organizational boundaries, members from the UNIA and the NOI enlisted and came to empathize with the PMEW and the DOO.[188]

The response of authorities to pro-Japan Black nationalist groups bore striking resemblance to the reactions of state actors to the Nation of Islam during the 1930s. From the PMEW's very beginning, the group received government scrutiny. The US Justice Department and War Department's Military Intelligence Division closely surveilled the PMEW starting in 1933 and continuing through the Second World War.[189] J. Edgar Hoover, who masterminded Garvey's takedown, was especially worried about the PMEW. Under Hoover's direction, authorities complied thousands of pages of surveillance files on PMEW activities in Chicago, Detroit, St. Louis, Omaha, Kansas City, Robbins, and Cairo, Illinois, as well as in New York.[190] Authorities also surveilled the DOO. To Hoover and white state actors, the PMEW's and DOO's Black working-class composition, call to arms, pro-Tokyo sympathies, and linkages with Asian activists were subversive. Given these fears, officials, in a move reminiscent of Marcus Garvey's plight, deported Takahashi in 1934 from the United States to Japan for lying to immigration officials about his background.[191] State suppression shut down neither the PMEW nor the DOO in the 1930s. Pearl Sherrod, a fervent Black nationalist and Takahashi's wife, took command of the DOO after his deportation, illustrating the ongoing visibility of women in leading heartland Black nationalist groups even while authorities targeted these organizations.[192]

At the same time that pro-Japan Black nationalists imagined a future world where Blacks and other people would be free from white supremacy, heartland-based neo-Garveyites upheld dominant ideas about middle-class respectability. The PMEW's constitution stipulated that the group's members "shall maintain respectability and decorum at all occasions where the organization is concerned."[193] The PME prohibited its officers from presiding over meetings while intoxicated and barred "vulgarity" in the organization.[194] Pro-Tokyo Black nationalists were determined to win freedom for African Americans through allying with Japan. But these organizations had no interest in undoing prevailing gender and class politics undergirding white supremacy.

Even more, Black nationalist admiration for Japan highlights the reoccurring tendency of Black nationalists to blur complex political realities and to promote alliances with authoritarian forces. While Black nationalists championed Japan, their Black leftist rivals framed the Empire of the Sun as a belligerent fascist country.[195] As Ernest Allen observes, African American communists in the 1930s consistently spoke out against the looming danger of Japanese fascism and warned about the ruse of Japan as the champion of the darker races.[196] Despite Black communists' best efforts in rebuking Black nationalists' claims about Japan, more Blacks joined pro-Tokyo groups than the US Communist Party. This fact underscores the wide appeal of pro-Japanese sentiment among African Americans across the United States. The significantly larger size of Black nationalist groups in contrast to African American membership in the Communist Party illustrates once again that nationalist aspirations remained prevalent in Black America, especially among the working poor in the urban heartland.[197]

The decision of Black nationalists to support Japan resembles the willingness of Mittie Maude Lena Gordon, Marcus Garvey, and other Black nationalists to collaborate with white supremacists in support of Liberian colonization. The UNIA and other neo-Garveyite groups understood race as a biological category at the core of structuring social relations and geopolitical power. Given this logic, pro-Tokyo Black nationalists believed humanity was divided into two groups—people of color and whites—and that capitalism and empire harnessed by the Japanese could be used to topple structural inequalities and to liberate the darker world. Black nationalists may have been naïve or willfully blind about Japanese military atrocities across Asia. However, Black Americans, especially dirt-poor southern newcomers to the Midwest, were aware of the racism, misery, violence, and injustice in Depression-era Jim Crow America. They could look abroad and see the knees of European colonial rulers on the necks of their subjects of color. From their vantage point, supporting the enemy of their enemy made sense. Pro-Japanese sentiment in Black America, centered in the heartland, speaks again to the paradoxical way Black nationalists imagined freedom and connected the Diasporic Midwest to the nonwhite world.

As the world teetered toward another global war, Midwest-based Black nationalists in the Garveyite tradition constituted the driving force in making the 1930s a dynamic moment in the history of Black nationalism, internationalism, and radicalism. The UNIA still counted thousands of active members in Chicago, Detroit, Cleveland, and around the African world from Garvey's deportation to his premature passing. Midwesterners remained a powerful constituency in the transnational UNIA. However, times had changed. Spawned by the racial conditions across the economically depressed Midwest and United States, the decline of the UNIA, and geopolitical events, new midwestern Garveyite front groups seized Garvey's torch and moved Black nationalism in exciting new directions. Globally minded, these groups forged an oppositional politics that captured the hopes of Black working-class people to the envy of UNIA officials and Black communists, to the consternation of the African

American establishment, and to the alarm of white US rulers. Viewing Black nationalists as a fundamental threat to the gendered racial status quo, US state actors sometimes brutally suppressed grassroots Garveyites, such as in the case of Louise Little and the Nation of Islam. Not without paradoxes, midwestern Black nationalists promoted patriarchy, Black settler colonialism, and a narrow racial nationalism that challenged and reinforced gendered racial capitalism and the global color line. Despite these paradoxes, Midwest-based Garveyites were well positioned to continue fighting for global Black freedom.

4

"ON DECEMBER 7 ONE BILLION BLACK

PEOPLE . . . STRUCK FOR FREEDOM"

Midwestern Garveyism during the 1940s

The conditions of life that Negroes have faced and are still facing in America are conducive to the highest degree to a nationalistic spirit. —THERESA E. YOUNG, "The Only Real Solution," *New Negro World*, September 1943

Mittie Maude Lena Gordon was headed for prison. On January 17, 1944, a federal judge in Chicago ordered her to the Federal Reformatory for Women in Alderson, West Virginia. Her incarceration soon thereafter marked the culmination of a long legal fight tied to her alleged response to the Second World War. On September 20, 1942, FBI agents arrested her in Chicago, along with her husband, William Green Gordon, and two PME officials. Authorities charged them with sedition and conspiracy. Government officials alleged that she had met with Japanese agents and had made racially inflammatory remarks at PME meetings in the Windy City in which she praised Japan as the champion of the darker races and dissuaded African Americans from serving in the US military. She denied these charges.[1] Inside Alderson, her health suffered immeasurably. Still, she bided her time until her release. She dreamed of returning to Chicago where she planned to resume fighting for Liberian colonization.[2]

Gordon's political persecution was part of a wartime nationwide government crackdown against alleged "foreign-inspired Agitation Among American

Negroes" fueled by Imperial Japan that sought to exploit Black American racial grievances and to gain favor through forging solidarity among the "darker" races. The Survey of Racial Conditions in the United States (RACON), established in 1940 by FBI director J. Edgar Hoover, carried out this work. He perceived wartime African American insurgency against Jim Crow and global white supremacy as a major threat to national security. Anticipating the Counter Intelligence Program of the Civil Rights–Black Power era, RACON surveilled wartime organizations affiliated with Black nationalists, civil rights, and communism for their alleged pro-Tokyo subversion.[3]

Chicago was ground zero of US government repression against Black militancy. Between September 19 and 21, 1942, authorities in the Windy City arrested Gordon, along with Elijah Muhammad; bibliophile, curator, and globetrotter F. H. Hammurabi Robb; and nearly ninety members of the PME, NOI, and Brotherhood of Liberty for Black People of America for their purported pro-Tokyo sympathies. They were political prisoners. Some Black nationalists like Robb evaded long prison sentences. Others such as Gordon and Muhammad were not so fortunate.[4] But neither Gordon nor Muhammad crumbled in the face of massive, wartime state repression. They remained determined to fight for the dignity and freedom of Black people everywhere during the 1940s.

Midwest-based Black nationalist groups in the Garveyite tradition were prominent in advancing a powerful and paradoxical Black diasporic right radicalism that contested and buttressed the gendered global color line and that linked the Diasporic Midwest to the world during the Second World War and early Cold War. The experience of the dialectic of opportunity and oppression, global events, and the long, complex history of Black resistance in the heartland shaped this work. The globally informed work of 1940s Black nationalist disciples of Garvey in and beyond the US heartland has been largely dismissed by scholars as irrelevant to wartime African Americans. Instead, scholars have framed wartime Black internationalism mainly as a leftist and liberal project in which East Coast and southern-based activists and intellectuals were prominent.[5]

Heartland Black nationalists in the 1940s forged grassroots Black opposition to the war; articulated searing critiques of global white supremacy; kept the legacy of Marcus Garvey alive; built racially autonomous institutions and communities; and cultivated transnational linkages between the heartland and the darker world. On the other hand, the Black diasporic right radicalism practiced by some heartland Garvey followers remained deeply rooted in nineteenth-century classical Black nationalism. For these reasons, some 1940s Black nationalists continued promoting Black capitalism, colonization, and in the most extreme cases alliances with white supremacists, as left-wing and more modern articulations of pan-Africanism gained ground across the Black world. Calling attention to the local and transnational work of 1940s midwestern Garveyites evinces once again the power and limitations of Black nationalism. Their politics provide a powerful lens for appreciating the ways the global visions of wartime Black nationalists, liberals, and leftists intersected and diverged in response to a momentous moment in twentieth-century world history. The 1940s also provide insight into the resilience of midwestern Garveyites such as Gordon, Elijah Muhammad, James Stewart, Goldie Stewart, Louise Little, and Malcolm Little, who endured extreme persecution and extralegal violence because of their racial defiance.

The Second World War and the Resurgent UNIA

The Second World War transformed Black America and Global Africa. In the United States, the Second Great Migration began and, between 1940 and 1970, five million African Americans migrated from the South to the urban North and West, with 1.6 million Blacks leaving Dixie between 1940 and 1950.[6] In the Midwest, Chicago's Black population increased from 277,731 in 1940 to 492,265 in 1950.[7] Detroit's Black population rose to 210,000 during the war.[8] In 1940, Cleveland counted 84,320 African Americans.[9] Nationally, the median income of Black wage earners and salaried workers of color rose from 41 percent of the white American median income in 1939 to 60 percent by 1950. The percentage of Black American women working in the industrial sector tripled while the percentage of domestics declined from 60 percent to 45 percent.[10] President Roosevelt's Four Freedoms, the Atlantic Charter, the establishment of the United Nations, and anticolonial fervor in Asia and Africa convinced many Black Americans that a "new world [was] a-coming."[11]

The war fueled Black American militancy. Prominent Black spokespersons called for a "Double Victory": the defeat of fascism abroad and Jim Crow at home, and the end of European colonial empires in Africa and Asia.[12] Nearly three million African Americans registered for US military service, and approximately 500,000 were stationed overseas.[13] Black labor leader A. Philip Randolph threatened to march on Washington, DC, for Black inclusion in war industries, and that forced President Franklin D. Roosevelt to issue Executive Order 8802 in June 1941. It barred racial discrimination in war industries and established the Fair Employment Practice Commission (FEPC) to implement the order.[14] Grassroots Black militancy pushed the NAACP, National Council of Negro Women, FOL, and other established Black civic organizations politically leftward.[15] The war witnessed the resurgence of the National Negro Congress and the formation of new Black protest groups such as the Congress of Racial Equality and the March on Washington Movement, which unapologetically called for direct action, boycotts, and mass protests.[16]

Despite significant wartime advances, the African-descended remained subjugated people in the United States and globally. In the Midwest, Chicago, Detroit, and Cleveland witnessed the formation of hypersegregated, underserved, majority-Black "second ghettos."[17] War industries in these cities relegated African Americans to the most menial jobs—if they were hired at all.[18] Wartime Detroit remained a hothouse of racial turmoil fueled by intraracial job competition, housing shortages, police brutality, white racist demagogues, the KKK, and mass white resistance to Black insurgence. The Detroit Riot of 1943 left twenty-five Blacks and nine whites dead, making it the deadliest racial disturbance in wartime America.[19]

Globally, the war fueled anticolonialism across Asia, Africa, and the Caribbean, as well as an emergent pan-Africanism and Black working-class political consciousness committed to decolonization, human rights, socialism, international solidarity, antifascism, trade unionism, secularism, and the liberation of the African-descended globally.[20] In the United States, the Council on African Affairs (CAA) best embodied this nascent Black leftist internationalism. Formed in 1937, the New York City–based CAA was a pioneering organization in forging African American understanding of African freedom struggles and in championing African liberation. In a break from classical Black nationalist civilizationism, formations such as the CAA increasingly looked to the African masses, not to Western-educated, middle-class New World Blacks, as the vanguard for African decolonization. African American activist-intellectuals, globetrotters, and cultural figures—Paul Robeson, Eslanda Robeson, Alphaeus Hunton, Max Yergan, and Marcus Garvey's old foe, W. E. B. Du Bois—led the CAA.[21] Council officials came to know and collaborate with a younger generation of Black leftists in the National Negro Congress and the Southern Negro Youth Congress. These groups shared the CAA's leftist global outlook. Women were visible in these organizations, practicing Black left feminism. It was within this local, national, and global context in which the wartime UNIA and midwestern Garveyite front carried out their work through a diasporic politics grounded in a nineteenth-century paradigm that overlapped and contrasted with the transnational politics advanced by Black liberals and leftists.

The transnational UNIA enjoyed a resurgence during the Second World War due in no small part to midwestern Garveyites. This was most evident in the ascension of James Stewart of Cleveland as the new UNIA president-general following the death of Marcus Garvey on June 10, 1940, in London. In August 1940, delegates at an extraordinary UNIA international meeting in New York elected Stewart as acting president-general. His years of dedicated service to the UNIA and his close relationship with Garvey generated enthusiastic support among conference delegates for Stewart's election. As the UNIA's acting president-general, he moved the Parent Body from its temporary headquarters in Harlem to Cleveland. Soon thereafter he was unanimously elected UNIA president-general.[22] From Cleveland's Liberty Hall, he attempted to revitalize the transnational UNIA. The Parent Body hosted UNIA international conferences. The UNIA published the *New Negro World* newspaper from the Forest City. Founded in 1940 and named after its famous predecessor, *New Negro World* covered UNIA and global affairs. The newspaper featured news about young African-descended activists committed to Garveyism, such as Nnamdi Azikiwe. Born in 1904 in Nigeria and educated at the historically Black Lincoln University outside of Philadelphia, he emerged during the war as a leading pan-African journalist, educator, and activist, who in 1960 became the first president of Nigeria. Later in life, he attributed his political awakening in the 1930s to reading *Negro World* and *The Philosophy and Opinions of Marcus Garvey* (1923, 1925), a two-volume set edited by Amy Jacques Garvey consisting of Marcus's essays, speeches, and sayings.[23] It is unclear if Stewart and Azikiwe ever met. What we know is that *New Negro World* praised the young Nigerian as "a devout believer in Garveyism," revealing the way the UNIA still connected multiple generations of Black people across the globe.[24] The circulation of *New Negro World* paled in comparison to its predecessor. Nonetheless, the newspaper being based in Cleveland signaled the city's continued importance to global Garveyism.[25]

UNIA women based in the Midwest played a vital role in leading the global Garvey movement in the 1940s. The veteran UNIA leader Ethel Collins of Jamaica moved to Cleveland during the war to assist Stewart.[26] From Robbins, Illinois, Elinor White remained actively involved in local and global UNIA affairs.[27] She was joined by a new generation of talented women from the heartland like Theresa E. Young of Cincinnati and Christina Lyons of Cleveland, both of whom held ranking UNIA posts in the 1940s.[28]

In keeping with the Black midwestern and Garveyite impulse of institution-building, the wartime UNIA under Stewart established Liberty Farm in 1943. The UNIA-owned farm was located on a fifty-eight-acre parcel of land in Oregonia, Ohio, a small town in Warren County. Stewart selected this site partially due to its proximity to Cincinnati, Columbus, Dayton, and Hamilton, cities home to sizable Black communities and loyal Garveyites.[29] Looking toward the future while keeping an eye on the past, he envisaged the farm as a stepping stone for preparing his family and Garveyites to emigrate to Liberia and to realize Garvey's unfulfilled dream of relocating the UNIA's headquarters to the West African republic. Stewart, along with his wife, Goldie, and four of their children, moved from Cleveland to Oregonia. They lived on the farm for almost six years. The Stewarts and other UNIA members constructed cabins and barns, dug wells, raised chickens, and grew vegetables for their own consumption and for sale in local markets. The farm hosted UNIA international conferences in which hundreds of faithful Garveyites from Cleveland, Chicago, Cincinnati, Dayton, Detroit, Gary, and St. Louis attended and generously donated money to the organization. Their willingness to support the UNIA and to travel to Oregonia show the ongoing importance of well-resourced heartland Garveyites to sustaining the UNIA.[30]

Liberty Farm connected the UNIA to the rich history of Black Ohio transnational resistance. Stewart did not articulate the property's mission in these terms. Nonetheless, the farm, like the nineteenth-century Colored Conventions held across the Buckeye State, signaled the long-standing importance that Black nationalists placed on self-reliance, Black capitalism, institution-building, landownership, farming, and emigration as strategies for Black self-determination.[31] This politics differed from those of Black liberals and leftists who believed that global Black freedom was inextricably linked to the expansion of the welfare state, interracialism, civil rights legislation, and, in some cases, socialism.

Life on Liberty Farm was dangerous for Garveyites. The property's location in southwestern Ohio placed it in a citadel of white anti-Black violence dating back to the antebellum era. Local whites perceived the Black-owned farm as a threat to white supremacy. Klansmen burned a cross in front of the farm and bombed a farm building. On another occasion, whites poured a slop bucket down a farm well, poisoning the water. No Garveyites were ever injured from these assaults. But they endured years of daily microaggressions from local whites, punctuated by occasional acts of extreme racial violence. This racism infuriated James Stewart and farm residents. Just like the Littles in Omaha, Stewart and his UNIA colleagues on the farm were ready to defend themselves with guns from racist midwestern whites who threatened their lives and property and detested their very existence.[32]

Encountering white hostility was hardly the only challenge facing Garveyites in Oregonia. The farm never turned a profit. Some UNIA members openly accused James Stewart of financial impropriety.[33] Frigid winters, sweltering summers, poisonous snakes, swarms of insects, and arduous farm labor tested the Garveyites' resolve. Despite these obstacles, the Stewarts and their colleagues never wavered in their beliefs.[34] The UNIA was a shadow of its glory days. Still, the UNIA marched on under the leadership of a Clevelander and through the organizational support of loyal midwestern Garveyites who propelled the transnational UNIA into its fourth decade.

Midwestern Black Nationalists and Japan

If the 1940s brought renewed visibility to the heartland in the UNIA, then these years also signaled the region's underappreciated importance as a bastion of US Black nationalist support for Japan and opposition to the Second World War, particularly to US involvement in the Asia-Pacific Theater. African American opposition to the war challenges popular memory and scholarly portrayals of Black Americans as uniformly supportive of the US war effort.[35] Antiwar sentiment found strong support in Black America across the political spectrum, with the exception of Blacks affiliated with the Communist Party who championed the war after the Nazi Germany invasion of the Soviet Union in June 1941.[36] In contrast to the Black left, Black nationalists read the war through their Black diasporic right radicalism. For this reason, the UNIA and the midwestern Garveyite front were at the front lines in opposing the war and sympathizing with Japan.[37] This sentiment hardened among Black nationalists following the Japanese surprise attack on Pearl Harbor in Hawai'i on December 7, 1941. The attack prompted the US declaration of war against Japan the following day and galvanized widespread (white) American support for the war through the rallying cry "Remember Pearl Harbor."[38] Pearl Harbor, together with a string of stunning Japanese victories between 1940 and 1942 over British, French, Dutch, and US forces across the Asia-Pacific, shattered the myth of European invincibility.[39] The pro-Tokyo position of midwestern Black nationalists not only speaks to the extent of wartime Black American opposition to the war but also illustrates the ideological differences among Black nationalists and their liberal and leftist counterparts, as well as the long-standing political paradoxes of Black nationalism in challenging the global color line.

Chicago-based Black nationalist organizations were at the forefront nationally in stoking pro-Japan sentiment among working-class African Americans. The PME's membership had decreased since the late 1930s. Still, the organization regularly drew excited crowds in the hundreds at mass meetings on the South Side.[40] At one meeting, Mittie Maude Lena Gordon celebrated the Japanese attack on Pearl Harbor by boasting that "on December 7 one billion Black people . . . struck for freedom."[41] Illustrating her Afro-Orientalism, she identified the Japanese as Black and the attack as a victory for people of color globally over whites. Given her pro-Japan stance, she discouraged her followers from serving in the US military. Liberian colonization, she contended, constituted Black America's "only hope."[42]

The Nation of Islam embraced a similar pro-Tokyo position. Elijah Muhammad proclaimed before his followers in Chicago that "the Japanese will slaughter the white man."[43] In keeping with the NOI's religious beliefs and refusal to recognize the United States as a sovereign authority over Black people, Muhammad dissuaded his followers from registering for the draft. The Messenger himself dodged the draft. Many Muslims followed his lead, making them the biggest group of African American war resisters.[44] Similarly, the Chicago-based MSTA encouraged its members to resist the war.[45] The St. Louis area, an epicenter of the PMEW, was another geographic center of pro-Japan grassroots support among African Americans.[46]

Black nationalists across the United States found receptive audiences to their pro-Japan message. However, racial terror facing Blacks in the Midwest was especially important for fostering pro-Japan sentiment among heartland Black nationalists. In the months before Pearl Harbor, James Stewart called for US government support for African American voluntary emigration to Africa in exchange for their loyalty in fighting against the Axis. However, in early 1942 the UNIA abruptly shifted its position on the war in response to the gruesome lynching of a twenty-six-year-old African American man named Cleo Wright in Sikeston, Missouri, a town located just north of the Missouri Bootheel. On January 25, 1942, a white mob savagely killed him on the town's street in broad daylight for allegedly trying to rape a white woman.[47] His lynching drew public outcry from African Americans nationwide. The Department of Justice investigated the case. The assailants went unpunished.[48]

Wright's lynching incensed Stewart, prompting him to end the UNIA's conditional support for the war and to express sympathy toward Tokyo. At a UNIA meeting in Cincinnati soon after Wright's grisly murder, Stewart declared: "'We will remember Missouri and then Pearl Harbor—To Hell with Pearl Harbor.'"[49] Wright's death trumped Stewart's support for the war. Rhetorically, his reference to Wright's death in relation to Pearl Harbor amounted to a skillful play on words that turned the US pro-war rallying cry on its head. Echoing Gordon's and Muhammad's pro-Japan sympathies, Stewart identified white America, not Japan, as the greatest threat to Black life and liberty. Unlike Gordon and Muhammad, Stewart neither called for Black men to dodge the draft nor claimed that African Americans would be better off living under Japan. Nonetheless, he predicted defeat for the allies so long as global white supremacy persisted.[50]

Midwestern Black nationalists' support for Japan illustrates the significant political differences between civil rights activists and Black diasporic right radicals toward the war. At the end of the day, the NAACP and Black mainstream media still pledged support for the war despite their grievances with US racism, believing in the possibilities of African Americans gaining their full freedom in the United States. Heartland Black nationalists rejected this position. Still fuming over the unfulfilled promises from the First World War "to make the world safe for democracy" and horrified by ongoing US racial terror, Black nationalists backed Japan and racial separation as the only realistic path to Black freedom.

While midwestern Garveyites rejected the US war effort, this politics also revealed the limits of their Black nationalism. Like the pro-Tokyo Black nationalist response in the 1930s, heartland Black nationalists in the early 1940s once again overlooked the oppressive reality of Japanese war-making and rule in the Asia-Pacific.[51] By championing Japan as an ally of people of color globally, Black nationalists in the heartland and across the United States in effect sanctioned the colonial subjugation of nonwhite people. The sense of alienation toward white America, quest for national belonging, and search for racial solidarity with the darker world distorted geopolitical realities and shrouded the suffering and national aspirations of conquered subjects of color living under Japanese rule. The midwestern Garveyites' pro-Tokyo stance contrasted from the position of Black leftists, who rejected empire and viewed Japan as a fascist nation. Black nationalists' support for Japan shows how much their global visions, still deeply informed by classical Black nationalism, aligned with Eurocentric ideas about race, empire, civilization, power, and knowledge.

At the same time, the Black nationalist pro-Japan line should not be dismissed. Midwestern Black nationalists arguably understood better than anyone else that the war had not significantly altered the lives of most Black Americans, especially in the heartland. Most Blacks in these cities continued to live in segregated ghettos, to work the dirtiest jobs, and to face police terror and white racial violence. Nationally, African Americans remained second-class citizens. Africa remained under European colonial rule. The war's lofty democratic promises compounded the sense of alienation among African Americans toward the United States and white world. Midwestern Black nationalists loathed the condition of Black people in America, and they had little faith in the war changing white people. For these reasons, heartland Black nationalists looked to imperial Japan as an agent for Black liberation.

Liberian Colonization and Pan-Africanism during the War

As heartland Black nationalists were at the forefront in galvanizing Black American grassroots opposition to the war, midwestern Garveyites also championed African American repatriation to Liberia during the 1940s. Mass Liberian colonization never again generated the support of millions of Black Americans. However, getting out of America for Liberia still enjoyed strong support among UNIA and neo-Garveyite groups across the United States, particularly in the heartland. Like the wartime pro-Tokyo Black nationalist position, calls for returning to Africa evidenced the possibilities and ambivalences of Black nationalism, as well as the ways 1940s Black diasporic right radicalism intersected and diverged from liberal and leftist Black internationalism. The PME's wartime endorsement of Theodore Bilbo's Greater Liberia Act is a case in point. On the eve of the war, Gordon still believed in Liberian colonization as the pathway for African American freedom.[52] The UNIA embraced a similar position. In the fall of 1940, James Stewart mandated all UNIA divisions in the United States to support the Greater Liberia Act.[53]

Midwestern-based UNIA women were some of the most vocal champions of Liberian emigration and racial purity during the war.[54] They used *New Negro World* as a platform for articulating this politics. In her heartfelt essay entitled "Arise," St. Louis UNIA leader Adelia Ireland praised James Stewart and UNIA assistant president Charles L. James for keeping alive Garvey's dream of a redeemed Africa. She called on Garveyite men to assume responsibility for leading Blacks back to "OUR MOTHERLAND."[55] Ethel Collins made a similar case for emigration in an impassioned 1942 article, "Liberty." Staunchly opposed to Black-white interracial sex, she wrote, "We are not seeking social equality; we do not seek inter-marriage." Instead, she emphasized, "We want the right to have a country of our own. The Pilgrim [*sic*] and colonists did it for America, and the New Negro can do it for Africa." Viewing the continent as "the legitimate, moral, and righteous home of the Black peoples of the world," she praised the UNIA for leading the charge "for the restoration of [Black] liberty and the land of our fathers."[56]

The wartime pan-Africanism of heartland Black nationalists was in conversation with the 1940s anticolonialism of Amy Jacques Garvey. From Jamaica, she was arguably the most revered Garveyite in the world after the passing of her husband, despite holding no formal leadership position in the UNIA. She held anticolonial and Black settler colonial views. During the war, she forged a broad network of pan-African contacts around the world, including Kwame Nkrumah, Nnamdi Azikiwe, W. E. B. Du Bois, and George Padmore. Even though she worked with leftists and liberals, she remained a staunch proponent of racialism and colonization.[57] This stance was evident in her anticolonial, pan-African tract *Memorandum Correlative of Africa, West Indies, and the Americas*. Self-published in 1944, she demanded United Nations support for postwar independence for African colonies.[58] In a controversial move, she endorsed the Greater Liberia Act. Like the PME and UNIA, she believed that Bilbo's bill still offered New World Blacks the best hope for African redemption and maintaining Black racial purity. She was cognizant of Bilbo's notorious racism. However, in a move resembling the response of Gordon to critics for her collaborations with Bilbo, Jacques Garvey urged her followers to separate the message from its racist messenger. Additionally, she proposed the creation of a postwar settler state from The Gambia to Nigeria governed by diasporic Blacks as an intermediary step toward full independence for Africa. James Stewart issued a similar call.[59]

Although Garveyites rejected European rule of Africa, many nonetheless followed the same complicated road traveled by Black nationalists since the nineteenth century through promoting settler colonialism and civilizationism. Collins framed European settlement of colonial New England—an encounter predicated on white settler genocidal conquest of Indigenous people—as a precedent for establishing diasporic settler colonies in Africa and for civilizing Indigenes.[60] The call by Jacques Garvey, the PME, and the UNIA for a Black settler colonial state was out of step with growing anticolonial sentiment across West Africa. It seems difficult to imagine Africans in the 1940s warmly receiving a large population of African American settlers. The violent nineteenth- and early twentieth-century history of Liberia attests to the resistance by Indigenous Africans to Black diasporic settlers. More broadly, the anticolonialism and pan-Africanism proffered by 1940s Black nationalists contrasted sharply with the global visions embraced by Black civil rights and leftist groups.[61]

Nowhere were wartime political differences among Black nationalists and Black liberals and radicals more apparent than in their responses to Bilbo. Black liberals and leftists loathed the Mississippi segregationist, comparing him with Adolf Hitler.[62] Echoing Garvey, Collins through *New Negro World* leveled familiar and disingenuous Black nationalist arguments against their Black ideological foes as being advocates of miscegenation. As the Second World War unfolded and as pro-independence sentiment intensified across the nascent Third World, the global politics of Black nationalists and their liberal and leftist counterparts continued growing steadily apart. The UNIA and PME remained wedded to Black diasporic right radicalism, a politics increasingly behind the times by the Second World War.

Meanwhile, the gender and sexual politics of 1940s heartland Black nationalists also differed from those of their liberal and leftist counterparts. As

Black left feminists and their Black male allies began thinking critically and collectively about the personal as political and challenging sexism in the public and private spheres, Black nationalists continued articulating Black freedom in heteropatriarchal terms. This perspective was evident in Adelia Ireland's call for Black men to assert their manly duty in leading the race back to Africa, showing that many Garveyite women remained deeply invested in the promise of patriarchy. Similarly, James Stewart espoused a masculinist understanding of freedom. In a May 1942 *New Negro World* editorial, he wrote, "The women of Africa must not be exposed as our women in America under the pretense of total war and Democracy." He added: "Black men needed to PAY THE PRICE OF FREEDOM . . . for the protection of our women."[63] He also opposed birth control. He made this point in a poem titled "Our Birth Control," published in *New Negro World* in February 1942:

Today I know that white men
do plan to take my hearth
And force on Blacks a birth control
to wipe them off the earth.
This earth was made for all men
and not for just a few
So why should white men take my land
and say what I must do.
To rule is man's ambition
And to serve befits a slave
If myself, on earth, I cannot rule
Dear GOD, better be my grave![64]

Stewart's antipathy toward birth control, a view widely shared at the time among Garveyite women and men, anticipated 1960s and 1970s Black nationalist framings of birth control as a conspiracy contrived by whites to eradicate Black people and to emasculate Black men.[65] His opposition to birth control and call for protection, grounded in religiosity, can be read as an effort to reassert Black men's control over African American women's bodies and livelihoods in a rapidly changing world.[66] So while he proffered a militant challenge to the racial oppression of Black men, his stance toward Black women's freedom was far less progressive. Garveyite heteropatriarchal articulations of African redemption foreclosed more critical readings of gender and imagining women as equal partners in the struggle for global Black freedom.

Organizationally, the UNIA's man-centered politics fractured the wartime UNIA. A bitter conflict between James Stewart and Ethel Collins is a case in point. In 1942, Stewart expelled Collins from the organization. He charged Collins, along with Philadelphia UNIA leader Thomas Harvey, with seeking to remove Stewart as UNIA president-general and to appoint Amy Jacques Garvey as the UNIA's new head. The dispute between Stewart and Collins became public and vicious. In *New Negro World*, he denounced her for allegedly "being totally disloyal" to him and the organization.[67] His accusations infuriated her. In an open letter to the UNIA, Collins wrote that it "was wicked for anyone" to accuse her of "being disloyal" because of her years of dedicated service to the Garvey movement. She alleged that he had "harassed and insulted" her for years.[68] As Stewart clashed with Collins, he battled with her close ally Amy Jacques Garvey. In a 1944 letter to him, she blasted Stewart for allegedly stealing the proceeds from copies of *The Philosophy and Opinions of Marcus Garvey* she had sent to him to sell. She also criticized Stewart for providing insufficient financial assistance to her two sons with Marcus Garvey—Marcus Garvey Jr. and Julius Garvey—whom she believed the UNIA was obligated to support.[69]

There is no record to indicate whether Stewart replied to Jacques Garvey's accusations or if they were true. Surely, there were two sides to this story. Friends and family remembered Stewart as an honest and austere man fiercely dedicated to his family and the UNIA.[70] What is certain is that his apparent masculinism and his public quarrels with Collins and Jacques Garvey helped sow the seeds for their break from Stewart and their support for a rival UNIA faction that came to be known as the Rehabilitating Committee. Formed in Philadelphia in 1943, the Rehabilitating Committee pledged to restore the UNIA based on the principles of Marcus Garvey that some Garveyites believed Stewart had abandoned.[71] In the coming years, prominent Garveyites such as Thomas Harvey, William Sherrill, and Ethel Collins moved into this rival group. Jacques Garvey backed the organization. Her support lent the Rehabilitating Committee an air of legitimacy. The tensions between Stewart and Collins and Jacques Garvey demonstrated again the impact of sexism in weakening the UNIA.[72]

It is important to note that Black male sexism was hardly unique to the UNIA. Heteropatriarchy was deeply entrenched in civil rights and communist-affiliated organizations as well. From the 1940s and onward, dynamic grass-roots civil rights organizer Ella Baker encountered persistent sexism from Black male civil rights leaders who never treated her as an equal.[73] In the Communist Party, Black women beginning in the 1920s vocally criticized their white male and female and Black male comrades for neglecting women of color.[74] Still, the communist left offered Black women unique space for thinking critically about the intersections among race, gender, and class, and for pursuing transgressive lifeways.

Just like their leftist and liberal rivals, wartime midwestern Black nationalists understood Global Africa's future as inextricably linked to the Second World War. But many of Garvey's heartland disciples continued subscribing to Black diasporic right radicalism. This stance enabled Black nationalists to build grassroots African American opposition to the war. But this politics in contrast to the Black left remained wedded to capitalism, racism, patriarchy, and empire. The wartime UNIA and midwestern Garveyite front pursued a complex politics both in opposition to and complicit with gendered racial capitalism and global white supremacy.

Wartime State Repression and the Personal Costs of Activism

Midwestern Black nationalists faced extreme government persecution for their opposition to the war and pro-Tokyo sympathies. Authorities surveilled and jailed Black civil rights and left-wing organizers across the United States during the war. However, government rulers viewed heartland Black nationalists as the most dangerous African Americans in the country as the possibility of an Axis victory loomed. For this reason, wartime government repression of midwestern Black nationalists was especially severe, highlighting the personal costs of activism for Garvey's disciples.[75]

The NOI bore a significant brunt of government persecution against Black nationalist organizations nationwide. On September 20, 1942, in Chicago, the FBI arrested Elijah Muhammad, along with seventy members of the Nation, for conspiracy to commit sedition and for evading the Selective Training and Service Act of 1940, a law requiring all able-bodied men between the ages of twenty-one and forty-five to register for the military draft.[76] Authorities found neither weapons nor incriminating evidence of direct connections between the NOI and Japanese agents. Nonetheless, on October 5, 1942, thirty-one rank-and-file Muslims pled guilty to charges of draft dodging. They received three-year prison sentences.[77] On December 18, 1942, a federal judge in Washington, DC, sentenced Muhammad to a one- to five-year prison term for sedition and draft evasion. Muhammad began his sentence on July 23, 1943, at the Federal Correctional Institution in Milan, Michigan, a town thirty miles southwest of Detroit.[78]

The Messenger's incarceration enhanced his reputation among his followers as a martyr persecuted by the diabolical white man.[79] While in prison, the Messenger and his son Emmanuel, who was also sentenced to Milan, converted several Black inmates to Islam. Muhammad came to realize that young, alienated, incarcerated African American men constituted fertile ground for increasing his flock. Upon his release from prison on August 24, 1946, he devoted special attention to recruiting these men into the NOI. His incarceration also impacted the Nation's future politics. Due in part to his jailing, the NOI in the coming years pursued a program predicated on avoiding political activism and direct confrontation with the government, which had characterized the Nation's work during the 1930s and 1940s.[80]

Gordon's response to her incarceration illustrates the resilience and paradoxes of wartime midwestern Black nationalists, as well as the personal costs of activism. Beginning in January 1944, she spent almost two years at the Alderson federal prison in West Virginia. Imprisonment broke neither her spirit nor her belief in Liberian colonization. She made this known in regular correspondences with her husband, PME associates, and, above all, Earnest Sevier Cox during her trial and imprisonment.[81] Letters between Gordon and Cox shed important light on their growing friendship and their interiority. In a 1943 letter to him, she framed herself as a political prisoner and martyr for the colonizationist cause whose plight, she believed, was worse than the "crucifixion" of Jesus.[82] There is no record of Cox's response to her claims. However, she saw him as a trusted ally.[83]

Gordon's imprisonment weakened the PME.[84] Her mental health and heart condition deteriorated while in Alderson, and her physical health never fully recovered after her release from prison in August 1945.[85] She shared the news about her declining health and desire for parole with Cox.[86] Worried about the deleterious effects of imprisonment on her health and wellness and her ability to agitate for Liberian colonization from behind bars, he lobbied prison and US government officials for her release.[87]

Self-interest seemingly played a role in motivating Cox's determined efforts to win Gordon's release from prison. He believed in racial separation, and he saw in Gordon an invaluable ally in pursuit of this objective. She too had her own agenda. Apparently, she believed the politically well-connected Cox could secure her freedom. Their correspondences also reveal that they genuinely cared about each other through forging a relationship based on mutual respect and after working together for ten years in support of Liberian colonization.[88] Their relationship illustrates a historical irony. At the very moment when the war discredited racialism and colonialism, Gordon and Cox found common ground through championing racialism and colonization, and she relied on a white supremacist man to free her from prison.

Whereas government repression landed heavy blows against the NOI and PME, law enforcement also targeted the UNIA. Government surveillance files reported information about UNIA activities across the country. James Stewart was of special concern to the FBI. From 1944 through 1953, the FBI accumulated 225 pages of surveillance files on him. Reports included information about his leadership of the UNIA, alleged "pro-Japanese" and "anti-white" sentiments, family life, and day-to-day activities.[89] During the war, white FBI agents interrogated Stewart at Liberty Hall in Cleveland about his work. Government harassment incensed him. He worried that the FBI might kill him or his family. These concerns contributed to his decision to relocate to Liberty Farm in southwestern Ohio and reaffirmed his determination to get to Liberia.[90] Politically, state harassment tempered his public statements opposing the war. By the summer of 1942, he dispensed with his "to hell with Pearl Harbor" refrain and pledged the UNIA's full support for the war.[91] He was no fool. Recognizing the immense punitive power of white US authorities, he apparently shifted the UNIA's stance toward the war to protect himself, his family, and the organization.

Wartime state repression decimated the Pacific Movement of the Eastern World. Fearful government officials came to believe that the PMEW, with the assistance of Japanese agents, planned to sabotage key infrastructure in St. Louis and to rally thousands of Black Americans in the Missouri Bootheel to take up arms to avenge the grisly lynching of Cleo Wright. The PMEW neither committed acts of sabotage nor ever fired a shot. Still, the government took no chances. Suffering a similar fate as Muhammad and Gordon, PMEW St. Louis–area leaders General Lee Butler and David Erwin were sentenced in 1942 to federal prison for allegedly conspiring to dodge the draft and for committing sedition. Authorities sentenced their faux Japanese associate Ashima Takis to federal prison for allegedly committing money fraud.[92] State repression shut down the PMEW.

As heartland Black nationalists encountered state persecution, they faced intense criticism from the mainstream African American press for apparently supporting Japan.[93] Echoing the hostile response of some Blacks toward Garvey and Black nationalists in the interwar years, the *Chicago Defender* excoriated the NOI and MSTA as subversive "cultists" and "'crack pot' organizations" with "illiterate followers" who foolishly believed Japan would liberate Black Americans. The Black press made similar charges about the PME.[94] Irrespective of what some Black middle-class spokespersons may have wished, segments of Black America sympathized with Tokyo, resisted the war, and embraced Black nationalism.

While high-profile, midwestern-based Black nationalists faced the wrath of the US government for opposing the war, state actors also targeted heartland, grassroots Garveyites for their apparent racial defiance. Arguably, no midwestern Garveyite felt the oppressive impact of state repression directed toward themselves and their family during the war more than Louise Little. The 1940s marked the first decade of her psychiatric institutionalization at the Kalamazoo State Hospital. If she was "driven toward madness" in the 1930s due in no small part by white social workers and court officials who read her racial pride and defiance, combined with her status as an Afro-Caribbean, working-class, widowed, single mother who had a child out of wedlock, as a sign of her alleged insanity and justification for her institutionalization, then her years at Kalamazoo State Hospital exacerbated her mental illness and highlighted her incapacitation as a form of state-sanctioned carcerality.

Louise's institutionalization beginning in January 1939 placed her in a physical and medical space where race, gender, class, psychiatry, science, punishment, politics, and power were inextricably connected. In his study of race and mental illness in nineteenth-century Washington, DC, historian Martin Summers argues that prevailing understandings of race were critical to shaping how mental health hospitals and workers understood mental illness and practiced therapeutic care.[95] Similarly, the work of historian Lynette Jackson on the Ingutsheni Mental Hospital in colonial Zimbabwe sheds important light on these connections among mental health hospitals, colonialism, and prisons. She writes that the asylum "differed from its cousin, the prison, only insofar as its inmates were the 'unintentional dangerous' and thus could not be held responsible for their transgressions" unlike apparently sane criminals. Mental hospitals in colonial Zimbabwe (and across the entire Western world, for that matter) served a similar social and political function as prisons: both institutions helped to (re)produce the dominant social order through incapacitating individuals deemed by white state actors as dangerous, criminal, deviant, and subversive.[96] These conclusions are useful for understanding Louise's quarter-century plight at the Kalamazoo Mental Hospital.

State actors held Louise in the first and largest mental health institution in Michigan. The hospital opened in 1859 as the Michigan Asylum for the Insane through the efforts of the state's governor, medical professionals, and social reformers. They envisioned the institution as an innovative hospital for leading the way nationally in treating mental illness, as the burgeoning medical field of psychiatry emerged in the mid-nineteenth-century in the United States and Europe.[97] The hospital's ornate buildings and wooded landscape made for an impressive sight. Located on 160 acres at the top of a hill, the hospital, with its 172-foot castle-like, brick water tower, became a landmark in the western Michigan city (see figure 4.1). The Kalamazoo State Hospital, as it was known during Little's residency, counted a patient load of 3,500 patients and 900 staff at the institution's peak in the mid-1950s. Most of the patients were white. Despite Kalamazoo State Hospital's noble intentions and impressive architecture, the

FIGURE 4.1. Kalamazoo Psychiatric Hospital, Kalamazoo, Michigan. Photo by the author.

institution from its very beginning earned an ignominious reputation for its inhumane treatment of patients.[98]

Little's time at the hospital was a living hell. Her institutionalization contributed to her emotional and physical decline. Over the years, hospital officials confined, isolated, spoon-fed, manhandled, and performed unnecessary dental work on her. They restricted her access to the outdoors and her family visits. Hospital workers mismedicated her, and they ignored real physical ailments from which she suffered.[99] Given her diagnosis of insanity, it seems likely that she received electroconvulsive therapy (ECT). The practice involved triggering seizures by stimulating the brain with small electric currents while the body was under general anesthesia. Health workers widely practiced this treatment of the mentally ill in the United States and globally beginning in the 1940s. Later, some psychiatrists condemned ECT as inhumane and torturous.[100] What we know is that years of confinement and medical mistreatment often left her in a catatonic state and separated her from her children and family.[101]

Little's thoughts about her institutionalization, like her battle in probate court in the late 1930s, have been mediated through hospital records and stories told by others. Still, existing evidence shows that Kalamazoo hospital workers continued to point to her family background and child (Robert) born out of wedlock as proof of her alleged insanity. She unequivocally rejected hospital officials' claim that she was insane.[102] She understood her institutionalization as a form of state-sanctioned punishment and incarceration for her attempt as a Black woman to live free. She made these points to hospital doctors and to family members when they visited her. Louise's second daughter, Yvonne Woodward, remembered that "she would beg us to get her outta there because, she said, 'They're going to take my land.'" For Louise, "they" referred to the white power structure. Her nightmare eventually came true. Judge McClellan, the same judge who ordered her children into placement into foster care and Little to the Kalamazoo mental hospital, seized her property. Given the importance of land to Little's sense of family, pride, and independence, losing her property was devastating.[103] Her family understood the magnitude of the injustice committed against her. In the *Autobiography*, Malcolm denounced the treatment of his mother by the courts and mental hospital as "nothing but legal, modern slavery—however kindly intentioned."[104]

Despite experiencing significant trauma and hardship, neither Louise nor her immediate and extended family relinquished hope of liberating her from the Kalamazoo State Hospital. During the war and onward, her children, including Malcolm, visited her at the hospital. Wilfred tirelessly lobbied state officials for his mother's release. From Montreal, Louise's Grenada-born uncle Edgerton Langdon wrote to hospital officials inquiring into the status of his beloved niece.[105] Her first cousin, Malcolm Orgias, who had migrated from Grenada to New York, visited her.[106] Family efforts to free her constituted a diasporic affair, revealing the way concern and support for Little's plight circulated across national boundaries among relatives in the United States, Canada, and Grenada. Their resolve, informed by family love and the desire to be free, speaks to their determination in rescuing Louise from state-sponsored incapacitation and suffering. Her experiences at the Kalamazoo State Hospital beginning in the 1940s were exceptionally cruel. However, her difficult journey was hardly unique. Elijah Muhammad, James Stewart, Mittie Maude Lena Gordon, and scores of other midwestern disciples of Garvey suffered mightily at the hands of state actors for their apparent racial defiance during the war. But all of them, through their resilience and support from their respective organizations and networks, weathered state repression and remained committed to living in a world where Black people could live independently and free from racial oppression.

"Detroit Red"

If the 1940s constituted a traumatic period in Louise Little's life, then these years also marked a significant turning point in the life of her son Malcolm. With his mother institutionalized and siblings separated, fifteen-year-old

Malcolm by early 1940 moved to Boston to live with his twenty-six-year-old half-sister, Ella Collins, in Roxbury, Boston's African American neighborhood. There, he gained his first real education into class divisions among African Americans and Black middle-class contempt for the Black working poor. Boston also provided his introduction to the wartime Black, urban, working-class hipster scene and the flamboyant, colorful zoot suit.[107] To earn a living, he worked for the Chicago-headquartered Pullman Car Company as a railyard worker, and as a porter and kitchen-staff person on passenger trains. Portering took him up and down the northeast corridor and provided him with keen insight into the exploitative, alienating, and racist nature of wage labor. He was especially appalled with the "Uncle Tomming"—a pejorative epithet for the behavior of an obsequious Black person—by African American porters "to get bigger tips" from racist white passengers.[108] He hated working low-paying, racially demeaning railroad jobs. His attitude resulted in him either quitting or getting fired.[109] By 1942, he moved to Harlem. There, he immersed himself in the hipster scene and bought his first zoot suit.[110]

The Autobiography of Malcolm X and prevailing accounts of his life during the 1940s often dismiss this period as an apolitical moment in his life. Looking back at these years through the ascetic prism of the Nation of Islam in the early 1960s, he framed his hipster days of wearing zoot suits, street hustling, drug use, involvement in prostitution and burglary, and hostility toward wage labor as vivid examples of his nihilism, apathy, and self-destructive behavior. These lifeways, he contended, led him to prison and to his political awakening and spiritual transformation through his conversion to Islam and mentoring under Elijah Muhammad. Robin Kelley challenges this interpretation of young Malcolm X's life through examining the zoot suit. Kelley frames the zoot suit as a symbol of Black urban, working-class male opposition against oppressors and as an escape from racism and dead-end, menial wage labor.[111] This was true for young Malcolm.[112]

Living in wartime Boston and Harlem certainly was critical to informing Malcolm's understanding of the plight of Black urban, working-class people in relation to wage labor, structural racism, white supremacy, and Black bourgeois cultural elitism. However, his midwestern Garveyite background also played a role in informing his identity and burgeoning oppositional politics during the 1940s. His nickname "Detroit Red" stands as the most visible marker of his linkages to the heartland. His Harlemite associates knew that he was from Michigan. But they "had never heard of Lansing," Malcolm recalled in his autobiography. So, they gave him the nickname "Detroit Red" because of his reddish hair color and skin complexion and his connections to the Great Lakes State.[113] He never lost touch with his Michigan roots. Throughout the war, he returned to Lansing and Detroit where he visited his relatives, worked in factories and bars, and engaged in petty crime. While his memoir provides little detail, it is certain that Malcolm visited Louise in the Kalamazoo State Hospital, indicating that he forgot neither his mother nor his ties to Michigan.[114] He was also proudly aware of his Garveyite roots, a fact also missing from the *Autobiography*. His Harlem associates recalled him sharing that his father had been a devoted follower of Marcus Garvey and that Garveyite principles could benefit Black people.[115]

Malcolm's midwestern Garveyite roots surely had an important role in informing his most political act as a hipster in Harlem: his decision in 1943 to dodge the draft and to feign support for Japan. In his autobiographical account of his wartime years, Malcolm recounted his fear of fighting and dying in what he perceived as a white man's war.[116] Subsequently, he concocted an outrageous scheme to evade the army through attaining 4F classification, a status designating a prospective recruit psychologically unfit to serve.[117] He began talking loudly around Harlem about his desire to join the Japanese Army. He hoped undercover white army intelligence officers would learn about his apparent pro-Tokyo sentiment and report him as unfit for duty. His boldest move came during his interview with a white psychiatrist at an army draft office in Harlem. Acting unhinged, Malcolm blurted: "Daddy-o . . . so don't you tell nobody . . . I want to get sent down South. Organize them nigger soldiers, you dig? Steal us some guns, and kill up crackers!"[118] His subterfuge worked. Shocked, the white psychiatrist immediately dismissed Malcolm from the interview. He received a 4F card by mail. Malcolm was one of perhaps thousands of zoot suiters in Harlem and across the country who dodged the draft because they had no desire to die in a white man's war.[119]

Although the *Autobiography* explains why Malcolm opposed joining the US army, his memoir does not provide a clear explanation of the origins of his apparent pro-Tokyo sympathies. Living in wartime Harlem, combined with his midwestern Garveyite background, surely informed his position. As a Harlem resident, he would have frequently heard Black nationalist street-corner orators such as Carlos Cooks, a well-known figure in the local Garvey movement, proclaim Japan as the defender of the darker races.[120] Given that Malcolm was raised by two globally informed Garveyite parents, pro-Japan Black nationalist messages would have struck a familiar chord. Additionally, the *Autobiography* neither explicitly connects the young Malcolm's opposition to the war with Muhammad's incarceration for draft dodging nor contextualizes their pro-Japanese sentiment in relation to wider Black nationalist sentiment in wartime Black America. Given that the *Autobiography* frames Malcolm's pre-prison years as apolitical, it is unsurprising that his memoir neither grounds Detroit Red's draft evasion in his Garveyite sensibility nor attributes his opposition to the war to growing Black militancy sweeping the United States.[121]

The *Autobiography* also fails to draw explicit connections between his mother's institutionalization and his arrest in Boston and imprisonment for burglary in 1946 as different forms of carceral punishment. Like his mother's ordeal, race, class, gender, sex, punishment, and power were at the heart of the events that led to his legal troubles and incarceration. In 1945, Malcolm, along with his white, blonde Armenian girlfriend, Bea Caragulian; her younger sister; another young Armenian woman; and his homeboys Malcolm "Shorty" Jarvis and Francis E. "Sonny" Brown, launched an ambitious burglary scheme to rob the homes of wealthy white Boston suburbanites. Police arrested the motley group for burglary in early January 1946. During the trial, the white district attorney attempted to convince the white women to testify against Malcolm and to accuse their Black male accomplices of rape. The district attorney hoped this testimony would possibly secure a life sentence for the Black men. The women did not accuse their Black male accomplices of rape. However, the women agreed to a plea deal. They received a short sentence for testifying that Malcolm coerced them into participating in the crime spree. Malcolm and Jarvis were not so lucky. They received an eight- to ten-year sentence in the Massachusetts state prison. Malcolm later learned that an average sentence for a first offender for burglary in Massachusetts was one to two years.[122]

Malcolm was aware of the connections among the criminal justice system, race, gender, class, sex, and power. Looking back, he remembered white court officials openly expressing their racist contempt for Malcolm and Jarvis for burglarizing and consorting with affluent white women. For these reasons, Malcolm believed the judge imposed an excessively long prison sentence on the two young Black male defendants for transgressing the status quo. Malcolm entered Charlestown Prison on February 27, 1946. He was not yet twenty-one. He would spend the next six and a half years in Massachusetts state prisons.[123] While his wartime life experiences contrasted from those of his mother, Malcolm, like Louise, suffered a terrible fate. They were both racially defiant, Black working-class people with deep connections to midwestern Garveyism whom white state actors feared and punished.

Midwestern Black Nationalism during the Early Global Cold War

As battlefields around the world fell silent following the defeat of the Axis by August 1945 and as the Cold War between the United States and Soviet Union began taking shape, Garveyites globally kept fighting for Black self-determination and African redemption. Heartland Black nationalists in the UNIA and midwestern Garveyite front were prominent in these efforts. Despite changing global times, their politics remained locked in the classical Black nationalist paradigm that had guided Garveyites since the UNIA's heyday and through the Second World War. For this reason, Black diasporic right radicalism remained, to varying degrees, central to the midwestern Garveyite program. This politics revealed the widening gap among Black nationalists and their counterparts in the NAACP, Council on African Affairs, and Fifth Pan-African Congress in imagining the prospects for global Black freedom in the postwar world.

Midwestern Black nationalists lived in a world devastated by the Second World War, the most deadly conflict in human history. This global conflict left upward of seventy-five million dead. The Holocaust resulted in the deaths of up to twelve million, exposing the moral bankruptcy of Western civilization and widely discrediting racialism. The US atomic bombings of the Japanese cities of Hiroshima and Nagasaki marked the beginning of the nuclear age and the possibility of a nuclear apocalypse.[124] If the war signaled the end of the Axis Powers, the Second World War also represented a key turning point in the drive toward decolonization in Asia and Africa and the emergence of what came to be known as the Third World. The United Nations, inaugurated in October 1945, constituted another significant event in the immediate postwar period and "the first time in history that the principle of human rights had been incorporated in an international legal document," observes historian Brenda Gayle Plummer.[125]

In the United States, the democratic and antiracist ideals of the Second World War, wartime social changes, formation of the UN, nascent global decolonization, and the aspirations of African Americans spawned the modern US Black Freedom Movement. As Black Americans struggled to secure their rights, the United States witnessed a spike in lynching and racial terror in the immediate postwar years. In June 1946, the Truman administration disbanded the Fair Employment Practices Committee in response to pressure from southern segregationists in Congress, who had feared the agency would initiate the dismantlement of Jim Crow.[126] The racism of Theodore Bilbo became even more extreme at the war's end. In his 1946 reelection bid for a third term in the US Senate, he unapologetically called for the lynching of Blacks, used explicitly racist language, and charged that desegregation was a Soviet-led conspiracy to promote interracial sex between Black men and white women. He won reelection in a landslide. But he died soon afterward. Still, even in death, Bilbo's racist politics lived on. In the coming years, segregationists echoed his charge that the Civil Rights Movement was a communist plot. These beliefs helped to fuel massive white resistance across the South against desegregation in the 1950s and 1960s.[127]

The nascent Cold War, combined with a white racial backlash, profoundly impacted the trajectory of the postwar US Black Freedom Movement and US life. Anticommunist repression, which came to be known in the early 1950s as "McCarthyism," targeted the Communist Party, trade unions, civil rights groups, women's organizations, and Black nationalists. US government persecution of Black leftists—W. E. B. Du Bois, Paul Robeson, Shirley Graham Du Bois, Eslanda Robeson, William L. Patterson, Claudia Jones, and Ferdinand Smith—for their antiracist, anticapitalist, anti-imperialist politics was especially fierce.[128] The US Red Scare was inextricably connected to the Cold War—the Manichean contest between the United States and the Soviet Union from 1945 and 1990 for global supremacy.[129] Fearful of Soviet criticism of American racism before the global stage, US Cold Warriors realized that Jim Crow constituted the "Achilles heel" for Washington's propaganda campaign to win the "hearts and minds" of people of color in newly emerging nations in Asia and Africa. The US ruling class acquiesced to civil rights reforms out of fear that segregation would invalidate the US claim of being the leader of the "democratic free world." In return, the NAACP and other Black liberals struck a Faustian bargain with US rulers whereby the former accepted US Cold War domestic and foreign policy and distanced themselves from Black leftists associated with the Council on African Affairs and US Communist Party.[130]

The end of the Second World War marked a key turning point in the global struggle for African liberation. These years signified a rapidly growing political rift between Black nationalists and leftists over the best path toward Black self-determination. The United Nations' inaugural conference, held in San Francisco from April 25 to June 26, 1945, was a key geographic site where competing visions of Black internationalism and pan-Africanism played out among Black nationalists, liberals, and leftists. Delegates from fifty Allied nations, representing 80 percent of the world's population, assembled at the gathering to build a better and more peaceful world.[131] During the conference, the Council on African Affairs and NAACP called for immediate self-governance and independence for Africa. However, Garveyites, wedded to the classical Black nationalist paradigm, did not demand immediate African colonial liberation. Instead, the UNIA issued a petition to the UN calling for a self-governing African territory under Black settler rule as a step toward full independence.[132]

The UNIA was serious about promoting Black settler colonialism at the UN inaugural conference. James Stewart assigned one of the UNIA's most venerable officials, William Sherrill of Detroit, to represent the organization at the gathering.[133] Upon arrival at the conference, he was not recognized as an official member of the US delegation. The State Department appointed no African Americans as official US representatives to the conference. However, Washington designated three NAACP officials—Walter White, W. E. B. Du Bois, and Mary McLeod Bethune—as consultant-observers. They worked closely with conference delegations from India and other emerging Third World nations in pushing the UN to center the status of colonized people and racial minorities in its agenda.[134] We know little about Sherrill's interactions with delegates of color at the San Francisco conference and his influence on the wider gathering. What is for sure is that he lobbied there for the UNIA's Black diasporic right radical vision for the future world.[135]

The San Francisco conference's official position announced at the end of the gathering infuriated Sherrill and the UNIA, as well as Black liberals and leftists alike. The UN refused to center global decolonization and racial equality in the new organization's mission.[136] Instead, the conference green-lighted European colonial powers to regain control of their rebellious overseas territories. The perceived failure of the San Francisco conference convinced the UNIA of the futility of working with the UN for African redemption. Believing the plight of Blacks in the postwar United States was hopeless, the UNIA doubled down in calling for voluntary repatriation to Liberia, and James Stewart continued to prepare to quit America for Africa (see figure 4.2).[137]

The UNIA's exuberance for Liberian colonization contrasted with growing sentiment among some Black thinkers about the West African's place in the global struggle for Black freedom. As historian Ibrahim Sundiata observes, a growing number of Black voices by the end of the Second World War perceived Liberia as standing on the wrong side of a looming, global anticolonial struggle.[138] Eslanda Robeson of the Council of African Affairs also subscribed to this position. After visiting Liberia in 1946 during her five-month journey across the continent, she came to regard the West African republic's Black settler elite as too cozy with the United States and ruthless in their treatment of Indigenes.[139]

The Fifth Pan-African Congress, held in Manchester, England, in October 1945, also signified the growing ideological divide between the Black

FIGURE 4.2. James R. and Goldie Stewart and family on the eve of their emigration to Liberia, Cleveland, Ohio, February 1949. Credit: Roberta Stewart Amos.

diasporic right radicalism of the postwar African world proffered by the UNIA and the Black left internationalism advanced at the conference. Approximately one hundred African-descended people from the continent, Anglophone Caribbean, and United States attended the Fifth Pan-African Congress, including future leaders of independent African states—Kwame Nkrumah of Ghana and Jomo Kenyatta of Kenya. Chaired by W. E. B. Du Bois and the Trinidad-born, former Communist Party leader George Padmore and organized in part as a response to the disappointment of the San Francisco conference, the Fifth Pan-African Congress dispensed with the reformism and civilizationism of earlier congresses and advanced the most radical Black internationalist positions in the history of Pan-African assemblies.[140] The Manchester conference declared: "We demand for Black Africa autonomy and independence." Vowing to use armed force if necessary to free Africa from European empires, conference delegates endorsed socialism, looked to workers and trade unions as key agents of transformative change, rejected white supremacy, and envisioned sovereign nations living peacefully under the UN charter.[141] The congress shifted the political trajectory of pan-Africanism. From Manchester forward and in a break from Garvey, Africa, not the Diaspora, constituted the geographical and political fulcrum in the struggle for global Black liberation. For African Americans and other New World Blacks, this meant taking a back seat to the aspirations of continental Africans.[142] There is no record of high-ranking UNIA officials in attendance at the Fifth Pan-African Congress. However, Amy Jacques Garvey and Amy Ashwood Garvey played crucial roles in organizing and leading the gathering, illustrating how some veteran Garveyites found common ground with Black leftists and a new generation of African militants. Still, neither Jacques Garvey nor Ashwood Garvey ever abandoned Black settler colonialism.[143]

The forceful move by some heartland Black nationalists to seize anticommunism and to collaborate with white supremacists best speaks to the paradoxes of the former's global politics and to the widening ideological differences between heartland Garveyites and their liberal and leftist counterparts in the early Cold War. This was the case with Mittie Maude Lena Gordon. Following in the footsteps of Marcus Garvey and moving in the opposite direction from Black liberals and leftists, she embraced the white supremacists Theodore Bilbo and Earnest Sevier Cox and anticommunism like never before after her release from federal prison and returning to Chicago in August 1945. She came home to a Chicago undergoing rapid transformations along the color line. The city's African American population increased from 277,731 in 1940 to 337,000 in 1944. Like those who came before them, the lure of good-paying jobs in the city's heavy industries and a new life brought them to Chicago.[144] But the Windy City remained an oppressive place for Black people. No major US city in the immediate postwar period experienced more racial violence than Chicago. Postwar housing shortages, job competition, and African American attempts to assert their right to the city by moving out of decrepit ghettoes and into all-white neighborhoods fueled the anxieties of white Chicagoans. Through homeowner associations, restrictive covenants, and rampant white anti-Black violence, often supported by the Catholic Church, realtors, police, and some elected officials, white Chicagoans sought to maintain the city's racial status quo.[145]

Black Chicagoans fought back on multiple fronts against the postwar white backlash. In 1942, Blacks on the South Side elected William L. Dawson to the US House of Representatives, making him for a moment the only African American in Congress.[146] The city's flourishing African American businesses and cultural and communal institutions signified Black Chicagoans' determination to live a life of dignity and autonomy. Perhaps no Black Chicago institution better embodied African American agency than the Johnson Publishing Company, founded in 1942 by Georgia migrant John H. Johnson. By the late 1940s, the Johnson Publishing Company, with its flagship publication *Ebony* magazine, was the world's largest Black-owned media company.[147] Thriving civic institutions and the dynamic culture scene in Black Chicago in the 1940s and early postwar years further cemented the city's prominence in the African world.[148]

Gordon's story reveals that Chicago Black nationalists remained active in the city, found grassroots support, and offered an alternative program to those of Black liberals and leftists. She was well aware of racial tension in Chicago and across the country in the immediate postwar years. She shared her thoughts about these trends with Cox. In a 1947 letter to him, she emphasized that "race tension [was] very high" in Chicago and that whites were "slugging every Colored person" who dared to venture into racially contested neighborhoods.[149] But she was still optimistic about the future. At a PME meeting in 1946 in the South Side, the group recruited five hundred new members. For her, these new recruits symbolized renewed grassroots support for Liberian colonization.[150]

Nothing infuriated Gordon more than the joyful responses of Black liberals and leftists to Bilbo's untimely death. In a mournful letter to Cox penned soon after Bilbo's death, she wrote, "We were bewildered because of the death of our Senator Bilbo."[151] She praised his recently published book *Take Your Choice: Separation or Mongrelization*. A racist diatribe, the book identified Black-white racial intermixture as "America's greatest domestic problem" and as a Soviet plot. Consequently, African American resettlement to Africa constituted a divine plan for ensuring Black and white racial purity and for safeguarding the United States from communism. Cox wrote the book's introduction.[152] In a letter from Gordon to Cox, she praised the book for its "wonderful message for this country." She hoped that all Americans—Black and white—would read it. In addition to lauding his book, she denounced the NAACP, *Chicago Defender*, and South Side churches for opposing colonization and for "rejoicing and celebrating the death" of Bilbo.[153] These celebrations, she believed, were part of a subversive nationwide "Communist element" who supported miscegenation.[154] Illustrating her long-held contempt for the Black elite, she charged that Bilbo's Black opponents were racial sellouts in bed with the Soviets and their US communist allies.

Garvey and other Black nationalists had leveled similar charges for decades. But the postwar years were different times than the 1920s and 1930s. The late 1940s witnessed the beginning of a Red Scare more repressive than the country had ever seen. Cold War repression in the United States crushed and suppressed organizations and individuals who advanced expansive global visions for social justice and racial equality. Segregationists were some of the staunchest anticommunists. They believed that the specter of interracial sex served as an effective weapon for maintaining the US racial status quo and in promoting domestic and foreign Cold War agendas.[155] In Gordon's case, her extreme anticommunism mirrored the virulent anti-Soviet rhetoric espoused by white supremacists. To her contemporary Black critics, she was a fanatical apologist for hard-core racists like Bilbo and a willing accomplice in her own people's oppression.[156] These conclusions were not unfounded. Although she envisioned herself as a Black liberator, her framing of colonization as a bulwark against communism and interracial sex, as well as her denouncement of Black leftists and liberals, echoed the positions of rabid segregationists hell-bent on holding back the postwar Black Freedom Movement and global decolonization.

It is indisputable that 1940s midwestern Black nationalists mounted serious and sincere efforts to upend global white supremacy. Through their activism, journalism, travel, institution-building, and lifeways, heartland Black nationalists generated grassroots resistance to US involvement in the Second World War, championed Japan as an ally of people of color around the world, built institutions such as Liberty Farm, lobbied for decolonization at the United Nations, advocated for emigration, and, above all, sought to build autonomous, racially proud Black communities. The distinct racial realities of the heartland helped to inform midwestern Garveyites' distinct response to local and global events. Their visibility and oppositional politics and lifeways made them easy targets for state persecution, as evident in the jailing of Mittie Maude Lena Gordon, Elijah Muhammad, and Malcolm Little, and in the institutionalization of Louise Little. Even more, the activism and lifeways of midwestern Black nationalists revealed ideological, political, and class cleavages within 1940s Black America and the African world. In contrast to Black liberals and leftists, midwestern Garveyites clung to older visions of freedom informed by Black diasporic right radicalism as the Cold War took shape. For this reason, the PME, most notably, adopted a fanatical anticommunism and collaborated with white supremacists as racialism became anathema in the postwar world. As the US Black Freedom Movement and global decolonization gained momentum in the 1950s, midwestern Black nationalists, despite rivalries, ideological paradoxes, and organizational limitations, remained determined to keep alive Garvey's legacy and fight for global Black freedom.

5

"NEW AFRICA FACES THE WORLD"

Midwestern Garveyism during the 1950s

It has been since the Bandung Conference that all dark people on earth have been striding toward freedom, but there are 20 million people here in America yet suffering the worst form of enslavement . . . mental bondage, mentally blinded by the white man, unable now to see that America is the citadel of white colonialism, the bulwark of white imperialism . . . the slave master of slave masters. —MALCOLM X, quoted in "Malcolm X Calls for Bandung Conference of Negro Leaders," *Los Angeles Herald Dispatch*, April 23, 1959

James Stewart was ecstatic. The second president-general of the Universal Negro Improvement Association eagerly followed news about the independence of Ghana, formerly known as the Gold Coast, on March 6, 1957, from his home on Liberty Farm, a UNIA commercial farm in Gbandela, a hamlet in rural central Liberia one hundred miles northeast of Monrovia. Since March 1949, he had resided in Liberia, along with his wife, Goldie, and several of their children; Margaret Davis, the UNIA secretary from Lebanon, Ohio; and a small number of UNIA members from Cleveland. They emigrated from Ohio to Liberia with the intention of fulfilling Marcus Garvey's dream of redeeming Africa from the continent.[1] Through living in Liberia, James Stewart succeeded where Marcus Garvey and countless New World Black nationalists had failed. Stewart set foot on the continent, made Liberia his home, and established the West African republic as the transnational UNIA's headquarters.[2]

Although Stewart neither attended Ghanaian independence ceremonies nor ever met the country's founder, Kwame Nkrumah, the UNIA president-general appreciated this new West African nation's broader significance to the Black world. He read Ghana's independence through Garveyite lenses. In *Stewart's Voice*, the UNIA's new official newspaper, he declared, "This [Ghana] is Garveyism. This is African Nationalism." He celebrated Ghana as "another step forward in the direction of African Redemption."[3] Stewart's move to West Africa signaled the way Black midwesterners since the nineteenth century stood at the forefront in promoting Liberian colonization and in championing worldwide Black freedom.

Stewart carried out his work in Liberia during an extraordinary moment in US and global history. In the United States, the postwar Black Freedom Movement gained momentum in 1954 after the Supreme Court ruled in the *Brown v. Board of Education of Topeka* case that separate but equal schools were unconstitutional, thereby overturning the infamous *Plessy v. Ferguson* decision of 1896. The twelve-month Montgomery Bus Boycott, launched in December 1955, marked the first major mass campaign of the Civil Rights Movement and signaled the emergence of Martin Luther King as an internationally known spokesperson for US racial equality.[4] In Africa, Libya won its independence from France in 1951, while Morocco and Tunisia gained their independence from France in 1956. A brutal eight-year war of national liberation began in Algeria against French rule in 1954, while two years later an armed revolt erupted in the British colony of Kenya that came to be known as the Mau Mau.[5] By the late 1950s, Ghana emerged as the torchbearer of pan-Africanism.[6]

The Afro-Asian Conference—or the Bandung Conference as it came to be known—held in Bandung, Indonesia, April 18–24, 1955, marked a sea change in the history of global decolonization and the postwar world. Twenty-nine newly and soon to be free nations from Africa and Asia assembled, with Indonesia, the People's Republic of China, India, Ceylon (Sri Lanka), Pakistan, and Burma spearheading the gathering.[7] Indonesia's first president, Sukarno, presided over the conference. As historian and commentator Vijay Prashad notes, the impetus for the gathering derived from a political position opposing colonialism and imperialism, not a belief in shared essential racial and cultural commonalities.[8] The conference called for global decolonization, Afro-Asian solidarities, and a new world order based on human rights, peace, and international cooperation. These principles served as the basis of what became known as the Third World and the "Bandung World," transnational political projects in which formerly colonized people in Africa, Asia, the Caribbean, and Latin

America dreamed of building a new world. The conference took place as the global Cold War intensified, with both the United States and Soviet Union vying for allies in the emerging Third World. This geopolitical reality positioned the Third World into a political bloc apart from the First World (the United States and its Western allies) and the Second World (the Soviet Union and the Eastern bloc), setting the stage for the Non-Aligned Movement.[9] The historical significance of the Bandung Conference was immediately apparent to the African American author, exile, ex-communist, and longtime Chicago resident Richard Wright who attended the gathering. In *The Color Curtain* (1956), his account of the conference, he wrote, "The despised, the insulted, the hurt, the dispossessed—in short, the underdogs of the human race were meeting" at Bandung.[10]

This chapter examines Black nationalism, internationalism, and racialism; the US heartland; Global Africa; and the nascent Bandung World of the 1950s through tracing the lives, sojourns, and activism of Black women and men in the Diasporic Midwest who remained deeply and consciously indebted to Garvey and Garveyism. Until recently, most scholarship on this period has looked at Black leftist and civil rights spokespersons such as W. E. B. Du Bois, Paul Robeson, Claudia Jones, Eslanda Robeson, Ella Baker, Walter White, and Thurgood Marshall, and at Black left and liberal formations such as the NAACP, Civil Rights Congress, Council on African Affairs, and the Sojourners for Truth and Justice.[11] Looking at the 1950s through the lens of midwestern Black nationalists tells a different story. Garveyism remained alive and well decades after Garvey arrived on the global scene. However, these years marked a turning point in the history of Garveyism. By the 1950s, the midwestern Garveyite front, not the UNIA, was clearly in the driver's seat in keeping Garvey's legacy alive and in moving Garveyism in new directions. A new generation of African Americans and some veteran Black nationalists outside of the UNIA forged a more modern Black (inter)nationalism linked to growing militancy across Black America, Africa, and the Bandung World. This was most evident in interest among Black people in the heartland in Ghana and Kwame Nkrumah, the ascendence of the Chicago-based Nation of Islam as the most dynamic US Black nationalist formation, and the rising profile of the Midwest-born and -reared Malcolm X. Calling attention to this history highlights the ideological variance and gender contours within Black nationalism and the US Black Freedom Movement, as well as the continued importance of the Diasporic Midwest as an engine for and crossroads of Black transnational politics as an old world gave birth to the Bandung World.

Grassroots Garveyism in the Midwest

The UNIA survived in 1950s Black communities in the Midwest and beyond due to Black women. Drawing from community feminism and the long tradition of Black nationalist women's grassroots organizing, heartland UNIA female officials such as Elinor White Neely of Robbins, Illinois, and Lillie Mae Gibson of Cleveland, Ohio, were critical to sustaining the UNIA long past Garvey's passing. From Robbins, White Neely served as vice president of Chicago UNIA Division 401.[12] Her role as an unofficial archivist of the UNIA constituted her most important contribution to postwar Garveyism. During the 1950s and 1960s, she self-published several pamphlets and books about Marcus Garvey and religious matters.[13] In addition to her UNIA work, White Neely was actively involved in Robbins civic life. Postwar suburban affluence bypassed the all-Black, working-class Chicago-area village that counted 4,776 residents in 1950. Robbins remained wedded to the Black nationalist principles of race pride, autonomy, and Christian brotherhood—ideals that had guided the village and other all-Black midwestern towns since the nineteenth century.[14] Respected in the community, she was elected village clerk in 1949, the first woman to hold this position. In a nod to her community feminism, she ran in 1953 for mayor for Robbins on the local Women's Party ticket. This local all-women's political party, headed by White Neely, ran a slate of candidates for village offices. It is unknown whether any of these women besides her were members of the UNIA. What we know is that the Women's Party called for honest government, criticized male politicians for their sexism, and urged women to come out to vote. Neely and her colleagues received national attention in the Black press, despite losing their bids for local office.[15] Still, her political campaign reveals the multiple sites—both inside and outside of the organizational structures of the UNIA—Garveyism survived in the Diasporic Midwest through the 1950s. The record has yet to reveal whether she was interested in ascendant US Black nationalist movements like the Nation of Islam and new liberation movements sweeping across the Bandung World. Her work and global politics remained rooted in older Black nationalist paradigms.

The activism of Lillie Mae Gibson also speaks to the visibility and community feminism of midwestern women in the 1950s transnational UNIA. She was one of the most visible leaders in the UNIA affiliated with James Stewart. Born in 1901 in Oakville, Alabama, and the sister of the famed Olympic sprinter Jessie Owens, she migrated to Cleveland. There, she became a leader in women's clubs and the church. A wife and mother of four, her middle-class social background provided her time and resources to engage in social activism and not to work outside her home. In June 1949, she joined the UNIA for unknown reasons, illustrating that the Garvey movement still attracted prominent social reformers and new members long after Garvey expired. In 1954, the UNIA board elected her as International Organizer and head of the American Field, a position once held by William Sherrill during the 1920s.[16] As the UNIA International Organizer, she corresponded from Cleveland with UNIA divisions around the world and traveled to Africa and the Caribbean. She attended UNIA international conferences in Liberia. After returning to Cleveland from the 1954 gathering, she wrote a message about the conference, which was published on the front page of *Stewart's Voice*. Praising James Stewart for his leadership, she wrote, the "Negro has begun to realize that if he is to have a place in the world, he must join hands with his African brother crying: 'Africa for the Africans, those at home and those abroad.'"[17] Like Stewart and White Neely, Gibson was committed to the classical Black nationalist idea of Liberia as the refuge for New World Blacks, and she echoed masculinist framings of Liberian colonization long upheld by Black spokespersons.

Although she sometimes articulated Black freedom in manly terms, Gibson was aware of the gendered hierarchy within the UNIA. Following a long line of Midwest-based UNIA women, Gibson refused to be silenced by UNIA men. At the 1958 international UNIA conference in Liberia, she excoriated Garveyite men for their sexism. She proclaimed: "The only complaint they have against me is that I am a woman. I cannot help that. I have served my Divisions; I have served my itinerary and each place I went, I went with peace."[18] She even challenged Stewart. In one correspondence to him, she stood her ground after he criticized her leadership. She wrote tersely: "I am well aware of my duties as head of the field."[19] Her confidence caught the attention of some UNIA men. A UNIA male leader from the Caribbean island of Aruba praised her: "I recognize in her a woman who is not afraid to stand up for the rights of her people and fight for their progress without preaching hate and revenge."[20] Her confrontation with UNIA men resembled those of Ethel Collins and Amy Jacques Garvey with James Stewart in the 1940s. But unlike those women, Gibson remained loyal to Stewart. The 1950s UNIA owed a tremendous debt to White Neely and Gibson. Their work further cemented the Midwest's visibility in global Garveyism and demonstrated once again that women in the US heartland, even decades after the UNIA's heyday, remained some of Garvey's most faithful disciples.

The UNIA, Liberia, and the Stewarts

If Liberia constituted a key site for Garvey's dream of African redemption during his lifetime and for Black nationalists during the interwar years, then the West African nation still captured the imaginations of post–Second World War Garveyites. The work of midwestern Garveyites, most notably of James and Goldie Stewart, was critical to advancing the transnational UNIA from Liberia during the 1950s. For Stewart, his fifteen years in Liberia marked the most important chapter of his life's work in pursuit of African redemption. In 1954, five years after arriving in West Africa, he declared, "I came here [Liberia] to lay a foundation for the building of the UNIA and I am not going to fail."[21] Goldie Stewart recounted decades later: "We went [to Liberia] in the interest of [the] UNIA."[22] There is no evidence of the Stewarts referencing the African journeys of the nineteenth-century classical Black nationalists Edward Wilmot Blyden, Martin Delany, and Henry McNeal Turner. Nonetheless, the Stewarts and their UNIA colleagues in Gbandela were Black diasporic right radicals dead-set on completing Garvey's unfinished pan-African work. The small band of Ohio Garveyites in Liberia highlights the transnational linkages between the Diasporic Midwest and West Africa; the possibilities, gendered contours, paradoxes, and continued resonance of Black settler colonialism; and the uneven results of Garveyism on the continent in challenging the global racial status quo.

The Stewarts and their peers arrived in Liberia at a propitious moment in the nation's history. Under the leadership of President William V. S. Tubman, Liberia underwent a process of modernization. Raised in an Americo-Liberian family and elected to office in 1944, he was the longest-serving Liberian president. He extended voting rights to women and Indigenes, and he sought close ties with the United States. In the early postwar years, he gained a reputation as an influential statesman who championed African decolonization and mentored young African nationalists such as Kwame Nkrumah.[23] The US government and corporations increased investment in the country. Monrovia counted sixty-five thousand inhabitants, making it one of the largest and most modern cities in West Africa.[24]

Stewart believed that his arrival in Liberia positioned him on the front lines of the struggle for African independence. He made this point in *Stewart's Voice*: "Those of us who can remember the hectic days of the early 20s when Garveyism was being forcibly brought to the attention of the world demanding the recognition for the rights of Asia and Africa. Today we see the spontaneous emergence of the continent of Africa and Asia from colonized rule." He cred-

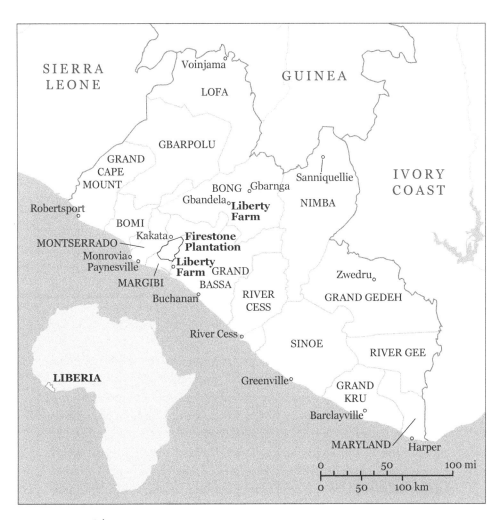

MAP 5.1. Liberia.

ited Garveyism for bringing "into fruition" African decolonization.[25] Immediately upon his arrival in Liberia, he put his plans into revitalizing the UNIA into action. He renounced his US citizenship and became a Liberian citizen.[26] This move anticipated a similar decision by Du Bois, who renounced his American citizenship and became a Ghanaian citizen on the eve of his death in that West African country in 1963.[27] Ever ambitious, Stewart befriended Tubman in May 1949, through a mutual acquaintance. Intrigued with the possibility of technically skilled diasporan Blacks coming to Liberia, Tubman endorsed Stewart's call for African American emigration to the West African republic.[28]

At the organizational level, Stewart moved forward with his plans for reviving the UNIA from Liberia and repatriating New World Blacks to Africa. This was no easy task. No UNIA division existed in Liberia when he arrived. Following Garvey's dream of building commercial farms in Liberia and extending the UNIA's work on Liberty Farm in Oregonia, Ohio, during the 1940s, Stewart, with the assistance of Tubman, bought two hundred acres of land in the village of Gbandela, located in the forested hills of present-day Bong County. There, Stewart established Liberty Farm in November 1949 in the heart of Kpelle country.[29] A Mandé language-speaking people, the Kpelle were the largest ethnolinguistic group in Liberia and an animist and peasant rice-farming people who, beginning in the sixteenth century, had established small chiefdoms across present-day central Liberia. The Liberian Frontier Force by the late 1920s pacified central Liberia, making it the last major Indigenous area to come under control of Monrovia.[30]

It is unknown if James and Goldie Stewart were aware of this recent violent history upon their settlement in Gbandela. What we can say is that James in the entrepreneurial spirit of Garvey envisioned Liberty Farm as an economic engine for Liberia, a model for pan-African economic self-sufficiency, and an agent of modernity. The Stewarts comanaged the farm and lived in a small farmhouse. The couple, together with their UNIA colleagues and local people, built four mudbrick buildings with electricity powered by a generator, planted cash crops such as peanuts and pineapples, and raised chickens. Hundreds of Indigenes worked on the farm.[31] Liberty Farm hosted three UNIA international conferences in Gbandela in 1950, 1954, and 1958.[32] The conferences, presided over by Stewart, counted twelve, eighteen, and sixteen delegates, respectively. Most attendees hailed from US heartland cities: Cleveland, Chicago, Dayton, Columbus, Youngstown, and Detroit. At the Twelfth International Convention of the UNIA in September 1954, the UNIA president-general declared the conference "the greatest Convention, ever held, not in number but in accomplishment."[33] The gatherings paled in size to UNIA conferences in New York, Kingston, and Toronto during the interwar years. However, the Gbandela conventions were the first UNIA conferences ever held on African soil.[34] The conferences and Liberty Farm received media attention in both the US Black mainstream and the nationalist press.[35] Besides operating Liberty Farm, Stewart with the assistance of Liberian and US officials established an elementary school in 1964 in Gbandela that bore his name.[36] In the United States, Cleveland remained a base of support for Stewart's transnational work due in part to Gibson. In 1954, two hundred members of the Cleveland UNIA held a jubilant fundraiser for twelve conference delegates headed for Liberia.[37] In 1958, Gibson's famous brother, Jesse Owens, spoke at a large send-off party in Cleveland for Gbandela conference delegates.[38] The large turnout demonstrates how well-resourced midwestern Garveyites remained a bedrock of the UNIA into the 1950s.[39]

Even as Stewart and his colleagues broke new ground for the UNIA in Liberia, their work remained rooted in the past at the very moment when a growing number of younger Black nationalists no longer looked to Liberia for inspiration for advancing global Black liberation.[40] Stewart supported Ghana and the Mau Mau.[41] However, no records have been found of him showing interest in newer forms of Black nationalism articulated by Malcolm X and the Nation of Islam or in the Bandung Conference and 1959 Cuban Revolution. Stewart was also out of step with a sizable portion of Black America. Echoing long-standing Garveyite framings of civil rights advocates as race traitors, he criticized the NAACP for "marching on Washington, praying, and begging for integration into a race and nation that was neither founded by them nor for them."[42] His position on civil rights echoed those of Malcolm X and veteran Black nationalist Audley "Queen Mother" Moore, who called the 1963 March on Washington for Jobs and Freedom the "Farce on Washington" for its apparent control by white liberals and the Kennedy administration.[43] However, there were important ideological differences between Stewart, Malcolm, and Queen Mother Moore. Even though the pre-Hajj Malcolm and Queen Mother Moore disparaged interracial sex, they looked to militant African states like Ghana and the Bandung World, not Liberia, as leaders of the burgeoning global Black revolution. Unlike Malcolm, Stewart did not lead an army of Black nationalists ready to die for their freedom.

Stewart and his ilk's embrace of Black diasporic right radicalism stands as another example of their seemingly unyielding resolve in holding on to a worldview of Africa linked to nineteenth-century classical Black nationalism. Following in the footsteps of Edward Wilmot Blyden, Henry McNeal Turner, and Marcus Garvey, Stewart understood his work in Liberia as a manly, capitalist, civilizationist, Black settler colonial venture. He made this position clear in a 1955 editorial published in *Stewart's Voice*: "The inhabitants of Liberia are made up of the civilized and uncivilized."[44] In an appeal to African Americans to settle in West Africa, he called on industrious "men" to come to and build Liberia.[45] The arrival of New World Black men, he charged, would fulfill Garvey's vision of a free Africa where "black men with dignity could invite the world's investors . . . to take part in the . . . development of the continent" and be "accepted as equals in the world's ruling class."[46] His articulation of African redemption resembled the prevailing US settler colonial discourse of rugged individualism, a highly gendered discourse forged through expansion by US settlers and gendered racial violence against Indigenous people across the so-called western frontier.[47] Stewart never called for the violent conquest of Indigenous Liberians, and he did not employ coercion in managing local Indigenous farm laborers. But he followed in the footsteps of nineteenth-century Black nationalists and Garvey. Like them, Stewart envisioned African redemption as a struggle between competing Black and white masculinities, and he believed that New World Blacks and Western-educated Africans possessed the right to rule Africa and to usher in modernity and capitalism. To this point, he neither learned Indigenous languages nor wore African garb. In many respects he remained culturally apart from local people and used his privileged position as an African American and connections with Tubman to exert authority over Indigenes.[48] His cultural distance from local people helps explain why he never prioritized the recruitment of Indigenes into the organization and why the small group of US Garveyites in Gbandela constituted the UNIA in Liberia. The Stewarts and their UNIA compatriots in rural Liberia, despite renouncing their US citizenship and foregoing the material comforts of postwar America, were still privileged settlers living among Indigenes.

The civilizationist impulse practiced by Stewart and other Garveyites speaks more broadly to the complicated relationship between Liberia and the African world in the mid-twentieth century. In the 1950s and 1960s, Tubman pursued a moderate foreign policy that sought to promote African independence while maintaining close relations with the United States. Liberia's foreign policy troubled African militants.[49] No evidence exists to show whether Stewart publicly criticized Liberia's domestic and foreign policy. But doing so would have been political suicide for him. Tubman would have turned against Stewart. Living in a West African nation founded on a civilizationist paradigm and befriending Tubman, a US Cold War ally, ensured that Stewart's pan-Africanism did not take a left-wing turn or become aligned with African and Third World militants. Stewart was a man with one foot in the present and the other in the past.

Stewart's collaborations with white supremacists represent the most glaring paradox of his Black nationalism in the 1950s. From Gbandela, the UNIA president-general endorsed the "Langer Bill" named after US Senator William Langer (R-ND), who introduced the legislation in May 1949. Resembling the Greater Liberia Act of 1939, the Langer Bill called for US federal government aid for African American emigration to Liberia. The Universal African Nationalist Movement, the PME, and the UNIA worked with Langer to secure its passage.[50] The longtime white supremacist Earnest Sevier Cox also championed the bill. Echoing positions made by emigration opponents since the nineteenth century, civil rights groups opposed the bill on the basis that African

Americans had earned their right to full citizenship in the land of their birth and that white supremacists backed the legislation. The Liberian government, whom Langer did not consult, objected to the bill on the grounds that the West African republic opposed large-scale immigration. The Langer Bill never became law.[51]

From Africa, Stewart endorsed the Langer Bill and corresponded with Cox about it.[52] Stewart's alignment with Cox was significant. In the 1950s, Cox became a patron saint to a new generation of US white supremacists who emerged in response to their opposition to desegregation, communism, and decolonization. His self-published book *Teutonic Unity: A Basis for Peace*, released in 1951, reemphasized his long-standing belief in white superiority and racial separation, and it enhanced his reputation among veteran Garveyites and won him new white racist supporters. In 1959, a neo-Nazi conference in Germany, which he attended, honored him.[53]

In fairness to Stewart, other veteran Garveyites—Amy Jacques Garvey, William Sherrill, and Mittie Maude Lena Gordon—collaborated with Cox in support of the Langer Bill.[54] The collaborations among Garveyites and white supremacists elucidate the underappreciated ideological complexities of diasporic politics as Jim Crow and colonialism were in retreat. Blacks across the political spectrum embraced African decolonization. However, old school Garveyites stood headstrong in their belief for racial purity and separation.[55] Given the long history of collaborations among Black nationalists and white supremacists, and the fact that Jacques Garvey, Stewart, Gordon, and Sherrill had worked with Cox for decades, it is unsurprising that Garveyites in the 1950s resorted to a familiar tactic.

While repatriating to West Africa and operating Liberty Farm created unique opportunities for Stewart to lead the transnational UNIA, his location in Liberia also weakened his power within the Garvey movement. His adversaries in the US-based Rehabilitating Committee—Thomas Harvey, William Sherrill, and Ethel Collins—took advantage of his emigration to Africa by breaking officially from Stewart. In a testament to the heartland's ongoing importance to the Garvey movement, the Rehabilitating Committee held its international convention in November 1951 in Detroit. The city remained a hub of Garveyism under Stewart's nemesis, Detroit UNIA president William Sherrill. More than thirty delegates from Chicago, Cincinnati, Dayton, Detroit, Montreal, New York, New Orleans, Philadelphia, and Toronto assembled at the conference. Renouncing Stewart for his alleged impropriety and misleadership, the Rehabilitating Committee declared itself the "legitimate" UNIA. Delegates elected Harvey, Sherrill, and Collins, as president-general, first assistant president-general, and secretary-general, respectively. In 1953, the new UNIA elected Sherrill as its president-general. This organization was initially based in Detroit before moving its headquarters to Philadelphia. Stewart dismissed his rivals as renegades.[56] Still, the infighting within the UNIA and the organizational weakness of the Stewart-led faction further weakened the global Garvey movement.

While the organizational work of Stewart in Liberia provides insight into the survival of classical Black nationalism, his time on the continent also illustrates the transformative power of living in West Africa on midwestern diasporic subjects. He was happy in Liberia. There, he was free from the US racism and government harassment he knew too well.[57] He passed away in Liberia in 1964 at the age of sixty-two. Goldie remained in Gbandela. Underscoring his belief in the importance of advancing global Black freedom from the continent, he was buried not in the country of his birth but in his beloved adopted homeland.[58]

Liberia forever changed Goldie Stewart's life. Her life in Gbandela demonstrates the continued centrality of women to the transnational UNIA, their practice of community feminism, and the ways classical Black nationalism survived into the 1950s. In a 1975 interview conducted in her hometown of Ravenna, Ohio, she explained: "I believe our work in the organization has awakened the black people to their identity.... We feel that Africa is the homeland of the blacks and that we should help to build it up and look back to Africa."[59] Articulating a belief that had animated US Black nationalists since the 1800s, she believed New World Blacks had a special obligation to uplift Africa. Given this belief, she comanaged Liberty Farm with her husband even though she did not hold a formal UNIA position.[60]

Looking at the longer history of African American women's diasporic encounters in Africa, Goldie Stewart's life in Liberia resembled and differed from the experiences of nineteenth-century Black American female missionaries on the continent. In her work on Black American women missionaries in turn-of-the-twentieth-century Congo, the historian Sylvia M. Jacobs argues that they played a significant role in spreading evangelical Protestantism in Africa. Missionary work in Africa often transformed Black American Christian women, prompting many to gain some acceptance of African Indigenous practices in order to better carry out their evangelism.[61] Goldie Stewart was not deeply religious.[62] Nonetheless, Jacobs's description of Black American female missionary work in Congo applies to Stewart and speaks to the way her life in Liberia affirmed and transgressed prevailing constructions of African American middle-class womanhood and female respectability. Emigrating with her family to West Africa was an unconventional move. Looking back, a Stewart family friend, Hanif Wahab of Cleveland, said, "She went to Black Africa when most people of her status would not have given it any thought."[63] He was right. In Gbandela, she lived with her family in a modest home without the comforts of electricity and running water. Plus, she willingly took her children to a remote part of an African nation, where the local population lived by Indigenous customs. Public nudity and polygyny were socially acceptable practices among the Kpelle. Stewart neither learned Kpelle nor wore African clothing. However, she was comfortable around local people.[64]

As a community feminist, she championed local women. Utilizing her extraordinary culinary skills, she taught them how to bake bread and to cook other foods for personal consumption and sale. She hoped that instilling entrepreneurship in Indigenous women would make them economically independent. Besides teaching local women how to cook, she established a small roadside restaurant in Gbandela. Through the farm and restaurant, she became affectionately known as "Ma Stewart" among locals and travelers who appreciated her warmth and generosity.[65] Her gendered title, "Ma Stewart," evidenced how her positionality as a mother, wife, and landowning New World Black Christian settler was critical to affording her power and privilege in rural central Liberia. She earned local people's respect. But she was not one of them. Her life in Gbandela, while in some respects unconventional, was also consistent with the long and complex encounters of Black Americans in Africa.

Goldie Stewart's life in Liberia provides insight into the range of African diasporic feminist practices during the 1950s. The politics of UNIA women resembled and contrasted with those of their sisters in newer Black nationalist formations like the Universal Association of Ethiopian Women (UAEW), formed in 1957 in New Orleans by Queen Mother Moore. Born in 1898 and coming of age in New Orleans, Moore stands as one of the most revered figures in twentieth-century Black nationalism, pan-Africanism, and communism. She was a lifelong Garveyite and a leading personality in the Communist Party in 1940s Harlem. In 1950, she broke from the Communist Party, reinventing herself as an ardent Black nationalist. By the early 1960s, she was critical in forging Black Power and the modern reparations movement. Under her leadership, the UAEW attempted to build mass movements for reparations, human rights, economic justice, welfare rights, the protection of Black women from rape and involuntary sterilization at the hands of white men, and the defense of Black men falsely accused of raping white women. There is no record of correspondence or collaboration between midwestern UNIA women and the UAEW. Goldie Stewart and Audley Moore would have agreed about the need for protecting Black women and the importance of Africa to global Black freedom. However, the former's Black nationalism remained locked in the Black settler colonial idea of Liberia, while the latter's Black nationalism evolved with changing times and embraced the politics of the Bandung World.[66] Additionally, the politics of 1950s Garveyite women differed from their counterparts in the Black left feminist formation, the Sojourners for Truth and Justice. Founded in 1951 and based in Harlem, the short-lived Sojourners was an all-Black women's left-wing protest organization committed to the full freedom of African-descended women globally.[67] In contrast to UNIA women, Sojourners such as Charlotta Bass, Louise Thompson Patterson, Claudia Jones, and Eslanda Robeson supported the Soviet Union and rejected narrow Black nationalism, middle-class respectability, and religiosity.[68]

African redemption remained a key concern for midwestern Garveyites. For James and Goldie Stewart, repatriating to Liberia was a critical piece in fulfilling Garvey's dream of redeeming Africa from the continent. Liberty Farm generated immense interest within the transnational UNIA, linking the Diasporic Midwest with Africa in new and exciting ways. Pursuing community feminism, midwestern Garveyite women like Goldie Stewart were critical to advancing the UNIA's transnational work. However, Liberty Farm was unsuccessful in revitalizing the organization. James Stewart's years in Liberia isolated him from Black communities he hoped to liberate, creating an opportunity for William Sherrill to usurp Stewart's influence. Still, the Stewarts accomplished what remained elusive for Garvey: moving the UNIA's headquarters to Africa.

Mittie Maude Lena Gordon and the PME

James and Goldie Stewart were not the only heartland Garveyites in the 1950s wedded to the classical Black nationalist dream of returning New World Blacks to Africa. Mittie Maude Lena Gordon and her Peace Movement of Ethiopia also held true to their Black diasporic right radicalism, forged in the 1930s by promoting African American emigration to Africa as the only solution to the problems facing the African-descended into the 1950s.[69] Given this politics, Gordon continued collaborating with Earnest Sevier Cox in support for African American emigration to Africa. In a 1961 letter to Cox, PME leaders Mittie Maude Lena Gordon and Alberta Spain railed against the Civil Rights Movement: "This Integration along with the sickening sit ins that is now going on in the South brought us to wits in [sic]." Instead, she expressed to her longtime white supremacist friend her continued desire to emigrate to Africa.[70] Her dream never came true. She passed away on June 16, 1961, in Chicago at the age of sixty-two without ever setting foot in Africa.[71] In a sorrowful letter from Cox to Alberta Spain, Gordon's successor, he lamented her passing as a great loss to the "cause of Negro Nationalism."[72] His grief was seemingly sincere. They had worked together for four decades on behalf of Liberian colonization. He had stood faithfully by her during the 1940s when federal authorities jailed her.

Cox's mournful words about Gordon's death speak to her extraordinary and complex life, the possibilities and limitations of Black nationalism, and the century-plus importance of the Midwest as a generative site of Black resistance and global politics. Under her leadership, the ex-Chicago UNIA member built the PME into the largest US Black nationalist organization during the Depression, forging nationwide African American mass support for Liberian colonization and preserving Garvey's legacy. Following her death, the PME continued to reject integration and to promote emigration through the 1960s. But the group now counted no more than a few dozen members, most of whom lived in Chicago.[73] By Gordon's death, the nineteenth-century Black classical nationalist dream of Liberian colonization no longer enjoyed widespread enthusiasm. Working with white supremacists seemed even more unfathomable to many Blacks in the era of civil rights and decolonization. As the PME and mass interest in Liberia colonization declined, newly independent Ghana and its founder, Kwame Nkrumah, mesmerized Black people across the Midwest and beyond and moved Garveyism in new directions.

Ghana, Kwame Nkrumah, the UNIA, and the US Heartland

As the work of the Stewarts and Gordon attests to the continued influence of classical Black nationalism in shaping Garveyite global imaginaries in the 1950s, Detroit UNIA leader William Sherrill's attendance of Ghanaian independence ceremonies and the grassroots enthusiasm among Black Chicagoans about Kwame Nkrumah's 1958 visit to the Windy City provide insight into the importance of Ghana to keeping Garveyism alive and to cultivating new diasporic sensibilities among Blacks in the Midwest and beyond in the Bandung era. The independence of Ghana from British colonial rule on March 6, 1957, electrified African-descended people around the world. On the eve of Ghana's independence, more than 500,000 euphoric people packed the Old Polo Grounds in the new nation's capital—Accra—to celebrate their freedom. As midnight of March 5, 1957, approached, Nkrumah and his top lieutenants gathered on a dais in front of the massive crowd. Soon after officials lowered the British Union Jack and raised the new Ghanaian flag, Nkrumah delivered an epic speech, filled with revolutionary bravado, in which he captured the historical significance of the moment. He proudly declared: "At long last, the battle has ended. At last, Ghana, your beloved country is free forever!" Appreciating Ghana's independence within the broader context of global Black freedom and decolonization, he stressed that their "independence is meaningless unless it is linked up with total liberation of the African continent." Cheers greeted Nkrumah throughout his speech.[74]

Nkrumah's powerful speech illustrated how Ghana and Nkrumah came to represent beacons of hope and possibility to African-descended people around the world as the Bandung era came to fruition.[75] As the first prime minister and president of Ghana, Nkrumah pursued nation-building predicated on the modernization of Ghana domestically and through positioning the West African state as a champion of pan-Africanism, the Third World, and the Non-Aligned Movement. By the early 1960s, he became increasingly outspoken in supporting socialism and in speaking out against Western neocolonialism in Africa and across the Third World.[76] Ghana inspired a new generation of African American activists and transformed popular perceptions of Africa among Black Americans, prompting them to embrace a modern, historically grounded understanding of the relation between Black America and the continent.[77]

Garveyism was critical to shaping Nkrumah and Ghana.[78] Like Nnamdi Azikiwe—the founder of Nigeria and an associate of Nkrumah—the founder of Ghana acknowledged "that of all the literature that I studied, the book that did more than any other to fire my enthusiasm was *Philosophy and Opinions of Marcus Garvey.*"[79] Nkrumah first encountered Garveyism as a student at Lincoln University during the late 1930s. Throughout his life, he considered himself a Garveyite and credited Garvey for stoking modern African nationalism. Nkrumah made this point during his Independence Day speech in Ghana.

> Here I wish I could quote Marcus Garvey. Once upon a time, he said, that he looked through the whole world to see if he could find a government of a black people. He looked around, he did not find one, and he said he was going to create one. Marcus Garvey did not succeed. But here today, the work of [Jean-Jacques] Rousseau, the work of Marcus Garvey, and the work of [James Kwegyir] Aggrey, the work of [Joseph Ephraim] Casely Hayford, the work of illustrious men who have gone before us has come to reality at this present moment.[80]

This address speaks to Nkrumah's understanding of Ghana as a fulfillment of modernity and the legacy of African and New World Black visionaries, not least Garvey. At Nkrumah's behest, Ghana's new national flag, with its red,

FIGURE 5.1. Black Star Gate, Accra, Ghana, March 2023. Photo by the author.

yellow, and green horizontal stripes and with a five-pointed black star at the center, resembled the UNIA banner conceived by Garvey in 1920 (see also the Black Star Gate in figure 5.1). The black star referenced the Black Star Line founded by Garvey. Nkrumah established a new Ghanaian commercial shipping company—the Black Star Line—named after its famous UNIA forebearer.[81] Nkrumah both embraced Garvey's dream of a free Africa and updated Garveyism to changing times.

The importance of Garveyism to birthing Ghana was not lost on midwestern UNIA spokespersons. As discussed, James Stewart celebrated Ghanaian independence. However, he did not travel to Accra. A chronic lack of funds may help to explain why he never left Liberia.[82] His absence from Ghanaian independence was symbolic of his isolation from new developments in the African world and the ways his pan-African vision remained rooted in the classical Black nationalist idea of Liberia as the beacon of hope for Black people globally.

No Midwest-based UNIA leader was moved more by Ghana's independence than William Sherrill (see figure 5.2). The Ghanaian government invited him to attend the independence ceremonies as the representative of the UNIA and as an official state guest. He remained in the newly independent West African

FIGURE 5.2.
William L. Sherrill,
circa 1950. Stuart A.
Rose Library Manu-
script, Archives, and
Rare Book Library,
Emory University,
Atlanta, Georgia.

nation for two weeks. Underscoring once again the importance of globetrotting to transforming Black diasporic subjects' internationalist sensibilities, traveling to Ghana marked one of the most exciting moments in his life. Even more, his trip, reported in the African American press, showcases the continued importance of Black midwesterners in keeping alive the memory of Garvey.[83]

Sherrill was exuberant on the eve of his trip. He shared this sentiment in a letter to Amy Jacques Garvey: "Since Africa has developed many able leaders I feel that the UNIA program in America should be geared to that of African leadership rather than expect them to gear theirs to the UNIA. [T]he leadership in Africa's struggle should come from Africa."[84] Amy Jacques Garvey did not attend Ghanaian independence ceremonies. However, she too viewed Ghana as the fulfillment of her husband's legacy.[85] Sherrill's and Jacques Garvey's enthusiasm about Ghana differed from Stewart's views about the UNIA and pan-Africanism. Stewart remained wedded to the belief that Liberia and Tubman represented beacons for African decolonization, whereas Sherrill and Jacques Garvey identified Ghana, Nkrumah, and the African masses as the agents of change for Global Africa. These contrasting conclusions about Ghana's significance to the Black world illustrate the ways Stewart's and Sherrill's divergent routes to and locations in West Africa informed their pan-Africanism.

Sherrill had never traveled to Africa before going to Ghana in March 1957. He was part of a larger delegation of African Americans whom Nkrumah invited to Ghana's independence ceremonies. The group included Martin Luther King Jr. and his wife, Coretta Scott King; educator Horace Mann Bond; labor activist Maida Springer; US congresspersons Charles Diggs (D-MI) and Adam Clayton Powell (D-NY); veteran civil rights and labor leader A. Philip Randolph; and diplomat Ralph Bunche. They traveled together from the United States to Ghana with Vice President Richard M. Nixon. Once there, King met privately with Nkrumah and Nixon.[86] There is no record of Sherrill meeting with prominent US civil rights leaders, Nixon, or Caribbean attendees such as Norman Manley of Jamaica, Grantley Adams of Barbados, and C. L. R. James of Trinidad.[87]

Sherrill's trip to Ghana exceeded his expectations. The Ghanaian government provided him with lavish hotel accommodations, a car and driver, and reserved seating at independence ceremonies. Meeting with Nkrumah constituted the highlight of Sherrill's trip to Africa. In a letter to the Detroit UNIA, Sherrill reported that he enjoyed "a long conference . . . [with Nkrumah] at which we went thoroughly into the UNIA's present program and his own program for the complete freedom of Africa."[88] Sherrill conferred with several Ghanaian officials, who, like Nkrumah, acknowledged "that Marcus Garvey did more to inspire Africa . . . than any single factor."[89] Energized by his trip, Sherrill concluded: "A new day has dawned for the UNIA. The African world is depending upon us to do the job abroad while they do the job at home."[90]

Sherrill viewed his trip as a propaganda coup for the UNIA. In a letter written from Accra to the Detroit UNIA, he stated: "My visit to Africa has brought the Universal Negro Improvement Association to the forefront again as the moving force for African liberation."[91] Sherrill claimed that "many big Negroes" from the United States did not receive the priority access he enjoyed in Accra.[92] He did not name specific African American leaders. It is possible he was referring to King. For sure, however, King echoed Sherrill's enthusiasm. Weeks after returning home from Ghana, King delivered a powerful sermon—"The Birth of a New Nation"—at the Dexter Avenue Baptist Church in Montgomery, Alabama, about observing Ghanaian independence.[93] Newly independent Ghana, King preached, represented a model for African American freedom, signaled a dying colonialism, and affirmed that the "forces of the universe [were] on the side of justice."[94] Sherrill would have agreed.

Journeying to Ghana afforded Sherrill an unparalleled chance to disseminate information about Ghana, Garveyism, and African nationalism into African

American communities following his return home to Detroit in April 1957. Energized by his trip, Sherrill spoke about his Ghana trip in churches and UNIA halls in Detroit, Toledo, Philadelphia, and New York.[95] In his speeches, he vividly described Ghanaian independence ceremonies. In his "I Saw a Nation Born" speech, Sherrill proclaimed: "I heard Garvey speak through the mouth of Nkrumah." In another address, Sherrill emphasized Nkrumah's public enthusiasm for the UNIA and Garveyism and criticized Martin Luther King. According to Sherrill, King "seemed a little stunned" that Nkrumah "did not say the NAACP, Urban League, but [the] Garvey movement" in discussing strategies for worldwide Black freedom. His remarks affirmed Sherrill's belief that Garveyism, not civil rights, represented the best program for Black freedom.[96]

Even though Sherrill and Stewart were bitter enemies by the 1950s, they found common ground in their Black nationalist opposition to King and civil rights. The staunchly pro-capitalist stance of Sherrill and Stewart differentiated them from civil rights spokespersons like King who came to embrace an anticapitalist perspective. Sherrill, like Stewart, remained wedded to civilizationism. In Sherrill's pamphlet *New Africa Faces the World*, published after his trip to Ghana, he writes, "There are parts of Africa where . . . African people have not embraced modern civilization but still follow their tribal laws and customs." These allegedly backward Africans "do not represent the New and awakened Africa."[97] Like Garvey, Stewart, and their nineteenth-century Black nationalist predecessors, Sherrill believed unquestionably in Western modernity, masculinism, racial purity, and emigration. He made this position clear in the pamphlet *Africa—Every Blackman's Business*, written just before his Ghana trip. Claiming that a "free and independent Africa will forever destroy the lie that Black men are inferior," he blasted civil rights proponents as advocates of "amalgamation" and "race suicide."[98] His support for racial purity explains why he endorsed the Langer Bill and corresponded with Cox. King rejected racial separatism and collaborating with white supremacists.

While Garveyites and civil rights leaders differed on matters of racial separatism, Sherrill and King both understood Ghanaian independence in highly gendered terms. In one address following his return from Ghana, Sherrill declared: "I saw freedom written in the eyes of Black men—I heard freedom in the voice of black men."[99] Similarly, King in his "The Birth of a New Nation" sermon, exclaimed: "To rob a man of his freedom is to take from him the essential basis of manhood."[100] For Sherrill and King, freedom meant redeeming Black manhood.

Sherrill's trip to Ghana produced mixed results for the UNIA. Like his adversary James Stewart, Sherrill was unable to translate the excitement generated by traveling to Africa into revitalizing the UNIA in Ghana or globally. The organizational weakness of Sherrill's group, combined with insufficient resources of the new Ghanaian government, prevented the UNIA from rebuilding the organization in West Africa.[101] He scored a propaganda victory with US civil rights leaders by garnering the praise of Nkrumah for Garveyism and the UNIA. Personally, visiting Ghana was a transformative experience for Sherrill. However, he never returned to Africa. He died two years after visiting Ghana.[102] Sherrill's journey and subsequent speaking tour across the United States show the prominence of the Midwest in keeping Garveyism alive into the 1950s. He never abandoned classical Black nationalism. However, like many young Black nationalists and even some veteran Garveyites, he looked to Ghana, not Liberia, as the new hope for African liberation as the Bandung World took shape.

While perhaps only hundreds of die-hard US Garveyites heard Sherrill speak about the miracle of Ghanaian independence, Nkrumah's whirlwind visit to Chicago from July 30 to 31, 1958, touched thousands of Black people in the Windy City and beyond.[103] The Ghanaian prime minister's trip to Chicago was part of his first state visit to the United States. US president Dwight D. Eisenhower had invited Nkrumah. Both leaders publicly framed Nkrumah's visit as a goodwill tour. However, Nkrumah and Eisenhower had their own ulterior motives. The Eisenhower administration sought to build good relations with newly independent African and Asian states to check the influence of the Soviet Union in the emerging Bandung World. For Nkrumah, the trip provided an excellent opportunity for him to lobby for economic investments for Ghana and for him to position himself as a global leader. Washington, DC, rolled out the red carpet for Nkrumah. He met with Eisenhower and addressed a joint session of Congress. After leaving Washington, Nkrumah visited Philadelphia, New York, and Chicago.[104]

Besides Harlem, no US city gave the Ghanaian prime minister a warmer welcome than Chicago. He visited this midwestern metropolis as it was undergoing profound racial transformations. In 1950, Chicago's population grew to its peak, 3,620,962. Chicago's African American population increased to 492,265, or 13.6 percent of the city's total population. Between 1950 and 1956, 270,000 whites left the city for the suburbs.[105] Racial tensions in the city persisted.[106] Politically, the 1955 mayoral election of Richard J. Daley, an Irish American Democrat, brought to power the city's most powerful and notorious machine politician.[107] Under Daley, slum clearance, highway construction, and police brutality, together with the mayor's control of the African American vote, opposition to open housing, and the nascent postindustrial economy further marginalized Black working-class people.[108] In response, Black Chicagoans, as they had since the nineteenth century, relied on their civic institutions and determination to live beyond the limitations of racism and discrimination imposed on them.

Nkrumah took Chicago by storm after his arrival at Midway Airport on July 30, 1958. A large delegation of local civic, business, and labor leaders, including Daley and US representative William L. Dawson of the South Side, greeted Nkrumah on the airport's tarmac.[109] From there, he traveled in a six-block-long motorcade along a twelve-mile route from the airport to downtown Chicago. Thousands of gleeful Black Chicagoans lined South Parkway (a main thoroughfare), proudly waved Garvey-inspired Ghanaian flags, and cheered as Nkrumah drove past them. The impressive spectacle may have reminded old-timers in the crowd of the UNIA's glory days in the 1920s when thousands of uniformed Garveyites paraded through South Side streets.[110] While in Chicago, Nkrumah dined with Daley and local officials. Chicago's heavy industrial character as the "candy capital" of the world played a role in bringing him to the Windy City.[111] Nkrumah attended the National Confectioner's Association annual conference, which had gathered there. Looking to secure foreign investment for his new nation, he lobbied the US confectionary industry to increase its imports of Ghanaian cocoa, the country's chief export.[112]

Chicago's dynamic, globally connected Black community was another important factor in drawing Nkrumah to the city. He met with African American media titan Claude Barnett.[113] The Ghanaian prime minister visited the Johnson Publishing Company, his only stop at a media firm during his US tour. St. Clair Drake, the preeminent Africana studies scholar based at Roosevelt University in Chicago, who was raised by a Garveyite parent, organized a reception for Nkrumah at the university on July 31, 1958 (see figure 5.3). African studies scholars from Roosevelt University, Northwestern University, and the University of Chicago attended the affair.[114] News about Nkrumah's Chicago tour traveled far beyond the city through the globally circulated *Chicago Defender*. The ebullient reception Nkrumah received in Chicago demonstrated the growing concern about African decolonization among African Americans locally and nationally. More broadly, the excitement in Black Chicago for Nkrumah's visit shows once again the Diasporic Midwest as an important political terrain where Garveyism not only resonated but also adapted to changing times and found new platforms for advancing global Black freedom. At the same time, the enthusiasm for Ghana and Nkrumah among Black Chicagoans provides insight into the ideological differences among Blacks in the heartland and beyond. Some veteran UNIA officials like Stewart and Sherrill celebrated Ghanaian independence

FIGURE 5.3. Kwame Nkrumah (*middle*) with (*L* to *R*) St. Clair Drake and Melville Herskovits at a reception at Roosevelt University, Chicago, Illinois, July 31, 1958. Roosevelt University Archives, Chicago.

while clinging to older classical Black nationalist paradigms. Younger Black nationalists and even some older ones, along with a growing number of everyday people based in the heartland and elsewhere, increasingly dispensed with Black settler colonialism and looked to Ghana, the Bandung World, and organizations outside of the UNIA as key agents for global Black freedom.

F. H. Hammurabi Robb and the House of Knowledge

While the UNIA carried on into the postwar years, it was through the midwestern Garveyite front where Black nationalism and the legacies of Garvey found new life, touched the lives of thousands of everyday African Americans across the heartland, and linked the Diasporic Midwest to a rapidly changing world in the Bandung era. An important grassroots site in conducting this work in postwar Chicago was the House of Knowledge (HOK), a South Side cultural center dedicated to chronicling Black life and history, established by Frederick H. Hammurabi Robb.[115] Charismatic, brilliant, and a tad scruffy, he was by the

1950s a living legend on the South Side as a world traveler, bibliophile, and public intellectual who believed in the transformative power of Black history. His life embodied the lived experiences of migration, transnationalism, and cosmopolitanism that had shaped Black midwestern life since the eighteenth century. Born in 1900 in Hartford, Connecticut, he graduated from Howard University and settled in 1924 in Chicago, where he earned a law degree from Northwestern University Law School.[116] His first significant public achievement came in 1927 with the publication of the *Intercollegian Wonder Book*, a survey of Black life in Chicago from 1779 to 1927. The book listed Marcus Garvey as one of the prominent Black spokespersons to have visited Chicago.[117] During the 1930s, Robb regularly wrote for the *Chicago Defender* about Black history, African nationalism, the Italo-Ethiopian War, and his numerous trips to Africa.[118] By 1936, he established the World Wide Friends of Africa, later renamed the House of Knowledge. His adoption in the 1930s of the surname Hammurabi, the name of the great ancient Babylonian king who codified the first legal codes in human history, and Robb's signature fez spoke to the ways that he, like countless Black midwesterners, forged an Afro-Orientalist subjectivity. Robb came to know leading Chicago Black nationalists of his day—Mittie Maude Lena Gordon, Elijah Muhammad, and probably Noble Drew Ali. Robb's Black nationalism engendered government scrutiny. In 1942, he was briefly jailed during the FBI's dragnet against Chicago Black nationalists for their alleged pro-Japanese sympathies.[119]

The House of Knowledge marked Robb's greatest life achievement and speaks to the long Black midwestern tradition of institution-building. The HOK embodied what cultural historian Ian Rocksborough-Smith calls "black public-history activism." He uses the term to describe the ways Black educators, journalists, visual artists, scholars, activists, and globetrotters in mid-twentieth-century Chicago advanced racial equality and social justice through celebrating and promoting African American, African, and Black diasporic culture and life.[120] The HOK sponsored lectures by Robb on his travels and Black history, published Black history books and calendars, held exhibits on African culture, and sponsored forums on the postwar US Black Freedom Movement and African decolonization.[121] The HOK was part of the larger Black Chicago Renaissance, a dynamic cultural movement from the 1930s through the 1950s on par with, if not surpassing, the earlier Harlem Renaissance in cultural production.[122] The HOK's location in the basement of a mansion at 3806 S. Michigan, owned by Margaret Taylor Goss Burroughs and Charles Burroughs, placed Robb at ground zero of the Black Chicago Renaissance. The Burroughs, a fixture in the Black Chicago Renaissance and the Black left, counted African American artists and radicals, such as Paul Robeson, Gwendolyn Brooks, Charles White, W. E. B. Du Bois, Shirley Graham Du Bois, Louise Thompson Patterson, Ishmael Flory, and William L. Patterson, as close friends. The Burroughs also admired Garvey.[123]

Celebrating Garvey was a crucial way the HOK advanced Black freedom. The center sponsored annual parades through the South Side in celebration of Garvey's birthday.[124] The HOK did not simply celebrate the glory days of Garvey and the UNIA. Robb adopted to changing times. Embracing modern Black nationalism, the HOK sponsored programs about African independence, including an event at the community center honoring Nkrumah during his Chicago tour.[125] Robb and the HOK effectively used public history for keeping Garvey's legacy alive, promoting modern Black nationalism, and forging linkages among everyday Black Chicagoans with Global Africa during the 1950s.

Moorish Science and the Persecution of Ahmad El

As the House of Knowledge disseminated Garveyism on the South Side, Black ethnic religions such as Moorish Science served as important sites for keeping alive and transforming the midwestern Garveyite tradition into the 1950s. Cities such as Chicago, Detroit, Cleveland, Gary, and Toledo remained Moorish Science strongholds even as the movement continued fracturing in the postwar years.[126] Cleveland was home to the most important Moorish Science formation established in the 1950s: the Clock of Destiny National Order of the Great Seal led by C. M. (Charles Mosley) Bey.[127] This group took shape as Cleveland's population peaked at 914,808 in 1950, making Cleveland the seventh-largest US city. Black Cleveland's population grew to approximately 146,000. Deindustrialization, redlining, government neglect, and white suburbanization aggravated racial disparities in the postwar Cleveland area.[128]

Travel and global understandings of Black freedom were critical to shaping Bey's life. Born in Chicago in 1897, he attended the University of Chicago, served in the US armed forces during the First World War, and studied at the University of the Yucatán in Mexico. It was in Mexico where he began to study "Moabite" people. Eventually making his way to Cleveland, he published the two-volume booklet *Clock of Destiny National Order of the Great Seal* in 1947. Combining the teachings of Noble Drew Ali, the Nation of Islam, Freemasonry, and astrology, *Clock of Destiny* proffered a new Moorish philosophy that served as the basis for an organization established by Bey in 1952 that bore the text's name.[129] The Clock of Destiny forged a theology more radical than the MSTA. Claiming "that the Moorish nation [was] free" and not under the jurisdiction of the US government, Bey instructed his followers not to enlist in the US military on the grounds that fighting for the United States violated the constitutional law of Moorish Science. He also directed his followers not to remove their red fezzes in court.[130] His teachings broke from MSTA doctrine, which neither explicitly called for its followers to dodge the draft nor framed African Americans as a sovereign nation unbound by US law.[131] His doctrine was transgressive, given that US armed forces became bogged down in the domestically unpopular Korean War and as the possibility of nuclear war with the Soviet Union loomed. His stance directly challenged US Cold War domestic and foreign policy and civil rights groups such as the NAACP who supported the Korean War on the grounds that the United States was justly fighting against communist aggression in Asia and that Blacks would win freedoms at home for their military service overseas. Instead, Bey's position bears some resemblance with those of Black leftists who viewed the Korean conflict as an unjust, racist, and imperialist war waged by the United States against a people of color fighting for self-determination.[132]

While Moorish Science attracted a loyal following in Cleveland and beyond, Moors also garnered state scrutiny as Cold War repression tightened its grip on 1950s America. African American Muslims in the 1950s and 1960s became prime targets of the FBI.[133] In 1952, a federal judge sentenced Clock of Destiny officials Robert Marcus-Bey and William Spearman-Bey, both of Cleveland, to five-year prison terms for refusing to fight in the Korean War.[134] Their incarcerations resembled the Cold War–era repression of Black leftists Paul Robeson, Claudia Jones, and W. E. B. Du Bois and speaks to the long tradition of state persecution of Black nationalists dating to the 1920s when J. Edgar Hoover took down Marcus Garvey.[135]

No Moor garnered more fear and anxiety among authorities and African American elites in 1950s Cleveland than the teacher and philosopher Ahmad El ("Tonelli"). His sensational trial and conviction in Cleveland in May 1954 for violating Ohio's white slavery law based on the Mann Act of 1910 generated national attention.[136] He was born in 1919 in Alabama. His life resembled the early years of Malcolm X. Ahmad El's racially proud family fled to the Forest City after his mother died during a shootout between his stepfather and Klanmen in Alabama. Like Malcolm in wartime Harlem, Ahmad El in 1940s Black Cleveland was a popular figure well known for his dancing skills, race pride, vegetarianism, and abstinence from tobacco, alcohol, and drugs. However, he was a complicated man. He was a notorious pimp, who had a penchant for wealthy white female lovers.[137] He also married a white woman. In the early 1950s, he became Bey's protégé, converted to Moorish Science, and adopted the name

FIGURE 5.4. Ahmad El, circa 1954. PG 268 Allen E. Cole Photographs, Western Reserve Historical Society, Cleveland, Ohio.

Ahmad El (see figure 5.4). There is no record of him ever joining the UNIA or the NOI. He became known as "The Prophet" among his followers. Proudly wearing a tasseled red fez and goatee, he encouraged African Americans to adopt clean lifeways and to reject the cultural values of white America. Despite his religious conversion, he stayed with his white wife, kept up his flamboyant lifeways, and remained known among Black Clevelanders as "Tonelli."[138]

Ahmad El's racial defiance, faith, flamboyance, and involvement in the underground economy threatened the racial status quo and alarmed Cleveland authorities. In April 1954, authorities charged him with raping a fifteen-year-old white girl from a wealthy suburb and with prostituting young Black and white women in Cleveland. Widely covered in the Black and mainstream press in Cleveland and nationwide, his religion and race became the focus of the trial. Prosecutors charged him with using his training in "occult sciences," drugs, and alcohol to seduce and lure white women into a life of prostitution, crime, and immorality.[139] These charges reflected growing nervousness within white America that linked African Americans with crime, drugs, and subversion.[140]

Throughout the contentious trial, Ahmad El, who represented himself, charged that the court unjustly persecuted him because he was Black, a Moor, and defiant.[141] Citing Moorish Science, Ahmad El wore his fez, portraying himself as a learned holy man and "Nationalist" who was a proud member of a sovereign nation immune from US jurisprudence.[142] He also charged that his case was a blatant example of racist state officials unjustly incarcerating Black urban, working-class men for crimes they did not commit. Ultimately, the court convicted Ahmad El on May 12, 1954, on eleven counts of pandering and rape and sentenced him to fourteen to sixty-eight years.[143] Declaring him "psychotic," the judge ordered Ahmad El to the Ohio State Hospital for the Criminally Insane in Lima, Ohio.[144] He spent the rest of his life in the state hospital. He died in 1999 at the age of eighty-nine, nearly forty-five years after his trial.[145]

Ahmad El's case sparked a moral panic among the Black Cleveland elite. *Call and Post* reporter Ralph Matthews rebuked "'the so-called prophet'" for his alleged immorality. Castigating Ahmad El and other Black Cleveland "pimps and hustlers . . . [as] moral lepers," Matthews worried that young Blacks would embrace the Moor as a role model.[146] His white wife titillated the *Call and Post*, which featured a front-page article describing her as a young, "pretty . . . buxom" woman who stood by her unjustly persecuted Black husband.[147] He embarrassed status-conscious Black middle-class Clevelanders. For them, his involvement in Moorish Science and the underground economy, sexual relations with white women, and outspokenness against racism affirmed the ways African American elites often sought to police the behaviors of Black working-class people through upholding respectability and stigmatizing interracial sex.[148] In fearing Ahmad El, Black elites found common ground with white authorities in ways similar to the ways both the Black press and white state actors in the 1930s demonized the Nation of Islam. Ahmad El's persecution also resembles the institutionalization of Louise Little for her alleged insanity for transgressing middle-class respectability and for resisting white authorities.

The popular memory in Cleveland of Ahmad El provides insight into the complexities of Black nationalism. During and after his trial, he emerged as a Black nationalist urban folk hero.[149] Looking back, Fredrick M. Brown Jr., a Black Cleveland autoworker whose family migrated from Alabama to the Forest City, recalled that "everyone wanted to be Tonelli." Brown added: "I have a lot of love for Tonelli, and the Marcus Garveys, and the Malcolm Xs. They kept saying no more; we ain't got to be bothered with them [whites]; we're

Kings and Queens."[150] For Brown, Ahmad El represented a link between Marcus Garvey and Malcolm X and a hero for Black midwesterners whose families had fled the Jim Crow South for the industrial heartland. In a familiar move, Brown read Ahmad El through a masculinist gaze. There is no question that he was a victim of racist state repression. However, he did sexually exploit women, including African American teenaged girls. The popular memory of Ahmad El in Black Cleveland contested white supremacy *and* celebrated patriarchy. His legendary status and misogyny highlight the survival of Garveyism decades after the UNIA's heyday and the complicated gender politics deeply embedded in the long history of Black nationalism.

The Early Ministry of Malcolm X, Sister Betty, and the Ascendency of the Nation of Islam

Midwestern Garveyism moved in its most exciting new directions in the 1950s through the Nation of Islam. The NOI, under Elijah Muhammad, continued to advance a Black diasporic right radicalism through its Black ethnic religious beliefs and organizational culture. However, a more modern revolutionary Black nationalism, informed by the legacy of Garvey and developments across the Bandung World, also found space in the Nation due in no small part to Malcolm X. Through his charisma, strong faith, indefatigable work, and devotion to the Messenger, Malcolm deserves significant credit for the NOI's emergence as the fastest-growing Black nationalist organization in the United States by the late 1950s.[151]

Malcolm's conversion to Islam and his meteoric rise in the Nation were inextricably linked to his continued interest in Garveyism and his family connections during his six-year prison term. Although not discussed in the *Autobiography*, Malcolm and his fellow inmates at the Charlestown Prison in Boston regularly discussed Garvey and the continued relevance of his ideas for freeing Black people.[152] Malcolm's first mentor in prison, an enigmatic figure whom the *Autobiography* names as "Bimbi," may have been an old-time Garveyite.[153] What is for sure is that the Michigan-based Little family played a crucial role in cultivating Malcolm's religious conversion, self-transformation, and entry into the NOI. Several of his siblings—Wilfred, Reginald, Philbert, and Wesley—joined the Nation's Temple No. 1 in Detroit around the time Malcolm was incarcerated.[154] The Little family's Garveyite roots informed the decisions of some of Malcolm's siblings to join the Nation. Wilfred recollected reading his first encounters with the Nation through his Garveyite worldview: "There really wasn't that much difference, except there was a little more religion emphasized than

Marcus Garvey had."[155] Wilfred converted to Islam. In no time, he emerged as a leading figure in Temple No. 1.[156]

Malcolm's first introduction to the NOI came through a correspondence in 1948 from Philbert soon after Malcolm had been transferred to Concord Reformatory outside of Boston. According to the *Autobiography*, Philbert told his younger brother that he "had discovered 'the natural religion of the black man'" through the Nation of Islam, which he had recently joined. Philbert insisted that Malcolm pray to Allah for deliverance.[157] Reginald followed up with a letter instructing his older brother to abstain from pork and smoking. Through correspondences and prison visits from Reginald and Hilda, Malcolm learned about W. D. Fard Muhammad, Elijah Muhammad, the story of Mr. Yacub, the wickedness of white "devils," and the principles of the Nation. Malcolm soon began corresponding daily with the Messenger, whom the young Muslim convert came to idolize as a surrogate father until his split from the Nation.[158]

Malcolm's critical thinking and correspondences with his siblings about Louise Little's institutionalization played a crucial role in decolonizing his mind and initiating his conversion to Islam. The *Autobiography* includes no discussion of this fact.[159] However, he made this point abundantly clear in a December 12, 1949, letter from Concord Prison to Philbert. In the letter, Malcolm recalled an instance during the Depression when Louise declined an offer of free pork from their neighbor to feed her hungry children. Malcolm wrote,

> It makes me feel good (incouragingly) [*sic*] to hear the Brothers there think I was in contact with Islam before my seclusion . . . for they are correct. We were taught Islam by Mom. Everything that happened to her happened because the devils knew she was not "deadening" our minds. When she refused those two pigs from Mr. Doane that time I thought she was crazy myself (as hungry as I was); and they sowed their lying seeds in our heads . . . but she suffered the abuse of all . . . even incurring the worse degree of the devils fury . . . unto death, all for our sake. Tis true, that my accomplishments are yours, and yours are mine . . . because we are all brothers and sisters . . . but *all* of our achievements are Mom's . . . for she was a most Faithful Servant of Truth years ago. *I* praise "Allah" for her. The love that exists in our family among us is strong—more so than in any other I know . . . and the devils kept us split up for years.[160]

This is a powerful and painful remembrance. The letter speaks to Malcolm's enduring love for his siblings and mother. The letter also challenges the commonly understood timeline of Malcolm's conversion. He asserted that his first introduction to the faith came during his childhood through Louise. According to him, her refusal to eat pork evidenced her Muslim beliefs. Did he truly believe that his mother was a Muslim even though by the mid-1930s she embraced Seventh Day Adventism, a faith that adhered to Abrahamic dietary codes? Was he aware of the long history of Islam within his family, dating to his West African Muslim progenitors? To be sure, Malcolm credited Louise for introducing the family to Islam and to instilling in them the search for truth long before his incarceration.

Even more, Malcolm's imprisonment and religious conversion prompted him to understand Louise as a survivor of racism and state repression. From his jail cell, he realized that his mother tried her best to protect her children from white racism, hunger, poverty, and state actors through upholding her religious faith and race pride, belief in self-reliance, and love for herself and her children. For her resistance, Malcolm now understood, Louise paid a terrible price. Truly sorry that he came to believe the lie concocted by white state actors that his mother was "crazy," he understood how he had internalized one of the diabolical white man's most insidious racist weapons—what the Nation called "tricknology." His internalized racism made him hate his mother and himself and blinded him to the systematic nature of Black oppression globally. In the coming years as a Muslim minister, he regularly condemned the pernicious psychological impact of white supremacy on Black people and the profound role of racism in shaping Western thought and social structures.[161]

Malcolm's adoption of the name "Malcolm X" by 1950 signified that his religious conversion and self-transformation were well underway. The young Black Muslim convert signed a letter "Malcolm X." For him, embracing the teachings of Elijah Muhammad and signing as "Malcolm X" constituted a powerful rejection of the white supremacy he and his family had known so well. Upon his parole from prison on August 7, 1952, the young Muslim was ready to set out on a new life journey.[162]

If Massachusetts prisons were key sites of his conversion, then Malcolm's Midwest-based family, combined with his experience of the unique dialectic of opportunity and oppression in Detroit, was instrumental in strengthening his new faith and making him into the Nation's leading minister and most eloquent champion for freedom and justice.[163] Per Hilda's insistence, Malcolm returned to Michigan. Initially, he lived with Wilfred's family in Inkster, a Black industrial suburb of Detroit.[164] He accompanied Malcolm to his first visit to Temple No. 1. Still located at 3408 Hastings Street in the heart of Black Bottom, the congregation consisted of about fifty members, while the national organization may have counted a few hundred members, most of whom were poor and working-class. In the summer of 1952, Malcolm traveled with Wilfred to Chicago, where he met Elijah and Clara Muhammad for the first time. The Messenger bestowed Malcolm with his "X." Recognizing the young Muslim's devotion, Muhammad appointed Malcolm as assistant minister to Temple No. 1 in June 1953. His early sermons contained the searing critiques of white America and global white supremacy that would become hallmarks of his life's work. Outside of the temple, he went "fishing" for new converts in the bars, pool halls, and street corners of Black Bottom.[165]

Malcolm began his ministry in Detroit as the mammoth industrial city was undergoing rapid racial and economic change. In 1950, Detroit's population peaked at 1.8 million people, and the city remained the fourth-largest US city.[166] The Motor City's Black population swelled to 350,000, making Detroit the fourth-largest Black urban community in the world.[167] Long-cherished dreams of finding a better life through the city's auto industries fueled ongoing African American migration from the Jim Crow South. The realities of deindustrialization and white racism in postwar Detroit shattered the hopes of many of the city's Black residents.[168] Between 1949 and 1960, Detroit experienced four major economic recessions. The city lost 134,000 manufacturing jobs between 1947 and 1963. Economic downturns, automation, and the relocation of plants to the suburbs and out of state forever changed the city's automobile industry and hit Black Detroiters disproportionately hard. Urban renewal and the construction of expressways forced growing numbers of African Americans out of Black Bottom and into previously all-white neighborhoods on Detroit's east and west sides. As in Chicago, the formation in Detroit of white homeowner associations, blockbusting, and restrictive covenants transformed racially contested neighborhoods into interracial war zones. Police brutality against African Americans remained endemic in Detroit.[169]

Malcolm knew firsthand what Blacks were experiencing in deindustrializing Detroit. In January 1953, he worked briefly at the Wayne Assembly Plant in suburban Detroit. Earning $1.80 per hour, his job was to guide automobile bodies on to chassis. Working in the plant automatically made him a member of United Automobile Workers Local 900, which had waged a series of strikes against speedups on the assembly line during the immediate postwar years. Grueling and mind-numbing work on the assembly line was too much for him. He quit after one week. After this job, he toiled at the Gar Wood plant in Detroit as a metal grinder. This job automatically placed him in the UAW Detroit Local 250. He then worked at the sprawling Ford Lincoln-Mercury Division plant in the Motor City until June 1953, when he began working full-time as an assistant minister in Temple No. 1.[170]

Most commentators and the *Autobiography* provide only cursory discussion of Malcolm's automobile factory work in Detroit. Recollections years later from Wilfred provide insight into Malcolm's thoughts about working in automobile plants. According to Wilfred, Malcolm often expressed feeling as if he were living and toiling "in the wilderness of America," a Nation of Islam expression about Muslims' understanding of white Christian America as a place of unbridled terror, violence, alienation, poverty, and misery for Black people.[171] Like Malcolm's experiences working as a railroad porter years earlier, factory work in Detroit alienated him. He could barely survive on his paltry wages. The grit, racism, monotony, noise, exploitation, and backbreaking working conditions of the automobile shop floor offered further proof to him that America offered no hope for Black people.[172] Only racial separatism and self-reliance could free Black America. He took these beliefs and lessons learned in Detroit to Philadelphia and then to Harlem after Elijah Muhammad appointed Malcolm minister of New York's Temple No. 7 in 1954. In the coming years, he gained national popularity within the NOI as one of its best ministers, as he established several temples, recruited new members like the heavyweight champion Muhammad Ali (Cassius Clay), and trained countless ministers across the country, most notably the future NOI head Louis Farrakhan (Louis Walcott / Louis X).[173]

Even though Malcolm relocated to Harlem, he never forgot lessons learned in the Midwest from his Garveyite parents, and he forged a nascent revolutionary nationalism that combined his admiration for Garvey with his interest in freedom struggles erupting across the African and Bandung worlds. Like his mother and father before him, the Muslim minister fearlessly stood up to white authorities and continued to embrace Garvey. This was evident in the case of Johnson Hinton, a Temple No. 7 member whom white police officers had jailed after viciously beating him on a Harlem street in April 1957. Malcolm secured Hinton's medical attention and release from a Harlem police station after the Muslim minister spontaneously confronted cops in the early morning with Fruit of Islam (FOI) at his side and thousands of angry Harlemites who gathered at the scene. Malcolm and the Nation won widespread respect and attention in Harlem for challenging the police and saving Hinton's life.[174] In August 1957, Malcolm spoke at a Marcus Garvey Day Celebration in Harlem sponsored by the United African Nationalist Movement. Acknowledging Garvey's importance to the ongoing African American freedom struggle, Malcolm railed against white supremacy and excoriated mainstream Black leaders as "puppets to the white man."[175] Malcolm's parents would have been proud.

In July 1958, Malcolm again spoke at the Marcus Garvey Day Celebration in Harlem, a massive outdoor rally at the intersection of 125th Street and Seventh Avenue, sponsored by the Universal African National Movement and the Marcus Garvey Day Committee. The event commemorated Marcus Garvey and honored Kwame Nkrumah during his US tour.[176] Speakers included Nkrumah, Malcolm X, Adam Clayton Powell, and Black nationalist Carlos Cooks.[177] Malcolm electrified the audience. Demanding the full freedom of Black people, he called on the crowd to identify not "as Republicans or Baptists but as black nationalists."[178] Given Nkrumah's respect for Garvey, the Ghanaian leader surely appreciated Malcolm's words. What is certain is that the event allowed Malcolm to interact with one of the world's foremost champions of Africa and the Bandung World.[179]

Malcolm's interest in the late 1950s in the emerging Third World was perhaps most apparent in his call at a Harlem community rally in April 1959 for a "Bandung Conference of Negro Leaders."[180] In his address, he praised African and Asian delegates at the 1955 Bandung Conference for "put[ting] aside religion and political differences" and for generating "sufficient force to break the bonds of colonialism, imperialism . . . [and] WHITE SUPREMACY." For him, the Bandung Conference served as a model for forging African American unity in pursuit of freedom.[181] His actions and words in Harlem speak to how he was connecting and reconfiguring the legacy of Garveyism with growing Black militancy in the United States and anticolonialism across the Bandung World.

While living and ministering in New York were critical to shaping Malcolm's ongoing political development and to raising his national profile within and beyond the NOI, so was speaking and spending time in the Midwest, especially Detroit. In the summer of 1957, he spent four weeks in the Motor City. During his extended stay there, he delivered several electrifying addresses before a packed Temple No. 1. Most people in attendance were not Muslims. Malcolm discussed the recent Hinton case and the Little Rock, Arkansas, public school desegregation crisis. Praising Elijah Muhammad for leading the "fastest-growing group of Freedom-seeking Black people in America today" and blasting civil rights leaders for their alleged timidity, Malcolm charged that the NOI provided the best vehicle for spiritual transformation and political freedom.[182] Given his childhood and adult lived experiences in Michigan, Malcolm was attuned to the dreams and nightmares of Black working-class Detroiters sick of persistent racism, joblessness, despair about deindustrializing Detroit, and white intransigence nationwide to desegregation. Malcolm's success in the Motor City, together with his five years of dedicated ministry, raised the NOI's national profile.[183]

Even though Malcolm spoke favorably of Garvey and the NOI bore his ideological influence, there were significant differences in beliefs and practices among the Nation, UNIA, and its spinoffs. Fundamentally, the NOI was a Black ethnic religious organization. The Nation called for racial separation and returning African Americans to Africa. However, the NOI, unlike the Garvey movement and the PME, never pursued concrete plans for emigration. Instead, Elijah Muhammad believed his divine mission was to lead the "Asiatic Black man" toward spiritual liberation, self-improvement, self-respect, discipline, community empowerment, and national identity through Islam. The NOI's organizational culture reflected these goals. The Nation was more hierarchical than the UNIA and "operated as a kind of military theocracy arranged along dictatorial lines."[184] Muhammad appointed all top leadership positions within the Nation and the principal officers within each NOI temple—ministers and captains. They attained their positions only through winning the complete trust of the Messenger and submitting to his wishes. These officials had to be members of the FOI and MGT-GCC. Temples (which were renamed mosques by 1963) were centers of NOI life. By 1959, the NOI operated perhaps thirty temples around the country. Temple No. 2 in Chicago counted the largest number of active members of about four hundred to six hundred believers, followed by Detroit, New York, Philadelphia, Washington, DC, and Los Angeles.[185]

NOI temples were busy places. They held required religious services three times a week. In addition to these services, the FOI and MGT-GCC held regular and mandatory programming inside and outside of temples throughout the week. Muslims regularly came together at NOI businesses, restaurants, and excursions. The Nation imposed a moral and social code on its members that was far more stringent than that of the UNIA and Moorish Science. The NOI often maintained strict gender separation at its events, discouraged its members from socializing with non-Muslims, and promoted a sense of superiority among its people bordering on conceit. Additionally, while the UNIA and other neo-Garveyite groups valued education and higher learning, the NOI was the only Black nationalist organization that established its own parochial schools.[186] Through the NOI's Black ethnic religious beliefs and distinct organizational culture, the group created a self-contained community of fervent followers fiercely loyal to the Messenger, whom they believed to be divine.

Even though Malcolm was at the forefront in advancing a more modern Black nationalism, he was still a member of an organization grounded in Black diasporic right radicalism. Many prospective followers found the Nation's beliefs bizarre and untenable. The NOI's staunch anticommunism and self-help philosophy prevented the group from forging a critical perspective on the linkages among racial oppression and capitalism.[187] His masculinism rooted him in the longer history of African-descended male spokespersons who understood Black freedom as synonymous with Black manhood redemption. A key part of the NOI's appeal rested in its ability to promote militant manhood and its success in transforming Black men beat down by racism into dignified and disciplined men.[188] Malcolm's sermons often called on Black men to serve as moral exemplars in their homes and communities and to provide and to protect African American women. Yet he promoted the NOI's heteropatriarchal position that "while a man must at all times respect his woman, at the same time he needs to understand that he must control her if he expects to get her respect."[189] He condemned lesbians as self-hating, pathological man-haters, and he often described women as naturally weak, deceitful, and domineering of men. After leaving the NOI, Malcolm admitted his misogyny earned him a reputation in the organization as "anti-woman."[190]

Although Malcolm and the NOI promoted militant manhood, Muslim women skillfully navigated the promise of patriarchy and found creative ways to assert their voices. Betty Shabazz's membership in the NOI and her marriage to Malcolm X speak to this truth. Myrlie Evers-Williams, the civil rights leader and widow of the slain NAACP official Medgar Evers, who came to know Shabazz years after Malcolm's assassination, described her dear friend as a "private woman . . . who was complex and yet simple in her wisdom."[191] These words powerfully captured Shabazz's brilliance and life journey, which, like her husband's life, also ended tragically. She died on June 23, 1997, from injuries sustained in a house fire accidentally ignited by her grandson, Malcolm.[192]

Like Louise Little, Betty Shabazz was more than a faithful wife and nurturing mother. She was Malcolm's intellectual partner, soulmate, and ally who made it possible for him to carry out his Black nationalist work. Born Betty Dean Sanders on May 28, 1934, in Pinehurst, Georgia, she migrated as a child to Detroit with her unwed working-class parents. At eleven, she was adopted by Lorenzo and Helen Malloy, a churchgoing, middle-class couple committed to racial uplift and respectability. She apparently was on the road toward a Black middle-class life when she enrolled in 1951 at her father's alma mater, the Tuskegee Institute in Alabama. But she felt suffocated living in Jim Crow Alabama. Given her frustrations and dreams, she transferred to the Tuskegee-affiliated Brooklyn State College of Nursing in New York in 1953. She graduated in 1955 and began working at the Montefiore Hospital in the Bronx.[193] Coming to New York forever changed Shabazz's life. She joined the NOI, becoming "Betty X" / "Sister Betty," met Malcolm, and married him in a civil ceremony in Lansing on January 12, 1958.[194]

Sister Betty was a devout Muslim and the wife of its most prominent minister. However, she did not blindly accept NOI doctrine or its promotion of patriarchy. Rather, she was a precocious young woman who thought critically about the Nation's strident call for racial separatism and women's subordination. She questioned these beliefs in a letter penned in October 1955 to a close female New York friend and fellow Muslim. Sister Betty was only twenty at the time. She wrote, "The minister stated that two things Allah would not forgive you for and that was 1. Eating pork 2. Indulging in copulation with a member of the devil race. So I was thinking in the car. What about socializing with them (e.g.) having coffee or tea with them . . . and participating in class projects like at the present my class."[195] Additionally, she noted that the unnamed minister, who most likely was her future husband, chastised her for socializing with her white colleagues and for not standing up to her parents who objected to her religious conversion. Privately, she took issue with the minister's rebuke. Noting that the minister "failed to realize that I am not self-supporting," she questioned his insensitivity to her plight and the practicality of the Nation's racial separatism as a young, single Black working woman. Given the patriarchal nature of the NOI, she apparently did not confront the minister. Instead, she shared this encounter only with her female confidante.[196] This would not be the last time that Sister Betty privately challenged male authority but publicly assumed the posture of a demure young woman.

Sister Betty's efforts to assert her independence in her marriage best illustrated the complex ways she navigated the male chauvinism of Malcolm and the NOI. Looking back four years after his assassination in 1965, Shabazz described her marriage as "hectic, beautiful, and unforgettable—the greatest thing in my life."[197] Keeping with NOI tenets about marriage and fearing being controlled by women, Malcolm could often be possessive and domineering of his wife. He objected to her aspirations to work outside of the house.[198] She hardly accepted his chauvinism. Looking back, she claimed: "The first time I told him what I expected of him as a husband, it came as a shock."[199] Over the course of her marriage, Sister Betty and Malcolm found a way to balance their respective needs and to forge a healthy marriage predicated on love, trust, and mutual respect.[200]

Sister Betty's journey into the NOI and marriage to Malcolm X shed light on the varied journeys of midwestern Black nationalist women during the 1950s. She shared much in common with Garveyite community feminists like Amy Jacques Garvey, Louise Little, Goldie Stewart, Elinor White Neely, and Lillie Mae Gibson. Like them, Sister Betty joined an organization steeped in patriarchy, married a man who embraced militant manhood, and cherished motherhood. At the same time, her life and outlook were different from those of her predecessors who came of age during the interwar years. She possessed a college degree, left her husband on multiple occasions, and desired to work outside of the home. In this respect, Sister Betty's outlook and life were more modern than her predecessors.

The 1950s marked an extraordinary moment for midwestern Black nationalism in the Garveyite tradition. Shifting racial formations in the deindustrializing urban Midwest, the emergent Civil Rights Movement, decolonization, and a global Cold War created the context in which Garveyism endured and transformed. Black nationalists from Chicago, Detroit, and Cleveland remained at the center of the transnational UNIA and midwestern Garveyite front years after Garvey's passing. The work and overseas journeying of James Stewart, Goldie Stewart, William Sherrill, and Lillie Mae Gibson forged concrete linkages between the heartland, Liberia, and Ghana. Garvey disciple Kwame Nkrumah mesmerized thousands of Black Chicagoans during his US tour. Grassroots cultural formations like the House of Knowledge celebrated Garvey. Moorish Science still captured the imaginations of thousands of working-class African Americans in the heartland and generated panic among the Black elite and the FBI. Goldie Stewart, Lillie Mae Gibson, and Elinor White Neely anchored the UNIA and promoted community feminism. At the same time, midwestern Garveyism underwent a profound transition in the late 1950s. An older generation of Garveyites, many of whom were born before the interwar years and whose politics reflected an earlier time, was no longer at the forefront of Black nationalism. James Stewart lived in Liberia. William Sherrill had passed away. The Nation of Islam filled this vacuum. By the late 1950s, the NOI emerged as the fastest-growing US Black nationalist organization, due in part to Malcolm X. His conversion to Islam and rising stardom in the Nation, shaped by his Garveyite roots and interest in the Bandung World, propelled his revolutionary Black nationalism. Betty Shabazz's religious conversion and marriage to Malcolm reveal the complicated ways Muslim women negotiated the promise of patriarchy.

As the 1960s dawned, a new generation of Black Americans shaped by the burgeoning Civil Rights Movement, Bandung World, and global Cold War looked beyond the PME, MSTA, and the UNIA. For these young people, the NOI, Malcolm X, and early Black Power formations in the heartland were their answer. These movements signaled once again the Diasporic Midwest as a hot spot in producing some of the most influential and radical movements in the Black world where the ghost of Garvey lived on.

6

"MESSAGE TO THE GRASS ROOTS"

The Nation of Islam, Malcolm X, and Early Black Power

Just as it took nationalism to remove colonialism from Asia and Africa, it'll take black nationalism today to remove colonialism from the backs and the minds of twenty-two million Afro-Americans in this country. —MALCOLM X, "The Ballot or the Bullet," speech delivered in Detroit, Michigan, April 12, 1964

It was January 23, 1963. Malcolm X was back home in Michigan. More than one thousand people packed the Erickson Kiva at Michigan State University in East Lansing to hear the dynamic Muslim minister and former Lansing resident speak. The university's chapter of the NAACP and the African Students Association had invited him to campus. The title of his provocative speech was "The Race Problem in America."[1] He did not disappoint his audience. He argued that the NOI, led by Elijah Muhammad, constituted the "fastest growing religious movement—among black people anywhere in the Western Hemisphere." Emphasizing Muhammad's position that racial "separation [was] our only solution," Malcolm argued that integration with white America was a fool's errand. Instead, he pointed to the Bandung Conference as the model for advancing Black American racial unity and freedom.[2] Through eloquently framing African American freedom in global terms, his speech connected his midwestern audience to the Bandung World. His talk evidenced his embrace of militant manhood, long upheld by Black nationalists. He exclaimed: "The only time the [race] problem is going to be solved is when a Black man can sit down like a Black man and a white man can sit down like a white man." Ridiculing Martin Luther King Jr. and other civil rights leaders as "twentieth-century Uncle Tom[s]," Malcolm called for self-defense.[3] His speech was personally meaningful. He recounted his childhood encounters in East Lansing with virulent racism. Illustrating his enduring connections to his Michigan family, Robert Little, Malcolm's youngest sibling who was a graduate student at Michigan State at the time, attended the talk. It was their first reunion in many years.[4]

Malcolm's Michigan State talk is significant for several reasons. The invitation for him to speak on campus affirmed his national prominence within the NOI and beyond as a leading US Black nationalist spokesperson. In September 1963, Elijah Muhammad appointed Malcolm as the National Representative of the NOI, making him the second highest official in the organization. At the same time, 1963 saw his growing political independence from the Nation. By this year, his speeches before non-Muslim audiences offered only perfunctory acknowledgment of Elijah Muhammad and focused more on politics and nonreligious matters. Additionally, his Michigan State address speaks to the continued and growing significance of the Midwest as a political terrain in shaping his ongoing political journey. His encounters in the final years of his life with militants of color either based in or with close ties to mid-America were critical to shaping his burgeoning revolutionary Black nationalism. Globally oriented, his revolutionary Black nationalism championed grassroots activism, mass action, decolonization, anti-imperialism, anticapitalism, armed self-defense, human rights, and Third Worldism—a politics foundational to the Black Power Movement of the 1960s and 1970s.[5]

Finally, Malcolm's Michigan State speech and growing national prominence reveal broader transformations within the long trajectory of Garveyism and the US Black Freedom Movement during the early 1960s. By 1963, the Chicago-based Nation of Islam was the preeminent Garveyite offshoot in the United States. Malcolm's charisma and hard work contributed to the NOI's meteoric growth and to the rise of early Black Power (see figure 6.1). While the Nation and Malcolm galvanized early Black Power organizations, there were significant political differences between the NOI and new Black nationalist formations. Mirroring Malcolm's move toward revolutionary Black nationalism before and following his official break from the Nation in March 1964, young Black midwestern militants promoted a politics that spurned many key components of Black diasporic right radicalism. Young Black militants also rejected the Nation's official position of nonpolitical intervention.

The prevailing coastal orientation of scholarship on the Black nationalist presence in the postwar US Black Freedom Movement has obscured the critical importance of the heartland in shaping the Civil Rights and early Black Power Movements in the late 1950s and early 1960s. The Nation and Malcolm, as well as early Black Power heartland-based militants and formations either based in or closely connected with Chicago, Detroit, and Cleveland—the Afro-American Institute (AAI), Group on Advanced Leadership (GOAL), Freedom Now Party, UHURU, the Congress for Racial Equality (CORE), Revolutionary Action Movement (RAM), and National Afro-American Organization—should be understood as constituent parts of the midwestern Garveyite front. These groups affirm a trend that had been developing for years. By the early 1960s, the Nation, Malcolm, and new midwestern Garveyite formations were at the vanguard in advancing Garveyism. The bulk of Black people in these groups came of age long after Garvey's heyday and never joined the UNIA. Still, they looked to Garvey as the progenitor of the twentieth-century global Black freedom struggle. At the same time, the NOI, Malcolm, and early Black Power militants looked to the Bandung World and the contemporary historical moment for inspiration. Subsequently, they refashioned Garveyism through adopting revolutionary Black nationalism; building vibrant, autonomous institutions; and cultivating ties of political solidarity with Africa and the Third World. Women played a pivotal role in building these heartland-connected Black movements, even as they grappled with sexism and masculine leadership. Tracing this history reveals the transformations, possibilities, and limitations of Garvey-inspired Black movements, and the continued importance of the Diasporic Midwest as a generative site and crossroads of Black transnational politics during a pivotal moment in the US Black Freedom Movement and global decolonization.

The NOI, Malcolm, and heartland-linked early Black Power groups forged their politics at a turning point in the postwar US Black Freedom Movement. Both the beginning of the "sit-in movement" across the South and the formation of the Student Non-Violent Coordinating Committee (SNCC) were in 1960. In 1961, CORE sponsored Freedom Rides, bus trips through the South led by groups of young Black and white civil rights activists committed to desegregating interstate public transportation. In the same year, Robert F. Williams, the militant head of the NAACP local in Monroe, North Carolina, who advocated armed Black self-defense, made international headlines when he and his wife, Mabel, absconded to Cuba to dodge arrest by the FBI.[6] The pace of the Civil Rights Movement accelerated in the spring of 1963 when thousands of African Americans, including children, heeded Martin Luther King's summons and took to the streets of Birmingham, Alabama, to protest Jim Crow. Growing

FIGURE 6.1. Photographs of Malcolm X and Betty Shabazz, Malcolm X College, Chicago, Illinois, November 2023. Photo by the author.

nationwide African American insurgence led to the famous March on Washington for Jobs and Freedom on August 23, 1963. The year 1964 marked a milestone in the US Black Freedom Movement. President Lyndon B. Johnson signed the landmark Civil Rights Act of 1964, which prohibited segregation in public accommodations and discrimination on the basis of race, color, religion, and sex. In 1965, Congress passed the Voting Rights Act, outlawing discriminatory voting practices across the South. Despite important legislative victories against de jure segregation, US racial oppression stubbornly persisted. In 1964, Black uprisings exploded in Harlem, Philadelphia, and Rochester, New York. Poor housing, unemployment, underfunded schools, police brutality, economic inequalities, persistent white racism, and growing Black militancy triggered this unrest.[7]

The early 1960s US Black Freedom Movement unfolded as the pace of global decolonization accelerated. In 1958, the People's Republic of China launched the Great Leap Forward, an ambitious plan to industrialize the communist nation.[8] The following year, the Cuban Revolution led by Fidel

Castro overthrew the US-backed dictator Fulgencio Batista and began moving the Caribbean nation toward socialism.[9] The Caribbean saw the establishment in 1958 of the short-lived West Indian Federation, a union of nine British Caribbean colonies that sought to gain independence as one sovereign nation. The federation collapsed due to internal divisions in 1962, but in the same year, Jamaica and Trinidad won their independence from Great Britain.[10] The United Nations designated 1960 as the "Year of Africa," as more than seventeen African nations gained their independence from European colonial powers.[11] Political independence, however, hardly freed Africa. South Africa's Apartheid regime became even more ruthless in its suppression of the country's nonwhite populations.[12] The Congo Crisis of 1960–1961 constituted a major global Cold War conflict on the continent. In January 1961, a US and Belgium–backed secessionist movement assassinated Patrice Lumumba, the democratically elected pan-African premier of the newly independent resource-rich Democratic Republic of Congo. His murder outraged African people around the world.[13] It was within this historical moment in which the UNIA—and other Black nationalist groups in the Garveyite tradition—carried out their work and linked the Diasporic Midwest to the global world.

The Ascendance of the NOI and Malcolm X

In a testament to the continued importance of the Midwest as a nexus of Black resistance and transnational politics, the NOI emerged by the late 1950s as the largest African American Muslim and Black nationalist organization in the United States. Contemporary outside observers diverged widely on the size of the group's membership, with estimates ranging from 10,000 to 250,000 members nationwide by the early 1960s. NOI officials claimed that the organization counted between five thousand and fifteen thousand registered members. The NOI counted more than fifty mosques across twenty-two states and US cities.[14] Large NOI rallies regularly drew thousands of people, many of whom were not Muslim. Major Black newspapers like the *Pittsburgh Courier* ran columns by Elijah Muhammad.[15] Like in the 1930s, most new NOI members were working-class men, who outnumbered women by 4 to 1. Male converts were often born in the North and raised by parents who hailed from the Deep South or the Caribbean. For these men, the Nation's apparent success in transforming its members' personal and spiritual lives remained a powerful draw. The NOI also saw an infusion of middle-class professionals, who joined the Nation beginning in the late 1950s in search of upward mobility through the organization's commercial enterprises.[16]

Scholars have long credited Malcolm for playing a key role in the Nation's phenomenal growth and for articulating the aspirations and nightmares of the Black masses in the urban North disaffected by the Civil Rights Movement and persistent racial oppression. Certainly, there is truth in these claims. However, the NOI's underappreciated effort in connecting itself to the legacy of Garvey and the long history of Black nationalism also helps explain the Nation's unprecedented growth in the early 1960s. By embracing and reconfiguring new and older forms of Black nationalism, the Nation positioned itself at the front lines of the Black freedom struggle and linked the Diasporic Midwest to the African and Bandung worlds. At the same time, these years saw a growing ideological divide between the Black diasporic right radicalism of Elijah Muhammad and the burgeoning revolutionary Black nationalism of Malcolm. The Nation's politics revealed the long-standing challenges that had bedeviled Black nationalists since the pre–Civil War years—masculinism, civilizationism, and collaborations with white racists.

The NOI's commitment to race pride, racial autonomy, self-help, territorial separation, self-defense, entrepreneurialism, institution-building, and internationalism shows the undeniable influence of Garvey and the UNIA on the Nation. Contemporary observers and NOI officials were quick to acknowledge these historical linkages. This fact is evident in Elijah Muhammad's most widely read book, *The Message to the Blackman in America*. Published in 1965, the book compiled the Messenger's teachings about religion, race, self-help, white supremacy, clean living, and freedom.[17] The book's foreword, "The Truth about Muhammad" by Black Chicago journalist Daniel Burley, framed Elijah Muhammad as the direct heir of Marcus Garvey. In the foreword's opening paragraph, Burley asserted: "It has been more than 40 years since a Negro has appeared on the national horizon of racial leadership with a program for his people as controversial and as clear cut as that of Elijah Muhammad's."[18] "Not since the days of Marcus Garvey" had African Americans been so electrified by a Black leader, who "like Marcus Garvey . . . is building his Religious group on a nonwhite basis and like Garvey has irrefutable reasons for excluding whites."[19] The Messenger's success, Burley added, rested in his uncompromising denouncement of white supremacy, as well as his ability, reminiscent of Garvey, to build an independent organization committed to advancing "race solidarity and unity."[20] The book's title—*Message to the Blackman in America*—invoked a masculinist understanding of African American freedom, a politics espoused by Garvey and Black nationalists long before him. Burley stressed that Muhammad "stirs up the masses in a way no one since the heyday of Marcus Garvey had done in telling them to stand up and be men!"[21] Muhammad neither mentioned his membership in the interwar UNIA nor referenced Garvey in the book's body chapters. However, the direct comparisons between Garvey and Muhammad in the book's foreword clearly show that the Messenger sought to position himself as the undisputed leader of Black America and as Garvey's successor.[22] At the same time, *Message to the Blackman in America* articulated a path toward freedom that diverged from Garvey. Drawing from the Nation's distinct religious beliefs and inspired by the whirlwind of global events of the early 1960s, Muhammad charged that only Islam and racial separation to a location in the United States, not emigration to Africa, would free "22 million" African Americans from the "devil race."[23]

The NOI's success in building long-lasting institutions best reflected the organization's connections to the Garvey movement and the long history of heartland Black nationalism. In 1957, the NOI purchased buildings for its new national headquarters, Mosque No. 2, and the University of Islam at 5333 S. Greenwood Ave. on the South Side of Chicago. In keeping with the organization's faith in Black capitalism and in the entrepreneurial spirit of Garvey, Mosque No. 2 operated a restaurant, bakery, grocery store, laundry, and auto repair shop. The memory of Garvey lived on in the Nation of Islam's newspaper, *Muhammad Speaks*. Spearheaded by Malcolm in 1961 and published in Chicago, the newspaper was one of the most militant Black American periodicals of its day and one of the best-known and longest-lasting NOI institutions. Within one year of its founding, the paper claimed a circulation of over 360,000 issues with more than 1.4 million readers, making it the most widely read Black nationalist newspaper since Garvey's *Negro World*.[24] *Muhammad Speaks* reflected a new militancy among African Americans in the early 1960s. With its masthead stating "Dedicated to Freedom, Justice, and Equality for the so-called Negro. The Earth Belongs to Allah," the newspaper positioned the NOI at the vanguard of the global Black freedom struggle. *Muhammad Speaks* covered breaking national news about civil rights, anti-Black racial violence, and electoral politics, and some of the most extensive reporting in the United States about Africa and the Bandung World. In contrast to the classical Black nationalist framings of global affairs still espoused by the UNIA and PME, *Muhammad Speaks* regularly ran articles that looked to Africa and the Third World as fulcrums of global transformative change.[25] Curiously, the newspaper's keen interest in Africa and the Bandung World contrasted with Elijah Muhammad's ambivalence toward the continent. In keeping with the teachings of W. D. Fard Muhammad, Elijah Muhammad continued to frame Black Americans as an "Asiatic" people whose ancestral home was Mecca. Given this perspective, *Message to the Blackman* did not contain explicit references to contemporary

African independence movements or to African Indigenous cultures. This tension within the Nation concerning African Americans' political and historical linkages to Africa helped to precipitate Malcolm's break from the NOI.

While scholars have correctly observed the cutting-edge Black internationalism featured in *Muhammad Speaks*, they have devoted less attention to the ways the newspaper connected the Nation and the early 1960s US Black freedom struggle with Garvey. In a January 1962 article, "Garvey Revisited," the newspaper asserted that "race conscious young Negroes" of the contemporary moment idolized Garvey for building a militant mass movement for African liberation.[26] The newspaper published a letter by Amy Ashwood Garvey from Liberia in which she praised Elijah Muhammad for leading a Black mass organization and for expressing "tremendous interest and love for Africa" in the spirit of Marcus Garvey.[27] In 1964, *Muhammad Speaks* celebrated the return of Garvey's remains from the United Kingdom to Jamaica.[28] In the same year, the newspaper published a letter from a Nation member, who had proudly joined the UNIA in the 1920s and who now lauded Elijah Muhammad as the "greatest" Black leader of all time.[29] For this veteran Garveyite, the Messenger and the NOI constituted the living embodiment of Garvey.

Like *Negro World*, *Muhammad Speaks* articulated Black freedom in highly gendered terms.[30] The paper regularly ran articles that equated the struggle for African American freedom with the redemption of Black manhood. Echoing the UNIA and MSTA, *Muhammad Speaks* extolled Black women's beauty, called for their protection, identified them as the "mother[s] of civilization," and featured articles related to women's domestic responsibilities as mothers and wives.[31] The newspaper reported the work and international travels of NOI female leaders like Clara Muhammad, her daughter Ethel Sharrieff, Christine Johnson, and Tynnetta Deanar. Nation women claimed a voice through *Muhammad Speaks*. The paper featured a regular column named "Women in Islam" by Tynnetta Deanar of Detroit, a young fervent follower of Elijah Muhammad.[32] Resembling Amy Jacques Garvey's "Our Women and What They Think" column of the 1920s, Deanar's "Women in Islam" featured articles about Muslim women's determined work in building the Nation, Elijah Muhammad's teachers, and Black women's feminine humility, beauty, and grace.[33] Her column did not mention Jacques Garvey or the UNIA. Still, Deanar's writings followed in Jacques Garvey's footsteps.

Meanwhile, the UOI, the Nation-operated elementary and parochial secondary schools founded in 1934, constituted another important site where the NOI found success in the 1960s in extending, reconfiguring, and advancing Black nationalism and to linking Black midwestern urban communities with people of color globally. In a testament to the Nation's growth, the NOI by the early 1960s operated eight UOI schools across the United States, with the two largest campuses in Chicago and Detroit. The Chicago UOI, the Nation's flagship school, counted 437 elementary and high school students and eight teachers in 1962. Most students hailed from working-class migrant families registered in the Nation. The UOI instilled NOI values of self-discipline, hard work, and self-reliance and offered a unique transnational space for connecting the school to Africa, global Islam, and the Bandung World. The Chicago UOI taught Arabic. Beginning in the 1950s, foreign guests from Muslim nations and the Third World regularly visited the school. The school celebrated independent nations in Asia and Africa.[34]

Women were critical to the success of the Chicago UOI in the early 1960s, most notably Christine C. Johnson. Commonly known in the Nation as Sister Christine, she was a dynamic educator, journalist, author, community activist, and globetrotter originally from Kentucky who made her way to Detroit and Chicago. She served as director and principal of the Chicago UOI from 1961 to 1965.[35] Her early life encounters in the Jim Crow South, combined with her adult experiences with racism and sexism as a Chicago public school teacher, led her to the Nation by the late 1950s.[36] Her directorship of the Chicago UOI stands as her most important work on behalf of the Nation. On her watch, the Chicago UOI's reputation as the NOI's premier school soared. Her work stretched far beyond the Chicago UOI's campus through her textbook *Muhammad's Children: A First Grade Reader*. Published in 1963 by the Nation, the book was pioneering in the history of African American education.[37] The book's title acknowledged the spiritual and intellectual debt she believed NOI members owed to the Messenger. She used lessons in phonics and grammar, as well as biographical sketches of famous Black people and information about Africa, to teach "self-love" and "self-respect."[38] *Muhammad's Children* made no explicit reference to Garvey. However, the book contained a biographical sketch of Kwame Nkrumah and included information about his historic 1958 trip to Chicago.[39] The book evidenced the long-held Black nationalist belief in the transformative power of race pride, self-knowledge, and global awareness to liberating Black people.

Sister Christine's work on behalf of the NOI speaks to the way Muslim women like her proffered new constructions of Black womanhood informed by developments across the Bandung World that anticipated new ideas about women, gender, and freedom during the Black Power era. According to historian Ashley Farmer, Black Power women forged four new tropes of womanhood—the "Revolutionary Black Woman," "African Woman," "Pan African Woman," and

"Third World Black Woman"—that challenged patriarchy, reimagined Black women's subjectivities, and promoted social justice on a global scale.[40] Sister Christine's work and subjectivity embodied all these tropes. A powerful orator, she won the respect of Elijah Muhammad and Malcolm and emerged as a national spokesperson for the Nation.[41] Her journalism in *Muhammad Speaks* emphasized the importance of Muslim women to advancing Black freedom globally.[42] Outside of the Nation, Sister Christine's commitment to African American public history and Black freedom evinced the "Revolutionary Black Woman." In 1958, she formed the Chicago-based African American Heritage Association (AAHA) with prominent South Side Communist Party leader Ishmael Flory and Margaret Burroughs. The AAHA sought to advance Black freedom, locally and globally, through celebrating Black public history.[43] Like the "African Woman," "Pan African Woman," and "Third World Black Woman" of the 1970s, Sister Christine centered Africa to her work.[44] Johnson visited the continent several times, but one of her most important visits occurred in June 1962, when she attended the Accra Assembly: The World Without the Bomb, held in Ghana. Delegates from Africa, Latin America, Europe, and the United States gathered for this weeklong peace conference.[45] While in Ghana, she conferred with Nkrumah. The conference placed her at the center of the global peace movement.[46] Personally, Sister Christine's decision to travel overseas unaccompanied by a husband was a transgressive move.[47] She occasionally went unveiled and wore African-styled clothing when most Black Americans were ashamed or ignorant about their ancestral homeland.[48] Through defying the Nation's dress code and gender protocols, she forged a multifaceted diasporic identity that openly embraced Africa, Islam, and the Bandung World and that claimed women's importance to advancing Black self-determination. Sister Christine was in many respects exceptional within the NOI. Nonetheless, her transnational activism and subjectivity illustrate how some women forged a cutting-edge transnational Black feminism within the patriarchal Nation.[49]

As much as Sister Christine forged new constructions of Black womanhood, her gender politics shared much in common with the community feminism of Amy Jacques Garvey, Bessie Bryce, Louise Little, and Goldie Stewart. Like her predecessors, Sister Christine embraced the idea that women's "natural" roles as wives and mothers best prepared them to build a nation. At the same time, her work illustrated generational differences among Black nationalist women. Her politics and deportment were more modern than those of older Black nationalist women such as Amy Jacques Garvey and Goldie Stewart. Sister Christine's gender politics also differed from those of prominent Nation women like Clara Muhammad, Ethel Sharrieff, and Tynnetta Deanar. They always wore veils and long white dresses in public, underscoring the varied ways NOI female members practiced Black womanhood. Despite differences among Black nationalist women in the UNIA and NOI, all operated within organizations in which men had the last word.[50] So while the 1960s Nation called for Black women's protection and produced female spokespersons like Clara Muhammad, Ethel Sharrieff, Tynnetta Deanar, and Sister Christine, the NOI simultaneously promoted women's subordination to men within the group.

The paradox of the NOI's treatment of women was most evident in the organization's silence around Elijah Muhammad's infidelity and sexual predatory behavior. By the early 1960s, it was an open secret among Nation officials and Muhammad's family that the Messenger had fathered numerous children with several of his underage secretaries. Malcolm recalled hearing rumors about Muhammad's extramarital sexual relations with young women as early as 1955, though Malcolm remained silent on the matter prior to his split from the NOI.[51] However, his disgust with Muhammad stemmed not from the Messenger's sexual infidelity per se, but from his apparent evasion of fatherly responsibilities. Malcolm's twisted patriarchal logic and staunch loyalty to Muhammad prevented him from fully grasping the depth of his actions and from publicly denouncing him prior to 1964.[52] Muhammad's sexual transgressions were part of a long history of sexual misconduct conducted by Black nationalist male leaders.

Patriarchy was not the only long-standing paradox within the early 1960s NOI. Like Edward Wilmot Blyden, Marcus Garvey, Mittie Maude Lena Gordon, and James Stewart, Malcolm and other Nation leaders collaborated in the early 1960s with white supremacists, most notably George Lincoln Rockwell, the leader of the American Nazi Party. A native of Bloomington, Illinois, and the father of American Nazism, he was vocally racist, antisemitic, and homophobic.[53] Despite his virulent racism, the NOI and Rockwell found common ground through their shared belief in racial separatism. The Nation hoped to form a Black nationalist–white supremacist united front with the American Nazi Party. Given these goals, the Nation invited Rockwell to attend a large NOI rally in Washington, DC, on July 25, 1961. He and ten stormtroopers dressed in swastika armbands attended the meeting as special guests. Malcolm presided over the rally and thanked the American Nazis for coming. They received tepid applause from the audience after Malcolm's introduction, suggesting that many rank-and-file Muslims were uncomfortable with the presence of Nazis and with the NOI collaborating with white racists.[54] This rally was not the first time Malcolm had associated with white supremacists. Per the instructions of Elijah Muhammad, Malcolm secretly conferred with KKK officials in

January 1961 in Atlanta. The meeting led to a tacit agreement between the NOI and KKK that the latter would not interfere with Muslims in the South.[55]

Malcolm's meeting with Klan leaders must be understood within the longue durée of Black nationalism. Like Garvey and other Black nationalists who sat down with white supremacists, Malcolm believed that it made sense to collaborate with them.[56] Following his break from the NOI, he regretted meeting with the Klan. For him, the Nation's collaborations with white supremacists evidenced the political and moral bankruptcy of Elijah Muhammad.[57]

Even as Malcolm embraced some of the Nation's most reactionary views, his revolutionary nationalism grew. In July 1959, he took his first trip to Africa and the Middle East, visiting Saudi Arabia, Egypt, Sudan, Nigeria, and Ghana as Elijah Muhammad's emissary.[58] The three-week trip transformed Malcolm's political vision. Through his encounters overseas, he became even more committed to forging concrete ties of political solidarity between Black America and the Bandung World.[59] In 1960, he met Cuban revolutionary leader Fidel Castro when he came to New York and spoke at the United Nations.[60] Malcolm's evolving global perspective enabled him to see Black Americans as a colonized people within the United States in solidarity with anticolonial struggles across the emerging Third World.[61]

If Malcolm's tireless work on behalf of the NOI brought him growing attention within the NOI, then his work also brought increased government security.[62] The FBI's surveillance file on the Nation and its leadership grew exponentially after 1959, as the bureau accumulated thousands of pages on the activities of the Nation, Muhammad, and Malcolm. Files detailed information about Muhammad's and Malcolm's family backgrounds, ministries, speaking engagements, domestic and international travel, and family lives, while reports on the NOI recorded information about its organizational history, membership, religious beliefs, program, businesses, and property holdings. Records also noted the historical connections between the UNIA of the 1920s and the contemporary NOI. In Chicago, the notorious Red Squad, a unit of Chicago's police department that used overt and covert tactics for surveilling and repressing Black Power, civil rights, leftist, religious, and labor organizations, surveilled the Nation.[63] The Red Squad compiled detailed information about the activities of Muhammad, Malcolm, Sister Christine, and other NOI officials; the property holdings of Mosque No. 2 and the size of its membership; and the University of Islam.[64] Similar to the conclusions authorities drew about civil rights leaders like Martin Luther King, Chicago cops and the FBI dismissed the Nation's legitimate grievances with US racism and the organization's separatist program as a subversive Soviet-inspired plot to overthrow white America. State actors misunderstood the NOI's aims. But they were correct in acknowledging the Nation's phenomenal growth and rising political influence among African Americans, especially in the urban North. Authorities also got it right by recognizing Malcolm's importance within and far beyond the Nation.

Malcolm and Early Black Power in Detroit and Cleveland

As the NOI enjoyed unprecedented growth by the early 1960s, Black militancy also took root in several trailblazing early Black Power groups either based or with strong support in Detroit and Cleveland. Early Black Power radicals in the heartland wanted nothing to do with mainstream civil rights liberalism, nonviolence, and integration. They wanted revolution. They saw themselves as the ideological descendants of Marcus Garvey and Elijah Muhammad. However, these young Black militants had no time for Garvey's and Muhammad's Black diasporic right radicalism. Instead, early Black Power militants forged a radical politics in line with the latest political currents flowing across the African and Bandung worlds. For this reason, they looked to Malcolm for revolutionary inspiration and as their most gifted spokesperson. At the same time, a multigenerational community of midwestern militants of color played an important role in radicalizing him.[65] These mutually informative relationships reveal the importance of Garveyism and Malcolm to early Black Power and to the region's continuing importance as a generative site of Black nationalism, internationalism, and radicalism. These political encounters, critical to facilitating his departure from the Nation, are absent in the *Autobiography* and from most accounts of his life.

Detroit, due to its distinct racial landscape, together with the city's long history of Black nationalism, militant Black trade unionism, and leftist organizing, offered Malcolm a receptive space for his burgeoning revolutionary Black nationalism.[66] He formulated this politics as the city experienced ongoing racial, political, and economic transformations. In 1960, the city's Black population swelled to 482,229, or nearly 29 percent of the city's 1.7 million residents.[67] African American political power in the city increased through local electoral politics and civil rights activity. Still, life remained extremely hard for most Black Detroiters in the early 1960s. Police brutality, poor housing, residential segregation, and deindustrialization immiserated substantial portions of Black Detroit. Black precarity in Detroit, combined with national and global developments, propelled Black protest in the city. Detroit was the site of the Walk to Freedom, a mass march led by Martin Luther King and local civil rights leaders that drew an estimated 125,000 people on June 23, 1963. The protest was the largest civil rights demonstration in US history at the time and the precursor to the March on Washington.[68]

As civil rights enjoyed strong support in Black Detroit, a dynamic group of early Black Power radicals in the Motor City forged mutually informative political ties with Malcolm.[69] At the center of this community were James (Jimmy) Boggs and Grace Lee Boggs. Jimmy was an African American auto-worker, labor activist, author, and autodidact, who was at the cutting edge of theorizing on the impact of deindustrialization, automation, and corporate unionism on African American life and working-class militancy. Grace was a Chinese American philosopher, author, and community organizer.[70] By 1963, the Boggses' living room in their home at 3061 Field Street became a popular hangout for militants from the Motor City and across the country, including Max Stanford and Don Freeman of the Revolutionary Action Movement; and Richard and Henry Milton of the Detroit-based Group on Advanced Leadership and Freedom Now Party, who later founded the Republic of New Afrika. Intense conversations about socialism, colonialism, armed struggle, decolonization, and the meaning of freedom often lasted late into the night in that living room. Malcolm's brother Wilfred, who still headed Mosque No. 1, was a regular at the Boggs home.[71] It was through Wilfred that Malcolm met the Boggses. Neither Grace nor Jimmy joined the Nation. But Grace was impressed with how the Nation initiated a process of cognitive liberation among the group's working-class faithful.[72] In addition, the Boggses worked closely with Reverend Albert B. Cleage, the militant pastor of the Central Congregational Church, later renamed the Shrine of the Black Madonna.[73]

Veteran Garveyites, together with the day-to-day experiences of Black Detroit autoworkers on the shop floor, played an important role in the late 1950s and early 1960s in radicalizing young Black militants who embraced Malcolm and who went on to become leading figures in Black Power. General Baker best fits this claim. A brilliant labor leader and organic intellectual, he is best known as a cofounder of the Detroit-based League of Revolutionary Black Workers founded in 1968. Born Gordon G. Baker Jr. in 1941 in Detroit to Georgia migrants, his entire life was inextricably shaped by the city's automobile industry. He took his first automobile factory job in 1958. Outside of the factory, he became involved in student activism while enrolled at Highland Park Community College in Highland Park, Michigan, an industrial suburb surrounded almost entirely by Detroit. At college, he joined the local NAACP and became aware of the Nation of Islam. He neither converted to Islam nor joined the Nation. However, he regularly attended Mosque No. 1 and befriended Wilfred X. Through Baker's encounters with Black nationalists, he came to identify himself as a Garveyite. For him, Garveyism constituted a powerful vision for Black self-determination and a link to the Black past.[74]

Working in Detroit auto plants bolstered Baker's nascent radicalism and interest in Garveyism. In 1963, he took a job in the Tool and Die Building at the massive River Rouge factory. The foundry was the site of the worst and most dangerous jobs in the plant and a preserve of African American workers due to the racism of white management and racially discriminatory rules regarding union seniority. Working in the foundry offered him keen insight into the horrific and exploitative working conditions facing Black auto laborers. The foundry also introduced him to longtime Detroit UNIA members, many of whom had toiled in the plant for decades. They recounted to him the UNIA's glory days. Despite his interest in Garvey, Baker never joined the UNIA. Old school Black nationalists, he believed, did not sufficiently engage in direct action. Still, he cherished what they taught him.[75]

By the early 1960s, Baker shed his Garveyite politics for revolutionary nationalism. Matriculating at Wayne State University, a public university near downtown Detroit and a cauldron of student activism, transformed his politics. In 1963, he cofounded the Black Marxist student group UHURU ("freedom" in Swahili). Baker and several UHURU members, including future League of Revolutionary Black Workers leaders Luke Tripp, Kenneth Cockrel, and John Watson, regularly frequented the Boggses' home. They also admired Malcolm for his outspoken opposition to racism, colonialism, and US imperialism.[76] Baker never met Malcolm. But Baker heard Malcolm deliver his famous "Message to the Grass Roots" speech in Detroit.[77]

Cleveland was a hub of the northern Civil Rights Movement and early Black Power. The Forest City, like other midwestern industrial cities, witnessed significant economic and racial shifts from the late 1950s onward. Cleveland's overall population decreased from 914,808 in 1950 to 810,858 in 1965, with more than 240,000 whites exiting the city for exclusively white suburbs. Cleveland's Black population increased from 147,847 in 1950 to 279,352 in 1965, accounting for 34.4 percent of the city's population. By 1965, 99 percent of Blacks lived in highly segregated neighborhoods on the city's east side.[78] Black Clevelanders fought back against second-class citizenship as they had since the antebellum era. On May 14, 1963, more than fifteen thousand people packed Cleveland's Cory Methodist Episcopal Church and filled the streets around it to hear Martin Luther King speak in the aftermath of the massive civil rights protests in Birmingham. His speech was the largest civil rights gathering in Cleveland's history. Perhaps there were people in the crowd who remembered when Marcus Garvey spoke decades earlier at the city's legendary Black church.[79]

Cleveland was home to nationally influential early Black Power groups who looked to Malcolm and Garvey for revolutionary inspiration.[80] No Cleveland Black radical was closer to Malcolm than Donald (Don) Freeman. A writer, teacher, theorist, organizer, and jazz enthusiast, whose involvement in radical movements would span more than seven decades, he stands as one of the most important figures in Black Power (see figure 6.2). He embodied a new generation of Midwest-linked Black radicals inspired by the Bandung World who embraced Garvey as a symbol of global Black freedom but who also pursued revolutionary nationalism. Freeman was born in Cleveland in 1939 and raised in public housing, and his working-class parents held unionized factory jobs. His political awakening began when he matriculated in 1957 at Western Reserve University in Cleveland. In 1958, he discovered Richard Wright's *The Color Curtain*. The book sparked Freeman's interest in global decolonization, as well as in W. E. B. Du Bois. Freeman became interested in Garvey while writing a paper in a political science class in 1959 on the independence movement in Nigeria. The paper led Freeman to Nnamdi Azikiwe and then to his inspiration: Marcus Garvey. Through writing on Nigeria and Azikiwe, Freeman came to appreciate the significance of Garvey to twentieth-century African liberation. Freeman's growing interest in Garvey, together with reading writings by Du Bois, Wright, and V. I. Lenin, led him to join the Western Reserve University's NAACP chapter, as well as the predominantly white Young People's Socialist League and Students for a Democratic Society. After graduating from college in 1961, he worked as a social studies teacher in a Central Area middle school. Like Christine Johnson, Freeman saw teaching Black youth as an important way of promoting Black liberation.[81]

Nineteen sixty-two marked a key year in Freeman's radicalization. In that year, he met Malcolm X for the first of five times.[82] Additionally, Freeman read Harold Cruse's influential 1962 essay "Revolutionary Nationalism and the Afro-American," which framed Black America as a domestic colony and the Black freedom struggle as the revolutionary force within the United States.[83] Ready to change the world, Freeman organized the Afro-American Institute (AAI) in October 1962. The first organization of its kind in Cleveland and one of the first early Black Power groups nationwide, the short-lived AAI forged a revolutionary Black nationalism by combining the pan-Africanism of Marcus Garvey with the socialism of Du Bois. The AAI counted around one hundred members in Cleveland.[84] Envisioning itself as a "vanguard" in the Black Freedom struggle, the AAI "embrace[d] the dynamic conception of Pan-Africanism encompassing the freedom movements of Africa and Afro-America . . . [as] . . . inextricably linked," Freeman wrote in an essay "The Cleveland Story" (1963),

FIGURE 6.2. Longtime Midwest-linked Black radicals Don Freeman, Norma Jean Freeman, and Muhammad Ahmad (Maxwell Stanford Jr.), Association for the Study of African American Life and History conference, Cincinnati, Ohio, September 2017. Photo by the author.

published in *The Liberator*, an influential early Black Power magazine based in New York.[85] Given this perspective, the AAI understood Black racial oppression in Cleveland and the United States as a form of colonialism. AAI pursued community organizing and coalition-building with the NOI, RAM, the Cleveland chapter of CORE, and trade unionists to promote Black political and economic power. Freeman and his early Black Power comrades were aware of Garvey's right-wing political turn. But for young Black militants his historical significance to inspiring global Black liberation initiatives outweighed his shortcomings. Malcolm neither joined nor spoke at AAI meetings. However, AAI members respected him for his unapologetic demand for human rights, armed self-defense, and self-determination.[86]

No early US Black Power organization bore Malcolm's influence more than RAM, which was a vanguard, semiclandestine, urban Black revolutionary organization that advocated armed self-defense, human rights, socialism, race pride, internationalism, and global decolonization. The group originated in 1962 at Central State University, a historically Black college in Wilberforce, Ohio. Central State students Max Stanford Jr. (Muhammad Ahmad) and

Wanda Marshall were driving forces in forming what became RAM. Philadelphia eventually became RAM's headquarters.[87] Although based in Philadelphia, RAM was in many respects a heartland formation. Midwesterners were prominent in the group's leadership. Don Freeman served as the executive chairman of RAM from 1964 to 1965, while the Boggses and Milton Henry held leadership positions.[88] RAM leadership regularly met at the Boggses' Detroit home. Black students, writers, and everyday people in Philadelphia, Cleveland, Detroit, Chicago, New York, and the Bay Area formed the core of RAM's rank-and-file members. RAM inspired the Black Panther Party and other Black Power groups across the United States.[89]

Like the AAI, RAM synthesized older and newer strains of Black nationalism into a potent Black revolutionary politics.[90] RAM acknowledged Marcus Garvey and Elijah Muhammad as progenitors of its program. The organization's motto, "One Purpose, One Aim, One Destiny," resembled the UNIA's motto. In Philadelphia, Max Stanford studied under UNIA president-general Thomas Harvey, Queen Mother Moore, and her Garveyite sister Eloise Moore. These veteran Black nationalists, along with Ethel Johnson, an associate of Robert Williams, schooled Stanford, Marshall, and other RAM members in the history of Garveyism.[91] As RAM looked to Garvey, the group also embraced Harold Cruse's "Revolutionary Nationalism and the Afro-American," Marxism-Leninism, Maoism, Third Worldism, and, above all, Malcolm. Still, as RAM charted new political ground, the group, like heartland Black protest formations since the antebellum years, remained mired in masculinism. RAM's executive board, apart from Grace Lee Boggs, was all male.[92]

While Malcolm inspired young Black midwestern militants, the heartland, especially Detroit, also served as key political terrain where a conjunction of events helped to set the stage for his break from the Nation. This development was apparent in Malcolm's "Message to the Grass Roots" speech, one of his most famous addresses and his last major speech as an NOI minister. He delivered the talk at the Group on Advanced Leadership–sponsored Northern Negro Grass Roots Leadership Conference in Detroit on November 10, 1963. Albert Cleage, Grace Lee Boggs, and Milton Henry organized the conference, held at the King Solomon Baptist Church, one of the city's largest and most politically active houses of worship.[93] Conference organizers envisioned the two-day gathering as a militant alternative to mainstream civil rights and as an event that would galvanize direct action for racial justice and equality nationwide. The audience at the conference, most of whom were non-Muslims, enthusiastically received Malcolm's radical message.[94] Rejecting Cold War liberalism and the domestic-centered civil rights agenda, he called for African Americans to look to the Bandung Conference and the global "black revolution" across Asia and Africa as models for Black American freedom. He made no reference to Garvey. But Malcolm's globally conscious talk embodied the spirit of Garvey.[95]

Although missing in most accounts of Malcolm's final years, Freeman deserves significant credit for shaping Malcolm's "Message to the Grass Roots" address. Freeman spoke immediately before Malcolm at the conference. In Freeman's address, he blasted the United States as a racist, capitalist, imperialist state "hell-bent" on achieving global hegemony. His talk so impressed Malcolm that he quickly rewrote his speech to reflect Freeman's revolutionary nationalism.[96] Malcolm's message and Freeman's influence on it signaled that the former's politics were rapidly evolving beyond the ideological boundaries of the Nation and that he was searching for answers outside the organization.

By 1963, Malcolm's growing national prominence both inside and outside of the Nation and his ongoing foray into secular Black politics alarmed Elijah Muhammad, some of his family members, and lieutenants. Given Muhammad's ailing health, some NOI insiders, many of whom were envious of Malcolm, feared that he would clean house if he succeeded the Messenger as the Nation's head.[97] Malcolm's notorious public statement in which he referred to the assassination of President John F. Kennedy on November 22, 1963, as a "case of the chickens coming home to roost" provided Muhammad the pretext for quelling Malcolm. On December 4, 1963, the Messenger banned Malcolm from public speaking for ninety days. Recognizing that his suspension from public speaking was likely permanent, Malcolm declared his independence from the Nation at a press conference on March 8, 1964, in New York. During his press conference, he announced the formation of Muslim Mosque, Inc., an organization he envisioned as the platform for advancing his new Black nationalist agenda.[98]

Though Muslim Mosque, Inc., was based in Harlem, the Midwest continued to serve as an important site where he moved in new political directions after splitting from the Nation. Cleveland was important to Malcolm's ongoing radicalization. On April 3, 1964, the Cleveland chapter of CORE invited Malcolm to speak at their public forum "The Negro Revolt—What Comes Next?" Formed in 1962, Cleveland CORE gained a national reputation for its use of direct action and protests for empowering the city's Black poor.[99] Before three thousand people at Cory Methodist Church, Malcolm delivered his most famous speech—"The Ballot or the Bullet." Extending ideas he had recently discussed at an address in Harlem, Malcolm in Cleveland framed Black America as an internal domestic colony of the United States and African American freedom as a struggle for human rights. Above all, he urged Black Americans to consider armed revolt if electoral politics failed to improve their plight and to look to the emergent Third World as allies. The location of his talk is significant. In 1920, Marcus Garvey spoke at Cory Methodist Church. Malcolm did not acknowledge Garvey. Malcolm may have been unaware of Garvey's visit to the city decades earlier. What is certain is that Malcolm's historic speech signaled Cleveland's longtime national and global importance to Black transnational radicalism.[100]

Malcolm made an even stronger case for his internationalist agenda for Black American freedom in another version of the "Ballot or the Bullet" speech, delivered before one thousand people on April 12, 1964, at the King Solomon Baptist Church in Detroit. The Group on Advanced Leadership sponsored this talk, heralded by scholars as the most mature articulation of his Black nationalist philosophy, just six months after he gave his "Message to the Grass Roots" speech at the same church.[101] This time in Detroit, he exclaimed, "Just as it took nationalism to remove colonialism from Asia and Africa, it'll take black nationalism today to remove colonialism from the backs and the minds of twenty-two million Afro-Americans in this country." Criticizing the United States as a "colonial power" stronger than its European counterparts, he charged that Black Americans had "suffered colonialism for the past four hundred years." Given these realities, he called for charging the United States before the United Nations with violating the human rights of African Americans.[102]

"The Ballot or the Bullet" signaled a clear break from the NOI's policy of nonpolitical intervention and represented the new political road he was now traveling. Even more, Malcolm's efforts in internationalizing the African American freedom struggle and framing it as a human rights struggle resembled campaigns in the late 1940s and early 1950s by Black left-wing radicals such as W. E. B. Du Bois, William L. Patterson, and Paul Robeson and organizations such as the NAACP, Civil Rights Congress, and Sojourners for Truth and Justice.[103] Like his predecessors, Malcolm believed that sympathetic Third World nations in the UN would sanction the United States for its second-class treatment of African Americans. He incorporated this strategy into the program of the Organization of Afro-American Unity, the Harlem-headquartered group he established in June 1964 to promote his internationalist approach for advancing African American freedom.[104]

While the *Autobiography* documents Malcolm's efforts in forming his own organizations after breaking from the Nation, neither the memoir nor most accounts of him discuss his enlistment in RAM in the spring of 1964. Impressed with the group's militancy, RAM was the only organization he joined other than those he established after leaving the NOI. Meetings at the Boggses' Detroit home were critical to bringing Malcolm into RAM and to helping him forge an explicitly anticapitalist position for Black liberation and global decolonization. Neither Malcolm nor RAM publicized his membership and elected position as International Spokesperson in the clandestine organization.[105] The fact that Malcolm joined RAM and delivered key speeches in Cleveland and Detroit shows the ongoing importance of the heartland as a political terrain in shaping and transforming his global outlook, especially in the final eighteen months of his life.

Alice Windom and Malcolm's 1964 African Sojourn

If Malcolm's collaborations with early Black Power militants in Detroit, Cleveland, and Chicago played an important role in accelerating his move toward revolutionary Black nationalism, then his underappreciated encounters in 1964 in Africa with African American female militants, such as the energetic social worker and globetrotter Alice Windom of Chicago, were critical to his adoption of a leftist Black internationalism in the final year of his life. Windom's family background and political journey embodied the long history of Black midwestern resistance, the ideological elasticity of Garveyism, and the importance of heartland, neo-Garveyite Black radical politics in shaping a new generation of Black militants. She was born in 1936 in Madison, Illinois, outside of St. Louis, and grew up in Texas and the Gateway City. Reared in a family with a long line of proud educators and with deep roots in southern Illinois, she became radicalized as an undergraduate at Central State University in Ohio in response to her growing interest in African liberation. After graduating in 1957, she enrolled in a master's program in social work at the University of Chicago.[106] Her radicalism blossomed there. She never joined the Communist Party. However, Marxism intrigued her for its critique of capitalism. At the same time, she immersed herself in Chicago's Black nationalist scene. She took classes in African history, Black nationalism, and current African affairs with F. H. Hammurabi Robb at the HOK. She also regularly attended NOI meetings. She never joined the organization, but she appreciated the NOI's fierce rejection of white supremacy. Through regularly attending Nation meetings in Chicago with her partner and fellow University of Chicago classmate E. U. Essien-Udom of Nigeria, she became an expert on the NOI. The couple's encounters with the Nation served as the basis of his 1962 monograph, *Black Nationalism: A Search for Identity in America*. An instant classic, *Black Nationalism* included extensive discussions about the NOI and located it within the long history of Black nationalism. Windom was actively involved in researching the book with

Essien-Udom. The couple interviewed Elijah and Clara Muhammad and Malcolm X.[107] Despite Windom's heavy involvement in researching and drafting *Black Nationalism*, she received no credit for writing it. Instead, Essien-Udom acknowledged only her role in typing two drafts of the manuscript.[108] His failure to acknowledge her work on the book speaks more broadly to the long-standing tendency of Black nationalist men, from Garvey to James Stewart to William Sherrill to Malcolm, to erase Black women's importance in shaping knowledge production about Black nationalism.

In 1962, Windom's life took a significant turn when she decided to move to Ghana. Looking back, she claimed that her disgust with racism back home and "the excite[ment] about the prospects of an independent Africa" brought her to the continent. In Accra, she joined the vibrant community of African American expatriates, which included Harlem leftist activist Vicki Garvin, aspiring author Maya Angelou, historian John Henrik Clarke, Julian Mayfield, W. E. B. Du Bois, and Shirley Graham Du Bois. Windom worked for Kwame Nkrumah's main speechwriter, although she never met the Ghanaian president.[109]

Windom reencountered Malcolm during his transformative trip to Ghana from May 10 to 17, 1964. He arrived there soon after taking his famous *hajj* to Mecca.[110] Like Stewart and Sherrill nearly ten years earlier, Malcolm appreciated Ghana as a symbol of global Black freedom and admired Nkrumah. In Accra, Malcolm conferred with Nkrumah for several hours about the importance of pan-Africanism to global Black liberation.[111] Malcolm also met Windom in Ghana. She played an impactful role in shaping his time in Ghana. She cofounded the Malcolm X Committee with African American activists Vicki Garvin and Maya Angelou; the Puerto Rican doctor Ana Livia Cordero and her husband, Julian Mayfield; and the Marxist writer Leslie Lacy. In the *Autobiography*, Malcolm explicitly credits Windom, Garvin, and Angelou with organizing the committee that arranged his meetings with diplomats based in Accra from Cuba, the People's Republic of China, Algeria, and other Third World nations. He left an indelible mark on those he encountered in Ghana.[112]

The work of radical women of color in Africa helped transform Malcolm's consciousness and propel him past the Nation's civilizationist outlook toward the continent. Following his return to the United States in May 1964, Malcolm embraced a revolutionary Black nationalism and categorically rejected Elijah Muhammad's Black diasporic right radicalism and description of Africans Americans as the "Asiatic Black Man."[113] This stance required Blacks in the diaspora to look to Africa as *the* ancestral home of Black people and as the agent for global Black liberation. This position also recognized the possibility of and necessity for coalition-building with non-Black people sincerely committed to fighting for Black self-determination, human rights, and social justice globally. By drawing these conclusions, Malcolm broke from the racialism of the NOI and the civilizationism deeply embedded in Black nationalism since the nineteenth century.

Similarly, Malcolm's international travels and exchanges with female revolutionaries of color overseas influenced his gender politics. Like Christine Johnson, Alice Windom personified new ideas about Black womanhood. Unmarried and child-free, she traveled alone to Ghana, wore African clothes, and immersed herself in a vibrant community of African American and Third World militants in Accra in which women were prominent. Underscoring the ways women of color were sometimes ahead of him on political matters, Malcolm began to adopt a more progressive gender outlook that appreciated women's status as the barometer by which to measure democracy at home and overseas. This shift is evident in his remarks to an interviewer in Paris in November 1964:

> One thing I became aware of in my traveling recently through Africa and the Middle East, in every country you go to, usually the degree of progress can never be separated from the woman. If you're in a country that's progressive, the woman is progressive. But in every backward country you'll find the women are backward. . . . So one of the things I became thoroughly convinced of in my recent travels is the importance of giving freedom to the woman. And I am frankly proud of the contributions our women have made in the struggle for freedom and I'm one person who's for giving them all the leeway possible because they've made a greater contribution than many of us men.[114]

Malcolm's 1964 comments reveal profound insight into his emergent thinking about the legacy of women in realizing revolutionary change. The first part of the passage links the status of women to social progress in Third World nations, while the latter portion of the statement acknowledges women as the backbone of the African American freedom struggle. These comments are a far cry from his days in the Nation when he angrily called for women's subservience to men. Still, this passage reveals contradictions in his new thinking about women and gender. Even as he testified to women's power and its importance, he exerted a kind of patriarchal control, insofar as he presented women's freedom as something for men to give. And when attributing power to the women themselves, he used the possessive—"our" women. Malcolm's gender politics were still evolving.[115] Nevertheless, he seemed more introspective about gender—at least in terms of his public remarks. His statement implies that realizing Black women's rights and dignity would actualize freedom for all African Americans and people across the Third World. His gender politics had come a long way in a short period of time, due in no small part to his encounters with African and Middle Eastern women and to his exchanges with US Black women radicals such as Alice Windom.

Women of color overseas played important roles in transforming Malcolm's politics and also shaped the knowledge production of his political and intellectual legacy after his assassination. This role remains largely invisible in Malcolm's life story told through the *Autobiography*. A detailed, six-page, single-spaced letter written by Alice Windom to NOI journalist Christine Wilson about Malcolm's sojourn to Ghana served as the basis for Alex Haley's discussion in the *Autobiography* of the former NOI minister's Ghana trip.[116] Windom penned the missive within days of his departure from Accra and mailed it to Wilson back home. Haley acquired a copy of the letter. Several paragraphs of Windom's letter appear almost verbatim in the *Autobiography*; however, he did not credit her. This move speaks not only to Black women's importance in keeping Malcolm's legacy alive after his death, but also to the exploitation of their intellectual property by Black (male) scholars and the erasure of their vital role in the production and dissemination of Malcolm's life story.[117] While contemporary male colleagues often overlooked their intellectual work, Black women radicals like Windom, confident in their abilities as organizers and thinkers, understood that they could advance global Black freedom by chronicling the work of prominent Black nationalist men for future generations, and, above all, through building militant African nations and through forging transnational political linkages among the African-descended on and off the continent. Coming of age in the Diasporic Midwest provided her with the foundations to carry out this work.

Malcolm, Family, and the Diasporic Midwest

As Malcolm's politics rapidly evolved and as his days became increasingly numbered after he broke from the Nation, his family remained a pillar of emotional and personal support. Growing scholarly attention has rightfully focused on his wife, Betty Shabazz. The most important person in his life, she was a supportive wife and brilliant thinker in her own right, who skillfully navigated the patriarchal expectations of her husband and the NOI. Without her intellectual support, counsel, and domestic labor, he would not have been able to travel extensively domestically and overseas or to forge his revolutionary Black nationalism in his final years.[118] While his wife and growing young family were at the center of his personal life, he did not lose touch with his midwestern Garveyite roots or with his Michigan and Caribbean family. The *Autobiography* and most narratives of his final years largely overlook these enduring family connections and his Garveyite foundations. Acknowledging these important dimensions of Malcolm's life complicates our understanding of his life. The ongoing importance of Garveyism and his Michigan and Caribbean family to him speaks more broadly to the transnational personal and political linkages that had informed the work and subjectivities of countless heartland-based Black freedom fighters since the nineteenth century.

Malcolm's short trip to Omaha in June 1964—not discussed in the *Autobiography*—played an important role in his pursuit of independence from the NOI and in reconnecting with his diasporic midwestern beginnings. In May 1964 in Chicago, he recounted his early childhood years in his birth city to Black journalist Charles Washington of the *Omaha Star*, Omaha's local African American newspaper. Malcolm shared the stories about Earl Little's involvement in the UNIA and Louise Little standing up to Klansmen at the doorway of the family's Omaha home while pregnant.[119] In late June 1964, local civil rights groups invited Malcolm to speak in Omaha. It was his first and only visit to Omaha since childhood. He received exuberant receptions from audiences at a prominent Black church and at a civic hall. His visit garnered favorable coverage in the *Omaha Star*.[120] His Omaha trip and his testimony about his family's Garveyite defiance there speak to his conscious effort to reconnect with his heartland Black nationalist roots after he left the NOI.[121]

As the *Autobiography* contains no discussion of his Omaha trip, Malcolm's memoir also fails to acknowledge his enduring connections to his Caribbean extended family, most notably his second cousin Malcolm Orgias of Grenada. Malcolm X had remained in touch with his Grenadian cousin who resided in Brooklyn.[122] As state surveillance and death threats from the Nation mounted against Malcolm, Orgias encouraged his cousin to abscond to Grenada for safety. For unknown reasons, Malcolm X declined the invitation. It is amazing to think how his life might have been different had he heeded his Caribbean cousin's advice.[123] Still, Orgias's invitation demonstrates that the descendants of Jupiter and Mary Jane Langdon, many of whom had supported Garvey, had not forgotten about their people even though relatives were now scattered across North America, the Caribbean, and Europe.

No relative did more to connect Malcolm to his diasporic family roots than Louise Little. Years after her institutionalization, Malcolm and his siblings continued fighting to win their mother's freedom. Louise's youngest daughter, Yvonne (Little) Jones Woodward, took the lead in freeing her.[124] Inspired by her Garveyite parents' commitment to justice and kin, Woodward believed that the family would not find peace so long as their mother remained in the hospital. After nearly twenty-five years of legal wrangling, the family secured Little's freedom from the Kalamazoo Psychiatric Hospital on August 21, 1963.[125]

Unfortunately, we know little about Louise's inner thoughts regarding her release and reunification with her family. What is certain is that her ability to survive a gross injustice and years-long confinement in a state mental hospital demonstrates her resilience and determination to survive. For Louise's children, her release from the hospital marked one of the most joyous events in their lives.[126] After leaving the hospital, she lived with her son Philbert X, who headed Lansing Mosque No. 16. Her reentry into the world was difficult. Her long institutionalization strained ties with family. Some of her grandchildren had never met their grandmother. This was the case for Deborah Jones, the middle child of Little's youngest daughter, Yvonne. Born in 1950 in Grand Rapids, Michigan, Deborah first met her grandmother in 1963 at her uncle Philbert's home. Looking back, Jones remembers her first encounter with Louise: "Grandma was quiet. She was very pleasant." In the coming years, Deborah—and her children and younger relatives—forged close relationships with Louise.[127] Deborah's uncle Malcolm saw his mother in Michigan at least once after her release from the hospital. But we know little about this encounter, and the *Autobiography* does not reference it.[128] Surely, the reunion between Louise and Malcolm was a complicated emotional moment filled with joy, sadness, grief, and relief. What is certain is that the Little family would soon face another violent and traumatic event: the assassination of Malcolm.

Assassination

Since Malcolm's tragic death on a cold wintry day at the Audubon Ballroom in Harlem on February 21, 1965, his family and supporters, scholars, and journalists have vigorously investigated and speculated about who assassinated him. There is a growing consensus that federal agencies and the New York Police Department played a crucial role in the murder.[129] The FBI and the NYPD had increased surveillance of Malcolm and planted agents within Muslim Mosque, Inc., the Organization of Afro-American Unity, and New York–area NOI mosques.[130] At the same time, the Nation helped to create a climate where "'death-talk' against [Malcolm] was filling the air for the first time" immediately after he announced his break from the Nation.[131] On April 10, 1964, *Muhammad Speaks* published Philbert Little's indictment of his brother alongside a cartoon showing Malcolm's severed head bouncing toward a pile of skulls. Pledging his allegiance to Muhammad, Philbert excoriated his brother for disobeying the Messenger. Philbert also dismissed Malcolm's accusations of sexual misconduct by Muhammad as slander and accused his brother of sexual predatory behavior with NOI women. Even more, Philbert asserted that Malcolm suffered from mental illness like Louise Little.[132] It is unknown if she was aware of Philbert's denouncement. In December 1964, *Muhammad Speaks* published an article attributed to Louis X (Farrakhan), who wrote that "Malcolm is worthy of death" for criticizing Elijah Muhammad.[133] In the early morning of February 14, 1965, unknown assailants firebombed Malcolm's Queens home. The family escaped unharmed. But the attack was reminiscent of the racist violence the Littles faced in Omaha and Lansing because of their Garveyite politics.[134]

The death threats, together with increased government surveillance, took a tremendous emotional toll on Malcolm. Given this threatening climate, he traveled with armed bodyguards.[135] His niece Deborah Jones remembered seeing her uncle when he visited her family in Grand Rapids, Michigan, in the summer of 1964. She met him on three previous occasions, with their first meeting in 1959 when he came with Sister Betty and their infant daughter, Attallah, to visit his sister Yvonne. Relaxed and avuncular, Malcolm encouraged his niece to be proud and confident. Times had changed since his previous family visits. "This time the [1964] visit was different," Jones recalled. Accompanied by bodyguards, Malcolm looked nervous and exhausted. He knew he was living on borrowed time. Jones never saw her uncle again.[136] Assailants murdered him months later while delivering an address at an Organization of Afro-American Unity meeting in New York in the presence of four hundred people, including a pregnant Betty Shabazz and her children.[137] Adding insult to injury, Elijah Muhammad, Louis X, and Muhammad Ali, as well as Malcolm's brothers Wilfred and Philbert, denounced Malcolm as a traitor at the Nation's annual Saviour's Day convention in Chicago just two days before his funeral. Years later, Wilfred and Philbert regretted their statements and claimed that the Nation pressured them into denouncing their brother.[138]

Malcolm's death devastated his wife, children, Ella Collins, his Michigan family, and close associates. Betty Shabazz and Malcolm's brother Robert and sister Yvonne attended the solemn funeral at Faith Temple of God and Christ in Harlem on February 27, 1965. They all kept their children home out of fear for their safety. Given their loyalty to Elijah Muhammad, Wilfred and Philbert did not attend their brother's funeral. Malcolm's death was excruciatingly painful for Betty Shabazz and her children. As Ilyasah Shabazz recalled in her memoir, "My mother herself never spoke to us about what happened on February 21, 1965 . . . ever." That day was simply too painful to discuss.[139] Aside from Betty

Shabazz and her children, perhaps no one took Malcolm's death harder than his mother. Louise Little's response to Philbert's and Wilfred's denunciations of their slain brother is unknown. However, she remarked to family soon after Malcolm's assassination that "he died violently just like his father." Apparently, she never spoke again about Malcolm's death. Following Louise Little's lead, her children grieved. For a woman who had suffered so much over the course of her life, the death of her fifth child, who had gained international fame for speaking out against US racism and global white supremacy, surely was unbearable.[140]

Malcolm's political transformation and tragic death marked a significant transition in the long history of Garveyism and Black nationalism in the heartland and beyond. By the early 1960s, the mood of Black America radically shifted as the Black Freedom Movement and global decolonization gained momentum. The Nation of Islam was at the forefront in galvanizing growing African American militancy, especially in the urban North. Malcolm's brilliance and hard work, combined with the Nation's success in positioning itself as the ideological and organizational heir of Garvey and the UNIA, contributed to the NOI's extraordinary growth across the United States beginning in the late 1950s. Malcolm, the Nation, and the legacy of Garvey, together with local and global events, helped to spawn cutting-edge, radical, heartland-linked early Black Power formations. These groups deeply respected and credited Garvey as the forerunner of contemporary global Black struggles. At the same time, Malcolm and Black midwestern militants were at the front lines in moving Black (inter)nationalism in new directions. Many Midwest-connected young Black militants like Don Freeman and Max Stanford came to Garvey through their leftist politics. Rejecting Cold War civil rights liberalism, they understood Black American freedom as a human rights struggle inextricably linked to global struggles against colonialism, imperialism, white supremacy, and capitalism. Malcolm's interactions with early Black Power groups in the Midwest played an important role in precipitating his split from the Nation and journey toward political independence in the final years of his life.

The politics of Malcolm and early Black Power formations in the heartland were not without their paradoxes and limitations. Like their forebearers, midwestern Black nationalist men proffered a hypermasculine vision for freedom. But women like Christine Johnson, Grace Lee Boggs, and Alice Windom held their own within Black formations. The possibilities and paradoxes of midwestern Garveyism as a liberatory project persisted through the 1960s as the US Black Freedom Movement and African decolonization reached their most radical phase.

7

"THE SECOND BATTLE FOR AFRICA HAS BEGUN"

Garveyism and Black Power in the Diasporic Midwest

G is for Garvey,
Who taught us to see
That Africa was home
For black you and me
—CHRISTINE C. JOHNSON, *ABC's of African History*, 1971

Rev. Clarence W. Harding Jr. was determined. It was August 1977 in Monrovia. Wearing a boubou and kufi, the Chicago-born Garveyite leader reviewed a parade of the Universal Negro Improvement Association along Broad Street, the Liberian capital's main thoroughfare.[1] Charismatic and austere, he was the president of the Monrovia-based Metropolitan Division of the UNIA. Uniformed and helmeted soldiers of the Universal African Legion, the UNIA's paramilitary force established in 1919, proudly led the parade and carried the Liberian flag and the UNIA tricolor banner.[2]

From Liberia, Harding played a pivotal role in leading a resurgent transnational UNIA and in forging a radical Black internationalist politics from the mid-1960s through the 1970s. He never explicitly used the term "Black Power" to describe his activism. However, his work was consistent with African-descended people around the world who used the slogan to call for Black pride, self-determination, autonomy, institution-building, global decolonization, Third World solidarity, and African liberation. This politics was illustrative in his transnational activism in Liberia. In early 1966, President-General Thomas Harvey of the Philadelphia-based UNIA appointed Harding as the UNIA High Commissioner of Africa. His primary responsibility was to direct the Africa Project. Conceived by Harvey and inspired by the longtime Garveyite dream of African redemption, the objective of the Africa Project was to advance "the liberation and restoration of Africa for the Africans at home and abroad" through the UNIA.[3] This initiative was to be based in Monrovia. Harvey envisioned the project as vital to rebuilding the transnational UNIA.[4] Harding did not disappoint Harvey. After moving to Liberia in 1966, the Africa Project, under the Chicago Garveyite's leadership, emerged as the most successful UNIA-led initiative on the continent during the organization's entire history. For the first time in the UNIA's history, the organization built a mass movement in Liberia with connections to the wider continent comprising primarily working-class Indigenes, students, and everyday people inspired by Garvey and committed to global Black freedom.[5] This fascinating story remains largely untold in prevailing narratives of Garveyism, African liberation, and Black Power.

This chapter challenges the widely held assumption that the UNIA and the afterlife of Garvey died by the 1970s. The Diasporic Midwest through the UNIA and midwestern Garveyite front constituted an important political terrain and international crossroads for birthing pathbreaking, globally oriented Black formations during the height of Black Power and the most radical phase in African decolonization. Black resistance dating back centuries, the heartland experience of the dialectic of opportunity and oppression, and global events shaped these movements. Through often embracing socialism and Third Worldism, Garvey's descendants forged a radical Black internationalism. This politics transcended the ideological, spiritual, and political parameters of the status quo and the Black diasporic right radicalism of Garvey. Their work once again reveals the ideological malleability of Garveyism and illustrates the contested meanings of Black freedom during the 1970s. Garveyism with its possibilities and paradoxes did not simply survive decades after Garvey's death. Garveyism found new life, touched more people than ever before, and enjoyed its finest and most radical hour through Black women, men, and youth directly and indirectly linked to the Diasporic Midwest during the Black Power era and height of African liberation.

The Resurgent Black Power–Era UNIA and Heartland Garveyite Female Activists

Although absent from standard narratives of global Garveyism and Black Power, the UNIA in the United States enjoyed a brief resurgence during the Black Power era due in no small part to the efforts of a new cadre of young Black, female Midwest-based militants—Mary Mason of Cleveland, Georgina Thornton of Youngstown, and Patricia Noni Gee of Detroit. These women highlighted the continued significance of the Diasporic Midwest as a global hub of Garveyism and of UNIA women for advancing a liberatory transnational Black radical politics. Just as Amy Jacques Garvey, Amy Ashwood Garvey, Henrietta Vinton Davis, Louise Little, Elinor White Neely, Goldie Stewart, and Lillie Mae Gibson worked hard in keeping the spirit of Garvey and the UNIA alive in their day, Mason, Thornton, and Gee did the same during the early 1970s. Through their movement-building, community organizing, and global travels, they brought new life to the UNIA and helped to raise its international profile.

Collectively, Black Power–era UNIA women joined a Garvey movement that remained bitterly divided between two organizations, both of which still claimed to be the legitimate UNIA. From Philadelphia, Thomas Harvey headed the larger faction formerly led by William Sherrill. Vernon Wilson of Chicago and later Mason Hargrave of Cleveland served as president-general of the smaller UNIA faction associated with the late James Stewart. By the late 1960s as Mason, Thornton, and Gee enlisted in the Garvey movement, many UNIA divisions around the world counted only a few dozen active members— many of whom had joined the Garvey movement decades earlier.[6]

One of the most exciting new UNIA recruits of the Black Power era was Mary Mason of Cleveland. A brilliant poet, playwright, nurse, and community activist, who was committed to freeing Black people, she joined Cleveland UNIA Division 133 by 1970. Utilizing her nursing skills, she participated in community home nursing care and youth antiviolence programs. In 1971, she lived for several weeks in rural Ghana. Journeying to Africa prompted Mason to appreciate the cultural connections among African-descended people on the continent and in the Diaspora.[7] In contrast to the Black diasporic right radicalism of Marcus Garvey, James Stewart, and Mittie Maude Lena Gordon, Mason looked to Africa not as a backward place but as the vanguard of global Black freedom. Changing times and sojourning to Africa rendered classical Black nationalism obsolete for Mason.

Underscoring her ability to operate in multiple organizations and to put her pan-Africanism into action, Mason became actively involved at the local and national levels in the International African Liberation Support Committee (ALSC). Formed in 1972 and inspired by national liberation wars in Guinea-Bissau, Angola, and Mozambique, and efforts to end white-minority rule in South Africa and Rhodesia (Zimbabwe), the Washington, DC–based ALSC forged a "Black united front" of African-descended people in the Americas against racism and imperialism in Africa and Asia.[8] The African Liberation Day (ALD) rally, held in Washington, DC, on May 27, 1972, gave birth to the ALSC. Thirty thousand people participated in the event, making it the largest demonstration in support of African liberation ever held in North America at the time. The legacy of Malcolm X and Marcus Garvey loomed large at the ALD. Betty Shabazz served on the ALD steering committee. On the day of the march, participants assembled at Washington, DC's Meridian Park (renamed Malcolm X Park by ALD marchers), located within miles of the US Capitol. Black Marxists, cultural nationalists, liberals, and revolutionary nationalists marched shoulder to shoulder in support of African liberation. A dashiki-adorned Charles Diggs Jr., the US House of Representatives member from Detroit, founder of the Congressional Black Caucus, whose father was a prominent 1920s Detroit UNIA leader, marched at the front of the procession. So did the revered Black nationalist Queen Mother Moore, underscoring how multiple generations of Black Americans across the ideological spectrum came together through the ALD.[9] In Cleveland, Mason played a crucial role in mobilizing African American community support for the ALD through chairing the local ALD arrangements committee and attending the march. It is unknown whether she met Queen Mother Moore. What we can say is that Mason saw no contradiction in joining the older UNIA and the new ALD. Her work in the UNIA, ALSC, and Cleveland demonstrates her pragmatic and coalitional approaches to organizing that resembled the activism of past midwestern Black nationalist women.[10]

As Mason raised the UNIA's profile in Cleveland, Georgina Thornton played a key role in revitalizing the organization at the local and transnational levels in the Black Power era (see figure 7.1). She was born in Chicago in 1939 and raised in a deeply religious working-class family in the steel-producing city of Warren, Ohio, near Youngstown. Her parents were not Garveyites. However, encountering racism and sexism as a child, watching her parents struggle to make ends meet, and living in a community where the bulk of Black men, including her husband, toiled in sweltering steel mills, and where Black women cleaned white women's homes, prepared the ground for her Garveyite activism as an adult. In 1970, she joined Youngstown UNIA Division 102 after receiving what she believed was a divine revelation from God instructing her to enlist in the UNIA. She came to believe that Blacks could not survive in the United States and that Garveyism provided Black people globally with the means for freeing themselves. She joined a UNIA division with a proud history. In the 1920s, Garvey had visited the Ohio steel town several times.[11] By the late 1960s, elderly Garveyites composed the bulk of the Youngstown UNIA's membership. She brought new life to this division. In 1971, she was elected lady president of Division 102 and third president-general of the UNIA affiliated with Harvey's Philadelphia-based faction.[12]

Thornton was a driving force in failed efforts to reunify the fractured Garvey movement in the early 1970s. Harvey deeply respected her leadership skills and commitment. For this reason, he appointed her to chair the Unification Council, a body organized to reunify the two rival UNIA factions. The council met on May 22, 1971, and June 19, 1971, in Youngstown. The UNIA presidents-general Thomas Harvey and Vernon Wilson agreed to meet there because they saw the city as a neutral site where the rival organizations could resolve their differences. Underscoring the ongoing importance of the Midwest to the transnational UNIA, most conference delegates hailed from the heartland, including young and veteran Garveyites like Raymond Kelley of Dayton; James R. Bennett, A. J. Carter, and Georgina Thornton of Youngstown; Hugh M. Kirkwood of Cleveland; and W. D. Anderson and Solomon Fitzhugh of Cincinnati. In the end, both factions failed to reach an accord in reconciling their differences. The UNIA remained splintered.[13]

Thornton focused special attention on empowering African-descended women globally. She did not consider herself a "feminist," a term that she, like so many Black women in the 1970s, associated with urban, middle-class white women.[14] Yet her concern for advancing the dignity and well-being of Black womanhood was apparent in her work. Through her activism in the UNIA and travels across the United States, she came to know and work with other young UNIA women like Mason and Gee. Thornton also came to respect Amy Jacques Garvey. Although they never met, Thornton looked to Jacques Garvey as a powerful symbol of Black womanhood and as an important link to early twentieth-century Black nationalism.[15] The young UNIA member was right in appreciating Jacques Garvey's importance to Garveyism, Black Power, and contemporary African nationalism. Jacques Garvey's pamphlet *Black Power in America*, published in 1968; the reissue in 1970 of her classic book *Garvey and Garveyism* and edited two-volume work *Philosophy and Opinions of Marcus Garvey*; and the publication in 1974 of *Marcus Garvey and the Vision of Africa*,

FIGURE 7.1. Georgina Thornton in her home, Youngstown, Ohio, October 2018. Photo by the author.

edited by John Henrik Clarke with the assistance of Jacques Garvey, reintroduced Garveyism and helped make her a living legend among a new generation of Black militants.[16]

In addition to respecting Jacques Garvey, Thornton came to know Queen Mother Moore. The elder Black nationalist invited Thornton to represent the UNIA at the historic All African Women's Conference (AAWC) in Dar es Salaam, Tanzania, from July 24 to 31, 1972. The AAWC sought to advance the dignity and freedom of African-descended women globally.[17] Thornton could not afford to travel to Tanzania, but she asked Moore to read a statement on behalf of the UNIA at the conference. Moore addressed the AAWC as its keynote speaker and delivered a powerful speech, "Africa for the Africans, at Home and Abroad." Her speech did not mention Marcus Garvey by name. However, the title of her address and its call for a liberated Africa invoked his spirit.[18] Garveyism as a liberatory, transnational politics lived on into the 1970s through multigenerational exchanges in which heartland Black nationalist women such as Thornton were prominent.

No young, midwestern, female Black nationalist better embodied the connections between older and younger UNIA women than educator, community activist, and world traveler Patricia (Noni) Gee of Detroit. She was born in 1947 in Los Angeles and was raised by a proud, single, working-class mother in Waterbury, Connecticut. By the late 1960s, Gee was ready to change the world. She joined a local chapter of the Black Panther Party. But she dreamed of moving to Detroit. For her, the Motor City represented "a mecca of Black Power" due to the national visibility of Detroit-based organizations like the Republic of New Afrika and the Nation of Islam. Given her enthusiasm for Detroit as a site of Black militancy, she packed her bags and headed for the Motor City.[19]

Moving to Detroit in 1969 changed her life and led her into the UNIA. Soon after her arrival, she worked in Detroit as a curator at what later became the Charles H. Wright Museum of African American History. The museum's legendary namesake assigned Gee and her future husband, (Nwalimu) Edward Michael Gee, to attend the UNIA Unification Council meeting in Youngstown in May 1971 as the museum's observers.[20] At the conference, Gee met young UNIA leaders like Thornton and veteran Garveyites like Harvey. Upon returning to Detroit, Gee and her future husband enlisted in UNIA Division 407 affiliated with the Harvey-led UNIA faction.[21]

Like Mason and Thornton, Gee did not self-identify as a feminist. But she was committed to the survival of Black people at home and abroad. She headed the Detroit UNIA Black Cross Nurses, which ran a neighborhood co-op and medical clinic. The gender politics of Gee and the Detroit BCN provides insight into the ideological range of African American women's activism during the 1970s. On the one hand, the gender politics of Gee and her UNIA sisters was more conventional than those of the pathbreaking Black queer socialist feminist of color organizations like the Third World Women's Alliance and Combahee River Collective. Committed to worldwide socialist change, these groups broke the silence about homophobia and sexism within communities of color, and they argued that sexualities, reproductive rights, domestic violence, and women's liberation were central issues in the struggle for Black liberation. Garveyite women did not share this perspective.[22]

Gee further challenged prevailing middle-class respectability. She lived with her boyfriend before they married. Soon after joining the UNIA, she adopted the Swahili name Noni, "Gift of God," to affirm her burgeoning "African" identity.[23] Her process of self-redefinition through Garveyism resembles what Robyn Spencer describes of the Black Panther Party in Oakland, California, whose members believed that transforming themselves was critical to transforming the world.[24]

Meanwhile, Gee's activism provides another example of young UNIA women in the heartland forging cross-generational connections among Black nationalist women across the Diaspora through Garveyism in the Black Power years. In June 1973, Gee traveled to Jamaica with another young Detroit UNIA member—Fabu Omari—to meet Amy Jacques Garvey. Like Thornton, Gee and Omari admired the veteran pan-Africanist. Even though Jacques Garvey suffered from terminal cancer, she generously opened her Kingston home to these young women. Jacques Garvey passed away at the age of seventy-seven within one week of Gee and Omari's visit. It was fitting that some of Jacques Garvey's last visitors were young Black women from the US heartland. The region had loomed large in her transnational activism since the 1920s when she spoke in Chicago, Detroit, Cleveland, and other heartland cities about African redemption and in defense of her persecuted husband. Following the Second World War, William Sherrill of Detroit emerged as one of her closest allies. Her association with Gee and Omari speaks again to the importance of Garveyism as a connective tissue linking Black nationalists across Global Africa and historical generations into the 1970s.[25]

Despite efforts by Garveyites to restore the UNIA's former glory, long-standing limitations of masculine leadership, ongoing internal divisions, and the emergence of new Black Power organizations proved too much for the Garvey movement to overcome. The fact that the UNIA survived and enjoyed a brief resurgence in the early 1970s points to the work of young, midwestern Garveyite female activists like Mason, Thornton, and Gee. These women, born after Garvey's death, kept the organization and his memory alive among the Garveyite faithful and a new generation of Black people. Even more, the work and subjectivities of Mason, Gee, and Thornton reveal how the Diasporic Midwest remained a stronghold of the transnational UNIA, established decades earlier, into the Black Power era.

Clarence Harding, Liberia, and the Africa Project

Black nationalists in the Midwest found their greatest success during the Black Power era in rekindling Garveyism and in pursuing a transnational Black politics through the Liberia-based Africa Project under the leadership of Harding. He led this transnational scheme at a very different historical moment from when nineteenth-century New World Blacks debated Liberian colonization, Garvey sought to build a Black settler colony in the West African republic in the 1920s, James and Goldie Stewart arrived on the continent in 1949, and Sherrill visited Ghana in 1957. By the late 1960s, Africa counted more than twenty-five independent states. Armed struggles against Portuguese colonialism raged in Guinea-Bissau, Angola, and Mozambique. The Organization of

African Unity (OAU), founded in 1963 in Addis Ababa, Ethiopia, pledged support for decolonization and greater cooperation among African states.[26] In Liberia, young people grew increasingly dissatisfied with the country's poverty and the growing authoritarianism of its president, William Tubman, who died in office in 1971. Vice President William R. Tolbert Jr., an Americo-Liberian, succeeded Tubman. Despite Tolbert's promising start, he failed to implement democratic reforms or to lift the country out of grinding poverty. By the late 1970s, mass antigovernment demonstrations rocked Monrovia. In 1980, Samuel K. Doe, an Indigenous Liberian and an army officer, led a military coup that killed Tolbert, plunging the country into years of bloody conflict. Within this context, Harding pursued his transnational UNIA work.[27]

Calling attention to Harding's life and times in Liberia challenges prevailing narratives about Black internationalism and Garveyism during the Black Power era. Scholars—most notably the historian Monique Bedasse—have identified Tanzania as "*the* mecca" of pan-Africanism on the continent from the late 1960s through the 1970s for Black radicals from around the world after the East African nation, under President Julius Nyerere, adopted an African socialist ideology for social and economic development called Ujamaa.[28] He claimed that cooperative economics and equitable exchange were intrinsic to African Indigenous societies. Given this position, Tanzania pursued a socialist model of development based on state-owned businesses and communal farming.[29] There is no question that Tanzania was an important site of 1970s Black internationalism. However, Harding's activism and the Africa Project reveal that Liberia, a nation so often thought of then and now as nothing more than a staid US Cold War ally and political backwater, was a thriving center of radical Black internationalism during the height of Black Power and African national liberation struggles. Harding and the Africa Project illustrate the continued visibility of Black midwesterners in advancing Black transnational politics. His work in Liberia marked something new in the history of the West African republic and global Garveyism. Through reconfiguring Garveyism and the idea of Liberia as a fulcrum for global Black freedom, Harding and his colleagues forged a radical Black internationalism that transcended Black diasporic right radicalism and made meaningful interventions into countless lives of African-descended people on both sides of the Atlantic.

Harding's lived experiences growing up in the Diasporic Midwest helped prepare the ground for his most important life's work. He was born in Des Moines, Iowa, around 1919. His Illinois-born father worked as a mail carrier. At a young age, Clarence Jr. moved with his family to the South Side of Chicago. His parents were staunch Garveyites. In the 1940s, Harding participated in

Chicago-based Black nationalist organizations. By the 1960s, he came to know F. H. Hammurabi Robb, served as president of Chicago UNIA Division 401, and gained the trust of Thomas Harvey.[30] Outside the UNIA, Harding ministered in the Kenwood United Church, a politically active Black church on the South Side affiliated with the multiracial United Church of Christ. When he departed for Liberia, Harding had acquired a reputation as a skilled, grassroots Garveyite leader.[31]

Harding began building a broad-based Garvey movement in Liberia the moment he set foot on the continent in May 1966. By July 1966, he founded the Metropolitan Division in Monrovia. At its peak in the early 1970s, the local counted around four hundred members, most of whom were Indigenous working-class people. No evidence has been found of Harding meeting or working closely with Goldie Stewart. Outside of Monrovia, Harding established divisions across Liberia and in Abidjan, Ivory Coast.[32] Emphasizing that "the second battle for Africa has begun," he stressed in a 1966 letter to UNIA members in West Africa that the Garvey movement, unlike its unsuccessful effort in the 1920s, would now find success in restoring the "ancient glory" of Africa and in freeing Black people globally.[33]

Harding's establishment of the Marcus Garvey Memorial Institute (MGMI), based in Monrovia, represented the most significant accomplishment of the Africa Project. Founded in 1966, the MGMI was an independent secondary school run by the UNIA and the only institution of its kind in the world at the time operated by the UNIA. Harding served as its principal over the course of the school's twelve-year operation. The MGMI enrolled more than five hundred students from seven African countries per year by the early 1970s. Young people, adults, and soldiers took courses at the school. The bulk of the MGMI's revenue came from student tuition and contributions from Garveyites in the United States, especially from financially well-endowed midwestern UNIA divisions in Detroit, Cleveland, and Chicago—locals that had generously supported the organization since the 1920s.[34] The Montreal UNIA, the division through which Louise Little joined the Garvey movement, and Henry J. Langdon, her cousin and the UNIA commissioner of Canada, also enthusiastically supported Harding's work in Africa.[35]

The MGMI was crucial to indigenizing the Garvey movement, disseminating pan-Africanism to the urban masses of Monrovia, and linking Liberia to Black liberation movements around the world. The MGMI student body president, Robert Ngateh, made this case. Praising Harding for bringing "a great change in the lives of many Liberians, especially the common man," Ngateh wrote, "the Garvey Memorial Institute is not just a mere school but it is a center

MAP 7.1. Africa in 1970.

for brotherhood, uniting young men and women both spiritually and socially. They are brought up to date with the progress of the race and the problem confronting black people everywhere around the world."[36] He was right. The MGMI provided a quality and affordable education in a nation where only about 20 percent of the population was literate (see figure 7.2).[37] Above all, the school helped students understand that Garvey was not a phantom from the distant past but a living spirit who provided essential lessons in advancing self-reliance, racial pride, and pan-African unity in the contemporary historical moment.[38]

FIGURE 7.2. Marcus Garvey Memorial Institute graduation in 1978, Monrovia, Liberia. Stuart A. Rose Library Manuscript, Archives, and Rare Book Library, Emory University, Atlanta, Georgia.

Looking beyond Liberia, Harding traveled across Africa to advance the Garveyite cause and to build the UNIA. In 1967 he received an invitation from Boubacar Diallo Telli, a Guinean diplomat and cofounder of the OAU, to discuss the UNIA and its role in African contemporary affairs at the OAU headquarters. Telli arranged meetings of Harding with President Joseph Mobutu of the Democratic Republic of Congo (DRC) and Kenyan president Jomo Kenyatta in Kinshasa and Nairobi, respectively. Mobutu and Kenyatta received Harding like a visiting head of state. Both African presidents shared their admiration for Garvey with Harding and welcomed the formation of UNIA divisions in their respective nations. Harding also journeyed to Addis Ababa, Ethiopia, where he addressed a one-day OAU conference on the UNIA and its relation to African decolonization. The conference agreed to support the UNIA program for African redemption.[39]

Like most previous UNIA-led efforts in West Africa, Harding's attempts to build the Garvey movement in the DRC and Kenya, as well as to shape OAU policy, were never realized. The UNIA apparently never established permanent divisions in the DRC or Kenya, and little sustained action seems to have come out of the OAU conference on the UNIA. The long-standing organizational weakness of the UNIA, together with the lack of resources and ideological divisions, contributed to this outcome.

As Harding cultivated the principles of Garveyism among students at the MGMI and traveled across the continent, he also mentored young Liberian militants in the Movement for Justice in Africa (MOJA). Formed in 1973, MOJA was initially composed of radical students at the University of Liberia, a hotbed of student activism, committed to supporting armed liberation struggles in Guinea-Bissau, Angola, and Mozambique, as well as to ending Apartheid in South Africa and white settler rule in Rhodesia. By the late 1970s, MOJA developed a multiethnic working-class base in Monrovia, advocated socialism and pan-Africanism, and emerged as one of the main popular opposition groups to the Tolbert administration. Outside of Liberia, MOJA established chapters in the Gambia and Ghana.[40]

The Midwest was critical to MOJA. The group's founder, Togba-Nah Tipoteh, a young Marxist economics professor at the University of Liberia, underwent his political awakening while studying at Ohio University and the Ohio State University during the 1960s. There, he became interested in Martin Luther King, Malcolm X, and the US Black Freedom Movement through friendships with Black and white college peers. However, he did not meet Malcolm X or associate with early Black Power groups. After graduating with a PhD in economics from the University of Nebraska, he returned to Liberia, committed to African liberation.[41]

The Midwest radicalized another important MOJA leader—Amos Sawyer, who later emerged as a leading Liberian scholar and the interim president of Liberia from 1990 to 1994. He was born in 1945 in the coastal town of Greenville. His family hailed from the continent and the Diaspora. He graduated with a bachelor's degree from the University of Liberia in 1966. His life changed when he came to the United States in the late 1960s and studied political science at Northwestern University in Evanston, Illinois, outside of Chicago. As a graduate student at Northwestern, he was first introduced to Garveyism and learned about Harding's work in Monrovia. Peers invited Sawyer to a UNIA meeting in Chicago. At this gathering, veteran Garveyites told Sawyer about Harding and encouraged the young Liberian to contact the Chicago-based Garveyite minister upon returning home. Sawyer followed their advice after earning his doctorate in 1973.[42]

After returning home, Sawyer accepted a teaching job at the University of Liberia and came to know Harding. Sawyer did not join the UNIA. But the veteran Garveyite became an important mentor to Sawyer. For him and other young African radicals, Harding represented a living connection to Garvey. In addition, Sawyer taught at the MGMI. One of his most famous students was future military coup leader Samuel K. Doe, who at the time was an enlisted army soldier. Doe did not join either MOJA or the UNIA, and he did not publicly credit the MGMI for shaping his politics after he came to power. But it seems possible that his education at the MGMI played a role in prompting his call for grassroots democracy and pan-Africanism during the early years of his rule.[43]

Harding was critical to MOJA's success. The group regularly held meetings at the MGMI, often with the Chicago Garveyite in attendance. He never joined the group. He was not interested in participating in local partisan politics. His primary focus was empowering ordinary Liberians.[44] His activism was not lost on the Liberian government, which surveilled the MGMI, MOJA, and the UNIA. Authorities never arrested Harding or Sawyer, but the government jailed some MOJA activists who taught at the MGMI following violent antigovernment protests in Monrovia in 1979.[45] Although it was not Harding's intention, he indirectly fomented mass opposition against the Tolbert government.

In addition to challenging Liberian domestic policy, the Monrovia UNIA under Harding's leadership defied the Tolbert administration's foreign policy by sending troops and material support to armed struggles against Portuguese colonialism in Mozambique and nearby Guinea-Bissau. In 1970, the Metropolitan Division formed a "battalion" of the Universal African Legion (see figures 7.3 and 7.4). The UAL was independent of the Liberian military. In 1972, the Liberian UAL lost two soldiers in action against Portuguese forces in Mozambique. The two fallen soldiers became local heroes in Monrovia.[46] The UAL's decision to deploy troops to Mozambique contrasted with the policy of the Liberian government, which did not send soldiers to Guinea-Bissau or Mozambique. In this regard, Liberian policy did not significantly differ from US foreign policy toward Africa, which supplied Portugal with arms used against African insurgents.[47] The deaths of Liberian UAL soldiers in Mozambique stand as the only time in UNIA history in which the UAL fought a military campaign against an imperial power. So, while Black Power groups in the United States often gave rhetorical support for national liberation struggles in Africa and across the Third World, the UNIA in Liberia under the direction of a Chicago Garveyite offered soldiers and real material support for Africans waging armed struggle against their oppressors.

Living in Monrovia and encountering young African revolutionaries at the height of the internationalist Black Power Movement prompted Harding to largely dispense with Black diasporic right radicalism. Upon his arrival to Libe-

FIGURE 7.3. Universal African Legion procession on Broad St., Monrovia, Liberia, August 1977. Stuart A. Rose Library Manuscript, Archives, and Rare Book Library, Emory University, Atlanta, Georgia.

ria, he embraced a Black settler colonial outlook like those of his predecessors.[48] In the coming years, he abandoned civilizationism, putting his faith in young African revolutionaries for liberating the continent. This was evident in his willingness to collaborate with MOJA and his strong support for African revolutionaries such as Amílcar Cabral, the brilliant Third World Marxist leader of the Partido Africano da Independência da Guiné e Cabo Verde (African Party for the Independence of Guinea and Cape Verde). The assassination in January 1973 of Cabral in Conakry, Guinea, at the hands of Black agents working for Portugal infuriated Harding.[49] In a report to Harvey, Harding called Cabral's assassination a "foul deed," placing the ultimate blame for his death on Portugal and the United States.[50] Harding neither became a Marxist nor disavowed emigration. But his politics diverged from Harvey and other veteran US-based UNIA officials, who, like Garvey, were anticommunist and, in some cases, collaborated with white racists in support of Liberian colonization.[51]

FIGURE 7.4. Reverend Clarence W. Harding inspecting UNIA Medical Battalion, Monrovia, Liberia, August 1977. Stuart A. Rose Library Manuscript, Archives, and Rare Book Library, Emory University, Atlanta, Georgia.

There is no evidence indicating that Harding corresponded with white separatists, and he did not embrace anticommunism while living in Liberia. Doing so would have been foolhardy given MOJA's socialist orientation.

Residing in Monrovia changed Harding's life. In a move marking his solidarity with the city's masses, he often wore African clothes and lived modestly in a working-class neighborhood. For him, living in Africa resembled the impact that sojourning across the continent had on Malcolm. There is no record of them ever meeting or of Harding expressing interest in Malcolm. But Africa transformed them both.

Even though Harding charted new political ground, he embraced a masculinist vision of freedom upheld by Black nationalist men since the antebellum period. In one report, he wrote, "For as long as Black Men Fight for Freedom in Angola, Mozambique, Rhodesia, and the Union of South Africa, our work is not done."[52] While men held the reins of power within the Africa Project, women nonetheless actively participated in the Monrovia UNIA. The BCN provided much-needed health services in West Point, Monrovia's large slum.

Women achieved visibility in MOJA, most notably Philomena Bloh Sayeh, who decades later became the director-general of the Center for National Documents and Records Agency in Monrovia.[53] In the United States, UNIA women leaders like Jean Slappy of Philadelphia, Georgina Thornton, Alma Gordon of Brooklyn, Elinor White Neely of Robbins, and Noni Gee coordinated grassroots support from Garveyites for Harding's work in Liberia.[54] Even though men dominated the formal leadership of the Monrovia UNIA, women on both sides of the Atlantic were essential to the Africa Project.

Harding's untimely death in Monrovia in 1978 from a fall and the subsequent closing of the MGMI soon afterward, together with the 1980 coup in Liberia and Goldie Stewart's return to the United States that same year, marked the end of an important chapter in the history of the UNIA in Africa.[55] Harding and the Africa Project were unsuccessful in revitalizing the UNIA globally. In this respect, his work resembled that of Stewart and Sherrill in West Africa. Still, Harding represented something new for the UNIA in Africa. Unlike his predecessors, he moved beyond nineteenth-century Black diasporic right radicalism. Drawing from decades of experience as a grassroots UNIA leader in Chicago and through forging a modern, radical pan-African politics, he touched the lives of thousands of young African people at the MGMI, affected national Liberian politics, and impacted anticolonial struggles across the continent. UNIA members from the US heartland were critical to Harding's unparalleled success in forging political exchanges between the Diasporic Midwest and Global Africa during the peak of Black Power and African liberation through Garveyism.

The Gary Convention

Beyond the UNIA, Garveyism in the 1970s survived and evolved in the midwestern Garveyite front, impacted Black American life, and linked the heartland to Global Africa during the height of Black Power. The historic National Black Political Convention, best known as the Gary convention, held from March 10 to 12, 1972, in Gary, Indiana, illustrates these connections. An estimated twelve thousand people assembled there. The convention adopted the "National Black Political Agenda," a sweeping manifesto that called for an independent Black political movement, the election of African American officials, and solidarity with Third World liberation movements.[56] Conference organizers selected Gary because it was a majority-Black city headed by an African American mayor, Richard G. Hatcher, who was an outspoken supporter of Black Power. He was elected as the city's first Black mayor on November 7, 1967—the same day Cleveland elected its first African American mayor, Carl B. Stokes. Hatcher and Stokes were the first two Black mayors of US cities of more than 100,000 people. The Second Great Migration, the steel industry, and white flight created the conditions for Hatcher's mayoral victory. Gary's Black population grew during the 1960s due to an ongoing influx of African American newcomers in search of a better life through the city's gargantuan steel industry. By 1970, African Americans constituted 52.8 percent of Gary's total population of 175,415.[57]

The National Black Political Convention connected Black Power to the legacy of Midwest-prominent Colored Conventions and the UNIA stronghold that was Gary. By 1972, the Gary UNIA was defunct. The UNIA played no apparent major role in the convention. Still, the spirit of Garvey and Malcolm resonated at the conference. Newark, New Jersey–based poet and playwright Amiri Baraka, who reinvented himself into a Black nationalist disciple of Malcolm after his assassination and who emerged as a key figure in the Black Power and Black Arts movements, was a driving force in organizing the gathering.[58] He co-convened the conference with Richard Hatcher and the Detroit Garveyite prodigy Charles Diggs. Queen Mother Moore, dressed in her trademark African clothing, beseeched conference delegates to demand reparations for slavery.[59] The National Black Political Agenda was never realized after the conference.[60] However, the Gary convention helped to set the stage for future African American campaigns for political office, most notably Jesse Jackson's unsuccessful bids for the US presidency in 1984 and 1988 and Barack Obama's historic presidential victory in 2008.[61]

While the National Black Political Convention blazed new ground on multiple fronts, its gender politics affirmed a long history of male chauvinism within Black movements.[62] Even though Coretta Scott King, Betty Shabazz, Moore, club woman leader Dorothy Height, poet Nikki Giovanni, and lawyer and feminist activist Florynce Kennedy attended the Gary convention, women were absent from the gathering's top leadership. Baraka was well known for his misogyny.[63] Undeniably, the convention was a major event in the longue durée of Black nationalism and showcased the heartland's ongoing importance to African American resistance. But its overt sexism speaks more broadly to African American women's long struggle against sexism in Black movements ranging from the Colored Conventions to the UNIA to Black Power.

Garveyism and Grassroots Black Power in Cleveland

If Gary provides insight into the complexities and the long history of Black nationalism in shaping a national Black Power political summit, then Cleveland highlights the impact of Garveyism in shaping local, grassroots, globally informed Black Power organizations in the United States and the city's national importance to precedent-setting state repression against US Black radicalism during the late 1960s. Black Power in Cleveland took shape at a decisive moment in the city's history. Cleveland made national headlines with the election of Carl B. Stokes on November 7, 1967, as the city's first African American mayor.[64] Born in Cleveland in 1927 and raised by a working-class widow in public housing in the Central neighborhood, he fought in the Second World War, graduated from law school, established a law firm, and served three terms in the Ohio House of Representatives from 1962 to 1967.[65] Stokes became Cleveland's mayor as life for the city's Black residents grew even more precarious. By 1967, Blacks made up 38 percent of the city's total population of approximately 750,000 people. Deindustrialization, high unemployment, suburbanization, poor housing, police brutality, and government neglect ravaged the city's African American neighborhoods of Hough and Glenville.[66] Racial violence erupted in Hough from July 18 to 24, 1966, resulting in four deaths.[67] Unlike many large US cities, Cleveland did not have a Black revolt after the assassination of Martin Luther King on April 4, 1968. Initially, Black militants supported the city's first Black mayor. Black Cleveland radicals Don Freeman and Ahmed Evans mobilized Black voters, who helped Stokes secure his narrow victory. There is no evidence of the Cleveland UNIA's involvement in campaigning for Stokes. His most successful collaboration with local Black militants came on July 20, 1968, when the mayor gleefully walked with rifle-carrying young Black nationalists—Harllel Jones, Omarr Majied, and Sababa Akili of the militant local group Afro-Set—in a peaceful parade through Hough commemorating the 1966 uprising in the neighborhood (see figure 7.5).[68] Stokes believed the absence of major civil unrest in Cleveland since 1966 testified to his political sagacity in steering the city toward tranquil racial waters. He was wrong. An uprising in Glenville just three days after Stokes's appearance with Black militants in Hough shattered the illusion of racial harmony in Cleveland.[69]

The "Glenville shootout," as it came to be called, marked a key turning point in Stokes's administration. The incident exposed the limitations of electoral politics for improving the lives of the Black urban masses, and it forever altered the course of Black Power in Cleveland and across the country. On July 23,

FIGURE 7.5. Cleveland mayor Carl Stokes (*middle*) with Black militants in procession through Hough, July 20, 1968. (*L* to *R* from Stokes) Omarr Majied to the left, Harllel Jones directly behind, and Sababa Akili to the right of Stokes. Cleveland Public Library, Ohio.

1968, a deadly firefight ensued between Ahmed Evans, members of his local Black nationalist group (the Republic of New Libya), and Cleveland police when cops attempted to arrest him in front of his apartment for allegedly planning an armed revolt. The shootout sparked a neighborhood-wide revolt. The unrest left eleven people dead—eight African Americans and three white police officers—and reduced portions of the neighborhood to smoldering ruins. The police captured Evans alive. He was tried and sentenced to death for killing police officers. Like the Cleveland Moorish leader Ahmad El of the 1950s, authorities and the mainstream media demonized Evans as a psychopathic Black nationalist responsible for the shootout. Evans met a similar fate as Ahmad El. Evans died in prison in 1978 before Ohio authorities could execute him.[70] Beyond Cleveland, the Glenville shootout occurred as the Black Panthers and their allies around the world organized the "Free Huey Campaign," an amnesty movement to free Black Panther leader Huey P. Newton from jail for the shooting death of a white Oakland, California, police officer in October 1967. Evans, like Newton, came to symbolize state repression of Black male militants who apparently posed an existential threat to America.[71]

National and local responses to Glenville contained ominous implications for Black Power across the country. According to the historian Yohuru Williams, the local mainstream media and white police officers, officials, and everyday people believed the Glenville shootout portended a looming, nationwide race war between whites and armed Black militants. In the coming years, police targeted Black militants in Chicago, Detroit, and Milwaukee "precisely because of their proximity to Cleveland."[72]

Despite the virulent repression and vilification meted out against Evans and the Republic of New Libya, Black militants in Cleveland fought on and connected their struggle to the legacy of Garvey and to contemporary struggles around the world against imperialism, white supremacy, capitalism, and colonialism. The Afro-Set Black Nationalist Party for Self-Defense, popularly known as Afro-Set, best exemplified this work. Founded in the summer of 1968 and patterned off the Black Panthers, Afro-Set was the largest Black Power organization in Cleveland. The group's founder and "prime minister," Harllel Jones (Harllel X), became one of the city's best-known Black radicals for decades. Afro-Set's members wore Black Panther–like military uniforms, and the group called for armed self-defense, cultural pride, community control, and worldwide Black liberation.[73]

Garvey was integral to Afro-Set. The group respected him as a symbol of global Black liberation. Afro-Set modeled its black, red, and green banner on the UNIA's tricolor flag. Afro-Set also possessed direct connections to the interwar UNIA. Afro-Set's minister of defense, Omarr Majied, who marched with Stokes in the commemoration of the 1966 Hough uprising, took pride in knowing his grandfather was a leader in the 1930s Cleveland UNIA. Like in other locales across the African world, the memory of Garvey served as an important link to earlier Black struggles.[74]

Afro-Set's complex gender politics resembled those of Black nationalist groups in the Midwest and around the world before and during Black Power. The Cleveland group's formal leadership was all male except for a "queen mother," a position held by a middle-aged African American woman who was responsible for overseeing the group's work related to women and children. Despite their exclusion from the group's formal leadership, women, like they had in Black formations since the early 1800s, found a way to make their presence known. Afro-Set's message inspired young Black women into action. One such person was Adenike (Miriam) Sharpley (see figure 7.6). She joined the group at the age of sixteen after her expulsion from high school for her involvement in Black Power activism. Afro-Set changed her life. The group provided her with a paid job in the group's office and an alternative education. The queen

FIGURE 7.6. Adenike Miriam Sharpley, Shaker Square, Cleveland, Ohio, December 2015. Photo by the author.

mother and Harllel Jones took Sharpley under their wing. A skilled dancer, Sharpley joined the group's dance team, which performed at Afro-Set community events in Hough. She came to be known as "Malaika." Her decision to adopt a new name, the move made most famously by Malcolm X to adopt a liberated persona, mirrored those of other Afro-Set members. Later in life, she enjoyed a successful professional career performing and teaching African-inspired dance at Oberlin College outside of Cleveland.[75] Her activism demonstrates how women asserted their voices in and transformed their identities through an organization that largely excluded them from formal leadership.

Like the UNIA in its prime and the Black Panthers, Afro-Set appreciated the importance of public space for contesting state power and the racial status quo. The group sponsored large rallies in public parks as well as marches that resembled processions sponsored by the Cleveland UNIA at its height.[76] Afro-Set not only touched thousands of Black Clevelanders but also terrified local authorities. Afro-Set and the police never exchanged gunfire. However, the police raided the group's office and harassed its members. The state of Ohio incarcerated Harllel Jones on a trumped-up murder charge, while federal authorities court-martialed and jailed Sababa Akili for refusing the military draft.[77] Political repression locally and nationally contributed to Afro-Set's demise.

Black radicalism and the violent state response to it in Cleveland offer profound insight into the possibilities and limitations of Black electoral politics in the Black Power era onward. The Glenville shootout sealed Stokes's political fate. He won reelection in 1969. But the optimism of his first term melted away, prompting his decision not to run again in 1971.[78] Living conditions for Black Clevelanders—and for African Americans in other midwestern cities—continued to deteriorate under Black mayors who were largely powerless in countering deindustrialization, the white backlash, population decline, and government disinvestment from urban America.[79] Moreover, Cleveland set a national precedent for virulent state repression against Black militancy. Given these realities, young Black Cleveland radicals understood perhaps better than anyone else in the United States that the road to global Black liberation would be far more difficult and longer than anyone could have imagined.

Black Power Student Protest in Lansing

As Garvey's legacy bore fruit in Black Power organizations in Cleveland, the shadow of Garvey cast itself in exciting ways on Black student radicalism in Lansing, Michigan, and Michigan State University in East Lansing, Michigan, during the late 1960s and early 1970s. Rarely discussed in conventional narratives of Black Power or Garveyism, the medium-sized industrial city of Lansing transformed into a hot spot of Black Power student protest. Through cutting-edge midwestern Garveyite front formations, such as the Black Liberation Front International, Malcolm X Communication Skills Academy, *Westside News*, Congress of African People and African Heritage Association, and Marcus Garvey Institute, Black youth in Lansing, inspired by Garvey, Malcolm X, and global upheavals, forged a cutting-edge Black radical diasporic politics committed to empowering local communities and to liberating Black people everywhere. Even more, Lansing Black Power groups showed once again how Midwest-based young Black militants were critical to preserving and retooling Garvey's ideas and to connecting the heartland to Global Africa.[80]

A Black Power student revolt in Lansing emerged in a deeply racially and economically divided city. In 1960, Lansing counted 6,745 African Americans out of a total population of 107,805. In 1969, the city's Black population and total population grew to 22,193 and approximately 130,000, respectively.[81] Lansing remained a major center of US automobile manufacturing. The auto industry dominated African American life in Lansing. For a significant portion of

Black men, working and earning good wages in local automobile plants, often right after high school, was a rite of passage. However, steady employment in the auto industry was elusive for Blacks. Plants regularly laid off thousands of workers. Racial biases of management and white union officials prevented African Americans from acquiring upwardly mobile factory jobs. Most wage-earning Black women in Lansing toiled at poorly paid service jobs.[82]

Even though the automobile companies in Lansing made millions of dollars in profit, the bulk of African Americans did not enjoy this prosperity. Most Blacks lived in a hypersegregated, underserved, working-class neighborhood on the city's west side.[83] Black frustration with racial oppression exploded on August 7, 1966. Violent civil unrest erupted for two days on Lansing's west side. No one was killed. However, the unrest further polarized racial divisions in the city.[84]

Michigan State was an active site of Black Power student protest in the United States during the late 1960s and early 1970s. As the historian Joy Ann Williamson observes, college campuses and Black students were crucibles of Black Power (see figure 7.7).[85] Dynamic Black student organizers and thinkers coalesced at MSU—Kimathi Mohammed, Belinda "Akosua" and Gary Good, Terry "Abdul" Johnson, Chui Karega, Maina wa Kinyatti, Kathie Stanley-House, Greg P. Kelley, Tony Martin, and Ronald Bailey. They believed that students and ordinary people possessed the knowledge and skills to change the world. Many Black MSU student radicals were either born in the South or raised in southern working-class families who had relocated to Lansing and Detroit. These young people knew they lived in Malcolm X's hometown.[86]

MSU was a tough place to be Black. The school counted only a few hundred African American students and a handful of Black professors. White administrators were indifferent to African American students' disgust with racism on and off campus. Beyond campus, many Black male MSU students worked in local automobile factories. Toiling on assembly lines opened their eyes to the grueling work conditions and superexploitation Black industrial workers faced on a global scale. Lansing's proximity to Detroit also stoked and radicalized Black Power protest at MSU. Young Black Lansing militants regularly traveled to Detroit, where they collaborated with James and Grace Lee Boggs, the League of Revolutionary Black Workers, Republic of New Afrika, Shrine of the Black Madonna, African Liberation Support Committee, and Communist Labor Party.[87]

Marcus Garvey, Malcolm X, and the long history of African-descended resistance in Michigan were integral in inspiring the radical political praxis pursued by Black Lansing militants.[88] Founded in 1970, the Marcus Garvey Institute for the Study of African Peoples (known among its members as the Marcus Garvey Institute) stands as the most important Black Power student-led organization in Lansing. The MGI had no formal organizational connections to the UNIA. The Marcus Garvey Institute and the Marcus Garvey Memorial Institute in Monrovia were unaware of each other, underscoring once again how Garveyism endured on multiple independent fronts long after Garvey's passing.[89] Initially, Black MSU and local high school students interested in studying Black history composed MGI's membership. However, the MGI evolved into a freedom school focused on winning control of the Lansing west side for its Black residents and connecting the local with liberation struggles in Africa, the Caribbean, and Asia. The MGI was the brainchild of Kimathi Mohammed (né Stanley McClinton). He stands as one of the most unheralded Black Power thinkers of his day. Born in 1948 and raised in a working-class family in Savannah, Georgia, he acquired a reputation as a tireless community organizer and brilliant theoretician as a student at MSU.[90]

Like with other local Black Lansing radical groups, Garvey was central to the MGI's praxis. The MGI named itself after Garvey because the group identified him as a key progenitor of pan-Africanism, illustrating how MGI members saw themselves as part of a diasporic radical political tradition. The title of the MGI's journal, *The New World*, was a clear reference to the UNIA's *Negro World*. Established in 1973, *The New World* featured articles about Garvey and Garveyism, as well as the latest news about liberation struggles in Africa, the Caribbean, and the Third World. Kimathi Mohammed wrote a front-page article titled "Pan-Africanism" with a photograph of the "Honorable Marcus Garvey." Tracing the history of pan-Africanism as a concept and transnational liberatory movement from the early twentieth century through the contemporary moment, Mohammed credited Garvey for establishing the idea that "Black people should know no national boundaries . . . and the idea that Black people needed to build an independent African government." Mohammed also acknowledged Garvey for "organizing the first mass movement based upon racial solidarity and Black Nationalism."[91]

Mohammed's essay did not refer to Garvey's shift toward the political right and alliances with white supremacists. However, like other Black Power militants, Mohammed and his comrades were aware of the contradictions and multiple political tendencies within Garveyism. However, the MGI was determined both to acknowledge and to rethink Garveyism through forging a Black radical praxis informed by the past and present.[92] In a break from Garvey, the MGI understood socialism as an essential component of global Black liberation. Unlike the UNIA, the MGI looked not to Liberia, but to Tanzania, Cuba, and Vietnam as revolutionary models for battling imperialism, capitalism, and racism.

MGI members studied Garvey. But they also studied W. E. B. Du Bois, Malcolm X, Kwame Nkrumah, Mao Zedong, Amílcar Cabral, George Padmore, and C. L. R. James. James was especially important to the MGI. The journalist, historian, and activist, originally from Trinidad, was a major figure in twentieth-century Marxism, anticolonialism, and Black liberation. By the late 1960s, young Black militants around the world revered James as an elder Black revolutionary theoretician. His rejection of the Marxist-Leninist vanguard party as the fulcrum for transformative change and his belief in the self-organization of ordinary African-descended people in liberating themselves deeply influenced young Black militants in Lansing, among other places.[93] In the 1970s, he regularly visited Lansing and Detroit where he gave lectures on Black history, dialectics, and global Black liberation through invitations from the MGI and other Black Power groups.[94]

The MGI and Black Power organizers at Michigan State produced groundbreaking work on Black politics, Black radicalism, and Garveyism. Kimathi Mohammed's book *Organization and Spontaneity: The Theory of the Vanguard Party and Its Application to the Black Movement in the U.S. Today* provides the best glimpse into his prescient thought. Published in 1974 and informed by collective conversations in the MGI, the book categorically rejected vanguardism and electoral politics as vehicles for Black liberation. Anticipating positions advanced decades later by Black Lives Matter / Movement for Black Lives, Mohammed emphasized the creativity and self-organization of everyday Black people and the importance of building democratic, nonhierarchical mass movements for advancing racial justice and transformative social change.[95] In addition, the graduate research at MSU by Tony Martin of Trinidad forever shaped the trajectory of Garvey studies. His dissertation on Garvey and the UNIA, completed in 1973, served as the basis of his groundbreaking monograph *Race First: The Ideological and Organizational Struggles of Marcus Garvey and the Universal Negro Improvement Association*, published three years later. Martin was a Black Power activist at MSU and an associate of Kimathi Mohammed. Conversations between Martin and other MSU Black Power groups informed Martin's dissertation.[96]

Lansing Black Power militants were serious community organizers dedicated to improving the lives of Black Lansing residents. The MGI sponsored community forums on Black history and collaborated with residents in securing better housing, schools, and food. The wages from well-paid MGI members who worked in automobile plants were critical to funding the organization's work and paying the rent for its three-story house on Lansing's west side.[97]

On the gender front, the MGI was no different from other midwestern Garveyite front organizations before and during the Black Power era. Men domi-

FIGURE 7.7. Black Student Union march led by eighteen-year-old Terry Johnson through the west side of Lansing, Michigan, 1971. Credit: Terry Johnson.

nated the MGI's leadership, and the group never devoted serious attention to combatting Black women's oppression. However, Black women still played an important role in the organization, most notably educator and world traveler Cynthia Hamilton, who enjoyed a distinguished academic career as a pioneering Africana studies scholar. She was born in New Orleans in 1950 and was reared in Los Angeles in a working-class family who deeply admired Garvey. After graduating high school in 1967, she studied at Stanford University under St. Clair Drake. He introduced her on campus to C. L. R. James and Robert A. Hill, a young Jamaican scholar and future luminary in Garvey studies. After a brief stint in the Black studies graduate program at Cornell University and working in Tanzania, she decided to pursue a career in education. Her passion for freeing Black people brought her to James. She worked as his secretary in his Washington, DC, home for almost two years. Recognizing her brilliance, he took her as his understudy with the intention of preparing her to teach at the MGI. She spent the summer of 1973 in Lansing teaching courses in dialectics at the MGI. Her male colleagues took her seriously and treated her with respect. Sexism existed within the MGI, but the organization neither relegated women to performing secretarial work nor expected them to provide sexual favors to men like in some other Black nationalist groups. Instead, women contributed to all aspects of the MGI's work, despite the organization's neglect of the special issues facing Black women.[98]

Meanwhile, the MGI and the MGMI in Monrovia provide insight into how Garvey-inspired Black radical movements across the 1970s African world evolved differently and independently from one another. On the one hand, these groups demonstrate the interest in and circulation of Garveyism among young Black militants across the Atlantic world. On the other hand, they show how social and geographic locations, nationalities, languages, and organizational affiliations positioned members of these formations differently vis-à-vis one another. MGI members were relatively more affluent than their counterparts in the MGMI even though African Americans in Lansing were positioned near the bottom of the socioeconomic ladder. MGI members resided in the world's most powerful and wealthy nation, while MGMI members lived in an underdeveloped, neocolonial West African state. Social and geographic locations, linguistic and global communication divides, and organizational boundaries were real. These factors help explain why neither the MGI nor the MGMI were aware of each other and why Garveyism in the 1970s acquired a distinct character in different locales.

The MGI and MGMI operated in two different worlds, oblivious of the other group's existence. Still, they shared a love for Garvey. They both confronted state repression. Like the MGMI in Monrovia, the MGI in Lansing made local authorities nervous. Automobile companies were especially concerned about the possibility of Black radicalism spilling into the plants. Management hired agents, who, along with the police, closely surveilled Black Lansing radicals. State repression neither triggered shootouts nor resulted in the deaths of African American militants in Lansing as they did in Cleveland and elsewhere. However, repression and the rightward national political turn, together with the departure of student organizers from the Lansing area after graduating from Michigan State, contributed to the demise of the MGI and Black militancy in Michigan's capital city.[99] Young Black Lansing radicals failed in overthrowing racial capitalism. That was a dream beyond their reach. However, they impacted the lives of ordinary people through institution-building and pursuing a groundbreaking, internationalist Black radical politics, informed by the racial landscape of Lansing, their respect for Garvey and Malcolm, and global events during the height of Black Power and Third World decolonization.

Black Midwestern Ethnic Religions in the Black Power Era

Midwestern Garveyism endured into the 1970s not only through Black Power protest groups but also through established and new midwestern Garveyite front religious formations in Chicago, Detroit, Cleveland, and elsewhere. Transnational in vision, these religious groups, like their early twentieth-century predecessors, provided their mostly working-class followers with a powerful sense of spiritual purpose and a strong racial identity for comprehending and resisting the political, material, and metaphysical forces they believed sought to annihilate Black people globally. Chicago-based Ethiopian Hebrews constituted one of the most important Black ethnic religious communities where Garveyism and the long history of Black nationalism evolved in the post–Second World War years. By the 1950s, Chicago was home to perhaps as many as ten thousand of the twenty-five thousand Ethiopian Hebrews in the United States.[100] Rabbis Abihu Ben Reuben and Joseph Lazarus, both of whom admired Garvey and came out of the interwar UNIA, were at the center of Ethiopian Hebrew life in Chicago. Reuben and Lazarus became Ethiopian Hebrews in response to their belief that Christianity was endemically racist. In 1952, Reuben and Lazarus established the Congregation of Ethiopian Hebrews on the South Side with the assistance of Wentworth A. Matthew, an Afro-Caribbean veteran Garveyite from St. Kitts and the leader of the Harlem-based Commandment Keepers of the Living God. Matthew was an associate of Arnold Josiah Ford of Barbados, a Garvey ally instrumental to orchestrating the pageantry of UNIA ceremonies.[101] Although the Congregation of Ethiopian Hebrews counted no more than one hundred members by the early 1960s, Black Israelites were visible in postwar Black Chicago. The *Chicago Defender* featured news about "Black Jews." Reuben was a fixture among Chicago Black nationalists and a regular speaker at F. H. Hammurabi Robb's HOK.[102]

The Black Power era marked a new chapter in Ethiopian Hebrew life in the United States, with Chicago as a global hub.[103] By the 1960s, many young African Americans, inspired by Black Power, adopted "Israelite" as part of a semantic shift to distinguish themselves from white Jews.[104] Arguably, the most important figure among Black Israelites from the 1960s through the early twenty-first century was the charismatic spiritual leader Ben Ammi Ben-Israel of Chicago. His religious beliefs and globetrotting embodied the possibilities and limitations embedded in Black nationalism from the nineteenth century to the UNIA to the movements Garvey spawned. Born Ben Carter in Chicago in 1939, his early years were difficult. After dropping out of high school, he served in the army. Like for other midwestern Black nationalists, the industrial shop floor was critical to radicalizing Ben-Israel. In the early 1960s, he worked as a metallurgist at a west side foundry. His life forever changed after a Black coworker told Ben-Israel that African Americans were the descendants of the biblical Israelites. Intrigued, he began studying the Bible, and he came to know Abihu Ben Reuben, who renamed him Ben Ammi Ben-Israel. His life took another unexpected turn in 1966 when he had a vision in which the biblical archangel Gabriel told Ben-Israel to lead an exodus of African Americans to the Promised Land—Israel. He was not prepared to lead Blacks to Israel. Instead, he set his eyes on Liberia as the destination for African Americans. A student of Black nationalism, he studied emigrationist Henry McNeal Turner, and he saw Liberia as a refuge for New World Blacks.[105]

Another significant turn in Ben-Israel's life occurred in 1967 when he founded the A-Beta Hebrew Israel Cultural Center, located on the South Side, to promote his religious and emigrationist beliefs. In the same year, Ben-Israel took more than three hundred of his followers to Liberia to initiate their spiritual rebirth and to return to their ancestral homeland. The Liberian government provided the group five hundred acres of land on which to settle in Bong County near Gbandela. It is unknown whether the Hebrew Israelites were familiar with the work of James and Goldie Stewart prior to arriving in Liberia or if the group came to know Clarence Harding in Monrovia. What is for sure is that some Hebrew Israelites befriended Goldie Stewart and some of her family in Gbandela.[106] Life was hard for Hebrew Israelites in the Liberian interior. Some perished from tropical diseases. Determined to fulfill his divine revelation, Ben-Israel took 150 followers to Israel in 1969. By 1972, more than 250 Black Israelites settled in Dimona, a town in the Negev Desert in southern Israel. They encountered racial discrimination from white Israeli government officials who viewed the group as foreign interlopers and as a dangerous cult. In response, Ben-Israel issued internationally circulated statements through the African American press condemning white Israeli racism.[107] Ultimately, the Israeli government granted the Hebrew Israelites visas. They came to regard Israel as home and as a beacon of hope for Black people globally. They also believed that Israel was an "African" nation located not in southwestern Asia but in northeastern Africa. In the coming years, Ben-Israel founded a spiritual organization that became the African Hebrew Israelites of Jerusalem (AHIJ). Hundreds of Black Americans—mostly from Chicago and Detroit—emigrated to Dimona, where they established a vibrant, largely autonomous community that came to be known as the Village of Peace. At the time of Ben-Israel's passing in 2014, the group counted more than three thousand members, half of whom were born in Israel. Today, Hebrew

Israelite communities continue to thrive in Israel. However, the citizenship status for some Hebrew Israelites in the Jewish state remains in limbo.[108]

The Hebrew Israelites' beliefs and travels speak to the long-standing complexities of Black internationalism practiced by US Black nationalists. Black Israelites moved to and claimed citizenship in pro-US settler colonial nations— Liberia and Israel. Black Israelites' decision to settle in Israel is curious, given the Jewish state's fraught history and political practice.[109] Nations across the Third World viewed Israel as a political pariah for occupying Palestinian territories captured during the Six-Day War of 1967. The Jewish state became a close ally of Apartheid South Africa, and Hebrew Israelites settled near the site of Israel's secret nuclear weapons program.[110] It would be a stretch to suggest that Liberia and Israel duped Hebrew Israelites. Instead, they truly believed that Liberia and Israel offered the best hope for oppressed Black people everywhere. They were hardly the first African Americans to draw these conclusions. As I discussed earlier in this book, Black nationalists since before the Civil War envisaged Liberia as a refuge for New World Blacks while at the same time endorsing Black diasporic conquest of Indigenes.

Hebrew Israelites interpreted the complex realities of Liberia and Israel through their lived experiences and spiritual beliefs as Black people forged in the United States. Their status as US citizens and access to the US media provided Black Israelites with a modicum of privilege not enjoyed by Arabs or Ethiopian Falasha Jews living in Israel. Hebrew Israelites understood that anti-Black racism existed in Israel. However, Hebrew Israelites believed that they, not European-descended Jews, were the true heirs of the ancient Israelites. Given this perspective, Hebrew Israelites believed they were best suited to realize Israel's divine prophecy as a redemptive homeland for all humanity. The journey of Ben-Israel and his Chicago followers to Liberia and Israel speaks again to the way Black internationalism often simultaneously challenged and upheld settler colonialism, racism, imperialism, and capitalism.

If Chicago constituted an Ethiopian Hebrew hub, then the Windy City also remained a center of African American Islam in the United States during the Black Power years. The long trajectory of Black nationalism lived on through the South Side–based Nation of Islam and its ailing leader Elijah Muhammad into the 1970s.[111] The memory of Malcolm X did not fare well in the Black Power–era NOI. The Nation continued denouncing him after his assassination. His protégé, Louis Farrakhan, who replaced Malcolm as minister of Mosque No. 7 in New York and as National Representative of the NOI, emerged as Muhammad's most loyal lieutenant and vocal critic of Malcolm.[112]

Malcolm's opponents were unsuccessful in completely erasing his legacy. Following Elijah Muhammad's passing at the age of seventy-seven in February 1975, his son Wallace D. Mohammed (Warith D. Mohammed), who had criticized his father's religious teachings and had allied with Malcolm before his split from the NOI, assumed leadership of the organization. Mohammed dissolved the Nation. In its place, he formed the Chicago-based World Community of al-Islam in the West. In a move that would have been unthinkable only a few years earlier, Mohammed's new group promoted a nonracial interpretation of Islam, upheld the practices and beliefs of Sunni Islam, and rejected the divinity of W. D. Fard Muhammad and Elijah Muhammad. W. D. Mohammed's reforms met stiff resistance from none other than Louis Farrakhan. In 1979, he reestablished the Nation of Islam.[113] The restoration of the NOI demonstrates the resilience of Black diasporic right radicalism and the visibility of the Diasporic Midwest in African American Islam decades after W. D. Fard Muhammad founded the neo-Garveyite organization.

Of all the religious figures in the midwestern Garveyite front during the Black Power era, arguably no one embraced Malcolm X more or promoted a more radical religious variant of Black nationalism than minister and theologian Albert B. Cleage of the Shrine of the Black Madonna (Central Congregation Church) of Detroit. By the late 1960s, he established himself as an internationally renowned Black Power theologian. He termed his theology "Black Christian nationalism."[114] Black Christian nationalism drew on the African American Christian prophetic tradition, the legacy of Marcus Garvey and Malcolm X, and Black Israelite beliefs.

Cleage argued that Jesus was the messiah *and* a revolutionary Black leader who sought to liberate the Black nation of biblical Israel from Roman foreign rule. Jesus in this interpretation sought to eradicate a colonial mentality among ancient Israelites. Imploring the African American church to abandon white supremacist theology, Cleage called on Black Christians to advance global Black liberation.[115]

Cleage's unshakable faith in the revolutionary power of the Black masses and embrace of the legacy of Malcolm were critical to shaping Black Christian nationalism. In a 1967 sermon and tribute to Malcolm, Cleage lauded the slain Muslim minister for "the power of [his] prophetic voice." According to Cleage, "The spoken word of Malcolm X was perhaps the most powerful thing for Black people in the twentieth century" for enabling them to understand that they were an oppressed nation entitled to self-determination. As the NOI denounced Malcolm, Cleage celebrated him as a Black nationalist prophet.[116]

Cleage's renaming the Central Congregational Church as the Shrine of the Black Madonna and the unveiling in the sanctuary of a large painting of a dark-skinned Black Madonna and child on Easter Sunday 1967 speaks to Cleage's ongoing embrace of Black Power. But this formulation also speaks to the long-standing, complex gender politics of Black nationalism.[117] The church's name and the painting amounted to powerful discursive and visual manifestos for venerating Black womanhood, rejecting white supremacist interpretations of Christianity, and decolonizing Black minds. At the same time, the portrait proffered a manly vision of racial advancement that framed African American women as subordinate to Black male authority and that defined Black women's beauty through patriarchal standards.[118] The portrait and the church's name simultaneously contested white supremacy, valorized Black womanhood, and affirmed Black patriarchal power. Additionally, Cleage, like Malcolm, often articulated the Black freedom struggle as a contest between "brothers" and "the white man," highlighting his masculinism.[119]

While Cleage's gender politics spoke to the long-standing masculinism embedded in Black nationalism, his work also illustrates his belief in Blacks' right to live in dignity in the Motor City.[120] This perspective was most evident in Cleage's response to the Detroit Rebellion of July 23–27, 1967. Black Detroiters' response to racial capitalism and state violence stoked the rebellion.

Deindustrialization, police brutality, poverty, residential segregation, poor housing, neglect from city hall, and white racism hit the city's 700,000 Black residents extremely hard. For five days, Black Detroiters raged against state violence, misery, and injustice, expropriated property from and burned down white-owned ghetto businesses, and shot back at authorities. US president Lyndon B. Johnson deployed the 82nd and 101st US army airborne divisions to assist local law enforcement and the National Guard in restoring order. The "Great Rebellion," as some Black Detroit and white radicals called it, was the deadliest and most destructive urban disorder to date in US history. At least forty-three people died, nearly two thousand people were injured, and one thousand buildings burned to the ground. State violence fell disproportionately on Black people. The police, National Guard, firefighters, and regular US soldiers killed thirty-three African Americans.[121]

The Detroit Rebellion was critical to shaping Cleage's Black nationalism for the rest of his life. The Shrine's proximity to the uprising's epicenter and the reverend's militancy provided him with a unique vantage point for understanding the unrest's significance. While local and national politicians and pundits often condemned Black Detroiters for using violence and blamed "outside agitators" and "criminals" for the unrest, Cleage from the pulpit praised the city's African American masses for forcibly resisting authorities and white racial oppression. Using masculinist discourse, he linked the Detroit uprising to a nationwide Black "rebellion" in which Blacks were "becom[ing] what God intended that we should be—free men with control of our destiny, the destiny of black men."[122] His perspective on the unrest in Detroit echoed those of other Black militants and white radicals who called the unrest a "Great Rebellion" instead of a "riot."[123] The Shrine's membership swelled after the rebellion, and his Black radical Christian message swept across Black America.[124]

Following the Detroit uprising, Cleage advanced his Black liberation theology through institution-building, grassroots political organizing, and transnational work informed by Garvey's legacy. In April 1970, the Shrine hosted the first Black Christian Nationalism conference, a UNIA-like international gathering attended by delegates from forty states and seven African countries ready to free Black people everywhere.

In a nod to Garvey, the Shrine operated a food co-op whose motto was "One Aim, One Purpose," while a nursery school run by the church celebrated August as "Marcus Garvey Month." Cleage and the Shrine played key roles in mobilizing strong Black support for Coleman Young, the city's first African American mayor elected in 1973.[125] In 1978, Cleage officially established a new denomination—the Pan African Orthodox Christian Church (PAOCC), whose name resembled Garvey's African Orthodox Church. Cleage changed the name of the Shrine of the Black Madonna to the Black Christian Nationalist Church.[126] There is no record of Cleage meeting Ben Ammi Ben-Israel and Clarence Harding. However, Harding and Ben-Israel would have agreed with Cleage in his claims that Jesus and the biblical Israelites were African people. Personally, the Black Power years transformed Cleage's life. In the early 1970s, he followed a path well traveled by Malcolm X and Black militants since the nineteenth century by adopting a new name—Jaramogi Abebe Agyeman ("Defender / Holy Man / Liberator of His People").[127] The Detroit theologian was part of a larger community of Black midwesterners who were at the forefront in the African world in forging powerful and complex Black ethnic religions during the Black Power era. Inspired by the spirit of Garvey, Malcolm, and the long history of Black nationalism and molded by the racial and material realities of the contemporary moment, heartland Black ethnic religious practitioners were ready to learn good, to seek justice, and to eradicate oppression everywhere.

Garvey and the Black Arts Movement in Chicago

As Garveyism enjoyed new life through heartland-based Black ethnic religions in the Black Power era, the Black Arts Movement in Chicago proved an important site for retooling and disseminating the long legacy of Black nationalism and Garvey in and far beyond the Windy City during the 1970s. The Black Arts Movement, the cultural arm of Black Power, understood the arts as a critical platform for advancing Black liberation. With the expression "Black Is Beautiful," the Black Arts Movement introduced a new Black cultural aesthetic premised on racial unity, positive community values, and the celebration of Blackness for advancing dignity, respect, and self-determination.[128] The Chicago Black Arts Movement emerged as the city's African American population increased in 1970 to 1,102,620, or 32.7 percent of the city's total population.[129] Scholars have correctly pointed out the importance of Chicago to the Black Arts Movement nationally. However, little attention has been given to the influence of Garvey on the Black arts scene in the Windy City.[130] The UNIA was not a major factor in shaping the Chicago Black Arts Movement. However, Chicago and other Black midwestern poets, scholars, journalists, visual artists, playwrights, and world travelers were at the forefront internationally in celebrating Garvey and Malcolm and in developing a new Black aesthetic that departed from the Black diasporic right radicalism of old.[131]

The educator, writer, and world traveler Christine Johnson was at the forefront in keeping Garvey's and Malcolm's legacies alive in Chicago and globally. She remained a close ally of Malcolm's after his split from the NOI. Following his assassination, she left the Nation.[132] After leaving the NOI, she celebrated Malcolm's life through her writing. Her poem "When You Died" was published in the landmark 1967 anthology *For Malcolm: Poems on the Life and Death of Malcolm X*. Coedited by Margaret Burroughs and Dudley Randall, the noted Detroit Black Arts poet and publisher of the Black independent publishing house Broadside Press, *For Malcolm* was one of the first published literary works about Malcolm. *For Malcolm* included poetry and essays by young and veteran Black cultural luminaries from across the United States and Black world.[133] Johnson's poem decried Malcolm's murder. But she also expressed confidence that his defiant call "For Rights, For Freedoms, and For Justice" would one day be realized.[134] Publishing "When You Died" was a brave move. She surely knew that she was putting herself in harm's way, given the Nation's denunciations of Malcolm and his followers. NOI members apparently never physically attacked her. But the poem amounted to a pledge of allegiance to Malcolm and a declaration of independence from the NOI.

Johnson combined her love for Malcolm with her veneration of Garvey. Her book *ABC's of African History* (1971) is a case in point. Like her groundbreaking children's textbook *Muhammad's Children* published a decade earlier, *ABC's of African History* was a trailblazing book for Black juvenile readers. The use of "African" instead of "Black" in the book's title reflected Johnson's deliberate effort to transform the subjectivities of her young readers. The book uses biographical sketches and illustrations of famous people of African descent to promote Black self-love and to celebrate the contributions of Black people to world history from the dawn of humanity in Africa millions of years ago to Ancient Egypt to the twentieth century.[135] Marcus Garvey and Malcolm X appear prominently. The vignette on Garvey features the famous photograph of him adorned in a plumed hat and military uniform at a UNIA parade in Harlem in 1924.[136] Similar to the MGI in Lansing and the MGMI in Monrovia, the book acknowledges Garvey as the forebearer of contemporary freedom struggles across the African world. Her biographical sketch of Malcolm stresses his self-transformation, global travels, and uncompromising commitment to the liberation of African and oppressed people everywhere. *ABC's of African History* made Garvey and Malcolm relevant to a new generation of young Black people during the 1970s. Johnson's cultural work illustrates how Black Chicago women were prominent in the local Black arts scene. The city's long tradition of African American women's activism and their visibility in the city's unique modern urban Black culture help explain this phenomenon.

While older Midwest-based Black cultural workers like Johnson kept the memory of Garvey and Malcolm alive, Chicago was home to countless young Black arts figures who understood their work within the longer history of Black struggle: Sylvia Abernathy, Gerald McWhorter (Abdul Alkalimat), Val Gray Ward, Hoyt Fuller, Carolyn Rogers, Conrad Kent Rivers, Haki Madhubuti, Phil Cohran, Useni Eugene Perkins, Myrna Weaver, Jeff Donaldson, and Carolyn Lawrence among others.[137] Arguably, Chicago-based poet Haki Madhubuti stands as the most important Black Arts Movement figure in the midwestern Garveyite front. A giant in the movement, Madhubuti had an extraordinary career, his work stretching from the late 1960s into the twenty-first century, that reflected his belief in the power of the creative arts and cultural institutions for promoting Black self-definition, self-love, and self-determination on a global scale. His career also illustrates the linkages between the Black Arts Movement, Malcolm X, and Marcus Garvey.[138] Born Donald Luther Lee in Little Rock, Arkansas, in 1942, he was reared in Detroit's Black Bottom and on Chicago's west side by a young, single, working-class mother. After serving four years in the US army, he returned to Chicago in 1963. In the coming years, veteran Black Chicago leftists Margaret and Charles Burroughs, as well as Gwendolyn Brooks, the Pulitzer Prize award-winning poet who embraced Black Power, mentored Madhubuti.[139] He never met Malcolm. However, looking back, Madhubuti claimed that "Malcolm X was the most important mentor I never met."[140] For Madhubuti, Malcolm represented "the perfect example of . . . a true revolutionary" due to his uncompromising rejection of white supremacy, imperialism, and colonialism, and commitment to self-transformation.[141] Madhubuti admired Garvey for building independent Black institutions and for advocating African liberation.[142]

In addition to his poetry, Madhubuti, following a long precedent of Black midwestern institution-building, understood the importance of establishing Black-controlled social infrastructures for advancing Black freedom. This belief was illustrative in Third World Press (TWP). Founded in 1967, Madhubuti launched the press from his South Side basement apartment. The press's name reflected the global perspective long upheld by Black midwesterners. TWP published work by leading Black Arts Movement intellectuals from Chicago and around the world, and the publishing house remains the oldest continuously operating Black independent press in the world.[143] Madhubuti was a national leader in establishing independent Black secondary schools. In 1969, he founded the Institute of Positive Education and the New Concept School three years later. These schools, operating in self-owned buildings on the South Side, reflected how Madhubuti—like Garvey, Louise Little, Clara Muhammad, Elijah Muhammad, Malcolm X, Harding, and Johnson—cherished African American–centered education and institution-building.[144]

Madhubuti's work existed within a larger Chicago Black arts universe of nationally and internationally influential institutions, public art, and literary works influenced by the legacies of Malcolm and Garvey—the Organization of Black American Culture (OBAC), Kuumba Theatre, AfriCOBRA, Association for the Advancement of Creative Musicians, Affro-Arts Theater, Malcolm X Black Hand Society, *Negro Digest / Black World*, Malcolm X College, and the Wall of Respect. Through promoting a Black Arts aesthetic, these Chicago-based initiatives found success in transforming the minds of Black people. Chicago Black Arts figures redefined public space, claimed the right for Black people to live in the city, and linked the local to the global through public art.[145] Most Chicago Black Arts Movement initiatives were short-lived. However, some endured for decades, most notably Malcolm X College (formerly Crane Junior College), a two-year college on Chicago's west side still open today. Founded in 1911, Crane Junior College was the first of the Chicago city colleges. By the late 1960s, most of its students were African Americans from the school's surrounding working-poor neighborhood. Frustrated with racism and inspired by Black Power, students along with Illinois Black Panthers and community members protested on campus. They demanded that the college hire a Black president and rename the school after Malcolm X. The Chicago City College board acquiesced to mass pressure by renaming the school Malcolm X College, making it the first college in the world named after Malcolm. The board hired William G. Hurston, a Howard University professor and Black Power champion, as the institution's president.[146]

Today, UNIA-inspired red, black, and green tricolors, and portraits and murals of Malcolm adorn Malcolm X College. Since its founding, the school has educated thousands of Black and brown working-class Chicagoans and has gained a reputation for training students in health sciences programs and other related fields that prepare them to pursue a four-year degree or a professional career.[147] Like the MGMI, MGI, Institute of Positive Education, and UOI, Malcolm X College empowered Black working-class people.

The success of Chicago Black Arts initiatives brought government scrutiny and surveillance. The Red Squad collected thousands of pages of surveillance files on Malcolm X College, the Illinois chapter of the Black Panther Party, and other Chicago neo-Garveyite groups, as well as on individuals such as Fred Hampton, Johnson, Madhubuti, and Val Gray Ward.[148] These files contained newspaper clippings, photographs, and reports about the politics, meetings, public protest, membership, and organizational structures of Black Power formations, as well as information about the private lives and travels of Black activists in the Windy City.[149] The police never raided Malcolm X College or arrested Madhubuti. But as in Cleveland, Lansing, Monrovia, and elsewhere, state repression helped to facilitate the demise of Black Power in Chicago.

The legacy of Garvey and the long history of Black nationalism lurked among young and old Black organizers, cultural workers, elected officials, students, factory workers, and everyday people into the 1970s through the UNIA and new political, cultural, and religious movements linked to the Diasporic Midwest. Garvey to varying degrees inspired these formations and their participants, and they profoundly shaped internationalist Black Power Movement and African liberation struggles raging across the continent. Black diasporic right radicalism for many Black Power militants, young and old, was a relic of the past. Countless militants refashioned Garveyism to keep it relevant to the realities and needs of the African-descended. The principles of and respect for Garvey also provided a common reference point for building multigenerational Black formations. Certainly, these groups understood freedom differently, and conflicts sometimes fractured them. Male chauvinism remained a problem in the UNIA and neo-Garveyite groups. But women like Mary Mason, Georgina Thornton, Noni Gee, Adenike Sharpley, Cynthia Hamilton, Queen Mother Moore, and Philomena Bloh Sayeh did more than simply hold their own. They challenged male leaders for their sexism and took the lead in building institutions, movements, and transnational political linkages. State repression, the death of Clarence Harding, the 1980 coup in Liberia, ongoing organizational weakness within the UNIA, the demise of Black Power, and a rightward geopolitical sea change, marked most significantly by the election of Ronald Reagan to the US presidency in 1980, signaled the end of a moment in the long trajectory of Garveyism. But it is undeniable that the US heartland, forged by its distinct racial, human, and geographical landscape, played an instrumental role in advancing global Black freedom and radical Black internationalism into the 1970s through formations and participants directly inspired by Garvey.

CONCLUSION. The Diasporic Midwest and Global Garveyism in a New Millennium

Garvey was the central force of inspiration for all the young revolutionaries who made an impact on the African continent. —EMMANUEL MULBAH JOHNSON, cofounder and former president of the James R. Stewart UNIA 435 Division, Monrovia, Liberia, September 6, 2022

Rabbi Capers C. Funnye Jr. was feeling the spirit. He was passionately preaching and his congregation was rocking on a wintry Saturday morning in Chicago in January 2017.[1] He is the African American chief rabbi of the Beth Shalom B'nai Zaken Ethiopian Hebrew Congregation (Beth Shalom), the oldest temple in the Chicago area serving the Black Israelite community and the largest congregation of its kind globally. The two-hundred-plus-member temple is located at 6601 S. Kedzie Avenue in the Chicago southwest side neighborhood of Marquette Park.[2] The neighborhood was once all-white. Its residents and the local Nazi Party bitterly resisted housing desegregation campaigns waged by Martin Luther King Jr. and the Chicago Freedom Movement in the mid-1960s. Today, Marquette Park is an overwhelmingly majority Black and brown neighborhood.[3]

Beth Shalom is a dynamic, transnational spiritual space connected to the long history of Garveyism, Black ethnic religions, and the Diasporic Midwest.

These linkages were evident in Funnye's sermon and the temple's Black Israelite spiritual beliefs and practices. In his sermon, delivered in the style of a southern African American Baptist preacher, he asserted that the congregants were the direct heirs of the ancient Israelites, who were Black. Parishioners cheered. He acknowledged that the temple's cofounding rabbis, Abihu Ben Reuben and Joseph Lazarus, were proud Garveyites and that the temple continues to live by their religious and political beliefs. Men adorned in yarmulkes and women in head coverings sat on separate sides of the temple. Worshippers rejoiced when Funnye took the Torah scrolls written in Hebrew out of the ornamental chamber—the Aron Kodesh. Assigned parishioners read aloud the Torah fluently in Hebrew to the congregation. During the service, choir members blew the shofar, the bugle typically made of a ram's horn, used for Jewish religious rituals. Unlike at white Jewish temple services, Beth Shalom choir members blew several shofars while the temple band feverishly played religious music reminiscent of contemporary gospel music, hip hop, and funk. The service, attended by more than one hundred people and packed with families with children, reflected the racial and ethnic diversity of the temple's surrounding neighborhood. Most of the congregants were African American working-class and lower middle-class people. However, there were a noticeable number of Latine in the temple, illustrating how the congregation temple speaks to its brown members' spiritual needs and has made inroads into the city's exponentially growing Latine population.[4] For Beth Shalom congregants, their beliefs are more than a religion. They are a "way of life" for guiding believers through all dimensions of life.[5]

Beth Shalom has gained national and international attention through its high-profile rabbi. Originally from South Carolina and a longtime resident of Chicago, Capers is the first cousin once removed of Michelle Obama, the first Black US First Lady and Barack Obama's wife. Beginning in 2008, US media outlets reported these family connections and the rabbi's globetrotting to Israel and Africa for spreading the faith.[6] The Garveyite principles of knowledge of self, race pride, institution-building, globality, and self-determination thrive not only at Beth Shalom. Garvey's legacy has forged a new generation of midwestern working-class people of color, determined to live spiritually healthy and socially meaningful lives, who are conscious of the world and history through their Black Israelite faith.[7]

This concluding chapter appreciates the ongoing global impact of the US heartland on Black lives and freedom-making through the UNIA and midwestern Garveyite front from the 1990s onward. Garveyism and the longue durée of Black nationalism have survived among formations, movements, institutions, and everyday people based in or linked to early twenty-first-century Chicago, Detroit, Cleveland, and other midwestern rural and urban locales. Garveyism, with its possibilities and paradoxes, continues to evolve in response to the heartland experience of the dialectic of opportunity and oppression, global events, and the burning desire of Black people to be free. The early twenty-first-century Diasporic Midwest remains a generative geographic terrain and transnational crossroads for powerful and complex Black movements informed by the afterlife of Garvey and committed to the full freedom of the African-descended everywhere.

The UNIA and Liberia in a New Millennium

It is undeniable that the present-day UNIA is a shadow of its former glory. The UNIA remains divided among several factions that claim to be the legitimate UNIA. The most visible UNIA faction, led by Jamaican-born Michael R. Duncan, who resides in Brooklyn, traces its lineage to the organization established in 1951 and once headed by William Sherrill, Thomas W. Harvey, and Charles L. James. Another UNIA faction, led by Cleophus Miller Jr., a retired Cleveland Browns professional football player, is based in Cleveland and is linked to the organization once headed by James Stewart. In 2020, a group calling itself the UNIA-ACL Rehabilitating Committee 2020 split from the Duncan-led UNIA. Relations between the three groups are complicated.[8] While tension exists among these competing Garveyite factions, the social class composition of the UNIA has remained the same since its founding. Like in the UNIA's heyday, most Garveyites today hail from working-class and lower middle-class backgrounds. One striking difference between the earlier and contemporary UNIA is the way many Garveyites today eschew Eurocentric lifeways for "African" ways of life. Highlighting the cultural impact of the Rastafari, Black Power, and Afrocentrism on the contemporary UNIA, many Garveyites don African clothing, take African names, and wear dreadlocks. Garvey's aversion to African Indigenous cultures is apparently of no major concern to present-day UNIA members. They appreciate him as the paragon of Africanity. Despite internecine rivalries, the contemporary UNIA remains vibrant and involved in global Black liberation initiatives.

Today, Liberia remains central to the UNIA's pan-African mission, underscoring the West African nation's continued importance to Black nationalism, internationalism, and radicalism. The political and social economic situation in early twenty-first-century Liberia is both remarkably like and different from the nation in the lifetime of Marcus Garvey, James and Goldie Stewart, and

Clarence Harding. Following the 1980 military coup led by Samuel K. Doe, the nation witnessed unprecedented social and political turmoil. Nineteen eighty-nine marked the beginning of the first Liberian civil war. Doe was executed one year later by rebel forces.[9] From 1990 and 1994, Amos Sawyer, a leader of the MOJA and an associate of the Chicago UNIA leader Clarence Harding in the 1970s, served as interim president of Liberia. Sawyer restored relative peace to the nation. However, armed civil conflict reignited in the ensuing years under Charles Taylor, a ruthless Liberian president initially backed by the United States. In 1998, popular opposition to his rule sparked the second Liberian civil war, a conflict known for widespread human rights violations, rape, and use of child soldiers.[10] The war ended in 2003. Two years later, Ellen Johnson Sirleaf was elected to the Liberian presidency, making her the first democratically elected female president of Liberia and in Africa. Her presidency was not easy. The Ebola epidemic of 2014 and 2015 ravaged Liberia and neighboring Sierra Leone and Guinea.[11] In 2022, Liberia counted 5,306,587 people, with 62 percent of its population under the age of twenty-four.[12] Despite years of turmoil, the Liberian people's determination got the nation through some of the world's worst civil conflicts and natural disasters since the late twentieth century.

The resilient spirit of young post–civil war Liberians is evident in the James R. Stewart UNIA Division 435 (JRS-D 435), based in Monrovia. Comprising students and young professionals, most of whom hail from the working poor, JRS-D 435 constitutes perhaps the most important and radical UNIA division in the world today. In the division's name and objectives, the organization connects itself in innovative and unexpected ways to the long trajectory of Garvey, the Diasporic Midwest, and Black radicalism in Liberia and across Global Africa. Like African-descended militants across the world since the interwar years, JRS-D 435 members identify Garvey as foundational to twentieth-century African liberation. However, they do not subscribe to Black diasporic right radicalism. Instead, they have formulated an idiosyncratic politics combining Garveyism, Marxism, Third Worldism, and pan-Africanism. In addition to Garvey, they look up to African revolutionary leaders such as Kwame Nkrumah, Agostinho Neto, Amílcar Cabral, and Thomas Sankara.[13]

Michael Duncan, UNIA's president-general, was instrumental to the founding of JRS D-435 in August 2015. He was in Liberia in part to recruit young people into the UNIA. He arranged a meeting with student organizers at the University of Liberia. They were knowledgeable about Marcus Garvey and James Stewart before encountering Duncan. His eloquence and urge for students to deepen their understanding of Garvey and Stewart impressed and prompted students to form JRS-D 435.[14] Given the local's staunch leftist politics, it might seem ironic that Liberian students chose to affiliate with the UNIA and to name their division after James Stewart, a staunch anticommunist and civilizationist, who battled in the 1950s with the UNIA faction now led by Michael Duncan. Politics can make for strange bedfellows. But JRS-D 435 members were neither taking liberties with history nor making a politically foolhardy decision. Instead, they made a politically savvy and strategic move. They wanted to change the world. But they possessed limited resources for advancing their dreams from chronically underdeveloped Liberia. By affiliating with the UNIA and naming their division after Stewart, young Liberian radicals acknowledged their country's complex diasporic heritage and secured organizational support for their local and transnational work through a legendary US-based pan-African movement. For New World Garveyites, JRS-D 435 restored the UNIA's presence in a nation identified by Black nationalists since the nineteenth century as the beachhead of global Black freedom (see figure C.1). The new division also provided the UNIA Parent Body with an entry point to youth in Liberia and across Africa. In 2019, the Duncan-led UNIA sought to extend the momentum of JRS-D 435 and to realize Garvey's and Stewart's desire for advancing the global Black struggle through staging the UNIA's sixty-second international conference in Monrovia. In the same year, Duncan established Liberty Farm, a UNIA-owned commercial farm in Grand Bassa County (see figure C.2), inspired by both Garvey's dream of operating commercial farms in Africa and James and Goldie Stewart's Liberty Farm in Bong County.[15]

Meanwhile, JRS-D 435 reflects the possibilities, continuities, and ruptures in the Garvey movement and its long-standing linkages to the US heartland. The division's cofounder and first president, Emmanuel Mulbah Johnson, embodies these connections. Raised in a large Indigenous family in Clara Town, a poor Monrovia neighborhood, he followed a similar road traveled by countless African-descended people since the early twentieth century who came to appreciate education and Garveyism as vehicles for self-transformation, upward mobility, and African liberation. His introduction to Garveyism came through self-study and student activism at the University of Liberia. After graduating and completing his term as JRS-D 435 president, he moved to Chicago, where in 2021 he earned his master's degree in international development and policy at the University of Chicago. He returned to Liberia. He served as the assistant minister of youth development for the Ministry of Youth and Sports and the national secretary-general of the Revolutionary National Youth League—Congress for Democratic Change, the ruling political party affiliated with Liberian former president George Weah.[16]

FIGURE C.I. Author (*back left corner*) with members of UNIA James R. Stewart Division 435, January 2016. Sammitta Entsua is the second woman from the left holding the UNIA flag. Emmanuel Mulbah Johnson is fourth from left in the back row. Photo by the author.

FIGURE C.2. Liberty Farm, Grand Bassa County, Liberia, March 2023. Photo by the author.

Women were just as vital to the UNIA now. One of the most important young Liberian Garveyites today is Sammitta Entsua. A dynamic leader, organizer, and university student from Monrovia's impoverished West Point district, she cofounded JRS-D 435. Like countless African-descended people long before her, she came to understand Garvey as "the father of pan-Africanism," illustrating how Black nationalists continue articulating pan-Africanism in gendered terms.[17] In 2019, she became the division's second president. On her watch, the local grew exponentially. She co-organized a memorial service on June 8, 2020, cosponsored by JRS-D 435 and other local radical youth groups, in front of the sprawling fortresslike US embassy in Monrovia, calling for justice for the African American George Floyd, murdered by a white police officer in Minneapolis, Minnesota, in May 2020.[18] More than fifty people attended this rally linked with global protests in solidarity with Floyd and in support of racial justice everywhere. Young Liberian demonstrators carried a banner adorned with Floyd's image and held photographs of Marcus Garvey, Malcolm X, Rosa Parks, and Martin Luther King. By taking to the streets, they defied the UNIA's unofficial policy of abstaining from social protests, denounced US racism, and tied their freedom dreams with those of Black people globally.[19]

Young Liberian Garveyites study history seriously. They are aware of the work of the young Amos Sawyer and MOJA. However, some know nothing about Clarence Harding and the Marcus Garvey Memorial Institute, let alone Black student radicalism through the Marcus Garvey Institute and the Black Liberation Front International in Black Power–era Lansing. Time, geographic distance, and national boundaries have severed some of the connections between JRS-D 335 and earlier Black struggles.

Beyond the formal organizational structures of the UNIA, the Stewarts' legacy survives through their descendants and those impacted by their work. Donna Cooper Hayford, the couple's second eldest daughter who in 1949 at the age of eighteen emigrated with her family to Liberia, made West Africa her home for the rest of her life. In the coming decades, she pursued a professional career, married, raised a family in Liberia and Ghana, and came to know leading figures in Liberian society.[20] Her older brother Victor was a decorated Second World War US army veteran, who served for decades with distinction as a colonel in the Liberian army.[21] Today, James and Goldie Stewart's immense number of descendants live in Liberia and across the United States. None of them became prominent Garveyites, but they are immensely proud of their family's rich history and midwestern and Liberian connections.

Outside of bustling contemporary Monrovia, their legacy also endures in tiny Gbandela in rural Bong County. It is here just off the Monrovia-Gbarnga

FIGURE C.3. Stewart family graveyard, Gbandela, Bong County, Liberia, March 2023. Photo by the author.

highway where the Ohio Garveyites are laid to rest in a tree-covered family graveyard. James has been buried there since 1964. The ashes of Goldie, who passed away in 1995 in Cleveland, were transported to her beloved Liberia and were interred in a small tomb on top of her husband's grave. Several of the couple's descendants are buried near them (see figure C.3).[22]

James Stewart's lasting achievement in Gbandela—the James R. Stewart Elementary School established in 1964—is still open (see figure C.4). A small staff of teachers instruct in English several hundred young and adolescent students whose first language is Kpelle. The open-air school building lacks electricity and running water. The underresourced school and the humble backgrounds of the students are metaphoric for the profound challenges facing contemporary Liberia *and* the resilience of its people. Despite difficult odds, thousands of Indigenous Liberians for decades have secured a brighter future and learned about the larger world through the school. As discussed earlier in this book, the Stewarts were unsuccessful in achieving Garvey's grand dream of building a powerful African super-state from rural central Liberia through the UNIA. But the Stewarts were not failures. The couple, inspired by their Garveyite convictions and with limited resources, made meaningful interventions

FIGURE C.4. Donna Cooper Hayford (*seated*) with teachers and students, James R. Stewart Elementary School, Gbandela, Bong, County, Liberia, February 2019. Photo by the author.

in the lives of countless everyday African-descended people in and far beyond Liberia. Today, scholars, activists, and UNIA members from around the world are discovering the Stewarts' extraordinary contributions to global Garveyism. Their work, as well as JRS D-435, illustrates the ongoing significance of Liberia to Black internationalism. The early twenty-first-century UNIA is not the early twentieth-century UNIA. Nonetheless, contemporary Garveyism remains sufficiently flexible in adapting to changing times, and the Diasporic Midwest still figures prominently in the transnational UNIA's present and future.

Garveyism in the Twenty-First-Century Heartland

Garveyism has endured in the twenty-first-century UNIA and Liberia, and Garvey's legacy also continues shaping Black life in the US heartland. The region has been hit especially hard by deindustrialization, globalization, and neo-liberalism since the late 1970s. Black communities have suffered under mass incarceration, increased state violence, the dismantlement of the welfare state, the full-scale assault on the victories won by the Civil Rights–Black Power Movements, and the rise of color-blind racial ideology, the prevailing racist ideology of the contemporary moment that denies the continued salience of racial oppression in shaping US life.[23] Globally, the past forty years witnessed the demise of the Soviet Union; the collapse of radical Third World regimes; the hypercapitalist turn of the People's Republic of China; the US-led "War on Terror"; growing socioeconomic inequalities; the rise of religious fundamentalism, heteropatriarchy, authoritarianism, and ethnonationalism; and the cascading effects of climate change. The turn of the twenty-first century, then, constituted a new historical conjuncture for Black people in the United States and globally.

Garvey's ghost survives in early twentieth-century Detroit. The city, once the marvel and global symbol of industrialization and modernity, is now the poster child of the so-called urban crisis. Today, Detroit is the largest Black-majority city in the United States. In 2022, the city counted 620,376 residents, a loss of more than 1.2 million people since 1950.[24] However, framing Detroit as an urban apocalypse shrouds the genius, resilience, and creativity of the city's African American residents. As Grace Lee Boggs, a longtime resident of Detroit and ally of Malcolm X, put it in 2010, Detroit today constitutes "a city of hope" for building a new society.[25] Black people inspired by Garvey are making this happen. The Detroit UNIA, like locals in Cleveland and Chicago, is largely inactive. However, Garvey lives in Detroit through grassroots organizations like D-Town Farm, the largest of the city's many gardens and farms, established in 2008 by Malik Yakini. A veteran community activist, he came of age in Black Power–era Detroit and deeply admires Garvey and Malcolm.[26] Reflecting their ideals, D-Town Farm advances community-building, self-reliance, "African self-determination," and "food sovereignty," a vision for creating a new world through equitable and sustainable production, distribution, and access to healthy food.[27] While D-Town Farm upholds Garveyite beliefs in self-reliance, the farm does not embrace Garvey's Black diasporic right radicalism. D-Town Farm envisions socialism as an essential component for Black liberation and global sustainability.[28]

Garvey's afterlife lives on in Chicago. Like Detroit and other midwestern cities, Chicago, once the greatest boomtown in the United States and a key terminus in the Great Migration, has been hit hard by deindustrialization, gentrification, divestment, gun violence, and neoliberalism. In 2022, the city counted 2,756,546 residents, making it the third-largest US city. Chicago's Black population has steadily declined by more than 350,000 since 1980, when the city counted its peak Black population of 1.2 million.[29] Despite facing immense challenges, Black Chicago continues to be an international center of Black life and culture. Third World Press and the Institute of Positive Education, the

Black Power–era brainchildren of Haki Madhubuti, along with the Betty Shabazz International Charter School, established by him in 1998, remain open.[30]
These institutions, like the UNIA and other midwestern Garveyite cultural
formations, embody the Black midwestern impulse of empowering working-
class Black people through institution-building and advancing transformative
knowledge. On the spiritual front, Chicago is still a center of several Garvey-
influenced Black ethnic religions—Moorish Science, Hebrew Israelites, and
the Nation of Islam. These religions still attract new believers across the heartland and beyond.[31]

Meanwhile, the Midwest was critical to shaping the most important Black
protest movement since the Civil Rights–Black Power Movements: Black Lives
Matter / Movement for Black Lives (BLM/M4BL). Neither the UNIA nor any
of its offshoots played a major role in organizing BLM/M4BL. It did not origi-
nate in the Midwest.[32] However, the killing of an unarmed African American
eighteen-year-old, Michael Brown, by a white police officer on August 9, 2014,
in midwestern Ferguson, Missouri, made Brown a household name and BLM/
M4BL a global phenomenon.[33] As scholar and public intellectual Keeanga-
Yamahtta Taylor argues, the massive protests in Ferguson and nationwide
shattered the illusion of a postracial America and highlighted the spontaneous
response of countless Black people and their allies across the country against
intensifying state violence and economic crisis faced by African Americans.[34]
It is no historical accident that Ferguson, an impoverished majority–African
American inner-ring suburb of St. Louis, was the site where BLM/M4BL truly
went global. Ferguson must be understood within the long arc of African
American life and resistance in the St. Louis area. The city is located about ten
miles from Brooklyn, Illinois, the oldest African American–incorporated US
municipality. Antebellum St. Louis was critical to white settler westward conquest and to slavery. The *Dred Scott* case, heard in St. Louis, was a major event
in the buildup to the Civil War. In the early and mid-twentieth century, the
St. Louis area was a stronghold of the UNIA and PMEW whose pro-Japanese
sympathies terrified US rulers during the Second World War. Postwar St. Louis
was a center for Black trade unionism, civil rights, and Black Power.[35] In recent
decades, Ferguson has been deeply impacted by deindustrialization, divestment, and heavy policing.[36]

While Ferguson was critical to raising BLM/M4BL's global profile, another
midwestern city—Cleveland—was essential to shaping this movement. In
July 2016, more than 1,500 Black activists from more than fifty grassroots Black
protest organizations from across the United States converged in Cleveland
at the historic National Convening of the Movement for Black Lives, the first

national BLM/M4BL conference.[37] There, they drafted the BLM/M4BL manifesto, "Vision for Black Lives: Policy Demands for Black Power, Freedom, and Justice." Transnational in scope and capacious in its conceptualization of freedom, the manifesto demanded Black political power, reparations, economic and environmental justice, prison abolition, food sovereignty, and the end of gender-based state and interpersonal violence and discrimination against women, girls, LGBTQIA+ people, and disabled people.[38] The fact that M4BL held its first national conference in this deindustrialized midwestern city, once an epicenter of the nineteenth-century Colored Conventions, the capital of the 1940s UNIA, and the site where Malcolm X delivered his seminal "Ballot or the Bullet" speech, demonstrates Cleveland's ongoing importance to global Black liberation initiatives.

In 2020, the Midwest was once again ground zero of BLM/M4BL. George Floyd's murder shook the world. In response to his death and amid the COVID-19 global pandemic, perhaps as many as twenty-six million people rallied under the "Black Lives Matter" slogan and participated in the largest protest movement in global history. People took to the streets, demonstrating against anti-Black police brutality and systemic racism in the United States and on every continent except Antarctica.[39] How much demonstrators knew about Garvey when they participated in BLM/M4BL actions is anyone's guess. However, it is undeniable that his ghost was on the streets of Ferguson, Minneapolis, and across the globe. Protestors on the streets and millions more around the world through media saw omnipresent UNIA-inspired red, black, and green flags and the Black Power clenched-fist salute at BLM/M4BL actions.[40]

The past lived on through BLM/M4BL. But young Black militants who rallied to Black Lives Matter deliberately broke new ideological and organizational ground in pursuit of racial justice and African American freedom. A key aspect of the historical significance of BLM/M4BL lies in the fact that for the "first time in the history of US social movements . . . Black feminist politics have defined the frame for a multi-issue, Black-led mass struggle that did not primarily or exclusively focus on women."[41] BLM/M4BL eschews respectability politics and symbolic empowerment through "Black faces in high places"—the election to office of African Americans and "historic firsts" women and people of color.[42] BLM/M4BL's politics is no accident. Through centering Black women, Black feminism, LGBTQIA+ people, and nonhierarchical approaches to organizing, BLM/M4BL rejects the heteropatriarchal, top-down social movement leadership model long practiced by countless Black nationalist, civil rights, and leftist formations. On the one hand, BLM/M4BL incorporated the political symbolism of the Garvey movement and stood on the shoulders of those who came before. On the other hand, BLM/M4BL proffered a vision of Black freedom far more expansive and inclusive than Garvey and his disciples could have ever imagined or desired. Still, BLM/M4BL has much to learn from Garveyism, namely its insistence on appreciating Black freedom in global terms and to centering Africa to Black liberation.

Unsilencing the Past: Louise Little, Garveyism, the
Diasporic Midwest, and the Politics of Possibility

This book ends near where it began, with a discussion of Louise Little and what her life and legacy hold for imagining a freer future world. As discussed, *The Autobiography of Malcolm X* and popular memory frame her as an apolitical, tragic figure whose life seemingly ended after her institutionalization at the Kalamazoo Psychiatric Hospital. Nothing could be further from the truth. Her life ended neither in the hospital nor immediately after her release from it in 1963. She lived for nearly another quarter-century after leaving the hospital. Her survival and legacy enriched her family, who never forgot the Garveyite lessons she instilled in her children. Throughout their entire lives, her sons Wilfred and Philbert continued searching for truth and self-discovery. After years of dedicated service to the Nation of Islam, both brothers left the NOI following Malcolm's assassination. Philbert embraced Sunni Islam and changed his name to Abdul Aziz Omar.[43] Wilfred, who re-adopted the family name "Little," became a community organizer in Detroit and a scholar of Malcolm and Little family history.[44] The life of Robert Little, Louise's youngest child, reflected her concern for nurturing future generations. After earning a graduate degree in social work from Michigan State University, Robert enjoyed a successful career as a pioneering scholar of family caregiving.[45] Wesley Little, too, maintained close ties to his family.[46]

Grassroots Garveyism and community feminism lived on in her daughters, Hilda Little and Yvonne Woodward. While neither woman converted to Islam or engaged in political activism, they both enjoyed long, productive lives. Hilda Little, who never married or had children, moved to Boston in the 1940s where she worked for years in an insurance company before returning to Michigan later in life. The family matriarch and the last surviving sibling of Malcolm X passed away in 2019.[47] Yvonne Woodward embodied the determination of her mother to build self-sufficient Black communities. Like her mother, Yvonne cherished landownership, self-help, and Black unity. In the 1960s, she and her family moved from Grand Rapids, Michigan, to Woodland Park, Michigan, a small Black resort town in central Michigan.[48] Resembling her mother's decision to live on their own land in Lansing, Yvonne purchased several parcels of land, opened a grocery store, and established a public park in Woodland Park. Hilda and several relatives, including her mother, moved to Woodland Park. It was in this quiet African American town where Louise spent her final years. She did not participate in grassroots Garveyite organizing or speak publicly about her world-famous child Malcolm. She was not stuck in a mournful past. Instead, she reconnected with her children and grew close to her grand- and great-grandchildren before her passing in 1989.[49] She had encountered state-sanctioned persecution, trauma, violence, confinement, injustice, and pain during her long life. However, her life should be remembered as a story of resilience, fortitude, determination, and family in the face of seemingly insurmountable odds and as a shining example of Midwest-based Black women's critical importance to the history of global Garveyism and Black struggle.

These factors help explain why Little has generated so much interest recently among organizers, scholars, journalists, artists, and everyday people of African descent and their allies across the United States, Canada, Europe, and Grenada. In Omaha, Louise's first stop in the Midwest, her legacy endures through the Malcolm X Memorial Foundation (MXMF). Located near the site of the Littles' former home at 3448 Pinkney Street, the MXMF is a nonprofit foundation dedicated to celebrating Malcolm's life and legacy and to promoting social change through sponsoring lectures, protests, and other community events.[50] The group has focused increased attention on Louise in recent years.[51] In Lansing, she has received growing interest among the city's Black community. In 2022, Sarah Anthony, a progressive African American Michigan state representative, spearheaded efforts in erecting a historic marker—"The Little Family Homesite"—near the site of the Littles' 1930s home on the city's outskirts. This marker was intended to replace a previous sign at the site, a "Malcolm X Homesite" marker erected in 1975, which focused exclusively on Malcolm. An automobile collision in 2021 had destroyed that sign. Anthony consulted with Deborah Jones, Ilyasah Shabazz, and Black Lansing community members about replacing the destroyed marker. Jones insisted that the new sign acknowledge the entire Little family.[52] Anthony agreed. "The Little Family Homesite" marker acknowledges all of Malcolm's siblings, Louise and Earl Little's Garveyite activism, and her herculean efforts to protect her children (see figure C.5).[53] Looking toward the future, Jones, Anthony, Shabazz, and others involved with designing the new marker hope it will educate the community about the Little family's history and inspire social change.[54]

Just as African Americans in Omaha and Lansing have recently taken steps to memorialize Louise Little and to promote social change through her life,

FIGURE C.5. Little Family Homesite marker, Lansing, Michigan, October 2022. Photo by the author.

Black activists in Montreal are doing the same. This is no easy task. Until recently, her life had been erased from historical memory in Montreal, the city where she first joined the UNIA. Her erasure from local popular memory is inseparable from the silencing of racism in Canada's past and present. Historian and poet activist Afua Cooper persuasively writes, "Canada was part of the New World, an *American* society. The New World was a slave society, and Canada shared that feature."[55] Despite slavery's long history in Canada, "the story of slavery in Canada is locked in the national closet—a well-guarded secret—so well guarded that even scholars who have made slavery their business do not know about the Canadian variant."[56] Accordingly, the silencing of Canadian slavery promotes a national mythology that frames Canada as a tolerant multicultural nation immune from the racism of its southern neighbor, the United States. This discourse conceals the inconvenient truth of Canada's settler colonial past and present, where Blacks, First Nation people, and other people of color and sexual minorities face ongoing state-sanctioned and extralegal violence and second-class citizenship.[57] Recovering Little's life, then, amounts to a process for resisting settler colonialism, empire, white supremacy, state violence, and sexual and gender-based violence in Canada, now and in the future.

In recent years, Black queer feminists in Montreal have been at the forefront in remembering and celebrating the life and legacy of Louise Little, most notably through the Black queer feminist organization Third Eye Collective. Formed in Montreal in 2013, comprising Black women from Canada, the Caribbean, Europe, and Africa, Third Eye Collective is a grassroots, multigenerational organization dedicated to fighting "against sexual, gender-based, intimate partner, and state and institutional violence" and for Black self-determination in Montreal and beyond through transformative and intersectional justice.[58] The group looks to and celebrates Little as a Black feminist queer progenitor and powerful symbol of resistance. Third Eye Collective member and Black queer feminist scholar-activist Délice Mugabo writes, "Her vision insists that we continue to create and nurture Black worlds that can imagine and bring forth Black freedoms that are beyond the 'possible.' Louise Langdon taught us to not wait for it but to make it."[59]

Robyn Maynard, a fellow Black Canadian, queer, feminist, prison abolitionist scholar-activist, draws similar conclusions about Little's significance to contemporary struggles around racial and gender justice locally and beyond. Maynard writes, "Langdon and her life in Montreal attest to a long-ignored history of Black resistance across [the city] and helps to remind us that just as antiblackness has no borders, neither does black resistance."[60] For Black Montreal feminists and queer activists, Little embodies Black women's historic struggle for freedom and the possibility of a freer future world.

Arguably, it is Little's erasure from historical memory in Grenada, her family's ancestral home, that speaks most powerfully to how prevailing historical narratives can silence the past and obscure revolutionary futurities for Black people on this Caribbean island and around the world. Today, many Grenadians know little if anything about her. This is not by accident. Her erasure from popular memory is linked in part to the contested meaning on the island of the Grenada Revolution (1979–1983) and to the US invasion of the country in October 1983 that toppled the revolution. At its core, the Grenada Revolution, led by Maurice Bishop (1944–1983), sought to create a new world through liberating the Grenadian people from centuries of foreign domination, slavery, colonialism, and underdevelopment. The Grenada Revolution had roots, partially anyhow, in Black Power. Like others in the Caribbean region, many key actors in the revolution, including Bishop, became politically active in the context of Black Power before embracing Marxism-Leninism. He credited Malcolm X, Kwame Nkrumah, Frantz Fanon, Che Guevara, and Fidel Castro for radicalizing him. In 1973, Bishop cofounded the New Jewel Movement (NJM), a Marxist-Leninist political formation in Grenada shaped by Black Power and

Third World movements.[61] On March 13, 1979, Bishop and his NJM comrades deposed Eric Gairy, Grenada's first prime minister, who led the country after it gained independence in 1974 from the United Kingdom. The NJM established the People's Revolutionary Government (PRG) and installed Bishop, deeply popular among Grenada's masses, as the island's new prime minister. Under the PRG, Grenada embraced socialism; promoted participatory democracy; established close relations with the radical Third World states of Cuba, Nicaragua, Mozambique, and Angola; and supported the transnational struggle against Apartheid South Africa.[62] Revolutionary Grenada generated excitement across the Caribbean, Third World, and Global Africa as a beacon of possibility and as a model for building a new world free from colonialism, imperialism, racism, and injustice. Bishop and his comrades were very interested in the African American situation. They traveled to the United States, where they met with exuberant Black audiences. Delegations of Black and white radicals from the United States eagerly traveled to Grenada to see a Black revolution in motion.[63] Given revolutionary Grenada's socialist orientation, Third World solidarities, and apparent pro-Soviet sympathies, the United States under Ronald Reagan, a sworn enemy of Black Power from his days as the governor of California and a rabid anticommunist, viewed the Black and English-speaking Caribbean island as a US national security threat. An ultra-leftist coup on October 12, 1983, deposed Bishop. Six days later, a firing squad summarily executed Bishop and his top lieutenants in the courtyard of Fort Rupert (Fort George)—the slave-built fortress atop St. George's Harbor that Little sailed past in 1917 en route to Canada (see figure C.6).[64] The United States used the coup as a pretext for launching a US-led multinational military invasion of the island on October 25, 1983. The invasion resulted in the installment of a pro-US parliamentary government in 1984.[65]

Today, Grenadians have yet to come to terms with the collective trauma and contested memory of the revolution, Bishop's overthrow and violent death, and US invasion—or "intervention"—as some Grenadians call the military action. Many local politicians and Grenadians still denigrate Bishop and the revolution and celebrate the US invasion.[66] This unresolved trauma and contested meaning of the revolution among Grenadians help explain Little's erasure from popular memory. Louise had helped to cultivate Malcolm's Black radicalism, and his work and legacy were instrumental in shaping Black Power and indirectly influencing the Grenada Revolution through Bishop. To acknowledge Louise would require recognizing Malcolm, therefore Bishop, and perhaps countless other resolute, proud, and cosmopolitan Black women in the mold of Louise Little living in Grenada, then and now. Rulers in contemporary Grenada

FIGURE C.6. Fort (Rupert) George, St. George's, Grenada, March 2015. Photo by the author.

reject Black Power, Third Worldism, and revolution—concepts they perceive as failed projects from a bygone past. They, like nearly all regimes today across what is now called the Global South, embrace neoliberalism and elite decision-making. Given this politics, postrevolution Grenadian rulers want nothing to do with the Black radicalism symbolized by Bishop and Malcolm by association with Little.

Additionally, the Grenada Revolution opened possibilities for discussions of Little and Black women's resistance in the context of Grenadian and Black diasporic history, even if those possibilities were not realized. As literary scholar Laurie Lambert has shown in her study of the Grenada Revolution, gender and sexuality were critical not only to shaping the revolution and women's and men's roles within it. Gender and sexualities are critical to framing how the revolution is remembered and represented today in Grenadian popular memory and literary work. Calling attention to the heteropatriarchal contours of the revolution and women's interpretations of it, Lambert argues, requires us to (re)consider the possibilities and corrosive aspects of revolutionary Grenada. As discussed, Little, fiercely proud of her Grenadian heritage, consciously defied racialized gender norms for Black women of her day through standing up to

Klansmen at her front door, her husband's male chauvinism, and white Michigan state authorities determined to incapacitate her and to break up her family. Acknowledging her life and resistance troubles heteropatriarchal interpretations of the Grenada Revolution that shroud its harmful aspects and rationalize contemporary gender and sexual inequalities in Grenada. Unsilencing and (re)telling her story offers the possibility for rethinking the past and envisaging radical futures for Black people in Grenada and everywhere, far beyond what the Grenada Revolution could have ever imagined.

Times are changing. A growing number of scholars, teachers, community organizers, and ordinary people of Grenadian descent on the island and globally are breaking the silence about Little's life.[67] Frustrated with neoliberalism, poverty, heteropatriarchy, and the unresolved legacies of slavery, imperialism, and colonialism, they see in her a symbol of resistance and possibility. Given this perspective, they are organizing initiatives to honor and explore her life and legacy. Terance Wilson, Louise's distant cousin who lives near La Digue, is critical to these efforts. He generously shares his unsurpassed knowledge of Louise and Langdon family history with scholars, writers, and community organizers from around the world. He also hopes to establish a memorial for her on the Langdon family land.[68] Local organizers have established the La Digue Community Heritage Honors Society. Founded in 2020, the group seeks to empower local youth and residents through raising awareness about Louise Little and Malcolm X.[69] Efforts are underway to rename Holy Innocents Anglican Primary School, the primary school in La Digue where she attended school, after her.[70] Contemporary initiatives in Grenada in recognizing her historical significance may not seem like revolutionary acts. But social transformation is a process, not an event. Arguably, through memorializing and raising consciousness about her, Grenadians are forging a new world and reckoning with a violent and traumatic past.

The story of Louise Little reveals the broader importance of the Diasporic Midwest to the ongoing history of Garveyism and Black resistance across Global Africa. Little, like other subjects and transnational movements explored in my book, illustrates the multidirectional flow of people, politics, and ideas that came together in unique and powerful ways in the US heartland. This region, vital to the development of US commercial capitalism and heavy industry and to the United States as a continental white settler nation and global superpower, profoundly impacted the twentieth-century Black world through Garveyism. Chicago, Detroit, Cleveland, Lansing, Gary, Youngstown, and other cities and rural parts of the North American middle were key strongholds of the transnational UNIA, the largest Black protest organization in

FIGURE C.7. Woodland Park, Michigan, October 2023. Our Hidden Gem LLC, Deborah Jones and Shawn Durr.

world history. Marcus Garvey acknowledged the heartland's importance to his organization. The experience of the dialectic of opportunity and oppression and Black agency made the region a bastion of the UNIA and the globally impactful formations it spawned. Garveyites like Louise Little made this happen. Born in Grenada within living memory of slavery and to a close-knit family whose progenitors came from Nigeria, she moved to Canada, where she married and enlisted in the UNIA before eventually settling in the US Midwest. In Michigan, she spent the greater part of her life and etched her name into history through her grassroots Garveyism; rearing eight, politically conscious Black children, most famously Malcolm; and surviving a quarter-century of cruel state incapacitation.

The lives and journeys of Louise Little and the countless number of Black people in the US heartland who joined Garvey-influenced movements contain broad implications for thinking in new directions about Garveyism, Black internationalism, Black nationalism, Black radicalism, diasporic feminisms, the Midwest, Black America, and Global Africa. Given this objective, I conceived the "Diasporic Midwest" framework to explicate the US heartland's underappreciated significance to the history of global Garveyism and to the modern Black world. The region was and remains a crucible of Black nationalism, internationalism, and radicalism. I hope *The Second Battle for Africa* will prompt scholars to look beyond the shores of the Atlantic, the Middle Passage, and oceanic crossings for examining diaspora-making, Blackness, and Black movements. I also hope this book helps scholars of Harlem, Haiti, the Low Country, the Chesapeake, Salvador, New Orleans, London, Paris, and other more commonly looked at places across the African world to appreciate these locales through a new light. The Diasporic Midwest shows that localities of race, space, and time are neither universal nor constant. Indeed, the lives, globetrotting, and organizing of Midwest-linked Black women, men, and youth, inspired by Garvey, provide unique insight into the genealogies of Black nationalism, contested meaning of freedom, gendered contours of Black movements, ideological variance within Black internationalism, Black feminism, the Black Radical Tradition, and the making of Diasporic communities. This is most apparent in Black diasporic right radicalism, an ideological tendency embedded in nineteenth-century classical Black nationalism and upheld by Garvey and many of his disciples. Midwestern Garveyite colonizationism, Afro-Asian solidarity, and religious organizations were some of the most vocal proponents of this politics. Despite their opposition to the dominant order, they often fell into the pitfalls of promoting a politics and worldview that (re)produced the status quo. Their dreams and nightmares, victories and losses, provide useful lessons for those of us committed to building a new world and remind us that "freedom is a constant struggle," requiring us to fight simultaneously on multiple fronts for human liberation.[71]

Finally, I hope this book inspires readers—African American midwesterners in particular but all people who live in and outside of the US heartland—to appreciate the region's Black radical heritage and potential to transform the world. This is the point St. Clair Drake and Horace Cayton boldly asserted in 1945 in *Black Metropolis*. They argued that the South Side of Chicago was a key battlefront in the unfinished global struggle between fascism and democracy. The same is true about the place of the Midwest in our present and future world. Climate change, resurgent white supremacy, growing economic disparities, creeping fascism, rising ethnonationalism, refugee crises, increasing violence against women and LGBTQIA+ people, endless wars, the high cost of living, food insecurity, and the possibilities of deadly global pandemics and nuclear holocaust loom over humanity. Black people have and will take the brunt of these crises. Whatever the future holds for the African-descended, it seems certain that the specters of Marcus Mosiah Garvey and the Black people he inspired will be present. Undoubtedly, the Diasporic Midwest, a fulcrum of Black transnational resistance and possibility for centuries, will remain a key geographic terrain where the battle for global Black liberation and human freedom will be waged and ultimately won.

INTRODUCTION

Portions of this introduction originated from McDuffie, "The Diasporic Journeys of Louise Little."

1. The original name of the organization was the Universal Negro Improvement and Conservation and African Communities (Imperial) League. However, the group later came to be known as the Universal Negro Improvement Association–African Communities League and then the Universal Negro Improvement Association–African Communities League (August 1929) of the World. For consistency, I will refer to the organization as the UNIA. The exact size of the UNIA's membership is difficult to quantify. It seems likely that the organization inflated the size of its membership. T. Martin, *Race First*, 6, 13–16, 18; Issa, "The Universal Negro Improvement Association in Louisiana," 17–41.

2. My understanding of pan-Africanism reflects Africana studies scholar Reiland Rabaka's definition of pan-Africanism as "*a simultaneously intellectual, cultural, social, political, economic and artistic project that calls for the unification of and liberation of all people of African ancestry, both on the continent and in the African Diaspora*" (emphasis in original). Rabaka, "Introduction," 8. Following the lead of historian George Shepperson, in my book, "Pan-Africanism" with an uppercase "P" designates the six major Pan-African Congresses held from 1919 to 1974, while "pan-Africanism" with a lowercase "p" refers to the project that Rabaka defines. Shepperson, "Pan-Africanism and 'Pan-Africanism,'" 346.

3. McDuffie, "'A New Day Has Dawned for the UNIA,'" 85–93.

4. My coinage and conceptualization of the midwestern Garveyite front is informed by what Garvey historian Adam Ewing calls the "Garveyist frontier." The Garveyite frontier refers to a loose array of interwar religious, educational, and political formations scattered across southern and eastern Africa, inspired, to varying degrees, by Garveyism and not directly affiliated with the UNIA. Ewing, *The Age of Garvey*, 162.

5. Malcolm X, *The Autobiography of Malcolm X*, 1 (hereafter, *AOMX*).

6. Rolinson, *Grassroots Garveyism*, 2, 72–160.

7. *AOMX*, 1.

8. Edozie and Stokes, "Malcolm X from Michigan."

9. Drake and Cayton, *Black Metropolis*, 97.

10. Drake and Cayton, *Black Metropolis*, 46–57.

11. Drake and Cayton, *Black Metropolis*, 767.

12. Drake and Cayton, *Black Metropolis*, 72, 751–53.

13. Drake, *The Redemption of Africa and Black Religion*, 5–6; McDuffie, "Chicago, Garveyism, and the History of the Diasporic Midwest," 133.

14. Defining the geographic parameters and the historical and cultural distinctiveness of the region now called the Midwest remains debated by scholars and pundits. The US Census Bureau divides the United States into four regions: the Northeast, Midwest, South, and West. The Midwest consists of twelve states—Ohio, Indiana, Illinois, Missouri, Michigan, Iowa, Wisconsin, Minnesota, Kansas, Nebraska, North Dakota, and South Dakota. "Census Regions and Divisions of the United States," https://www2 .census.gov/geo/pdfs/maps-data/maps/reference/us_regdiv.pdf (accessed October 12, 2023). For discussions of what constitutes the Midwest, see Madison, "The States of the Midwest," 1–8; and Ford, *A Brick and a Bible*, 3–4.

15. Trotter, *River Jordan*, xiii.

16. Drake and Cayton, *Black Metropolis*; Bush, *We Are Not What We Seem*, 88–93; Baldwin, *Chicago's New Negroes*, 1–20.

17. Bates, *The Making of Black Detroit*, 199–249; Blocker, *A Little More Freedom*, 1–35.

18. W. Cronon, *Nature's Metropolis*, xv–xxv, 5–54.

19. Murphy, *Great Lakes Creoles*, 1–23.

20. Hine and McCluskey, *The Black Chicago Renaissance*; Phillips, *AlabamaNorth*, 98–126, 161–89.

21. W. Johnson, *The Broken Heart of America*, 1–105; Campney, *Hostile Heartland*, 1–34.

22. Campney, *Hostile Heartland*, 1–34.

23. Drake and Cayton, *Black Metropolis*, 214–62; Sugrue, *The Origins of the Urban Crisis*, 125–52.

24. Ford, *A Brick and a Bible*, 24–26; Wolcott, *Remaking Respectability*, 18–31; Drake and Cayton, *Black Metropolis*, 242–47.

25. Howard, "Prairie Fires," 13, 17–18.

26. "'The Rebellious Life of Mrs. Rosa Parks': New Film Explores Untold Radical Life of Civil Rights Icon," *Democracy Now!*, October 17, 2022, https://www.democracynow .org/2022/10/17/the_rebellious_life_of_mrs_rosa; Theoharis, *The Rebellious Life of Mrs. Rosa Parks*, xii, xiii.

27. I take the phrase "the institution-building impulse in the Midwest" from historian James Smethurst in his study of the Black Arts Movement. He argues that institution-building constituted a key feature of African American midwestern life. *The Black Arts Movement*, 247.

28. Stein, *The World of Marcus Garvey*, 229.

29. I am not suggesting that other regions across the African world did not see the development of long-lasting institutions. However, the Midwest was home to some of the largest and most capitalized Black businesses and institutions on the planet. Chambers, "A Master Strategist"; Reed, *The Rise of Chicago's Black Metropolis*, 71–117.

30. For a history of the origins of the term "Rust Belt" in contemporary US vernacular, see Trubek, *Voices from the Rust Belt*.

31. Ben Austen, "The Post-Post-Apocalyptic Detroit," *New York Times* (hereafter, *NYT*), July 11, 2014, https://www.nytimes.com/2014/07/13/magazine/the-post-post-apocalyptic-detroit.html; Sugrue, *The Origins of the Urban Crisis*; Kurashige, *The Fifty-Year Rebellion*, 3.

32. Anne Trubek, "Our Collective Ignorance about the Rust Belt Is Getting Dangerous," *Time*, April 3, 2018, https://time.com/5225497/rust-belt-history/.

33. G. Boggs, *The Next American Revolution*, 105.

34. Lauck, *The Lost Region*, 1–28; Jon Lauck, email to author, December 13, 2022.

35. Midwestern History Association, http://www.midwesternhistory.com (accessed October 15, 2023).

36. Miles, *The Dawn of Detroit*, 1–64; W. Johnson, *The Broken Heart of America*, 1–71; Sarmiento, Castellanos, and Perreira, "Introduction," 7–17.

37. Hoganson, *The Heartland*; Manalansan, Nadeau, Rodríguez, and Somerville, "Introduction."

38. Hoganson, *The Heartland*, xiv.

39. Manalansan, Nadeau, Rodríguez, and Somerville, "Introduction," 11–12; Tamara Winfrey-Harris, "Stop Pretending Black Midwesterners Don't Exist," *NYT*, June 16, 2018, SR 7.

40. This new generation of Black midwestern studies scholars include Davarian Baldwin, Jonathan Fenderson, Melissa Ford, Tanisha Ford, Stephanie Fortado, Nishani Frazier, Olivia Hagedorn, Ashley Howard, Courtney Pierre Joseph, Crystal Marie Moten, Kerry Pimblott, Christy Clark-Pujara, Jamala Rogers, Stephanie Sulik, Jazma Sutton, Nikki Taylor, Alonzo Ward, and Terrion Williamson, among others. The Black Midwest Initiative, based at the University of Illinois at Chicago and founded by Terrion Williamson, constitutes one of the most important academic collective efforts in studying and writing about Black life in the heartland. See https://www.theblackmidwest.com.

41. Hartman, *Lose Your Mother*, 1–18.

42. Blain and Gill, "Introduction: Black Women and the Complexities of Internationalism," 1–12; Umoren, *Race Women Internationalists*, 5–10; Joseph-Gabriel, *Reimagining Liberation*, 5–28.

43. Paul Gilroy's *The Black Atlantic: Modernity and Double Consciousness* stands perhaps as the most well-known iteration of Black transoceanic frameworks.

44. For a small sampling of scholarship on these topics, see M. Bowen, *For Land and Liberty*; K. Butler, *Freedoms Given, Freedoms Won*; Cooper, *The Hanging of Angélique*; Gomez, *Exchanging Our Country Marks*; Harrison, *Outsider Within*; Henson, *Emergent Quilombos*; Hine, Keaton, and Small, *Black Europe*; Horne, *The Dawning of the Apocalypse*; Patterson and Kelley, "Unfinished Migrations"; Putnam, *Radical Moves*; J. Scott, *The Common Wind*; Swan, *Pasifika Black*.

45. Blocker, *A Little More Freedom*, 1–182.

46. Makalani, "Diaspora and the Localities of Race," 1–7.

47. This new generation of scholars includes Keisha Blain, Nicole Bourbonnais, Natanya Duncan, Adam Ewing, José Andrés Fernández Montés de Oca, Kerri Greenidge, Claudrena Harold, Jahi Issa, Leslie James, Brian Kwoba, Asia Leeds, John Maynard, Courtney Morris, Mary Rolinson, Holly Roose, Ronald Stephens, Frances Peace Sullivan, Stephanie Sulik, Ula Taylor, Robert Trent Vinson, and Michael O. West.

48. These scholars include Amy Ashwood Garvey, Amy Jacques Garvey, Robert A. Hill, Tony Martin, Barbara Bair, Horace Campbell, Rupert Lewis, Emory Tolbert, and Jeannette Smith-Irvin. Stephens and Ewing, *Global Garveyism*, 2, 10, 12.

49. Robinson understands the Black Radical Tradition as a shared revolutionary consciousness and vision rooted in African-descended people's ontological opposition to racial capitalism, slavery, colonialism, and imperialism. Robinson, *Black Marxism*, 1, 2. See also Kelley, foreword to *Black Marxism*, xvii–xix.

50. Stephens and Ewing, *Global Garveyism*, 7.

51. Stephens and Ewing, *Global Garveyism*, 11.

52. Stephens and Ewing, *Global Garveyism*, 12.

53. West, "Garveyism Root and Branch," 15.

54. In *Worldmaking after Empire: The Rise and Fall of Self-Determination*, political scientist Adom Getachew uses the term "worldmaking" to describe the ways mid-twentieth-century anticolonial nationalists—Nnamdi Azikiwe, W. E. B. Du Bois, Michael Manley, Kwame Nkrumah, Julius Nyerere, George Padmore, and Eric Williams—theorized and agitated against empire and imagined and advanced self-determination for Africa and the Caribbean through nation state-building, international political federations, and the United Nations. Midwestern Garveyites provide insight into how twentieth-century African-descended women, men, and youth forged an expansive vision for worldmaking encompassing not only nation state-building and international relations but also religion, culture, education, identity, lifeways, entrepreneurialism, and a politics of solidarity.

55. Burden-Stelly and Horne, "From Pan-Africanism to Black Internationalism," 69, 70.

56. Bedasse et al., "*AHR* Conversation," 1716, 1730.

57. Makalani, *In the Cause of Freedom*, 62–69.

58. Robinson, *Black Marxism* (1983), 2.

59. For important studies of the origins and ideological contours of Black nationalism, see Stuckey, *Slave Culture*; Moses, *The Golden Age of Black Nationalism*; Henderson, *The Revolution Will Not Be Theorized*.

60. Moses, *Classical Black Nationalism*, 2. Not all classical Black nationalists called for the establishment of a separate or autonomous geographic territory or nation-state. Henderson, *The Revolution Will Not Be Theorized*, 42–72.

61. Moses, *The Golden Age of Black Nationalism*, 20–22.

62. S. Johnson, *African American Religions*, 7, 205.

63. S. Johnson, *African American Religions*, 205.

64. Moses, *The Golden Age of Black Nationalism*, 59–145, 197–219; Vinson, *The Americans Are Coming!*, 34–50.

65. M. Stephens, *Black Empire*, 84.

66. M. Stephens, *Black Empire*, 84.

67. Mills, "'The United States of Africa,'" 92, 97–105.

68. Clegg, *The Price of Liberty*, 6. By the end of the nineteenth century, Liberia counted one million Indigenes, 16,428 free African Americans; 5,722 "recaptured Africans"—Africans liberated from slave ships bound for the Americas who came to be known as "Congoes"—and 346 emigrants from Barbados. Liberian Studies Association,

"Statement by the Historical Society of Liberia on the Bicentennial of Free Blacks in Liberia, 1822–2022," email, October 3, 2021.

69. Clegg, *The Price of Liberty*, 5.

70. Adeleke, *UnAfrican Americans*, 111, 152.

71. Moses, *The Golden Age of Black Nationalism*, 103–31; Moses, *Classical Black Nationalism*, 221–50.

72. K. Butler, *Freedoms Given, Freedoms Won*, 210–27.

73. T. Martin, *Race First*, 344–55.

74. Ewing, *The Age of Garvey*, 186–237.

75. West and Martin, "From Toussaint to Tupac," 10–12; Kornweibel, *"Seeing Red,"* 100–131; Vinson, *The Americans Are Coming!*, 82.

76. Kornweibel, *"Seeing Red,"* 100–131; Hill, *The FBI's RACON*, 507–50; Evanzz, *The Judas Factor*, xiii–xxiv.

77. Vinson, *The Americans Are Coming!*, 3.

78. Umoren, *Race Women Internationalists*, 7.

79. My understanding of the Diasporic Midwest as a key site of Black radicalism resembles what historian Melissa Ford describes as "Midwestern Black radicalism," a distinct oppositional politics forged by Depression-era African Americans in cities like Chicago, Detroit, Cleveland, and St. Louis in response to the "unique racial, political, geographic, economic, gendered, and spatial characteristics that make up the American heartland" (*A Brick and a Bible*, 3). Her analysis focuses on African American midwestern radicalism primarily in local settings through the communist left and trade unions. Heartland Garveyites illustrate the significance of Black nationalist formations, operating in local and transnational settings, as incubators of Black radicalism.

80. My commitment to explicating the significance of Liberia to Black internationalism is influenced by the Liberian historian William Ezra Allen, who emphasizes grounding the complex history of the West African republic within the broader Atlantic world. W. Allen, "Liberia and the Atlantic World in the Nineteenth Century." See also Brooks Marmon, "The Decline of Liberia in Black Internationalism," April 22, 2021, https://africasacountry .com/2021/04/the-decline-of-liberia-in-black-internationalism.

81. Alexander, *Fear of a Black Republic*; Byrd, *The Black Republic*.

82. Gaines, *American Africans in Ghana*; Bedasse, *Jah Kingdom*; Byrne, *Mecca of Revolution*.

83. Marmon, "The Decline of Liberia in Black Internationalism."

84. Marmon, "The Decline of Liberia in Black Internationalism."

85. I am not suggesting scholars interested in Black internationalism in relation to Haiti, Ghana, and Tanzania are naive or uncritical in their assessments of these nations. However, no nation in the African world is arguably more paradoxical than Liberia. Johnson Sirleaf, *This Child Will Be Great*, 1.

86. U. Taylor, *The Veiled Garvey*, 64–90. I also draw on the work of historians Keisha Blain, Ashley Farmer, Natanya Duncan, Asia Leeds, Margaret Stevens, and Kerri Greenidge on women, gender, the UNIA, and Black nationalist movements.

87. Carew, *Ghosts in Our Blood*, 109.

88. *AOMX*, 2–22.

89. McDuffie and Woodard, "'If You're in a Country That's Progressive,'" 509, 512.

90. For recent work on Louise Little, see M. Collins, *Ocean Stirrings*; Russell, *The Life of Louise Norton Little*; Tubbs, *The Three Mothers*.

91. Trouillot, *Silencing the Past*, xxiii, 1–30.

92. Boyce Davies, "Sisters Outside."

93. J. James, "Resting in Our Mother's Garden," 4.

94. J. James, "Resting in Our Mother's Garden," 4.

95. Fletcher, "Manning Marable and the Malcolm X Biography Controversy," 127.

96. Marable, *Malcolm X*, 9; Kelley, *Race Rebels*, 161–81; Norrell, *Alex Haley*, 95.

97. Payne and Payne, *The Dead Are Arising*; Edozie and Stokes, *Malcolm X's Michigan Worldview*; Young, "Detroit's Red."

98. Kelley, *Race Rebels*, 181.

99. Horne, "Toward a Transnational Research Agenda," 288–89.

100. William L. Sherrill to Kwame Nkrumah, April 10, 1957, UNIA Records, box 7, folder 3, Stuart A. Rose Manuscript, Archives, and Rare Book Library, Emory University, Atlanta, GA (hereafter, UNIA Records RL). I have yet to find the invitation for William Sherrill to attend Ghanaian independence ceremonies.

101. The works on this topic by a wide range of inter- and multidisciplinary scholars of color, such as Saidiya Hartman, Jennifer Morgan, Marissa Fuentes, and Françoise Hamlin, are especially important to my thinking about "the white supremacist heteropatriarchal archive in the history of Black nationalism." These scholars focus on the ways historical archives are not only essential to knowledge production. They emphasize how the archive is critical to (re)producing historical narratives that erase and disfigure the knowledge, subjectivities, and resistance of African-descended women by telling their stories through their oppressors. These narratives, in effect, commit epistemological violence against African-descended women and promote historical narratives that rationalize the past and contemporary status quo. Despite the tremendous problems the archive holds for Black women's history, the lives and voices of the African-descended are hardly irrecoverable from the past. In her pathbreaking article "Venus in Two Acts," Saidiya Hartman proffered the theory of "critical fabulation," an approach drawing from fiction and critical theory to fill in the silences of the archive. Hartman, "Venus in Two Acts," 12–13; Fuentes *Dispossessed Lives*, 1–12; Hamlin, "History Unclassified."

102. The phrase "Black archival practice" describes an interdisciplinary approach for "explor[ing] how the social meanings—past, present, and future—of . . . Black life and Black lives . . . get imagined, contested, and negotiated within traditional archival spaces and in spaces intentionally coded as Black." Collier and Sutherland, "Introduction," 1.

103. Hill, *The Marcus Garvey and the Universal Negro Improvement Association Papers* (hereafter, *MGP*), 2:xxxii.

104. "The right to the city" refers to a concept and call to action formulated by sociologist and philosopher Henri Lefebrve that emphasizes the power and right of working-class and marginalized communities to live in dignity and to transform urban social spaces into inclusive, democratic spaces. C. Butler, *Henri Lefebvre*, 133–59.

105. McKittrick and Woods, *Black Geographies and the Politics of Place*; LaRoche, *The Geography of Resistance*; Pile and Keith, *Geographies of Resistance*.

1. "WE ARE A NATION WITHIN A NATION"

1. *Minutes and Address of the Convention of the Colored Citizens of Ohio* (hereafter, Convention of the Colored Citizens of Ohio), 1, 7–10.

2. Foreman, "Black Organizing," 21–58.

3. Cheek and Cheek, *John Mercer Langston*, 1–4.

4. Convention of the Colored Citizens of Ohio, 8.

5. Convention of the Colored Citizens of Ohio, 11.

6. Woo, "Deleted Name: But Indelible Body," 180.

7. Casey, Foreman, and Patterson, "How to Use This Book," 8.

8. Lauck, *The Lost Region*, 27.

9. Hansel and McKay, "Quaternary Period"; Larson and Schaetzl, "Origin and Evolution of the Great Lakes," 518.

10. Ray, "Geomorphology and Quaternary Geology of the Glaciated Ohio River Valley—A Reconnaissance Study."

11. Dick, "Oak-Hickory Forest," CW Dick Lab blog, March 27, 2016, https://sites.lsa.umich.edu/cwdick-lab/2016/03/27/oak-hickory-forest-a-vestige-of-native-american-land-use/.

12. "The Tallgrass Prairie in Illinois," https://www.inhs.illinois.edu/animals-plants/prairie/tallgrass (accessed July 22, 2021).

13. W. Cronon, *Nature's Metropolis*, 25.

14. Trotter, "Cahokia," 1–4.

15. Richter, *Before the Revolution*, 20–23; "Cahokia Mounds," https://cahokiamounds.org (accessed July 24, 2021).

16. Writers' Program, Works Project Administration in the State of Nebraska, *The Negroes of Nebraska*, 6.

17. Hannah-Jones et al., *The 1619 Project*.

18. Miles, *The Dawn of Detroit*, 2.

19. Neal Rubin, "Monuments to Detroit Area's Past Seen in New, Troubling Light: Slavery," *Detroit News*, June 16, 2020, https://www.detroitnews.com/story/news/local/detroit-city/2020/06/17/monuments-detroit-areas-past-seen-new-troubling-light-slavery/5341800002.

20. City of Detroit Recreation Department, "The Black Presence in Detroit."

21. Mayor's Interracial Committee, *The Negro in Detroit*, pt. 2, "Population," 1–2; Miles, *The Dawn of Detroit*, 12.

22. Quoted in Dolinar, *The Negro in Illinois*, 6.

23. "First, the French," Illinois Writers Project, the Negro in Illinois, box 2, folder 1, Chicago Public Library, Vivian G. Harsh Research Collection, Woodson Regional Library, Chicago.

24. Lauck, *The Lost Region*, 14.

25. Drake and Cayton, *Black Metropolis*, 31–32.

26. Drake and Cayton, *Black Metropolis*, 31.

27. Cain, "Ou Ayisyen?," 6.

28. A. Cox, *The Bone and Sinew of the Land*, 22.

29. A. Cox, *The Bone and Sinew of the Land*, xvii, 3, 24.

30. A. Cox, *The Bone and Sinew of the Land*, 3, 24.

31. Saler, *The Settlers' Empire*, 1, 115.

32. W. Johnson, *The Broken Heart of America*, 41–71.

33. Middleton, *The Black Laws in the Old Northwest*, xxi–xxvii, 84.

34. Kaba, *We Do This 'Til We Free Us*.

35. Gilmore, *Golden Gulag*, 2.

36. Gilmore, *Golden Gulag*, 241–48; Kaba, *We Do This 'Til We Free Us*, 2–28.

37. Middleton, *The Black Laws in the Old Northwest*, xv.

38. Middleton, *The Black Laws in the Old Northwest*, xxvi.

39. Mayor's Interracial Committee, *The Negro in Detroit*, pt. 2, p. 1.

40. Mayor's Interracial Committee, *The Negro in Detroit*, xv.

41. Gerber, *Black Ohio and the Color Line*, 9.

42. Middleton, *The Black Laws in the Northwest*, 13.

43. Middleton, *The Black Laws in the Northwest*, 15–18.

44. Middleton, *The Black Laws in the Northwest*, 33–40, 47–49.

45. Berwanger, *The Frontier against Slavery*, 44.

46. Dolinar, *The Negro in Illinois*, 10–12; Campney, *Hostile Heartland*, 14, 42–43.

47. Berwanger, *The Frontier against Slavery*, 40, 41.

48. N. Taylor, *Frontiers of Freedom*, 28.

49. Pfeifer, "Introduction," 8.

50. Berwanger, *The Frontier against Slavery*, 20.

51. N. Taylor, *Frontiers of Freedom*, 21.

52. Trotter, *River Jordan*, 3.

53. N. Taylor, *Frontiers of Freedom*, 14, 15, 16, 19.

54. N. Taylor, *Frontiers of Freedom*, 28; Gerber, *Black Ohio and the Color Line*, 274.

55. Trotter, *River Jordan*, 28; N. Taylor, *Frontiers of Freedom*, 26.

56. LaRoche, *The Geography of Resistance*, xii; N. Taylor, *Frontiers of Freedom*, 139.

57. Rose, *Cleveland*, 26.

58. "Forest City," *Encyclopedia of Cleveland History*, https://case.edu/ech/articles/f/forest-city (accessed March 15, 2024).

59. Russell Davis, *Black Americans in Cleveland*, 270.

60. "Western Reserve," *Encyclopedia of Cleveland History*, https://case.edu/ech/articles/w/western-reserve (accessed March 15, 2024).

61. Russell Davis, *Black Americans in Cleveland*, 67–69, 102; Gerber, *Black Ohio and the Color Line*, 13–14; Kusmer, *A Ghetto Takes Shape*, 188.

62. N. Taylor, *Frontiers of Freedom*, 36.

63. Gerber, *Black Ohio and the Color Line*, 18.

64. Miles, *The Dawn of Detroit*, 1–64.

65. Mayor's Interracial Committee, *Negro in Detroit*, pt. 2, p. 3.

66. R. Thomas, *Life for Us Is What We Make It*, 2, 4.

67. R. Thomas, *Life for Us Is What We Make It*, 2; Frost and Tucker, *A Fluid Frontier*, xii.

68. R. Thomas, *Life for Us Is What We Make It*, 10; Smith, "Worship Way Stations in Detroit," 103–15.

69. Asaka, *Tropical Freedom*, 53.

70. Landon, "Amherstburg," 1–3.

71. E. Williams, *Capitalism and Slavery*, 197–208.

72. "Celebration of West India Emancipation," *Democratic Free Press*, August 3, 1847, p. 2; "West India Emancipation," *Detroit Free Press*, August 2, 1851, p. 3.

73. R. Thomas, *Life for Us Is What We Make It*, 10.

74. Reed, *Black Chicago's First Century*, 43.

75. Reed, *Black Chicago's First Century*, 54, 67–68; A. Ward, "The Specter of Black Labor," 61–63.

76. Reed, *Black Chicago's First Century*, 43.

77. W. Cronon, *Nature's Metropolis*, 33, 55–81; Reed, *Black Chicago's First Century*, 69.

78. A. Cox, *The Bone and Sinew of the Land*, 5.

79. Jazma Sutton, "African American Women's Work in the Underground Railroad," October 31, 2019, http://www.processhistory.org/sutton-beyond-harriet (accessed August 26, 2021).

80. Cha-Jua, *America's First Black Town*, 5, 3.

81. Cha-Jua, *America's First Black Town*, 17–28, 219.

82. Painter, *Exodusters*; Cha-Jua, *America's First Black Town*, 217–19.

83. N. Taylor, *Frontiers of Freedom*, 64–65, 109–12, 118–26.

84. Campney, *Hostile Heartland*, 25.

85. Campney, *Hostile Heartland*, 13–14, 21.

86. W. Johnson, *The Broken Heart of America*, 73–74.

87. Dolinar, *The Negro in Illinois*, 15–18; W. Johnson, *The Broken Heart of America*, 76.

88. Campney, *Hostile Heartland*, 30, 35–47.

89. Blackett, *The Captive's Quest for Freedom*, xi–xv, 3–4; Comminey, "National Black Conventions," 11.

90. Campney, *Hostile Heartland*, 23–24, 41, 45–46.

91. W. Johnson, *The Broken Heart of America*, 104.

92. W. Johnson, *The Broken Heart of America*, 104–5.

93. E. Williams, *Capitalism and Slavery*, v–vi, 209–12.

94. Horne, *The Deepest South*, 17–65, 151–71; Ferrer, *Insurgent Cuba*, 1–12.

95. Bell, *Minutes of the Proceedings of the National Negro Conventions*, 5.

96. Foreman, "Black Organizing," 21.

97. Bell, *Minutes of the Proceedings of the National Negro Conventions*, 5, 9–12.

98. Foreman, "Black Organizing," 28–30.

99. Woo, "Deleted Name: But Indelible Body," 180.

100. *Proceedings of the National Emigration Convention of Colored People*, cover.

101. Adeleke, *In the Service of God and Humanity*, 2–6, 34–36.

102. *Proceedings of the National Emigration Convention of Colored People*, 16–18.

103. Quoted in Ullman, *Martin R. Delany*, 154.

104. Tibebu, *Edward Wilmot Blyden*, 14.

105. *Proceedings of the National Emigration Convention of Colored People*, 35 (emphasis in original).

106. *Proceedings of the National Emigration Convention of Colored People*, 37.

107. Delany, *The Condition, Elevation, Emigration, and Destiny*, 169.

108. Adeleke, *In the Service of God and Humanity*, 40.

109. Ullman, *Martin R. Delany*, 155.

110. Woo, "Deleted Name: But Indelible Body," 180.

111. Delany, *Official Report of the Niger River Valley*, 70 (emphasis in original).

112. Adeleke, *In the Service of God and Humanity*, 38.

113. Adeleke, *In the Service of God and Humanity*, 38.

114. Bennett, "The Negro Colonization Movement in Ohio," 52; "Charles McMicken's Legacy," https://www.artsci.uc.edu/about/history/slavery-research/charles-mcmickens-legacy.html (accessed September 3, 2021).

115. "Charles McMicken's Legacy."

116. "Anti-Colonization," *The North Star*, March 20, 1851, 3.

117. McPherson, *The Negro's Civil War*, 79–99.

118. Du Bois, *Black Reconstruction*, 55–127.

119. McPherson, *The Negro's Civil War*, 145–243.

120. Adeleke, *In the Service of God and Humanity*, 4–5, 122–38; Cheek and Cheek, *John Mercer Langston*, 349–417.

121. Du Bois, *Black Reconstruction*, 30, 670–710.

122. Moses, *The Golden Age of Black Nationalism*, 50–55; Campbell, *Middle Passages*, 99–135.

123. Olson, *Chicago Renaissance*, 1–6.

124. Reed, *Black Chicago's First Century*, 230; Drake and Cayton, *Black Metropolis*, 9; Gerber, *Black Ohio and the Color Line*, 274.

125. "African Americans," *Encyclopedia of Chicago*, http://www.encyclopedia.chicagohistory.org/pages/27.html (accessed March 15, 2024).

126. Weems and Chambers, introduction to *Building the Black Metropolis*, 13.

127. A. Ward, "The Specter of Black Labor," 16.

128. Reed, "Early Black Chicago Entrepreneurial and Business Activities from the Frontier Era to the Great Migration," 34, 36–38; Hendricks, *Fannie Barrier Williams*, 50–68; Duster, *Crusade for Justice*, xxii–xxxii; Ashbaugh, *Lucy Parsons*, 16–71.

129. Gaines, *Uplifting the Race*, 14.

130. Reed, *"All the World Is Here!,"* xxi, 3.

131. Rydell, *The Reason Why*, xi, xii–xiii.

132. Rydell, *The Reason Why*, xxix.

133. Rydell, *The Reason Why*, 7.

134. Reed *"All the World Is Here!,"* 172–78.

135. Reed, *"All the World Is Here!,"* 179.

136. Reed, *"All the World Is Here!,"* xxiii, 179–90.

137. Quoted in Noble, *The Chicago Congress on Africa*, 315; Reed, *"All the World Is Here!,"* 180.

138. The Berlin Conference of 1884 and 1885, called by German Chancellor Otto von Bismarck, divided Africa among European colonial powers in order to exploit the continent's immense resources, find new markets for European goods, and avoid imperial rivalries among Western nations. Hochschild, *King Leopold's Ghost*, 84–86.

139. Noble, *The Chicago Congress on Africa*, 316.

140. Reed, *"All the World Is Here!,"* xxxiii–xxxv, 182. There is no evidence that W. E. B. Du Bois attended the Congress on Africa. However, Booker T. Washington addressed the International Labor congress held in Chicago in conjunction with the World's Fair.

His invited talk anticipated his famous address at the 1895 Atlanta Exposition that vaulted him into international fame as the foremost African American spokesperson and champion of racial accommodationism. Rydell, *The Reason Why*, xxxvii.

141. Quoted in Noble, *The Chicago Congress on Africa*, 316; Campbell, *Middle Passages*, 103–26.

142. "Congress of Peace," *The Daily Inter Ocean*, August 16, 1893, p. 8; "Language of Africa," *The Daily Inter Ocean*, August 17, 1893, p. 8; "Union of Peoples," *Daily Inter Ocean*, August 19, 1893, p. 9.

143. Reed, *"All the World Is Here!,"* 53.

144. "The Dark Continent," *Daily Inter Ocean*, August 15, 1893, p. 8.

145. Noble, *The Chicago Congress on Africa*, 291.

146. Ida B. Wells, "Afro-Americans and Africa," *AME Church Review* 9, no. 1 (July 1892): 40–44, in Ida B. Wells Papers, box 8, folder 9, University of Chicago.

147. Reed, *"All the World Is Here!,"* 194, 196–97.

148. Tamale, "Research and Theorising Sexualities," 15.

149. Moses, *Afrotopia*, 131–33; Higginbotham, *Righteous Discontent*, 185–229.

150. Campbell, *Middle Passages*, 172–83.

151. Noble, *The Chicago Congress on Africa*, 282.

152. Noble, *The Chicago Congress on Africa*, 286.

153. Noble, *The Chicago Congress on Africa*, 314.

154. Campbell, *Middle Passages*, 96.

155. Blyden, *The Origin and Purpose of African Colonization*, 5.

156. Tibebu, *Edward Wilmot Blyden*, 20.

157. A. Ward, "The Specter of Black Labor," 298.

158. A. Ward, "The Specter of Black Labor"; Cha-Jua, "The Cry of the Negro"; Campney, *Hostile Heartland*, 1.

159. D. Lewis, *W. E. B. Du Bois: The Fight for Equality and the American Century*, 37–84.

160. "Descendants of Ham," *Detroit Free Press*, March 4, 1895, p. 5; "Revival Services," *Detroit Free Press*, February 2, 1896, p. 4; Second Baptist Church, "Our History," https://www.secondbaptistdetroit.org/copy-of-second-baptist-history (accessed April 22, 2021).

161. Reed, *The Rise of Chicago's Black Metropolis*, 101–13.

162. "Biographical Facts of Jane Edna Hunter," Jane Edna Hunter Papers, Western Reserve Historical Society, Cleveland, OH, box 1, folder 1; Kusmer, *A Ghetto Takes Shape*, 148–50.

163. "Now a Law," *Cleveland Gazette*, February 3, 1894, p. 1; Kusmer, *A Ghetto Takes Shape*, 130–32.

164. Gerber, *Black Ohio and the Color Line*, 371.

2. STRONGHOLD

Portions of chapter 2 originated from McDuffie, "The Diasporic Journeys of Louise Little."

1. *Passenger Lists, 1865–1935*, Microfilm Publications T-479 to T-520, T-4689 to T-4874, T-14700 to T-14939, and C-4511 to C-4542, Library and Archives Canada, n.d., RG 76-C, Department of Employment and Immigration fonds. Library and Archives Canada, Ottawa, Ontario. Courtesy of Jessica Russell.

2. J. Martin, *A–Z of Grenada Heritage*, 83–84.

3. Russell, *The Life of Louise Norton Little*, 42–43.

4. I borrow the phrase "personal costs of activism" from historian Chana Kai Lee's biography of the civil rights activist Fannie Lou Hamer, who endured years of state-sanctioned sexualized racial violence for her political activism as a Black woman living in the Jim Crow South. *For Freedom's Sake*, xi.

5. Garvey was originally named after his father, Malchus. Birth certificate, September 6, 1887, 1B/5/77/1, Jamaica Archives, Central Government Spanish Town, Spanish Town, Jamaica.

6. E. Williams, *Capitalism and Slavery*, 51–84.

7. Robinson, *Black Marxism* (2021), 135–37, 160–64.

8. Grant, *Negro with a Hat*, 7–10.

9. T. Martin, *Race First*, 3–4, 111–12.

10. Hill, *MGP*, 1:lix–lxvi.

11. A. Garvey, *Philosophy and Opinions of Marcus Garvey*, 1:126.

12. Hill, *MGP*, 1:62.

13. Grant, *Negro with a Hat*, 68–70.

14. J. Perry, *Hubert Harrison: The Voice of Harlem Radicalism*, 243–80; Kelley, "'But a Local Phase of a World Problem,'" 1055–66; Bush, *We Are Not What We Seem*, 90–120.

15. K. Butler, *Freedoms Given, Freedoms Won*, 88–167; Ranger, *Bulawayo Burning*, 38–52.

16. Makalani, *In the Cause of Freedom*, 23–67.

17. J. Perry, *Hubert Harrison: The Voice of Harlem Radicalism*, 10, 141–219.

18. J. Perry, *Hubert Harrison: The Voice of Harlem Radicalism*, 281–327.

19. J. Perry, *Hubert Harrison: The Voice of Harlem Radicalism*, 281–327; J. Perry, *A Hubert Harrison Reader*, 182–83.

20. Hill, *MGP*, 1:391.

21. Hill, *MGP*, 1:391.

22. Hill, *MGP*, 1:lxx–lxxi; 2:500.

23. Kwoba, "Pebbles and Ripples," 396–423.

24. Hill, *MGP*, 2:478.

25. Hill, *MGP*, 2:479, 571–75.

26. Bandele, *Black Star*, 14, 151–67.

27. Burkett, *Garveyism as a Religious Movement*, 7.

28. Turner, *Islam in the African-American Experience*, 87–90.

29. Bair, "True Women, Real Men," 155; U. Taylor, *Veiled Garvey*, 64–90.

30. Bair, "True Women, Real Men," 155.

31. U. Taylor, *Veiled Garvey*, 44, 45.

32. Bair, "True Women, Real Men," 156–57.

33. Hill, *MGP*, 2:xlix, l, li; Kornweibel, *"Seeing Red,"* 100.

34. Vinson, *The Americans Are Coming!*, 88–89.

35. Hill, *MGP*, 4:xxxii; Kornweibel, *"Seeing Red,"* 100–31.

36. Hill, *MGP*, 5:liii.

37. Coolidge commuted Garvey's sentence in response to legal actions by his attorneys and international public pressure. However, Coolidge ordered Garvey's immediate deportation out of fear that his continued presence in the United States would stoke Black militancy. Hill, *MGP*, 6:xxxvi–xxxviii, lxvii, 609–11.

38. Kornweibel, *"Seeing Red,"* 182.

39. Grant, *Negro with a Hat*, 268–97.

40. A. Garvey, *Philosophy and Opinions of Marcus Garvey*, 1:351–412.

41. Hill, *MGP*, 10:152–54, 176–78; Sundiata, *Brothers and Strangers*, 31–41.

42. [Charles D. B. King?] to US Ambassador, August 25, 1922, President King Collection, Department of State, Government of Liberia Presidential Records, Center for National Documents and Records Archive, Monrovia, Liberia.

43. Hill, *MGP*, 10:152–54, 176–78; Sundiata, *Brothers and Strangers*, 31–41.

44. Sundiata, *Brothers and Strangers*, 47.

45. Ronald Davis, "The Liberian Struggle for Authority on the Kru Coast."

46. Nevin, "In Search of the Historical Madam Suakoko."

47. A. Garvey, *Philosophy and Opinions of Marcus Garvey*, 1:59.

48. Makalani, *In the Cause of Freedom*, 62, 68.

49. A. Garvey, *Philosophy and Opinions of Marcus Garvey*, 2:81.

50. D. Lewis, *W. E. B. Du Bois: The Fight for Equality*, 82, 83.

51. Makalani, *In the Cause of Freedom*, 60–69.

52. T. Martin, *Race First*, 344–60.

53. T. Martin, *Race First*, 346.

54. D. Lewis, *W. E. B. Du Bois: The Fight for Equality*, 149.

55. T. Martin, *Race First*, 344–46.

56. Hill, *MGP*, 6:lxii, 42–48.

57. K. Jackson, *The Ku Klux Klan in the City*, 251.

58. Gordon, *The Second Coming of the KKK*, 11–24; Fox, *Everyday Klansfolk*, 20.

59. Bates, *The Making of Black Detroit*, 82.

60. For the best biographical account of Cox, see Hedlin, "Earnest Cox and Colonization."

61. E. Cox, *Let My People Go*, 6–7.

62. Marcus Garvey (hereafter, MG) to Earnest Sevier Cox (hereafter, ESC), August 27, 1925, box 2, folder 5, Earnest Sevier Cox Papers, David M. Rubenstein Rare Book and Manuscript Library, Duke University, Durham, NC (hereafter, ESC Papers).

63. Amy Jacques Garvey (hereafter, AJG) to ESC, December 2, 1925, box 2, folder 6, ESC Papers.

64. MG to ESC, January 9, 1926, box 3, folder 1, ESC Papers; Hill, *MGP*, 5:169n2.

65. Powell received a warm welcome at the UNIA's Liberty Hall when he spoke there on October 28, 1925. The same cannot be said of the reception Cox received at a UNIA-sponsored meeting at Sharon Baptist Church in Richmond on September 10, 1925. The audience ran him out of the church, illustrating that many rank-and-file Garveyites did not share the Jamaican Black nationalist's warm feelings toward Cox. A. Garvey, *Philosophy and Opinions of Marcus Garvey*, 2:339; Rev. Roger H. Johnson to ESC, September 11, 1925, box 2, folder 6, ESC Papers.

66. AJG to ESC, November 18, 1925, December 2, 1925, December 14, 1925, all in box 2, folder 6, ESC Papers.

67. Osofsky, *Harlem*, 128.

68. Osofsky, *Harlem*, 128, 131; Watkins-Owens, *Blood Relations*, 10–29.

69. Hill, *MGP*, 2:405.

70. Rolinson, *Grassroots Garveyism*, 48–71, 96–102, 135–41; Harold, *The Rise and Fall of the Garvey Movement in the Urban South*, 2–8, 19–28, 91–114.

71. Tolbert, *The UNIA and Black Los Angeles*, 5–22, 49–82; Roose, *Black Star Rising*, xvii–xxiii, 74–130.

72. Roose, *Black Star Rising*, 33.

73. Drake and Cayton, *Black Metropolis*, 8.

74. Drake and Cayton, *Black Metropolis*, 8, 12.

75. Esch, *The Color Line and the Assembly Line*, 33–49.

76. Wolcott, "Defending the Home," 23; Bates, *The Making of Black Detroit*, 15–16.

77. R. Thomas, *Life for Us Is What We Make It*, 26.

78. Bates, *The Making of Black Detroit*, 16.

79. Stein, *The World of Marcus Garvey*, 229.

80. Bates, *The Making of Black Detroit*, 39; R. Thomas, *Life for Us Is What We Make It*, 29–31.

81. Phillips, *AlabamaNorth*, 59, 60.

82. Ford, *A Brick and a Bible*, 169.

83. Drake and Cayton, *Black Metropolis*, 77–83.

84. Bates, *The Making of Black Detroit*, 95–103.

85. Kusmer, *A Ghetto Takes Shape*, 88–89, 195.

86. Esch, *The Color Line and the Assembly Line*, 18–19, 92–100.

87. Tuttle, *Race Riot*, 159, 242; Drake and Cayton, *Black Metropolis*, 64.

88. K. Jackson, *The Ku Klux Klan in the City*, 90.

89. In comparison to East Coast cities, Philadelphia and New York counted thirty-five thousand and sixteen thousand Klan members, respectively. K. Jackson, *The Ku Klux Klan in the City*, 236.

90. Wolcott, "Defending the Home," 25.

91. Palella, "The Black Legion," 81; Bates, *The Making of Black Detroit*, 61.

92. Fox, *Everyday Klansfolk*, xxv.

93. Kusmer, *A Ghetto Takes Shape*, 152–53.

94. "Report on the Negro Migration and Its Effects," circa 1926, box 2, Charles W. Chesnutt Papers, Western Reserve Historical Society, Cleveland; Drake and Cayton, *Black Metropolis*, 73–75; E. Frazier, *The Negro Family in Chicago*, 238.

95. Drake and Cayton, *Black Metropolis*, 830, 76.

96. "Paradise Valley," *Encyclopedia of Detroit*, https://detroithistorical.org/learn/encyclopedia-of-detroit/paradise-valley (accessed October 1, 2020).

97. "Spingarn Medal," n.d., box 2, Charles W. Chesnutt Papers, Western Reserve Historical Society, Cleveland; "Biographical Facts of Jane Edna Hunter," box 1, folder 1, Jane Edna Hunter Papers, Western Reserve Historical Society, Cleveland.

98. Hill, *MGP*, 2:340.

99. Hill, *MGP*, 4:260–61.

100. Bates, *The Making of Black Detroit*, 71.

101. Hill, *MGP*, 3:340; Kusmer, *A Ghetto Takes Shape*, 229.

102. T. Martin, *Race First*, 366; Sulik, "Waving the Red, Black, and Green"; Christian, "Marcus Garvey."

103. Phillips, *AlabamaNorth*, 186–87.

104. Stein, *The World of Marcus Garvey*, 229.

105. Mayor's Interracial Committee, *The Negro in Detroit*, section 11, p. 6.

106. Smith-Irvin, *Marcus Garvey's Footsoldiers*, 59–63.

107. "Mr. Garvey in Detroit," *Negro World* (hereafter, *NW*), December 15, 1923, 5. The article neither quotes nor provides an extensive account of Chandler's remarks.

108. It is unclear what job Zampty worked at the FMC. Smith-Irvin, *Marcus Garvey's Footsoldiers*, 36–47.

109. Joseph A. Craigen Reading Room File, Burton Historical Collection, Detroit Public Library, Detroit, MI.

110. Hill, *MGP*, 5:661.

111. Hill, *MGP*, 5:661.

112. Hill, *MGP*, 6:lviii.

113. Hill, *MGP*, 3:164.

114. "Cleveland Sixth City," *Cleveland Gazette*, February 10, 1917, p. 3; "Big Mass Meeting," March 1917, box 10, file 10, Amy Garvey Memorial Collection of Marcus Garvey, Special Collections and Archives, Fisk University, Nashville (hereafter, *AJG* Papers); "Long Awaited Answer to Critics Made by Hon. Marcus Garvey," *NW*, February 26, 1921, 3, 4.

115. Smith-Irvin, *Marcus Garvey's Footsoldiers*, 47–48.

116. U. Taylor, *Veiled Garvey*.

117. Hill, *MGP*, 2:902.

118. Grant, *Negro with a Hat*, 173.

119. Redmond, "Citizens of Sound," 25.

120. Levine, *Black Culture and Black Consciousness*, 121.

121. "Detroit Members Visit Chicago," *NW*, August 8, 1925, p. 6; "Detroit, Mich.," *NW*, November 28, 1925, p. 6.

122. Duster, *Crusade for Justice*, 389–90.

123. Division 59, organizational minutes, March 19, 1924, roll 11, folder 69, UNIA Papers WRHS.

124. Division 59 organizational minutes, April 6, 1926, July 12, 1926, both in roll 11, folder 69, UNIA Papers WRHS.

125. "What Does the Garvey Movement Mean to Negro Womanhood?," *NW*, August 8, 1921, p. 8.

126. "The UNIA Indorsed [*sic*] in Chicago," *NW*, April 16, 1921, p. 10.

127. A. Garvey, *Philosophy and Opinions of Marcus Garvey*, 2:342.

128. S. A. Davis to [ESC?], September 17, 1925, box 2, folder 6, ESC Papers; Cox, *Let My People Go*; Clarence Bascome to ESC, September 9, 1925; Isiah Davis to ESC, October 5, 1925; Mrs. W. Corbin to ESC, October 15, 1925; Mrs. W. O. Sampson, October 15, 1925; UNIA Puerto Cortes Division to ESC, November 20, 1925, all in box 2, folder 6, ESC Papers.

129. Grant, *Negro with a Hat*, 374.

130. William L. Sherrill death certificate, Office of the Wayne County Clerk, Detroit. No US southern state sent more emigrants in the late nineteenth century to Liberia than Arkansas. Barnes, *Journey of Hope*.

131. Hill, *MGP*, 4:1000.

132. Hill, *MGP*, 6:386–87.

133. "UNIA Torn by Internal Dissension," *Norfolk New Journal and Guide*, March 6, 1926, p. 1.

134. Hill, *MGP*, 6:lxvi.

135. Lindsay, *Atlantic Bonds*, 236.

136. Terance Wilson, personal conversation with author, La Digue, Grenada, March 14, 2015.

137. *AOMX*, 2.

138. Jupiter Langdon died at the age of seventy-five in 1901, while Mary Jane Langdon passed away at the age of sixty-eight in 1916. Jupiter Langdon and Mary Jane Langdon death certificates, Terance Wilson Personal Papers, in Wilson's possession, Madeys, Grenada (hereafter, TW Papers).

139. Anderson and Lovejoy, *Liberated Africans*.

140. R. Thompson, *Flash of the Spirit*, xv.

141. Terance Wilson, telephone conversation with author, April 7, 2016.

142. Birth certificates of Langdon family members, TW Papers; Wilson, conversation with author, January 13, 2015; Wilson, telephone conversation with author, April 7, 2016.

143. Wilson, telephone conversation with author, April 7, 2016.

144. Gomez, *Black Crescent*, 343.

145. *AOMX*, 156, 155–90.

146. Wilson, conversation with author, La Digue, Grenada, January 13, 2015.

147. Wilson, conversation with author, January 13, 2015.

148. Death certificate of Mary Jane Langdon, 1916, and marriage certificate of Gertrude Langdon, 1919, both in TW Papers; Wilson, telephone conversation with author, April 7, 2016.

149. Wilson, conversation with author, January 13, 2015; Gloria Chitterman and Fitzroy Walcott, conversation with author, La Digue, Grenada, January 15, 2015; J. Martin, *Island Caribs*, 17; U. Taylor, *Veiled Garvey*, 15–16.

150. J. Martin, *Island Caribs*, 296–307.

151. Wilson, conversation with author, January 13, 2015; Carew, *Ghosts in Our Blood*, 125.

152. Wilson, conversations with author, January 13 and March 14, 2015; Putnam, *Radical Moves*, 1, 23–39.

153. D. Williams, *Blacks in Montreal*, 21–41.

154. Carew, *Ghosts in Our Blood*, 131.

155. Henry J. Langdon to Thomas W. Harvey (hereafter, TWH), May 27, 1968, box 12, folder 4, UNIA Papers RL; Bertley, "The Universal Negro Improvement Association," 51–55; Marano, "'For the Freedom of the Black People,'" 1; T. Martin, *Race First*, 16.

156. Steven Jones and Talib El Amin, interview with author, June 9, 2014, Grand Rapids, MI; State of Michigan, "Certificate of Death: Earl Little," Division of Vital Records, Ingham County Courthouse, Lansing, file no. 545; Carew, *Ghosts in Our Blood*, x, 131.

157. Haley, *No Mercy Here*, 11–13.

158. *AOMX*, 2.

159. *AOMX*, 2.

160. R. Collins, *Seventh Child*, 5.

161. Gomez, *African Dominion*.

162. Gomez, *Black Crescent*, 143, 159.

163. R. Collins, *Seventh Child*, 6.

164. *AOMX*, 199.

165. R. Collins, *Seventh Child*, 3–4.

166. W. James, *Holding Aloft the Banner of Ethiopia*, 8.

167. Marable, *Malcolm X*, 20–22; Strickland and Greene, *Malcolm X*, 9–10.

168. Q. Taylor, *In Search of the Racial Frontier*, 204–5.

169. Menard, "Lest We Forget."

170. Hill, *MGP*, 1:43.

171. "Omaha, Nebraska," *NW*, January 9, 1926, p. 6; Steven Jones and Talib El Amin, interview with author, June 9, 2014.

172. "Omaha, Neb.," *NW*, May 22, 1926, p. 6; Louise Little, "Omaha, Nebraska," *NW*, June 19, 1926, p. 6; Louise Little, "Omaha, Neb.," *NW*, July 3, 1926, p. 6.

173. Armstrong, *Mary Turner*.

174. Jones and El Amin, interview with author, June 9, 2014.

175. Douglas K. Meyer, "Growth of Lansing's Negro Community," *Peninsular* (1969), 10, Forest Park Library and Archives, Central Capital Area District Libraries, Lansing, MI.

176. Strickland and Greene, *Malcolm X*, 16–17.

177. *AOMX*, 3; Strickland and Greene, *Malcolm X*, 19.

178. *AOMX*, 6–7, 10–11; Strickland and Greene, *Malcolm X*, 23.

179. Payne and Payne, *The Dead Are Arising*, 108.

180. J. Martin, *A–Z of Grenada Heritage*, 157–58.

181. Deborah Jones, interview with author, February 19, 2015, East Lansing, MI.

182. *AOMX*, 10; Marable, *Malcolm X*, 27.

183. Little, "Our Family from the Inside," 10.

184. Hill, *MGP*, 4:801–2; Burkett, *Garveyism as a Religious Movement*, 114–17, 129–30.

185. S. Johnson, *African American Religions*, 274.

186. Weisenfeld, *New World A-Coming*, 5.

187. Weisenfeld, *New World A-Coming*, 5.

188. S. Johnson, *African American Religions*, 274.

189. Dorman, *Chosen People*, 4–5.

190. Dorman, *Chosen People*, 2.

191. Hill, "Black Zionism," 42.

192. Hill, "Black Zionism," 40–42.

193. Hill, *MGP*, 3:692n3, 693–94n4.

194. Hill, "Black Zionism," 40–42; T. Martin, *Race First*, 243.

195. Burkett, "The Baptist Church in Years of Crisis."

196. P. Bowen, "The African American Islamic Renaissance," 4, 156.

197. Dorman, *The Princess and the Prophet*, 181–201.

198. Certification of MSTA with State of Illinois, November 29, 1926, box 1, folder 3, Moorish Science Temple of America Collection, Schomburg Center for Research in Black Culture, New York, NY (hereafter, MSTA Papers).

199. Mullen, *Afro-Orientalism*, xv, xvi.

200. Mullen, *Afro-Orientalism*, xiii–xxvi; Dorman, *The Princess and the Prophet*, 6–7.

201. Ali, *The Holy Koran of the Moorish Science Temple of America*.

202. P. Bowen, "The African American Islamic Renaissance," 154–75.

203. Moorish Science Temple of America, "The Divine Constitution and By-Laws," box 1, folder 3, MSTA Papers; Ali, *The Holy Koran of the Moorish Science Temple of America*; Turner, *Islam in the African-American Experience*, 90–99.

204. Gomez, *Black Crescent*, 203.

205. Gomez, *Black Crescent*, 203, 274.

206. Gomez, *Black Crescent*, 203, 221.

207. Gomez, *Black Crescent*, 203, 93.

208. Ali, *The Holy Koran of the Moorish Science Temple of America*, 59.

209. "Noble Drew Ali Returns after Long Visit South," *Chicago Defender* (hereafter, *CD*), November 19, 1927, p. 5.

210. Gomez, *Black Crescent*, 266, 274.

211. Hill, *The FBI's RACON*, 92; P. Bowen, "The African American Islamic Renaissance," 176–77n425.

212. Turner, *Islam in the African-American Experience*, 100.

213. A physical altercation between Ali and the Chicago police did occur shortly before his death. The police severely beat him. Turner, *Islam in the African-American Experience*, 99, 100.

214. Chatelain, *South Side Girls*, 94.

215. Ali, *The Holy Koran of the Moorish Science Temple of America*, 32–34.

216. Chatelain, *South Side Girls*, 78–88.

217. Passed in 1910, the Mann Act made it illegal to traffic women across state lines "for the purpose of prostitution or debauchery, or for any other immoral purpose." "Mann Act," *Dictionary of American History*, www.encyclopedia.com (accessed October 21, 2013).

218. Chatelain, *South Side Girls*, 88–90.

219. Gomez, *Black Crescent*, 272.

3. NEW DIRECTIONS

Portions of chapter 3 originated from McDuffie, "The Diasporic Journeys of Louise Little."

1. "Hon. Theodore Bilbo of Mississippi to Present Farce in U.S. Senate," *PC*, April 22, 1939, p. 2; "President of Liberia Encourages Migration of Select Race Group: They Backed Bilbo's 'Exodus to Liberia,'" *CD*, May 6, 1939, p. 3.

2. US Congress, Senate, Committee on Foreign Relations, *Greater Liberia Act*, S 2231, 76th Congress, introduced in Senate, April 24, 1939, reel 3, box 8, folder D5, UNIA NY Division Papers, Schomburg Center for Research in Black Culture, New York; Sundiata, *Brothers and Strangers*, 311.

3. "Sen. Bilbo Plans 'Back to Africa' Bill," *PC*, April 22, 1939, 1; "President of Liberia Encourages Migration of Select Race Groups"; Fitzgerald, "'We Have Found a Moses,'" 309.

4. Blain, *Set the World on Fire*, 48.

5. Fitzgerald, "'We Have Found a Moses,'" 315, 316.

6. E. Allen, "When Japan Was 'Champion of the Darker Races,'" 39.

7. "United States Steel Corporation," https://www.referenceforbusiness.com/businesses/M-Z/United-States-Steel-Corporation.html (accessed March 19, 2021).

8. Lane, *"City of the Century,"* 36, 105–29.

9. Stein, *The World of Marcus Garvey*, 242–43.

10. Lane, *"City of the Century,"* 69–71; Mohl, "The Evolution of Racism," 59–60.

11. K. Jackson, *The Ku Klux Klan in the City*, 97.

12. Mohl, "The Evolution of Racism," 60–62.

13. "Gary Division of the UNIA and ACL," *NW*, June 25, 1921, p. 9; "Gary, Indiana," *NW*, March 25, 1922; "Gary, IND," *NW*, July 11, 1925, p. 6.

14. Stein, *The World of Marcus Garvey*, 242–43.

15. Mwariama Kamau, text message with author, November 19, 2023.

16. Official Minutes of the Midwestern Conference, April 8–9, 1950, box 4, folder 13, Marcus Garvey and the Universal Negro Improvement Association Collection (formerly the Wahab Papers), Charles H. Wright Museum of African American History, Detroit (hereafter, UNIA Collection CHWM); Smith-Irvin, *Marcus Garvey's Footsoldiers*, 64–65.

17. Tyrone Haymore, interview by author, October 6, 2017, Robbins, IL; *Historic Robbins, Illinois: Souvenir Journal* (Robbins, IL: Robbins History Museum).

18. Robbins is best known today as the home of the country's first African American–owned airport. Constructed in 1931, the airport's owner-aviators trained several pilots who later became the legendary Tuskegee airmen during the Second World War. *Historic Robbins, Illinois: Souvenir Journal*; Andrew Wiese, "Robbins, IL," *Encyclopedia of Chicago*, http://encyclopedia.chicagohistory.org/pages/1083.html (accessed May 28, 2021); Haymore, interview by author.

19. W. M. Hinton, "Robbins, IL," *NW*, October 3, 1925, p. 6; Haymore, interview by author.

20. Throughout this book, I refer to her as Elinor White, her name prior to her marriage to her second husband, John Neely, until 1951. Elinor White Neely marriage certificate, Office of County Clerk, Cook County, IL.

21. Elinor Neely White death certificate, Cook County Clerk's Office, Chicago; Haymore, interview by author; Hill, *MGP*, 10:604n2.

22. Smith-Irvin, *Marcus Garvey's Footsoldiers*, 48.

23. Jolly, *"By Our Own Strength,"* 96.

24. William H. Ferris, "Former Boxer Succeeds Garvey as UNIA Head," *CD*, August 31, 1940, p. 2; Roberta Stewart Amos, telephone conversation with author, January 25, 2013.

25. James R. Stewart, "Message from the President General," *Stewart's Voice* (November 1953), 1, container 6, roll 15, folder 93, Universal Negro Improvement Association Papers, Western Reserve Historical Society, Cleveland, OH (hereafter, UNIA Papers WRHS).

26. Ferris, "Former Boxer Succeeds Garvey as UNIA Head."

27. Sulik, "Waving the Red, Black, and Green," 69.

28. Goldie M. Stewart to Department of Vital Statistics, New Castle, Pennsylvania, October 15, 1980, Roberta Stewart Amos Personal Papers, Shaker Heights, OH.

29. Goldie Stewart's four children with James Stewart were born in Ravenna, Ohio. Goldie was the stepmother of Victor Stewart, James Stewart's child from a previous marriage. Roberta Stewart Amos, telephone conversations with author, January 25, 2013, and June 13, 2013.

30. Roberta Stewart Amos, telephone conversation with author, July 29, 2014.

31. "Jacob Goldsmith House," *Encyclopedia of Cleveland History*, https://case.edu/ech/articles/j/jacob-goldsmith-house (accessed July 23, 2009).

32. Minutes of September 29, 1935, officers meeting, roll 12, folder 71, UNIA Papers WRHS.

33. Future Outlook League, Minutes of Meeting, May 25, 1938, container 1, folder 3, Future Outlook League Papers, Western Reserve Historical Society, Cleveland; Phillips, *AlabamaNorth*, 190–225.

34. Informed by Garveyism and drafted at the Sixth Communist International Congress in Moscow in 1928, the "Black Belt Thesis," as the policy came to be known, framed African Americans in the South as a nation within a nation entitled to self-determination, and it directed US communists to champion racial equality, with special focus on fighting against Jim Crow and lynching. Horne, *Black Revolutionary*, 29–40.

35. Horne, *Black Revolutionary*, 41–66.

36. Gellman, *Death Blow to Jim Crow*, 5, 36

37. Storch, *Red Chicago*, 96.

38. Hill, *MGP*, 7:307n1.

39. Hill, *MGP*, 7:xl–xliii.

40. R. Stephens, "Marcus M. Garvey," 122, 123.

41. Hill, *MGP*, 7:xlvii.

42. W. Scott, *The Sons of Sheba's Race*, xi–xii, 3–37, 106–20.

43. Makalani, *In the Cause of Freedom*, 3, 203–12.

44. Hill, *MGP*, 7:681–84, 687.

45. T. Martin, *Race First*, 60.

46. Hill, *MGP*, 7:xlvi, 539.

47. Gilroy, "Black Fascism," 73.

48. Hill, *MGP*, 7:xlvii, 666–67, 668.

49. Grant, *Negro with a Hat*, 441.

50. Toronto was the site of the First Regional UNIA Conference and Eighth International UNIA Convention, held in August 1936 and August 1938, respectively. Hill, *MGP*, 7:967–68, 969–70.

51. Hill, *MGP*, 7:770n1.

52. Hill, *MGP*, 7:769.

53. Only two graduates, Philadelphia UNIA leaders Thomas W. Harvey and Sara Isaac, resided on the US East Coast. The two other graduates—Arthur Clement Moore and Abraham R. Roberts—lived in Toronto. "The School of African Philosophy: First Graduate," *The Black Man* 2, 8 (December 1937): 4–5, box 6, file 6, AJG Papers.

54. "Marcus Garvey Speaks at BME Church," *Windsor Daily Star*, September 18, 1937, 11; Mary-Lou Gelissen, email to author, March 18, 2021; Adjetey, *Cross-Border Cosmopolitans*, 84–86.

55. Hill, *MGP*, 7:781–82.

56. Hill, *MGP*, 7:781, 782, 784, 786, 787.

57. *AOMX*, 1–22.

58. Steven Jones, phone interview by author, October 10, 2014.

59. *AOMX*, 11, 13, 22, 28.

60. I borrow the phrase "driven toward madness" from the study by Nikki Taylor of Margaret Garner, a self-emancipated African American woman, who in 1856 fled Kentucky for Cincinnati with slave catchers on her heels. After being cornered in a building, Garner, to the shock and horror of her assailants, slit the throat of her infant daughter to prevent the child from being reenslaved. N. Taylor, *Driven toward Madness*, 1–23.

61. Malcolm X (hereafter, MX) to Philbert Little, December 12, 1949, box 3, folder 1, Malcolm X Collection, Schomburg Center for Research in Black Culture, Harlem, NY (hereafter, MX Collection).

62. *AOMX*, 17.

63. Quoted in Dr. Geo. R. Clinton, Ingham County Probate Court file, January 3, 1939; Dr. E. F. Hoffman, Ingham County Probate Court file, January 3, 1939, both in Louise Little Probate File, B-4398, Lansing, MI.

64. R. A. Morter to John McClellan, January 31, 1939, Louise Little Probate File; *AOMX*, 22; Deborah Jones, interviews with author, February 18 and 19, 2015; Deborah Jones, email correspondence with author, March 11, 2015.

65. Gross, *Colored Amazons*, 128.

66. Kalamazoo State Hospital, circa 1963, Deborah Jones Personal Papers.

67. P. Bowen, "The African American Islamic Renaissance," 196–204.

68. P. Bowen, *A History of Conversion to Islam in the United States*, 240, 326.

69. Finley, "'The Secret . . . of Who the Devil Is,'" 155.

70. Bates, *The Making of Black Detroit*, 120, 121, 156.

71. Bald, *Bengali Harlem*, 120.

72. Warren, *Radio Priest*, 2.

73. Bald, *Bengali Harlem*, 120.

74. Bald, *Bengali Harlem*, 156; Gardezi, *Chains to Lose*, 1:i–xviii.

75. Bald, *Bengali Harlem*, 157; Gardezi, *Chains to Lose*, 2:446–90.

76. Clegg, *An Original Man*, 2.

77. Finley, *In and Out of This World*, 1–73; Gomez, *Black Crescent*, 276–330.

78. Gomez, *Black Crescent*, 276; Lincoln, *The Black Muslims in America*, 62.

79. Beynon, "The Voodoo Cult," 896.

80. Macuzzi, "Going Back," 72; Evanzz, *The Messenger*, 73; Muhammad, *The Message to the Blackman in America*, 3, 52–54; Nation of Islam, "Brief History on Origin of the Nation of Islam," https://noi.org/noi-history (accessed March 28, 2024).

81. Muhammad, *The Message to the Blackman in America*, 3, 52–54; Gomez, *Black Crescent*, 297, 299–300.

82. Gomez, *Black Crescent*, 302.

83. Muhammad, *The Message to the Blackman in America*, 51, 1–30, 50–54.

84. Gomez, *Black Crescent*, 319.

85. Muhammad, *The Message to the Blackman in America*, 44–50; P. Bowen, *A History of the Conversion to Islam in the United States*, 293–97.

86. U. Taylor, *The Promise of Patriarchy*, 2.

87. *AOMX*, 199.

88. Gomez, *Black Crescent*, 321–22.

89. Gomez, *Black Crescent*, 276.

90. P. Bowen, "The African American Islamic Renaissance," 306n89.

91. Beynon, "The Voodoo Cult," 907; P. Bowen, "The African American Islamic Renaissance," 307.

92. Beynon, "The Voodoo Cult," 900, 905.

93. Clegg, *An Original Man*, 13.

94. Smith-Irvin, *Marcus Garvey's Footsoldiers*, 72; Gomez, *Black Crescent*, 296.

95. U. Taylor, *The Promise of Patriarchy*, 27.

96. Gomez, *Black Crescent*, 287.

97. *AOMX*, 161.

98. Gomez, *Black Crescent*, 292–93.

99. U. Taylor, *The Promise of Patriarchy*, 1–6.

100. U. Taylor, *The Promise of Patriarchy*, 75, 22.

101. U. Taylor, *The Promise of Patriarchy*, 22.

102. U. Taylor, *The Promise of Patriarchy*, 16.

103. U. Taylor, *The Promise of Patriarchy*, 16.

104. "400 Youths at Cult School," *Atlanta Daily World*, April 24, 1934, p. 1.

105. Clegg, *An Original Man*, 101.

106. U. Taylor, *The Promise of Patriarchy*, 15.

107. Beynon, "The Voodoo Cult," 907.

108. Felber, *Those Who Know Don't Say*, 1.

109. P. Bowen, "The African American Islamic Renaissance," 312–13.

110. "Leader of Cult Admits Slaying at Home 'Altar,'" *Detroit Free Press*, November 21, 1932, 1.

111. "Raided Temple Bares Grip of Voodoo in City," *Detroit Free Press*, November 23, 1932, 1.

112. Russell J. Cowans, "Fears More Murders in Queer Order," *CD*, December 3, 1932, p. 1.

113. "400 Youths at Cult School"; Taylor, *Promise of Patriarchy*, 28.

114. Quoted in *Norfolk New Journal and Guide*, April 28, 1934, A14; "500 Join March to Ask Voodoo Kings' Freedom," *Detroit Free Press*, November 25, 1932, p. 1; U. Taylor, *The Promise of Patriarchy*, 28.

115. Felber, *Those Who Know Don't Say*, 13.

116. "Cultists Riot in Court; One Death, 41 Hurt," *Chicago Daily Tribune*, March 6, 1935, 1; U. Taylor, *The Promise of Patriarchy*, 51.

117. "Cultists Riot in Court."

118. "Moors Battle in Court; 40 Hurt," *CD*, March 9, 1935, 1.

119. "Moors Battle in Court."

120. U. Taylor, *The Promise of Patriarchy*, 51, 53.

121. "Forty Cultists Put in Jail for Courtroom Riot," *Chicago Daily Tribune*, March 7, 1935, p. 13; "Cultists Riot in Court."

122. "Moors Battle in Court," 2.

123. U. Taylor, *The Promise of Patriarchy*, 56.

124. Mittie Maude Lena Gordon (hereafter, MMLG) to ESC, October 27, 1939, box 5, folder 2, ESC Papers.

125. McLaughlin, "Reconsidering the East St. Louis Race Riot of 1917," 187, 194–203.

126. Hill, *MGP*, 1:213.

127. Blain, *Set the World on Fire*, 50–51.

128. MMLG to ESC, October 27, 1939.

129. "Peace Movement of Ethiopia," FBI, Chicago Bureau, File 100-8932, September 30, 1942.

130. Blain, *Set the World on Fire*, 62–63.

131. Constitution of the Peace Movement of Ethiopia, box 30, PME folder, ESC Papers; Blain, *Set the World on Fire*, 64.

132. Horne, *Facing the Rising Sun*, 66–67.

133. Horne, *Facing the Rising Sun*, 66–67 (emphasis in original).

134. Blain, *Set the World on Fire*, 59–60.

135. Horne, *Facing the Rising Sun*, 66–67.

136. MMLG to ESC, March 7, 1934, box 4, folder 1, ESC Papers.

137. PME Memorial, box 30, PME folder, ESC Papers.

138. Blain, *Set the World on Fire*, 73–74.

139. Brief History of the Petition of the Peace Movement of Ethiopia, box 30, PME folder, ESC Papers.

140. PME Memorial; Blain, *Set the World on Fire*, 61.

141. Blain, *Set the World on Fire*, 105.

142. ESC to Peace Movement of Ethiopia (hereafter, PME), March 10, 1934, box 4, folder 1, ESC Papers.

143. MMLG to ESC, March 15, 1934, box 4, folder 1.

144. MMLG to ESC, October 10, 1934, box 4, folder 1, ESC Papers.

145. Theodore G. Bilbo, "Voluntary Resettlement of African Negroes in Africa," *Congressional Record*, April 24, 1939, box 1089, folder 12, Theodore G. Bilbo Papers, McCain Library and Archives, University of Southern Mississippi, Hattiesburg (hereafter, TGB Papers).

146. Kelley, *Hammer and Hoe*, 79.

147. Theodore G. Bilbo (hereafter, TGB) to MMLG, October 16, 1939, box 1090, folder 9, TGB Papers.

148. "She's 1939 'Moses,'" *Afro-American* (hereafter, *AA*), April 29, 1939, p. 24.

149. E. Cronon, *Black Moses*, 4; Sernett, *Harriet Tubman*, 41–72.

150. Blain, *Set the World on Fire*, 128.

151. Hill, *MGP*, 10:851.

152. MG to TGB, August 13, 1938, box 1091, folder 9, TGB Papers; MG to ESC, March 9, 1938, box 4, folder 1, ESC Papers; Hill, *MGP*, 10:884n2.

153. James R. Stewart (hereafter, JRS) to TGB, December 9, 1938, box 1091, folder 3, TGB Papers; Ethel Waddell to ESC, May 1, 1938, box 4, folder 1, ESC Papers.

154. Hill, *MGP*, 10:893, 912–13.

155. Blain, *Set the World on Fire*, 47.

156. Sundiata, *Brothers and Strangers*, 312.

157. "Hon. Theodore Bilbo of Mississippi to Present Farce," 2; "President of Liberia Exchange Encourages Migration," 3.

158. MMLG to TGB, August 10, 1938, box 1091, folder 10, TGB Papers.

159. MMLG to TGB, August 10, 1938, box 1091, folder 10, TGB Papers.

160. Blain, *Set the World on Fire*, 121, 141.

161. "Peace Movement of Ethiopia"; Blain, *Set the World on Fire*, 124.

162. Hill, *MGP*, 10:917–20.

163. Katznelson, *Fear Itself*, 85–87.

164. ESC to Thomas Dixon, February 26, 1939, box 5, folder 2, ESC Papers.

165. *The Peace Movement of Ethiopia, A Corporation v. Mittie Maude Gordon, William Gordon, William Meriwether, and Joseph Rockmore*, Counter-Complaint, Superior Court of Cook County, May 6, 1940, box 1089, folder 2, TGB Papers; Hill, *MGP*, 7:894–95n5; Blain, *Set the World on Fire*, 75–103.

166. Kuumba, *Gender and Social Movements*, 57.

167. Constitution of the Peace Movement of Ethiopia, 17.

168. Gordon did not accompany the two-person PME delegation to Liberia. The PME never established a colony in West Africa. Constitution of the Peace Movement of Ethiopia, 16.

169. Blain, *Set the World on Fire*, 129–30.

170. E. Frances White, "Africa on My Mind," 76–77.

171. McDuffie, "'I Wanted a Communist Philosophy,'" 183.

172. Prominent Black left feminists include Claudia Jones, Louise Thompson Patterson, Audley "Queen Mother" Moore, Esther Cooper Jackson, Thyra Edwards, Eslanda Robeson, Shirley Graham Du Bois, Alice Childress, Lorraine Hansberry, Vicki Garvin, and Grace Campbell. McDuffie, *Sojourning for Freedom*, 3–6; Hagedorn, "'Chicago's Renaissance Woman,'" 1–14.

173. McDuffie, *Sojourning for Freedom*, 3–6.

174. McDuffie, *Sojourning for Freedom*, 64, 68–69, 147–51.

175. T. Martin, *Amy Ashwood Garvey*, 46–75; U. Taylor, *Veiled Garvey*, 29.

176. U. Taylor, *Veiled Garvey*, 125–42.

177. Mullen, *Afro-Orientalism*, xii.

178. Horne, *Race War*, 43.

179. Horne, *Facing the Rising Sun*, 12–13, 41.

180. Horne, *Facing the Rising Sun*, 59.

181. "UNIA Mass Meeting of the St. Louis Division Well Attended," *NW*, March 26, 1921, p. 9; L. G. Chambers, "East St. Louis," *NW*, September 6, 1924, 6; "UNIA Closes District Meet at St. Louis," *CD*, December 6, 1941, p. 6; Charles L. James, "Travels and Expenditures," n.d., box 5, folder 25, UNIA Collection CHWM.

182. Hill, *MGP*, 10:717.

183. E. Allen, "When Japan Was 'Champion of the Darker Races,'" 24, 29–30.

184. Horne, *Facing the Rising Sun*, 64, 65.

185. Hill, *The FBI's RACON*, 514–17.

186. E. Allen, "Waiting for Tojo," 43.

187. Horne, *Facing the Rising Sun*, 59.

188. "Voodoo Probe in City Widens," *Detroit Free Press*, January 20, 1937, p. 4; Blain, "'For the Rights of Dark People,'" 94; Turner, *Islam in the African-American Experience*, 168.

189. J. E. Hoover to Assistant Attorney General Keenan, November 10, 1933, file 146-10-2, class 146-10 (Japanese Propaganda) Litigation Case Files and Enclosures, 1940–1955, entry AI-COR 146-10, box 4301, folder 235408, Record Group 60, Pacific Movement of the Eastern World, National Archives, Index Cards, National Archives at College Park, MD (hereafter, PMEW).

190. There are countless surveillance records of PMEW activities in these cities throughout the PMEW files. See, for example, "Peace Movement of Ethiopia," St. Louis FBI file 65-305, April 23, 1943, file 146-10-2, class 146-10 (Japanese Propaganda), Litigation Case Files and Enclosures, 1940–1955, entry AI-COR) 146-10, box 2, folder 1, PMEW.

191. Kearney, *Solidarity or Sedition?*, 80.

192. Blain, "'For the Rights of Dark People,'" 94.

193. Constitution and By-Laws of the PMEW, circa November 1933, FBI File, Record Group 60, folder 146-10-2 (sect. 1), PMEW.

194. Constitution of the Peace Movement of Ethiopia, 8.

195. Negro Commission, *Is Japan the Champion of the Colored Races?*

196. E. Allen, "When Japan Was 'Champion of the Darker Races,'" 39.

197. Horne, *Facing the Rising Sun*, 12.

4. "ON DECEMBER 7 . . ."

Portions of chapter 4 originated from McDuffie, "The Diasporic Journeys of Louise Little."

1. "FBI Accuses 80 in Chicago of Part in Seditious Activities," *Afro-American* (hereafter, *AA*), September 26, 1942, p. 1; Blain, *Set the World on Fire*, 152–54.

2. For correspondences between MMLG and ESC related to her arrest and incarceration, see box 6, folders 1 and 2, ESC Papers.

3. Hill, *The FBI's RACON*, xvii.

4. David H. Orro, "Cultists Remain Undaunted," *CD*, October 24, 1942, p. 4; "25 Chi Cultists Get 3-Year Prison Terms," *AA*, October 31, 1942, p. 3.

5. Plummer, *Rising Wind*, 124.

6. Marable, *Race, Reform, and Rebellion*, 10, 13–27.

7. Hirsch, *Making of the Second Ghetto*, 17.

8. Widick, *Detroit*, 90.

9. Ford, *A Brick and a Bible*, 169.

10. Marable, *Race, Reform, and Rebellion*, 15.

11. Ottley, *"New World A-Coming,"* 84–85.

12. Singh, *Black Is a Country*, 102–3, 123.

13. Marable, *Race, Reform, and Rebellion*, 13–14.

14. Singh, *Black Is a Country*, 99–109.

15. Untitled History of Housewives League, box 1, history folder, Housewives League of Detroit Papers, Burton Historical Collection, Detroit Public Library, Detroit; Phillips, *AlabamaNorth*, 226–52.

16. Lucander, *Winning the War for Democracy*, 2.

17. Hirsch, *Making of the Second Ghetto*; Widick, *Detroit*, 88–112.

18. Phillips, *AlabamaNorth*, 226–32.

19. Widick, *Detroit*, 99–112.

20. Von Eschen, *Race against Empire*, 22–68.

21. Von Eschen, *Race against Empire*, 20, 70–95.

22. Hill, *MGP*, 7:957n1.

23. Azikiwe, *My Odyssey*, 34, 66.

24. "Editorials," *New Negro World* (hereafter, *NNW*), January 1942, p. 3, roll 15, folder 91, UNIA Papers WRHS.

25. Hill, *MGP*, 7:958n3.

26. JRS to UNIA Officers, October 19, 1940, roll 1, folder 3, UNIA Papers WRHS.

27. "Official Minutes of Tenth International Convention of the Universal Negro Improvement Association," August 16–24, 1946, box 4, folder 5, UNIA Papers CHWM; "Official Minutes of the National Conference of the Universal Negro Improvement Association," August 30–September 1, 1947, roll 8, folder 40, UNIA Papers WRHS.

28. "Official Minutes of Midwestern and Southern Regional Conference of the Universal Negro Improvement Association," 2015 Papers, UNIA Collection CHWM; Blain, *Set the World on Fire*, 137.

29. "Official Minutes of the National Conference"; "Liberty Farm," *NNW*, November–December 1942, p. 13–14, roll 15, folder 92, UNIA Papers WRHS; untitled caption, *NNW*, September 1943, p. 12, roll 15, folder 92, UNIA Papers WRHS.

30. "Launching the Five Year Plan: Liberty Farm," flyer, n.d., box 15, folder 95, UNIA Papers WRHS; "UNIA Conference Great Success," *NNW*, September 1943, p. 5, roll 15, folder 92, UNIA Papers WRHS; Roberta Stewart Amos, telephone interview with author, July 28, 2014.

31. B. Smith, *Food Power Politics*, 1–16.

32. Roberta Stewart Amos, telephone conversation with author, July 22, 2019.

33. "Official Minutes of Tenth International Convention."

34. Amos, telephone conversation with author, July 22, 2019.

35. Kearney, *Solidarity or Sedition?*, xxxvi, 92–127.

36. Horne, *Red Seas*, 81–120.

37. Horne, *Facing the Rising Sun*, 10; Kearney, *Solidarity or Sedition?*, xxxvi, 92–127.

38. Dixon, *African Americans and the Pacific War*, 22.

39. Horne, *Race War*, 243.

40. Hill, *The FBI's RACON*, 93, 526.

41. "Peace Movement of Ethiopia," FBI, Chicago Bureau file 100-124410-4, May 10, 1942, p. 3.

42. Horne, *Facing the Rising Sun*, 100.

43. Horne, *Facing the Rising Sun*, 102.

44. Felber, *Those Who Know Don't Say*, 22; Horne, *Facing the Rising Sun*, 88–97.

45. P. Bowen, "The African-American Islamic Renaissance," 232; Horne, *Facing the Rising Sun*, 12.

46. Horne, *Facing the Rising Sun*, 12–15, 112–18.

47. Capeci, *The Lynching of Cleo Wright*.

48. Hill, *The FBI's RACON*, 699.

49. Hill, *The FBI's RACON*, 101.

50. JRS, untitled article, *NNW*, March 1942, p. 2, roll 15, folder 91, UNIA Papers WRHS.

51. Negro Commission, *Is Japan the Champion of the Colored Races?*, 7–17.

52. MMLG to ESC, December 31, 1940, box 6, folder 1, ESC Papers.

53. "Bilbo Bill Helps Negro," *NNW*, November 16, 1940, pp. 1, 5, box 6, folder 3, ESC Papers.

54. Blain, "'We Want to Set the World on Fire,'" 195.

55. Adelia Ireland, "Arise," *NNW*, July 1942, p. 16, roll 15, box 91, UNIA Papers WRHS (emphasis in original).

56. Ethel Collins, "Liberty," *NNW*, January 1942, p. 8, roll 15, box 91, UNIA Papers WRHS.

57. Goldthree, "Amy Jacques Garvey," 156; U. Taylor, *The Veiled Garvey*, 165–93.

58. A. Garvey, *Memorandum Correlative of Africa, West Indies, and the Americas*, May 1944, box 13, folder 7, Amy Jacques Garvey Memorial Collection on Marcus Garvey, Special Collections and Archives, Fisk University, Nashville (hereafter, AJG Papers).

59. A. Garvey, *Memorandum*; A. Garvey, African Study Circle of the World [November 1944?], box 10, folder 5, AJG Papers; AJG to James A. Blades, box 1, folder 3, AJG Papers.

60. Greer, *Property and Dispossession*, 191–240; Blain, *Set the World on Fire*, 141.

61. Goldthree, "Amy Jacques Garvey," 158. The archive has yet to reveal direct conversations between James Stewart and Amy Jacques Garvey about colonization. She did, however, admire Mittie Maude Lena Gordon for her continued efforts to pass the Greater Liberia Bill, indicating how the support for colonization circulated among Black nationalists globally. Blain, *Set the World on Fire*, 154.

62. "Report of Esther V. Cooper," circa 1946, box 3, folder 5, Edward Strong Papers, Moorland-Spingarn Research Center, Howard University, Washington, DC.

63. JRS, untitled editorial, *NNW*, May 1942, p. 2, roll 15, folder 91, UNIA Papers WRHS (emphasis in original).

64. JRS, "Our Birth Control," *NNW*, February 1942, p. 1, box 31, folder 2, ESC Papers.

65. JRS, "Our Birth Control."

66. U. Taylor, *The Promise of Patriarchy*, 161.

67. "To the Officers, Members, and Friends of the Association and of the Race," *NNW*, March 1943, p. 11, roll 15, folder 92, UNIA Papers WRHS.

68. EMC to the Officers, Members, and Friends of the UNIA and of the Race, August 15, 1943, box 1, file 5, AJG Papers.

69. AJG to JRS, April 5, 1944, box 3, folder 5, AJG Papers.

70. Roberta Stewart Amos, telephone conversation with author, April 9, 2013.

71. "Tentative Agenda for Conference of the Rehabilitating Committee, Philadelphia, August 1–2, 1943," box 16, folder 18, UNIA Papers RL.

72. "Minutes of the International Convention of the UNIA & ACL," box 15, folder 53, UNIA Papers RL.

73. Ransby, *Ella Baker*, 105–47, 170–95.

74. C. Jones, "An End to the Neglect of the Problems of the Negro Woman!"; McDuffie, *Sojourning for Freedom*, 118–52, 166–68.

75. It should be noted that the arrest of Black nationalists in Chicago followed a government roundup of Black nationalists in New York City and Kansas City in spring 1942.

In December 1942, authorities arrested twenty suspected pro-Japanese Black militants in New Orleans. Horne, *Facing the Rising Sun*, 95, 112–18.

76. Clegg, *An Original Man*, 82–83.

77. Clegg, *An Original Man*, 91–92.

78. Clegg, *An Original Man*, 88–97.

79. Clegg, *An Original Man*, 88–97; Turner, *Islam in the African-American Experience*, 169.

80. Turner, *Islam in the African-American Experience*, 168, 182–83; Clegg, *An Original Man*, 97, 98.

81. Rosie Lee Gearring to ESC, January 26, 1944, and June 6, 1944, both in box 6, folder 2, ESC Papers.

82. MMLG to ESC, May 7, 1943, box 6, folder 1, ESC Papers.

83. MMLG to ESC, August 14, 1944, box 6, folder 2, ESC Papers.

84. Rosie Lee Gearring to ESC, January 26, 1944, and June 6, 1944, both in box 6, folder 2, ESC Papers.

85. MMLG to ESC, August 28, 1945, box 6, folder 2, ESC Papers.

86. ESC to MMLG, March 31, 1944, box 6, folder 2, ESC Papers.

87. ESC to US Board of Parole, November 6, 1944; ESC to MMLG, March 31, 1944; ESC to Helen C. Hironimus, June 8, 1944, and June 10, 1944, all in box 6, folder 2, ESC Papers.

88. MMLG to ESC, January 27, 1942, box 6, folder 1, ESC Papers.

89. Hill, *The FBI's RACON*, 97.

90. Roberta Stewart Amos, telephone conversation with author, December 4, 2017.

91. "UNIA Pledges Loyalty to Uncle Sam," *CD*, September 12, 1942, p. 2.

92. Horne, *Facing the Rising Sun*, 112–18.

93. Horne, *Facing the Rising Sun*, 120.

94. "Cultists Wait Evasion Trial in Motor City," *CD*, May 30, 1942, p. 2; "Grand Jury Probes Jap-Backed Negro Culturists in Chicago," *Call and Post* (Cleveland) (hereafter *CCP*), October 17, 1942, p. 14.

95. Summers, *Madness in the City*, 3.

96. L. Jackson, *Surfacing Up*, 44.

97. In 1978, the hospital was renamed the Kalamazoo Regional Hospital. In 1995, the institution's name changed to the Kalamazoo Psychiatric Hospital. At the time of this book's publication, the asylum remains open and operated by the Michigan Department of Health and Human Services. "Kalamazoo Psychiatric Hospital: The Largest Mental Health Institute in Michigan," https://www.kpl.gov/local-history/kalamazoo-history/health/kalamazoo-psychiatric-hospital (accessed November 14, 2013).

98. Marable, *Malcolm X*, 36.

99. Russell, *The Life of Louise Norton Little*, 233–306.

100. Mark L. Ruffalo, "A Brief History of Electroconvulsive Therapy," *Psychology Today* November 3, 2018, https://www.psychologytoday.com/us/blog/freud-fluoxetine/201811/brief-history-electroconvulsive-therapy.

101. Marable, *Malcolm X*, 36.

102. Russell, *The Life of Louise Norton Little*, 209.

103. Strickland and Greene, *Malcolm X*, 33.

104. *AOMX*, 21.

105. Edgerton Langdon to Muriel Rumbey, May 15, 1939, Deborah Jones Personal Papers; Russell, *The Life of Louise Norton Little*, 260, 267.

106. Like other Langdon family members, Malcolm Orgias was steeped in Garveyism. His father, Joseph Orgias, who married Gertrude Langdon, Louise's mother's sister, was an ardent supporter of Marcus Garvey. Orgias raised funds in Grenada for the UNIA. He sent the money to his brother-in-law Edgerton Langdon in Montreal. Terance Wilson, telephone conversation with author, January 21, 2022; Russell, *The Life of Louise Norton Little*, 249.

107. *AOMX*, 38–69.

108. *AOMX*, 75.

109. *AOMX*, 75–78; Pullman Employment Record for Malcolm Little, Newberry's Pullman Company Archives, 1926–68, Newberry Library, Chicago.

110. *AOMX*, 40–41, 59, 76.

111. Kelley, *Race Rebels*, 166.

112. Kelley, *Race Rebels*, 171.

113. *AOMX*, 96.

114. Marable, *Malcolm X*, 64–65.

115. Marable, *Malcolm X*, 52.

116. *AOMX*, 104.

117. Kelley, *Race Rebels*, 172.

118. *AOMX*, 106.

119. Kelley, *Race Rebels*, 172.

120. Ottley, *"New World A-Coming,"* 129, 134.

121. *AOMX*, 209.

122. *AOMX*, 142–50; Marable, *Malcolm X*, 64–69.

123. Goldman, *The Death and Life of Malcolm X*, 32.

124. Bessel, "Unnatural Deaths," 301–21.

125. Plummer, *Rising Wind*, 140.

126. Garfinkel, *When Negroes March*, 148–61.

127. "The Election Case of Theodore G. Bilbo of Mississippi," 1947, https://www.senate.gov/artandhistory/history/common/contested_elections/126Theodore_Bilbo.htm (accessed June 19, 2019).

128. Horne, *Black and Red*.

129. Westad, *The Global Cold War*.

130. Horne, *Black Revolutionary*, 1–14.

131. Plummer, *Rising Wind*, 125–26.

132. Petition of the UNIA to the United Nations, San Francisco Conference, April 1945, box 15, folder 3, UNIA Papers RL. No record of the UN's response to the UNIA's proposal has yet been found. "The San Francisco Conference and the Colonial Issue: Statement of the Council on African Affairs," n.d., reel 57, 1377–83, W. E. B. Du Bois Papers microfilm, History, Philosophy, and Newspaper Library, University of Illinois at Urbana-Champaign; Anderson, *Bourgeois Radicals*, 57–60.

133. Short Biography of William L. Sherrill Sr., box 21, folder 5, UNIA Papers RL.

134. Plummer, *Rising Wind*, 132.

135. Von Eschen, *Race against Empire*, 81–82; Plummer, *Rising Wind*, 176.

136. Untitled report, box 21, folder 10, UNIA Papers RL; Plummer, *Rising Wind*, 150–51.

137. *The Black Pilot*, February 3, 1948, roll 15, folder 90, UNIA Papers WRHS; JRS to ESC, February 1, 1949, box 7, folder 2, ESC Papers.

138. Sundiata, *Brothers and Strangers*, 333.

139. Robeson, *African Journey*, 28.

140. Getachew, *Worldmaking after Empire*, 72.

141. Adi and Sherwood, *The 1945 Manchester Pan-African Congress Revisited*, 55.

142. Plummer, *Rising Wind*, 160.

143. U. Taylor, *The Veiled Garvey*, 165–74; T. Martin, *Amy Ashwood Garvey*, 196–230.

144. Drake and Cayton, *Black Metropolis*, 8.

145. Hirsch, *Making of the Second Ghetto*, 40, 41; Balto, *Occupied Territory*, 91–153.

146. "Victory Sign of Loyalty," CD, November 14, 1942, p. 3.

147. Chambers, "A Master Strategist," 142.

148. Green, *Selling the Race*, 45.

149. MMLG to ESC, September 7, 1947, box 6, folder 5, ESC Papers.

150. MMLG to ESC, August 5, 1946, box 6, folder 4, ESC Papers.

151. MMLG to ESC, September 7, 1947. The UNIA expressed similar sentiments about Bilbo's death. "That Man Bilbo," *The Black Pilot*, February 21, 1948, 3, box 15, folder 90, UNIA Papers WRHS.

152. Bilbo, *Take Your Choice*, ii, 154.

153. MMLG to ESC, September 7, 1947. James Stewart's position on Bilbo's passing and historical significance mirrored Gordon's. JRS, "That Man Bilbo."

154. MMLG to ESC, September 7, 1947; MMLG to ESC, May 30, 1946, box 6, folder 4, ESC Papers.

155. Lieberman and Lang, "Introduction," 7.

156. "Link Bilbo to Sedition Trial," ADW, January 31, 1943, p. 1; "Jap Payoffs to Cult at Trial" CD, February 6, 1943, p. 3.

5. "NEW AFRICA FACES THE WORLD"

Portions of chapter 5 originated from McDuffie, "'A New Day Has Dawned for the UNIA.'"

1. "President General's Message to *Stewart's Voice*," *Stewart's Voice* (hereafter, SV), October 1957, pp. 1, 2, roll 15, folder 93, UNIA Papers WRHS; Ghana Independence Celebrations, March 1957, UNIA Papers RL.

2. John B. Nanah, conversation with author, Gbandela, Liberia, January 14, 2014; Roberta Stewart Amos, telephone conversation with author, January 25, 2013; Hill, MGP, 7:957–58n1.

3. "President General's Message," SV, October 1957, pp. 1, 2, box 15, folder 93, UNIA Papers WRHS; "President General's Message to *Stewart's Voice*," SV, April 1957, p. 1, box 5, folder 6, UNIA Collection CHWM.

4. R. Williams, *Concrete Demands*, 48–86.

5. Horne, *Mau Mau in Harlem*, 115–28.

6. Gaines, *American Africans in Ghana*, 2.

7. Six African independent and to-be-independent nations attended the Bandung Conference: Egypt, Ethiopia, Gold Coast (Ghana), Liberia, and Libya.

8. Prashad, *The Darker Nations*, 34.

9. Prashad, *The Darker Nations*, xv–xix; Prashad, *The Poorer Nations*, 1–3; Padmore, *Pan-Africanism or Communism?*, 418–27.

10. Wright, *The Color Curtain*, 12.

11. Horne, *Black and Red*, 201–53.

12. N. H. Grissom to AJG, June 24, 1949, box 2, file 2, AJG Papers; "Minutes of the International Convention of the UNIA & ACL," Detroit, August 26–September 1951, box 15, folder 53, UNIA Papers RL.

13. Hill and Bair, *Marcus Garvey*, 441–42.

14. Quoted in *Robbins Eagle*, April 18, 1953; see also *Robbins Eagle*, March 28, 1953; Tyrone Haymore, interview by author, October 6, 2017, Robbins, IL.

15. "Women Seek Rule of All-Negro Town," *Jet*, April 9, 1953, p. 22.

16. "Lillie Mae Owens Gibson: International Organizer," 1961, box 5, folder 30, UNIA Collection CHWM; Ledger Book, 158, box 6, folder 31, UNIA Collection CHWM; "Lillie Mae Owens Gibson: International Organizer," *CCP*, May 12, 1962, p. 5.

17. Lillie Mae Gibson (hereafter, LMG), "Thanksgiving Message," *SV*, circa November 1954, p. 1, box 5, folder 10, UNIA Collection CHWM.

18. "Minutes of the Thirteenth International Convention of the Universal Negro Improvement Association," Gbandela, Liberia, August 1–17, 1958, box 4, folder 6, UNIA Collection CHWM.

19. LMG to JRS, September 10, 1959, reel 6, folder 32, UNIA Papers WRHS.

20. "Lillie Mae Owens Gibson," 1961.

21. "Minutes of the Twelfth International Convention of the UNIA," Gbandela, Liberia, 1954, box 15, folder 56, UNIA Papers RL.

22. Wahab, *I Have the Honor of Being*, 65.

23. Dunn, *The Foreign Policy of Liberia*, 51–67; Nkrumah, *Ghana*, 180–83.

24. E. Thompson, *Africa*, 19–25; *The Liberian Age*, March 23, 1956, box 1, folder 1, Griffith J. Davis Papers, Rubenstein Library, Duke University, Durham, NC.

25. JRS, "Stewart's Voice," *SV*, November 1956, p. 1, roll 15, folder 93, UNIA Papers WRHS.

26. Goldie Stewart and the Stewart children also adopted Liberian citizenship. Roberta Stewart Amos, conversation with author, April 9, 2013.

27. Marable, *W. E. B. Du Bois*, 213.

28. "Exact Quotations from Letters Received from the Hon. James R. Stewart," Sara R. Isaac Collection, box 1, folder 21, Charles L. Blockson Collection, Philadelphia.

29. Stewart purchased the land in his name on behalf of the UNIA. The initial parcel was one hundred acres in size. In the coming years, James Stewart purchased additional land. Florence E. Pitters, "My Observations of Liberia," *SV*, April 1955, p. 2, roll 15, 93, UNIA Papers WRHS; Receipt Bureau of Internal Revenues, Liberia, to JRS, November 17, 1949, Donna Cooper Hayford Personal Papers, Paynesville, Liberia.

30. Nevin, "In Search of the Historical Madam Suakoko."

31. "Pittsburgh Garveyites behind Plan to Set Up Liberian 'Liberty Farms,'" *Pittsburgh Courier* (hereafter, *PC*), January 21, 1950, p. 2; "Garveyites Prospering in Liberia," *SV*,

June 1953, reel 15, folder 93, p. 3; Pitters, "My Observations of Liberia," pp. 1–2, all in UNIA Papers WRHS.

32. "Minutes, UNIA Eleventh International Convention, October 1950," Isaac Collection, box 1, folder 21, UNIA Collection CHWM; "Minutes of the Twelfth International Convention of the UNIA"; "Minutes of Thirteenth International Convention of the UNIA."

33. "Minutes of the Twelfth International Convention of the UNIA."

34. Fifteen delegates attended the 1953 International Convention of the Sherrill-led UNIA in Detroit. "Minutes of the Twelfth International Convention of the UNIA."

35. "Pittsburgh Garveyites behind Plans to Set Up Liberian 'Liberty Farms,'" *PC*, January 21, 1950, p. 2; Harold I. Keith, "Facts about Africa," *PC*, October 9, 1954, p. 21; JRS, "Convention in Africa," *African Opinion* 3, nos. 7–8 (June–July 1954), 2; "Machinery Shipped," *African Opinion* 3, nos. 9–10 (October–November 1954): 3, 14; "Garveyites Backing Africa," *African Opinion* 3, nos. 9–10 (October–November 1954): 5–6, "Garvey Movement Ends Convention," *African Opinion* 3, nos. 11–12 (May–June 1955): 9; "Liberian Visits U.S. Mother," *African Opinion* 4, nos. 11–12 (March–April 1959): 5, all in box 8, folder 3, F. H. Hammurabi Papers, Archives and Special Collections, Chicago State University.

36. Roberta Stewart Amos, telephone conversation with author, April 8, 2013; death certification of James R. Stewart, National Public Health Service of the Republic of Liberia, May 4, 1964, in Roberta Stewart Amos Papers, in possession of author.

37. "200 Leave Soon for Liberia; Won't Return," *CCP*, June 26, 1954, p. 1-A.

38. "Jesse Owens to Speak to UNIA Fete, Sunday," *CCP*, June 14, 1958.

39. R. C. Rockmore, "An Announcement," *SV*, March 1956, p. 2, box 5, folder 5, UNIA Collection CHWM.

40. Blain, *Set the World on Fire*, 179.

41. "President General's Message," *SV*, October 1957, pp. 1–2; "President General's Message to Stewart Voice," *SV*, April 1957, p. 1; "April 8-Day Crisis in Kenya," *SV*, May 1953, p. 2, reel 15, folder 93, UNIA Papers WRHS.

42. JRS, "President General's Message to Stewart's Voice," *SV*, August 1957, p. 2, box 5, folder 6, UNIA Collection CHWM.

43. *AOMX*, 278; A. *Moore, Why Reparations?*

44. JRS, untitled article, *SV*, April 1955, p. 1, reel 15, folder 93, UNIA Papers WRHS.

45. "Pittsburgh Garveyites behind Plans."

46. JRS, "President General's Message to *Stewart's Voice*," *SV*, July 1, 1957, roll 8, folder 44, UNIA Papers WRHS.

47. A. Smith *Conquest.*

48. Roberta Stewart Amos, conversation with author, July 28, 2014.

49. Dunn, *Liberia and the United States during the Cold War*, 31.

50. S. 276, January 10, 1955, box 10, folder 3, ESC Papers; "Pittsburgh Garveyites behind Plans."

51. "What's Senator Langer's Story," *PC*, January 21, 1950, p. 16; Plummer, *In Search of Power*, 36–37.

52. ESC to JRS, June 9, 1951, box 8, folder 4, ESC Papers.

53. For material on the collaborations between ESC and white supremacist organizations during the 1950s and 1960s, see box 10, folder 6, and box 14, folder 1, ESC Papers; E. Cox, *Teutonic Unity*, 197–221.

54. AJG to ESC, July 5, 1949, box 7, folder 3, ESC Papers.

55. Plummer, *In Search of Power*, 36–39.

56. "A Proclamation by the Universal Negro Improvement Association 1929 of the World," circa 1951, box 15, folder 53, UNIA Papers RL; William L. Sherrill (hereafter, WLS) to AJG, September 4, 1953, box 1, folder 7, UNIA Papers RL.

57. Donna Cooper Hayford, telephone conversation with author, January 14, 2013.

58. Stewart Amos, telephone conversation, April 8, 2013; death certification of James R. Stewart.

59. Dotty Lane, "Fete Liberian Visitor," *Record-Courier* (Kent, OH), August 4, 1975, in Roberta Stewart Amos Papers.

60. Stewart Amos, telephone conversation with author, July 28, 2014.

61. Jacobs, "Three African American Women Missionaries in the Congo," 318, 320.

62. Cheryl Cooper Morgan, text to author, February 6, 2022.

63. Donald Freeman, Norma Jean Freeman, and Hanif Wahab, interview by author, August 11, 2017, Cleveland, OH.

64. Stewart Amos, telephone conversation, July 29, 2014; Wahab, *I Have the Honor of Being*, 67, 73.

65. Victor J. Stewart Jr., conversation with author, February 1, 2019, Gbandela, Liberia; Victor J. Stewart Jr., interview by author, December 20, 2014, Beachwood, OH.

66. Farmer, "Reframing African American Women's Grassroots Organizing"; McDuffie, *Sojourning for Freedom*, 207, 208.

67. McDuffie, "A 'New Freedom Movement of Negro Women,'" 85–106.

68. McDuffie, *Sojourning for Freedom*, 6, 10–11, 64–65, 147–51; Ransby, *Eslanda*, 1–11, 64–69.

69. Blain, *Set the World on Fire*, 181.

70. MMLG and Alberta Spain to ESC, March 3, 1961, box 14, folder 3, ESC Papers.

71. State of Illinois Death Certificate for MMLG, 41729, June 19, 1961.

72. ESC to Alberta Spain, June 21, 1961, box 14, folder 3, ESC Papers.

73. Blain, *Set the World on Fire*, 194–95.

74. "Prime Minister's Midnight Speech on the Eve of Independence," March 6, 1957, box 14, folder 21, Kwame Nkrumah Papers, Moorland-Spingarn Research Center, Howard University, Washington, DC; Gaines, *American Africans in Ghana*, 1–3.

75. Gaines, *American Africans in Ghana*, 2–4.

76. Ahlman, *Living with Nkrumahism*, 49–203.

77. Meriwether, *Proudly We Can Be Africans*, 159.

78. Ahlman, *Kwame Nkrumah*, 75.

79. Nkrumah, *Ghana*, 45.

80. "Prime Minister's Midnight Speech on the Eve of Independence."

81. "Report of the Commission Appointed under the Commission of Enquiry Act," 1964 (Act 250 to Enquire into the Affairs of the Black Star Line), Public Records and Archives Administration Department, Accra, Ghana (hereafter, PRAAD); Hill, *MGP*, 3:765.

82. Nkrumah, *Ghana*, 180–83.

83. "Visits Ghana," *Michigan Chronicle*, March 16, 1957, p. 23; "Nkrumah Praises Garvey Movement," *CD*, March 30, 1957, p. 12.

84. WLS to AJG, February 11, 1957.

85. AJG to Kwame Nkrumah, February 18, 1957, box 2, folder 10, AJG Papers.

86. Gaines, *American Africans in Ghana*, 80–81; "Martin Luther King, Jr., Ghana Trip," Martin Luther King Jr. Research and Education Institute, https://kinginstitute.stanford .edu/ghana-trip (accessed October 27, 2017).

87. T. E. Sealy, "Manley . . . Everyone Will Remember Forever," *Daily Gleaner*, March 7, 1957, p. 1; T. W. Sealy, "Reactions from Some Other West Indians," *Daily Gleaner*, March 7, 1957, p. 1.

88. WLS to the Members of the Division, March 15, 1957, box 7, folder 1, UNIA Papers RL.

89. Quoted in "Nkrumah Praises Garvey Movement"; WLS to AJG, April 5, 1957, box 7, folder 1, UNIA Papers RL.

90. WLS to the Members of the Division, March 15, 1957.

91. WLS to the Members of the Division, March 15, 1957.

92. WLS to the Members of the Division, March 15, 1957.

93. King delivered the sermon on April 7, 1957. Carson, Carson, and Clay, *The Papers of Martin Luther King Jr.*, 155.

94. Carson, Carson, and Clay, *The Papers of Martin Luther King Jr.*, 160, 164.

95. "Program," Sunday, April 7, 1957, William L. Sherrill, Isaac Collection, box 1, folder 36.

96. WLS, "To Build Speech," n.d., box 21, folder 8, UNIA Papers RL.

97. WLS, *New Africa Faces the World*, circa 1957, box 22, folder 10, UNIA Papers RL.

98. WLS, *Africa—Every Blackman's Business* (Philadelphia: Universal Negro Improvement Association, n.d.), box 22, folder 13, UNIA Papers RL.

99. WLS, "I Saw a Nation Born," speech, n.d., box 21, folder 8, UNIA Papers RL.

100. King, "'The Birth of a New Nation,'" 156.

101. "The African Land Project," box 22, folder 47, UNIA Papers RL; Jolly, *"By Our Own Strength,"* 207.

102. Jolly, *"By Our Own Strength,"* 236; *Michigan Chronicle*, March 14, 1959; Certificate of Death, 1882, William L. Sherrill, Office of the Wayne County Clerk, April 15, 1959.

103. "City Prepares for Visit by Dr. Nkrumah," CD, July 26, 1958, p. 1; "Nkrumah Visit Schedule: Hour by Hour," DF, July 29, 1958, p. 1; Greg Harris, "Throngs Hail Nkrumah Here," DF, July 31, 1958, p. 1; Charles J. Livingston, "Nkrumah Africa's Man of the Hour," DF, August 2, 1958; "Chicago Gives Nkrumah Colorful Reception," CD, August 9, 1958, p. 12.

104. "Program for the Visit to the United States of America of the Honorable Dr. Kwame Nkrumah, M.P., Prime Minister of Ghana, July 23 to August 2, 1958," PRAAD; address delivered by Dr. Kwame Nkrumah to US Senate, July 24, 1958, Nkrumah Papers, box 14, folder 48; Schwar and Shaloff, *Foreign Relations of the United States*, 646–52; Meriwether, *Proudly We Can Be Africans*, 172–73.

105. Hirsch, *Making of the Second Ghetto*, 16, 17, 28.

106. Hirsch, *Making of the Second Ghetto*, 171–258; J. Williams, *From the Bullet to the Ballot*, 19.

107. J. Williams, *From the Bullet to the Ballot*, 29.

108. J. Williams, *From the Bullet to the Ballot*, 28–42.

109. Nkrumah's Complete Schedule: Welcome," CD, July 30, 1958, p. 1.

110. "Chicago Gives Nkrumah Colorful Reception"; "Program for the Visit to the United States of America of the Honorable Dr. Kwame Nkrumah"; Kwame Nkrumah to Claude Barnett, August 1, 1958, all in GH/PRAAD/RG 17/1/1, 20, PRAAD.

111. "Nkrumah Visit Schedule: Hour by Hour."

112. "Chicago Puts Out Red Carpet for Ghana's Nkrumah," CD, August 9, 1958, p. 1.

113. KN to Claude Barnett, August 1, 1958, GH/PRAAD/RG 17/1/120, PRAAD.

114. For documentation about Nkrumah's meeting at Roosevelt University with African studies scholars, see box 70, folder 43, St. Clair Drake Papers; "University to Honor Nkrumah," DF, July 29, 1958, p. 9; Rosa, "St. Clair Drake, the Formative Years," 53–58.

115. Throughout his life, Robb went by several names. For consistency, I will refer to him as F. H. Hammurabi Robb (hereafter, FHHR).

116. FHHR funeral program, April 2, 1978, box 1, folder 15, Arthur L. Logan Papers, Vivian G. Harsh Collection of Afro-American History and Literature, Chicago.

117. Robb, *Intercollegian Wonder Book*, 129.

118. FHHR, "What Do Colleges Offer Our Race," CD, June 17, 1933, p. 11; FHHR, "Africa's Charm Described by One of Its Wandering Sons," CD, February 29, 1936, p. 11; FHHR, "Historically Ethiopia Is Destined to Win Conflict," CD, March 14, 1936, p. 11; FHHR, "Hammurabi Robb Starts New Feature Series for Defender," CD, August 1, 1936, p. 24.

119. David H. Orro, "Seek Indictments of Sedition Suspects," CD, October 3, 1942, p. 4; "Cultists Remain Undaunted," CD, October 24, 1942, p. 13.

120. Rocksborough-Smith, *Black Public History*, 1–14.

121. "Publish 4th Edition of 'New Era," ADW, January 18, 1957, p. 2; "History Unfolds through Calendar," CD, March 4, 1956, p. 10.

122. Hine, introduction to *The Black Chicago Renaissance*, xv–xxi.

123. Feldman, *The Birth and the Building of the DuSable Museum*, 31, 77–86, 108; Hagedorn, "'Chicago's Renaissance Woman,'" 1–3, 6–8; Hine, introduction to *The Black Chicago Renaissance*, xv.

124. "History Unfolds through Calendar," CD, February 4, 1956, p. 10.

125. "House of Knowledge Has World Program," DF, March 7, 1957, p. 23; "Honor Nkrumah at House of Knowledge," DF, September 24, 1958, p. A4; "Job Forum Set at House of Knowledge," DF, November 20, 1958, p. A4.

126. "Minutes of the 1946 MSTA 19th Annual Convention" and "Minutes of the 1958 31st Annual Convention, Chicago, September 15–20, 1958," both in box 1, folder 4, MSTA Collection; P. Bowen, "The African American Islamic Renaissance," 413.

127. "C. M. Bey Dead at 76," CCP, July 7, 1973, p. 4.

128. L. Moore, *Carl B. Stokes*, 18; Freedom Fighters' Platform, box 2, folder 13, Congress of Racial Equality, Cleveland Chapter Records, Western Reserve Historical Society.

129. Bey, *Clock of Destiny*; Ahmad Drake-El, interview, September 3, 2016, Shaker Heights, OH; "Culture Club Has Meeting," CCP, August 23, 1952, p. 3; letter from Sheba Marcus-Bey to author, August 10, 2017, in author's possession.

130. Quoted in photo caption, CCP, January 23, 1958, p. 6. See also Bob Williams, "'Moors' Say They Are Not Bound by U.S. Constitution," CCP, January 23, 1958, p. 6.

131. Clock of Destiny, http://clockofdestiny.com/index.php/cm-bey (accessed November 21, 2016); Ahmad Drake-El, interview, September 3, 2016.

132. R. Frazier, *The East Is Black*, 78–81; McDuffie, *Sojourning for Freedom*, 160, 165.

133. S. Johnson, *African American Religions*, 323.

134. FBI, "MSTA," Chicago Bureau File, 25-371604-3, July 20, 1953; "Culture Club Has Meeting"; Dannin, *Black Pilgrimage*, 32. C. M. Bey apparently never went to jail. However, the FBI did acquire a nine-page file on his activities.

135. Horne, *Black and Red*.

136. Alvin Ward, "17 Years Later: Stay for Medical Treatment," *CP*, December 11, 1971, p. 4A; "Sidelights: From Tonelli Trial," *CCP*, May 15, 1954, p. 7. Passed in 1910, the Mann Act made it illegal to traffic women across state lines "for the purpose of prostitution or debauchery, or for any other immoral purpose." "Mann Act," *Dictionary of American History*, www.encyclopedia.com (accessed October 21, 2013).

137. Ahmad Drake-El, interview, September 3, 2016.

138. Ward, "17 Years Later"; Ahmad Drake-El, interview, September 3, 2016.

139. Ryan Miday, "Cleveland Legend Emmet Cobb, a.k.a. 'Tonelli,'" https://docshare.tips/1733-cleveland-legend-ahmed-el_5750368cb6d87f3a138b4571.html (accessed January 11, 2017); "11 Accuse Prophet: Hypnotized into Crime Girls Say Defendant Held in $35,000 Bail after Indictment," *AA*, April 24, 1954, p. 1; "Fez Nets Prophet Test for Sanity," *AA*, May 15, 1954, p. 3.

140. Reiss, *We Sell Drugs*, 192, 195.

141. Miday, "Cleveland Legend."

142. Woody L. Taylor, "Bitter 'Prophet' Snarls in Cell: Tonelli Rebukes Reporter, Spurns Aid Toward Appeal," *CCP*, May 29, 1954, p. 1-A.

143. Taylor, "Bitter 'Prophet' Snarls in Cell"; Woody L. Taylor, "Tonelli Denies Charges; Will Be Own Lawyer," *CCP*, April 24, 1954, p. 1-A; Woody L. Taylor, "Tonelli Gets 14 to 68 Years," *CCP*, May 15, 1954, p. 1-A.

144. "Judge Sends Tonelli to Lima," *CCP*, May 29, 1954, p. 3-A.

145. Miday, "Cleveland Legend."

146. Ralph Matthews, "Tonelli Case Puts Spotlight on Cleveland Panderes [*sic*]: Will His Conviction Curb Other Pimps and Hustlers?," *CCP*, May 22, 1954, p. 1-D.

147. Marty Richards, "White Wife Says Tonelli 'Framed' Because of Race," *CCP*, April 17, 1954, p. 1-A.

148. R. Shabazz, *Spatializing Blackness*, 27.

149. M. A. Shaheed, telephone conversation with author, January 13, 2017; "Death Ends Long Battle for Her Brother's Freedom," *CCP*, March 6, 1971, p. 6A; Ulf Goebel, "Released from Lima: Tonelli's Trial Reversed after 17 Years in Hell," *CCP*, May 22, 1971, p. 1A; Ward, "17 Years Later."

150. Miday, "Cleveland Legend."

151. P. Bowen, "The African American Islamic Renaissance," 377–78.

152. Gambino, "The Transgression of a Laborer," 14.

153. Gambino, "The Transgression of a Laborer"; *AOMX*, 153–55.

154. Payne and Payne, *The Dead Are Arising*, 230.

155. Payne and Payne, *The Dead Are Arising*, 265.

156. Payne and Payne, *The Dead Are Arising*, 265–67.

157. *AOMX*, 155.

158. *AOMX*, 156–68.

159. *AOMX*, 157; Carson, *Malcolm X*, 60.

160. MX to Philbert Little, December 12, 1949, box 3, folder 1, MX Collection (emphasis in original).

161. *AOMX*, 182.

162. Quoted in MX to Philbert Little, letter, January 29, 1950, box 3, folder 1, MX Collection. This letter is the first document in the collection in which he signed his name "Malcolm X." *AOMX*, 170.

163. Payne and Payne, *The Dead Are Arising*, 270.

164. *AOMX*, 193–94.

165. *AOMX*, 201.

166. Christine MacDonald, "Detroit Population Rank Is Lowest since 1850," *Detroit News*, May 19, 2016, http://www.detroitnews.com/story/news/local/detroit-city/2016/05/19/detroit-population-rank-lowest-since/84574198.

167. Detroit Urban League, *For a New Day in Human Relations*.

168. Sugrue, *The Origins of the Urban Crisis*, 124.

169. Sugrue, *The Origins of the Urban Crisis*, 126, 127, 143–44, 209–58; Clark, *Disruption in Detroit*, 90–178.

170. Gambino, "The Transgression of a Laborer," 22; Marable and Felber, *The Portable Malcolm X Reader*, 22, 48.

171. Muhammad, *The Message to the Blackman in America*, 174, 230.

172. *AOMX*, 192–93, 211.

173. *AOMX*, 293–97; Marable, *Malcolm X*, 100–29.

174. *AOMX*, 233–35.

175. "Moslem Speaker Electrifies Garvey Crowd," *Amsterdam News* (New York) (hereafter, *AN*), August 10, 1957, p. 4.

176. *AOMX*, 273; Sherwood, *Malcolm X*, 34–61; *AN*, July 11, 1959, p. 18.

177. Meriwether, *Proudly We Can Be Africans*, 212.

178. Quoted in "Jack, Powell, Brown All Agree on Garvey," *AN*, August 9, 1958, p. 22; "Garvey Day Celebration Set," *AN*, July 26, 1958, p. 4 (emphasis in original).

179. *AOMX*, 356–57.

180. Carson, *Malcolm X File*, 174–75.

181. Carson, *Malcolm X File*, 175.

182. "Malcolm X Making Hit in Detroit," *AN*, September 7, 1957, p. 16.

183. Joseph, *Waiting 'Til the Midnight Hour*, 57; Essien-Udom, *Black Nationalism*, 71.

184. Clegg, *An Original Man*, 103.

185. Clegg, *An Original Man*, 114.

186. Essien-Udom, *Black Nationalism*, 231.

187. Essien-Udom, *Black Nationalism*, 197–99.

188. R. Shabazz, *Spatializing Blackness*, 90.

189. *AOMX*, 226, 201–22.

190. *AOMX*, 294.

191. Rickford, *Betty Shabazz*, xi.

192. Robert D. McFadden, "Betty Shabazz, a Rights Voice, Dies of Burns," *NYT*, June 24, 1997, pp. A1, D20.

193. B. Shabazz and Taylor, "Loving and Losing Malcolm."

194. *AOMX*; Rickford, *Betty Shabazz*, 55, 69–74.

195. Betty X to Yvonne Molette, October 8, 1955, box 2, folder 1, MX Collection.

196. Betty X to Yvonne Molette, October 8, 1955.

197. Quoted in B. Shabazz, "The Legacy of My Husband," 182; Rickford, *Betty Shabazz*, xxi.

198. Rickford, *Betty Shabazz*, 29.

199. Rickford, *Betty Shabazz*, 29, 86.

200. B. Shabazz and Taylor, "Loving and Losing Malcolm," 50; I. Shabazz and McLarin, *Growing Up X*, 82, 86–87, 107–8, 124–27.

6. "MESSAGE TO THE GRASS ROOTS"

1. *State News* (East Lansing, MI), January 24, 1963, http://archive.lib.msu.edu/DMC/state_news/1963/state_news_19630124.pdf.

2. B. Perry, ed., *Malcolm X: The Last Speeches*, 25, 45, 43, 30, 31, 51.

3. B. Perry, ed., *Malcolm X: The Last Speeches*, 40.

4. *AOMX*, 3–4.

5. According to historian Peniel Joseph, Black Power "at its core . . . attempted to radically redefine the relationship between blacks and American society. Black Power activists trumpeted a militant new race consciousness that placed black identity as the soul of a new radicalism." Joseph, "Introduction," 2–3; *AOMX*, 194–235; Marable, *Malcolm X*, 210–68.

6. R. Williams, *Concrete Demands*, 66–69, 75, 76, 77.

7. Marable, *Race, Reform, and Rebellion*, 59–83.

8. R. Frazier, *The East Is Black*, 49–51.

9. Pérez-Stable, *The Cuban Revolution*, 66–84.

10. Getachew, *Worldmaking after Empire*, 125–31.

11. Benjamin Talton, "The Challenge of Decolonization of Africa," http://exhibitions.nypl.org/africanaage/essay-challenge-of-decolonization-africa.html#year (accessed October 11, 2017).

12. "Sharpeville Massacre," South African History Online, http://www.sahistory.org.za/article/sharpeville; "Rivonia Trial, 1963–1964," South African History Online, http://www.sahistory.org.za/article/rivonia-trial-1963-1964 (both accessed November 29, 2017).

13. Plummer, *Rising Wind*, 300–304.

14. List of NOI mosques, circa 1962, box 9, folder 326, Alfred Balk Papers, Newberry Library, Chicago (hereafter, Balk Papers); Essien-Udom, *Black Nationalism*, 70–71; P. Bowen, "The African American Islamic Renaissance," 422; Clegg, *An Original Man*, 114–15.

15. Clegg, *An Original Man*, 116.

16. William Worthy, "The Angriest Negroes," *Esquire*, February 1961, pp. 102–6; Clegg, *An Original Man*, 111–13.

17. Muhammad, *The Message to the Blackman in America*; Clegg, *An Original Man*, 178–79.

18. Muhammad, *The Message to the Blackman in America*, xiii.

19. Muhammad, *The Message to the Blackman in America*, xiii.

20. Muhammad, *The Message to the Blackman in America*, xvii.

21. Muhammad, *The Message to the Blackman in America*, xvii.

22. Muhammad, *The Message to the Blackman in America*, xvii, xix.

23. Muhammad, *The Message to the Blackman in America*, 220.

24. Khuram Hussain, "The Radical Black Press: A Forgotten Legacy of Malcolm X," http://blackpressresearchcollective.org/tag/muhammad-speaks (accessed March 30, 2018).

25. *Muhammad Speaks* (hereafter, MS), February 1962; Clegg, *An Original Man*, 159–60.

26. "Garvey Revisited," MS, January 1962, p. 20. See also "Garvey to Come 'Home,'" MS, September 25, 1964, p. 11.

27. "Letter to Mr. Muhammad—from the Wife of the Late Marcus Garvey," MS, June 7, 1963, p. 2.

28. "Garvey to Come 'Home,'" p. 11.

29. "Letters to the Editor," MS, October 23, 1964, p. 8.

30. Haywood, "The Nation of Islam, Black Masculinity, and Selling *Muhammad Speaks*," 10.

31. "First Lady Visits Son in Cairo," MS, June 1962, p. 3; MS, December 1961, p. 15.

32. Curtis, *Black Muslim Religion in the Nation of Islam*, 63, 64, 65; U. Taylor, *The Promise of Patriarchy*, 138.

33. Tynnetta Deanar, "Women in Islam," MS, July 5, 1963, p. 16; Tynnetta Deanar, "Women in Islam," MS, April 10, 1964, p. 17.

34. Essien-Udom, *Black Nationalism*, 234.

35. Johnson used multiple names over the course of her long public career. They included Christine Johnson, Christine Johnson X, Christine Muhammad, and Sister Christine. I will refer to her as "Sister Christine" when referring to her time in the NOI. Jeffries, *A Nation Can Rise No Higher Than Its Women*, 122.

36. "University of Islam Add to Faculty," MS, November–December 1961, p. 9.

37. Hussain, "Born of Necessities," 119.

38. C. Johnson, *Muhammad's Children*, 9.

39. Untitled photo with caption, *Daily Defender* (Chicago) (hereafter, DF) July 24, 1958, p. 7.

40. "Revolutionary Black Woman" describes the organizational and community work as well as cultural representations of Black women in the Black Panther Party who championed racial and gender equality and transformative social change. The "African Woman" refers to Black women's efforts in cultural nationalist formations such as the US organization to counter patriarchal definitions of "African" women and to center women in struggles against Eurocentrism. Embodying a commitment to Black women's freedom and diasporic and African liberation, the "Pan African Woman" emerged from the All-African Women's Conference of 1972 and the Sixth Pan-African Congress of 1974—both of which were held in Dar Es Salaam, Tanzania. Finally, the "Third World Black Woman" described a radical transnational feminist coalition politics associated with the Third World Women's Alliance. Farmer, *Remaking Black Power*, 50–51, 93–94, 127–28, 159–61.

41. Kenneth C. Field, "Muhammad Tells 'Role of Negro,'" CD, March 11, 1961, p. 12; "Muslim Leader Addresses Huge Rally in New York," CD, September 12, 1961, p. 19.

42. Christine Johnson, untitled article, MS, February 1962.

43. Rocksborough-Smith, *Black Public History in Chicago*, 75–100.

44. "Muslim Leader Addresses Huge Rally in New York," *DD*, September 12, 1961, p. 19; "Attended Ban Bomb Confab," *AN*, July 28, 1962, p. 4.

45. "55 Nation Peace Assembly Spurred by Nkrumah Crusade for International Justice" and untitled photograph of Christine Muhammad with Kwame Nkrumah, both in *MS*, August 31, 1962, pp. 11–13; Allman, "Nuclear Imperialism."

46. "Attended Ban Bomb Confab."

47. Sister Christine married Earl Johnson. It is unclear if they had children. What is certain is that *Muhammad Speaks* and other African American newspapers did not mention Sister Christine being accompanied overseas by a husband or with children.

48. "Admire African Art," *DD*, August 18, 1959, p. 14; Kelley, *Yo' Mama's Disfunktional*, 30.

49. Untitled photo of Muhammad with Nkrumah.

50. U. Taylor, *The Promise of Patriarchy*, 177.

51. *AOMX*, 295.

52. U. Taylor, *The Promise of Patriarchy*, 133, 175; Clegg, *An Original Man*, 186–88.

53. Lois Beckett, "George Lincoln Rockwell, Father of American Nazis, Still in Vogue," *Guardian*, August 27, 2017, https://www.theguardian.com/world/2017/aug/27/george-lincoln-rockwell-american-nazi-party-alt-right-charlottesville.

54. Marable, *Malcolm X*, 198–200.

55. Clegg, *An Original Man*, 152–53.

56. Marable, *Malcolm X*, 199.

57. Carson, *Malcolm X*, 29.

58. Gomez, *Black Crescent*, 349–50.

59. *AOMX*, 238.

60. Marable, *Malcolm X*, 172–73.

61. Gomez, *Black Crescent*, 349.

62. Evanzz, *The Judas Factor*, 81–96, 115–16.

63. S. Johnson, "Red Squads and Black Radicals," 390–94.

64. Surveillance report, Intelligence Divisions, Bureau of Inspection Services, Chicago Police Department, May 24, 1962, box 9, folder 326, Balk Papers; S. Johnson, "Red Squads and Black Radicals," 390–94.

65. R. Williams, *Concrete Demands*, 81.

66. Young, "Detroit's Red," 20.

67. S. Ward, *In Love and Struggle*.

68. H. Thompson, *Whose Detroit?*, 28; Joseph, *Waiting 'Til the Midnight Hour*, 62, 81–84.

69. S. Ward, *In Love and Struggle*, 3, 290–92.

70. G. Boggs, *The Next American Revolution*, 2–9, 82–84; S. Ward, *In Love and Struggle*, 1.

71. Grace Lee Boggs, interview by author, January 12, 2012, Detroit.

72. "Grace Lee Boggs on Malcolm X: 'He Was a Person Always Searching to Transform Himself,'" *Democracy Now!*, February 20, 2015, https://www.democracynow.org/2015/2/20/grace_lee_boggs_on_malcolm_x.

73. Dillard, *Faith in the City*, 23, 287–305.

74. General Baker, telephone interview by author, August 29, 2013.

75. General Baker, telephone interview by author, August 29, 2013.

76. Luke Tripp, telephone interview by author, June 27, 2017.

77. Baker, interview by author.

78. L. Moore, *Carl B. Stokes*, 19–20.

79. Howard Allen, "Dr. King Overwhelms 15,000 Clevelanders," *CCP*, May 18, 1963, pp. 1-A, 2-A; Al Sweeney, "Biggest Civil Rights Rally Ever Predicted: Dr. Martin King and Aides at Cory Tuesday," *CCP*, May 11, 1963, p. 1-A.

80. Donald Freeman, "The Cleveland Story," *Liberator* 3, no. 6 (June 1963): 7, 18.

81. Freeman, *Reflections of a Resolute Radical*, 1–50; Donald Freeman, phone interview by author, June 29, 2011; Donald Freeman, phone conversation with author, May 18, 2023.

82. Freeman met Malcolm for the first time in April 1962 through a mutual friend at Mosque No. 7 in Harlem. Freeman, interview by author, June 29, 2011; Don Freeman, interview by author, December 31, 2013, Cleveland.

83. Cruse, "Revolutionary Nationalism and the Afro-American," 13, 19, 25; Joseph, *Waiting 'Til the Midnight Hour*, 31.

84. Freeman, "The Cleveland Story."

85. Freeman, "The Cleveland Story," 18; Tinson, *Radical Intellect*.

86. Donald Freeman and Norma Jean Freeman, interview with author, August 2, 2013, Cleveland; Freeman, phone conversation with author, May 18, 2023.

87. Ahmad, *We Will Return in the Whirlwind*, 95–98, 104; Muhammad Ahmad, telephone conversation with author, September 30, 2016; Donald Freeman and Norma Jean Freeman, interview by author, December 31, 2015, Cleveland.

88. Ahmad, *We Will Return in the Whirlwind*, 123.

89. Stanford, "Revolutionary Action Movement," 66–118; Don Freeman, "Black Youth and Afro-American Liberation," *Black America* (Fall 1964): 15–16.

90. Joseph, *Waiting 'Til the Midnight Hour*, 60.

91. Ahmad, *We Will Return in the Whirlwind*, 100; Stanford, "Towards Revolutionary Action Movement Manifesto," 508–13.

92. Ahmad, *We Will Return in the Whirlwind*, 98, 100, 123.

93. Malcolm and Elijah Muhammad had previously spoken at King Solomon. "Historic King Solomon Baptist Church," http://www.therevcw.com/hksmbchistory (accessed May 10, 2018).

94. Breitman, *Malcolm X Speaks*, 3.

95. Breitman, *Malcolm X Speaks*, 7, 8, 9, 12; Grace Lee Boggs, interview by author, January 12, 2012, Detroit.

96. Freeman, *Reflections of a Resolute Radical*, 71.

97. *AOMX*, 198, 288, 290–98; Clegg, *An Original Man*, 179–80, 190–94.

98. Breitman, *Malcolm X Speaks*, 20.

99. N. Frazier, *Harambee City*, xxv–xxxvi, 52–135.

100. Breitman, *Malcolm X Speaks*, 22.

101. Malcolm X, "The Ballot or the Bullet."

102. Malcolm X, "The Ballot or the Bullet," 9, 10, 17.

103. C. Anderson, *Eyes off the Prize*, 92–96, 101–12, 166–209; McDuffie, *Sojourning for Freedom*, 178.

104. Breitman, *Malcolm X Speaks*, 72–87.

105. John Bracey Jr., telephone interview by author, December 20, 2013; Muhammad Ahmad, telephone conversation with author, February 8, 2018; Ahmad, *We Will Return in the Whirlwind*, 95, 123; Don Freeman, telephone conversation with author, August 15, 2017.

106. Alice Windom, telephone interview with author, January 9, 2012; "Alice Windom," *History Makers*, http://www.thehistorymakers.org/biography/alice-windom-41 (accessed July 22, 2017); Kenya Vaughn, "'African Patriot,' Activist and Community Leader Alice Windom Passes at 85," *St. Louis American*, February 19, 2022, https://www.stlamerican.com/news/local_news/african-patriot-activist-and-community-leader-alice-windom-passes-at-85/article_63798a12-8abd-11ec-a2cf-6f517ff5f446.html.

107. Essien-Udom, *Black Nationalism*, x.

108. Essien-Udom, *Black Nationalism*.

109. Windom, telephone interview with author, January 9, 2012.

110. From May 1 to 21, 1964, Malcolm visited Algeria, Egypt, Ethiopia, Ghana, Kenya, Liberia, Morocco, Nigeria, Senegal, and Tanzania. He journeyed to Africa again in July that year. Sherwood, *Malcolm X*, 25–64, 121–37.

111. *AOMX*, 356–57.

112. *AOMX*, 353.

113. Mazucci, "Going Back," 76–80.

114. Malcolm X, *By Any Means Necessary*, 214.

115. P. Collins, "Learning to Think for Ourselves," 79.

116. Christine Wilson, "Black Woman Who Came Home to Islam Discovered Muhammad While Abroad," MS, May 19, 1967, p. 11.

117. Alice Windom to Christine Wilson, May 1964, box 24, folder 33, John Henrik Clarke Papers, Schomburg Center for Research in Black Culture, New York.

118. Rickford, *Betty Shabazz*, 140–202.

119. Charles Washington, "Omaha-Born Malcolm X Says: 'Whites Should Thank God Daily Negro Doesn't Hate More," May 29, 1964, 1, box 16, folder 1, MX Collection.

120. Hickey et al., *Nebraska Moments*, 325–26; Duane Snodgrass, "Malcolm X Declares Anything Whites Do Blacks Can Do Better," *Omaha World-Herald*, July 1, 1964, p. 1; "'Negro Must Prepare to Defend Himself or Continue at the Mercy of Racist Mob,'" *Omaha Star*, July 3, 1964, p. 1.

121. Sherwood, *Malcolm X*, 69–145.

122. Similarly, Malcolm remained close with his half-sister Ella Collins, who converted to Islam and briefly joined the NOI. A. Peter Bailey, telephone conversation with author, June 14, 2018.

123. Terance Wilson, telephone conversations with author, March 5, 2018, and June 12, 2018.

124. Deborah Jones, telephone interview with author, February 18, 2015.

125. Undated Kalamazoo State Hospital Record, Deborah Jones Personal Papers, Grand Rapids, MI; State of Michigan, "Louise Little," Probate Court of Ingham County, file no. 13132-39, January 11, 1967.

126. Carew, *Ghosts in Our Blood*, x.

127. Deborah Jones, telephone conversation with author, April 26, 2018.

128. Jones, conversation with author, April 26, 2018.

129. Jonah E. Bromwich, Ashley Southall, and Troy Closson, "Exoneration Is 'Bittersweet' for Men Cleared in Malcolm's Murder," *NYT*, November 18, 2021, https://www.nytimes.com/2021/11/18/nyregion/khalil-islam-muhammad-aziz-exonerated.html; Evanzz, *The Judas Factor*, xiii–xxiv.

130. Ashley Southall, "Man Exonerated in Malcolm's Murder Sues U.S. over His Conviction," *NYT*, November 16, 2023, https://www.nytimes.com/2023/11/16/nyregion/malcolm-x-muhammad-aziz-exonerated-lawsuit.html.

131. I. Shabazz and McLarin, *Growing Up X*, 27.

132. "Malcolm Exposed by Brother," *MS*, April 10, 1964, p. 1.

133. Evanzz, *The Judas Factor*, 264.

134. Marable, *Malcolm X*, 344–47, 416–17.

135. Evanzz, *The Judas Factor*, 290, 309.

136. Deborah Jones, telephone interview with author, February 18, 2015.

137. For detailed descriptions of Malcolm's final days and assassination, see I. Shabazz and McLarin, *Growing Up X*, 12–19; Evanzz, *The Judas Factor*, 277–99; and Marable, *Malcolm X*, 6–7, 418–49.

138. Evanzz, *The Judas Factor*, 300–305.

139. Deborah Jones, telephone conversation with author, January 22, 2017; I. Shabazz and McLarin, *Growing Up X*, 17, 18.

140. Jones, telephone conversation with author, February 18, 2015.

7. "THE SECOND BATTLE FOR AFRICA HAS BEGUN"

Portions of chapter 7 appeared in Stephens and Ewing, *Global Garveyism*. Also, McDuffie, "'A New Day Has Dawned for the UNIA,'" provides the basis of much discussion in chapter 7.

1. A boubou is a loose-fitting, wide-sleeved robe traditionally worn by people across West Africa. A kufi is a short, rounded cap worn by people across West and North Africa, the Middle East, and India.

2. "Annual Inspection and Review—August 1977," photo, box 19, folder 27, and Allison P. Tarlue (Monrovia) to TWH, July 3, 1966, both in box 12, folder 3, UNIA Records RL; Amos Sawyer, interview with author, January 11, 2016, Monrovia, Liberia.

3. TWH, form letter, September 18, 1967, box 12, folder 3, UNIA Papers RL.

4. Spadey and Wright, "Jean Harvey Slappy's Philosophy," 60.

5. Clarence W. Harding (hereafter, CWH) to TWH, May 14, 1966, box 12, folder 2, UNIA Records RL.

6. UNIA Papers WRHS guide, 2.

7. "Cleveland Nurses Go to Africa," *CCP*, February 20, 1971, p. 1A; Roland Forte, "Local Poet, Mary Mason Writes African Trilogy," *CCP*, March 4, 1972, p. 18A.

8. "Statement of Principles of African Liberation Support Committee," in Kadalie, *Internationalism*, 621.

9. Woodard, *A Nation within a Nation*, 176n35, 289; Farmer, *Remaking Black Power*, 131.

10. "African Liberation Coordinator Speaks," *CCP*, June 17, 1972, p. 12B.

11. Kenneth King, email to author, May 9, 2022; "The Youngstown, Ohio, UNIA Holds Rousing Meeting," *NW*, February 18, 1922, p. 7; "Youngstown Division Holds Mass

Meeting," *NW*, July 15, 1922, p. 8; W. S. Vaughn, "Youngstown Division," *NW*, May 5, 1923, p. 8; "Garvey Promoter of Famous Black Star Line, Deported to Jamaica," (Youngstown) *Sunday Vindicator*, December 11, 1927, p. 10.

12. "UNIA Officers at Youngstown Meet," *Garvey's Voice* 20, no. 1 (January 1972); minutes of UNIA executive meeting, October 23, 1971; TWH to Georgina Thornton, May 8, 1972; and Gina Thornton, "UNIA Together Now," July 27, 1971, all in Georgina Thornton Personal Papers, Youngstown, OH (hereafter, GT Personal Papers); Georgina Thornton and Kenneth King, interview with author, October 18, 2018, Youngstown, OH.

13. Minutes of the Meeting for the Unification Council, May 22, 1971, box 16, folder 13, UNIA Papers RL; Unification Council Agenda, June 19, 1971, GT Papers; Thornton and King, interview with author.

14. Springer, *Living for the Revolution*, 28–37.

15. Thornton and King, interview with author.

16. A. Garvey, *Black Power in America*; Clarke, *Marcus Garvey and the Vision of Africa*.

17. The AAWC launched in Accra, Ghana, in 1958. The 1972 AAWC marked the first time that it invited African-descended women from the United States to attend the gathering. Third Congress of African Women's Conference, "Statutes of the All African Women's Conference," Simons Collection, Collection: Women's Organisations, R 13.3, All African Women's Conference, 1964–1974 folder, Manuscripts and Archives, University of Cape Town, Cape Town, South Africa; Farmer, *Remaking Black Power*, 133–38.

18. Georgina Thornton to Queen Mother Moore, June 28, 1972, box 12, folder 8, UNIA Papers RL; Queen Mother Moore, "Africa for the Africans, at Home and Abroad," Simons Collection: Women's Organisations, R 13.3, All African Women's Conference, 1964–1974 folder.

19. Patricia Noni Gee, telephone interview with author, September 12, 2018.

20. Overview of the Charles H. Wright Museum, https://thewright.org/index.php /explore/about-the-museum/overview-history (accessed September 19, 2018).

21. Gee, telephone interview with author, September 12, 2018.

22. Farmer, *Remaking Black Power*, 159–92.

23. Patricia Noni Gee, telephone conversation with author, October 9, 2018.

24. Spencer, *The Revolution Has Come*, 4.

25. Gee, telephone conversation with author, October 9, 2018; Mensah Saleem and Noni Patricia Gee, interview by author, January 12, 2012, Detroit; U. Taylor, *The Veiled Garvey*, 233–34.

26. Talton, *In This Land of Plenty*, 9–43; African Union, "About the African Union," https://au.int/en/overview (accessed April 1, 2024).

27. Dunn, *Liberia and the United States during the Cold War*, 84–85, 87–137; Johnson Sirleaf, *This Child Will Be Great*, 93–136.

28. Bedasse, *Jah Kingdom*, 49.

29. Bedasse, *Jah Kingdom*, 49; Nyerere, *Ujamaa*, 1–12, 76–90, 107–44.

30. United States Census 1920, https://familysearch.org/ark:/61903/1:1:MDM7-NVT; United States Census 1930, https://familysearch.org/search/collection/results?count=20 &query=%2Bgivenname%3AClarence~%20%2Bsurname%3AHarding~%20%2Bresidence _place%3AChicago~%20%2Bgender%3AM%20%2Brace%3ABlack&collection._id=1810731

(both accessed April 11, 2016); "House of Knowledge Sets Bible Show," CD, 20 May 1961, p. 7; "African Speakers Will Be Honored at Round-Up,'" CD, 15 July 1961, p. 5.

31. "Doomed Second Time, Francis Gets Parole Board Hearing," *Atlanta Daily World*, February 26, 1947, 1; "Film on Peace Corps," CD, September 26, 1964, p. 5; "2 S. Siders Join Area Poverty Plan," September 21, 1965, p. 10; Amos Sawyer, telephone conversation with author, November 22, 2014; "What We Believe: A Statement of Faith," http://www.ucc.org/about-us_what-we-believe (accessed December 4, 2018).

32. CWH to TWH, May 14, 1966, and Benny J. Whitefield to Elinor White, June 24, 1966, both in box 12, folder 2, UNIA Records RL.

33. CWH to the Presidents, Officers and Members of all West African Divisions of the UNIA, December 1966, box 12, folder 2, UNIA Records RL.

34. CWH to TWH, August 4, 1969; box 12, folder 4; Isaac Mialo to TWH, March 15, 1971, box 12, folder 7, and CWH to John Vincent, September 27, 1972, box 12, folder 8; all in UNIA Records RL; Amos Sawyer, email to author, November 14, 2014.

35. E. J. Tucker to TWH, March 7, 1968; Henry J. Langdon to TWH, May 27, 1968, both in box 12, folder 4, UNIA Records RL.

36. David K. Franklin, "History of Marcus Garvey Memorial Institute," March 1972, box 19, folder 410, Dabu Gizenga Collection on Kwame Nkrumah, Moorland-Spingarn Research Center, Howard University, Washington, DC.

37. Sawyer, *What Is the Total Political Involvement in Liberia?*, 3, in Movement for Justice in Africa Vertical File, Africana Collection, Northwestern University, Evanston, IL.

38. Graduating Class of 1978, MGMI, Monrovia (photograph), box 19, folder 28, UNIA Records RL; Sawyer, interview with author, January 11, 2016.

39. CWH to TWH, September 25, 1967, and CWH to Arnold L. Crawford, September 27, 1967, both in box 12, folder 3, UNIA Records RL.

40. "Movement for Justice in Africa (MOJA)"; Dunn, *Liberia and the United States during the Cold War*, 92; Amos Sawyer, email to author, November 15, 2014.

41. Sawyer, interview with author.

42. Sawyer, "Social Stratification"; Sawyer, interview with author.

43. Sawyer, email to author, November 15, 2014; John Stewart and Emmanuel Moses, interview with author, January 13, 2014, Monrovia, Liberia.

44. Sawyer, interview with author; "Sawyer, Amos Claudius."

45. Stewart and Moses, interview with author; "Secret Message Codes," box 18, folder 28, UNIA Records RL; Johnson Sirleaf, *This Child Will Be Great*, 86–90.

46. John Stewart, telephone conversation with author, October 21, 2014; CWH to John Vincent, September 27, 1972, box 12, folder 8, UNIA Records RL.

47. Stewart, telephone conversation with author.

48. CWH to TWH, October 23, 1966, box 12, folder 2, UNIA Records RL.

49. Davidson, *No Fist Is Big Enough to Hide the Sky*, 87n18.

50. CWH to TWH, February 5, 1973, box 12, folder 9, UNIA Records RL.

51. Charles W. Connelly Jr. to TWH, May 26, 1969; TWH to Charles W. Connelly Jr., June 21, 1968, both in box 12, folder 5, UNIA Records RL.

52. CWH, "A Special Message to All West African Divisions of the UNIA," July 1966, box 12, folder 2, UNIA Records RL.

53. Sawyer, telephone conversation with author, November 24, 2014; Philomena Bloh Sayeh, interview with author, January 8, 2016, Monrovia.

54. Jean Slappy to Elinor White, Raymond Kelley, Solomon Fitzhugh, and Oquine Jackson, October 14, 1966, and Benny J. Whitefield to Elinor White, June 24, 1966, box 12, folder 2, UNIA Records RL; CWH to Georgina Thornton, April 12, 1972, and Alma Golden to TWH, May 22, 1972, both in box 12, folder 8, UNIA Records RL; Gee, telephone interview with author, September 12, 2018.

55. Given his love for Africa, Clarence Harding—like James Stewart—was buried in the West African republic. Sawyer, interview with author, January 11, 2016.

56. Marable, *Race, Reform, and Rebellion*, 130.

57. Catlin, *Racial Politics and Urban Planning*: 17–27, 39.

58. Woodard, *A Nation within a Nation*, 59–63.

59. Farmer, "Audley Moore and the Modern Reparations Movement," 108–24; Joseph, *Waiting 'Til the Midnight Hour*, 279.

60. Woodard, *A Nation within a Nation*, 184–218.

61. Joseph, *Dark Days, Bright Nights*, 171–79.

62. Winslow, *Shirley Chisholm*, 103.

63. Winslow, *Shirley Chisholm*, 103–5.

64. Biles, *Mayor Harold Washington*, 53.

65. L. Moore, *Carl B. Stokes*, 9–60.

66. United States Department of Commerce, *Census Tracts: Cleveland, Ohio: Standard Metropolitan Statistical Area* (1970), https://www2.census.gov/library/publications /decennial/1970/phc-1/39204513p5ch03.pdf (accessed May 15, 2019); N. Frazier, *Harambee City*, 160; Seawell, "The Black Freedom Movement," 192–94.

67. L. Moore, *Carl B. Stokes*, 46–51. The Hough rebellion was part of a wave of more than 250 Black urban rebellions that erupted in Harlem, Los Angeles, Omaha, Newark, Detroit, and other cities across the United States between 1964 and 1972. Marable, *Race, Reform, and Rebellion*, 90–91.

68. "Hough Memorial Rally Saturday," *Plain Dealer* (Cleveland) (hereafter, *PD*), July 18, 1968, p. 18.

69. L. Moore, *Carl B. Stokes*, 77–78.

70. L. Moore, *Carl B. Stokes*, 79–99; "Ahmed Evans Eulogized," *CCP*, March 11, 1978, p. 4A.

71. Joseph, *Waiting 'Til the Midnight Hour*, 205–40.

72. Y. Williams, "'Give Them a Cause to Die For,'" 248.

73. Adenike (Miriam) Sharpley, interview by author, September 4, 2015, Cleveland.

74. Marcus Greenwood, interview by author, March 24, 2015, Garfield Heights, OH.

75. Sharpley, interview by author, September 4, 2015.

76. "Afro Set Marches to Aid Panther Clinic," *PD*, August 22, 1971, p. 16-A.

77. "Black Nationalists Here Condemn Pressures on Blacks Not Natural," *CCP*, October 5, 1968, pp. 1A, 16A; "Afro Set Shop Raided," *CCP*, October 5, 1968, p. 7A; Alvin Ward, "Akil Claims He's a Political Prisoner," *CCP*, May 24, 1969, p. 16A.

78. R. Williams, *Concrete Demands*, 173.

79. L. Moore, *Carl B. Stokes*, 191–92.

80. Terry Johnson, telephone interview by author, November 29, 2012.

81. Meyer, "Evolution of a Permanent Negro Community in Lansing," 143.

82. "Telling It Like It Is: Oldsmobile and the Lansing Community," *Inner City Times*, May 21, 1969, p. 3; Terry Johnson, telephone interview by author, November 12, 2012.

83. Hawkings, "The Destruction of a Black Community."

84. "Young Negroes Claim Whites Triggered Riots," *State News* (East Lansing, MI), August 10, 1966, pp. 1, 4, https://archive.lib.msu.edu/DMC/state_news/1966/state_news_19660810/state_news_19660810.pdf.

85. J. Williamson, *Black Power on Campus*, 1.

86. Terry Johnson, telephone conversation with author, March 20, 2019; Cynthia Hamilton, telephone interview by author, May 10, 2019.

87. Johnson, telephone interview by author, November 29, 2012; Johnson, interview by author, March 20, 2019.

88. Terry Johnson, text message to author, May 27, 2022; Johnson, telephone interview by author, November 29, 2012; Johnson, telephone conversation with author, March 20, 2019.

89. Terry Johnson, text to author, January 30, 2019.

90. Johnson, interview by author, March 20, 2019; Kimathi Mohammed and Maina Kinyatti, "Tunataka Uhura Na Mashamba: Freedom and Land," *Black World / Negro Digest* 19, 10 (August 1970): 22, 94–98.

91. Kimathi Mohammed, "Pan-Africanism," *New World* (circa 1973): 1, 2.

92. Terry Johnson, text to author, May 15, 2023.

93. Mohammed, *Organization and Spontaneity*, 116; Johnson, interview by author, March 20, 2019.

94. Johnson, interview by author, March 20, 2019; Johnson, telephone interview by author, November 29, 2012.

95. Mohammed, *Organization and Spontaneity*, 9–10, 32–37.

96. Mohammed, *Organization and Spontaneity*, 108; T. Martin, "The Emancipation of a Race"; Johnson, interview by author, March 20, 2019.

97. Modibo Kadalie, telephone interview by author, February 20, 2019; Hamilton, telephone interview by author, May 10, 2019.

98. Hamilton, telephone interview by author, May 10, 2019; Kathie Stanley-House, telephone interview by author, May 19, 2019.

99. Johnson, interview by author, March 20, 2019.

100. Robert McClory, "Chicago Is Capital of Black Jews Movement," CD, March 10, 1973, p. 28.

101. Teresa Wiltz, "Pioneer Black Rabbi in Chicago," *Chicago Tribune*, February 9, 1991, p. N13; "Rabbi in Chicago to Start Hebrew School," CD, December 27, 1952, 2; Capers Funnye Jr., interview by author, June 30, 2015, Chicago.

102. "The Black Jews of the Southside," CD, January 28, 1963, pp. 1, 9; Arnold Rosenzweig, "Are Most Negroes of Jewish Decent [*sic*]?," CD, January 31, 1963, pp. 1, 11; Arnold Rosenzweig, "Hebrews Here Find Link to Ethiopian Past," CD, February 2, 1963, pp. 1, 2; "'Emerging Africa,' Dark Liberators at H of K," CD, February 15, 1962, p. 6; program, Beth Shalom B'nai Zaken Ethiopian Hebrew Congregation (January 2017), in author's possession; Landing, *Black Judaism*, 316, 334n10.

103. McClory, "Chicago Is Capital of Black Jews Movement."

104. Jacob Dorman, email to author, June 4, 2022.

105. "African Hebrew Israelites of Jerusalem," https://africanhebrewisraelitesofjerusa lem.com (accessed July 30, 2022); Kenneth Chang, "Ben Ammi Ben-Israel Dies at 75: Led Black Americans in Migration to Israel," *NYT*, December 31, 2014, https://www.nytimes .com/2015/01/01/world/middleeast/ben-ammi-ben-israel-leader-of-black-americans -who-migrated-to-israel-dies-at-75.html.

106. Donna Cooper Hayford, email to author, April 4, 2019.

107. Landing, *Black Judaism*, 387–410.

108. In April 2021, the Israeli government announced deportation orders for fifty-one Hebrew Israelites, some of whom were born in Israel, on the grounds that they had overstayed their visas. "51 Members of Hebrew Israelites Community Ordered to Leave Israel by Sept. 23," *Times of Israel*, September 12, 2021, https://www.timesofisrael.com/51 -members-of-hebrew-israelites-community-ordered-to-leave-israel-by-sept-23.

109. Salaita, *Israel's Dead Soul*, 3.

110. Cohen, *The Whistleblower of Dimona*, 1–26.

111. Clegg, *An Original Man*, 239.

112. Clegg, *An Original Man*, 249–51.

113. Douglas Martin, "W. Deen Mohammed, 74, Top U.S. Imam, Dies," *NYT*, September 9, 2008; Gardell, *In the Name of Elijah Muhammad*, 99–143.

114. Cleage, *Black Christian Nationalism*, xv–xxxvii, 3–20.

115. Alta Harrison (Fundi Difie), "A History of the Shrine of the Black Madonna with a Focus on the Development of Printed, Audio, and Visual Media," circa 1980s, box 4, Shrine of Black Madonna history folder, Albert Cleage Papers, Bentley Historical Library, University of Michigan, Ann Arbor (hereafter, ABC Papers); Dillard, *Faith in the City*, 290.

116. Tribute to Malcolm X, February 26, 1967, box 11, Tribute to Malcolm X folder, ABC Papers.

117. The church officially adopted the name the Shrine of the Black Madonna in 1970. Harrison, "A History of the Shrine of the Black Madonna," 13.

118. P. Collins, "Malcolm X's Black Nationalism Reconsidered," 76.

119. Tribute to Malcolm X.

120. H. Thompson, *Whose Detroit?*, 85.

121. Darden and Thomas, *Detroit*, 1.

122. Darden and Thomas, *Detroit*, 9.

123. Georgakas and Surkin, *Detroit: I Do Mind Dying*, xv.

124. H. Thompson, *Whose Detroit?*, 84–85.

125. H. Thompson, *Whose Detroit?*, 192–98.

126. The First Annual Convention of the Black Christian National Movement and the Black Preacher's Conference and the Conference of Black Youth, April 1–5, 1970, box 1, folder about Cleage and his Church 1950–2004, ABC Papers; brochure of the Ashanti Cooperative Inc., box 4, Ashanti Co-Op / Black Star Co-Op Supermarket folder, ABC Papers; Articles of Association, Constitution and By-Laws of the Pan-African Orthodox Church, 1978, box 4, PAOOC 1978 folder, ABC Papers.

127. Harrison, "A History of the Shrine of the Black Madonna," 21.

128. Alkalimat, "Black Liberation," 101, 104.

129. Alkalimat, "Black Chicago," 79.

130. Smethurst, *The Black Arts Movement*, 179–246.

131. Smethurst, *The Black Arts Movement*, 83.

132. Hagedorn, "'Call Me African,'" 153, 197.

133. Contributors included Gwendolyn Brooks, Ossie Davis, Keorapetse William Kgositsile, LeRoi Jones, Ted Jones, Don L. Lee, Sonia Sanchez, and Margaret Walker.

134. Dudley and Burroughs, *For Malcolm X*.

135. C. Johnson, *ABC's of African History*, preface, 13–16.

136. C. Johnson, *ABC's of African History*, 36, 37.

137. Alkalimat, "Black Liberation."

138. Madhubuti, *Liberation Narratives*, xxiii.

139. Madhubuti, *YellowBlack*, 3–91, 129–51, 231–35.

140. Haki R. Madhubuti, interview by author, December 21, 2016, Chicago.

141. Madhubuti, interview by author, December 21, 2016; Madhubuti, *YellowBlack*, 232, 236, 237.

142. Madhubuti, interview by author, December 21, 2016.

143. Madhubuti, interview by author, December 21, 2016.

144. "Celebrating the Life and Work of Haki R. Madhubuti," event program in author's possession.

145. Alkalimat, "Black Chicago."

146. E. Davis, "Liberation and Transformation."

147. "About the College," https://www.ccc.edu/colleges/malcolm-x/menu/Pages/About-the-College.aspx (accessed August 31, 2022).

148. Randi Storch, "Red Squad," *Encyclopedia of Chicago*, http://www.encyclopedia.chicagohistory.org/pages/1049.html (accessed September 1, 2022).

149. For surveillance files on Black Chicago radicals, see box 118, folder 1034 in box 183, and folder 1109 in box 224, all in Chicago Police Department Red Squad Papers, Chicago History Museum, Chicago, IL.

CONCLUSION

Portions of this conclusion originated from McDuffie, "The Diasporic Journeys of Louise Little."

1. The descriptions of this service are the author's firsthand observations of Beth Shalom on January 14, 2017, Chicago.

2. Beth Shalom B'nai Zaken Ethiopian Hebrew Congregation, "Our History" (accessed September 3, 2022); Zev Chafets, "Obama's Rabbi," *New York Times Magazine*, April 2, 2009, https://www.nytimes.com/2009/04/05/magazine/05rabbi-t.html.

3. "Race and Ethnicity in Marquette Park," https://statisticalatlas.com/neighborhood/Illinois/Chicago/Marquette-Park/Race-and-Ethnicity (accessed September 3, 2022); Niko Koppel, "Black Rabbi Reaches Out to Mainstream of His Faith," *NYT*, March 16, 2008, https://www.nytimes.com/2008/03/16/us/16rabbi.html.

4. Alden Loury and Esther Yoon-Ji Kang, "Latinos Have Surpassed African Americans as Chicago's Second Largest Racial or Ethnic Group," WBEZ Chicago, August 13, 2021, https://www.wbez.org/stories/latinos-are-now-chicagos-second-largest-racial-group/5377b600-8927-4700-bc92-f23fc99780d4.

5. James Brazelton, (Yahath) Mahalia Koroma, Brenda Ross, and Candice Smith, interview by author, December 17, 2015, Chicago.

6. Chafets, "Obama's Rabbi."

7. Rabbi Capers C. Funnye Jr., interview by author, June 30, 2015, Chicago; author's firsthand observations of Beth Shalom.

8. Mwariama Kamau, phone conversation with author, September 6, 2022; UNIA-ACL Rehabilitating Committee, https://www.facebook.com/uniarehabilitatingcommittee2020 (accessed September 6, 2022); Cleophus Miller Jr., interview by author, August 12, 2017, Warrensville Heights, OH.

9. Gershoni, *Liberia under Samuel Doe*, 3–67, 317–18; Johnson Sirleaf, *This Child Will Be Great*, 93–194.

10. Johnson Sirleaf, *This Child Will Be Great*, 137–244.

11. "Help Us: Liberian President Writes a Touching Letter to the World on Ebola," *African Leadership Magazine*, October 23, 2014, https://www.africanleadershipmagazine.co.uk/help-us-liberian-president-writes-a-touching-letter-to-the-world-on-ebola; "Ebola: A Touching Letter to the World by President Ellen J. Sirleaf," November 17, 2014, http://www.smwf.org/2014/11/letter-to-the-world-on-ebola-by-president-sirleaf.

12. United Nations Population Dashboard, "World Population Dashboard Liberia," https://www.unfpa.org/data/world-population/LR; "Liberia Population 2022 (Live)," https://worldpopulationreview.com/countries/liberia-population (both accessed September 9, 2022).

13. Emmanuel Mulbah Johnson, telephone interview by author, September 6, 2022.

14. Proposal to the Parent Body of the UNIA-ACL for the Establishment of the James Robert Stewart Division 435, circa June 2015, in email from JRS-D 435 to author, December 9, 2015; Senghor Jawara Baye to JRS-D 435 (n.d.) in email from James R. Stewart Division to author, December 9, 2015; E. Johnson, telephone interview by author, September 6, 2022; Sammitta Entsua, telephone interview by author, September 12, 2022.

15. Liberty Farm in Grand Bassa County is located along the Farmington River across from Roberts International Airport and approximately forty miles east of Monrovia. Michael R. Duncan and Rosemarie James, interview by author, March 9, 2023, Grand Bassa County, Liberia.

16. Duncan and James, interview by author, March 9, 2023.

17. Entsua, telephone interview by author, September 12, 2022.

18. Entsua, telephone interview by author, September 12, 2022; J. H. Webster, "Liberians Memorialize George Floyd as a Call for an End to Racial Violence in America," *Front Page Africa*, June 9, 2020, https://frontpageafricaonline.com/news/liberians-memorialize-george-floyd-as-a-call-for-an-end-to-racial-violence-in-america.

19. Daughters of the African Revolution Facebook page, https://m.facebook.com/permalink.php?id=311675508995406&story_fbid=1528653210630957 (accessed September 8, 2022).

20. Untitled article, *SV*, September 1953, 2, reel 6, folder 93, UNIA Papers WRHS.

21. Jonathan Stewart and Emmanuel Moses, interview by author, January 13, 2014, Monrovia, Liberia; "Victor Stewart, 69, Was Officer in Liberian Army," *PD*, November 24, 1993, p. 9B.

22. Victor Stewart Jr. and Cheryl Morgan, conversation with author, January 29, 2019, Monrovia, Liberia.

23. Cha-Jua, "The Changing Same," 27–39.

24. US Census Bureau QuickFacts, https://www.census.gov/quickfacts/fact/table /detroitcitymichigan,MI/PST045222 (accessed October 23, 2023).

25. G. Boggs, *The Next American Revolution*, 105.

26. Malik Yakini, interview by author, June 23, 2016, Detroit.

27. D-Town Farm, "D-Town Farm," https://www.dbcfsn.org/educational-youth-pro-grams (accessed September 14, 2022); B. Smith, *Food Power Politics*, 8, 9.

28. Yakini, interview by author, June 23, 2016.

29. "UIC Report Examines Black Population Loss in Chicago," January 30, 2022, https://www.newswise.com/articles/uic-report-examines-black-population-loss-in -chicago.

30. Haki R. Madhubuti, interview by author, December 21, 2016, Chicago; Betty Shabazz International Charter Schools, "History," https://www.bsics.org/apps/pages/index .jsp?uREC_ID=179003&type=d (accessed September 15, 2022).

31. Rosemary Marcus-Bey, interview by author, December 29, 2016, Cleveland; Jazmine Jackson, interview by author, December 29, 2016, East Cleveland; Benjamin Satter-Bey, interview by author, June 18, 2016, Chicago.

32. Ransby, *Making All Black Lives Matter*, 1–2.

33. Ransby, *Making All Black Lives Matter*, 47–80.

34. K. Taylor, *From #Blacklivesmatter to Black Liberation*, 13–15.

35. Ervin, *Gateway to Equality*, 145–86; Lipsitz, *A Life in the Struggle*, 93–197.

36. W. Johnson, *The Broken Heart of America*, 416–31.

37. Robin D. G. Kelley, "What Does Black Lives Matter Want?," *Boston Review*, August 17, 2016, https://bostonreview.net/articles/robin-d-g-kelley-movement-black-lives -vision.

38. "Vision for Black Lives," https://m4bl.org/policy-platforms (accessed November 18, 2023).

39. Javier C. Hernández and Benjamin Mueller, "Global Anger Grows over George Floyd Death, and Becomes an Anti-Trump Cudgel," *NYT*, June 1, 2020, https://www.nytimes.com /2020/06/01/world/asia/george-floyd-protest-global.html.

40. The UNIA apparently was not a presence in Minneapolis during the Garvey movement's heyday.

41. Ransby, *Making All Black Lives Matter*, 3.

42. Ransby, *Making All Black Lives Matter*, 3; K. Taylor, *From #Blacklivesmatter to Black Liberation*, 75–106.

43. Strickland and Greene, *Malcolm X*, 212.

44. "Wilfred Little, 78, Brother of Malcolm X," *NYT*, May 21, 1998; Little, "Our Family from the Inside," 1–41.

45. Gary Anderson, telephone interview by author, May 14, 2015; "Robert Little: Youngest Brother of Malcolm X," *Detroit News*, November 28, 1999; Crumbley and Little, *Relatives Raising Children*.

46. Steven Jones and Talib El Amin, interview with author, 2014.

47. Steven Jones, telephone interview with author, February 18 and 19, 2015; Steven Jones and Talib El Amin, interview with author, 2014.

48. S. Jones, "Woodland Park."

49. Deborah Jones and Shahara Brown, interview with author, July 12, 2018, Grand Rapids, MI; Jones, telephone interview with author, February 18 and 19, 2015.

50. The Little home was demolished by 1970. "Nebraska: Malcolm X House Site of Omaha," https://www.nps.gov/places/nebraska-malcolm-x-house-site-omaha.htm (accessed October 11, 2022).

51. Walter Brooks, interview by author, May 15, 2015, Omaha; Malcolm X Foundation, https://www.malcolmxfoundation.org (accessed October 11, 2022).

52. Deborah Jones, phone conversation with author, November 5, 2023; Jace Harper, "Lansing Historic Marker Honors Family of Malcolm X," WILX (Lansing, MI), May 20, 2022, https://www.wilx.com/2022/05/21/lansing-historic-marker-honors-family -malcolm-x.

53. Willie Davis, "News Spotlight: A Michigan Historical Site-Unveiling of the Little Family Homesite and Malcolm X (Little) Marker," *New Citizens Press*, June 10, 2022.

54. Jones, phone conversation with author, November 5, 2023; "Lansing Historic Marker Honors Family of Malcolm X."

55. Cooper, *The Hanging of Angélique*, 11 (emphasis in original). The first African captive arrived in Canada in 1628, just nine years after Africans arrived in Virginia, marking the beginning of a 206-year history of slavery in Canada. Cooper, *The Hanging of Angélique*, 70–71.

56. Cooper, "A New Biography of the African Diaspora," 47.

57. Maynard, *Policing Black Lives*, 1–16.

58. Third Eye Collective, https://thirdeyecollective.wordpress.com (accessed November 9, 2017).

59. Délice Mugabo, text to author, November 9, 2017.

60. Robyn Maynard, text to author, November 9, 2017.

61. Marcus and Taber, *Maurice Bishop Speaks*, 1–15, 21–23; "The Revolution in Grenada," 51–53.

62. Marcus and Taber, *Maurice Bishop Speaks*, 1–15, 21–23, viii, xii–xvii.

63. D. Scott, *Omens of Adversity*, 16; Marcus and Taber, *Maurice Bishop Speaks*, 287–311.

64. Marcus and Taber, *Maurice Bishop Speaks*, vii, xxxvii.

65. Military forces from seven Caribbean nations opposed to the Grenada Revolution also participated in the US-led invasion of Grenada. "Invasion of Grenada," NYT, October 26, 1983, p. B1.

66. Puri, *The Grenada Revolution in the Caribbean Present*, 12, 1.

67. These scholars include Merle Collins, Nicole Phillip-Dowe, and Tesfa Aki Peterson.

68. Terance Wilson, interview by author, March 14, 2015, La Digue, Grenada.

69. La Digue Community Support and Honors Interim Team/Committee Notes, circa September 2019; La Digue Heritage Honors Remembrance Memorial Day flyer, February 2021, both in author's possession.

70. Gloria Chitterman and Fitzroy Walcott, interview by author, January 15, 2015, La Digue, Grenada.

71. A. Davis, *Freedom Is a Constant Struggle*.

This bibliography is divided into five sections: "Manuscripts and Photograph Collections"; "Government Publications"; "Newspapers, Magazines, and Other Media"; "Oral Histories and Interviews"; and "Books, Chapters, Dissertations, and Journal Articles."

MANUSCRIPTS AND PHOTOGRAPH COLLECTIONS

Abbott-Sengstacke Family Papers. Vivian G. Harsh Research Collection of Afro-American History and Literature, Woodson Regional Library, Chicago.

Amos, Roberta Stewart. Personal collection. Shaker Heights, OH.

Ashtabula County Female Anti-Slavery Society Records. Western Reserve Historical Society, Cleveland.

Balk, Alfred. Papers. Newberry Library, Chicago.

Banda, H. K. Archive. Herman B. Wells Library, Indiana University, Bloomington.

Barnett, Claude A. Papers. Associated Negro Press, 1918–1967 (microfilm). History, Philosophy, and Newspaper Library, University of Illinois at Urbana-Champaign, Urbana.

Bilbo, Theodore G. Papers. McCain Library and Archives, University of Southern Mississippi, Hattiesburg.

Black, Timuel D. Papers. Vivian G. Harsh Research Collection of Afro-American History and Literature, Woodson Regional Library, Chicago.

Black Power Movement. Part 3, Papers of the Revolutionary Action Movement (microfilm). History, Philosophy, and Newspaper Library, University of Illinois at Urbana-Champaign, Urbana.

Boggs, James and Grace Lee Boggs. Papers. Walter P. Reuther Library, Wayne State University, Detroit.

Bond, Horace Mann. Papers (microfilm). History, Philosophy, and Newspaper Library, University of Illinois at Urbana-Champaign, Urbana.

Brooks, Gwendolyn. Papers. Rare Book and Manuscript Library, University of Illinois at Urbana-Champaign, Urbana.

Brotherhood of Sleeping Car Porters, Chicago Division Records. Chicago History Museum, Chicago.

Burns, Ben. Collection. Vivian G. Harsh Research Collection of Afro-American History and Literature, Woodson Regional Library, Chicago.

Canton Ladies Anti-Slavery Society Records. Western Reserve Historical Society, Cleveland.

Chesnutt, Charles W. Papers (microfilm). Western Reserve Historical Society, Cleveland.

Chicago Federation of Labor: John Fitzpatrick Papers. Chicago Historical Museum, Chicago.

Cincinnati Human Relations Commission Records. Archives and Rare Books Library, University of Cincinnati, Cincinnati.

Clarke, John Henrik. Papers. Schomburg Center for Research in Black Culture, New York Public Library, New York.

Class, 146-10 (Japanese Propaganda) Litigation Case Files and Enclosures, 1940–1955, Entry AI-COR 146-10, Record Group 60. Department of Justice and Civil Division, Criminal Division. National Archives and Records. College Park, MD.

Cleage, Albert B., Jr. Papers. Bentley Historical Library, University of Michigan, Ann Arbor.

Cleveland Documents Microfilm Project. Cleveland Public Library, Cleveland.

Cleveland Public Library Photograph Collection. Cleveland Public Library, Cleveland.

Cole, Allen E. Papers. Western Reserve Historical Society, Cleveland.

Cole, Allen E. Photograph Collection. Western Reserve Historical Society, Cleveland.

Congress of Racial Equality, Cleveland Chapter Records. Western Reserve Historical Society, Cleveland.

Conroy, Jack. Papers. Newberry Library, Chicago.

Cooper, Donna Hayford. Personal collection. Paynesville, Liberia.

Cox, Earnest Sevier. Papers. David M. Rubenstein Rare Book and Manuscript Library, Duke University, Durham, NC.

Craigen, Joseph A. Papers. Burton Historical Collection, Detroit Public Library, Detroit.

Davis, Griffin A. Papers. David M. Rubenstein Rare Book and Manuscript Library, Duke University, Durham, NC.

Detroit Revolutionary Movements Records. Walter P. Reuther Library, Wayne State University, Detroit.

Detroit Urban League Records. Bentley Historical Library, University of Michigan, Ann Arbor.

Drake, St. Clair. Papers. Schomburg Center for Research in Black Culture, New York Public Library, New York.

Du Bois, W. E. B. Papers (microfilm). History, Philosophy, and Newspaper Library, University of Illinois at Urbana-Champaign, Urbana.

Durham, Richard. Papers. Vivian G. Harsh Research Collection of Afro-American History and Literature, Woodson Regional Library, Chicago.

Flewellan, Icabod. Collection. East Cleveland Public Library, Cleveland.

Franklin, Clarence LaVaughn. Papers. Bentley Historical Library, University of Michigan, Ann Arbor.

Future Outlook League Records. Western Reserve Historical Association, Cleveland.

Garvey, Amy Ashwood. Collection. National Library of Jamaica, Kingston, Jamaica.

Garvey, Amy Ashwood. Memorabilia collection. Alma Jordan Library, University of West Indies, St. Augustine, Trinidad and Tobago.

Garvey, Amy Jacques. Collection. Charles L. Blockson Afro-American Collection, Temple University, Philadelphia.

Garvey, Amy Jacques. Memorial collection on Marcus Garvey. Special Collections and Archives, Fisk University, Nashville.

Garvey, Marcus, and the Universal Negro Improvement Association. Collection (formerly the Wahab Collection). Charles H. Wright Museum of African American History, Detroit.

Gizenga, Dabu. Collection on Kwame Nkrumah. Moorland-Spingarn Research Center, Howard University, Washington, DC.

Goldsmith, Jacob. Family Papers. Western Reserve Historical Society, Cleveland.

Hammurabi, F. H. Papers. Archives and Special Collections, Chicago State University, Chicago.

Hill, Robert A. Collection of the Marcus Garvey and Universal Negro Improvement Association Papers Project Records. David M. Rubenstein Rare Book and Manuscript Library, Duke University, Durham, NC.

Housewives Leave of Detroit Records. Bentley Historical Library, University of Michigan, Ann Arbor.

Hunter, Jane Edna. Papers. Western Reserve Historical Society, Cleveland.

Hunton, William Alphaeus. Papers. Schomburg Center for Research in Black Culture, New York Public Library, New York.

Illinois Writers Project. The "Negro in Illinois" Papers. Vivian G. Harsh Research Collection of Afro-American History and Literature, Woodson Regional Library, Chicago.

Isaac, Sara R. Collection. Charles L. Blockson Afro-American Collection, Temple University, Philadelphia.

Jack, Homer A. Papers. Swarthmore College Peace Collection, Swarthmore College, Swarthmore, PA.

Klunder, Bruce. Papers. Western Reserve Historical Society, Cleveland.

Langdon, Victor. Personal collection. Montreal, Canada.

Liberian Presidential Records. Center for National Documents and Records Archive, Monrovia, Liberia.

Logan, Arthur. Papers. Vivian G. Harsh Research Collection of Afro-American History and Literature, Woodson Regional Library, Chicago.

Malcolm X Collection. Papers, 1948–1965. Schomburg Center for Research in Black Culture, New York Public Library, New York.

Malcolm X Collection. Stuart A. Rose Manuscript, Archives, and Rare Book Library, Emory University, Atlanta.

Malcolm X Collection. Charles H. Wright Museum of African American History, Detroit.

Malcolm X. Miscellaneous files. Federal Bureau of Investigation.

Matthews, Wentworth A. Collection. Schomburg Center for Research in Black Culture, New York Public Library, New York.

Moorish Science Temple of America Collection. Schomburg Center for Research in Black Culture, New York Public Library, New York.

Moorish Science Temple of America Photograph Collection. Schomburg Center for Research in Black Culture, New York Public Library, New York.

Movement for Justice in Africa, Vertical File. Africana Collection, Northwestern University Library, Evanston, IL.

Nation of Islam. Miscellaneous files. Federal Bureau of Investigation.

Nation of Islam Collection. Schomburg Center for Research in Black Culture, New York Public Library, New York.

National Association for the Advancement of Colored People Papers (microfilm). Western Reserve Historical Association, Cleveland.

Newman, Richard, and Laura Adorkor Kofi. Collection. Schomburg Center for Research in Black Culture, New York Public Library, New York.

Nkrumah, Kwame. Papers. Moorland-Spingarn Research Center, Howard University, Washington, DC.

Northeast Ohio Broadcast Archives. John Carroll University, University Heights, OH.

Operation Black Unity Records. Western Reserve Historical Society, Cleveland.

Photograph Collection. Roosevelt University Archives, Roosevelt University, Chicago.

Prints and Photographs Division. Library of Congress, Washington, DC.

Pullman Company Records. Newberry Library, Chicago.

Reed, Christopher Robert. Papers. Roosevelt University Archives, Roosevelt University, Chicago.

Robbins History Museum. Archival records. Robbins, IL.

Sawyer, Amos. Vertical file. Africana Collection, Northwestern University Library, Northwestern University, Evanston, IL.

Second Baptist Church. Records. Bentley Historical Library, University of Michigan, Ann Arbor.

Simons Collection: Women's Organisations Manuscripts and Archives, University of Cape Town, Cape Town, South Africa.

Spanish Town Archives. Jamaica Archives and Records Department, Spanish Town, Jamaica.

Strong, Edward. Papers. Moorland-Spingarn Research Center, Howard University, Washington, DC.

Toward Freedom. Papers. Africana Collection, Northwestern University Library, Northwestern University, Evanston, IL.

Tubman, William V. S. Papers (microfilm). Liberian Collections, Indiana University Libraries, Bloomington, IN.

Universal Negro Improvement Association Central Division Records. Schomburg Center for Research in Black Culture, New York Public Library, New York.

Universal Negro Improvement Association Records (microfilm). Western Reserve Historical Society, Cleveland.

Universal Negro Improvement Association Records. Stuart A. Rose Manuscript, Archives, and Rare Book Library, Emory University, Atlanta.

Wash, Leonard. Papers. Vivian G. Harsh Research Collection of Afro-American History and Literature, Woodson Regional Library, Chicago.

Wells, Ida B. Papers (online). Hanna Holborn Gray Special Collections Research Center, University of Chicago, Chicago.

Western Anti-Slavery Society Records. Western Reserve Historical Society, Cleveland.

Wheatley, Phyllis. Association records. Western Reserve Historical Society, Cleveland.

Williams, Robert F. Papers (microfilm). History, Philosophy, and Newspaper Library, University of Illinois at Urbana-Champaign, Urbana.

Wilson, Terance. Personal collection. Maydes, Grenada.

GOVERNMENT PUBLICATIONS

US Thirteenth Census, 1910
US Fourteenth Census, 1920
US Fifteenth Census, 1930

NEWSPAPERS, MAGAZINES, AND OTHER MEDIA

African Leadership Magazine
African Opinion
Amsterdam News
Atlanta Daily World
Boston Review
Call and Post (Cleveland)
Chicago Crusader
Chicago Daily Defender
Chicago Daily Tribune
Chicago Defender
Chicago Tribune
Cleveland Gazette
Daily Gleaner (Kingston, Jamaica)
Daily Inter Ocean (Chicago)
Democracy Now!
Democratic Free Press (Detroit)
Detroit Free Press
Detroit News
Ebony
Esquire
Essence
Frontpage Africa (Monrovia, Liberia)
Inter City Times (Lansing, MI)
Jerusalem Post
Los Angeles Sentinel
Michigan Chronicle
Muhammad Speaks
National Public Radio
Negro World

New Citizens Press (Lansing, MI)
New Negro World
New World (Lansing, MI)
New York Times
Norfolk New Guide and Journal (VA)
North Star
Omaha World-Herald
Ottawa Citizen (Lansing, MI)
Pittsburgh Courier
Plain Dealer (Cleveland)
Robbins Eagle (Robbins, IL)
St. Louis American
State News (East Lansing, MI)
Stewart's Voice
Time
USA Today
Vindicator (Youngstown, OH)
wbez (Chicago)
Windsor Daily Star (Windsor, Ontario)

ORAL HISTORIES AND INTERVIEWS

Allen, Armstead. Interview by author, 27 February 2018. Chicago.

Amadu, Amissata. Interview by author, 14 January 2016. Monrovia, Liberia.

Amiel, Prince Sar. Interview by author, 29 May 2019. Chicago.

Amos, Roberta Stewart. Interview by author, 18 May 2012. Shaker Heights, OH.

Amos, Roberta Stewart. Phone conversations with author, 25 January 2013, 9 April 2013, 11 February 2014, 24 August 2015, 4 December 2017, 9 December 2020.

Anderson, Gary. Phone interview by author, 14 May 2015.

Asomi, Yasin A. Interview by author, 30 December 2015. Detroit.

Atkins, Russell. Interview by author, 3 September 2015. Bedford Heights, OH.

Avellano, Lizabet. Interview by author, 16 May 2015. Omaha.

Bailey, A. Peter. Phone interviews by author, 7 February 2012, 30 June 2017.

Baker, General. Phone interview by author, 23 August 2013.

Baptiste, Deydra. Interview by author, 12 November 2016. Montreal, Canada.

Ben Asiel, Prince Yosef. Interview by author, 29 May 2019. Chicago.

Bettjes, Kim. Phone interview by author, 22 May 2015.

Boggs, Grace Lee. Interview by author, 12 January 2012. Detroit.

Bracey, John H., Jr. Phone interview by author, 20 December 2013.

Brazelton, James, (Yahath) Mahalia Koroma, Brenda Ross, and Candice Smith. Interview by author, 17 December 2015. Chicago.

Brooks, Walter. Interview by author, 15 May 2015. Omaha.

Brown, Shahara. Interview by author, 7 April 2016. Chicago.

Burroughs, Margaret. Interview by author, 26 February 2003. New York.

Chitterman, Gloria, and Fitzroy Walcott. Interview by author, 15 January 2015. La Digue, Grenada.

Colliste, James. Interview by author, 14 March 2015. Grenada.

Cooper Hayford, Donna. Interviews by author, 22 June 2013, 29 January 2018. Monrovia, Liberia; 9 March 2023, Paynesville, Liberia.

Coxoll, Wilson. Interview by author, 14 March 2015. La Digue, Grenada.

Crowe, Larry. Interview by author, 27 May 2016. Dayton, OH.

Doeteh, Emmanuel S. Interview by author, 8 January 2016. Monrovia, Liberia.

Drake-El, Ahmad. Interview by author, 3 September 2016. Shaker Heights, OH.

Duncan, Michael R., and Rosemarie James. Interview by author, 9 March 2023. Grand Bassa County, Liberia.

El Amin, Talib. Interview by author, 9 June 2014. Grand Rapids, MI.

Entsua, Sammitta B. Interviews by author, 14 January 2016, 13 March 2023. Monrovia, Liberia.

Entsua, Sammitta B. Phone interview by author, 12 September 2022.

Fannoh, J. Sabastian. Interview by author, 2 February 2018. Monrovia, Liberia.

Freeman, Don. Interview by author, 31 December 2013. Cleveland, as well as numerous phone conversations.

Freeman, Donald, Norma Jean Freeman, and Hanif Wahab. Interview by author, 11 August 2017. Cleveland.

Freeman, Norma Jean. Interview by author, 31 December 2013. Cleveland.

Funnye, Rabbi Capers C., Jr. Interview by author, 30 June 2015. Chicago.

Gbah, Eddie S., Jr. Interview by author, 14 January 2016. Monrovia, Liberia.

Gee, Patricia Noni. Phone interviews by author, 12 September 2018 and 9 October 2018.

Gingrich, Linda. Interview by author, 26 May 2016. Lebanon, OH.

Greenwood, Joyce. Interview by author, 25 March 2015. Garfield Hills, OH.

Greenwood, Marcus. Interview by author, 24 March 2015. Garfield Hills, OH.

Habeebah, Amatul Aleem. Interview by author, 27 May 2016. Dayton, OH.

Hamilton, Cynthia. Phone interview by author, 10 May 2019.

Hayford, Donna Cooper. Phone interview by author, 14 January 2013.

Haymore, Tyrone. Interview by author, 6 October 2017. Robbins, IL.

Jackson, Jazmine. Interview by author, 29 December 2016. East Cleveland, OH.

Jasper, Robert J. Interview by author, 8 January 2016. Monrovia, Liberia.

Joe, Abraham J. Interview by author, 14 January 2016. Monrovia, Liberia.

Johnson, Emmanuel Mulbah. Interview by author, 8 January 2016, 14 March 2023. Monrovia, Liberia.

Johnson, Emmanuel Mulbah. Phone interview by author, 6 September 2022.

Johnson, Keith. Interview by author, 23 October 2015. Detroit.

Johnson, Mechail R. Interview by author, 2 February 2018. Monrovia, Liberia.

Johnson, Terry. Phone interviews by author, 29 November 2012, 29 November 2019, as well as numerous phone conversations and electronic communications.

Jones, Deborah. Interviews by author, 20 March 2015, East Lansing, MI; 20 September 2017, Kalamazoo, MI, as well as numerous phone conversations and electronic communications.

Jones, Steven. Phone interviews by author, 4 February 2014, 10 October 2014.

Jones, Steven, and Talib El Amin. Interview by author, 9 June 2014. Grand Rapids, MI.

Kaba, Makonddy. Interview by author, 14 January 2016. Monrovia, Liberia.

Kadalie, Modibo. Phone interview by author, 20 February 2019.

Kamau, Mwariama. Phone interview by author, 6 September 2022.

Kendig, Diane. Interview by author, 3 September 2015. Bedford, OH.

Kollie, Jacob A. D. Interview by author, 14 January 2016. Monrovia, Liberia.

Langdon Brookings, Agnes. Interview by author, 14 January 2015. True Blue, Grenada.

Langdon Strakev, Rita. Skype interview by author, 13 March 2015.

Langdon, Victor. Interview by author, 13 November 2016. Montreal, Canada.

Lawiru, Sharif. Interview by author, 16 May 2015. Omaha.

Madhubuti, Haki. Interview by author, 21 December 2016. Chicago.

Mahn, Solomon G. Interview by author, 8 January 2016. Monrovia, Liberia.

Marcus-Bey, Rosemary. Interview by author, 29 December 2016. East Cleveland, OH.

Massaquoi, Siafa J. Interview by author, 2 February 2018. Monrovia, Liberia.

McCant, Bill. Interview by author, 11 June 2014. Detroit.

McGee, James. Interview by author, 2 February 2018. Monrovia, Liberia.

Miller, Cleophus. Interview by author, 12 August 2017. Warrensville Heights, OH.

Morgan, Cheryl. Interview by author, 29 January 2018. Monrovia, Liberia. As well as numerous conversations and electronic communications.

Mullbah, Cyrus. Interview by author, 2 February 2018. Monrovia, Liberia.

Nanah, John B. Interview by author, 14 January 2014. Gbandela, Liberia.

Neewhord, Abel T. Interview by author, 8 January 2016. Monrovia, Liberia.

Perot Turner, Ruth. Phone interview by author, 1 November 2018.

Pettway, Quill. Phone interview by author, 11 November 2013.

Pitt, Bertrand. Interview by author, 14 January 2015. Lance Aux Epines, Grenada.

Purcell, Joan. Interviews by author, 15 and 16 January 2015. Grand Anse, Grenada.

Saleem, Mensah and Noni Patricia Gee. Interview by author, 12 January 2012. Detroit.

Sanneh, Tepitapia. Interview by author, 2 February 2018. Monrovia, Liberia.

Satter-Bey, Benjamin. Interview by author, 18 June 2016. Chicago.

Sawyer, Amos. Interview by author, 11 January 2016. Monrovia, Liberia.

Sawyer, Amos. Phone interview by author, 22 November 2014.

Sayeh, Philomena Bloh. Interview by author, 8 January 2016. Monrovia, Liberia.

Saylee, Martin B. Interview by author, 14 January 2016. Monrovia, Liberia.

Sayoh, Hamedu Patrick, III. Interview by author, 14 January 2016. Monrovia, Liberia.

Sesay, Haja S. Interview by author, 14 January 2016. Monrovia, Liberia.

Shaheed, Mutawaf A. Interview by author, 3 September 2015. Bedford, OH.

Shaheed, Mutawaf A. Phone interview by author, 13 January 2017.

Sharpley, Miriam Adenike. Interview by author, 4 September 2015. Cleveland.

Shaw, Christian S. W. Interview by author, 2 February 2018. Monrovia, Liberia.

Siafa, Bondu S. Interview by author, 14 January 2016. Monrovia, Liberia.

Sneh, Kamizoe T., Jr. Interview by author, 2 February 2018. Monrovia, Liberia.

Stanley-House, Kathie. Phone interview by author, 20 May 2019.

Stewart, John. Phone interview by author, 21 October 2014.

Stewart, John, and Emmanuel Moses. Interview by author, 13 January 2014. Monrovia, Liberia.

Stewart, Roberta H. Interview by author, 15 August 2013. Grand Rapids, MI.

Stewart, Victor, Jr. Interview by author, 20 December 2014. Beachwood, OH.

Taweh, Tom. Interview by author, 12 January 2016. Monrovia, Liberia.

Taylor, Alfred W. Interview by author, 2 February 2018. Monrovia, Liberia.

Taylor, Marshall. Interview by author, 16 May 2015. Omaha.

Thornton, Georgina, and Kenneth King. Interview by author, 17 October 2018. Youngstown, OH.

Tipoteh, Togba-Nah. Interviews by author, 11 January 2016, 2 March 2023. Monrovia, Liberia, as well as numerous conversations.

Tripp, Luke. Phone interview by author, 26 July 2017.

Wahab, Hanif. Interview by author, 29 December 2016. Cleveland Heights, OH.

Walcott, Fitzroy. Interview by author, 15 January 2015. La Digue, Grenada.

Watson, Abraham Kenneh. Interview by author, 14 January 2016. Monrovia, Liberia.

Wilson, Terance V. Interviews by author, 13 and 15 January 2015, 14 March 2015. La Digue, Grenada, as well as numerous phone conversations and electronic communications.

Yakini, Malik. Interview by author, 23 June 2016. Detroit.

Yeargar, Platoi B. Interview by author, 2 February 2018. Monrovia, Liberia.

BOOKS, CHAPTERS, DISSERTATIONS, AND JOURNAL ARTICLES

Adeleke, Tunde. *In the Service of God and Humanity: Conscience, Reason, and the Mind of Martin R. Delany*. Columbia: University of South Carolina Press, 2021.

Adeleke, Tunde. *UnAfrican Americans: Nineteenth-Century Black Nationalists and the Civilizing Mission*. Lexington: University of Kentucky Press, 1998.

Adjetey, Wendell Nii Laryea. *Cross-Border Cosmopolitans: The Making of Pan-African North America*. Chapel Hill: University of North Carolina Press, 2023.

Adi, Hakim, and Marika Sherwood, eds. *The 1945 Manchester Pan-African Congress Revisited*. London: New Beacon, 1995.

Ahlman, Jeffrey S. *Kwame Nkrumah: Visions of Liberation*. Athens: Ohio University Press, 2021.

Ahlman, Jeffrey S. *Living with Nkrumahism: Nation, State, and Pan-Africanism in Ghana*. Athens: Ohio University Press, 2017.

Ahmad, Muhammad. *We Will Return in the Whirlwind: Black Radical Organizations, 1960–1975*. Chicago: Charles H. Kerr, 2007.

Alexander, Leslie M. *Fear of a Black Republic: Haiti and the Birth of Black Internationalism in the United States*. Urbana: University of Illinois Press, 2022.

Ali, Noble Drew. *The Holy Koran of the Moorish Science Temple of America*. Self-published, 1927.

Alkalimat, Abdul. "Black Chicago: The Context for the Wall of Respect." In *The Wall of Respect: Public Art and Black Liberation in 1960s Chicago*, edited by Abdul Alkalimat, Romi Crawford, and Rebecca Zorach, 75–92. Evanston, IL: Northwestern University Press, 2017.

Alkalimat, Abdul. "Black Liberation: OBAC and the Makers of the Wall of Respect." In *The Wall of Respect: Public Art and Black Liberation in 1960s Chicago*, edited by Abdul

Alkalimat, Romi Crawford, and Rebecca Zorach, 93–109. Evanston, IL: Northwestern University Press, 2017.

Allen, Ernest, Jr. "Waiting for Tojo: The Pro-Japan Vigil of Black Missourians, 1932–1943." *Gateway Heritage* (Fall 1995): 16–33.

Allen, Ernest, Jr. "When Japan was 'Champion of the Darker Races': Satokata Takahashi and the Flowering of Black Messianic Nationalism." *Black Scholar* 24, no. 1 (Winter 1994): 23–46.

Allen, William E. "Liberia and the Atlantic World in the Nineteenth Century: Convergence and Effects." *History in Africa* 37 (2020): 7–49.

Allman, Jean. "Nuclear Imperialism and the Pan-African Struggle for Peace and Freedom, Ghana 1959–1962." *Souls* 10, no. 2 (April–June 2008): 83–102.

Anderson, Carol A. *Bourgeois Radicals: The NAACP and the Struggle for Colonial Liberation, 1941–1960*. Cambridge: Cambridge University Press, 2014.

Anderson, Carol A. *Eyes Off the Prize: The United Nations and the African American Freedom Struggle for Human Rights, 1944–1955*. Cambridge: Cambridge University Press, 2009.

Anderson, Richard, and Henry B. Lovejoy, eds. *Liberated Africans and the Abolition of the Slave Trade, 1807–1896*. Rochester, NY: University of Rochester Press, 2020.

Andrews, Gregg. *Thyra J. Edwards: Black Activist in the Global Freedom Struggle*. Columbia: University of Missouri Press, 2011.

Aptheker, Bettina. *Communists in Closets: Queering the History 1930s–1990s*. New York: Routledge, 2023.

Armstrong, Julie Buckner. *Mary Turner and the Memory of Lynching*. Athens: University of Georgia Press, 2011.

Asaka, Ikuko. *Tropical Freedom: Climate, Settler Colonialism, and Black Exclusion in the Age of Emancipation*. Durham, NC: Duke University Press, 2017.

Ashbaugh, Carolyn. *Lucy Parsons: An American Revolutionary*. Chicago: Haymarket, 2012.

Azikiwe, Nnamdi. *My Odyssey: An Autobiography*. New York: Praeger, 1970.

Bair, Barbara. "True Women, Real Men: Gender, Ideology, and Social Roles in the Garvey Movement." In *Gendered Domains: Rethinking Public and Private in Women's History: Essays from the Seventh Berkshire Conference on the History of Women*, edited by Dorothy O. Helly and Susan M. Reverby, 154–166. Ithaca, NY: Cornell University Press, 1990.

Bald, Vivek. *Bengali Harlem and the Lost Histories of South Asian America*. Cambridge, MA: Harvard University Press, 2015.

Baldwin, Davarian L. *Chicago's New Negroes: Modernity, the Great Migration, and Black Urban Life*. Chapel Hill: University of North Carolina Press, 2007.

Baldwin, Davarian L., and Minkah Makalani, eds. *Escape from New York: The New Negro Renaissance beyond Harlem*. Minneapolis: University of Minnesota Press, 2013.

Ball, Jared A., and Todd Steven Burroughs, eds. *A Lie of Reinvention: Correcting Manning Marable's Malcolm X*. Baltimore: Black Classic, 2012.

Balto, Simon. *Occupied Territory: Policing Black Chicago from Red Summer to Black Power*. Chapel Hill: University of North Carolina Press, 2019.

Bandele, Ramla M. *Black Star: African American Activism in the International Political Economy*. Urbana: University of Illinois Press, 2008.

Banton, Caree A. *More Auspicious Shores: Barbadian Migration to Liberia, Blackness, and the Making of an African Republic*. Cambridge: Cambridge University Press, 2019.

Barnes, Kenneth C. *Journey of Hope: The Back-to-Africa Movement in Arkansas in the Late 1880s*. Chapel Hill: University of North Carolina Press, 2004.

Bates, Beth Tompkins. *The Making of Black Detroit in the Age of Henry Ford*. Chapel Hill: University of North Carolina Press, 2012.

Bedasse, Monique A. *Jah Kingdom: Rastafarians, Tanzania, and Pan-Africanism in the Age of Decolonization*. Chapel Hill: University of North Carolina Press, 2017.

Bedasse, Monique A., Kim D. Butler, Carlos Fernandes, Dennis Laumann, Tejasvi Nagaraja, Benjamin Talton, and Kira Thurman. "*AHR* Conversation: Black Internationalism." *American Historical Review* 125, no. 5 (December 2020): 1699–1739.

Bell, Howard Holman. *Minutes of the Proceedings of the National Negro Conventions, 1830–1864*. New York: Arno, 1969.

Bennett, Charles Raymond. "The Negro Colonization Movement in Ohio: 1827–1860." Master's thesis, University of Dayton, 1969.

Bertley, Leo W. "The Universal Negro Improvement Association of Montreal, 1917–1979." PhD diss., Concordia University, 1980.

Berwanger, Eugene H. *The Frontier against Slavery: Western Anti-Negro Prejudice and the Slavery Extension Controversy*. Urbana: University of Illinois Press, 2002.

Bessel, Richard. "Unnatural Deaths." In *Oxford History of World War II*, edited by Richard Overy, 301–21. New York: Oxford University Press, 2023.

Bey, C. M. *Clock of Destiny*. Vols. 1 and 2. Cleveland: C. M. Bey, 1947.

Beynon, Erdmann D. "The Voodoo Cult among Negro Migrants in Detroit." *American Journal of Sociology* 43, no. 6 (May 1938): 894–907.

Bilbo, Theodore G. *Take Your Choice: Separation or Mongrelization*. Poplarville, MS: Dream House, 1947.

Biles, Roger. *Mayor Harold Washington: Champion of Race and Reform in Chicago*. Urbana: University of Illinois Press, 2018.

Blackett, R. J. M. *The Captive's Quest for Freedom: Fugitive Slaves, the 1850 Fugitive Slave Law, and the Politics of Slavery*. Cambridge: Cambridge University Press, 2018.

Blain, Keisha N. "'Confraternity among All Dark Races': Mittie Maude Lena Gordon and the Practice of Black (Inter)nationalism in Chicago, 1932–1922." *Palimpsest: A Journal on Women, Gender, and the Black International* 5, no. 2 (Fall 2016): 151–81.

Blain, Keisha N. "'For the Rights of Dark People in Every Part of the World': Pearl Sherrod, Black Internationalist Feminism, and Afro-Asian Politics during the 1930s." *Souls* 17, no. 1–2 (January–June 2015): 90–112.

Blain, Keisha N. *Set the World on Fire: Black Nationalist Women and the Global Struggle for Freedom*. Philadelphia: University of Pennsylvania Press, 2018.

Blain, Keisha N. "'We Want to Set the World on Fire': Black Nationalist Women and Diasporic Politics in the New Negro World, 1940–1944." *Journal of Social History* 49, no. 1 (2015): 194–212.

Blain, Keisha N. and Tiffany M. Gill. "Introduction: Black Women and the Complexities of Internationalism." In *To Turn the Whole World Over: Black Women and Internationalism,* edited by Keisha N. Blain and Tiffany M. Gill, 1–12. Urbana: University of Illinois Press, 2019.

Blain, Keisha N., and Tiffany M. Gill, eds. *To Turn the Whole World Over: Black Women and Internationalism*. Urbana: University of Illinois Press, 2019.

Blocker, Jack S. *A Little More Freedom: African Americans Enter the Urban Midwest, 1860–1930*. Columbus: The Ohio State University Press, 2008.

Blyden, Edward W. *Christianity, Islam and the Negro Race*. Baltimore: Black Classic, 1994.

Blyden, Edward W. *The Origin and Purpose of African Colonization*. London: Forgotten Books, 1883.

Boggs, Grace Lee, with Scott Kurashige. *The Next American Revolution: Sustainable Activism for the Twenty-First Century*. Berkeley: University of California Press, 2012.

Boggs, James. *The American Revolution: Pages from a Negro Worker's Notebook*. New York: Monthly Review Press, 1963.

Bowen, Merle L. *For Land and Liberty: Black Struggles in Rural Brazil*. Cambridge: Cambridge University Press, 2021.

Bowen, Patrick Denis. "The African American Islamic Renaissance and the Rise of the Nation of Islam." PhD diss., University of Denver, 2013.

Bowen, Patrick D. *A History of Conversion to Islam in the United States, Vol. 2: The African American Islamic Renaissance, 1920–1975*. Leiden: Brill, 2017.

Boyce Davies, Carole. *Left of Karl Marx: The Political Life of the Black Communist Claudia Jones*. Durham, NC: Duke University Press, 2008.

Boyce Davies, Carole. "Sisters Outside: Tracing the Caribbean/Black Radical Intellectual Tradition." *Small Axe* 13, no. 1 (March 2009): 217–29.

Boyd, Herb, Ron Daniels, Maulana Karenga, and Haki R. Madhubuti, eds. *By Any Means Necessary: Malcolm X—Real, Not Reinvented*. Chicago: Third World, 2012.

Breitman, George, ed. *Malcolm X Speaks*. New York: Pathfinder, 1965.

Burden-Stelly, Charisse, and Gerald Horne. "From Pan-Africanism to Black Internationalism." In *Routledge Handbook of Pan-Africanism*, edited by Reiland Rabaka, 69–86. New York: Routledge, 2020.

Burkett, Randall K. "The Baptist Church in Years of Crisis: J. C. Austin and Pilgrim Baptist Church, 1926–1950." In *African-American Religion: Interpretive Essays in History and Culture*, edited by Timothy E. Fulop and Albert Raboteau, 316–29. New York: Routledge, 1997.

Burkett, Randall K. *Garveyism as a Religious Movement: The Institutionalization of a Black Civil Religion*. Metuchen, NJ: Scarecrow, 1978.

Bush, Roderick D. *We Are Not What We Seem: Black Nationalism and Class Struggle in the American Century*. New York: New York University Press, 1999.

Butler, Chris. *Henri Lefebvre: Spatial Politics, Everyday Life and the Right to the City*. New York: Routledge, 2012.

Butler, Kim D. *Freedoms Given, Freedoms Won: Afro-Brazilians in Post-Abolition São Paulo and Salvador*. New Brunswick, NJ: Rutgers University Press, 1998.

Byrd, Brandon R. *The Black Republic: African Americans and the Fate of Haiti*. Philadelphia: University of Pennsylvania Press, 2020.

Byrne, Jeffrey James. *Mecca of Revolution: Algeria, Decolonization, and the Third World Order*. New York: Oxford University Press, 2016.

Cain, Courtney. "Ou Ayisyen? The Making of a Haitian Diasporic Community in Chicago, 1933–2010." PhD diss., University of Illinois at Urbana-Champaign, 2017.

Campbell, James T. *Middle Passages: African American Journeys to Africa, 1787–2005.* New York: Penguin, 2006.

Campney, Brent M. S. *Hostile Heartland: Racism, Repression, and Resistance in the Midwest.* Urbana: University of Illinois Press, 2019.

Capeci, Dominic J. *The Lynching of Cleo Wright.* Lexington: University Press of Kentucky, 1998.

Carew, Jan. *Ghosts in Our Blood: With Malcolm X in Africa, England, and the Caribbean.* Chicago: Lawrence Hill, 1994.

Carson, Clayborne. *Malcolm X: The FBI File.* New York: Carroll and Graf, 1991.

Carson, Clayborne, Susan Carson, and Adrienne Clay, eds. *The Papers of Martin Luther King Jr.* Vol. 4. Berkeley: University of California Press, 2000.

Casey, Jim, P. Gabrielle Foreman, and Sarah Lynn Patterson. "How to Use This Book and Its Digital Companions: Approaches to and Afterlives of the Colored Conventions." In *The Colored Conventions: Black Organizing in the Nineteenth Century*, edited by P. Gabrielle Foreman and Sarah Lynn Patterson, 1–17. Chapel Hill: University of North Carolina Press, 2021.

Catlin, Robert A. *Racial Politics and Urban Planning: Gary, Indiana, 1980–1989.* Lexington: University Press of Kentucky, 1993.

Cayton, Andrew R. L., and Susan E. Gray, eds. *The American Midwest: Essays on Regional History.* Bloomington: Indiana University Press, 2001.

Cha-Jua, Sundiata Keita. *America's First Black Town: Brooklyn, Illinois, 1830–1915.* Urbana: University of Illinois Press, 2000.

Cha-Jua, Sundiata Keita. "The Changing Same: Black Racial Formation and Transformation as a Theory of the African American Experience." In *Race Struggles*, edited by Theodore Koditschek, Sundiata Keita Cha-Jua, and Helen A. Neville, 9–47. Urbana: University of Illinois Press, 2009.

Cha-Jua, Sundiata Keita. "'The Cry of the Negro Should Not Be Remember the Maine, but Remember the Hanging of Bush': African American Responses to Lynching in Decatur, Illinois, 1893." In *Lynching beyond Dixie: American Mob Violence Outside the South*, edited by Michael J. Pfeifer, 165–89. Urbana: University of Illinois Press, 2013.

Chambers, Jason P. "A Master Strategist: John H. Johnson and the Development of Chicago as a Center for Black Business Enterprise." In *Building the Black Metropolis: African American Entrepreneurship in Chicago*, edited by Robert E. Weems Jr. and Jason Chambers, 122–146. Urbana: University of Illinois Press, 2017.

Chatelain, Marcia. *South Side Girls: Growing Up in the Great Migration.* Durham, NC: Duke University Press, 2015.

Cheek, William, and Aimee Lee Cheek. *John Mercer Langston and the Fight for Black Freedom, 1829–65.* Urbana: University of Illinois Press, 1989.

Christian, Mark. "Marcus Garvey and the Universal Negro Improvement Association (UNIA): With Special Reference to the 'Lost' Parade in Columbus, Ohio, September 25, 1923." *Western Journal of Black Studies* 28, no. 3 (Fall 2004): 424–34.

City of Detroit Recreation Department. "The Black Presence in Detroit." Historical marker, 1989. Available at the Historical Marker Database, https://www.hmdb.org/m.asp?m=33483 (last updated April 7, 2023).

Clark, Daniel J. *Disruption in Detroit: Autoworkers and the Elusive Postwar Boom.* Urbana: University of Illinois Press, 2018.

Clarke, John Henrik. *Marcus Garvey and the Vision of Africa.* New York: Vintage, 1974.

Cleage, Albert B., Jr. *Black Christian Nationalism: New Directions for the Black Church.* New York: William Morrow, 1972.

Clegg, Claude A., III. *An Original Man: The Life and Times of Elijah Muhammad.* New York: St. Martin's, 1997.

Clegg, Claude A., III. *The Price of Liberty: African Americans and the Making of Liberia.* Chapel Hill: University of North Carolina Press, 2004.

Cohen, Yoel. *The Whistleblower of Dimona: Israel, Vanunu, and the Bomb.* New York: Holmes and Meier, 2003.

Collier, Zakiya, and Tonia Sutherland. "Introduction: The Promise and Possibility of Black Archival Practice." *Black Scholar* 52, no. 2 (April 2022): 1–6.

Collins, Merle. "Louise Langdon Norton Little, Mother of Malcolm X." *Caribbean Quarterly* 66, no. 3 (2020): 346–369.

Collins, Merle. *Ocean Stirrings: A Work of Fiction in Tribute to Louise Langdon Norton Little, Working Mother and Activist, Mother of Malcolm X and Seven Siblings.* Leeds, UK: Peepal Tree, 2023.

Collins, Patricia Hill. "Learning to Think for Ourselves: Malcolm X's Black Nationalism Reconsidered." In *Malcolm X: In Our Own Image,* edited by Joe Wood, 59–85. New York: Anchor, 1992.

Collins, Rodnell P., with A. Peter Bailey. *Seventh Child: A Family Memoir of Malcolm X.* Secaucus, NJ: Birch Lane, 1998.

Comminey, Shawn C. "National Black Conventions and the Quest for African American Freedom and Progress." *International Social Science Review* 91, no. 1 (2015): 1–18.

Cooper, Afua. *The Hanging of Angélique: The Untold Story of Canadian Slavery and the Burning of Old Montréal.* Athens: University of Georgia Press, 2007.

Cooper, Afua. "A New Biography of the African Diaspora: The Life and Death of Marie-Joseph Angélique, Black Portuguese Slave Woman in New France, 1725–1734." In *Extending the Diaspora: New Histories of Black People,* edited by Dawne Y. Curry, Eric D. Duke, and Marshanda A. Smith, 46–76. Urbana: University of Illinois Press, 2009.

Cooper, Afua. "The Voice of the Fugitive: A Transnational Abolitionist Organ." In *A Fluid Frontier: Slavery, Resistance, and the Underground Railroad in the Detroit River Borderland,* edited by Karolyn Smardz Frost and Veta Smith Tucker, 135–53. Detroit: Wayne State University Press, 2016.

Cox, Anna-Lisa. *The Bone and Sinew of the Land: America's Forgotten Black Pioneers and the Struggle for Equality.* New York: Public Affairs, 2018.

Cox, Earnest Sevier. *Let My People Go.* Richmond, VA: White America Society, 1925.

Cox, Earnest Sevier. *Teutonic Unity.* Self-published, 1951.

Cox, Earnest Sevier. *White America.* Richmond, VA: White America Society, 1925.

Cronon, E. David. *Black Moses: The Story of Marcus Garvey and the Universal Negro Improvement Association.* Madison: University of Wisconsin Press, 1955.

Cronon, William. *Nature's Metropolis: Chicago and the Great West.* New York: W. W. Norton, 1991.

Crumbley, Joseph, and Robert L. Little, eds. *Relatives Raising Children: An Overview of Kinship Care*. Washington, DC: Child Welfare League of America, 1997.

Cruse, Harold. "Revolutionary Nationalism and the Afro-American." *Studies on the Left* 2, no. 3 (1962): 12–25.

Curtis, Edward E., IV. *Black Muslim Religion in the Nation of Islam, 1960–1975*. Chapel Hill: University of North Carolina Press, 2006.

Dannin, Robert. *Black Pilgrimage to Islam*. New York: Oxford University Press, 2002.

Darden, Joe T., and Richard W. Thomas. *Detroit: Race Riots, Racial Conflicts, and Efforts to Bridge the Racial Divide*. East Lansing: Michigan State University Press, 2013.

Davidson, Basil. *No Fist Is Big Enough to Hide the Sky: The Liberation of Guinea-Bissau and Cape Verde, 1963–1974*. London: Zed, 2017.

Davis, Angela Y. *Freedom Is a Constant Struggle: Ferguson, Palestine, and the Foundations of a Movement*. Chicago: Haymarket, 2016.

Davis, Edward C., IV. "Liberation and Transformation through Education: Black Studies at Malcolm X College, Chicago." In *Malcolm X's Michigan Worldview: An Exemplar for Contemporary Black Studies*, edited by Rita Kiki Edozie and Curtis Stokes, 135–52. East Lansing: Michigan State University, 2015.

Davis, Ronald W. "The Liberian Struggle for Authority on the Kru Coast." *International Journal of African Historical Studies* 8, no. 2 (1975): 222–65.

Davis, Russell H. *Black Americans in Cleveland*. Washington, DC: Association for the Study of Negro Life and History, 1972.

Delany, Martin R. *The Condition, Elevation, Emigration, and Destiny of the Colored People of the United States*. Baltimore: Black Classic, 1993.

Delany, Martin R. *Official Report of the Niger River Valley Exploring Party*. New York: T. Hamilton, 1861.

Detroit Urban League. *For a New Day in Human Relations*. Detroit: James P. Chapman, 1952.

Dillard, Angela D. *Faith in the City: Preaching Radical Social Change in Detroit*. Ann Arbor: University of Michigan Press, 2007.

Dixon, Chris. *African Americans and the Pacific War, 1941–1945: Race, Nationality, and the Fight for Freedom*. Cambridge: Cambridge University Press, 2018.

Dolinar, Brian, ed. *The Negro in Illinois: The WPA Papers*. Urbana: University of Illinois Press, 2013.

Dorman, Jacob S. *Chosen People: The Rise of American Black Israelite Religions*. New York: Oxford University Press, 2013.

Dorman, Jacob S. *The Princess and the Prophet: The Secret History of Magic, Race, and Moorish Muslims in America*. Boston: Beacon, 2020.

Dorman, Jacob S. "'Western Civilization through Eastern Spectacles': Dusé Mohamed Ali, Black Orientalist Imposture, and Black Internationalism." *Journal of African American History* 108, no. 1 (Winter 2023): 23–49.

Drake, St. Clair. *The Redemption of Africa and Black Religion*. Chicago: Third World, 1991.

Drake, St. Clair, and Horace Cayton. *Black Metropolis: A Study of Negro Life in a Northern City*. Revised ed. Chicago: University of Chicago Press, 1993.

Du Bois, W. E. B. *Black Reconstruction in America. 1860–1880*. New York: Atheneum, 1992.

Dudley, Randall, and Margaret Burroughs, eds. *For Malcolm X: Poems on the Life and Death of Malcolm X.* Detroit: Broadside, 1967.

Duncan, Natanya. "The 'Efficient Womanhood' of the Universal Negro Improvement Association, 1919–1930." PhD diss., University of Florida, 2009.

Dunn, D. Elwood. *The Foreign Policy of Liberia during the Tubman Era, 1944–1971.* London: Hutchinson Benham, 1979.

Dunn, D. Elwood. *Liberia and the United States during the Cold War.* New York: Palgrave Macmillan, 2009.

Duster, Alfreda M., ed. *Crusade for Justice: The Autobiography of Ida B. Wells.* Chicago: University of Chicago Press, 1970.

Dworkin, Ira. *Congo Love Song: African American Culture and the Crisis of the Colonial State.* Chapel Hill: University of North Carolina Press, 2017.

Edozie, Rita Kiki, and Curtis Stokes. "Malcolm X from Michigan: Race, Identity, and Community across the Black World." In *Malcolm X's Michigan Worldview: An Exemplar for Contemporary Black Studies*, edited by Rita Kiki Edozie and Curtis Stokes, 3–34. East Lansing: Michigan State University Press, 2015.

Edozie, Rita Kiki, and Curtis Stokes. *Malcolm X's Michigan Worldview: An Exemplar for Contemporary Black Studies.* East Lansing: Michigan State University Press, 2015.

Eltis, David. "The Diaspora of Yoruba Speakers, 1650–1865: Dimensions and Implications." In *The Yoruba Diaspora in the Atlantic World*, edited by Toyin Falola and Matt D. Childs, 17–39. Bloomington: Indiana University Press, 2004.

Ervin, Keona K. *Gateway to Equality: Black Women and the Struggle for Economic Justice in St. Louis.* Lexington: University Press of Kentucky, 2017.

Esch, Elizabeth D. *The Color Line and the Assembly Line: Managing Race in the Ford Empire.* Chapel Hill: University of North Carolina Press, 2018.

Essien-Udom, E. U. *Black Nationalism: A Search for an Identity in America.* Chicago: University of Chicago Press, 1962.

Evanzz, Karl. *The Judas Factor: The Plot to Kill Malcolm X.* New York: Thunder's Mouth, 1992.

Evanzz, Karl. *The Messenger: The Rise and Fall of Elijah Muhammad.* New York: Pantheon, 1999.

Ewing, Adam. *The Age of Garvey: How a Jamaican Activist Created a Mass Movement and Changed Global Black Politics.* Princeton, NJ: Princeton University Press, 2014.

Farmer, Ashley D. "Reframing African American Women's Grassroots Organizing: Audley Moore and the Universal Association of Ethiopian Women, 1957–1963." *Journal of African American History* 101, no. 1/2 (Winter/Spring 2016): 69–96.

Farmer, Ashley D. *Remaking Black Power: How Black Women Transformed an Era.* Chapel Hill: University of North Carolina Press, 2017.

Farmer, Ashley D. "'Somebody Has to Pay': Audley Moore and the Modern Reparations Movement." *Palimpsest: A Journal on Women, Gender, and the Black International* 7, no. 2 (2018): 108–34.

Felber, Garrett. *Those Who Know Don't Say: The Nation of Islam, the Black Freedom Movement, and the Carceral State.* Chapel Hill: University of North Carolina Press, 2020.

Feldman, Eugene. *The Birth and the Building of the DuSable Museum.* Chicago: DuSable Museum Press, 1981.

Fenderson, Jonathan. *Building the Black Arts Movement: Hoyt Fuller and the Cultural Politics of the 1960s.* Urbana: University of Illinois Press, 2019.

Ferrer, Ada. *Freedom's Mirror: Cuba and Haiti in the Age of Revolution.* Cambridge: Cambridge University Press, 2014.

Ferrer, Ada. *Insurgent Cuba: Race, Nation, and Revolution, 1868–1898.* Chapel Hill: University of North Carolina Press, 1999.

Finley, Stephen C. *In and Out of This World: Material and Extraterrestrial Bodies in the Nation of Islam.* Durham, NC: Duke University Press, 2022.

Finley, Stephen C. "'The Secret . . . of Who the Devil Is': Elijah Muhammad, the Nation of Islam, and Theological Phenomenology." In *New Perspectives on the Nation of Islam,* edited by Dawn-Marie Gibson and Herbert Berg, 154–73. New York: Routledge, 2017.

Fitzgerald, Michael W. "'We Have Found a Moses': Theodore Bilbo, Black Nationalism, and the Greater Liberia Bill of 1939." *Journal of Southern History* 63, no. 2 (May 1997): 293–320.

Fletcher, Bill, Jr. "Manning Marable and the Malcolm X Biography Controversy: A Response to the Critics." In *By Any Means Necessary: Malcolm X—Real, Not Reinvented,* edited by Herb Boyd, Ron Daniels, Maulana Karenga, and Haki R. Madhubuti, 121–35. Chicago: Third World, 2012.

Ford, Melissa. *A Brick and a Bible: Black Women's Radical Activism in the Midwest during the Great Depression.* Carbondale: Southern Illinois University Press, 2022.

Foreman, P. Gabrielle. "Black Organizing, Print Advocacy, and Collective Authorship: The Long History of the Colored Conventions Movement." In *The Colored Conventions Movement: Black Organizing in the Nineteenth Century,* edited by P. Gabrielle Foreman, Jim Casey, and Sarah Lynn Patterson, 21–71. Chapel Hill: University of North Carolina Press, 2021.

Foreman, P. Gabrielle, Jim Casey, and Sarah Lynn Patterson, eds. *The Colored Conventions Movement: Black Organizing in the Nineteenth Century.* Chapel Hill: University of North Carolina Press, 2021.

Fox, Craig. *Everyday Klansfolk: White Protestant Life and the KKK in 1920s Michigan.* East Lansing: Michigan State University Press, 2011.

Frazier, E. Franklin. *The Negro Family in Chicago.* Chicago: University of Chicago Press, 1932.

Frazier, Nishani. *Harambee City: The Congress of Racial Equality in Cleveland and the Rise of Black Power Populism.* Fayetteville: University of Arkansas Press, 2017.

Frazier, Robeson Taz. *The East Is Black: Cold War China in the Black Radical Imagination.* Durham, NC: Duke University Press, 2016.

Freeman, Don. *Reflections of a Resolute Radical.* Self-published, 2017.

Frost, Karolyn Smardz, and Veta Smith Tucker, eds. *A Fluid Frontier: Slavery, Resistance, and the Underground Railroad in the Detroit River Borderland.* Detroit: Wayne State University Press, 2016.

Fuentes, Marisa J. *Dispossessed Lives: Enslaved Women, Violence, and the Archive.* Philadelphia: University of Pennsylvania Press, 2016.

Gaines, Kevin K. *American Africans in Ghana: Black Expatriates and the Civil Rights Era.* Chapel Hill: University of North Carolina Press, 2003.

Gaines, Kevin K. *Uplifting the Race: Black Leadership, Politics, and Culture in the Twentieth Century*. Chapel Hill: University of North Carolina Press, 1996.

Gambino, Ferruccio. "The Transgression of a Laborer: Malcolm X in the Wilderness of America." *Radical History Review* 55 (1993): 7–31.

Garb, Margaret. *Freedom's Ballot: African American Political Struggles in Chicago from Abolition to the Great Migration*. Chicago: University of Chicago Press, 2014.

Gardell, Mattias. *In the Name of Elijah Muhammad: Louis Farrakhan and the Nation of Islam*. Durham, NC: Duke University Press, 1996.

Gardezi, Hasan N., ed. *Chains to Lose: Life and Struggles of a Revolutionary, Memoirs of Dada Amir Haider Khan*. Vols. 1 and 2. Karachi: Pakistan Study Centre, 2007.

Garfinkel, Herbert. *When Negroes March: The March on Washington Movement in the Organizational Politics for FEPC*. New York: Atheneum, 1969.

Garvey, Amy Jacques. *Black Power in America: Marcus Garvey's Impact on Jamaica and Africa*. Self-published, 1968.

Garvey, Amy Jacques. *Garvey and Garveyism*. New York: Collier, 1970.

Garvey, Amy Jacques. *The Philosophy and Opinions of Marcus Garvey*. Vols. 1 and 2. Dover, MA: Majority, 1986.

Gellman, Erik S. *Death Blow to Jim Crow: The National Negro Congress and the Rise of Militant Civil Rights*. Chapel Hill: University of North Carolina Press, 2012.

Georgakas, Dan, and Marvin Surkin. *Detroit: I Do Mind Dying: A Study in Urban Revolution*. Chicago: Haymarket, 2012.

Gerber, David A. *Black Ohio and the Color Line, 1860–1915*. Urbana: University of Illinois Press, 1976.

Gershoni, Yekutiel. *Liberia under Samuel Doe, 1980–1985: The Politics of Personal Rule*. Lanham, MD: Lexington, 2022.

Getachew, Adom. *Worldmaking after Empire: The Rise and Fall of Self-Determination*. Princeton, NJ: Princeton University Press, 2019.

Giddings, Paula. *Ida, a Sword among Lions: Ida B. Wells and the Campaign against Lynching*. New York: Amistad, 2008.

Giffin, William W. *African Americans and the Color Line in Ohio, 1915–1930*. Columbus: The Ohio State University Press, 2005.

Gilmore, Ruth Wilson. *Golden Gulag: Prisons, Surplus, Crisis, and Opposition in Globalizing California*. Berkeley: University of California Press, 2007.

Gilroy, Paul. *The Black Atlantic: Modernity and Double Consciousness*. Cambridge, MA: Harvard University Press, 1993.

Gilroy, Paul. "Black Fascism." *Transition* 81–82 (2000): 70–91.

Gilyard, Keith. *Louise Thompson Patterson: A Life of Struggle for Justice*. Durham, NC: Duke University Press, 2017.

Gitlin, Jay, Robert Michael Morrissey, and Peter J. Kastor, eds. *French St. Louis: Landscapes, Contexts, and Legacy*. Lincoln: University of Nebraska Press, 2021.

Goldman, Peter. *The Death and Life of Malcolm X*. 3rd ed. Urbana: University of Illinois Press, 2013.

Goldthree, Reena N. "Amy Jacques Garvey, Theodore Bilbo, and the Paradoxes of Black Nationalism." In *Global Circuits of Blackness: Interrogating the African Diaspora*, edited by Jean Muteba Rahier, Percy Hintzen, and Felipe Smith, 152–173. Urbana: University of Illinois Press, 2010.

Gomez, Michael A. *African Dominion: A New History of Empire in Early and Medieval West Africa.* Princeton, NJ: Princeton University Press, 2018.

Gomez, Michael A. *Black Crescent: The Experience and Legacy of African Muslims in the Americas.* Cambridge: Cambridge University Press, 2005.

Gomez, Michael A. *Exchanging Our Country Marks: The Transformation of African Identities in the Colonial and Antebellum South.* Chapel Hill: University of North Carolina Press, 1998.

Goodman, James. *Stories of Scottsboro.* New York: Vintage, 1994.

Gordon, Linda. *The Second Coming of the KKK: The Ku Klux Klan of the 1920s and the American Political Tradition.* New York: W. W. Norton, 2017.

Gore, Dayo F. *Radicalism at the Crossroads: African American Women Activists in the Cold War.* New York: New York University Press, 2011.

Goulding, Marc C. "Colonial Mutiny and the Black Radical Atlantic: Sierra Leone, 1939." *African and Black Diaspora: An International Journal* 8, no. 2 (2015): 171–177.

Grant, Colin. *Negro with a Hat: The Rise and Fall of Marcus Garvey.* New York: Vintage, 2003.

Green, Adam. *Selling the Race: Culture, Community and Black Chicago, 1940–1955.* Chicago: University of Chicago Press, 2007.

Greer, Allan. *Property and Dispossession: Natives, Empires and Land in Early Modern North America.* Cambridge: Cambridge University Press, 2017.

Gross, Kali N. *Colored Amazons: Crime, Violence, and Black Women in the City of Brotherly Love, 1880–1910.* Durham, NC: Duke University Press, 2006.

Grossman, James R. *Land of Hope: Chicago, Black Southerners, and the Great Migration.* Chicago: University of Chicago Press, 1989.

Grout, Lewis. *The Place and Power of Each Family of African Languages as Factors in the Development of Africa: An Essay at the Chicago Congress on Africa, August 1893.* Chicago: Congress of Africa, 1893.

Guridy, Frank Andre. *Forging Diaspora: Afro-Cubans and African Americans in a World of Empire and Jim Crow.* Chapel Hill: University of North Carolina Press, 2010.

Hagedorn, Olivia M. "'Call Me African': Black Women and Diasporic Cultural Feminism in Chicago, 1930–1980." PhD diss., University of Illinois at Urbana-Champaign, 2022.

Hagedorn, Olivia M. "'Chicago's Renaissance Woman': The Life, Activism, and Diasporic Cultural Feminism of Dr. Margaret Taylor Goss Burroughs." *African and Black Diaspora: An International Journal* 13, no. 2 (2020): 296–313.

Hahn, Steven. *A Nation under Our Feet: Black Political Struggles in the Rural South from Slavery to the Great Migration.* Cambridge, MA: Harvard University Press, 2003.

Haley, Sarah. *No Mercy Here: Gender, Punishment, and the Making of Jim Crow Modernity.* Chapel Hill: University of North Carolina Press, 2016.

Hamlin, Françoise. "History Unclassified, Historians and Ethics: Finding Anne Moody." *American Historical Review* 125, no. 2 (April 2020): 487–497.

Hannah-Jones, Nikole, Caitlin Roper, Ilena Silverman, and Jake Silverstein, eds. *The 1619 Project: A New Origin Story.* New York: One World, 2021.

Hansel, Ardith K., and E. Donald McKay III. "Quaternary Period." In *Geology of Illinois*, edited by Dennis R. Kolata and Cheryl K. Nimz, 216–247. Champaign: Illinois State Geological Survey, 2010.

Harold, Claudrena N. *The Rise and Fall of the Garvey Movement in the Urban South, 1918–1942*. New York: Routledge, 2007.

Harrison, Faye V. *Outsider Within: Reworking Anthropology in the Global Age*. Urbana: University of Illinois Press, 2008.

Hartman, Saidiya. *Lose Your Mother: A Journey along the Atlantic Slave Route*. New York: Farrar, Straus and Giroux, 2007.

Hartman, Saidiya. "Venus in Two Acts." *Small Axe* 26, no. 2 (June 2008): 1–14.

Hawkins, Homer C. "The Destruction of a Black Community: A Case Study of Lansing, Michigan." In *Blacks and Chicanos in Urban Michigan*, edited by Homer C. Hawkins and Richard W. Thomas, 28–43. Lansing: Michigan History Division, Michigan Department of State, 1979.

Haywood, D'Weston. *Let Us Make Men: The Twentieth-Century Black Press and a Manly Vision for Racial Advancement*. Chapel Hill: University of North Carolina Press, 2018.

Haywood, D'Weston L. "'Superb Sales Force ... the Men of Muhammad': The Nation of Islam, Black Masculinity, and Selling *Muhammad Speaks* in the Era of Black Power." In *New Perspectives on the Nation of Islam*, edited by Dawn-Marie Gibson and Herbert Berg, 9–30. New York: Routledge, 2017.

Hedlin, Ethel W. "Earnest Cox and Colonization: A White Racist's Response to Black Repatriation, 1923–1966." PhD diss., Duke University Press, 1974.

Henderson, Errol A. *The Revolution Will Not Be Theorized: Cultural Revolution in the Black Power Era*. Albany: State University of New York Press, 2019.

Hendricks, Wanda A. *Fannie Barrier Williams: Crossing the Borders of Region and Race*. Urbana: University of Illinois Press, 2014.

Henson, Bryce. *Emergent Quilombos: Black Life and Hip-Hop in Brazil*. Austin: University of Texas Press, 2024.

Hickey, Donald R., Susan A. Wunder, and John R. Wunder. *Nebraska Moments*. New Edition. Lincoln: University of Nebraska Press, 2007.

Higginbotham, Evelyn Brooks. *Righteous Discontent: The Women's Movement in the Black Baptist Church, 1880–1920*. Cambridge: Harvard University Press, 1993.

Hill, Robert A. "Black Zionism: Marcus Garvey and the Jewish Question." In *African Americans and Jews in the Twentieth Century: Studies in Convergence and Conflict*, edited by V. P. Franklin, Nancy L. Grant, Harold M. Kletnick, and Genna Rae McNeil, 40–53. Columbia: University of Missouri Press, 1998.

Hill, Robert A., ed. *The FBI's RACON: Racial Conditions in America during World War II*. Boston: Northeastern University Press, 1995.

Hill, Robert A., ed. *The Marcus Garvey and the Universal Negro Improvement Association Papers*. Vol. 1. Berkeley: University of California Press, 1983.

Hill, Robert A., ed. *The Marcus Garvey and the Universal Negro Improvement Association Papers*. Vol. 2. Berkeley: University of California Press, 1983.

Hill, Robert A., ed. *The Marcus Garvey and the Universal Negro Improvement Association Papers*. Vol. 3. Berkeley: University of California Press, 1984.

Hill, Robert A., ed. *The Marcus Garvey and the Universal Negro Improvement Association Papers*. Vol. 4. Berkeley: University of California Press, 1985.

Hill, Robert A., ed. *The Marcus Garvey and the Universal Negro Improvement Association Papers*. Vol. 5. Berkeley: University of California Press, 1986.

Hill, Robert A., ed. *The Marcus Garvey and the Universal Negro Improvement Association Papers*. Vol. 6. Berkeley: University of California Press, 1989.

Hill, Robert A., ed. *The Marcus Garvey and the Universal Negro Improvement Association Papers*. Vol. 7. Berkeley: University of California Press, 1990.

Hill, Robert A., ed. *The Marcus Garvey and the Universal Negro Improvement Association Papers*. Vol. 8. Berkeley: University of California Press, 1995.

Hill, Robert A., ed. *The Marcus Garvey and the Universal Negro Improvement Association Papers*. Vol. 9. Berkeley: University of California Press, 1995.

Hill, Robert A., ed. *The Marcus Garvey and the Universal Negro Improvement Association Papers*. Vol. 10. Berkeley: University of California Press, 2006.

Hill, Robert A., ed. *The Marcus Garvey and the Universal Negro Improvement Association Papers*. Vol. 11. Durham, NC: Duke University Press, 2011.

Hill, Robert A., ed. *The Marcus Garvey and the Universal Negro Improvement Association Papers*. Vol. 12. Durham, NC: Duke University Press, 2014.

Hill, Robert A., ed. *The Marcus Garvey and the Universal Negro Improvement Association Papers*. Vol. 13. Durham, NC: Duke University Press, 2016.

Hill, Robert A., and Barbara Bair, eds. *Marcus Garvey: Life and Lessons*. Berkeley: University of California Press, 1987.

Hine, Darlene Clark. "Black Migration to the Urban Midwest." In *The New African American Urban History*, edited by Kenneth W. Goings and Raymond Mohl, 240–265. Thousand Oaks, CA: Sage, 1996.

Hine, Darlene Clark. Introduction to *The Black Chicago Renaissance*, edited by Darlene Clarke Hine and John McCluskey Jr., xv–xxxiii. Urbana: University of Illinois Press, 2012.

Hine, Darlene Clark, Trica Danielle Keaton, and Stephen Small, eds. *Black Europe and the African Diaspora*. Urbana: University of Illinois Press, 2009.

Hine, Darlene Clark, and John McCluskey, eds. *The Black Chicago Renaissance*. Urbana: University of Illinois Press, 2012.

Hirsch, Arnold R. *Making of the Second Ghetto: Race and Housing in Chicago, 1940–1960*. Chicago: University of Chicago Press, 1998.

Hochschild, Adam. *King Leopold's Ghost: A Story of Greed, Terror, and Heroism in Colonial Africa*. New York: Houghton Mifflin, 1999.

Hoganson, Kristin L. *The Heartland: An American History*. New York: Penguin, 2019.

Horne, Gerald. *Black and Red: W. E. B. Du Bois and the Afro-American Response to the Cold War*. Albany: State University of New York Press, 1986.

Horne, Gerald. *Black Revolutionary: William Patterson and the Globalization of the African American Freedom Struggle*. Urbana: University of Illinois Press, 2013.

Horne, Gerald. *The Dawning of the Apocalypse: The Roots of Slavery, White Supremacy, Settler Colonialism, and Capitalism in the Long Sixteenth Century*. New York: Monthly Review Press, 2020.

Horne, Gerald. *The Deepest South: The United States, Brazil, and the African Slave Trade*. New York: New York University Press, 2007.

Horne, Gerald. *Facing the Rising Sun: African Americans, Japan, and the Rise of Afro-Asian Solidarity*. New York: New York University Press, 2018.

Horne, Gerald. *Mau Mau in Harlem? The U.S. and the Liberation of Kenya*. New York: Palgrave McMillan, 2009.

Horne, Gerald. *Race War: White Supremacy and the Japanese Attack on the British Empire*. New York: New York University Press, 2004.

Horne, Gerald. *Red Seas: Ferdinand Smith and Radical Black Sailors in the United States and Jamaica*. New York: New York University Press, 2005.

Horne, Gerald. "Toward a Transnational Research Agenda for African American History in the 21st Century." *Journal of African American History* 91, no. 3 (2006): 288–303.

Howard, Ashley M. "Prairie Fires: Urban Rebellions as Black Working Class Politics in Three Midwestern Cities." PhD diss., University of Illinois, 2012.

Howard, Ashley M. "Then the Burnings Began: Omaha's Urban Revolts and the Meaning of Political Violence." *Nebraska History* 98, no. 2 (Summer 2017): 82–97.

Hussain, Khuram. "Born of Our Necessities: 'Muhammad Speaks' Vision of School Reform." In *Critical Perspectives on Black Education: Spirituality, Religion, and Social Justice*, edited by Noelle Witherspoon Arnold, Melanie Brooks, and Bruce Makoto Arnold, 109–40. Charlotte, NC: Information Age, 2014.

Issa, Jahi U. "The Universal Negro Improvement Association in Louisiana: Creating a Provisional Government in Exile." PhD diss., Howard University, 2005.

Jackson, Kenneth T. *The Ku Klux Klan in the City: 1915–1930*. New York: Oxford University Press, 1967.

Jackson, Lynette. *Surfacing Up: Psychiatry and Social Order in Colonial Zimbabwe, 1908–1968*. Ithaca, NY: Cornell University Press, 2005.

Jacobs, Sylvia M. "Three African American Women Missionaries in the Congo, 1887–1899: The Confluence of Race, Culture, Identity, and Nationality." In *Competing Kingdoms: Women, Mission, Nation, and the American Protestant Empire, 1812–1960*, edited by Barbara Reeves-Ellington, Kathryn Kish Sklar, and Connie A. Shemo, 318–41. Durham, NC: Duke University Press, 2010.

James, C. Boyd. *Garvey, Garveyism, and the Antinomies in Black Redemption*. Trenton, NJ: Africa World, 2009.

James, Joy. "Resting in Our Mother's Garden, Battling in Deserts: Black Women's Activism." *Black Scholar* 29 (1999): 3–5.

James, Leslie. "Blood Brothers: Colonialism and Fascism as Relations in the Interwar Caribbean and West Africa." *American Historical Review* 127, no. 2 (June 2022): 634–663.

James, Winston. *Claude McKay: The Making of a Black Bolshevik*. New York: Columbia University Press, 2022.

James, Winston. *Holding Aloft the Banner of Ethiopia: Caribbean Radicalism in Early-Twentieth Century America*. London: Verso, 1998.

Jeffries, Bayyinah S. *A Nation Can Rise No Higher Than Its Women: African American Muslim Women in the Movement for Black Self-Determination, 1950–1975*. Lanham, MD: Lexington, 2014.

Johnson, Christine C. *ABC's of African History*. New York: Vantage, 1971.

Johnson, Christine C. *Muhammad's Children: A Reader*. Self-published, 1963.

Johnson, Eric Eugene. *Ohio's Black Soldiers Who Served in the Civil War*. Bellville: Ohio Genealogical Society, 2014.

Johnson, Gaye Theresa, and Alex Lubin, eds. *Futures of Black Radicalism*. London: Verso, 2017.

Johnson, Michele A., and Funké Aladejebi, eds. *Unsettling The Great White North: Black Canadian History*. Toronto: University of Toronto Press, 2022.

Johnson, Sylvester A. *African American Religions, 1500–2000: Colonialism, Democracy, and Freedom*. New York: Cambridge University Press, 2015.

Johnson, Sylvester A. "Red Squads and Black Radicals: Reading Agency in the Archive." *Journal of the American Academy of Religion* 88, no. 2 (June 2020): 387–406.

Johnson, Walter. *The Broken Heart of America: St. Louis and the Violent History of the United States*. New York: Basic Books, 2020.

Johnson Sirleaf, Ellen. *This Child Will Be Great: Memoir of a Remarkable Life by Africa's First Woman President*. New York: HarperCollins, 2009.

Jolly, Kenneth S. *"By Our Own Strength": William Sherrill, the UNIA, and the Fight for African American Self-Determination in Detroit*. New York: Peter Lang, 2013.

Jones, Claudia. "An End to the Neglect of the Problems of the Negro Woman!" *Political Affairs* 28, no. 6 (June 1949): 51–67.

Jones, Steven Frederick, Sr. "Woodland Park: Newaygo County's Hidden Black Gem." *Michigan History* (March/April 2010): 40–46.

Joseph, Peniel E. *Dark Days, Bright Nights: From Black Power to Barack Obama*. New York: Basic Civitas, 2010.

Joseph, Peniel E. "Introduction: Toward a Historiography of the Black Power Movement." In *The Black Power Movement: Rethinking the Civil Rights–Black Power Era*, edited by Peniel E. Joseph, 1–25. New York: Routledge, 2006.

Joseph, Peniel E. *Waiting 'Til the Midnight Hour: A Narrative History of Black Power in America*. New York: W. W. Norton, 2006.

Joseph-Gabriel, Annette K. *Reimagining Liberation: How Black Women Transformed Citizenship in the French Empire*. Urbana: University of Illinois Press, 2020.

Kaba, Mariame, ed. *We Do This 'Til We Free Us: Abolitionist Organizing and Transforming Justice*. Chicago: Haymarket, 2021.

Kadalie, Modibo M. *Internationalism, Pan-Africanism, and the Struggle of Social Classes*. Savannah, GA: One Quest, 2000.

Katzman, David M. *Before the Ghetto: Black Detroit in the Nineteenth Century*. Urbana: University of Illinois Press, 1972.

Katznelson, Ira. *Fear Itself: The New Deal and the Origins of Our Time*. New York: Liveright, 2013.

Kearney, Reginald. *Solidarity or Sedition? African American Views of the Japanese*. Albany: State University Press of New York, 1998.

Kelley, Robin D. G. "'But a Local Phase of a World Problem': Black History's Global Vision, 1883–1950." *Journal of American History* 86, no. 3 (1999): 1045–77.

Kelley, Robin D. G. Foreword to *Black Marxism: The Making of the Black Radical Tradition*. Rev. 3rd ed., edited by Cedric Robinson, xi–xxxiii. Chapel Hill: University of North Carolina Press, 2021.

Kelley, Robin D. G. *Freedom Dreams: The Black Radical Imagination*. Boston: Beacon, 2002.

Kelley, Robin D. G. *Hammer and Hoe: Alabama Communists during the Great Depression.* Chapel Hill: University of North Carolina Press, 1990.

Kelley, Robin D. G. *Race Rebels: Culture, Politics, and the Black Working Class.* New York: Free Press, 1994.

Kelley, Robin D. G. *Yo' Mama's Disfunktional: Fighting the Cultural Wars in Urban America.* Boston: Beacon, 1997.

King, Martin Luther, Jr. "'The Birth of a New Nation,' Sermon Delivered at Dexter Avenue Baptist Church." [April 7, 1957?] Martin Luther King, Jr. Research and Education Institute, Stanford University, Palo Alto, CA. https://kinginstitute.stanford.edu/king -papers/documents/birth-new-nation-sermon-delivered-dexter-avenue-baptist-church (accessed March 30, 2024).

Kornweibel, Theodore, Jr. *"Seeing Red": Federal Campaigns against Black Militancy, 1919–1925.* Bloomington: Indiana University Press, 1998.

Kurashige, Scott. *The Fifty-Year Rebellion: How the U.S. Political Crisis Began in Detroit.* Berkeley: University of California Press, 2017.

Kusmer, Kenneth L. *A Ghetto Takes Shape: Black Cleveland, 1870–1930.* Urbana: University of Illinois Press, 1976.

Kuumba, M. Bahati. *Gender and Social Movements.* Walnut Creek, CA: Altamira, 2001.

Kwoba, Brian. "Pebbles and Ripples: Hubert Harrison and the Rise of the Garvey Movement." *Journal of African American History* 105, no. 3 (2020): 396–423.

Lambert, Laurie R. *Comrade Sister: Caribbean Feminist Revisions of the Grenada Revolution.* Charlottesville: University of Virginia Press, 2020.

Landing, James E. *Black Judaism: Story of an American Movement.* Durham, NC: Carolina Academic Press, 2002.

Landon, Fred. "Amherstburg, Terminus of the Underground Railroad." *Journal of Negro History* 10, no. 1 (January 1925): 1–9.

Lane, James B. *"City of the Century": A History of Gary, Indiana.* Bloomington: Indiana University Press, 1978.

Lang, Clarence. *Grassroots at the Gateway: Class Politics and Black Freedom Struggle in St. Louis, 1936–75.* Ann Arbor: University of Michigan Press, 2009.

LaRoche, Cheryl Janifer. *Free Black Communities and the Underground Railroad: The Geography of Resistance.* Urbana: University of Illinois Press, 2014.

Larson, Grahame, and Randall Schaetzl. "Origin and Evolution of the Great Lakes." *Journal of Great Lakes Research* 27, no. 4 (2001): 518–46.

Lauck, Jon K., ed. *The Lost Region: Toward a Revival of Midwestern History.* Iowa City: University of Iowa Press, 2013.

Lauck, Jon K. *The Making of the Midwest: Essays on the Formation of Midwestern Identity, 1787–1900.* Hastings, NE: Hastings College Press, 2020.

Lee, Chana Kai. *For Freedom's Sake: The Life of Fannie Lou Hamer.* Urbana: University of Illinois Press, 1999.

Leeds, Asia. "Toward the 'Higher Type of Womanhood': The Gendered Contours of Garveyism and the Making of Redemptive Geographies in Costa Rica, 1922–1941." *Palimpsest: A Journal on Women, Gender, and the Black International* 2, no. 1 (2013): 1–27.

Levine, Lawrence W. *Black Culture and Black Consciousness.* New York: Oxford University Press, 2007.

Levy, Peter B. *The Great Uprising: Race Riots in Urban America during the 1960s*. Cambridge: Cambridge University Press, 2018.

Lewis, David L. *W. E. B. Du Bois: The Fight for Equality and the American Century, 1919–1963*. New York: Henry Holt, 2000.

Lewis, David L. *W. E. B. Du Bois, 1868–1919: Biography of a Race*. New York: Henry Holt, 1994.

Lewis, Robert. *Chicago Made: Factory Networks in the Industrial Metropolis*. Chicago: University of Chicago Press, 2008.

Lieberman, Robbie, and Clarence Lang. "Introduction." In *"Another Side of the Story": Anticommunism and the African American Freedom Movement*, edited by Robbie Lieberman and Clarence Lang, 1–15. New York: Palgrave Macmillan, 2009.

Lincoln, C. Eric. *The Black Muslims in America*. Trenton, NJ: Africa World, 1994.

Lindsay, Lisa A. *Atlantic Bonds: A Nineteenth-Century Odyssey from America to Africa*. Chapel Hill: University of North Carolina Press, 2017.

Lipsitz, George. *A Life in the Struggle: Ivory Perry and the Culture of Opposition*. Philadelphia: Temple University Press, 1988.

Little, Wilfred. "Our Family from the Inside: Growing Up with Malcolm X." *Contributions in Black Studies: A Journal in African and Afro-American Studies* 13 (1995). http://scholarworks.umass.edu/cibs/vol13/iss1/2.10.

Lucander, David. *Winning the War for Democracy: The March on Washington Movement, 1941–1946*. Urbana: University of Illinois Press, 2014.

Madhubuti, Haki R. *Liberation Narratives: New and Collected Poems, 1966–2009*. Chicago: Third World, 2009.

Madhubuti, Haki R. *YellowBlack: The First Twenty-One Years of a Poet's Life*. Chicago: Third World, 2005.

Madison, James H. "The States of the Midwest: An Introduction." In *Heartland: Comparative Histories of the Midwestern States*, edited by James H. Madison, 1–8. Bloomington: Indiana University Press, 1988.

Makalani, Minkah. "Diaspora and the Localities of Race." *Social Text* 27, no. 1 (2009): 1–9.

Makalani, Minkah. *In the Cause of Freedom: Radical Black Internationalism from Harlem to London, 1917–1939*. Chapel Hill: University of North Carolina Press, 2011.

Malcolm X. *The Autobiography of Malcolm X*. New York: Ballantine, 1965.

Malcolm X. "The Ballot or the Bullet, 1964." In *Say It Loud: Great Speeches on Civil Rights and African American Identity*, edited by Catherine Ellis and Stephen Drury Smith, 1–18. New York: New Press, 2010.

Malcolm X. *By Any Means Necessary*. New York: Pathfinder, 1970.

Manalansan, Martin F., IV, Chantal Nadeau, Richard T. Rodríguez, and Siobhan B. Somerville. "Introduction: Queering the Middle." *GLQ: A Journal of Lesbian and Gay Studies* 20, no. 1–2 (2014): 1–12.

Marable, Manning. *Malcolm X: A Life of Reinvention*. New York: Viking, 2011.

Marable, Manning. *Race, Reform, and Rebellion: The Second Reconstruction and Beyond in Black America*. Jackson: University Press of Mississippi, 2007.

Marable, Manning. *W. E. B. Du Bois: Black Radical Democrat*. Boston: Twayne, 1986.

Marable, Manning, and Garrett Felber, eds. *The Portable Malcolm X Reader: A Man Who Stands for Nothing Will Fall for Anything*. New York: Penguin, 2013.

Marano, Carla. "'For the Freedom of the Black People': Case Studies on the Universal Negro Improvement Association in Canada, 1900–1950." PhD diss., University of Waterloo, Ontario, 2018.

Marcus, Bruce, and Michael Taber. *Maurice Bishop Speaks: The Grenada Revolution and Its Overthrow, 1979–1983.* New York: Pathfinder, 1983.

Martin, John Angus. *A–Z of Grenada Heritage.* Oxford: Macmillan Caribbean, 2007.

Martin, John Angus. *Island Caribs and French Settlers in Grenada.* St. George's: Grenada National Museum Press, 2013.

Martin, Tony. *Amy Ashwood Garvey: Pan-Africanist, Feminist, and Mrs. Marcus Garvey No. 1 or, A Tale of Two Amies.* Dover, MA: Majority, 2007.

Martin, Tony. "The Emancipation of a Race Being an Account of the Career and Ideas of Marcus Mosiah Garvey, together with an Examination of Diverse Ideological and Organizational Struggles in Which He Became Involved." PhD diss., Michigan State University, 1973.

Martin, Tony. *Race First: The Ideological and Organizational Struggles of Marcus Garvey and the Universal Negro Improvement Association.* Dover, MA: Majority, 1976.

Maynard, Robyn. *Policing Black Lives: State Violence in Canada from Slavery to the Present.* Halifax: Fernwood, 2017.

Mayor's Interracial Committee (Rev. Reinhold Niebuhr et al., under the direction of Governmental Research, Inc.). *The Negro in Detroit.* Detroit: Detroit Bureau of Governmental Research, 1926.

Mazucci, Liz. "Going Back to Our Own: Interpreting Malcolm X's Transition from 'Black Asiatic' to 'Afro-American.'" *Souls* 7, no. 1 (2005): 66–83.

McDuffie, Erik S. "'Chicago, Garveyism, and the History of the Diasporic Midwest." *African and Black Diaspora: An International Journal* 8, no. 2 (June 2015): 129–45.

McDuffie, Erik S. "The Diasporic Journeys of Louise Little: Grassroots Garveyism, the Midwest, and Community Feminism." *Women, Gender, and Families of Color* 4, no. 2 (Fall 2016): 146–70.

McDuffie, Erik S. "Garveyism in Cleveland, Ohio and the History of the Diasporic Midwest, 1920–1975." *African Identities* 9, no. 2 (May 2011): 163–81.

McDuffie, Erik S. "'I Wanted a Communist Philosophy, but I Wanted a Chance to Organize Our People': The Diasporic Radicalism of Queen Mother Moore and the Origins of Black Power." *African and Black Diaspora: An International Journal* 3, no. 2 (2010): 181–95.

McDuffie, Erik S. "'A New Day Has Dawned for the UNIA': Garveyism, the Diasporic Midwest, and West Africa, 1949–1957." *Journal of West African History* 2, no. 1 (Spring 2016): 73–114.

McDuffie, Erik S. "A 'New Freedom Movement of Negro Women': Sojourning for Truth, Justice, and Human Rights during the Early Cold War." *Radical History Review* 101 (Spring 2008): 81–106.

McDuffie, Erik S. "'The Second Battle for Africa Has Begun': Rev. Clarence W. Harding Jr., Garveyism, Liberia, and the Diasporic Midwest, 1966–1978." In *Global Garveyism*, edited by Ronald J. Stephens and Adam Ewing, 89–113. Gainesville: University Press of Florida, 2019.

McDuffie, Erik S. *Sojourning for Freedom: Black Women, American Communism, and the Making of Black Left Feminism*. Durham, NC: Duke University Press, 2011.

McDuffie, Erik S. and Komozi Woodard. "'If You're in a Country That's Progressive, the Woman Is Progressive': Black Women Radicals and the Making of the Politics and Legacy of Malcolm X." *Biography* 36, no. 3 (Summer 2013): 507–39.

McKinnis, Leonard. *The Black Coptic Church: Race and Imagination in a New Religion*. New York: New York University Press, 2023.

McKittrick, Katherine, and Clyde Woods, eds. *Black Geographies and the Politics of Place*. Cambridge, MA: South End, 2007.

McLaughlin, Malcolm. "Reconsidering the East St. Louis Race Riot of 1917." *International Review of Social History* 47, no. 2 (August 2002): 187–212.

McPherson, James M. *The Negro's Civil War: How American Blacks Felt and Acted during the War for the Union*. New York: Ballantine, 1965.

Menard, Orville D. "Lest We Forget: The Lynching of Will Brown, Omaha's 1919 Race Riot." *Nebraska History* 91 (2010): 152–165.

Meriwether, James H. *Proudly We Can Be Africans: Black Americans and Africa, 1935–1961*. Chapel Hill: University of North Carolina Press, 2003.

Meyer, Douglas K. "Evolution of a Permanent Negro Community in Lansing." *Michigan History* (Summer 1971): 141–154.

Middleton, Stephen. *The Black Laws in the Old Northwest: A Documentary History*. Westport, CT: Greenwood, 1993.

Miles, Tiya. *The Dawn of Detroit: A Chronicle of Slavery and Freedom in the City of the Straits*. New York: New Press, 2017.

Mills, Brandon. "'The United States of Africa': Liberian Independence and the Contested Meaning of a Black Republic." *Journal of the Early Republic* 34, no. 1 (Spring 2014): 79–107.

Milne, June. *Kwame Nkrumah: The Conakry Years: His Life and Letters*. London: Panaf, 1990.

Minutes and Address of the Convention of the Colored Citizens of Ohio. Oberlin, OH: J. M. Fitch's Power Press, 1849.

Miraftab, Faranak. *Global Heartland: Displaced Labor, Transnational Lives, and Local Placemaking*. Bloomington: Indiana University Press, 2016.

Mohammed, Kimathi. *Organization and Spontaneity: The Theory of the Vanguard Party and Its Application to the Black Movement in the U.S. Today*. Atlanta: On Our Own Authority!, 2013.

Mohammed, Kimathi, and Maina Kinyatti. "Tunataka Uhura Na Mashamba: Freedom and Land." *Black World / Negro Digest* 19, no. 10 (August 1970): 22, 94–98.

Mohl, Raymond A. "The Evolution of Racism in an Industrial City, 1906–1940: A Case Study of Gary, Indiana." *Journal of Negro History* 59, no. 1 (January 1974): 51–64.

Moore, Audley. *Why Reparations? "Reparations Is the Battle Cry for the Economic and Social Freedom of More Than 25 Million Descendants of American Slaves."* Los Angeles: Reparations Committee for the Descendants of American Slaves, [1963?].

Moore, Leonard. *Carl B. Stokes and the Rise of Black Political Power*. Urbana: University of Illinois Press, 2003.

Morgan, Jennifer L. "Archives and Histories of Racial Capitalism: An Afterword." *Social Text* 33, no. 4 (2015): 153–161.

Morrissey, Robert Michael. *Empire by Collaboration: Indians, Colonists, and Governments in Colonial Illinois Country*. Philadelphia: University of Pennsylvania Press, 2015.

Moses, Wilson Jeremiah. *Afrotopia: The Roots of African American Popular History*. Cambridge: Cambridge University Press, 1998.

Moses, Wilson Jeremiah, ed. *Classical Black Nationalism from the American Revolution to Marcus Garvey*. New York: New York University Press, 1996.

Moses, Wilson Jeremiah. *The Golden Age of Black Nationalism, 1850–1925*. New York: Oxford University Press, 1978.

"Movement for Justice in Africa (MOJA)." In *Historical Dictionary of Liberia*, edited by D. Elwood Dunn, Amos J. Beyan, and Carl Patrick Burrowes, 237–238. Lanham, MD: Scarecrow, 2000.

Muhammad, Elijah. *The Message to the Blackman in America*. Newport News, VA: United Brothers Communications Systems, 1965.

Mullen, Bill V. *Afro-Orientalism*. Minneapolis: University of Minnesota Press, 2004.

Murphy, Lucy Eldersveld. *Great Lakes Creoles: A French-Indian Community on the Northern Borderlands, Prairie du Chien, 1750–1860*. New York: Cambridge University Press, 2014.

Negro Commission, National Committee of the Communist Party, USA. *Is Japan the Champion of the Colored Races? The Negro's Stake in Democracy*. New York: Workers Library, 1938.

Nevin, Timothy D. L. "In Search of the Historical Madam Suakoko: Liberia's Renowned Female Kpelle Chief." *Journal of West Africa* 3, no. 2 (2017): 1–38.

Nkrumah, Kwame. *Ghana: The Autobiography of Kwame Nkrumah*. New York: International Publishers, 1957.

Nkrumah, Kwame. *Neocolonialism: The Last State of Imperialism*. New York: International Publishers, 1965.

Noble, Frederick Perry. *The Chicago Congress on Africa*. Chicago: Congress on Africa, 1893.

Norrell, Robert J. *Alex Haley and the Books That Changed a Nation*. New York: St. Martin's, 2015.

Nyerere, Julius K. *Ujamaa: Essays on Socialism*. London: Oxford University Press, 1968.

Odamtten, Harry Nii. *Edward W. Blyden's Intellectual Transformations: Afropublicanism, Pan-Africanism, Islam, and the Indigenous West African Church*. East Lansing: Michigan State University Press, 2019.

Okonkwo, R. L. "The Garvey Movement in British West Africa." *Journal of African History* 21, no. 1 (1980): 105–17.

Olson, Liesl. *Chicago Renaissance: Literature and Art in the Midwest Metropolis*. New Haven, CT: Yale University Press, 2017.

Onaci, Edward. *Free the Land: The Republic of New Afrika and the Pursuit of a Black Nation-State*. Chapel Hill: University of North Carolina Press, 2020.

Opie, Frederick D. "Garveyism and Labor Organization on the Caribbean Coast of Guatemala." *Journal of African American History* 94, no. 2 (2009): 153–71.

Osofsky, Gilbert. *Harlem: The Making of a Ghetto: Negro New York, 1890–1930*. New York: Harper and Row, 1966.

Ottley, Roi. *"New World A-Coming": Inside Black America*. Boston: Houghton Mifflin, 1943.

"Outline for Petition to the United Nations Charging Genocide against 22 Million Black Americans." In *Malcolm X: The Man and His Times*, edited by John Henrik Clarke, 343–351. Trenton, NJ: African New World, 1990.

Padmore, George. *Pan-Africanism or Communism?* Garden City, NY: Anchor, 1972.

Painter, Nell Irvin. *Exodusters: Black Migration to Kansas after Reconstruction*. New York: Knopf, 1977.

Palella, Andrew G. "The Black Legion: J. Edgar Hoover and Fascism in the Depression Era." *Journal for the Study of Radicalism* 12, no. 2 (Fall 2018): 81–106.

Parish, Ryan M., and Charles H. McNutt. *Cahokia in Context: Hegemony and Diaspora*. Gainesville: University of Florida Press, 2020.

Patterson, Tiffany Ruby, and Robin D. G. Kelley. "Unfinished Migrations: Reflections on the African Diaspora and the Making of the Modern World." *African Studies Review* 43, no. 1 (April 2001): 11–45.

Payne, Les, and Tamara Payne. *The Dead Are Arising: The Life of Malcolm X*. New York: Liveright, 2020.

Pérez-Stable, Marifeli. *The Cuban Revolution: Origins, Course, and Legacy*. New York: Oxford University Press, 1999.

Perry, Bruce. *Malcolm: The Life of a Man Who Changed Black America*. New York: Station Hill, 1991.

Perry, Bruce, ed. *Malcolm X: The Last Speeches*. New York: Pathfinder, 1989.

Perry, Jeffrey B. *Hubert Harrison: The Struggle for Equality, 1918–1927*. New York: Columbia University Press, 2021.

Perry, Jeffrey B. *Hubert Harrison: The Voice of Harlem Radicalism, 1883–1918*. New York: Columbia University Press, 2009.

Perry, Jeffrey B., ed. *A Hubert Harrison Reader*. Middletown, CT: Wesleyan University Press, 2001.

Pfeifer, Michael J., ed. "Introduction." In *Lynching beyond Dixie: American Mob Violence Outside the South*, edited by Michael J. Pfeifer, 1–17. Urbana: University of Illinois Press, 2013.

Phillips, Kimberley. *AlabamaNorth: African-American Migrants, Community, and Working-Class Activism in Cleveland, 1915–1945*. Urbana: University of Illinois Press, 1999.

Pile, Steve, and Michael Keith, eds. *Geographies of Resistance*. New York: Routledge, 1997.

Plummer, Brenda Gayle. *In Search of Power: African Americans in the Era of Decolonization, 1956–1974*. Cambridge: Cambridge University Press, 2013.

Plummer, Brenda Gayle. *Rising Wind: Black Americans and U.S. Foreign Affairs, 1935–1960*. Chapel Hill: University of North Carolina Press, 1996.

Power-Greene, Ousmane K. *Against Wind and Tide: The African American Struggle against the Colonization Movement*. New York: New York University Press, 2014.

Prashad, Vijay. *The Darker Nations: A People's History of the Third World*. New York: New Press, 2007.

Prashad, Vijay. *The Poorer Nations: A Possible History of the Global South*. London: Verso, 2012.

Proceedings of the National Emigration Convention of Colored People Held at Cleveland, Ohio, on Thursday, Friday and Saturday, the 24th, 25th and 26th of August, 1854. Pittsburgh: A. A. Anderson, 1854.

Puri, Shalini. *The Grenada Revolution in the Caribbean Present: Operation Urgent Memory*. New York: Macmillan, 2014.

Putnam, Lara. *Radical Moves: Caribbean Migrants and the Politics of Race in the Jazz Age*. Chapel Hill: University of North Carolina Press, 2013.

Rabaka, Reiland. "Introduction: On the Intellectual Elasticity and Political Plurality of Pan-Africanism." In *The Routledge Handbook of Pan-Africanism*, edited by Reiland Rabaka, 1–32. London: Routledge, 2020.

Ranger, Terence. *Bulawayo Burning: The Social History of a Southern African City, 1893–1960*. Woodbridge, UK: James Currey, 2010.

Ransby, Barbara. *Ella Baker and the Black Freedom Movement: A Radical Democratic Vision*. Chapel Hill: University of North Carolina Press, 2003.

Ransby, Barbara. *Eslanda: The Large and Unconventional Life of Mrs. Paul Robeson*. New Haven, CT: Yale University Press, 2013.

Ransby, Barbara. *Making All Black Lives Matter: Reimagining Freedom in the 21st Century*. Berkeley: University of California Press, 2018.

Ray, Louis. L. "Geomorphology and Quaternary Geology of the Glaciated Ohio River Valley; A Reconnaissance Study." Washington: United States Government Printing Office, 1974, 1–75.

Reddock, Rhoda. "The First Mrs. Garvey: Pan-Africanism and Feminism in the Early 20th Century British Colonial Caribbean." *Feminist Africa* 19 (2014): 58–77.

Redmond, Shana L. *Anthem: Social Movements and the Sound of Solidarity in the African Diaspora*. New York: New York University Press, 2014.

Redmond, Shana L. "Citizens of Sound: Negotiations of Race and Diaspora in the Anthems of the UNIA and NAACP." *African and Black Diaspora: An International Journal* 4, no. 1 (January 2011): 19–39.

Reed, Christopher Robert. *"All the World Is Here!" The Black Presence at White City*. Bloomington: Indiana University Press, 2000.

Reed, Christopher Robert. *Black Chicago's First Century*. Vol. 1, *1833–1900*. Columbia: University of Missouri Press, 2005.

Reed, Christopher Robert. *The Rise of Chicago's Black Metropolis*. Urbana: University of Chicago Press, 2011.

Reiss, Suzanna. *We Sell Drugs: The Alchemy of U.S. Empire*. Berkeley: University of California Press, 2014.

"The Revolution in Grenada: An Interview with Maurice Bishop." *Black Scholar* 11, no. 3 (January–February 1980): 50–58.

Richter, Daniel K. *Before the Revolution: America's Ancient Pasts*. Cambridge, MA: Harvard University Press, 2011.

Rickford, Russell J. *Betty Shabazz: A Remarkable Story of Survival and Faith before and after Malcolm X*. Naperville, IL: Sourcebook, 2003.

Robb, Fredric H. *Intercollegian Wonder Book, or, 1779—the Negro in Chicago—1927*. Chicago: Washington Intercollegiate Club of Chicago, 1927.

Robeson, Eslanda Goode. *African Journey*. New York: John Day, 1945.

Robinson, Cedric J. *Black Marxism: The Making of the Black Radical Tradition*. London: Zed, 1983.

Robinson, Cedric J. *Black Marxism: The Making of the Black Radical Tradition*. Rev. ed. Chapel Hill: University of North Carolina Press, 2000.

Robinson, Cedric J. *Black Marxism: The Making of the Black Radical Tradition*. Rev. 3rd ed. Chapel Hill: University of North Carolina Press, 2021.

Rocksborough-Smith, Ian. *Black Public History in Chicago: Civil Rights Activism from World War II into the Cold War*. Urbana: University of Illinois Press, 2018.

Rolinson, Mary G. *Grassroots Garveyism: The Universal Negro Improvement Association in the Rural South, 1920–1927*. Chapel Hill: University of North Carolina Press, 2007.

Roose, Holly M. *Black Star Rising: Garveyism in the West*. Lubbock: Texas Tech University Press, 2022.

Rosa, Andrew J. "The Roots and Routes of 'Imperium in Imperio': St. Clair Drake, the Formative Years." *American Studies* 52, no. 1 (2012): 49–75.

Rose, William Ganson. *Cleveland: The Making of a City*. Cleveland: World Publishing, 1950.

Runstedtler, Theresa. *Jack Johnson: Rebel Sojourner*. Berkeley: University of California Press, 2012.

Russell, Jessica, with Hilda Little and Steve Jones Sr. *The Life of Louise Norton Little: An Extraordinary Woman: Mother of Malcolm X and His 7 Siblings*. Self-published, 2021.

Rydell, Robert W., ed. *The Reason Why the Colored American Is Not in the World's Columbian Exposition*. Urbana: University of Illinois Press, 1999.

Salaita, Steven. *Israel's Dead Soul*. Philadelphia: Temple University Press, 2011.

Saler, Bethel. *The Settlers' Empire: Colonialism and State Formation in America's Old Northwest*. Philadelphia: University of Pennsylvania Press, 2015.

Sarmiento, Thomas Xavier, M. Bianet Castellanos, and Christopher Perreira. "Introduction: Unsettling Global Midwests." *American Studies* 62, no. 3 (Fall 2023): 7–19.

Sawyer, Amos. "Social Stratification and Orientation toward National Development: A Case of Liberia." PhD diss., Northwestern University, 1973.

Sawyer, Amos. *What Is the Total Political Involvement in Liberia?* Monrovia, Liberia: Movement for Justice for Africa, 1979.

"Sawyer, Amos Claudius." In *Historical Dictionary of Liberia*, edited by D. Elwood Dunn, Amos J. Beyan, and Carl Patrick Burrowes, 293. Lanham, MD: Scarecrow, 2000.

Schwar, Harriet Dashiell, and Stanley Shaloff, eds. *Foreign Relations of the United States, 1958–1960*. Vol. 14. Washington, DC: United States Government Printing Office, 1992.

Scott, David. *Omens of Adversity: Tragedy, Time, Memory, Justice*. Durham, NC: Duke University Press, 2014.

Scott, Julius S. *The Common Wind: Afro-American Currents in the Age of the Haitian Revolution*. London: Verso, 2018.

Scott, William R. *The Sons of Sheba's Race: African-Americans and the Italo-Ethiopian War, 1935–1941*. Bloomington: Indiana University Press, 1993.

Seawell, Stephanie L. "The Black Freedom Movement and Community Planning in Urban Parks in Cleveland, Ohio, 1945–1977." PhD diss., University of Illinois at Urbana-Champaign, 2014.

Sernett, Milton C. *Harriet Tubman: Myth, Memory, and History*. Durham, NC: Duke University Press, 2007.

Shabazz, Betty. "The Legacy of My Husband." *Ebony*, June 1969, 172–82.

Shabazz, Betty, and Susan L. Taylor. "Loving and Losing Malcolm." *Essence* 22, no. 10 (February 1992): 50.

Shabazz, Ilyasah, and Kim McLarin. *Growing Up X: A Memoir by the Daughter of Malcolm X.* New York: One World, 2002.

Shabazz, Rashad. *Spatializing Blackness: Architectures of Confinement and Black Masculinity in Chicago.* Urbana: University of Illinois Press, 2015.

Shepperson, George. "Pan-Africanism and 'Pan-Africanism': Some Historical Notes." *Phylon* 23, no. 4 (1962): 346–358.

Sherwood, Marika. *Malcolm X: Visits Abroad (April 1964–February 1965).* Hollywood, CA: Tsehai, 2011.

Singh, Nikhil Pal. *Black Is a Country: Race and the Unfinished Struggle for Democracy.* Cambridge, MA: Harvard University Press, 2004.

Sleeper-Smith, Susan. *Indigenous Prosperity and American Conquest: Indian Women of the Ohio River Valley, 1690–1792.* Chapel Hill: University of North Carolina Press, 2019.

Smethurst, James Edward. *The Black Arts Movement: Literary Nationalism in the 1960s and 1970s.* Chapel Hill: University of North Carolina Press, 2005.

Smith, Andrea. *Conquest: Sexual Violence and American Indian Genocide.* Boston: South End, 2005.

Smith, Barbara Hughes. "Worship Way Stations in Detroit." In *A Fluid Frontier: Slavery, Resistance, and the Underground Railroad in the Detroit River Borderland*, edited by Karolyn Smardz Frost and Veta Smith Tucker, 103–19. Detroit: Wayne State University Press, 2016.

Smith, Bobby J., II. *Food Power Politics: The Food Story of the Mississippi Civil Rights Movement.* Chapel Hill: University of North Carolina Press, 2023.

Smith-Irvin, Jeannette. *Marcus Garvey's Footsoldiers of the Universal Negro Improvement Association.* Trenton, NJ: Africa World, 1989.

Spadey, James G. *Marcus Garvey: Jazz, Reggae, Hip Hop, and the African Diaspora.* Philadelphia: Marcus Garvey Foundation, 2011.

Spadey, James G., and Giles R. Wright. "Jean Harvey Slappy's Philosophy and the Tradition of Marcus Garvey and Thomas W. Harvey." *American Philosophical Association Newsletters* 2, no. 2 (Spring 2003): 57–61.

Spencer, Robyn C. *The Revolution Has Come: Black Power, Gender, and the Black Panther Party in Oakland.* Durham, NC: Duke University Press, 2016.

Springer, Kimberly. *Living for the Revolution: Black Feminist Organizations, 1968–1980.* Durham, NC: Duke University Press, 2005.

Stanford, Maxwell C. "Revolutionary Action Movement (RAM): A Case Study of an Urban Revolutionary Movement in Western Capitalist Society." Master's thesis, Atlanta University, 1986.

Stanford, Maxwell C. "Towards Revolutionary Action Movement Manifesto." In *Black Nationalism in America*, edited by John H. Bracey Jr. and August Meier and Elliot Rudwick, 508–13. Indianapolis: Macmillan, 1970.

Stein, Judith. *The World of Marcus Garvey: Race and Class in Modern Society.* Baton Rouge: Louisiana State University Press, 1986.

Stephens, Michelle A. *Black Empire: The Masculine Global Imaginary of Caribbean Intellectuals in the United States, 1914–1962*. Durham, NC: Duke University Press, 2005.

Stephens, Ronald J. "Marcus M. Garvey and Joseph Craigen: Collaborations and Conflicts." In *Global Garveyism*, edited by Ronald J. Stephens and Adam Ewing, 114–38. Gainesville: University Press of Florida, 2019.

Stephens, Ronald J., and Adam Ewing, eds. *Global Garveyism*. Gainesville: University Press of Florida, 2019.

Storch, Randi. *Red Chicago: American Communism at Its Grassroots, 1928–1935*. Urbana: University of Illinois Press, 2009.

Strickland, William, and Cheryll Greene. *Malcolm X: Make It Plain*. New York: Viking, 1994.

Stuckey, Sterling. *Slave Culture: Nationalist Theory and the Foundations of Black America*. 2nd ed. New York: Oxford University Press, 2013.

Sugrue, Thomas. *The Origins of the Urban Crisis: Race and Inequality in Postwar Detroit*. Princeton, NJ: Princeton University Press, 2014.

Sulik, Stephanie Theresa. "Waving the Red, Black, and Green: The Local and Global Vision of the Universal Negro Improvement Association in Akron and Barberton, Ohio." PhD diss., University of Texas at Arlington, 2020.

Summers, Martin. *Madness in the City of Magnificent Intentions: A History of Race and Mental Illness in the Nation's Capital*. New York: Oxford University Press, 2019.

Sundiata, Ibrahim. *Brothers and Strangers: Black Zion, Black Slavery, 1914–1940*. Durham, NC: Duke University Press, 2004.

Swan, Quito. *Pasifika Black: Oceania, Anti-colonialism, and the African World*. New York: New York University Press, 2022.

Talton, Benjamin. *In This Land of Plenty: Mickey Leland and Africa in American Politics*. Philadelphia: University of Pennsylvania Press, 2019.

Tamale, Sylvia. "Researching and Theorising Sexualities in Africa." In *African Sexualities: A Reader*, edited by Sylvia Tamale, 11–36. Cape Town: Pambazuka, 2011.

Taylor, Keeanga-Yamahtta. *From #Blacklivesmatter to Black Liberation*. Chicago: Haymarket, 2016.

Taylor, Keeanga-Yamahtta. *Race for Profit: How Banks and the Real Estate Industry Undermined Black Homeownership*. Chapel Hill: University of North Carolina Press, 2019.

Taylor, Nikki M. *Driven toward Madness: The Fugitive Slave Margaret Garner and the Tragedy on the Ohio*. Athens: Ohio University Press, 2016.

Taylor, Nikki M. *Frontiers of Freedom: Cincinnati's Black Community, 1802–1868*. Columbus: Ohio University Press, 2005.

Taylor, Quintard. *In Search of the Racial Frontier: African Americans in the American West*. New York: W. W. Norton, 1998.

Taylor, Ula Y. *The Promise of Patriarchy: Women and the Nation of Islam*. Chapel Hill: University of North Carolina Press, 2017.

Taylor, Ula Y. *The Veiled Garvey: The Life and Times of Amy Jacques Garvey*. Chapel Hill: University of North Carolina Press, 2002.

Theoharis, Jeanne. *The Rebellious Life of Mrs. Rosa Parks*. Boston: Beacon, 2013.

Thomas, Darryl C. "Cedric J. Robinson's Mediation on Malcolm X's Black Internationalism and the Future of the Black Radical Tradition." In *Futures of Black Radicalism*, edited by Gaye Theresa Johnson and Alex Lubin, 148–70. London, Verso, 2017.

Thomas, Richard W. *Life for Us Is What We Make It: Building Black Community in Detroit, 1915–1945*. Bloomington: Indiana University Press, 1992.

Thompson, Era Bell. *Africa: Land of My Fathers*. Garden City, NY: Doubleday, 1954.

Thompson, Heather Ann. *Whose Detroit? Politics, Labor, and Race in a Modern American City*. Ithaca: Cornell University Press, 2001.

Thompson, Robert Farris. *Flash of the Spirit: African and Afro-American Art and Philosophy*. New York: Vintage, 1983.

Tibebu, Teshale. *Edward Wilmot Blyden and the Racial Nationalist Imagination*. Rochester, NY: University of Rochester Press, 2012.

Tinson, Christopher M. *Radical Intellect: Liberator Magazine and Black Activism in the 1960s*. Chapel Hill: University of North Carolina Press, 2017.

Tolbert, Emory J. *The UNIA and Black Los Angeles: Ideology and Community in the American Garvey Movement*. Los Angeles: Center for Afro-American Studies, 1980.

Trotter, Joe William, Jr. *Black Milwaukee: The Making of an Industrial Proletariat, 1915–45*. 2nd ed. Urbana: University of Illinois Press, 2007.

Trotter, Joe William, Jr. *River Jordan: African American Life in the Ohio Valley*. Lexington: University Press of Kentucky, 1998.

Trotter, Joseph A. "Cahokia: Urbanization, Metabolism, and Collapse." *Frontiers in Sustainable Cities* 1 (December 2019): 1–16.

Trouillot, Michel-Rolph. *Silencing the Past: Power and the Production of History*. Boston: Beacon, 1995.

Trubek, Anne, ed. *Voices from the Rust Belt*. New York: Picador, 2018.

Tubbs, Anna Malaika. *The Three Mothers: How the Mothers of Martin Luther King, Jr., Malcolm X, and James Baldwin Shaped a Nation*. New York: Flatiron, 2021.

Turner, Richard Brent. *Islam in the African-American Experience*. 2nd ed. Bloomington: Indiana University Press, 2003.

Tuttle, William M., Jr. *Race Riot: Chicago in the Red Summer of 1919*. New York: Atheneum, 1970.

Ullman, Victor. *Martin R. Delany: The Beginnings of Black Nationalism*. Boston: Beacon, 1971.

Umoja, Akinyele Omowale. *We Will Shoot Back: Armed Resistance in the Mississippi Freedom Movement*. New York: New York University Press, 2013.

Umoren, Imaobong D. *Race Women Internationalists: Activist-Intellectuals and Global Freedom Struggles*. Berkeley: University of California Press, 2018.

Vance, J. D. *Hillbilly Elegy: A Memoir of a Family and Culture in Crisis*. New York: Harper, 2016.

Vinson, Robert Trent. *The Americans Are Coming! Dreams of African American Liberation in Segregationist South Africa*. Athens: Ohio University Press, 2012.

Von Eschen, Penny M. *Race against Empire: Black Americans and Anticolonialism, 1937–1957*. Ithaca, NY: Cornell University Press, 1997.

Wahab, Hanif. *I Have the Honor of Being*. Self-published, 2015.

Ward, Alonzo M. "The Specter of Black Labor: African American Workers in Illinois before the Great Migration, 1847–1910." PhD diss., University of Illinois at Urbana-Champaign, 2016.

Ward, Stephen M. *In Love and Struggle: The Revolutionary Lives of James and Grace Lee Boggs.* Chapel Hill: University of North Carolina Press, 2016.

Warren, Donald I. *Radio Priest: Charles Coughlin, the Father of Hate Radio.* New York: Free Press, 1996.

Watkins-Owens, Irma. *Blood Relations: Caribbean Immigrants and the Harlem Community, 1900–1930.* Bloomington: Indiana University Press, 1996.

Weems, Robert E, Jr. and Jason P. Chambers, eds. Introduction to *Building the Black Metropolis: African American Entrepreneurship in Chicago*, edited by Robert E. Weems Jr. and Jason P. Chambers, 1–26. Urbana: University of Illinois Press, 2017.

Weisenfeld, Judith. *New World A-Coming: Black Religion and Racial Identity during the Great Migration.* New York: New York University Press, 2016.

West, Michael O. "Decolonization, Desegregation, and Black Power: Garveyism in Another Era." In *Global Garveyism*, edited by Ronald J. Stephens and Adam Ewing, 265–286. Gainesville: University Press of Florida, 2019.

West, Michael O. "Garveyism Root and Branch: From the Age of Revolution to the Onset of Black Power." In *Global Garveyism*, edited by Ronald J. Stephens and Adam Ewing, 15–58. Gainesville: University Press of Florida, 2019.

West, Michael, and William G. Martin. "From Toussaint to Tupac: Contours of the Black International." In *From Toussaint to Tupac: The Black International since the Age of Revolution*, edited by Michael O. West, William G. Martin, and Fanon Che Wilkins, 1–44. Chapel Hill: University of North Carolina Press, 2009.

Westad, Odd Arne. *The Global Cold War: Third World Interventions and the Making of Our Times.* Cambridge: Cambridge University Press, 2005.

White, Deborah Gray. *Too Heavy a Load: Black Women in Defense of Themselves.* New York: W. W. Norton, 1999.

White, E. Frances. "Africa on My Mind: Gender, Counter Discourse and African-American Nationalism." *Journal of Women's History* 2, no. 1 (Spring 1990): 73–97.

White, Monica M. *Freedom Farmers: Agricultural Resistance and the Black Freedom Movement.* Chapel Hill: University of North Carolina Press, 2018.

White, Richard. *The Middle Ground: Indians, Empires, and Republics in the Great Lakes Region, 1650–1815.* New York: Cambridge University Press, 2011.

Widick, B. J. *Detroit: City of Race and Class Violence.* Detroit: Wayne State University, 1989.

Wiese, Andrew. "Robbins, IL," *Encyclopedia of Chicago*, http://encyclopedia .chicagohistory.org/pages/1083.html (accessed May 28, 2021).

Williams, Dorothy W. *Blacks in Montreal, 1628–1986: An Urban Demography.* Cowansville, Quebec: Les Éditions Yvon Blais, 1989.

Williams, Eric. *Capitalism and Slavery.* London: Andre Deutsch, 1964.

Williams, Jakobi S. *From the Bullet to the Ballot: The Illinois Chapter of the Black Panther Party and Racial Coalition Politics in Chicago.* Chapel Hill: University of North Carolina Press, 2013.

Williams, Rhonda Y. *Concrete Demands: The Search for Black Power in the 20th Century.* New York: Routledge, 2015.

Williams, Yohuru. "'Give Them a Cause to Die For': The Black Panther Party in Milwaukee, 1969–77." In *Liberated Territory: Untold Local Perspectives on the Black Panther Party,* edited by Yohuru Williams and Jama Lazerow, 232–64. Durham, NC: Duke University Press, 2008.

Williamson, Joy Ann. *Black Power on Campus: The University of Illinois, 1965–1975.* Urbana: University of Illinois Press, 2003.

Williamson, Terrion L., ed. *Black in the Middle: An Anthology of the Black Midwest.* Cleveland: Belt, 2020.

Winslow, Barbara. *Shirley Chisholm: Catalyst for Change, 1926–2005.* Boulder, CO: Westview Press, 2014.

Wolcott, Victoria W. "Defending the Home: Ossian Sweet and the Struggle against Segregation in 1920s Detroit." *OAH Magazine of History* 7, no. 4 (1993): 23–27.

Wolcott, Victoria W. *Remaking Respectability: African American Women in Interwar Detroit.* Chapel Hill: University of North Carolina Press, 2001.

Woo, Jewon. "Deleted Name: But Indelible Body; Black Women at the Colored Conventions in Antebellum Ohio." In *The Colored Conventions Movement: Black Organizing in the Nineteenth Century,* edited by P. Gabrielle Foreman, Jim Casey, and Sarah Lynn Patterson, 179–92. Chapel Hill: University of North Carolina Press, 2021.

Woodard, Komozi. *A Nation within a Nation: Amiri Baraka (LeRoi Jones) and Black Power Politics.* Chapel Hill: University of North Carolina Press, 1999.

Woodruff, Nan Elizabeth. *American Congo: The African American Freedom Struggle in the Delta.* Chapel Hill: University of North Carolina Press, 2012.

Work, Monroe N. *Negro Year Book, 1921–1922.* Tuskegee, AL: Negro Year, 1922.

Wright, Richard. *The Color Curtain: A Report on the Bandung Conference.* Jackson: University Press of Mississippi, 1994.

Writers' Program, Works Project Administration in the State of Nebraska. *The Negroes of Nebraska.* Lincoln, NE: Woodruff, 1940.

Young, Jasmine. "Detroit's Red: Black Radical Detroit and the Political Development of Malcolm." *Souls* 12, no. 1 (2010): 14–31.

Zeleza, Paul Tiyambe. "Rewriting the African Diaspora: Beyond the Black Atlantic." *African Affairs* 104, no. 414 (2005): 35–68.

nium, 285–91; organizational history, 69–80; Philadelphia move by, 188; records of, 29, 31; resurgence in Black Power era, 245–50; resurgence of, 149–53; Sherrill and, 89–90; splits in, 118; state repression and, 161–62; street parades and, 87; surveillance of, 74–75; Unification Council, 247, 249; UN inaugural conference and, 171; women and, 289

Universal Negro Improvement Association and African Communities League, 118

UOI, 222–23

Up from Slavery (Washington), 70

Urban League, 72

US Black Freedom Movement, 169–70, 175, 178–79, 200, 216–18, 242

US Constitution: fugitive slave clause of, 44; Thirteenth Amendment, 45

US Nazi Party, 10, 30

US Postal Service, 75

US Supreme Court, 52, 57

Vance, J. D., 13

Van Pelt, Louis, 88

Voting Rights Act (1965), 218

Waddell, Ethel, 140

Wahab, Hanif, 189

Walk to Freedom, 227

Wallace, William A., 121–22

Wallace-Johnson, I. T. A., 119

Ware, William, 90–91, 118

War on Terror, 292

Washington, Booker T., 19, 60, 63, 70, 142

Washington, Charles, 239

Watson, John, 229

Weaks, Dorothy, xiv

Weisenfeld, Judith, 103

Wells, Ida B., 19, 58–62; Garvey, Marcus, and, 88

West, Michael O., 17

West Coast, Garveyism in, 81

Western Indian (newspaper), 101

West Indian Federation, 101, 219

Westside News (newspaper), 265

"What We Believe" (Garvey, Marcus), 78

"When You Died" (Johnson, C.), 277

White, E. Frances, 141

White, Elinor, 27, 115–16, 151

White, Walter, 171, 179

White America (Cox), 79, 89

white mob violence, 63

white supremacists, 10, 79, 100, 161, 173; Liberia and, 20; NOI and, 225–26

Wilfred X, 228, 241–42

Williams, Fannie Barrier, 58

Williams, Robert F., 217, 232

Williams, Yohuru, 263

Williamson, Joy Ann, 265

Wilson, Christine, 238

Wilson, Terance, 31, 33, 93, 301

Wilson, Vernon, 245, 247

Windom, Alice, 25, 27, 242; *Black Nationalism* and, 235–36; Black womanhood and, 237; Ghana and, 236–38; Malcolm X and, 238

Windsor, Ontario, 121

women: Black internationalism scholarship and, 25; in Black Panther Party, 343n40; Black Power movement and, 223–24; heartland Garveyite activists, 245–50; knowledge production and, 236, 238; MOJA and, 259; *Muhammad Speaks* and, 222; NOI and, 222, 225; UNIA and, 289

Women's Party, 180

women's protection agencies, 64

Woodward, Yvonne, 165, 239, 241, 295–96

World Community of al-Islam in the West, 274

worldmaking, 17, 308n54

World's Columbian Exposition, 57–63

World War I, 63

World Wide Friends of Africa. *See* House of Knowledge

Wright, Cleo, 154, 162

Wright, Richard, 18, 179, 230

Yakini, Malik, 292

Yergan, Max, 150

Young, Coleman, xiv, 276

Young People's Socialist League, 230

Zampty, John Charles, 85

Zionism, 103

zoot suits, 166